INSTRUCTIONAL TECHNOLOGY FOR TEACHING AND LEARNING

Designing Instruction, Integrating Computers, and Using Media

TIMOTHY J. NEWBY
Purdue University

DONALD A. STEPICH
Northeast Illinois University

JAMES D. LEHMAN
Purdue University

JAMES D. RUSSELL
Purdue University

Merrill, an imprint of Prentice Hall
Englewood Cliffs, New Jersey   Columbus, Ohio

Library of Congress Cataloging-in-Publication Data
Instructional technology for teaching and learning:
designing instruction,
     integrating computers, and using media / Timothy J.
Newby . . . [et al.].
          p.   cm.
     Includes bibliographical references and index.
     ISBN 0-02-386695-0
     1. Instructional systems—Design. 2. Educational
technology—Planning.
     3. Computer-assisted instruction. I. Newby, Timothy J.
LB1028.38.I587   1996
371.3′078—dc20   95-25380
                                       CIP

All photos by Scott Cunningham/Merrill/Prentice Hall
except the following, courtesy of Apple Computer, Inc.,
p. 249; The Bettmann Archive, p. 318 (bottom); Andy
Brunk/Merrill/Prentice Hall, p. 196; Computer-Based
Education Research Library, University of Illinois, p. 321;
IBM Archives, p. 320; Missouri Historical Society, p. 318
(top); Proxima, p. 213; John Underwood, Center for
Instructional Services, Purdue University, pp. 21, 61, 78,
105, 127, 157, 190, 210, 217, 253, 260, 264, 331; UPI/
Bettmann, p. 316; Anne Vega/Merrill/Prentice Hall,
pp. 47, 144, 174, 205, 244, 285; Tom Watson/Merrill/
Prentice Hall, pp. 201, 269.

Cover illustration and design: Proof Positive/Farrowlyne
     & Assoc., Inc.
Editor: Debra A. Stollenwerk
Developmental Editor: Linda Ashe Montgomery
Production Editor: Julie Anderson Peters
Photo Editor: Anne Vega
Design Coordinator: Jill E. Bonar
Text Design: Anne Flanagan Book Design
Production Manager: Pamela D. Bennett
Electronic Text Management: Marilyn Wilson Phelps,
     Matthew Williams, Karen L. Bretz, Tracey Ward
Illustrations: Jane Lopez, Tom Kennedy

This book was set in Zapf Calligraphic by Prentice Hall
and was printed and bound by Von Hoffman Press, Inc.
The cover was printed by Von Hoffman Press, Inc.

© 1996 by Prentice-Hall, Inc.
A Simon & Schuster Company
Englewood Cliffs, New Jersey 07632

Printed in the United States of America

10 9 8 7 6 5 4 3 2 1

ISBN: 0-02-386695-0

Prentice-Hall International (UK) Limited, *London*
Prentice-Hall of Australia Pty. Limited, *Sydney*
Prentice-Hall of Canada, Inc., *Toronto*
Prentice-Hall Hispanoamericana, S. A., *Mexico*
Prentice-Hall of India Private Limited, *New Delhi*
Prentice-Hall of Japan, Inc., *Tokyo*
Simon & Schuster Asia Pte. Ltd., *Singapore*
Editora Prentice-Hall do Brasil, Ltda., *Rio de Janeiro*

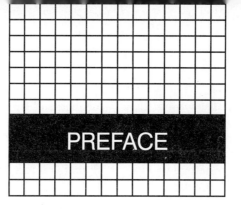

PREFACE

As we began to create *Instructional Technology for Teaching and Learning*, we turned to some "guiding principles" on which to base our work. Those principles include the following.

Those who teach (whether in public school or elsewhere) need:

- to be proficient in selecting, modifying, and designing instructional materials. They need to know how to plan instruction that addresses and solves complex learning problems for individual students.

- to have a repertoire of instructional approaches and media from which to draw in order to select and utilize those which most effectively and efficiently impact student learning.

- to be familiar with the computer as a tool for development of instructional materials, as well as an asset for the delivery and management of those materials.

Traditionally, pre-service teachers needed to take separate courses in instructional design, instructional media, and instructional computing in order to gain the competencies which addressed each of the principles listed above. For most, course availability and time severely limited or blocked this possibility. *Instructional Technology for Teaching and Learning* has been designed as a single, integrated source that introduces students to the basic principles of effective instructional material planning, to different types of media and how they are best utilized, and to the computer as a powerful tool that can be used to plan, as well as, deliver effective instructional materials.

Organization of the Text

To facilitate this integration approach, the text is designed around a *Plan, Implement, Evaluate* model. Following introductory chapters that pro-

vide the needed background on learning, instructional approaches, and media, the book focuses on helping students discover how to plan effective and efficient instructional materials. While providing students with guidance on gathering the needed information about the learner, content, setting, and what is needed to create an instructional plan, students are also introduced to computer software that can increase their capabilities to accomplish these tasks (e.g., word processing, telecommunications, database management).

The implementation phase focuses on how the instructional materials are experienced by the students. Here, proper utilization techniques for various forms of media are given and practiced, and (based on the size of the group of learners) different instructional approaches are described and discussed. The utility of the computer is again emphasized to show how instructional materials can be effectively delivered through this electronic medium—whether through large screen projection, small group workstations, or individual computer-assisted instructional software. Moreover, the computer's value within distance education is explored.

Chapters 12 and 13 examine the evaluation of both students and instructional materials. We examine how evaluation can be used continuously to improve the abilities and skill of the students as well as the effectiveness of the instructional materials. The function of the computer as a calculating tool (e.g., electronic grade book, spreadsheet) and a management tool to manage instruction (e.g. Computer Managed Instruction) is brought to the forefront in this section.

Special Features

To facilitate the process of learning from this text, several pedagogical features have been included. For example, throughout the text hundreds of examples are inserted to illustrate how the principles described have been implemented within the classroom setting. One example is ongoing throughout the text. Toward the conclusion of each chapter this extended example follows one teacher (Ms. Janette Moreno) as she **integrates technology** within her specific classroom situation. Additionally, extensive **use of analogies**, classroom scenarios, and practical applications are incorporated throughout the text to help those unfamiliar with a specific topic to relate it to something more familiar. In various sections of the text, specific instructional techniques or strategies are also highlighted. These are special inserts that give further information and references about a specific type of technique or strategy that is currently being used within the text (e.g., progressive disclosure, concept maps, use of analogies). These are referred to as **Technology Integration Prompts** (or TIPs for short). Finally, to illustrate the different roles the computer plays throughout the process of planning, implementing, and evaluating instruction, various **Computer Use Essentials (CUEs)** are placed at the conclusion of most chapters. CUEs discuss topics from the basics of computer hardware and software to the use of various applications (e.g., word processing, database, spreadsheet) to the various ways the computer can be implemented (e.g., distance education, Internet access, hypermedia) integrated, and managed within an educational setting.

In summary, we hope this text will provide preservice and inservice teachers with a solid foundation regarding how one goes about planning, implementing, and evaluating instruction. By integrating the principles of instructional design, by selecting and utilizing relevant instructional media, and by making appropriate use of the computer, this teaching-learning process can become more effective, efficient, and appealing.

Notes to Course Instructors

- This text has an accompanying *Instructor's Guide*. For each chapter, the guide includes: (a) ideas on how to model the use of the various technological tools; (b) ideas for introducing each of the main concepts of the chapter; (c) an integrated application section which includes items such as suggested applied activities for individuals, case studies, cooperative activities for both small and large groups, discussion starters, and suggested topics for a concurrent computer lab; (d) suggestions for assessment and feedback—which include an extensive test bank, portfolio project suggestions, minute paper ideas, suggestions for the use of reflective journal entries; and (e) a set of

overhead transparency masters. If you have not yet received a copy, please contact your Merrill/ Prentice Hall representative (or send us an e-mail message [note address below] and we will see that you receive a copy).

- As authors, we believe wholeheartedly in communication and feedback. If you have a question, let us know. Encourage your students to send us e-mail messages. We will make every attempt to respond in a timely fashion. Additionally, we are available for live telelectures if you so desire. There won't be any cost—other than the long- distance phone charge.

- Because of the frequent changes that occur within the computer industry, much of the information within this text will be periodically updated. We can't put out new editions of the text each month (the publisher doesn't like that idea), so the next best thing we can do is keep you informed through e-mail and our home page on the World Wide Web. As new changes, ideas, and suggestions come to us, we will be posting them for you to access electronically. If you do not have that capability, send us a postcard with your name and address (see our address listed below) and we will send you a hardcopy of any and all information that will be available over the Internet. Likewise, as you come across relevant products, literature, effective teaching activities, etc., we encourage *you* to share those with us. Think of it as an interactive user exchange.

Where to reach the authors:

e-mail address: newby@sage.cc.purdue.edu
telephone: 317-494-5672
address: 1442 LAEB, Purdue University, W. Lafayette, IN 47907–1442

Acknowledgments

This textbook, like anything of value, could not have been possible without the combined efforts of many individuals. We really appreciate all of those who have contributed in one way or another to the writing of this book. In particular:

- Our families who put up with missed vacations, deadlines, word processing late at night and early in the morning, and extended times of grumpy insecurity.

- Peg Ertmer—the toughest graduate student four professors ever had to work for! Words cannot express what her critical eye and reflective ideas have meant for this book. Thanks for being a wonderful colleague and friend to us all.

- Janette Moreno and the cohorts from McCutcheon High School: Brice Barrett, Melissa Barrett, Sommer Bennett, Amber Bowman, Rob Cain, Laura Davis, Mandi Farrell, Maria Martin, Jenny Merritt, Maria Miller, Timbre Newby, and Chris Young.

- The crew at Merrill/Prentice Hall:

  Debbie Stollenwerk, our Senior Editor and motivator and a delight to talk to on the phone—she always knows how to make us laugh

  Linda Montgomery, our Developmental Editor who contributed great ideas from concept to layout, especially insights into what's really important for the classroom teacher

  Julie Peters, our Production Editor who added the organization and fire to make sure the deadlines were met—even if it meant only taking one day off for her own wedding, just so our text could stay on schedule

  Anne Vega, our Photo Editor who did a great job identifying and locating pictures no one thought even existed

  Jonathan Lawrence, our copyeditor who has an exactness for detail and consistency—how he finds those tiny little inconsistencies no one will ever know.

- Reviewers and their hours of work on a book that they didn't know who was writing. You will never know how much time and energy was spent considering all of your comments and suggestions and how those suggestions helped to form the final work. The reviewers of this edition are:

  Morris I. Beers, State of University of New York at Brockport

  Richard A. Couch, Clarion University of Pennsylvania

  Leticia Ekhaml, West Georgia College

  Chip Fischer, The University of Texas at Tyler

  Mark A. Horney, University of Oregon

  Bonnie H. Keller, Valdosta State University

  Hilary McLellan, Kansas State University

  Jeanne Ormrod, University of Northern Colorado

  Don Pease, California State University at Fullerton

  Gregory C. Sales, University of Minnesota

  Janice R. Sandiford, Florida International University

  Neal Studler, University of Nevada—Las Vegas

  Nancy H. Vick, Longwood College

  M. C. Ware, State University of New York at Cortland

  Barbara Watson, Eastern Michigan University

- Our current and past students—for asking the questions that required us to reflect on what really is useful, relevant, and important.

Tim Newby
Don Stepich
Jim Lehman
Jim Russell

CONTENTS

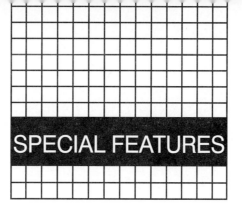

SPECIAL FEATURES

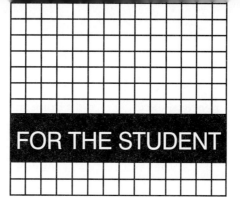

FOR THE STUDENT

A few years ago a small group of students and their instructor (one of the authors of this text) were discussing the upcoming final exam for their graduate seminar. The course consisted of many wide-ranging discussions on various topics related to a central theme. During the discussion, one of the students asked the professor, "If you were going to study for this exam, how would you go about it?" In response, the professor reflected on the overall course and then sat at the word processor and wrote a "few" notes to his students. His notes began with the simple statement, *If I were studying for this exam, I would . . .* followed by a list of items for the students to consider. The goal was not to provide a list of specific items to memorize, rather it was to guide them through some suggestions of what to think about so they could draw their own conclusions. The students found the notes helpful and several commented later that this was "the best part of the course." In subsequent semesters those "notes" became even more effective when they were introduced early in the course.

For most of you, you are reading this at the beginning of your course. But for us as authors these are the last few words we will write for this edition. We have looked at the book as a whole now, repeatedly reviewed and edited earlier drafts, and have pondered and reflected on the content to share some of our insights, thoughts, and reflections we offer the following points for your consideration. These are our "notes" to you.

If we were studying this textbook, we would:

- *Read and reflect on the subtitle of the text.* It is important to realize that the purpose of this textbook is to show how instructional design, instructional media, and instructional computing become powerful teaching and learning tools when they are integrated. No longer should these be seen as separate areas of study. Throughout the book you should note how an instructional expert strives to integrate all three to increase instructional effectiveness, efficiency, and appeal.

- *Pay close attention to the plan, implement, and evaluate model.* (Study the inside text cover.) The main parts of the book have been structured around these three elements and thus provide a basic framework from which to work. Whenever you approach learning (from either a teacher's or student's perspective) you need to think about how the planning will occur, how the learning will be experienced, and how assessment measures will indicate what worked and what needs improvement. Refer frequently to the inside cover of this text and the list of question offered there. These will help you recall important features of each part of the model.

- *Realize that learning is not a simple process.* There are no set prescriptions to ensure that it will consistently occur. Every time you attempt to learn, or help someone else learn, you will encounter a different situation, with new content, and a variety of learners with a multitude of past experiences. You must be prepared to solve unique problems and to draw solutions from a repertoire of possible techniques, strategies, approaches, and media. Many of these are described within this text. Additionally, don't be afraid to mix and match. Because there are few exact answers, you may need to experiment—this is what makes learning challenging and fun. If you see that one approach or tool is not overly helpful, reflect on what it is lacking and try to determine what would be more effective.

- *Reflect on how the textbook material can be applied.* We have included hundreds of examples throughout the text. They will be most relevant if you incorporate them within your own situation and compare them to your own experiences. Reflect on the similarities and differences. Think about what you can learn from each of them.

- *Realize that this book has been designed to serve as a foundation.* It will not teach you everything about instructional design, instructional media, or instructional computing. This book will give you the fundamental knowledge and skills you need in order to effectively use these tools for your own learning and future teaching. Building on this foundation, you will be able to gain needed information on other design features, additional techniques with various media formats, and especially more information on the power and use of the computer and its various applications.

- *Do not underestimate the power of the computer.* Unlike many media formats that are mainly used to present information, the computer can be used by both learner and teacher during the planning and the evaluation phases as well. Moreover, when the computer is used in the implementation phase, it provides a platform for combining a number of different approaches and media formats (e.g., multimedia) to give learners more enriched learning experiences.

- *Learn to appreciate the power of the computer as a teaching and learning tool, but do not be overwhelmed by it.* Don't fall into the trap of thinking that the computer is the savior of education. Remember, the computer is not the most important tool in *all* learning situations. It is a tool that, like any other tool, can facilitate your work when used in the proper manner and at the proper time. In addition, don't think that the computer is such a complex tool that you cannot master it. Through examples and practice you will learn to use it to accomplish many valuable tasks. You may even find that undertaking and completing tasks on the computer become quite enjoyable.

- *Reflect and question.* Take time to reflect and think about what is presented in this text and, more importantly, how you can *use* it. When a principle is presented, imagine how, when, and why you might apply it.

- *Ask for help.* As you reflect and question, feel free to contact us directly. Instead of just learning about the "information superhighway"—try using it. We would love to hear your thoughts, address your questions, and listen to your concerns pertaining to this textbook. We appreciate and desire feedback. To contact us you can use any of the following methods (Note: e-mail is generally the fastest and most reliable):

Electronic mail (e-mail):
>   newby@sage.cc.purdue.edu

Regular mail:
>   Authors of ITTL—Attention: Tim Newby
>   1442 LAEB
>   Purdue University
>   W. Lafayette, IN 47907–1442

Telephone: 1-317-494-5669

We found this textbook a challenge to write—but the benefits of what we have learned have been well worth the time. Hopefully, you will now be challenged and experience the satisfaction and fun of learning.

A little help from you:

If you turn to the last couple pages of this text you will find a short evaluation form. We feel the best way to improve this text is to hear from those who have used it. After reading and studying this text for your course, you will be exactly the type of individual we would like to hear from. Fill out the sheet and mail it to us. For your time and effort we will be happy to send you a disk with a hypertext version of the chapter summaries and glossary.

Something About Us

Tim Newby is an Associate Professor of Instructional Research and Development at Purdue University. He teaches introductory courses in instructional design, computing, and media, as well as advanced courses in instructional design research, foundations of instructional design theory, and instructional strategies. His primary research efforts are directed toward examining the impact of learning and instructional strategies on students' learning and on defining/ investigating instructional conditions which foster and support the development of expert learners. Tim is particularly interested in the use of analogies and their impact on learning and memory. Thus, throughout this book, you will note the use of something familiar to explain something new. Tim's other life consists of chasing four active children and trying to keep up with an overly committed wife. Watching, coaching, and cheering for little kids as they learn to catch, throw, hit, and kick various forms of "ball" is a passion.

Don Stepich is currently an Associate Professor in the Human Resource Development Program at Northeastern Illinois University in Chicago where he teaches courses in instructional design, instructional media, and presentation skills for both graduate and undergraduate students. As an instructional designer, Don is interested in the use of interactive strategies to help students learn and in the improvement of instructional materials through continuous evaluation. He is particularly interested in the impact of analogies on learning and their effective use in instructional materials. Together with Tim Newby, Don is a frequent presenter at professional conferences where their workshops on analogies have drawn wide critical acclaim. In a former life Don was a professional social worker in a mental health center and in private counseling practice. In fact, it was his counseling work that led him into education. He found that he was spending a lot of time teaching—assertiveness, active listening, communication skills, etc.—which led him back to school to study learning and instructional design.

Jim Lehman is an Associate Professor of Educational Computing and Co-Director of the Technology Resources Center in the School of Education at Purdue University. He teaches classes on the educational applications of personal computers, integration and management of computers in education, computer software design, and interactive video and multimedia. His research interests include integration of computer technology into subject matter instruction especially in the sciences, interactive multimedia design and implementation, and computer mediated communication for distance education. He works extensively with colleagues in the K-12 schools on the integration of computers and related technologies. In his spare time, Jim is raising two daughters, Lauren and Katie, and he likes gardening.

Jim Russell is Professor of Curriculum and Instruction at Purdue University. A former high school mathematics and physics teacher, Jim teaches courses on media utilization, instructional design, instructional delivery systems, and principles of adult education. He was honored as his department's Outstanding Teacher in 1993. Jim is also involved with Purdue's Center of Instructional Services where he conducts workshops on teaching techniques for faculty and graduate assistants. His specialty areas are presentation skills and using media and technology in classrooms. When away from the university, Jim finds time to put together plastic model race cars and is an announcer for the Nationwide Demolition Derby circuit. His wife Nancy is a nurse and his daughter Jennifer is a high school teacher.

In Conclusion

This text has been designed to provide you with a source of information on instructional technology. Our desire is for you to be challenged by what is here—but not to be frustrated or overwhelmed. If you have questions or problems or even some suggestions, please contact us. Learning should be a marvelous adventure, whether you accomplish it personally or assist in helping others experience it. As you learn about instructional technology and begin to see its potential impact for you personally, we hope you will become as excited as we are.

All the best,
Tim, Don, Jim & Jim

Section I

Introduction to Instructional Technology

Have you opened a computer software program or its accompanying manual lately? If so, you may have noticed a little section or file entitled "READ ME FIRST." This attention-getter is included because the authors want to tell you something important about the materials *before* you head off into some trial-and-error learning process. In similar fashion, we think it is important for you to know a few things about this text in general, and the first section in particular, before you dive into the initial chapters. We think that if you know what we envisioned while writing the text, you can benefit from this vision while you are reading it.

First, it would be helpful to know *why* this textbook was put together. We believe that many individuals, especially those within teacher education, need to know (1) how instruction is designed, developed, and improved; (2) the types and uses of different media formats—especially the use of the personal computer; and (3) how the design of the instruction and the media are integrated to promote student learning. Meeting these three needs requires an integration of the three general areas of instructional design, instructional media, and instructional computing within the pages of a single textbook. Traditionally, these have been taught through individual texts and separate courses; however, the teacher has to apply them in an integrated fashion in order to have maximum impact on student learning. Our goal is to help you understand the critical principles and application benefits of each of the separate areas of instructional design, media, and computing—but even more importantly, to help you understand the benefits of integrating these areas in such a way as to facilitate your and your students' growth.

Second, it is useful to know that this text is organized around a simple Plan, Implement, Evaluate (PIE) model. The main sections of the text (Sections II, III, and IV), which follow the four introductory chapters, are all based on this model. All of the different aspects of instructional design, instructional media, and instructional computing are discussed within this structure, as it provides a simple, convenient, and relevant way to demonstrate how to integrate those areas.

Third, there are a number of special features within this text designed to facilitate your learning.

This is a text on instructional technology, one that focuses on the approaches, strategies, and techniques that can increase the effectiveness, efficiency, and appeal of instruction. We explain how, when, and why these techniques are best developed and also include examples to encourage their use. Therefore, we have integrated these techniques throughout this text as a means to help you assimilate the text's information; moreover, these same techniques can be used as reference examples as you attempt to use them within your own teaching. To help in this regard, we have inserted Technology Integration Prompts (TIPs), which are special highlighted sections describing the learning technique or feature that is currently being used within the text (e.g., an explanation of analogies and why and when they are effectively used within instructional materials). We also use TIPs to suggest how different forms of media (especially computers) can be integrated at specific points within instruction to increase its effectiveness. These suggestions serve as reminders of how the computer can be used, what types of software may be needed, and why

this technology might be applicable at this point. Relevant supporting research is also included. We hope you will see how these tools have been used successfully by others and will consider how you can apply them in your future work.

Similar to these TIPs are a number of other features that focus specifically on the computer. To use the computer within an instructional setting, you need some basic information about it and its applications. In most of the chapters, explanations of relevant computer applications (e.g., word processing, database management, spreadsheets) are included. Computer Use Essentials (CUEs) provide information regarding what the specific application is and how it can be used, and offer examples of how it can be integrated and when and why it should or should not be used. We have also included an ongoing example of a particular classroom teacher who has struggled with the use of technology and found ways to improve her performance, and the performance of her students, through its integration.

Several other features that occur within each chapter should help you learn this information.

You should note that each chapter begins with a section consisting of the chapter outline, key words and concepts, instructional outcomes, and a brief introduction to the chapter content. The outline provides an overview of the chapter by depicting the sequence of the material, highlighting the relationship among the major points and supplying a tool for later review. The key words and concepts supply a ready reference to new concepts and terms introduced in the chapter and indicate which are defined in the text's glossary. The instructional outcomes indicate what we hope you will achieve from reading and studying the chapter content. Finally, we set the stage for each of the chapters with a short scenario, an analogy, or some type of problem situation that helps illustrate the importance or relevance of the chapter's information. Note how this introductory material is repeatedly referred to throughout the chapter and how closely it is tied to the reflective questions and activities found in the final pages of each chapter.

You should note that analogies, examples, and extended examples are frequently used throughout each of the chapters. We realize that there are many new concepts and that you will need to see many examples of how they are applied and integrated in a classroom. Pay close attention to the analogies and examples. These are often used to illustrate how to adapt and change your teaching strategies given different situations, learners, and content. We will inform you when you should refer back to a specific example and will indicate where that original citation is located. It may take a few extra moments to refresh your memory, but the benefits of seeing the different applications and adaptations should more than compensate for the effort.

At the end of each chapter we summarize what has been discussed in the chapter, describe how the information relates to both the previous and subsequent chapters of the text, and provide activities and questions to think about, work through, and complete. Each chapter closes with a list of suggested further readings on the topics discussed.

It is our desire that you be actively involved throughout this entire text, so we frequently ask questions, present ideas for you to ponder, and describe problems that need thoughtful analysis and synthesis in order to be adequately worked through. This is our attempt to get you involved and to help you to remember and use the presented information for a long time to come.

We would like to introduce you to the first chapter of the text. We call it "Learning and Instructional Technology: An Introduction," because it is exactly that—an introduction to the field of instructional technology and the supporting contributions of instructional design, media, and computing. Central to this chapter is the concept of *learning* and how it can be enhanced through the use of instructional technology. At the conclusion of Chapter 1 we introduce you to Ms. Janette Moreno and her high school Spanish class. Ms. Moreno's work is referred to and elaborated on throughout the entire text.

In Chapter 2 we explore the theoretical foundations of teaching and learning. We look at learning from a number of different angles to enable you to consider which teaching and learning orientation might be best, given a particular topic, situation, and/or type of learner. To increase the usefulness of this theoretical background, realize that the emphasis is not simply on knowing the different perspectives of learning but on understanding how each perspective applies to real students in actual classroom settings. Through examples and reflective activities we challenge you to understand the unique relevance of and need for each of these different perspectives.

Finally, Chapters 3 and 4 have been designed to supply important prerequisite information. Before you begin to plan and prepare instruction, you need some prerequisite knowledge—that is, knowledge regarding alternative approaches, media, materials, and so on—so that when the time comes, you can make good decisions. Two critical decisions deal with the instructional approaches (Chapter 3) and instructional media (Chapter 4) that will be used. In both cases, it is important to know that there are many alternative approaches (e.g., tutorial, cooperative learning, presentation), as well as a wide range of media (e.g., computer software, overhead transparencies, multipurpose boards) that can be used. Before you can choose them wisely, however, you must know that they exist, what their strengths and limitations are, and when, why, and how they are best used. These two chapters provide that information so that, as you plan instruction, you can determine the optimal instructional approach and media format to utilize for specific content, individual learners, and particular situations. These introductory chapters present a wide range of alternatives that subsequently will be explored in much greater depth in the remaining sections and chapters of the text.

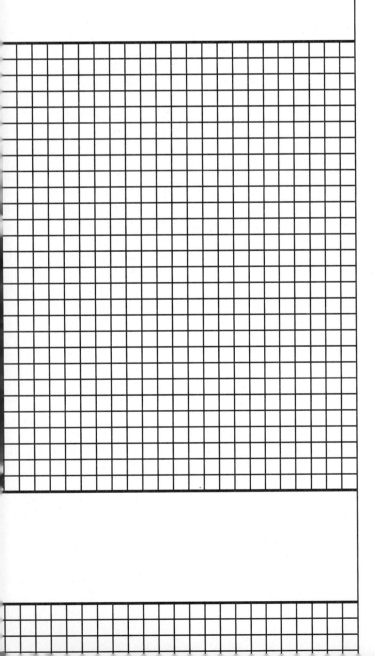

Chapter 1

Learning and Instructional Technology: An Introduction

KEY WORDS AND CONCEPTS

Learning	Evaluation
Analogizing	Technology
Instructional effectiveness	Instructional technology
Instructional efficiency	Instructional design
Instructional appeal	Instructional plan
Planning	Instructional media
Implementation	Instructional computing

OUTCOMES

After reading and studying this chapter, you will be able to:

- Define *learning* and explain its relationship to instructional technology.

- Describe why an understanding of the learning process is important for the teacher and the student and what outcomes could result from its study.

- Explain the difficulties involved in gaining an understanding of the learning process.

- Explain the roles of the teacher, the learner, and technology in the learning process.

- Discuss how planning, implementation, and evaluation are important for the teacher and the learner.

- Generate relevant questions to pose during the planning, implementation, and evaluation phases of the development and use of instructional materials.

- Explain how instructional design, instructional media, and instructional computing contribute to learning.

- Describe the relationships among instructional design, instructional media, and instructional computing.

- Describe the purpose of an instructional plan and explain its position within instructional technology.

■ INTRODUCTION

Have you ever had the opportunity to watch an expert craftsperson at work? Perhaps you have observed an artist take a plain white canvas and create a stunning portrait, or watched a fashion designer bring together different types of materials to produce a beautiful evening gown. If you ever attempted to replicate such fine work, you undoubtedly soon realized that it was not a simple task. That is, basic differences probably existed in the manner in which the experts approached their work and in what you attempted to do. For example, if you observed an expert cabinetmaker build a customized bookcase and then compared that performance with a novice attempting to make the same thing, you would likely note one or more of the following differences. First, before ever touching a tool, the expert typically spends time planning and preparing for the creation. Although this effort is not always recorded on paper, productive time is spent visualizing the final product, planning for its creation, and considering alternative approaches. The expert visualizes not just the end result but the process of creation as well—what materials will be needed, which tools will be most useful, how and when those tools should be used, and even what can be done if certain problems are encountered. To some degree even novices plan their work, but it appears that experts take more time, are more thorough, and are more effective with their planning.

A second difference regards the expert cabinetmaker's overall knowledge of the available tools. Experts seem to know exactly which tool is correct for every situation that is encountered. Even if they run into an unexpected problem that renders their first choice ineffective, they can quickly determine the next-best alternative. The customized bookcase, for example, may have a unique recessed panel design that can be created with the standard router and blade; however, the expert may realize that a stationary wood shaper would provide a cleaner, more precise cut. The less experienced novice, on the other hand, may select a familiar, favorite tool and use it even if it doesn't work quite right.

One additional difference—and perhaps the biggest—is the way experts continually review and monitor how their work is progressing. During the actual production they constantly check and recheck their work to make sure any problems are handled early on. Experts don't wait until little problems become big headaches. For example, if the initial pieces of the bookcase are not properly squared, serious problems will result later with misaligned joints and uneven shelves. Experienced woodworkers frequently measure and monitor their work and fix problems as they develop. As the project nears completion, experts also spend time reviewing the creation process—what steps were taken, how close the final product matched what was originally conceived, what problems were encountered, and what could have been improved.

At this point you may be wondering why a text on instructional technology begins with an example of building a bookcase. Our primary interest is not woodworking but how the transition from novice to expert is made and how this transformation can be facilitated through the effective use of technology and the application of its tools. The purpose of this text is to describe what these technologies are, as well as how, when, and why they can be used to support the learning of your students. It is our belief that this transition from novice to expert can be facilitated through the proper use of technology. ■

LEARNING

The novice-to-expert transition depends on learning. Therefore, a central focus of this text is on human learning and how it is accomplished. Even though most of us are quite familiar with the "learning experience" and we know we have "learned" in the past, there are still important questions to address, such as

- What exactly is learning?
- Why is the study of learning important?
- What are the major phases of learning?
- Who or what plays a key role in the learning process?

What Exactly Is Learning?

It is relatively easy to cite examples of learning; however, generating a simple definition is somewhat more difficult. For example, reflect on the past few days or weeks and think about something you learned. Maybe it was something that necessitated concerted time and effort, such as learning how to write a specific type of research paper. Or you learned something that required less effort or time, such as the location of the closest parking facility for your new night class. Or possibly your learning occurred without your consciously realizing it, such as learning verbatim two full verses of an obnoxious jingle on a television commercial. The time, effort, and purpose involved in each of these examples varied considerably. However, in each case learning occurred.

Even though learning is quite common and examples can be readily recalled, the descriptions and explanations of what actually transpires in order for it to occur are not as easily discerned. For centuries the causes, processes, and consequences of learning have been researched and debated with a less-than-complete consensus. In fact, one noted psychologist, after years of studying this phenomenon, wrote, "In reviewing the evidence . . . the necessary conclusion is that learning just is not possible at all. Nevertheless, in spite of such evidence against it, learning does sometimes occur" (Lashley, 1960, p. 501).

Difficulties

What makes the study of learning so difficult? First, learning occurs across a wide variety of situations and tasks. For example, reciting the Gettysburg Address requires learning, but so does using a nine-iron to get over a sand trap. Analyzing a problem to determine the amount of radiation to give a cancer patient requires learning, as does the attitude of choosing to be reverent during a church service. With such broad topics and situations, identifying how to maximize learning, as well as how to measure the amount and quality of learning that has occurred, is difficult.

Second, learning is heavily influenced by the previous experience of the individual. That is, two individuals with the same task to be learned, in the same setting, and with the same consequences for achievement will not necessarily learn the same thing. Differences in backgrounds and experiences have an impact on what is perceived, how it is associated within memory, and how and under what conditions it is recalled. Moreover, not only are the differences between individuals difficult to predict, but variances within a single individual also frequently impact learning over time. We've all experienced "good" and "not-so-good" learning days. Our experiences and backgrounds influence the manner in which each task is approached and the way in which each is accomplished, making it difficult to predict what will occur during a single learning episode.

Finally, it is difficult to study learning because of the inherent problems in its observation and measurement. Because no two learning situations are alike, the indications of when and to what degree learning has been accomplished are open to discussion and interpretation. Although it would be nice if they were, students are not equipped with standardized "learn-o-meters" that indicate when and to what degree learning has been accomplished (Figure 1.1). Without such a standard or tool, interpreting learning's occurrence can often be subjective and difficult.

Definitions

Compare the following definitions of learning:

- Learning is a "persisting change in human performance or performance potential . . . [brought] about as a result of the learner's interaction with the environment" (Driscoll, 1994, pp. 8–9).
- "Learning is the relatively permanent change in a person's knowledge or behavior due to experience" (Mayer, 1982, p. 1040).
- "Learning is an enduring change in behavior, or in the capacity to behave in a given fashion, which results from practice or other forms of experience" (Shuell, 1986, p. 412).

Even though difficulties of observation and measurement are inherent within the study of human learning, it is important and helpful to identify the common criteria used to signify that learning has

Figure 1.1 A "learn-o-meter" would help us understand when learning occurs

transpired. Using these and similar definitions, Schunk (1991, p. 2) outlined the process of **learning** in the following way:

1. a change, or the capacity for such a change, occurs in the learner's behavior

2. the change, or its capacity, results from practice or other forms of experience (e.g., observing others)

3. the change, or its capacity, endures over time (i.e., it is not something temporarily induced by fatigue, drugs, or illness)

The key word in these definitions is *change*. To learn is to change (or have the capacity to change) one's level of ability or knowledge. Typically, learning is measured by the amount of change that occurs within an individual's level of performance or behavior. As Schunk points out, this change endures over time and generally results from specific experiences such as practice.

Why Is the Study of Learning Important?

More than 60 years ago, Thorndike answered this question by saying, "Man's power to change himself, that is, to learn, is perhaps the most impressive thing about him" (1931, p. 3). The study of learning is important for both those who will be learning and

those who will be helping, guiding, and facilitating learning in others. The basic premise behind the answer to the question, Why should it be studied? lies in the belief that specific actions, techniques, and technologies can have an impact on the quantity and quality of what is learned. That is, by knowing what learning is, how it occurs, and what factors combine to influence the learning process, we are in a position to change and influence the levels of ability and knowledge within the learner—whether that learner is oneself or another individual.

The emphasis of this text is on what teachers and learners can do to positively impact learning. Such things relate to

- the planning required to ensure that instruction is designed, developed, and sequenced in a manner effectively processed by the learner

- the delivery and reception of the instruction

- the evaluation of both the implemented instruction and the resultant learning by the student

This emphasis can be compared to those differences between the expert and novice craftspersons mentioned earlier. The expert cabinetmaker was noted for planning, for understanding the strengths and weaknesses of various tools given different situations and outcome desires, and for reflecting on and evaluating the effectiveness of the tools throughout the entire design and construction process. A similar emphasis on planning, implementing, and evaluating will be made throughout this text. Our goal is that those who design, develop, and use instruction will attain similar levels of expertise.

Desired Outcome

For those involved in teaching and learning (which includes almost everyone), one or more of the following positive outcomes can justify the investment of effort in the creation and use of instruction.

- *Increased **instructional effectiveness.*** In this case the student actually learns in a better way than would have been accomplished without the experience. Increased effectiveness includes increased levels of recall accuracy, longer retention, and better transfer and generalization of the skills and knowledge to similar or not-so-similar situations.

- *Increased **instructional efficiency.*** Here the focus is on time. Increased efficiency could mean that the same amount of learning occurred, but in a shorter period of time. Efficiency may be gained through reducing the amount of time required

USING ANALOGIES, SIMILES, AND METAPHORS

During the opening paragraphs of this chapter, we referred to a master cabinetmaker and his or her need to plan, implement, and evaluate. You may have asked yourself, What is the value of reading about a cabinetmaker? The value has to do with an instructional technique known as **analogizing.** Its purpose is to help you learn by comparing some new, to-be-learned concept with something that is perhaps more familiar or concrete. An analogy (which includes similes, metaphors, and analogies) consists of four basic parts:

1. the to-be-learned information (subject)
2. the familiar knowledge to which the new information is compared (analogue)
3. the means by which the analogue and subject are compared (connector)
4. a description of the similarities between the subject and the analogue (ground)

In the opening paragraphs of this chapter, the differences between how expert and novice cabinetmakers would go about creating a bookcase (analogue—that which is fairly concrete and/or familiar) are highlighted. These are later compared (connector) to teachers and the learning process (subject—less familiar or concrete) and how one can progress by gaining knowledge in how to plan, implement, and evaluate (ground).

Similes, analogies, and metaphors have repeatedly been found to be effective in teaching all types of subject matter (West, Farmer, & Wolff, 1991). To facilitate your own analogizing, see Table 1.1 for a simple ABCDE method of constructing an analogy.

Table 1.1 The ABCDEs of analogizing

A	**A**nalyze the subject.	What is it that you most want the learners to understand about this subject?
B	**B**rainstorm potential analogues.	What concrete items share the important feature(s) you have identified?
C	**C**hoose the analogue.	Which candidate analogue has the best combination of the following characteristics: • *Familiarity*—Will the learners recognize the analogue? • *Accuracy*—Does the analogue accurately reflect the identified feature? • *Memorability*—Is the analogue vivid; will the learner remember it? • *Concreteness*—Is the analogue something that is directly perceived?
D	**D**escribe the connector and ground.	How are the subject and analogue alike? How are they different?
E	**E**valuate the analogy.	Does the analogy work with the intended audience?

Adapted from Kearny, Newby, and Stepich, 1995.

to design and develop the instruction. It could also be gained through better or quicker means of instructional delivery. Or it could also be related to the manner in which the skills and knowledge were assimilated by the learners, such that the amount of time they needed to learn the new information was reduced.

• *Increased **instructional appeal**.* Another outcome—often neglected and forgotten but critical to the success of the instruction—is its appeal to the teacher and the student. Increasing the appeal enhances the possibility that students will devote time and energy to the learning task and increases the likelihood they will return to review and work on the material at other times. Appeal is strongly associated with learners' attitudes toward the information and the motivation the learners will have for the subject being studied.

To summarize, a major reason why the study of learning is important is that its understanding leads to the development of increasingly more effective, efficient, and appealing instruction.

What Are the Phases of Learning?

The phases of learning discussed within this text are similar to the major points brought out by the cabinetmaker analogy. As shown in Figure 1.2, they consist of the planning phase, the implementation phase, and the evaluation phase. All three are highly interdependent. Using this same structure, this text is divided into sections devoted to planning, implementation, and evaluation.

The Planning Phase. This phase focuses on what should be or needs to be learned and how this learning might be accomplished, as well as when and why. The final outcome is an outline, lesson plan, or blueprint of what is to be developed and what should be implemented in order to achieve the desired goal. This plan helps to delineate what the learners presently know or can do and what they should know or be able to do, and it suggests means to reduce the difference between those two states. This plan highly influences the manner in which the information is developed, presented, and received by the learner.

The Implementation Phase. The focus during this phase is on actually using the plan and putting it into action. Based on what is to be learned and what situational constraints have been determined, implementation may require the selection, assembly, or

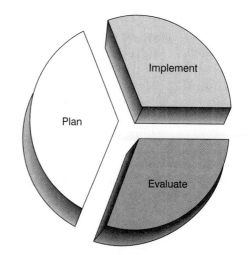

Figure 1.2   Plan, implement, and evaluate: The phases of learning

creation of instructional materials using various instructional approaches, techniques, and media. Once determined, these materials can then be used.

The Evaluation Phase. The emphasis during this phase is on the evaluation of both the effectiveness of the materials and the overall learning accomplished by the students. The plan and its development and use are reviewed to ensure that all needed changes are considered. This is a time to reflect on and review what was accomplished, to compare that with the desired goal, to suggest changes to be made to the planning and implementation phases, and to complete suggested revisions and fix-ups.

Who or What Plays a Key Role in the Learning Process?

Many factors contribute to the actual accomplishment of learning. Those critical within the classroom include the learner, the teacher, and technology.

The Learner

As can be expected within any learning task, the individual doing the learning plays a central role. Although some view the learner as an empty, passive vessel waiting to be filled, others see the learner as one who actively constructs and processes new information (Ertmer & Newby, 1993). Of central concern here is what the individual can do that will facilitate the overall learning process. Through the observation and study of various "strategic" or "expert" learners (Weinstein & Van Mater Stone, 1993), several important learner actions can be highlighted that assist the learning process.

First, when given a new, to-be-learned task, the strategic learner, just like an expert craftsperson, frequently spends time **planning** and preparing a course of action. This preparation often includes the review of personal cognitive and motivational resources, such as past strategies and tactics used to encode and retrieve new information (e.g., using simple rehearsal techniques for memorizing passages of information, or using analogies to highlight how the new information is similar to what is already known). It may also include reviewing familiar motivational strategies used to instigate and maintain task interest and levels of effort (e.g., determining one's reasons for learning the new material). Additionally, the task and the environment may be analyzed to determine if the task requires a specific type of strategy or technique (e.g., summarizing the main idea of each paragraph, paraphrasing new definitions) or if the environment contains any obstacles that must be overcome in order to accomplish the task (e.g., distracting background noises, insufficient light).

This planning phase will differ considerably depending on the abilities and previous experiences of the learners. Although the expert may readily review his or her resources and select the appropriate strategy based on past experiences, many young, novice, or less sophisticated learners may have few resources on which to draw, little experience in analyzing what a new task requires, and/or inadequate ability to match current resources with the needs of the task. As shown through the work of Weinstein and Van Mater Stone (1993), novices can learn these types of strategies and selection mechanisms in order to become more strategic learners. In this case the focus is not just on learning the content of the task but also on *learning how to learn* this and similar content.

A second important action occurs during the **implementation** of the plan. Here the strategic learner concentrates on actually developing what was planned and on using and monitoring the effects of selected learning and motivational strategies. During this phase the learner monitors learning and motivational progress, making revisions to selected strategies as obstacles are encountered. Additionally, he or she monitors the means by which the to-be-learned materials are presented, the amount and speed of information presented, the sequence of its presentation, and how well attention and motivation are maintained.

And finally, the strategic learner spends time **evaluating** the impact of the experience and the effectiveness of the employed strategies. This is a period of reflecting, revamping, and revising as needed. If the desired level of learning has not been achieved, redirection to additional planning and implementation may be needed.

As shown in Table 1.2, key questions can be asked during each of the planning, implementation, and evaluation phases to focus on what the individual can do to facilitate learning. These questions should be asked by students before, during, and after they attempt the learning task. Additionally, the teacher can use these questions to prompt and cue novice learners as they encounter new tasks. We suggest you consider these questions as you attempt to learn the materials found within this text.

The Teacher

Another key ingredient within the learning process is the teacher. In North American educational systems, the teacher assumes many duties. The teacher has been assigned the jobs of chief motivator, leader, counselor, model, and surrogate parent. At the same time, the teacher is asked to serve as an advisor for school administration, management, and curriculum development. The most important duty or function of the teacher, however, is that which Woolfolk (1990) refers to as the "instructional expert." In this capacity the teacher plans, implements, and evaluates instructional activities that are used to teach and influence the learning of the students. The involvement of the instructional expert can range from one of little actual interaction with the students (e.g., where the teacher's time and efforts are devoted to designing materials and developing independent learning activities) to one requiring a high amount of group or individual interaction (e.g., when presenting new materials to the students in a lecture or discussion format).

Although varying duties and responsibilities have been shifted to and from the teacher over the years, the functions of a teacher as the instructional expert have remained relatively constant. Whether direct or indirect, good or bad, what the student experiences and subsequently learns in the classroom is largely influenced by the teacher. Even in situations where the students have more control (e.g., a discovery/exploratory environment, individualized instruction), the teacher selects or arranges the activities and gives subtle guidance and clarifications. Because of this critical role, *this text will focus on what you as an instructional expert should know and do and how those things can be accomplished.*

Similar to those things outlined for the student, the things to be learned by the teacher are based on the phases of learning: planning the instruction; developing, implementing, and delivering the instruction; and evaluating, revising, and managing the instruction.

Table 1.2 Questions the learner should ask during each learning phase

Planning

- What is the goal of this task (i.e., What am I supposed to learn?)?
- What will I need to learn this task (e.g., learning strategies, assistance from others, time, effort)?
- In what ways can my previous learning experiences help?
- What obstacles and problems could hinder me from learning this task?
- How will my motivation and effort in this task be generated and maintained (e.g., Am I good at this kind of task? Do I like this kind of work?)?
- How should I attempt this task in order to effectively learn the materials while maintaining my motivation and overcoming presented obstacles (e.g., Does this type of activity require a great deal of concentration?)?

Implementation

- How do I assemble or create what is needed to carry out the plan?
- How do I begin and follow the planned learning strategies?
- Is this going the way I planned?
- Do I understand what I am doing?
- What outside materials or resources should be added?
- What should I look for in order to tell if learning is occurring?
- How can I tell if my task motivation is being maintained?

Evaluation

- Was the quality and quantity of learning at the needed level?
- What did I do when the selected tactics and learning strategies didn't work?
- What obstacles were encountered, and what strategies were or were not effective in overcoming those problems?
- What have I learned from this experience that could be used at other times for different tasks?
- What improvements could I make for future learning tasks?

As defined by Reigeluth (1983), the role of **planning** involves "the process of deciding what methods of instruction are best for bringing about desired changes in student knowledge and skills for a specific course content and a specific student population" (p. 7). Teachers need to identify the instructional needs of their students by identifying any existing gaps between current and desired levels of skills and knowledge. After these gaps have been identified, instructional approaches and strategies are selected to overcome them. The principal result is a plan or blueprint of instruction. It includes the content as well as an indication of which strategies and activities should be used and when and how they should be structured. Table 1.3 identifies several key questions that the teacher should ask at or during this stage. Note that the questions asked do not dictate a single role for the teacher. In some cases the instruction is planned, presented, and controlled by the instructor, but in others it may be controlled totally by the individual learner.

Another role frequently played by the teacher is that of **implementer** of the instruction. After the teacher assembles or produces the needed instructional materials, he or she then delivers the material. In the ideal situation the teacher follows a previously completed plan or one suggested by other teachers or curriculum experts, and the needed instruction is brought together or developed into a finished product. The finished product may be in the form of lecture notes, videotapes, reading assignments, small-group activities, computer programs, or guided discovery activities.

At this point the teacher becomes a "director of learning activities" (Ausubel, Novak, & Hanesian, 1978). This may require the teacher to personally disseminate the information through some form of expository lecture, inquiry discussion, or demonstration, or to serve as manager of other means (e.g., video presentation, small-group discussion) used as the primary vehicle for the transfer of information to the student. The primary outcome is that the student has experienced the instruction.

Table 1.3 Questions the teacher should ask during each learning phase

Planning

- What task must the students be able to do, and how can I determine when it has been accomplished?
- What do the students already know that will assist in learning this task?
- What resources, facilities, and equipment are available and accessible?
- What information should be included in the instructional materials or activities?
- What is the most effective, efficient, and appealing manner in which the to-be-learned task can be acquired by the students?
- In what order should the learning activities be sequenced?
- What is the best medium to assist students in learning the new information?
- What can be done to help this learning be transferred to other similar situations?

Implementation

- Are there relevant instructional materials (or parts thereof) that already exist? Which materials will need some adaptation? Which materials will need to be created?
- Based on need and practicality, what approaches and media should I include or have students include within the instruction?
- During the learning process, how will my students' attention and motivation be maintained?

Evaluation

- How can I determine if (and to what degree) the students have learned the material?
- What types of remediation or enrichment activities may be necessary for my students?
- In what ways can these instructional materials and activities be improved for repeated or adapted use?

The final role of the instructional expert is that of **evaluator** of both the learners and the instruction. In this case the teacher measures both the learning of the students and the overall effectiveness, efficiency, and appeal of the instruction. This is typically completed by examining how well the students completed the lesson and by determining if the students have attained the desired level of performance. This phase should also be a time to reflect on the successes achieved and problems encountered. The result of the evaluation is a description of the strengths and weaknesses of the program, which can be used for instructional improvement and increased student learning.

For most teachers, the planning, implementation, and evaluation of instruction is an ongoing process. On any given day a teacher may plan and develop several future lessons, monitor current topics to ensure that they are being properly addressed, and reflect on completed lessons and the results they produced.

Technology

An important concept addressed throughout this text is "technology"—particularly the role it plays within education. Formally stated, **technology** is defined as "the systematic application of scientific or other organized knowledge to practical tasks" (Galbraith, 1967, p. 12). In this sense technology performs a bridging function between research and theoretical explorations on the one side and the real-world problems faced by practitioners on the other (Figure 1.3). Although the information from research and theory is critical, the practitioner frequently has neither time nor expertise to study and understand how that information could be applied to practical situations. Likewise, from the standpoint of researchers, time and energy are often not devoted to explaining how their theories and experimental findings can be applied. This difference is often referred to as the "scientist/practitioner problem." This problem illustrates the necessity for a technology bridge.

Figure 1.3 The bridge of technology between research and practical problems

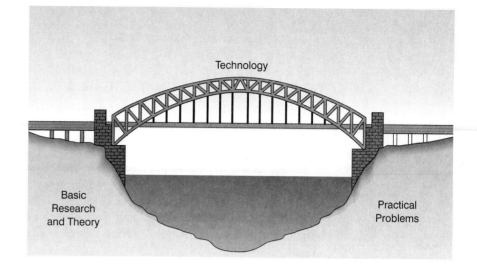

This bridging function requires the technologist/translator to (1) understand the basic research and theory, (2) have a working knowledge of the practical task (e.g., constraints imposed by the situation, needs, etc.), and (3) translate the research into a form that can be used by the practitioner to complete the task. The space industry offers a good example. Numerous practical problems have been encountered as man has traveled in space (e.g., How does one breathe in a place devoid of oxygen? What is needed to propel one into space? How does one reenter an atmosphere at the proper place and speed?). In order to answer such practical questions, contributions from such fields as physics and materials science had to be translated in a way that could be applied to those practical problems. In many cases the results of those applications were tangible products such as space shuttles, space suits, and advanced telecommunications capabili-

ties. In other situations those tools and products have taken not-so-tangible forms such as enhanced safety procedures, formulas for reentry projections, and backup contingency plans. In each instance, scientific knowledge was reviewed and applied to answer specific practical problems.

Just as there is a space technology, an engineering technology, and a medical technology that bridge basic research and practical problem areas in these specialized areas, there is also instructional technology. Generalizing from the previous definition, **instructional technology** has been defined as "applying scientific knowledge about human learning to the practical tasks of teaching and learning" (Heinich, Molenda, & Russell, 1993, p. 16). Specifically, instructional technology is the bridge between those who conduct research on human learning (e.g., psychologists, linguists) and those who are teaching and learning (Figure 1.4). That is, instruc-

Figure 1.4 The bridge of instructional technology between research on learning and practical teaching and learning problems

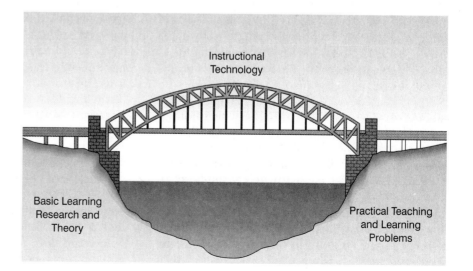

TIP

TECHNOLOGY INTEGRATION PROMPT

CLARIFYING THE DEFINITION OF "TECHNOLOGY"

Take a moment and think about the following statement: "Technology has allowed us to make great advances."

If you were given this as the topic of an oral report, what would you talk about? That is, what would be your main focus? Before reading on, think about this and jot a couple of notes on a scrap piece of paper.

In most cases, the topics selected for the oral presentation have included "things" such as computers, airplanes, lightbulbs, televisions, automobiles, and lasers. It has been our experience that most, if not all, of the attention is given to such hardware, machines, or tangible items. However, if we revisit the definition of technology ("the systematic application of scientific or other organized knowledge to practical tasks"), we will see that such a "hardware" view is not the whole story. As brought out in this definition, a critical part of technology is the *process* of applying knowledge. Using the bridge analogy of Figure 1.3, technology should be viewed not only as the tangible bridge itself but also as the bridging process. To fully comprehend technology and its ramifications, you must come to understand and appreciate that the hardware of technology is typically the result or product of the process of technology; that is, the process controls the resultant product.

In this text we will introduce you to hardware such as the computer, the overhead projector, the VCR, the CD player, and so on, but more importantly, we will show you how the effectiveness of these products is controlled by the principles underlying the instructional plan and how that process dictates what hardware should be selected or developed, when and how it should be used, and why it should be effective, efficient, and appealing. From this point on, do not limit yourself by thinking only of the technology hardware; think also of the principles and processes that direct the use of the hardware, since this is where the true advances have been generated.

tional technology translates and applies basic research on human learning to produce methods (processes) and tools (products) that teachers and students can use to increase learning effectiveness. It isn't just the resultant hardware. (See Chapter 14 for additional insights into the background and history of instructional technology.)

In this text the focus will be on the educationally relevant processes and products of technology available to teachers and students, how these processes and products are effectively selected, and when and under what conditions they are best employed. As demonstrated in the example taken from the space industry, technology may be in the form of tangible equipment (e.g., overhead projectors, computers) or less tangible processes and procedures (e.g., cognitive learning strategies, media selection strategies). In a general sense, instructional

technology has been directed at the processes and hardware used to *produce* instructional materials (i.e., those used by the teacher to design an instructional experience; those used by the learner to prepare to learn new materials) and the processes and hardware used to *present* the instructional materials (i.e., those means used to convey and present the to-be-learned material and experiences to the learner).

Just as craftspersons view their tools as being necessary for the successful completion of many tasks, so too the student and teacher must see the use of available tools that have been derived from instructional research and applied through the bridge of technology as needed within the field of education. This text will explore these two uses of instructional technology and demonstrate how, when, and why they are relevant to both learners and teachers as they go about planning, implementing, and evaluating the learning process. It is our desire to show that just as the cabinetmaker can increase his or her level of performance through the correct selection and use of trade tools, students and teachers can elevate their level of performance with the proper use of tools designed for the improvement of human learning. As in other professions, these tools may be tangible equipment such as computers, cellular telephones, or even voice-activated videotape recorders; however, they also include less noted—but equally important—process technologies, such as lesson plans and instructional techniques.

Questions pertaining to the role of technology within the learning process should also be addressed. These questions (Table 1.4) can help us focus on how technology and its processes and products can be used during the planning, implementation, and evaluation phases of learning and teaching.

LEARNING AND INSTRUCTIONAL TECHNOLOGY: POTENTIAL CONTRIBUTIONS OF INSTRUCTIONAL DESIGN, MEDIA, AND COMPUTING

As outlined in the previous discussion, instructional technology can and should play a key role in the learning process. Based on research in human learn-ing, communications, and related fields, technology can provide products and procedures to facilitate the teaching and learning process. Instructional technology revolves around three areas of study:

- instructional design
- instructional media
- instructional computing

Not only do all of these make important individual contributions, but also they can be successfully inte-grated when working toward the common goal of learner achievement.

Instructional Design

Instructional design has been defined as "the sys-tematic process of translating principles of learning and instruction into plans for instructional materi-als and activities" (Smith & Ragan, 1993, p. 2). The emphasis within instructional design is on creating a plan for developing instructional materials that increases the learning of an individual. Reigeluth (1983) compared this task with that of the architect. The architect produces a blueprint or plan that effectively integrates the needs of those who will purchase and use the facility, the environment in

Table 1.4 Questions to ask about technology within each learning phase

Planning

- In what ways can instructional technology effectively impact how a student addresses a learning task?
- In what ways can instructional technology effectively impact how a teacher designs and creates instructional materials?
- How can instructional technology be utilized by students and/or teachers to improve learner attention and topic motivation?
- How can instructional technology improve the efficiency of student learning and/or teacher preparation?

Implementation

- In what ways can technology assist and impact the manner in which the instruction is experienced by the student?
- In what ways can technology be employed to increase teacher efficiency dur-ing the delivery of instruction?

Evaluation

- How can instructional technology be used to determine the degree of student learning that has occurred?
- How can instructional technology be used to generate teacher and student feedback?
- In what ways can instructional technology be used to measure the effective-ness, efficiency, and appeal of the implemented instructional materials?

which it will be placed, the costs involved, the appropriate materials, and other design specifications for functionality, safety, and aesthetics. Similarly, instructional designers produce a plan for the development of instructional materials based on analyses of the learners, the situation, and the task to be learned. These designers focus on the principles of learning and how they can be incorporated.

Although a builder may attempt to build (and may at times even succeed in building) a structure without the use of the architect's plans or blueprints, several problems may be encountered that could have been avoided had a plan been used. For example, the walls may be in the wrong location, electrical outlets forgotten or misplaced, or improper materials purchased. As with any plan, the major benefit of instructional design is the guidance it gives to the individuals developing instructional materials. By following the plan, a reliable result should occur. This does not mean that all instruction should be designed based on a single set of plans (like a subdivision of one-style homes) but rather that specific principles can be used to solve different instructional problems and to produce unique answers in a variety of situations.

In summary, the potential contributions of instructional design for teachers and learners include

- the overall instructional plan—what should be included and how the components should be arranged

- various analysis techniques and methods that help determine both the current skill level of the learner and the level needed to accomplish the task

- analysis techniques to determine what the information to be learned is and what should receive the focus of the instruction

- a repertoire of strategies, tactics, and techniques, based on principles of learning and communication, that can be used to increase learning by the student (these may include when and why to use examples, analogies, or summaries, or even when it would be most effective to use repetition versus other forms of memory aids)

- strategies for sequencing instructional materials so that the learner gets the proper amount of information when needed (these strategies may be directed at a single lesson about a specific topic or may be at a more global level that involves a set of curriculum materials)

- an emphasis on evaluation to ensure that what was completed and accomplished was attribut-

able to the instructional materials (this ensures that the materials are effective and efficient and appropriate for the students' overall learning)

This text explains these contributions of instructional design and indicates how the learner and teacher can benefit from knowledge of and use of its principles.

Power of the Plan

The overall **instructional plan** plays a critical role in directing the selection and use of all other tools within the learning environment. Just as the cabinetmaker uses a plan to determine what materials and woodworking tools to select and use, so too the teacher and the learner should use a plan to determine which approach, technique, and media to use; how and when to present specific sets of information; and when additional information is required.

Even though the benefits of the plan focus on giving the teacher direction in the selection of materials, the plan should not be perceived as a rigid structure that dictates regimented, systematic procedures written in stone. Whenever learning is required, different types of learners, tasks, and situations all interact, requiring flexibility. The plan provides a means to review possible alternative solutions to instructional problems, assess their potential, and then confidently select the best alternatives. If and when those alternatives do not produce desired levels of learning, the plan can be revised and additional alternatives can be selected. The goal is for the best alternatives to be selected, and if and when those do not succeed the next-best alternatives can be chosen. Robinson (1981) noted that expert anglers usually outperform those of lesser ability, not because they know the best alternative bait for a given fish on a specific day, but because they also know the second- and third-best alternatives. Similarly, the power of the instructional plan is that it suggests alternatives and a means whereby those alternatives can be investigated and evaluated before time and money are invested in the development of the final products.

Instructional Media

Instructional media are "the different ways and means by which information can be delivered to a learner" (Heinich et al., 1993, p. 5). In one case the selected medium may be a video, in another it may be a teacher delivering the instruction, and in still another it may be the use of an overhead transparency. Each medium represents a means of presenting information to the learner. Important questions involving the manner in which information is delivered include the following:

- What forms of media are available?
- What impact, if any, do the different forms of media have on student learning?
- Under what conditions can this potential impact be altered?
- How is each media format most effectively selected and used?

When investigating the answers to these and similar questions, research in the areas of perception, cognition, communication, and instructional theory comes to the forefront. For every learner and teacher, the central concerns are how information can be transmitted and what happens to the information once it has been received by the individual learner. Research shows that various forms of media and their respective selection and utilization processes directly impact what the learner perceives and how information is retained and recalled (Kozma, 1991).

Instructional media for teachers and learners have the potential to

- present the materials in a manner readily perceived, used, and assimilated by the learner (e.g., a video can clearly illustrate how cells divide in the early stages of reproduction)
- deliver materials in a teacher-independent manner, thus allowing students some independence and control over how much of the material they will experience and when (e.g., students can rewind or fast-forward portions of an audiotape to match their own needs for learning)
- allow learners to experience the materials through various senses (e.g., seeing the projected pictures, reading the textual materials, and hearing a verbal description of the same content)
- provide learners with repeated and varied experiences with subject matter in order that they construct their own understanding or meaning
- gain and maintain learners' attention to the subject matter
- motivate students toward some goal
- present information in a manner that otherwise could not be experienced by the individual learner (e.g., events can be speeded up or slowed down, objects can be decreased in size [e.g., the universe] or increased in size [e.g., an atom])
- accommodate varying sizes of audiences in an effective and efficient manner

As will be pointed out in Chapter 4, instructional media are generally viewed as tangible presentation tools such as overhead transparencies, real objects, slides, videotapes, and computer programs. Throughout the text we will emphasize the importance of the correct selection and utilization of these various forms of media. It is critical to keep in mind that no matter how good the medium, learning will be hindered if the message is poorly designed. Likewise, if the message is well designed but delivered in such a fashion that the learner can't understand or interpret it correctly, similar poor outcomes will result. For most of us it is not hard to think of past learning situations in which either a good message was unusable because of the poor or inadequate manner in which it was delivered (e.g., an outdated film of poor technical quality) or a well-delivered message was found to be worthless because of a lack of attention to how the instructional message was planned, structured, and developed (e.g., a fancy computer math program that put in lots of bells, whistles, and graphics but neglected to give feedback at critical junctures). In both cases, learning was inhibited or not achieved.

Instructional Computing

The computer has made a tremendous impact throughout our society, and that impact has been particularly strong within the field of education. **Instructional computing** is defined as the use of the computer in the design, development, delivery, and evaluation of instruction. The computer's power within education revolves around its versatility as both a production tool and a presentation tool. Although it is a form of media and should be considered as such, the computer's capability to be *both* a presentation tool and a production tool sets it apart from other media formats (e.g., slides, videos). For example, in a single day a classroom computer may be used to write a creative short story about a character from the Wild West, to link with a telecommunications system that allows one to monitor the current shape and velocity of a tropical storm in the Caribbean, to enter and store scores from the last social studies assignment, and to look up information on John F. Kennedy and listen to parts of major speeches he made while in office. These examples illustrate the power of the computer and how it can be manipulated and used in the teaching and learning process.

Because of its current impact and tremendous potential, it is imperative that classroom teachers understand the power of the computer and how it can be used and adapted for learning. Throughout this text, sections are devoted to the explanation of how the computer can be used, when and why it is a valuable asset, and how to integrate it in the classroom to ensure the maximum effect on teacher performance and student learning.

Instructional computing for teachers and learners has the potential to

- enhance the quality of instructional materials using the electronic capabilities of the computer
- reduce the time required to design, produce, and reproduce instructional materials
- increase the overall effectiveness of instructional materials through enhanced presentations
- combine graphics, video, audio, and textual forms of media into a single integrated instructional presentation
- store and quickly access huge amounts of information and data
- communicate with other computers at both near and distant locations
- function as a learner in which the student programs the computer to complete a task or solve a problem
- function as an instructional expert in which the computer makes decisions about levels of student learning, suggests media and experiences needed by the students, and then selects and presents those missing learning experiences

Integrating Instructional Design, Media, and Computing

The goal of instructional technology is to bring together the tools, potential research applications, and contributions from the areas of design, media, and computing in order that the teacher's efforts and the students' learning are both maximized. Reaching this goal requires the classroom teacher to have a basic understanding of each area of study, of what each has to offer, and, most importantly, of how they are interrelated. The extent to which teaching and learning can be impacted is determined by the degree to which these individual tools are related and used interdependently.

In many cases individuals take one course to learn how to design and develop instructional materials, another course to learn about different forms of media and proper utilization techniques, and still another to learn how to use the computer in the classroom. Although such a disjointed approach may give students a solid background in all of the individual areas of study, it may limit their ability to see how each can be used to expand the effectiveness of the others. We feel that such an approach, while better than not having any courses, can be improved by emphasizing the relationships among those individual areas of study. It is only through this integrated approach that the more difficult problems of human learning can be identified and solved by the classroom teacher. Through such an integrated approach the teacher should readily see how the computer can contribute to the design of the instructional plan and the development of the instructional materials, how the design directs the selection of media, and, likewise, how the utilization of the media impacts the interpretation and acceptance of the designed instructional message. Although instructional design, media, and computing can be studied independently, when they are viewed as an interrelated whole their potential worth for teacher and student alike is magnified. The scenario below illustrates the benefits of interrelating these functions.

INTEGRATING TECHNOLOGY
One Teacher's Story

We'd like to introduce you to a very special high school teacher, Ms. Janette Moreno. Ms. Moreno has been teaching high school Spanish for 8 years and has earned a reputation as a challenging, stimulating, and enjoyable teacher. What we find particularly remarkable about Ms. Moreno is the constant effort she makes to keep her courses exciting and effective. She continually evaluates her students' interest and performance in her courses and seeks innovative ways to improve those areas that seem weak. Over the last few years, Ms. Moreno has turned more and more to the instructional technology literature for ideas regarding course upgrades. We'd like to share with you some of the things we have learned from Ms. Moreno and describe how she has gradually integrated a number of new technologies into her Spanish Conversation course. We'll discuss some of the benefits that have resulted, as well as some of the difficulties she has encountered along the way. We think Ms. Moreno has a lot to offer her Spanish students, and we think you will enjoy, and benefit from, her story

Ms. Janette Moreno is teaching students in her Spanish Conversation class.

as well. For this reason we have decided to include parts of her story throughout this text, specifically as they relate to topics being discussed in each chapter.

Ms. Moreno learned, in her preservice courses, about the importance of establishing learning goals for her students and of planning and preparing ways to help students achieve those goals. So whenever Ms. Moreno begins planning a new course, one of the first things she does is to ask herself some questions: What should students be able to do when they finish this course? How can I assess whether they have accomplished these goals? To determine what students should know at the end of a course, Ms. Moreno gathers information from a variety of sources: personal experiences, other teachers, the designated textbook, literature in the field, the required curriculum, and the students themselves. After determining what the students should take away from the course, she spends time identifying the level at which they are entering the course. What are students' current skills and knowledge? What level of motivation do they bring to the course?

It didn't take long for Ms. Moreno to realize that there was a critical need for individualized instruction in her language courses. Students are never all at the same level when they enter a class. Each student brings unique strengths and weaknesses to the course and works at his or her own pace through the selected materials and activities. This seemed particularly true in Ms. Moreno's Spanish Conversation course. Students needed multiple opportunities for practicing conversational skills in the context of person-to-person interchanges, followed by accurate feedback, in order to build authentic conversational skills. How could a single

teacher manage such diverse individual needs in a class of 25 to 30 students that met for only 55 minutes a day?

Ms. Moreno admits that this initially posed a major dilemma for her. She had tried a buddy system during her first couple years of teaching, but she found that peers often provided poor role models and/or inappropriate feedback. She realized that she could not tackle the whole gamut of "conversational skills" with one course revision, so she looked for ways to increase students' word-recognition skills first. She developed some short audiotaped lessons that students could listen to using small recorders and earphones. These lessons weren't fancy or flashy, but they gave students the opportunity to hear a wide variety of words and phrases being enunciated correctly. Later, students began recording their own voices so they could compare their enunciations with hers.

Ms. Moreno might have been satisfied with the benefits realized from these small changes, yet one of her students, a few terms ago, mentioned how helpful it would be if she could see the person who was talking. Ms. Moreno asked a fellow teacher, Mr. Bauer, if he would be willing to help her experiment with the school's camcorder to videotape some of her lessons. It wasn't too much later that the students started videotaping each other's Spanish conversations and playing them back to evaluate their own performances. These weren't polished productions, but the kids acted as though they were on Broadway. They begged to take the videotapes home to show them off to their families,

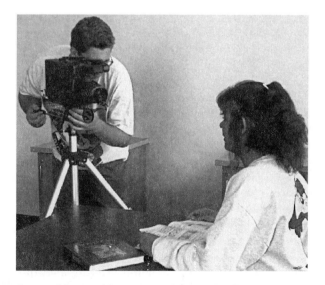

Some of Janette Moreno's students in the Spanish Conversation class are taping conversations for later review and evaluation.

and, not surprisingly, the quality of students' conversations grew by leaps and bounds. Ms. Moreno felt pleased with this first major change. Students were learning good conversational skills, and they were excited about it!

After students' enunciations became clearer, Ms. Moreno decided to try to improve their *range* of vocabulary use. Specified course objectives indicated that students should leave her course with a command of words beyond the basic first-year words. Flashcards offered a fairly simple means to increase students' vocabulary skills, but students found them boring and Ms. Moreno thought they were pretty inefficient. Following the advice of the school's technology coordinator, she decided to try a computer software program that a previous teacher had ordered. This particular drill-and-practice program used an arcade theme to make learning vocabulary humorous and stimulating. Different games within the program allowed students to work at increasingly difficult levels. The first level simply presented a word and asked students to recognize the proper translation. Other levels required students to identify synonyms, to find correct responses to questions, or to arrange words into proper sentences. This particular program allowed Ms. Moreno to periodically update the lists of words included so that even the easier levels could become more advanced. By utilizing a sophisticated review pool, the computer could replace a newly mastered word with an unfamiliar one. After a specific time period, the computer reintroduced a previous word so that students would not forget it.

When Ted Mellette worked as Ms. Moreno's student teacher last year, he asked if he could create a hypertext program out of these vocabulary words. He had taken a course in hypermedia and was anxious to use some of his new skills. The advantage to putting all of the vocabulary into a hypertext format was that it allowed specific words and phrases to be linked to other information in the program. For example, when students were given a word they didn't know, they could use the mouse to click on the word and immediately access a definition, a translation, or an example of the word in context. If the students already knew the presented word, they had the option to continue on in the program without accessing this additional information. This way they controlled the information they accessed.

After Ted got the basic hypertext program debugged and running smoothly, he extended the program to include written paragraphs. Now, as the students read through a passage, specific words are highlighted, indicating that additional information can be obtained about those words. If they aren't sure about one of the new words being introduced, they can click on that word to get a definition, synonym, or example. Recently, Ms. Moreno has been thinking about creating an oral version of the words within this hypertext program by incorporating the computer's audio digitizer, but this is still in the works. She is excited about the possibility, however, knowing that conversation depends on clear speaking skills as much as on extensive vocabulary skills.

One of the things we admire most about Ms. Moreno is her continual striving for improvement. Even after she finds an acceptable solution to an instructional dilemma, she continues to search for new and better ways to help her students learn. Using course goals as her basis, she creates an instructional plan to direct her choice of learning activities and guide the selection of appropriate media for developing and implementing those activities. Periodic course evaluations provide information regarding students' perceptions of the strengths and weaknesses of her choices. Ms. Moreno reminds us of a watchdog—constantly looking for any indications that something might be amiss and then taking immediate measures to thwart potential problems. Ms. Moreno's Spanish Conversation course was not created overnight in one grand moment of insight. It evolved gradually as additional information was gained from students, colleagues, and other educators. As you will see throughout this text, that evolution is still occurring to this day.

SUMMARY

A number of key concepts are presented in this chapter. First, learning is defined as a change or potential to change in one's level of skill or knowledge, and it is of central concern for both students and teachers. The text emphasizes that learning can be facilitated through the design and use of effective, efficient, and appealing instruction.

Second, learning is difficult to measure and to consistently achieve because of the inherent differences in learners, content, and contexts. Facilitating learning requires an active knowledge of a variety of tools and techniques plus an understanding of how, when, and why they should be appropriately used. Technology, and particularly instructional technology, provides not only tangible tools (e.g., computers, overhead projectors, videos, CD players) for the delivery of important instruction, but also effective guidelines for planning, implementing, and evaluating instruction.

Third, learners, teachers, and technology all play key roles in the learning process. Furthermore, each of these roles shifts as the instructional focus changes from planning, to implementing, to evaluating instruction.

REFLECTIVE QUESTIONS AND ACTIVITIES

1. Reflect on things you have learned in the past and note the impact of the technologies that were used. What planning was involved? What media were used? What went especially well (e.g., What did you grasp from the very beginning?)? What other methods could have been as effective, if not better?

2. If you were asked to give a talk (e.g., on the care of pets) to a class of third graders, what questions would you ask yourself during the planning, implementation, and evaluation phases of this presentation?

3. Convince a skeptic of the benefits of reflecting on and evaluating instructional materials. Explain why this is such a needed endeavor.

4. Keep a notebook/diary for the next two weeks on the instructional technologies that you encounter. Note the type of instruction, how it was planned and sequenced, what type of media was used in the delivery, and what forms of evalua-

tion you believe were used. Also note the level of effectiveness you felt the instruction achieved.

INTEGRATION AND SYNTHESIS

This chapter sets the stage for what is to come by introducing the planning, implementation, and evaluation phases of learning as the instructional model used throughout the other sections of this text. In particular, we have highlighted the role of instructional technology as a bridge between research and theory on human learning and its application to practical learning situations. Chapter 2 explores these theoretical foundations in greater depth. Chapters 3 and 4 then give a broad picture of the different media and instructional approaches available to both teacher and student. This information serves as the foundation on which the remaining chapters are built.

SUGGESTED READINGS

Driscoll, M. P. (1994). *Psychology of learning for instruction.* Boston: Allyn & Bacon. (Chapter 1)

Kemp, J. E., Morrison, G. R., & Ross, S. M. (1994). *Designing effective instruction.* Englewood Cliffs, NJ: Merrill/Prentice Hall. (Chapter 1)

Seels, B. B., & Richey, R. C. (1994). *Instructional technology: The definition and domains of the field.* Washington, DC: Association for Educational Communications and Technology. (Chapter 1)

Chapter 2

Theory into Application

KEY WORDS AND CONCEPTS

Instruction	Encoding
Theory	Retrieval
Learning theory	Focusing question
Antecedent	Highlighting
Behavior	Analogy
Consequence	Mnemonic
Contingencies	Communication
Instructional program	Filter
Frame	Interference
Attention	System

OUTCOMES

After reading and studying this chapter, you will be able to:

- Define *instruction,* including its essential characteristics.
- Define *theory.*
- Discuss the role of the instructional expert from three theoretical perspectives on learning.
- Discuss the transactional nature of communication.
- Define *system* and provide an example.
- Diagram an example of an instructional system.
- Describe an instructional application of communication theory and general systems theory.

■ INTRODUCTION

Cynthia, a friend of ours, has been a teacher for a number of years. Over lunch one day the conversation turned naturally to the subject of teaching. We mentioned that a lot had been written about educational theory over the years and asked her what theoretical principles she found most useful. Cynthia laughed and said, "The only thing I remember about any theory is that I'm supposed to bribe the kids with candy." She went on to explain that in the "real world" teachers have too much to do to spend much time thinking about theory. "In the first place," she said, "there are so many theories out there that it's difficult to keep track of them, much less make sense of them all. In the second place, the theories are so abstract and artificial that they don't seem relevant to what goes on in my classroom. They just don't seem to offer much in the way of practical advice."

Cynthia has raised a legitimate question about the practical relevance of theory: Is it important for teachers to understand theory? Initially you might think the answer is "No." After all, teachers are practitioners who are rightly concerned with what happens in real classrooms with real students. And as our friend has said, theory often seems too abstract and artificial to be applicable to the practical concerns of classroom life. In addition, if instructional technology serves as a bridge between theory and practice, as described in Chapter 1, is it necessary for teachers to understand both theory *and* practice? Given the variety of duties that fill teachers' days, isn't it enough that they know the tools and techniques available to them and use those tools and techniques effectively? (This is, after all,

what the rest of the book is about.) Is it really necessary to take the time to study theory?

We recognize that teachers often work under significant time constraints. However, we also believe that understanding theory has *practical* value that will more than compensate for the time spent studying it. As illustrated in Table 2.1, every profession, including teaching, is built on a foundation of theoretical knowledge that allows practitioners to respond adaptively and flexibly to the unique characteristics of a particular situation.

This chapter describes the theoretical foundations for the practice of teaching. There are two essential points to keep in mind throughout the chapter. First, the purpose of teaching is learning, and the teacher's primary role in the learning process is that of an instructional expert. Second, theory informs practice and, as a result, helps teachers effectively fulfill their roles as instructional experts.

We first describe the nature of instruction and teachers' primary role in it. Then, for the major portion of the chapter, we focus on several of the building blocks that make up the theoretical foundation for teaching practice: learning theory, communication theory, and general systems theory. ■

THE NATURE OF INSTRUCTION

Chapter 1 defined learning as a change in human performance or performance potential that results from practice or other experience and endures over time. As indicated earlier, learning occurs in a variety of situations and can be the result of either deliberate effort or unintended circumstance.

In simple terms, **instruction** refers to that which is done to help students learn. More specifically, instruction refers to the

- selection and arrangement of information, activities, approaches, and media
- by an instructional expert
- to help students
- meet predetermined learning goals.

People—adults as well as children—learn through instruction in a wide variety of situations. But while students, goals, teaching techniques, and media may differ, the essential similarity in all instruction is a deliberate effort to help a group of students learn. Consider the differences and the essential similarities in the following examples:

Learning to create plural words. Third graders are learning how to change words into their plural

Table 2.1   Examples of professions and their
theoretical foundations

Profession	Theoretical Foundations
Architecture	Materials
	Mechanics
	Visual design
Medicine	Biochemistry
	Anatomy
	Phyciology
Teaching	Learning theory
	Communication theory
	General systems theory

forms. The teacher gives students a set of rules (e.g., when a word ends in "ss" or "sh," add "es") and shows examples of these rules. A workbook gives the students practice exercises to do, either in class or as homework assignments. Periodically, students are given tests that gradually increase in difficulty. After each practice exercise or test, students are given feedback so they can see how well they're doing. The teacher also uses the feedback to monitor students' progress, prescribing additional practice when needed.

Learning to interview job applicants. Because of the Americans with Disabilities Act (ADA), recruiters for companies must change the way they interview job applicants. The goal of a company-sponsored workshop is to learn how to conduct legal application interviews. A workshop packet gives recruiters information about the background and requirements of the ADA, along with suggested interviewing guidelines. During the workshop, recruiters are asked to critique a sequence of videotaped interviews and identify those questions that are allowed and not allowed by the ADA. Finally, in a series of role plays, each recruiter interviews applicants who may or may not be disabled. Each role play is followed by feedback from the workshop facilitator and other recruiters that identifies the strengths and weaknesses of the recruiter's interviewing techniques.

Learning to use word-processing computer software. A computer owner has just purchased a word-processing program for a home computer. The goal is to learn how to use the software. In addition to a manual, the software comes with a tutorial on a diskette. After following the procedures in the manual to load the software onto the computer's hard drive, the owner starts the tutorial. The tutorial combines text information, demonstrations, and exercises shown on the computer screen. Each demonstration shows a new function of the word processor and is followed by an exercise in which the owner is asked to use that function. The exercises build on one another to allow the owner to use the functions of the word processor to create, change, save, and print various types of documents. The owner works through the tutorial gradually, going back over functions that aren't clear the first time through.

As shown in Table 2.2, these situations appear to be quite different. The students, learning goals, instructional approaches, and media differ in each situation. However, each situation also involves a deliberate effort to help a group of students learn. For the third graders, the deliberate effort took the form of a series of classroom and workbook activities intended to help them learn how to create plural words. For the recruiters, the deliberate effort took the form of a combination of videotaped and live role plays intended to help them learn how to interview job applicants. For the computer owner, the deliberate effort took the form of an on-line tutorial intended to help the owner learn how to use the new word-processing software. So, while the situations differ in some ways, in each case information, instructional approaches, and media were selected, arranged, and presented to particular students in a way intended to help them achieve learning goals that were specified in advance.

These situations are similar in one other, less obvious, way: the instruction was invariably the responsibility of a teacher functioning as an instructional expert. The teacher's role in implementing instruction varies. For example, in the third graders' language lesson, the teacher is directly involved

Table 2.2   A comparison of three instructional situations

Students	Learning Goal	Teaching Technique	Media
Third graders	Creating plural words	Demonstration	Print
Professional recruiters	Interviewing techniques	Simulation	Videotape
Computer owner	Word processing	Tutorial	Computer

with the students in many ways: presenting information, guiding their practice, giving them feedback, and monitoring their progress. In the interviewing workshop, the teacher is again directly involved with the students but in a somewhat different role, serving primarily as a facilitator of the discussion rather than as a presenter of information. In the word-processing tutorial, in contrast, it is the computer that is presenting the information, providing practice exercises, and giving feedback.

However, while the teacher is not always responsible for implementing the instruction, he or she is responsible for planning the instruction. This involves two closely related tasks: first, accurately diagnosing the learning needs of particular students, and second, prescribing the instructional techniques and activities that will help students meet their diagnosed learning needs. This diagnosis and prescription seems clear in the third graders' language lesson. For example, the teacher determined the rules to be included in the lesson, identified examples of those rules, and selected workbook exercises for the students to complete. It is only somewhat less obvious in the interviewing workshop. For example, the teacher (facilitator) selected the videotaped interviews for the recruiters to critique, selected the role-play scenarios, and guided the feedback, identifying the strengths and weaknesses of individual recruiters. Even in the case of the word-processing tutorial, it was an "instructional expert" who diagnosed what the "students" (the computer owners) needed to know about the software, who prescribed a tutorial as the most effective way to present the instruction, who developed the information, examples, and exercises to be included in the tutorial, and who will probably evaluate the effectiveness or usefulness of the tutorial.

The teacher's primary role, then, is that of an instructional expert, planning instruction to meet students' learning needs. The foundation for that expertise, just as in any other profession, is theory.

THEORETICAL FOUNDATIONS
Introduction

A **theory** is a set of related principles explaining the cause-and-effect relationships among events (Richey, 1986). As observations about causes and their effects accumulate, a theory is suggested to explain those observations. Based on that explanation, the theory makes predictions in the form of "If x, then y" statements that can be tested, resulting in more cause-and-effect observations. These new observations may verify the theory or require modifications to the theory. In either case, the result is additional predictions, which can also be tested, resulting in additional observations, leading to further verification or modification of the theory, and so on. As an example, the theory of evolution was Charles Darwin's attempt to explain the physiological differences he noticed among the birds on a remote island in the Pacific Ocean (Asimov, 1966). He hypothesized that the differences were caused by "natural selection," referring to an increased capacity for survival that individual birds had gained from characteristics they had acquired by chance. As another example, the theory of immunity to disease was Edward Jenner's attempt to explain why milkmaids in early-19th-century England were less likely to catch smallpox than most other people (Asimov, 1966). Jenner noticed that the milkmaids were *more* likely to catch cowpox, a similar but relatively minor disease. He hypothesized that the cowpox virus caused the body to develop a natural immunity to the disease that also protected the person from the smallpox virus.

That's what a theory is. But the question is, *What is the practical value of theory?* It's important to note that a theory both explains and predicts. Particularly because of its ability to predict, theory informs practice (Driscoll, 1994). This means that theoretical principles can be translated into practical guidelines. This is important because *effective* professional practice requires more than knowing what tools and techniques are available and how to use them. The hallmark of professional practice is the ability to select and use those tools and techniques in order to create a unique solution for a unique problem, that is, to devise a solution that meets the demands of the particular situation. This requires the flexibility and adaptability that come from understanding at the deeper level of theoretical principle rather than at the more superficial level of technique.

Theory informs practice in every profession. For example, physicians routinely provide vaccinations as protection against infectious diseases. The relevant principle from biology is that the body naturally develops antibodies to many of the diseases it encounters. As a result, vaccines contain weakened or dead organisms that cause the disease. The vaccine is injected, and our bodies develop antibodies that protect us when we are exposed to the disease at a later time. This is what happens when we get flu shots or have our children vaccinated against diseases such as smallpox, diphtheria, and whooping cough. As another example, architects routinely design buildings and bridges that sway back and forth like trees in the wind. The relevant principle from physics is that a flexible structure is often stronger than a rigid structure. As a result, architects often place buildings and bridges on shock absorbers or other devices that allow them to flex under the stress of earthquakes or high winds.

Similarly, theory informs practice in the classroom. For example, Chapter 1 described Ms. Moreno's high school Spanish Conversation class, in which she sought better ways to help students acquire the ability to correctly pronounce a growing repertoire of Spanish words. The problem was that when students practiced with one another their progress was limited or hindered because of the poor feedback they gave one another. The relevant principle from learning theory is that students learn best when they have frequent practice followed by immediate and *accurate* feedback. Applying this principle, Ms. Moreno devised a number of activities to encourage students to practice frequently and to provide them with accurate feedback about their pronunciation. At first, audiotape was used to allow students to compare their pronunciations with hers. This was changed to videotape to provide students with more complete information about the physical aspects of forming the words. The point is that, while new and better learning activities were devised, they were invariably based on the same theoretical principle: students learn best when they receive immediate and accurate feedback.

In summary, theory is not simply a collection of abstractions that have no relevance to the real world of practice. Theory has *practical* value for the teacher. As in other professions, the principles that form the theoretical foundation for teaching can be translated into guidelines that help teachers select and use the practical tools and techniques provided by instructional technology. Our task for the remainder of this chapter, then, is to describe the theories that inform instructional practice and to describe the practical guidelines provided by those theories.

Before we begin, however, there are two caveats. First, teaching, like other professions, is built on a foundation that is made up of many building blocks (refer back to Table 2.1). We haven't tried to include all of the theories that inform teaching practice. That would make this book much too long. Instead, we have selected three theories (or, more accurately, three categories of theory) that we believe inform teaching practice in essential ways. One theory, learning theory, is an obvious choice. The other two, communication theory and general systems theory, have been selected because they inform teaching practice in ways that are as impor-

tant as, though less obvious than, the ways learning theory informs teaching practice.

Second, our purpose here is *not* to provide a definitive statement of any theory. This is a practical book, and lengthy descriptions of theory are beyond its scope. Our intention here is to provide a highlight reel rather than a feature film. We want to outline some of the key features of these theories, with an emphasis on how they inform instructional practice. Thus, each theory will be described briefly in terms of its growth and development, its central principles, and its practical applications.

Learning Theory

We will begin with learning theory because it is the cornerstone of instructional practice: the way we teach is governed by what we know about how people learn. Learning has been defined as a change in human performance or performance potential. A theory has been defined as a set of related principles explaining the cause-and-effect relationships among events. A **learning theory**, then, is a set of related principles explaining changes in human performance or performance potential in terms of the causes of those changes.

But we can't simply describe learning theory as a single entity. Learning has been studied for hundreds (perhaps thousands) of years, and many theories have been proposed to explain the learning process (see Driscoll, 1994; Ormrod, 1995; Schunk, 1991). Of the many theories that have been presented over the years, we have selected three broad theoretical perspectives: behavioral, information processing, and constructivist. These perspectives represent major trends or themes in the way learning is conceptualized and provide some distinctly different practical guidelines for instructional practice.

It's important to note that these perspectives are presented in roughly historical order rather than their order of importance. Each perspective is alive and well today and can claim adherents within both the population of theoreticians and the population of practitioners.

The Behavioral Perspective

To begin our discussion of the behavioral perspective, imagine Ms. Moreno's Spanish class. The students are working at computer terminals on a vocabulary lesson. The computer presents students with an increasingly difficult series of sentences in Spanish. Each sentence contains a blank space, and students are asked to use the computer keyboard to enter a Spanish word or phrase that fits into the sentence. For example:

¿_____ te llamas?
¿_____ vive María?
¿_____ Ud. de Mexico, señora?

After a student enters a response, the computer gives him or her feedback about the appropriateness of the word or phrase he or she has selected. The computer allows for a number of "correct" responses for each sentence. When the response is "correct," students move on to the next sentence. When the response is "incorrect," the computer gives them a hint regarding how to translate the sentence and asks again for a response. As before, a "correct" response leads to the next sentence. However, if the response is again "incorrect" the computer translates the sentence and provides several appropriate responses.

Why does this instructional technique work? In what ways is it informed by theory? Let's consider the development, principles, and practices of the behavioral perspective and then revisit this classroom.

Background.   Behaviorism began in the early part of the 20th century with the argument that "the subject matter of human psychology is the behavior *or activities of the human being*" (Watson, 1924, p. 3) rather than the mental phenomena, such as consciousness, that had been the subject of study during the latter part of the 19th century. In education, behaviorism is most closely associated with the work of B. F. Skinner. In contrast to other forms of behaviorism (e.g., Pavlov's classical conditioning), Skinner focused on the voluntary, deliberate behaviors that he believed made up most of an individual's behavioral repertoire. These behaviors, which he termed "operants" because they are the individual's way of operating on, or influencing, the environment, are affected by what follows them, as well as what precedes them. Understanding this type of behavior, therefore, involves understanding all of the environmental events surrounding it—what comes after, as well as what comes before. Skinner developed his principles of "operant conditioning" during the 1930s and began applying them to an increasingly broad array of human problems, including education, during the 1950s. He believed that, by applying the "technology of teaching" (Skinner, 1968), "the school system of any large American city could be so redesigned, at little or no additional cost, that students would come to school and apply themselves to their work with a mini-

mum of punitive coercion and, with very rare exceptions, learn to read with reasonable ease, express themselves well in speech and writing, and solve a fair range of mathematical problems" (Skinner, 1984, p. 948).

Theoretical Principles.   The primary focus of the behavioral perspective is on behavior and the influence of the external environment in shaping the individual's behavior. Learning is described as a change in the probability of a particular behavior occurring in a particular situation (Ertmer & Newby, 1993). Since this probability can't be measured directly, it is inferred from the frequency of the behavior.

An A → B → C model can be used to explain how behaviorists view the learning process (Woolfolk, 1990). Briefly stated, the environment presents an **antecedent** (A) that prompts a **behavior** (B) that is followed by some **consequence** (C) that then determines whether the behavior will occur again. Learning is said to have occurred when the student consistently behaves in the desired way in response to the specific antecedent, that is, when A consistently results in B.

According to Skinner, instruction refers to the "arrangement of contingencies under which students learn"; students learn without instruction, but instruction provides "special contingencies which expedite learning" (1968, p. 64). These **contingencies** refer to the environmental conditions that shape an individual's behavior. There are two types of contingencies: antecedents, or what comes before the behavior; and consequences, or what comes after the behavior.

These contingencies are arranged and presented to students in the form of an **instructional program** (Bell-Gredler, 1986), made up of a series of **frames.** In generic terms, each frame presents students with some information and a question or problem (A) that requires a response (B), which is then followed by feedback (C) based on the response. In explaining the value of the instructional program, Skinner stressed that it neither replaces the teacher nor depersonalizes instruction. Instead, he argued (1968) that a well-designed program allows teachers to concentrate on those aspects of the learning situation that are "uniquely human": diagnosing learning needs and providing encouragement, support, and guidance.

Instructional programs have taken many forms over the years, from the simple teaching machines and programmed textbooks used during the 1950s to the much more complex computer programs that are common today.

Practical Applications.   The emphasis in the behavioral perspective is on the role of the external environment as the primary determinant of behavior. Instruction, then, refers to the environmental conditions that are arranged and presented to students. From the behavioral perspective, the primary responsibility of the instructional expert is to identify and sequence the contingencies (antecedents and consequences) that will help students learn. In order to carry out this responsibility, the behavioral perspective suggests that teachers follow certain guidelines. First, teachers should state the objectives of the instruction as learner behaviors. Learning is inferred from behavior, so it's important to identify the specific behaviors that will allow a reasonable inference that students have acquired the desired knowledge or skill. In addition to identifying the goal behavior, this involves breaking that goal down into a set of simpler behaviors and arranging them in a sequence of frames that will help students progress toward the goal.

Second, teachers should use cues to guide students to the desired behavior. Behavior is determined by the antecedent. Incorporating a cue, or hint, into the antecedent will help ensure students' success by guiding them to the desired behavior.

Third, teachers should use consequences to reinforce the desired behavior. Behaviors that are reinforced are more likely to be repeated. Using consequences effectively involves two tasks. The first task is to select the reinforcers. Unfortunately, selecting reinforcers isn't always an easy matter. Reinforcement is defined solely in terms of its effects on students' behavior and can often be determined, therefore, only after the fact. When students repeat the behavior, the consequence was a reinforcer. However, when the behavior is not repeated, the consequence was not a reinforcer. In addition, different students are reinforced by different things, and, to make matters even more complicated, the same student may be reinforced by different things in different subjects or be reinforced differently on different days in the same subject. The point is that selecting reinforcers for a particular situation is often a matter of trial and error. The second task is to arrange the selected consequences so that they reinforce the desired behavior. Timing is critical. To be effective, the consequence should immediately follow the behavior it is meant to reinforce. Otherwise it may reinforce an unintended behavior that doesn't help students progress toward the goal.

Now let's revisit Ms. Moreno's Spanish classroom. In the situation described at the beginning of this section, the students are working through a structured program developed by an instructional expert to help them increase their Spanish vocabulary. Each frame in the program presents students with a problem in the form of a sentence to complete (antecedent). Students enter a word or phrase that they think will complete the sentence (behavior), and the computer tells them immediately whether they are "correct" (consequence). If the initial response isn't "correct," students are given a cue in the form of help in translating the sentence and asked to enter a new response. Students can be said to have learned a new set of Spanish words when they can consistently use them correctly in sentences.

Table 2.3 summarizes the theoretical principles and practical applications from the behavioral perspective.

The Information Processing Perspective

Let's imagine another lesson in Ms. Moreno's Spanish class. Students are working on another vocabulary lesson, but this time they are using a written workbook. For each new Spanish word, students are presented with an English translation and, to help them remember the meanings of the words, a visual image based on a familiar English word that sounds like part of the Spanish word. For example, the Spanish word *silla* (chair) sounds similar to the English word *sea*. A simple picture of a chair float-

Table 2.3 Practical applications of principles from the behavioral perspective

Theoretical Principle	Practical Application
Learning is inferred from the behavior of the students.	State the objectives of the instruction as learner behaviors.
Behavior is determined by the antecedents that precede it.	Use cues to guide students to the desired behavior.
Whether a behavior will be repeated depends on the consequences that follow it.	Select consequences that will reinforce the desired behavior. Arrange the consequences to immediately follow the desired behavior.

ing on the sea is used to quickly associate the Spanish word with a similar-sounding word in English and the English translation (Figure 2.1). For the first set of new words, the workbook provides the images. For subsequent sets of new words, students are asked to create their own images and draw them into their workbooks. At the end of each set of words, students are quizzed on the meanings of the words they have just learned. As part of the directions for the quiz, students are advised to use their images to help them remember the meanings of the new words.

Why does this instructional technique work? In what ways is it informed by theory? Let's consider the development, principles, and practices of the information processing perspective and then revisit this classroom.

Background. Behaviorism developed as a reaction to the study of mental phenomena, such as consciousness, that had characterized 19th-century psychology. In a similar way, cognitive psychology developed as a reaction to behaviorism. Cognitive psychology "was officially recognized around 1956" (Gardner, 1985, p. 28), in large part because of a growing dissatisfaction with behaviorism's inability to adequately explain complex behaviors such as language acquisition. For example, at a 1948 symposium on "Cerebral Mechanisms in Behavior," Karl Lashley argued that when people use language their behavior is so rapid and continuous that it could not possibly be controlled by external prompts alone, as behaviorism would suggest (Gardner, 1985). Their behavior must be organized and planned in advance using processes that occur internally in the mind. Lashley used language as his primary example, but he argued that most human behavior is similarly complex and governed by mental processes.

The perceived limitations of behaviorism led to a search for new ways of explaining human behavior. At the same time, rapid technological advances led to the development of the high-speed computer as a mechanism for swiftly manipulating large amounts of information. As these two trends came together, one result was the development of the information processing view of human cognition, using the computer as a model for the way humans think. While this view isn't the only one that has developed from cognitive psychology (see Driscoll, 1994, for descriptions of other cognitive theories of learning), it has been a prominent view that has influenced instructional practice. Using the computer as a model has provided a means for looking inside the mind by equating human thought with the way a computer works. That is, the mind takes information in, organizes it, stores it for later use, and retrieves it from memory in a way that can be compared to the computer. With the growth of cognitive psychology the focus was again on the mind, as it had been before the advent of behaviorism. However, using computer models and other laboratory methods (e.g., reaction time tests), cognitive scientists were now able to quantify mental functions with dramatically increased scientific rigor.

Theoretical Principles. The behavioral perspective has an external focus. Learning is defined as a change in the probability of an observable behavior, with the emphasis on the influence of the external environment. In contrast, the information processing perspective has an internal focus. Learning is described as a change in knowledge stored in memory. The central principle is that most behavior, including learning, is governed by internal memory processes rather than external circumstances. Understanding behavior, therefore, requires understanding how memory works.

Human memory has two essential characteristics. First, it is organized rather than random. As an illustration, try this simple exercise: Ask several people to write down the names of as many of the 50 United States as they can. Give them about 15 seconds and then examine the results. The lists are likely to be different, but virtually all of them will be organized in some way. The most common organizing schemes are alphabetic (Alabama, Alaska, Arizona, Arkansas, etc.) and geographic (Washington, Oregon, Idaho, California, etc.). Some lists may be organized in a way that isn't readily apparent

SILLA

Figure 2.1 An example of the use of a visual image as an aid in remembering the English translations of Spanish words

and may make sense only to the person who wrote the list (Florida, Virginia, Wyoming, Kentucky, etc.—states someone has visited on vacation). But each list will be organized in some way. The same can be said for all the knowledge we have accumulated: it is organized in memory.

The second essential characteristic of human memory is that it is active rather than passive. Memory doesn't simply receive information. It actively synthesizes information, looking for, and usually finding, order in new information and integrating it with knowledge already stored in memory. Memory as an active synthesizer involves three processes: attention, encoding, and retrieval (Bell-Gredler, 1986). **Attention** refers to the process of selectively receiving information from the environment. **Encoding** refers to the process of translating information into some meaningful form that can be remembered. **Retrieval** refers to the process of identifying and recalling information for a particular purpose. Learning is said to have occurred when new information has been encoded or when existing information has been recoded in some new way. In both cases, the individual can easily recall information from memory and effectively use it in a particular situation.

As a way of understanding how these memory processes work together, imagine a library receiving new books and subsequently making them accessible to its patrons (Stepich & Newby, 1988a). A library continually receives information about new books and selects some of those books for addition to its collection (attention). When a library receives new books, they are cataloged using a classification scheme such as the Dewey Decimal System (encoding). This places the new books into coherent categories and allows related books to be placed on the shelves near one another. It also provides a search cue that can be used to find the books at a later time. To locate a particular book in the library, the individual begins with the search cue provided by the catalog number and searches the shelves for the desired book, perhaps at the same time scanning the shelves for other relevant books (retrieval).

Memory works in a similar way. Humans are constantly bombarded with information from the environment and select only some of it to remember (attention). New information is considered in light of what is already known and integrated into existing information whenever possible (encoding). This creates a coherent organization that makes new information more meaningful and allows related information to be linked together. It also

provides a "search cue" that makes it easier to find information at a later time. In order to recall some information from memory, the individual begins with the "search cue" provided by the organizing scheme and searches memory for the desired information, perhaps at the same time "scanning" memory for other relevant information (retrieval).

There is, of course, at least one significant difference between memory and a library. A library keeps physical objects (books) in specific places (shelves). In contrast, the facts and ideas that make up memory aren't physical objects, and we can't yet pinpoint where specific memories are kept. However, the processes involved in using memory are similar to those involved in using a library.

Practical Applications.   The emphasis in the information processing perspective is on students' cognitive processes and on the critical role memory plays in helping them translate new information into a meaningful form that can be remembered and used. Instruction, then, refers to the deliberate effort to guide and support those cognitive processes. The primary responsibility of the instructional expert is to arrange external conditions that will help students attend to, encode, and retrieve information. In order to carry out this responsibility, the information processing perspective suggests that teachers do the following:

First, organize new information. Knowledge in memory is organized, and humans actively seek order in information as a way of making sense of it. Because of this, new information will be easier to encode, and therefore easier to retrieve, if it is also organized.

Second, carefully link new information to existing knowledge. Learning is influenced primarily by students' existing knowledge that is stored in memory. New information that is linked to this existing knowledge will be more meaningful to students and therefore more easily and effectively learned.

Third, use techniques to guide and support students' attention, encoding, and retrieval. A wide variety of techniques can be used (see Baine, 1986), but we will briefly describe a few. (The Technology Integration Prompts, or TIPs, used throughout this book provide further illustration of a number of these techniques.) To guide students' attention, use focusing questions and highlighting. To guide students' encoding and retrieval, use analogies and mnemonic devices.

- *Focusing questions.* A **focusing question** is used, typically at the beginning of a lesson, to direct students' attention to particularly important aspects of the new information. For example, at the beginning of a lesson on the American Revolution, students might be asked, What were the arguments supporting the revolution? Who made those arguments? What were the arguments against the revolution? Who made those arguments?

- *Highlighting.* **Highlighting** refers to various techniques designed to direct students' attention to certain aspects of information. Written information can be highlighted through the use of **bold print,** underlining, or *italics.* Pictorial information can be highlighted through the use of color, labels, and arrows. Verbal information can be highlighted by speaking more loudly or more slowly, or by repetition.

- *Analogies.* An **analogy** likens something new to something familiar. Analogies are typically used either to make abstract information more concrete or to organize information that is complex. For example, imagine that you wanted beginning biology students to learn the function of red blood cells. You might use the following analogy: "Red blood cells work like trucks, carrying needed materials from a central distribution point for delivery throughout the body" (Stepich & Newby, 1988a, p. 136). This analogy uses a familiar object (trucks) to direct students' attention to the critical (at least for this lesson) feature of red blood cells: their function as carriers of essential materials. In addition, the analogy uses the familiar object as a guide to help students encode new information about red blood cells. Finally, the analogy provides students with a retrieval cue, allowing them to recall their new knowledge about red blood cells. This retrieval process might begin with the analogy itself (red blood cells are like trucks). Students might then recall how red blood cells are like trucks (they carry things), and this might be followed by their recalling what red blood cells carry (oxygen).

- *Mnemonics.* In general terms, any practical device used to make information easier to remember can be called a **mnemonic.** To illustrate some of the many different mnemonics, answer the following questions:

How many days does March have in it? Perhaps, like many people, you answered this question by thinking, "Thirty days hath September, April, June, and November . . . " This is an example of using a rhyme as a mnemonic.

What are the names of the five Great Lakes? One way to answer this question is by thinking of the word "homes" (Huron, Ontario, Michigan, Erie, Superior). This is an example of an acronym, in which a single word is made up of the first letters of a group of words.

What are the names of the lines on the musical staff? This question can be answered by thinking of the sentence "Every good boy deserves fudge." This is an example of an acrostic, in which letters in the new information (E, G, B, D, F) are used as the first letters of the words in a sentence or phrase.

Now, let's revisit our Spanish classroom. In this latest situation we saw students using a type of mnemonic called a keyword (Ormrod, 1989) to learn the meanings of new Spanish words. Creating a keyword involves two steps. First an unfamiliar word is linked to a similar-sounding familiar keyword. Then the keyword is used to create a visual image that incorporates the meaning of the new word. Like other types of mnemonics, a keyword helps students encode the new words in a way that makes it easier to retrieve them at a later time.

Table 2.4 summarizes the theoretical principles and practical applications from the information processing perspective.

Table 2.4 Practical applications of principles from the information processing perspective

Theoretical Principle	Practical Applications
Knowledge is organized in memory.	Organize new information for presentation.
Learning is influenced by students' existing knowledge.	Carefully link new information to existing knowledge.
Learning is made up of the component processes of attention, encoding, and retrieval.	Use a variety of techniques to guide and support students' learning processes, including focusing questions, highlighting, analogies, and mnemonics.

The Constructivist Perspective

We have been visiting Ms. Moreno's classes throughout this section on learning, so let's see one more lesson. In this class students have been divided into small groups, and each group is acting out a real-life scenario in Spanish. There is no set script for any of the scenarios. Each student has been given a description of a situation, a role to play, and a task to accomplish. The students' task is simply to make themselves understood in order to carry out their assigned role, using only Spanish. Examples could include finding a lost child who only speaks Spanish, asking a policeman in Madrid for directions, and convincing an airline baggage assistant at the Mexico City International Airport that the bag you have claimed is indeed your own.

Why does this instructional technique work? In what ways is it informed by theory? Let's consider the development, principles, and practices of the constructivist perspective and then revisit this classroom.

Background. *Constructivism* is a relatively recent term used to represent a collection of theories, including (among others) generative learning (Wittrock, 1990), discovery learning (Bruner, 1961), and situated learning (Brown, Collins, & Duguid, 1989). The common thread among these theories is the idea that individuals actively construct knowledge by working to solve realistic problems, usually in collaboration with others (Duffy, Lowyck, & Jonassen, 1993).

While the label is relatively recent, the ideas that make up constructivism have been around for a long time. As early as 1897, for example, Dewey argued that "education must be conceived as a continuing reconstruction of experience" (p. 91) that occurs through "the stimulation of the child's powers by the demands of the social situations in which he finds himself" (p. 84). In the middle of the 20th century, the idea that knowledge is constructed through social collaboration shows up in the theories of Piaget, Bruner, and Vygotsky (Driscoll, 1994).

The constructivist perspective represents a marriage of principles from a number of disciplines. Cognitive psychology has contributed the idea that the mind "actively constructs its own interpretations of information and draws inferences from them" (Wittrock, 1990, p. 348). Developmental psychology has contributed the idea that an individual's constructions vary predictably according to the person's cognitive development (Driscoll, 1994). Anthropology has contributed the idea that learning is a naturally occurring sociocultural process in which individuals enter a "community of practice" where they work together to accomplish meaningful tasks and solve meaningful problems (Brown et al., 1989).

Theoretical Principles. The constructivist perspective describes learning as a change in meaning constructed from experience. On the surface this seems the same as the information processing definition of learning, but there's a critical difference in the way the two perspectives define knowledge (Jonassen, 1991). The information processing perspective defines knowledge as an *objective representation* of our experience, whereas the constructivist perspective defines knowledge as an *individual interpretation* of experience.

An analogy will help to illustrate this critical difference. In the information processing perspective, the mind is like a mirror, accurately reflecting the objects and events in our experience. The assumption is that knowledge is objective and can be described as separate from the knower. In other words, regardless of whose mirror is used, the picture in the mirror is essentially the same. Learning, then, refers to the acquisition of new representations. In the constructivist perspective, on the other hand, the mind is like a lens. When we look through our lens, some aspects of our experience are in sharp focus, some are fuzzy, and some can't be seen at all. The assumption in the constructivist perspective is that knowledge is constructed by the knower and therefore *cannot* be separated from the knower. In other words, the picture we see is determined by the lens we use. Learning, then, refers to the construction of new interpretations.

Thus, knowledge construction is a process of thinking about and interpreting experience. And because each individual has a unique set of experiences, seen through a unique lens, each individual constructs a unique body of understanding. Learning is said to have occurred when our knowledge has changed in a way that allows us to interpret our experience in a way that is more complete, complex, or refined, that is, when our lens allows us to see something we couldn't see before or to see things in sharper focus.

Practical Applications. According to the constructivist perspective, learning is determined by the complex interplay among students' existing knowledge, the social context, and the problem to be solved. Instruction, then, refers to providing students with a collaborative situation in which they have both the means and the opportunity to construct "new and situationally-specific understandings by assembling prior knowledge from diverse sources" (Ertmer & Newby, 1993, p. 63). Various authors have described the characteristics of constructivist instruction (e.g., Brooks & Brooks, 1993; Cognition and Technology Group at Vanderbilt [CTGV], 1993; Collins, Brown, & Holum, 1991; Honebein, Duffy, & Fishman, 1993). Two characteristics seem to be central to these descriptions:

1. *"Good" problems.* According to the constructivist perspective, knowledge is like a muscle; it grows when it's used. Therefore, constructivist instruction asks students to use their knowledge to solve problems that are meaningful and realistically complex. The idea is that when they work to apply their knowledge to a specific problem, students will naturally explore their knowledge, and this will, in turn, lead to the continual refinement of that knowledge. However, not all problems are equally effective. "Good" problems are required to stimulate the exploration and reflection necessary for knowledge construction. According to Brooks and Brooks (1993), a "good" problem is one that

- requires students to make and test a prediction. Like a theory, knowledge is constructed as it is used to explain what has happened and to predict what will happen.
- can be solved with inexpensive equipment. Sophisticated equipment can be used, but the focus should be on the problem rather than the equipment.
- is realistically complex. Complex problems are more likely to trigger the different experiences of students and, therefore, promote different approaches to a solution.
- benefits from group effort. The problem should generate dialogue and negotiation, which encourage the exploration of alternative interpretations.
- is seen as relevant and interesting by students. Students are likely to invest more effort in problems they perceive as relevant.

2. *Collaboration.* According to the constructivist perspective, students learn through interaction with others. This collaboration has two basic aspects. The first involves the relationships among students. Students work together as peers, applying their combined knowledge to the solution of the problem. The dialogue that results from this combined effort provides students with the opportunity to test and refine their understanding in an ongoing process.

The second aspect of collaboration involves the role of the teacher. Constructivist instruction has been likened to an apprenticeship (e.g., Collins et al., 1991; Rogoff, 1990) in which teachers participate *with* students in the solution of meaningful and realistic problems. This doesn't mean that teachers know "the answer" to the problem. In fact, the problem may be just as new to the teacher as it is to the students. However, teachers are probably more familiar with the processes of solving problems and constructing knowledge. Teachers, therefore, serve as models and guides, showing students how to reflect on their evolving knowledge and providing direction when the students are having difficulty. Learning is shared (teachers are likely to learn as much as students) and responsibility for the instruction is shared. The amount of guidance provided by the teacher will depend on the knowledge level and experience of the students.

The emphasis in the constructivist perspective is on students' evolving knowledge and the critical role social negotiation plays in helping students interpret their experiences. From a constructivist perspective, the primary responsibility of the instructional expert is to create and maintain a collaborative problem-solving environment. In order to carry out this responsibility, the constructivist perspective suggests that teachers

- pose "good" problems. Learning occurs as knowledge is applied to the solution of problems that are realistically complex and personally meaningful to students.
- create group learning activities. Learning can be equated with social dialogue in which students and teacher participate in a "community of inquiry" (CTGV, 1993) to explore and apply their combined knowledge.
- model and guide the knowledge construction process. In constructivist instruction, the relationship of students to teachers is like that of apprentices to masters. Students and teachers work together to solve problems, with teachers providing direction consistent with the experiences and knowledge levels of their students.

Let's revisit our last Spanish lesson. In this situation, students are engaged in a problem that meets the criteria for a "good" problem: they must use their knowledge of Spanish vocabulary and pronunciation to make themselves understood; the situation makes use of very little, if any, equipment; the problems are complex enough to allow for a number of different conversations; accomplishing the task is a cooperative effort; and the situations stimulate the curiosity and interest of the students.

Table 2.5   Practical applications of principles from the constructivist perspective

Theoretical Principle	Practical Applications
Learning occurs through the application of knowledge to the solution of problems.	Pose "good" problems.
Learning occurs through interaction with others.	Create group learning activities.
Constructing knowledge can be thought of as an apprenticeship process.	Model and guide the knowledge construction process.

Table 2.5 summarizes theoretical principles and practical applications from the constructivist perspective.

Learning Theory Summary

Learning theory has been defined as an attempt to explain how people acquire new knowledge and skills. We have presented three perspectives of learning, summarized in Table 2.6. Because these three theoretical perspectives view learning in distinctly different ways, you might ask, *Which theory is best?* While this is a natural question, we believe it isn't the right question to ask. It's like asking, Which food is best? The inevitable answer is that no one food is best. We should eat a variety of foods, because each one contributes something to good nutrition. Similarly, we believe that teachers should understand a variety of theoretical perspectives because each perspective contributes something to good instruction.

Some theoretical principles are virtually universal. For example, reinforcement (from the behavioral perspective), organized information (from the information processing perspective), and learning from one another (from the constructivist perspective) are principles that will be useful in virtually every instructional situation. However, these theoretical perspectives focus on different aspects of the learning process. It's possible, therefore, to use a combination of theoretical principles, depending on the demands of the specific instructional situation. Ertmer and Newby (1993) suggest a heuristic guideline, shown in Figure 2.2, based on two factors: the knowledge level of students and the amount of thought and reflection required by the learning tasks. As the figure shows, students with little knowledge of the content are likely to profit from

Table 2.6   A comparison of three theoretical perspectives of learning

	Behavioral Perspective	Information Processing Perspective	Constructivist Perspective
What is learning?	A change in the probability of a behavior occurring	A change in knowledge stored in memory	A change in meaning constructed from experience
What is the learning process?	Antecedent → behavior → consequence	Attention → encoding → retrieval of information from memory	Repeated group dialogue and collaborative problem solving
What is the teacher's primary role in the learning process?	Arrange external contingencies.	Arrange conditions to support memory processes.	Model and guide.
What can the teacher do to carry out that role?	• State objectives. • Guide student behavior with cues. • Arrange reinforcing consequences to immediately follow students' behavior.	• Organize new information. • Link new information to existing knowledge. • Use a variety of attention, encoding, and retrieval aids.	• Pose "good" problems. • Create group learning activities. • Model and guide the process of construction knowledge.

Figure 2.2 A heuristic guide for selecting principles from the three theoretical perspectives on learning

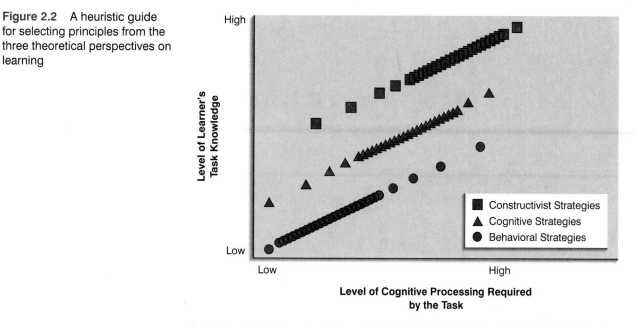

Level of Cognitive Processing Required by the Task

■ Constructivist Strategies
▲ Cognitive Strategies
● Behavioral Strategies

Note. © 1993 by the Learning Systems Institute, Florida State University, 205 Dodd Hall R-19, Tallahassee, FL 32306. Reprinted by permission from Performance Improvement Quarterly.

strategies based on behavioral principles. As students' knowledge grows, the emphasis may shift to information processing and then constructivist principles. At the same time, learning tasks requiring little thought and reflection (e.g., memorizing facts, following a rote procedure) are likely to profit from behavioral strategies. As the amount of thought and reflection required by the learning tasks increases, the emphasis may shift to information processing and then constructivist strategies (e.g., finding unique solutions to "old" problems, inductive reasoning, creative thinking).

While learning theory is the cornerstone of instructional practice, it isn't the only building block in the foundation. There are two other theories that inform instructional practice in important ways: communication theory and general systems theory. We turn our attention to these theories in the next two sections.

Communication Theory

Background. The study of communication dates back to the beginning of human civilization; the first recorded communication theories were developed by Plato and Aristotle during the 5th century B.C. (Trenholm, 1991). It became a recognized field of study, however, in the 1940s with the development of models describing the communication process. Just as it gave a boost to manufacturing, World War II facilitated the development of communication theory. The machine technologies and telecommunications systems developed during the 1940s led to mathematical models of communication (see Shannon & Weaver, 1949) that were designed to provide precise descriptions of the mechanics of transmitting a message, without regard to the content or meaning of the message. Later models put communication in a human context (see Schramm, 1954) and focused on the meaning of a message as a vital aspect of the process. Communication theory continues to evolve, with increasing emphasis being placed on its social dimension (Trenholm, 1991).

Theoretical Principles. **Communication** refers to the "process of creating a meaning between two or more people" (Tubbs & Moss, 1994, p. 6). Many models have been proposed to describe this process (Trenholm, 1991). We will focus on the "transactional" model because of its currency and its strong links to learning theory. Tubbs and Moss (1994) present one version of the transactional model, shown in Figure 2.3. In this model, communication occurs when two or more individuals send messages to one another and receive messages from one another, using one or more channels, or means of transmission, to carry the messages. The messages are subject to distortion. **Filters** in the sender (e.g., inadequate vocabulary, lack of organization or clarity, biases) distort a message as it is sent. Filters in the receiver (e.g., fatigue, daydreaming, limited knowledge about the topic) distort a message as it is received.

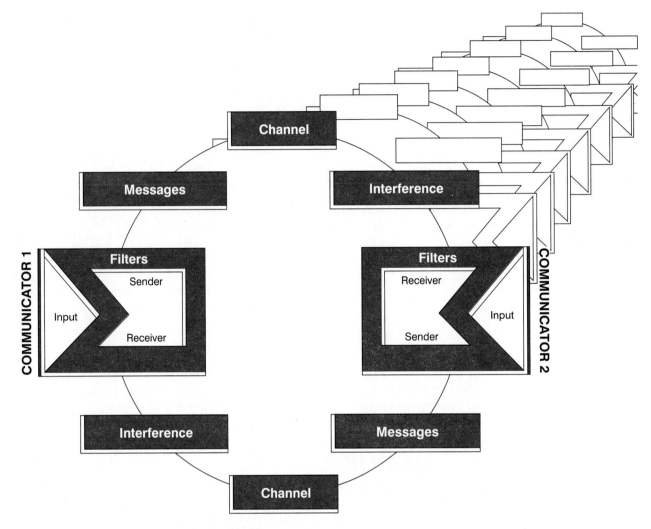

Figure 2.3   The Tubbs Communication Model

Note. From *Human Communication* (7th ed.) (p. 7), by S. L. Tubbs and S. Moss, 1994, New York: McGraw-Hill. Copyright 1994 by McGraw-Hill. Used by permission of the publisher.

Interference (e.g., distracting noises, harsh lighting) distorts a message as it passes from the sender to the receiver.

The transactional model emphasizes several essential characteristics of communication. One way to understand these characteristics is to liken communication to ballroom dancing. First, communication is a continuous process. When dancing, both partners move together, and their steps flow into one another so that, in practice, they are parts of a single action. Similarly, when communicating, everyone involved is both sending and receiving, and at virtually the same time. It's possible, for the sake of analysis, to break down the process into its component messages, but the breakdown would be largely arbitrary. In actuality the process has no discrete parts.

Second, communication is a dynamic process. As dance partners move around the dance floor, they continually adjust their steps to fit the music, the space, and each other. Similarly, communication is a continually changing process, more of "an uncoiled spring" than a circle (Tubbs & Moss, 1994, p. 14). As the communication continues, the participants adjust their messages to fit their changing understanding of one another.

Third, the communication process has many variations. Dancing is a complex human interaction that is influenced by a number of factors. As a result, there is no single best way to dance, and the steps will vary depending on the music, the setting, and the abilities and preferences of the partners. Similarly, communication is a complex human interaction that is influenced by a number of factors, including the complexity of the messages, the experiences and preferences of the communicators, and the existing filters and interference. As a result, there is no single best way to communicate. Communicators choose the messages and methods that work best for them in a particular situation.

Practical Applications. Instruction, as defined at the beginning of the chapter, is a form of transactional communication. It creates meaning by sending messages about a particular topic back and forth along various channels among students, teachers, and technology. The value of communication theory is that it provides a framework for understanding this complex transaction. For example, Figure 2.4 shows the Tubbs Communication Model modified to represent an instructional situation.

From the perspective of communication theory, the primary responsibility of the instructional expert is to maintain the transactional nature of the instruction. In order to carry out this responsibility, communication theory makes a number of suggestions for teachers. First, communicate *with* students rather than *to* them. Even in very traditional classrooms, in which teachers are seen primarily as a source of information, teachers should communicate *with* students. Recall that communication is a continuous and dynamic process. For example, at the same time that the teacher is sending messages about the topic, students are invariably sending messages about their understanding of the topic and their interest (or lack of interest) in it. This interplay of messages makes learning a two-way street. The messages from students will allow the teacher to modify the nature of the instruction in order to maintain students' attention and further their understanding. At the same time, and just as importantly, students may have a unique way of talking about the topic that will help the teacher develop a new or different understanding of the topic.

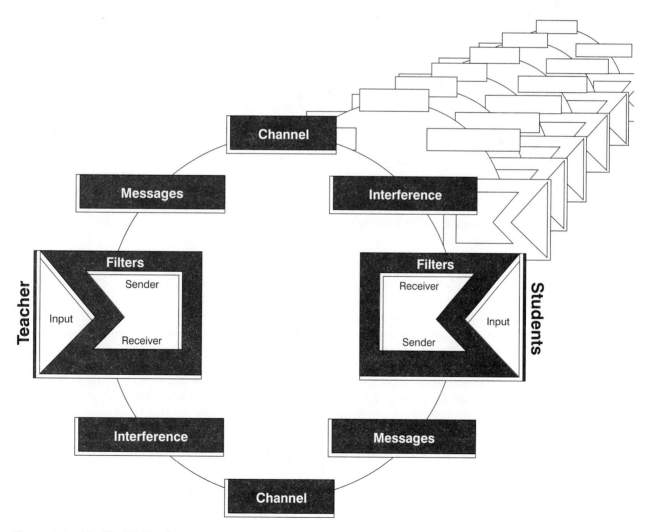

Figure 2.4 Modified Tubbs Communication Model

(a)   (b)

Effective communication requires talking (a) <u>with</u> *students rather than (b)* <u>to</u> *them.*

Second, identify the filters and interference (actual and potential), and reduce them as much as possible. Communication theory suggests where to look for barriers that might make learning difficult. Interference is often the easiest barrier to identify. It's relatively easy to determine whether some aspect of the physical surroundings (e.g., noise, lighting) is interfering with learning and to reduce or eliminate the interference. It's more difficult, though perhaps more important, to identify the filters that might make learning more difficult. For example, instruction that contains unfamiliar technical jargon will make learning more difficult because some information will be filtered out because of the technical language. Similarly, students who are anticipating an after-school activity will find learning more difficult because some information will be filtered out by their preoccupation. The point is that when we know where to look for potential barriers it is easier to find them, and this makes it easier to avoid or eliminate them.

Finally, use more than one channel to communicate with students. A channel is something that helps transmit or carry a message or series of messages between two or more communicators. It is natural for communication to involve multiple channels. For example, think about a recent conversation you had with a friend. The messages were carried by the words that were said and by the gestures and vocal intonations that accompanied those words. Even if the conversation took place over the telephone, tone of voice helped carry the messages, and the words and vocal intonation communicated more together than either channel could by itself. Multiple channels can also be used by teachers to help their students learn. (In teaching, communication channels can be equated with instructional media, and Chapter 4 will provide detailed infor-

mation about a variety of media.) As in everyday conversation, communication among students and teachers will be more effective (i.e., the messages are more likely to be received) when more than one channel is used. For example, imagine explaining the principle of leverage to students in a physics class. The principle says that the efficiency of a lever is directly related to the distance between the fulcrum (pivot point) and the weight of the load on the lever. The principle might be explained, for example, orally or in written text. But in either case, the explanation will be clearer if it is accompanied by a diagram that shows how the efficiency of the lever is affected by moving the fulcrum. The words and pictures both help to transmit the message, and together they communicate more than either could by itself. We will return to the advantage of using multiple communication channels in Chapter 4.

Table 2.7 summarizes the theoretical principles and practical applications from communication theory.

General Systems Theory

Background. The growth of general systems theory was fueled by the practical necessities of building complex machines during World War II. Faced with the need, for example, to produce a large number of combat airplanes in a relatively short period of time, aircraft designers first tried to add various military equipment (guns, bombs, etc.) to existing airplanes. They soon discovered, however, that they had changed the performance capabilities of the airplanes in ways they hadn't anticipated (Banathy, 1968). This led to the realization that the airplane was, in reality, a unitary piece of equipment rather than a collection of independent parts. It had to be produced as an integrated system. With

Table 2.7 Practical applications of principles from communication theory

Theoretical Principle	Practical Application
Communication is a continuous two-way transaction.	Communicate *with* students rather than *to* them.
Filters and interference distort the message.	Identify the filters and interference (actual and potential), and reduce them as much as possible.
There is no single best way to communicate.	Use more than one channel to communicate with students.

this realization, designers began to build new airplanes, designing them from the ground up beginning with a precise set of specifications that defined the airplane's purpose and the performance that was expected of it.

Theoretical Principles.   The basic premise of general systems theory is that the world is an inherently ordered place (Richey, 1986) that allows for rational decision making based on what we want to accomplish. Within this ordered world, a **system** (such as an airplane) is a set of parts that depend on one another and work together toward a common goal. The goal defines the reason for the existence of the system and drives its operations. The parts interact; that is, they work together to accomplish the goal, with each part playing a role. The parts are also interdependent; that is, they affect one another. A change in one part of a system inevitably leads to changes in the other parts.

Many things can be seen as systems. For example, a tree is a natural system designed to grow and propagate through the process of photosynthesis (the production of sugars from carbon dioxide, water, and sunlight). In order to accomplish this goal, the tree has roots that absorb water and minerals from the ground, sapwood that carries water from the roots to the leaves, leaves that carry out the photosynthesis, and bark that protects the tree from the elements. There are many other systems in nature, including biological cells, digestive systems, volcanoes, and ecosystems.

In addition to natural systems, people build systems to accomplish a variety of purposes they consider important. For example, a lightbulb is an artificial system designed to provide illumination on demand through the process of incandescence (glowing as a result of intense heat). To accomplish this goal, the lightbulb has a filament that glows when it's heated, a wire frame that holds the filament in place, a globe that provides a vacuum in which the filament can be heated efficiently, and a base that connects the filament to a source of electricity. A

large number of other systems help people accomplish other important goals. For example: automobiles provide transportation, libraries store documents, telephones provide communication across long distances, governments mediate interpersonal interactions, and parcel companies deliver packages.

Practical Applications.   Instruction, as defined at the beginning of the chapter, is a complex phenomenon. It blends students, learning goals, information, teaching techniques, activities, and media in a myriad of combinations. The value of general systems theory is that it provides a framework for understanding this complex phenomenon. Instruction can be viewed as an artificial system, bringing together a set of interacting and interdependent parts to accomplish the common goal of learning. For example, Kemp, Morrison, and Ross (1994) define an instructional system in terms of four components: learners, methods, objectives, and evaluation (see Figure 2.5). The goal of an instructional system like the one in Figure 2.5 is the acquisition

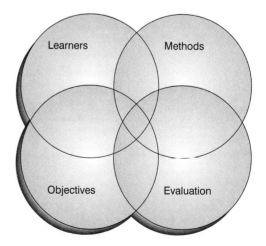

Figure 2.5   An instructional system
Note. From *Designing Effective Instruction* (p. 8), by J. E. Kemp, G. R. Morrison, and S. M. Ross, 1994, Englewood Cliffs, NJ: Merrill/Prentice Hall. Copyright 1994 by Merrill/Prentice Hall. Reprinted with permission.

of some new knowledge or skills by a group of students. Each part of the system plays an important role in accomplishing this goal. Learners provide curiosity, interest, and prior knowledge. The methods present the new information to the students and provide opportunities for them to use that information. The objectives define the goal more specifically in terms of the performance(s) expected of the system and communicate those expectations to all parts of the system. Evaluation provides a means for determining whether learning has taken place and, therefore, a means for revising the system.

From the perspective of general systems theory, the primary responsibility of the instructional expert is to coordinate the efforts of the system's parts. In order to carry out this responsibility, general systems theory suggests that teachers follow three guidelines.

First, they should identify the goal of the system. What is the purpose for this instruction? Specifically, what new knowledge or skills are students to acquire? A goal that is clearly identified will provide a focal point for the system and make it easier for the system's parts to combine their efforts to accomplish the goal.

Second, teachers should identify the parts of the system and the role each part plays in accomplishing the goal. What interests and prior knowledge do students bring to the instruction? What methods will be used to present new information to students? What techniques will be used to determine whether students have learned? Clearly identifying what all parts of the system contribute will make it easier to coordinate their efforts.

Third, when changes occur in one part of the system, teachers should maintain the system's balance by making corresponding changes in the other parts of the system. General systems theory suggests that, because the parts of an instructional system are mutually dependent, a change in one part of the system will lead to changes in other parts. Changing the students may require different instructional methods, even when the objectives remain constant. For example, when the objective requires students to be able to explain the physical principle "Force equals mass times acceleration" ($F = MA$), the instructional methods will change depending on whether the students are 4th or 10th graders. Similarly, changing the objective will require a different form of evaluation, even when the students remain constant. For example, when the objective requires students to be able to apply $F = MA$ to the solution of a physics problem, a different form of evaluation will be needed than when the objective requires students to be able to recall the principle.

Table 2.8 summarizes the theoretical principles and practical applications from general systems theory.

SUMMARY

In reviewing this chapter, there are several points that should be highlighted. First, while learning may be the responsibility of students, instruction is the responsibility of teachers. Instruction is invariably a deliberate effort on the part of the teacher, functioning as an instructional expert, to help particular students meet particular learning goals. Instructional experts aren't always responsible for implementing instruction, but they are always responsible for planning instruction, that is, diagnosing students' learning needs and prescribing the information and activities that will meet those needs.

Second, functioning as an instructional expert is based on a theoretical foundation. In every profession, including teaching, theory informs practice. This means that theory offers a set of consistent principles that can be used to create solutions to a variety of unique problems. As in other professions, understanding theory allows teachers to select the

Table 2.8 Practical applications of principles from general systems theory

Theoretical Principle	Practical Application
The goal drives the system.	Identify the goal of the instructional system.
Each part of the system plays a role in accomplishing the goal.	Identify parts of the system and the specific role each plays in accomplishing the goal.
The parts of a system are mutually interdependent.	When changes occur in one part of the system, maintain the system's balance by making corresponding changes in the other parts of the system.

tools and techniques that will work best with specific students and learning goals, apply those principles in a coherent manner, and adapt the instruction as the needs of students change.

Third, instructional practice is built on a diverse theoretical foundation, including learning theory, communication theory, and general systems theory. Each theory has been described in terms of its central principles and its practical applications to the role of the instructional expert. Learning theory is the cornerstone of this theoretical foundation. Three broad theoretical perspectives (behavioral, information processing, and constructivist) have been included because, just as different foods contribute to good nutrition, different learning theories contribute to good instruction.

REFLECTIVE QUESTIONS AND ACTIVITIES

1. Write a letter to a skeptical friend explaining why the time you spend studying theory will help you become a better teacher.

2. Consider a class you have been in from the behavioral perspective. Were objectives stated as learner behaviors? What cues and consequences were used? How might the class be made more consistent with the behavioral perspective?

3. Consider the same class from the information processing perspective. Was new information organized? Was it clearly linked to existing knowledge? What techniques were used to make information processing easier (e.g., focusing questions, analogies, mnemonics)? How might the class be made more consistent with the information processing perspective?

4. Consider the same class from the constructivist perspective. Were "good" problems presented? Was collaborative learning emphasized? Did the teacher serve as a model and guide? How might the class be made more consistent with the constructivist perspective?

5. Think about one of the systems you are a part of. What is the goal of the system? What is your part in accomplishing that goal?

6. Think back on a learning situation you have been in. Identify as many of the sources of interference as you can. Briefly indicate how you would reduce the distortion caused by each source.

INTEGRATION AND SYNTHESIS

This chapter is the second within the introductory section of the book. The focus in Chapter 1 was on the learning process and the role of instructional technology in that process. In this chapter the focus was on instruction, its relationship to the learning process, and the theories that form the foundation for instructional practice.

This information, together with information on instructional approaches (Chapter 3) and instructional media (Chapter 4), relates directly to Chapter 6, in which the learning plan is described. In creating a learning plan, the instructional expert makes a number of decisions, including selecting, modifying, and/or creating instructional materials to help students learn (Chapter 7). The decisions that are made in creating the learning plan are based, in large part, on the theoretical foundation described in this chapter. In fact, it's important to remember throughout the remainder of the book that, because theory informs practice, planning instruction (Section II), implementing instruction (Section III), and evaluating instruction (Section IV) should all be based on a sound theoretical foundation.

SUGGESTED READINGS

For learning theory

Driscoll, M. P. (1994). *Psychology of learning for instruction.* Boston: Allyn & Bacon.

Ertmer, P. A., & Newby, T. J. (1993). Behaviorism, cognitivism, constructivism: Comparing critical features from an instructional design perspective. *Performance Improvement Quarterly, 6*(4), 50–72.

For communication theory

Tubbs, S. L., & Moss, S. (1994). *Human communication* (7th ed.). New York: McGraw-Hill.

For general systems theory

Richey, R. (1986). *The theoretical and conceptual bases of instructional design.* London: Kogan Page.

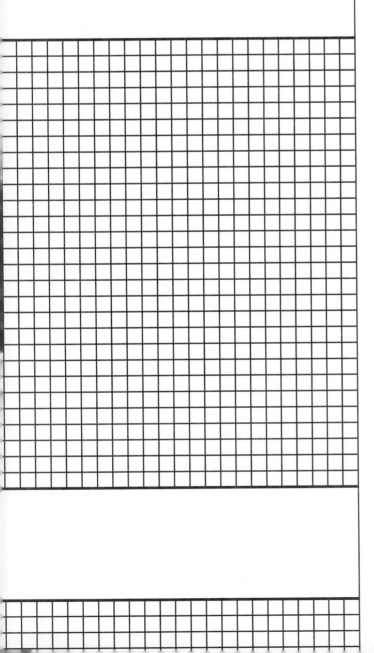

Chapter 3

Instructional Approaches

KEY WORDS AND CONCEPTS

Instructional approaches	Cognitive domain
Presentation	Problem solving
Demonstration	Instructional games
Discussion	Simulation
Cooperative learning	Drill and practice
Discovery	Programmed instruction
Intrinsic motivation	Tutorial

OUTCOMES

After reading and studying this chapter, you will be able to:

- Relate instructional approaches to the message or lesson, students, and media.
- Describe all of the approaches, including the key attributes of each.
- Discuss an application of each approach in a discipline you plan to teach.
- Classify each approach in terms of its level of interactivity and its appropriate group size.
- Select an approach for a given instructional situation based on the criteria given in this chapter, and be able to justify your selection.

▉ INTRODUCTION

Imagine going into a particular hardware store for the very first time. You are in need of a ladder, and as you enter you immediately notice that they have ladders—in fact, ladders are *all* they carry. Wall-to-wall ladders. No hammers, nails, saws, or electrical equipment—just ladders. When you approach the sales clerk you mention your amazement, and he replies that their ladders are of the highest quality and that if you need one, they certainly could help. You mention that your project requires a 12-foot extension ladder. Apologetically, the clerk responds that his store only carries 6-foot aluminum stepladders, but he would be happy to sell you two of those. You shake your head and say that won't do. Then you ask the clerk why they sell only a single product. He explains that it makes it very easy to display the merchandise, simplifies ordering, and makes training the sales clerks quick and efficient. He also mentions, however, that it does have its drawbacks—most people come in, look around for only a couple of minutes, and then leave. Very little repeat business occurs.

How does this story relate to our study of instructional technology? Think about the variety of learning problems or challenges faced by teachers and students each day. In most of these cases, specific instructional tools are needed in order to accomplish what is required. From a teacher's perspective, if you are limited in the number of tools you have access to or which you have expertise in using, could this limit your overall effectiveness? It is our contention that instructional experts do not limit themselves to a single instructional approach (Chapter 3) or a single form of instructional media (Chapter 4) but have knowledge of a number of effective tools and the ability to use them correctly at the appropriate time. Limiting your knowledge to a single tool may result in situations in which you will not be able to get the desired results. In this and the following chapters we will introduce you to a number of instructional tools. We have designed these chapters to supply background and prerequisite materials that will be critical for the proper planning, implementation, and evaluation of instructional materials. ▉

INSTRUCTIONAL APPROACHES: AN ANALOGY

Traditionally, **instructional approaches** have been described as "presentation forms" such as lecture and discussion. **Approaches,** sometimes called methods, are the procedures of instruction that are selected to help students achieve the stated outcomes or to understand the content or message of the instruction.

To help us understand instructional approaches, let's use an analogy. This analogy will help us here, as well as when we discuss various types of instructional media in Chapter 4. Assume you have a package you wish to send to a friend. You can choose from a number of delivery systems, all of which vary in cost and speed. Possible choices would include the U.S. Postal System, United Parcel Service (UPS), and Federal Express. After you choose a carrier, such as UPS, they would determine the appropriate vehicle and route to deliver your package, depending on a number of factors, such as how quickly (time) you want it to get to your friend, how much you are willing to pay (cost), where your friend lives (location), the size and weight of the package (contents), the vehicles available to them, and possible routes. UPS has small delivery trucks, over-the-road tractors with tandem trailers, and airplanes. The routes might include interstate highways to an air terminal, air routes to a distant city, and city streets to your friend's home (Figure 3.1).

In some situations, your friend may not want to wait for the package to be delivered. She may go to the delivery company's office to pick it up or come to your home to get it, thereby determining her own route and vehicle to use. Some packages are delivered after they are requested or ordered by the receiver, as in the case of mail-order sales. In other cases, individuals go out and get the necessary components to assemble materials into a unique, personal package.

How does this relate to classroom instruction? You have a message or lesson (package) to deliver

Figure 3.1 Different types of delivery routes are available for sending a package

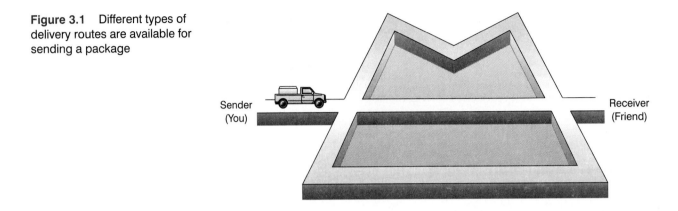

Sender
(You)

Receiver
(Friend)

to your students. You have a certain amount of time to deliver the contents. There is a budget available for instruction. The instruction has unique characteristics in terms of subject matter and complexity (contents). Different students in your class have various backgrounds and learning styles (locations). You have a variety of vehicles—we call these media—available to you, such as real objects, textbooks, overhead transparencies, slides, videotapes, and computer programs (these are described in Chapter 4). You also have various routes or paths available to reach your students. We call these instructional approaches.

In this chapter we describe ten instructional approaches that are applicable to students of all ages: presentation, demonstration, discussion, cooperative learning, discovery, problem solving, instructional games, simulation, drill and practice, and tutorial. Students may determine for themselves which media and approaches to use—similar to picking up their own packages. And just as in mail-order sales, students may control the delivery of instruction by requesting the content and sequence that they desire. Other students can go out and get the content they need using the school library media center or by conducting computer searches for information throughout the world. They can assemble the information in a way that is meaningful to them.

In Chapter 6 we help you develop instructional plans, which include your selection of instructional approaches and media. Your selection of approaches depends on your learners, the available resources, and the message. Because of the complexity of the various delivery tasks, no one route will work every time, no matter how good it is.

As a teacher you need to be able to use a variety of approaches to reach your students. As we mentioned in the opening paragraphs of this chapter, if you know only one way to present the content (e.g., lecture) you may run into trouble, just like the learner who knows only one way to learn (e.g.,

memorization). Sometimes you will not be able to deliver the lesson because you don't have the right path. However, if you have many different approaches available you have a greater likelihood of reaching your students wherever they are.

Planning a good route involves judgment. Judgment implies choices, and choices imply having alternatives to choose from. When more routes are available to you, it will be easier to identify one that matches the situation and to modify the route if the demands of the situation change (much like detours on the highway). We have chosen to present this information (and that within Chapter 4) during this text's introductory section in order to build a foundation that will support you as you make decisions about the design, production, and implementation of instructional materials.

The ten instructional approaches described in this chapter will be presented in the following format:

- *Description.* First we describe the approach. You will learn what it is and how it is different from other approaches. At least one example is included with the description. Other examples and applications are included after the approach's attributes are discussed.

- *Attributes.* The attributes, or characteristics, of each approach include some advantages and limitations; that is, its potential benefits and possible pitfalls. Many of the pitfalls can be avoided by proper selection and utilization of the approach. By knowing the attributes of each approach, you will be able to select the approaches that are most appropriate for any given instructional situation.

- *Applications.* We present several possible applications of each approach. The applications provide examples of *when* to use a particular approach. *How* to use each of the approaches will be discussed in Chapters 9 and 10.

THE INSTRUCTIONAL APPROACHES

Presentation

Description

In the **presentation** approach a source relates, dramatizes, or otherwise disseminates information to learners. This approach makes use of verbal information and/or visual symbols to convey material quickly. Presentations are typically made so students will learn essential background information. It's a one-way communication method controlled by the source, with no immediate response from, or interaction with, the learners. The source may be a textbook, an audiotape, a video, a film, an instructor, and so on.

Examples of the presentation approach are reading a book, listening to an audiotape, viewing a film or videotape, and attending a lecture. During a visit to a museum, you might check out a cassette tape and player with private headphones. The audiotape and accompanying map would guide you through the museum and present information about each of the exhibits and displays.

Attributes

The presentation approach

- affords greater control for the teacher in terms of content, pace, and meeting the needs of the majority of the students
- can be used with groups of all sizes
- gives all students the opportunity to see and hear the same information

- provides students with an organized perspective of the content to be learned (i.e., the information is structured and relationships among concepts are illustrated)
- can be used to present a lot of content quickly
- often includes an aural component, which is particularly helpful for auditory learners
- requires little activity on the part of learners (students' mental involvement is difficult to assess during a presentation)
- doesn't provide feedback to learners since, by definition, presentation is a one-way approach

Applications

A presentation can introduce a new topic, provide an overview, and motivate students to learn. For example, a fourth-grade teacher presents an overview of a unit on dinosaurs with models and visuals to motivate her students to follow up with their own investigations of the topic. Presentations can provide background information and material for other approaches (e.g., information to be discussed). For example, a middle school social studies teacher shows a videotape on environmental pollution to stimulate discussion. Teachers or students can use a brief presentation to summarize the content studied during a lesson. In a senior history class, a small group of students do a mediated presentation on the origin and meaning of the Bill of Rights to share what they learned with the rest of the class.

Presentation is an effective approach for presenting certain information to a group of students.

Demonstration

Description

Demonstrations show students how to do a task as well as why, when, and where it is done. In this approach students view a real or lifelike example of the skill or procedure to be learned. Demonstrations may be recorded and played back by means of a video or computer. If two-way interaction or learner practice with feedback is desired, a live instructor or a computer is needed. The desired outcome may be for the learner to imitate a physical performance, such as swinging a golf club or changing the oil in a car, or to adopt the attitudes or values exemplified by a respected model.

Attributes

The demonstration approach

- utilizes several senses; students can see, hear, and possibly experience an actual event
- makes verbal explanations more concrete by illustrating ideas, principles, and concepts for which words are inadequate
- has dramatic appeal if the presenter uses good showmanship techniques, such as demonstrating an unexpected result or a discrepant event
- arouses and maintains interest
- is essential when teaching a psychomotor procedure (such as jumping rope) or an interpersonal skill (such as participating in a discussion)
- provides a holistic perspective by showing a complete performance before students learn to do part or all of it
- reduces hazards and trial-and-error learning of students conducting an experiment or procedure involving materials and equipment (as in science labs, shops, and home economics classes)
- can set performance standards for student work; by demonstrating how to properly perform a task, teachers establish the criteria students are expected to meet
- can be used by teachers or students
- is time-consuming if demonstrations are done live, and may not go as planned

Applications

The demonstration approach can be used to illustrate how something works, to show how to perform a task, or to teach safety procedures. For example, a student in a science class demonstrates the effect of heat on a bimetallic strip, or a lab instructor demonstrates the manipulative skill of bending glass tubing in the chemistry lab. Cooking instructors use demonstrations to show how procedures should be followed to create the perfect German chocolate cake. And the band leader shows the trumpet players how the correct posture can make a difference in the quality and volume of sound they produce.

Interpersonal skills can also be demonstrated. An important aspect of a business class may be to have the teacher show students how to respond to questions during a job interview. Likewise, a demonstration can be used with many safety procedures. A gym teacher may introduce her students to the correct use of the free weights by showing how the use of spotters is critical, while the shop instructor may demonstrate the use of the emergency shutdown switch on the power table saw. Finally, role models such as famous sports figures sometimes use demonstrations to help individuals adopt an attitude or value—such as influencing young people to stay in school, volunteer their time, or stay away from drugs and alcohol.

Discussion

Description

Discussion is a dynamic approach that encourages classroom rapport and actively involves students in learning. Students talk together, share information, and work toward a solution or consensus. They are given the opportunity to apply principles and information through verbal discourse. This approach introduces students to different beliefs and opinions, encouraging them to evaluate the logic of, and evidence for, their own and others' opinions. It provides teachers with immediate feedback on students' understanding of course material.

There are three important skills associated with the discussion approach: asking students questions, managing the flow of answers to your questions, and responding to students' questions. Discussion among students or between students and teacher can make a significant contribution throughout the learning process, whether in tutorials, small groups, or large groups. It is a useful way of assessing the knowledge, skills, and attitudes of a group of students. Discussion can help an instructor establish rapport both with and among a new group in a way that fosters collaborative and cooperative learning.

A discussion prior to the presentation of media may help guide students' attention during the presentation. For example, a third-grade teacher may lead a discussion on the meaning of Thanksgiving Day in preparing his students to attend a Thanksgiving play presented by high school students. A dis-

Discussion facilitates students learning content and interpersonal skills.

cussion after a presentation is helpful in answering students' questions and ensuring that everyone understood what was presented. In combination with written forms of evaluation, discussion can also be used to evaluate the effectiveness of instruction.

Attributes

The discussion approach

- teaches content as well as processes such as group dynamics, interpersonal skills, and oral communication
- allows students to actively practice problem-solving, critical-thinking, and higher-level thinking skills
- is interesting and stimulating for teachers and students alike
- can change attitudes and behavior
- makes effective use of students' backgrounds and experiences
- provides teachers with information about students, including how much students know about the content
- allows students to benefit from the contributions of others
- requires the teacher to prepare and to practice leading an effective discussion

Applications

Discussion can be used to access the knowledge, skills, and attitudes of a group of students, to determine how well students understand concepts and principles, and to determine student progress. It can also be used to prepare for a presentation (as described in the Thanksgiving example above), to provide interaction during a presentation, or to follow up on a presentation.

Discussions can encourage imaginative solutions to problems and secure active student participation. They stimulate interest and thinking—because students state their ideas aloud, they reinforce their own understanding of the topic. For example, a discussion on proper care of the family cat can be an effective way for lower elementary students to begin to learn about responsibility. Likewise, having middle school students discuss their tactics and techniques for preparing for essay examinations can help them clarify what the most effective strategies are.

After students have read *To Kill a Mockingbird,* the teacher leads a discussion so students can exchange views on how the characters dealt with specific situations and examine how class members might act under similar circumstances. After students participate in a game on parts of speech, the high school teacher uses discussion to evaluate the effectiveness of the game and to determine what content still needs to be covered using other approaches.

Cooperative Learning
Description

Cooperative learning involves small heterogeneous groups of students working together to learn collaborative and social skills while working toward a common academic goal or task. It is an approach in which students apply communication and criti-

QUESTIONING

One cornerstone technique that is incorporated within all forms of instruction pertains to the ability to generate and ask questions. Questions can be used to gain attention, maintain focus, pique interest, probe for depth of understanding, increase relevance for a topic of focus, or evaluate the quality of the instructional materials. Questions may be generated by the teacher or student, and answers can range from simple, to difficult, to unknown.

Several guidelines can help you incorporate productive questions into your instructional lessons (Dallmann-Jones, 1994; Wasserman, 1992).

When planning and developing questions:

- Determine why the question will be asked. Make sure each serves an important purpose.
- Determine if the question will be used to stimulate remembering, reasoning, evaluating, or creative thinking.
- Use "who," "what," "when," and "where" questions to check information for review purposes. "Why" and "how" questions encourage higher levels of thought. Ask students to provide in-depth explanations or additional examples.
- State each question as clearly as possible.
- Frame questions to invite, rather than intimidate. Help students feel safe to express their thoughts. Questions and responses should be respectful, nonthreatening, and productive.
- Structure, in advance, the questions to be used. Write them down so you can deliver the questions appropriately.

When using questions:

- Sample class responses randomly; that is, ask questions of all students equally.
- Take time to pause after asking a question, thus providing students with time to think.
- Listen to students' responses before formulating your response so you can accurately reflect the students' ideas.
- Respond positively to appropriate responses, but never belittle incorrect answers.
- Allow students the chance to formulate questions in response to comments from the teacher or other students.
- When a student repeatedly provides incorrect answers, coach that individual during one-on-one sessions. Provide him or her with opportunities to answer questions that you have previously discussed during your session.

---

cal-thinking skills to solve problems or to engage in meaningful work together.

Many educators have criticized the competitive atmosphere that dominates some classrooms. They believe that pitting student against student in the attainment of grades is contrary to the societal requirements of on-the-job teamwork. Teacher and students often find themselves in an adversarial relationship in the cat-and-mouse game of test-taking and grading. Competition in the classroom interferes with students learning from each other.

Critics of competitive learning recommend an emphasis on cooperative learning as an instructional approach. They argue that learners need to develop skills in working and learning together because their eventual workplaces will require teamwork. A growing body of research supports the claim that students learn from each other when they work on projects as a team (Slavin, 1990a, 1990b). Two or three students at a computer terminal learn more as they cooperate while working through an assigned problem. Some computer programs, such as *Aspects* and Lotus's *Notes,* make it possible for several students to work interactively while at separate computers.

Students can learn cooperatively not only through discussion of media presentations but also by producing media. For example, the design and production of a video or a slide set as a curriculum project presents an excellent opportunity for cooperative learning. The teacher should work as a partner with the students in a cooperative learning situation.

Attributes

The cooperative learning approach

- promotes positive interdependence, individual accountability, collaborative and social skills, and group processing
- encourages trust-building, communication, and leadership skills
- facilitates student learning in academic as well as social areas
- can be motivational when students enjoy working together
- involves students in active learning
- requires a compatible group of students (this may be difficult to form)
- takes more time to cover the same amount of content than other approaches
- is less appealing to individuals who prefer to work alone

Applications

A second-grade teacher divides her students into cooperative learning spelling groups. Each week those within the groups work together to learn the spelling words and are graded based on their group's overall performance.

In the science lab, groups of three middle school students work together as detectives to determine the nature of an unknown substance. Some are assigned to go to the public library to complete some background research, others focus on designing and running experiments on the substance, while others work to locate someone who may be familiar with the substance. Together they pool their information to come to a combined, cooperative solution.

A type of computer courseware called groupware has been developed to facilitate decision making and problem solving. Tom Snyder Productions distributes a series of computer groupware titled *Decisions, Decisions* (Figure 3.2) Each program begins with a description of a problem scenario. The students gather information about the problem, discuss alternative solutions as a group, and make decisions.

Discovery
Description

The **discovery** approach enables and encourages students to find "answers" for themselves. The

Figure 3.2 Screen from Tom Snyder Productions' *Decisions, Decisions: Substance Abuse*

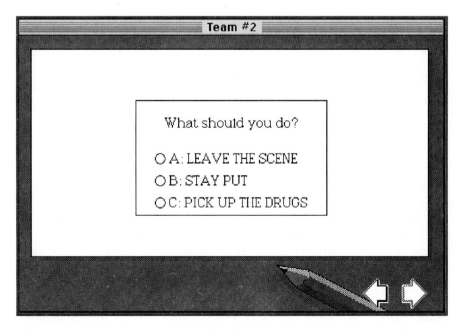

teacher may arrange the environment so the "discovery" can occur. A principle of discovery learning is that students learn best by doing rather than by just hearing and reading about a concept.

This approach uses an inductive, or inquiry, approach to learning; it presents problems to be solved through trial and error. The aim of a discovery approach is to foster a deeper understanding of the content through active involvement with it. The rule or procedure that learners discover may be derived from previous experience, based on information in reference books, or stored in a computer database.

Instructional media can help promote discovery or inquiry learning. For discovery teaching in the physical sciences, students might view a video to observe the relationships represented and then go on to discover the principles that explain those relationships. For example, by viewing something as simple as a balloon being weighed before and after being filled with air, students discover that air has weight.

Attributes

The discovery approach

- allows students to use raw data and operate in the manner required by the nature of the discipline (e.g., rather than studying science, students are "sciencing")

- helps students learn how to follow leads and clues, record findings, and use logic

- provides **intrinsic motivation** (where merely participating in the task itself is rewarding) to discover the "answer"

- develops the skills and attitudes essential for self-directed learning

- usually results in increased retention of knowledge and processes, because students have processed the information and not simply memorized it

- encourages thinking at the higher levels of the **cognitive domain** because students are required to analyze and synthesize information rather than memorize low-level facts

- allows for the discovery of "incorrect" or unintended information

- can be very time-consuming

Applications

A primary-level teacher uses discovery learning to introduce the concept of colors and their relation-

ships to each other. Rather than telling students that blue and yellow make green, she provides paper, paints, and brushes. Then she asks, "What happens when you mix different colors, such as blue and yellow?" A middle school math teacher uses the computer courseware *Geometric Supposer* to allow students to manipulate lines and angles to discover the relationships among the number of sides and the angles of a regular geometric shape inscribed within a circle.

Consumer science students study data to determine the relationship between the supply of and demand for various household products and their costs. A similar application has high school and middle school students "playing" the stock market with $100,000 in play money. Students work in teams to gain the most from their "investments." Their success or failure is determined by the rise and fall of the real stock market during the time they are "playing." Students discover how outside forces, such as the Federal Reserve, impact the value of stocks.

Problem Solving
Description

In the **problem-solving** approach learners use previously mastered skills to resolve a challenging problem. Problem solving is based on the scientific method of inquiry. The usual steps are (1) define the problem and all major components, (2) formulate hypotheses, (3) collect and analyze data, (4) derive conclusions and/or solutions, and (5) verify conclusions and/or solutions. Learners must define the problem more clearly (perhaps state a hypothesis), examine data (possibly with the aid of a computer), and generate a solution. Through this process learners can be expected to arrive at a higher level of understanding of the phenomenon under study.

One type of problem-solving method commonly used is the case study. Students in a business class are given information about a situation at a small manufacturing firm and asked to design a solution for the problem of low production. After gathering further data about the situation, they determine whether the solution should involve training or, perhaps, changing the environment or attitudes of the workers.

Attributes

The problem-solving approach

- increases comprehension and retention because students are required to work with everyday problems and to apply theory to practice

TECHNOLOGY INTEGRATION PROMPT

CASE STUDIES The case study is a teaching approach that requires students to actively participate in real or hypothetical problem situations that reflect the types of experiences actually encountered in the discipline under study. The following are examples
of case studies. After you read them, reflect on the type of problem solving that
could be generated from their use.

> You are a botanist working to preserve the waters of Everglades National Park in Florida,
> the nation's third-largest national park, established in 1947. You have already documented
> the extent of the damage from surrounding farm chemicals that run off into the Everglades'
> vast swamps, saw grasses, and coastal mangrove forest. But recent attempts to reach
> agreement on the part of government and farmers' organizations have failed. How can you
> work to preserve these natural wonders of the country? (Barell, 1995, p. 126)

> Aurora is experiencing an increase in the crime rate. Currently, 30 percent of the cases
> admitted to hospital emergency rooms are victims of violent crimes, compared with a rate
> of 25 percent two years ago. What steps should the city take to find a solution to the prob-
> lem? (from Gallaher, Stepien, & Rosenthal, 1992, as cited in Barell, 1995, p. 126)

The case "report" contains relevant (but not conclusive) data and can be either
presented to the students or developed by them. Individual or group work follows
the case presentation, allowing students to analyze data, evaluate the nature of the
problem(s), decide on applicable principles, and recommend a solution or course of
action. A case discussion follows, which is considered useful in developing critical-
thinking, problem-solving, and interpersonal skills. Although case methods may have
strategies in common with other teaching techniques (particularly simulations and
instructional games), the focus in all case methods is a specific set of circumstances
and events. Whereas case methods are generally motivating to students due to the
high level of involvement and can help bridge the gap between the "real" world and
life in the classroom, they tend to be time-consuming and require good management
skills on the part of the discussion leader.

- involves higher-level learning since problems cannot be solved by simple memorization and regurgitation

- develops responsibility as students learn to think independently

- should be designed so that problems have multiple solutions, not a single right answer

- should utilize resources other than textbooks

- provides students with the opportunity to learn from their mistakes

- allows students to practice strategy development and logical thinking, including both inductive and deductive reasoning

Applications

Problem solving can be applied to everyday life. Students may choose to examine problems at school,
such as dealing with litter on the playground or
selecting more nutritious foods in the cafeteria. In
physics classes, the students may solve story prob-

lems in a systematic manner by first drawing a
visual representation of the situation described.
The known elements are listed and the unknowns
or questions are identified. An equation relating the
knowns to the unknowns is then selected.

A computer program called *Thinkin' Things*
makes use of various problem-solving strategies,
such as working backwards, analyzing a process,
determining a sequence, and thinking creatively.
The software provides the user with a factory that
produces creative-looking feathered friends (see
Figure 3.3). The preschool-aged child selects from a
set of options in order to create the next appropriate bird in the sequence.

Instructional Games
Description

Instructional games provide an appealing environment in which learners follow prescribed rules as
they strive to attain a challenging goal. It is a highly
motivating approach, especially for tedious and

Figure 3.3 *Thinkin' Things* allows the student to create a feathered friend based on a specific pattern and sequence.

Source: Thinkin' Things, Edmark Corporation. Reprinted with permission.

repetitive content. The game may involve one learner or a group of learners. Games often require learners to use problem-solving skills or demonstrate mastery of specific content.

Where in the World is Carmen Sandiego? is a popular computer game that develops students' understanding of geography and world culture. Players assume the role of detectives who must track down a thief who has stolen a national treasure from somewhere in the world. By gathering clues and conducting research, players are able to track the thief around the world, learning about geography as they go (see Figure 10.3).

Attributes

The instructional game approach

- can be incorporated into many instructional situations in order to increase student motivation and levels of effort for specific learning tasks
- actively involves students and encourages social interaction through the necessary communication among players
- provides the opportunity for practice of skills with immediate feedback
- provides a clearly defined set of rules that outlines how the game will be played, what actions are and are not allowed, and what constitutes winning

- includes elements of competition or challenge wherein players compete against themselves, against other individuals, or against an objective standard
- helps students learn to deal with unpredictable circumstances
- may involve students with the competition more than the content
- can be impossible to play if pieces are lost or damaged
- can be time-consuming to set up if games have many components

Applications

Games can be used to improve decision-making skills, to learn basic concepts, to practice human relations and interpersonal skills, to develop leadership skills, and to foster cooperation and teamwork. Through competitive repetition within individual or team games, elementary students can learn basic concepts like math facts and vocabulary words. Spelling bees and speed math facts (e.g., a student is given many problems to attempt during a short time period and points are awarded for accuracy and speed) are common instructional games used in the elementary classroom to teach basic skills. Other games, such as *Trivial Pursuit* and *Jeopardy,* can be easily adapted to contain relevant subject-matter content and at the same time retain the benefits of the game structure.

Some instructional games have been produced to help learners acquire specific motor skills. For example, for practice with keyboarding, several computer programs have been developed in which the learner is pitted against invading aliens and required to type a specific set of letters in the right order and within the correct time period in order to shoot down the aliens and keep them from taking over the world. As one progresses through the program, the required level of speed and accuracy increases in difficulty.

Other games that have been effective in fostering the development and practice of both decision-making and interpersonal skills include what are known as survival games. In this format, groups of four or five students are given a scenario in which they are lost at sea in a small rubber raft (other variations include being trapped in a bomb shelter following a nuclear war or being trapped on the moon following an emergency lunar landing). The participants are given a list of items that they must rank in order of importance (e.g., sextant, shaving mirror, 5-gallon container of water, maps of the Pacific Ocean) for their survival. After reviewing the list, the group must come to a consensus on the ranking. The final rankings are compared with those of other groups and with those completed by members of the U.S. Coast Guard.

Simulation
Description

Using the **simulation** approach, learners confront a scaled-down approximation of a real-life situation. Simulation allows realistic practice without the

Instructional games provide a challenging approach to experiencing a variety of activities.

expense or the risks otherwise involved. The simulation may involve participant dialogue, manipulation of materials and equipment, or interaction with a computer.

Interpersonal skills and laboratory experiments in the physical sciences are popular subjects for simulations. In some simulations learners manipulate mathematical models to determine the effect of changing certain variables, such as those affecting the control of a nuclear power plant.

Sim City is a popular simulation program for personal computers. The program allows students to simulate the management of a city, including such elements as budget, construction of infrastructure, traffic, pollution, and crime. Students can build their own city from scratch or manage one of several well-known cities around the world.

Attributes

The simulation approach

- can be used for acquisition of information, improvement of new processes, and identification of alternatives in decision making
- can promote cognitive, affective, and interpersonal skills that emphasize response accuracy, speed, self-pacing, and convergent questioning abilities
- provides practice and experimentation with skills to be learned
- provides immediate feedback on actions and decisions
- simplifies the complexities of the real world and focuses on important attributes or characteristics
- is appealing, motivates intense effort, and increases learning
- helps students develop decision-making skills
- can cause deep emotional involvement (e.g., students in veterinary school get very attached to "sick" animals they diagnose and attempt to "save," even though the animals exist only within the simulation)
- can be time-consuming for both the setup and the debriefing

Applications

Simulations can promote decision making and build positive values and attitudes by putting students in roles with which they are not familiar. High school students can pretend that they are operating a household. They have an "income" from which

ROLE PLAYING

One type of instructional simulation is known as *role playing*. Role playing is like a drama in which each participant is assigned a character to depict; however, individuals portraying specific roles improvise their responses to the situation. Examples include learning how to interview for a job, managing a situation in which a hostile student threatens a teacher, discussing a questionable call with an umpire during a championship baseball game, and establishing a personal relationship.

Role playing encourages creativity and allows students to express their feelings and attitudes. It's an effective means to develop and practice social skills, and it can help students learn to organize thoughts and responses instantly while reacting to a situation or question.

Consider the following guidelines when designing and implementing role play in the classroom (see Dallmann-Jones, 1994; McKeachie, 1994):

- Design the situation in sufficient detail prior to class.
- Define participants' roles in terms of the situation.
- Ask for volunteers rather than choosing participants—volunteers are less likely to feel like they've been put on the spot.
- Allow the participants a short time to get their thoughts together.
- Brief students before the role play begins. Describe the situation and indicate what nonparticipants should look for.
- Don't let the role play "run" too long. Three to six minutes is usually sufficient to accomplish its purpose.
- Stop the role play and reverse roles if a "hot" topic is encountered and emotions begin to get out of hand.
- Conduct a follow-up discussion to analyze the group process. To avoid defensiveness, allow players to discuss their perceptions and emotional reactions first.

they "pay" for housing, food, transportation, and recreation. Periodically they draw a "life event" card, which gives them extra income or leads to a financial setback. These simulated experiences give them insight into how they might respond in similar situations and provide them with an opportunity to explore their own values and actions.

In a similar way, upper elementary students can learn about the law of supply and demand by operating a school "store." They learn how to order items, how to exchange money for their products, and how item prices can fluctuate based on the availability of the product and how much demand there is for it.

To learn interpersonal skills such as those needed for job interviews, senior high school students can be placed within a job interview simulation in which they can practice and develop the skills. Likewise, students desiring to learn how to safely drive a car or fly an airplane frequently use simulators to practice and develop the needed skills. In both cases, the simulations can be very realistic yet offer a safe environment for skill development.

Drill and Practice

Description

In **drill and practice**, learners are led through a series of practice exercises designed to increase fluency in a new skill or to refresh an existing one. Use of this approach assumes that learners have previously received some instruction on the concept, principle, or procedure that is to be practiced. To be effective, drill-and-practice exercises should include corrective feedback to remediate errors that learners might make along the way.

Drill and practice is commonly used for such tasks as math facts, foreign language learning, and vocabulary building. Certain media formats and delivery systems lend themselves particularly well to drill-and-practice exercises. For example, learning-laboratory instruction and **programmed instruction** (see Chapter 10) are well suited to these purposes. Audiotapes can be used effectively for drill and practice in spelling, arithmetic, and language instruction.

Attributes

The drill-and-practice approach

- provides repetitive practice in basic skills to enhance memorization, build competency, and attain mastery
- is applicable for psychomotor and low-level cognitive skills
- is appropriate for information not learned by a single exposure
- is helpful when speed and accuracy are necessary
- can be perceived as boring
- may lead to student confusion as to when and how to apply the facts learned

Applications

When facts need to be memorized and readily recalled, the use of drill and practice is frequently found to be beneficial. To learn math facts to a level of automatic recall, students frequently employ flashcards. On one side of the card can be a simple arithmetic problem, on the other the answer. Students attempt to answer the problem and then flip the card and compare their answer to the correct solution. This format can be used for learning states and their capitals, the names of animals and their young (e.g., goose and gosling, kangaroo and joey), and foreign words and their translation, to name just a few.

Drill and practice is an integral part of developing many types of skills. Golfers visit driving ranges to hit the golf ball over and over, each time attempting to improve the manner in which they hold the club, keep their head down, and complete the follow through. Musicians constantly drill on musical pieces, playing them repeatedly to make sure the instrument is held properly and that the sound is produced in the proper manner. And finally, have you ever wondered why the key person in a Marine bootcamp is called a "drill" sergeant? It's because of the fact that he repeatedly works the recruits over the same basic maneuvers and drills until they can perform them in their sleep.

Tutorial

Description

A tutor—in the form of a person, computer, or special print materials—presents the content, poses a question or problem, requests learner response, analyzes the response, supplies appropriate feedback, and provides practice until the learner demonstrates a predetermined level of competency. Tutor-

ing is most often done on a one-to-one basis and is frequently used to teach basic skills such as reading and arithmetic, although it can be used for higher-level skills as well.

Tutorial arrangements include instructor to learner (e.g., Socratic dialogue), learner to learner (e.g., tutoring or programmed tutoring), computer to learner (e.g., computer-assisted tutorial software), and print to learner (e.g., programmed instruction). The computer is especially well suited to play the role of tutor because of its ability to quickly deliver a complex menu of responses to different learner inputs.

Attributes

The tutorial approach

- provides optimum individualized instruction; all students get the individual attention they need
- provides for the highest degree of student participation
- expands the number of "teachers" in the classroom by using students as tutors
- frequently benefits student tutors as much as or more than the tutees
- introduces new concepts in a sequenced, interactive way
- may be impractical in some cases because the appropriate tutor or tutorial material may not be available to meet the needs of an individual learner
- may encourage student dependency on the human tutor, such that students may become reluctant to work on their own

Applications

Tutorials can be used for learning all types of content. Unlike the drill-and-practice approach, which simply goes over previously presented information again and again, tutorials can be used to introduce new material to the student. For example, a sixth-grade math teacher teaches her class how to calculate the area of a rectangle through a tutorial approach. First she helps them recall the relevant information that they have studied in previous lessons (e.g., the concepts of rectangle, length, height, and multiplication). Then she introduces and explains the concept of area as the product of the length of the rectangle multiplied by its height. She then demonstrates and shows a number of examples of how the area of different sizes of rectangles can be determined. The students are then given the opportunity to attempt some novel problems using the same format described by the teacher. Finally, feedback is given on the students' performance.

This same type of approach could be completed through a computer-assisted format, with the computer cueing the recall of prerequisite knowledge, presenting the new content and the practice problems, and supplying feedback to the students on their performances. At other times it may be more appropriate for advanced students to perform the role of the tutor. The tutors in this case often find that they learn as much as or more than those they teach.

Not only can the manner in which the tutorial is delivered vary, but the content taught within the tutorial approach can also range from topics such as determining the area of a rectangle, to bird identification, to computer literacy, to the history of the Industrial Revolution, and even to the study of the human central nervous system.

CLASSIFICATION OF APPROACHES

Now that we have looked at a variety of approaches to instruction, let's look at ways to classify them. As shown in the matrix of instructional approach characteristics (Figure 3.4), they vary in their interactivity. Presentations and demonstrations are low in interactivity, while drill and practice and tutorials are highly interactive. As you can see from the figure, most approaches lend themselves to small-group instruction, while presentations and demonstrations are most effective for larger groups and tutorials and drill and practice are best for individuals

(utilization procedures for large and small groups are discussed in Chapter 9, while techniques for using approaches with individual students are described in Chapter 10).

Let's return to our delivery-system analogy presented at the beginning of this chapter. Approaches to learning are analogous to routes (air, water, highways) that lead to different destinations (outcomes). Learning materials and media described in the next chapter are analogous to different vehicles. Certain vehicles "fit" different routes better (e.g., ship—water; plane—air), and students may need to travel several different routes and use several different vehicles to reach their destination. Some students may progress more rapidly by different routes and with different vehicles. Likewise, approaches and media are different and can be used in a large variety of combinations.

INSTRUCTIONAL APPROACH SELECTION PROCESS

In any instructional situation, a variety of approaches can and should be used. Most of the approaches described here could be used to teach any content to any group of learners. However, some approaches seem better suited for certain content or certain learners. Trying the various approaches with actual students will determine which approach or combination of approaches is most effective. Consider using a variety of approaches to keep instruction interesting.

Figure 3.5 presents some of the criteria to be considered when you select an approach for a specific instructional situation. All the factors listed in the

Figure 3.4   Instructional approach characteristics

Approach	Level of Interactivity			Group Size		
	Low	Medium	High	Large (20+)	Small (2–20)	Individual
Presentation	●			●	●	
Demonstration	●			●	●	
Discussion		●			●	
Cooperative learning		●			●	
Discovery		●			●	●
Problem solving		●			●	●
Instructional games		●			●	●
Simulation		●			●	●
Drill and practice			●			●
Tutorial			●			●

Figure 3.5 Instructional approach selection checklist

Students

- ❑ General characteristics: age, grade level, socioeconomic backgrounds, experiences, and physical or mental challenges
- ❑ Specific knowledge/skills: prerequisites
- ❑ Learning styles: preferences
- ❑ Perceptual preferences: audio, visual, personal interaction, and/or tactile (hands-on)
- ❑ Group size: number of learners per group

Content

- ❑ Learning outcomes
- ❑ Types of learning tasks

Context or Setting (environment)

- ❑ Physical environment: facilities, room arrangement (flexibility), equipment
- ❑ Psychological environment: students' attitudes toward the content and their desire to learn

Resources and Constraints

- ❑ Costs and funds available
- ❑ Time

    to produce the necessary materials: _____ minutes

    to prepare to use materials/approach: _____ minutes

    to present materials and approach: _____ minutes

Approaches

- ❑ Presentation
- ❑ Demonstration
- ❑ Discussion
- ❑ Cooperative learning
- ❑ Discovery
- ❑ Problem solving
- ❑ Instructional games
- ❑ Simulation
- ❑ Drill and practice
- ❑ Tutorial

Characteristics of Approaches

- ❑ Active student involvement: including interactivity, and learner practice with feedback
- ❑ Group size: total number of students. Can the students be conveniently divided into groups of appropriate sizes for approach? (See Figure 3.3)
- ❑ Ability to arouse and maintain interest
- ❑ Structure/organization: inductive or deductive
- ❑ Degree of reality

Strengths

- ❑ Interest
- ❑ Ease of use
- ❑ Best match for students
- ❑ Best match for content

Weaknesses

- ❑ What to overcome
- ❑ How to overcome

checklist—students, content, context, resources and constraints, the approaches and their characteristics—should be considered. After taking all these factors into consideration, list the strengths of the possible approach(es) selected. Then identify any weaknesses of the selected approach(es) and describe how these weaknesses can be overcome. Let's look at all of the factors in some detail.

Your students are an important consideration in your planning and selection of approach(es). What are their general characteristics? Consider age, grade level, socioeconomic backgrounds, experiences, and any physical or mental disabilities. What specific skills or knowledge do they bring to the instructional situation? Do they have the prerequisites? What are their learning styles? How do they learn best? What are their preferences? Do they prefer audio materials, visuals, interpersonal experiences, or hands-on learning? How many students do you have to deal with at a time? Can you conveniently divide them into small groups? Can they work individually?

Another important consideration is the content to be learned. What outcomes do you expect? What types of learning tasks need to be accomplished? What are the cognitive demands of the task? In what sequence should the content be given or experienced?

The context, setting, or environment must also be considered. There are two types of contexts, the physical context and the psychological context. The first refers to the facilities, the arrangement of tables and chairs, and the size of the instructional environment (classroom, auditorium, gymnasium, or outdoor setting). What equipment is available and/or needed? What audiovisual equipment is needed to present mediated materials? The psychological environment refers to students' attitudes toward the content and their desire to learn. Do they want to be there? Are they disturbed by family troubles or distracted by other interpersonal concerns?

What resources do you have at your disposal, and what constraints are there on what you can do? Resources include materials, equipment, and funds. An important resource or constraint is time. In instructional situations there are three types of time to consider: the time needed to produce the materials necessary for a particular approach, the time needed to prepare to use the approach (getting the materials together, going over your role in the approach, etc.), and the actual time needed to complete the activity associated with the approach.

Of course, you'll need to consider all the approaches described in this chapter. How actively will the students be involved (refer to Figure 3.4)? Will they have the opportunity to practice important skills and content and receive feedback? Can they be divided into groups of a size appropriate for the approach to be used? If not, select a different approach. Will the approach arouse and maintain interest? Does the approach use an inductive sequence, or a deductive one? Which will be most effective for the content? Does the approach provide the degree of realism appropriate for the expected outcomes?

Finally, list the strengths of the various approaches and identify their weaknesses. Can identified weaknesses be overcome? If so, how? List ways to overcome them to assist you in your future planning. When you have taken all these factors into consideration, you are ready to make your approach selection. It is not an easy decision and will require judgment on your part. If you make the wrong decision, you will realize it when you use the lesson. You can select a different approach before the next time. The ability to select the "best" approach for your situation will come with experience. There is no perfectly objective way (i.e., add up the numbers) to select instructional materials, media, or approaches. All instructional situations involve unique circumstances and problems and thus require an understanding of the different approaches and what they offer before the "best" selection can be made.

INTEGRATING TECHNOLOGY
The Story Continues

Janette Moreno told us recently about a panel she was asked to serve on at a statewide media conference. The topic being discussed was "Effective Instructional Approaches for Language Teaching in the High School." Ms. Moreno knew that another panelist, Mr. Trebella, would be emphasizing computer applications, so she decided to speak about other approaches that had been successful in her Spanish Conversation class. Do you recall the variety of approaches she used that were described in Chapter 1? Remember how she first presented new vocabulary to her students? Can you recall how early approaches were modified, or enhanced, based on students' suggestions? Can you think of any approaches that weren't particularly successful? What other approaches might Ms. Moreno use in the future to teach conversational Spanish?

Ms. Moreno's students learn to communicate in Spanish using a multimedia simulation.

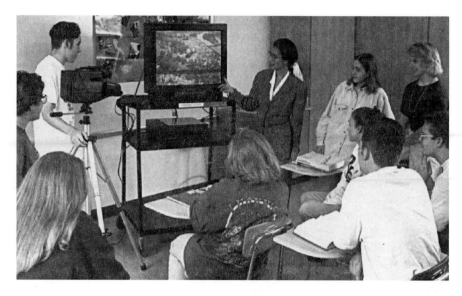

Were you able to identify at least four different instructional approaches that Ms. Moreno used in her Spanish class? As you read the remaining chapters of this text, and our references to this particular teacher, note how she varies her approaches in response to changing instructional conditions and individual learner's needs.

SUMMARY

We began this chapter by discussing the importance of knowing more than a single approach to teaching and learning. Because the requirements for learning often change based on the learner and the learning environment, it was shown to be important for the teacher to have a knowledge of several different instructional approaches (e.g., presentation, demonstration, simulation, drill and practice, tutorials), as well as when and how they should be used. To illustrate this point, an analogy was made comparing instructional approaches for the teacher with the various routes that can be taken by a parcel delivery service in order to take a package from one location to another. Similar to the delivery service, different approaches are required based on the situation, needs, and desires of the individuals involved.

In this chapter we explored ten different approaches to teaching and learning, describing each one in terms of its attributes and presenting examples of how each one can be used in the classroom. We classified each approach according to its interactivity and the group size for which it is appropriate. To facilitate the process of selecting

the appropriate instructional approach, we presented a checklist that identifies the many factors to be considered.

REFLECTIVE QUESTIONS AND ACTIVITIES

1. Why is selecting the proper approach important to the learning process? Be sure to consider all the factors listed in Figure 3.5.

2. How could Ms. Moreno have used demonstration, discovery, discussion, cooperative learning, problem solving, or instructional games to teach conversational Spanish? If any of these approaches are not appropriate, explain why.

3. Think of an instructional situation for which you might have to select an instructional approach. Describe the situation in some detail. Which approach would you use, and why?

4. Consider a recent learning experience you personally encountered. Decipher how the instructional approach was used and determine if it was appropriate or if additional learning could have occurred given a different or additional approach.

INTEGRATION AND SYNTHESIS

As we explained in the introduction to Section I, this chapter was intended to help you see and understand the variety of instructional approaches available for your use as a classroom teacher. This information must be closely synchronized with the selection and use of the instructional media format, which we will discuss in Chapter 4. Just as the type of route that leads from the source to the receiver dictates the type of vehicle that can be used by the parcel delivery company, so too the approach should impact the selection of the media format. Moreover, this combined information is a critical prerequisite for the successful completion of the instructional plan, which we outline in Chapter 6.

SUGGESTED READINGS

Dallmann-Jones, A. S. (1994). *The expert educator: A reference manual of teaching strategies for quality education.* Fond du Lac, WI: Three Blue Herons.

Wasserman, S. (1993). *Getting down to cases: Learning to teach with case studies.* New York: Teachers College Press.

Chapter 4

Instructional Media for Learning

KEY WORDS AND CONCEPTS

Medium

Compact disc (CD)

Video

Videotape

Videodisc

Computer-based
  instruction (CBI)

Computer-assisted
  instruction (CAI)

Computer-assisted
  learning (CAL)

Multimedia

Interactive multimedia

Hypermedia

Hypertext

Interactive videodisc

CD-ROM

Hardware	Scanner
Software	Digitizer
Computer	Output
Computer system	Output device
Mainframe computer	Monitor
Supercomputer	CRT
Minicomputer	LCD screen
Personal computer	Pixel
CPU	Printer
Microprocessor	Hard copy
Bit	Dot matrix printer
Byte	Letter-quality printer
Internal (main) memory	Ink-jet printer
ROM	Laser printer
RAM	Mass or external storage
Megabyte	Floppy disk/diskette
Peripheral	Hard (fixed) disk
I/O device	Gigabyte
Interface	Computer program
Input	Systems software
Input device	Operating system
Keyboard	Graphical user interface (GUI)
Cursor	
Mouse	Applications software
Modem	Icon
Graphics tablet	

OUTCOMES

After reading and studying this chapter, you will be able to:

- Define *instructional media.*
- Describe the roles of instructional media and their importance in the learning process.
- Identify different forms of media and generate examples of applications of each.
- Generate instructional situations in which one form of media would be more beneficial than another, based on individual attributes.
- Discuss how computers have proven educationally beneficial as teachers, tools, and learners.
- Define *multimedia* and *hypermedia.*

- Compare and contrast common interactive multimedia systems.
- Identify and describe the function of various input and output devices in a computer system.
- Describe the purpose of each of the main parts of a computer system (the CPU, internal memory, mass storage, input and output devices).
- Diagram the interactions and relationships among the parts of a computer system.
- Differentiate between systems software and applications software.

■ INTRODUCTION

Recently a mother lamented that three of her children had been ill. When she took them to the doctor they were all diagnosed with basically the same problem—an inner ear infection. To fight the infection, the doctor prescribed a similar antibiotic for each. Her 2-year-old got a pink liquid medicine that smelled like bubble gum and tasted like chalk, the 6-year-old got chewable tablets with a similar smell and taste, and the 14-year-old received her medication through an injection. She didn't smell it, but she did mention that it wasn't much fun. All of the kids had similar needs and all received similar medication; however, in each case the medicine was delivered through different means.

If you examine the drug industry, it's easy to see that they have concentrated not only on the development of new, effective medications, but also on the ways in which those drugs are delivered (e.g., liquids, tablets, capsules, caplets, injections, skin patches). In each case, their goal is to effectively and efficiently deliver medicine to the person in need. The selection of the means by which to deliver the medicine is determined by a number of criteria. Some of these include the characteristics of the drug itself, the physical and mental characteristics of the individual receiving the drug, and the situation or environment in which the drug is to be delivered (e.g., who will be administering it, where it will be delivered, how often it must be given).

Similar to those in the drug industry, instructional experts realize that not only must they develop effective instructional materials, but also they must determine the most effective and efficient means for learners to receive the instruction. Based on the type of learning experience desired, the characteristics of the students, and the situation in which the learning will occur, appropriate delivery means must be determined.

In this chapter we will introduce some of the media available for helping students learn. They include such things as computer software, slides, videotapes, and field trips. To make sense out of all of this "stuff," we return to the analogy introduced in the opening paragraphs of Chapter 3. In that chapter, getting an instructional message to a learner was compared to sending a package to a friend. We discussed the different routes, paths, or approaches that could be taken. In this chapter we wish to expand on that analogy and discuss the different ways in which the message could actually be transported between the sender and the receiver. As shown in Figure 4.1, just as there are different routes or approaches between you and your friend, there are also different vehicles needed to carry the package over those paths. In the instructional situation these vehicles are known as instructional media.

As we also discussed in Chapter 3, selecting the most beneficial approach is based on the situation (e.g., where the receiver is in relation to the package, what paths are available, and which are obstructed) as well as the type of package being sent. In this chapter we will also use these criteria to determine the medium or combination of media that will ensure that the message is delivered in the most effective, efficient, and appealing manner. ■

WHY STUDY MEDIA?

If media are merely the vehicles by which instructional messages are delivered to students, why bother to learn much about them? After all, isn't the message the critical element, and isn't the medium just a carrier of that message, relatively unimportant by itself? Richard Clark (1983), a prominent critic of media comparison studies, has argued that the specific medium has no more impact on instructional effectiveness than a delivery truck has on the nutritional value of the groceries it carries to market.

We believe that media *are* important to instruction. Different media can impact learning in different ways. Let's extend our delivery vehicle analogy a little further. Does the delivery vehicle impact the end result? In many circumstances the choice of delivery vehicle impacts efficiency. A package delivery company does not use a jet plane to transport a package across town. Likewise, a semi-trailer does

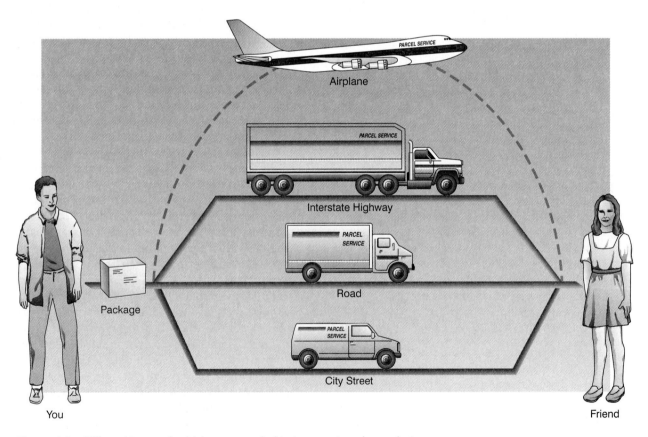

Figure 4.1   Different types of vehicles are needed to transport packages between various locations

not make a good door-to-door delivery vehicle. These are obvious examples of inefficient uses of delivery vehicles. Likewise, some educational media may be more efficient than others in particular circumstances. For example, interactive multimedia is well suited to some educational problems, but it is an inefficient solution to a problem that needs nothing more than a short set of printed instructions.

What about instructional effectiveness? Does the medium matter? In many cases, it may not. Your package, sent through a normal delivery company, may get to its destination just as well via a panel truck or a step van. However, there are circumstances in which the delivery vehicle does affect its contents. When fresh milk is being delivered from the dairy to local grocery stores, a refrigerated truck has significant advantages over a nonrefrigerated vehicle in terms of the wholesomeness and nutritional value of the contents. In this case, the medium does make a difference.

To further explore the role of media in teaching and learning we now need to step away from our vehicle analogy. Analogies are very useful educational tools. Frequently, however, analogies fail to fully reflect the reality they are trying to represent. So it is with our vehicle analogy. It does a good job of conveying the ideas of instructional delivery systems and approaches. But in a very fundamental way, learning is unlike package delivery. Learning is more complicated.

When a package is delivered to you, all you have to do is receive it. The transaction is complete; the job is done. The delivery vehicle simply carries the package from one point to another. In learning, however, the learner must construct meaning from the delivered instructional message. This is a complex process that occurs throughout an instructional session. Furthermore, it is an active process that involves an interplay between the learner and the instructional medium. Every individual learner actively constructs his or her understanding through this interplay.

Robert Kozma (1991) points out that different media possess different attributes or characteristics. One obvious attribute of a medium is its hardware (e.g., a television set, a computer, an overhead projector). Media can also be distinguished by the manner in which they represent information (e.g., text, symbols, spoken words, still or moving images). Learners may capitalize on or benefit from the particular attributes of a medium while constructing meaning from an instructional message. For example, readers make use of the stable quality of information presented in the traditional textbook. When they encounter a difficult passage, learners can slow down, reread portions of the text, skip back and forth, refer to pictures or diagrams, and so on. In other words, as learners struggle to create meaning from the information in a textbook, they actively interact with the textbook in a way that is dependent, to a great extent, on the characteristics of that medium.

Each medium has its own set of unique characteristics, and people interact with the message in ways that are shaped by the particular attributes of the medium. For that reason, it is important to understand what each medium can contribute to the learning environment. For example, in contrast to the printed page, video has a very fluid or transitory character. People watching television tend to sample from this fluid stream of information frequently, and thus their attention may shift toward or away from it. Instructional applications of video, however, can be manipulated to capitalize on its unique elements (e.g., pacing, presentation style, music, narration) to increase the level of viewer attention.

Video and accompanying audio can represent information in multiple ways, including textual, visual, and audiolinguistic (sounds and language) formats. When more than one representation system is employed to deliver information, the effects are greater than with a single system. People learn more when the same message is presented by both visual and aural means. Now that integrated multimedia systems are becoming more common, this is particularly important. Today it is possible to draw on different types of media or combinations of media to address a particular teaching or learning problem. Thus it is even more important to utilize media wisely.

INSTRUCTIONAL MEDIA

A **medium** is a channel of communication. Derived from the Latin word meaning "between," the term refers to that which carries information between a source and a receiver. Examples of media include slides, videotapes, diagrams, printed materials, and computer software. These are considered instructional media when they carry messages with an instructional purpose. The purpose of instructional media is to facilitate communication and enhance learning.

Media can serve a variety of roles in education. Their primary role is to facilitate student learning. One way they do this is by providing a stimulus-rich environment. Media can provide and extend experiences vicariously. A student doesn't have to go to a foreign country to "see" it. Visuals give meaning to words. The student can see what a new invention looks like, not just hear or read a verbal description of it. Motion media and sequential still visuals can demonstrate a process. It is better if, when learning a skill, a learner sees it demonstrated before being asked to practice it. The demonstration can be live, captured on videotape, or presented through a series of photographs. In addition, color, sound, and motion can increase student interest and motivation to learn.

Another role of media often overlooked is their use in the evaluation process. Students can be asked to identify an object or parts of an object in a photograph. They can be required to describe the movements in a musical composition recorded on audiotape. Videotapes can present the events leading up to a problem situation, and the students can be asked to describe their responses to the problem.

Some of the media commonly used in elementary and secondary schools include real objects and models, text, visuals, display boards, overhead transparencies, slides and filmstrips, audio, video and film, television, and computer software. We will take a look at each of these, along with examples of possible classroom applications.

Real Objects and Models

A way to bring the outside world into the classroom is by using real objects and models. Real objects, such as coins, tools, plants, and animals, are some of the most accessible media available to promote student learning. Models are three-dimensional representations of real objects. Compared with the object it represents, a model may be larger, smaller, or the same size. It may be complete in detail or simplified for instructional purposes. Models of almost everything are available from teacher supply companies and toy stores.

Objects and models can bring the real world into the classroom.

A new topic can often be introduced with a real object or a model. Invite the students to see and handle it. Both elementary and secondary students can learn about objects in their own environment and those from foreign cultures and other times. Real objects and models add relevance for the students and can be used to generate interest and enthusiasm for a topic. If the real things cannot be brought into the classrooms, a field trip can take students to them. Another effective use of these materials occurs during evaluation as students classify objects, describe their functions, and identify their components.

Instructional Applications

Science

- Elementary students create a terrarium to observe how the water cycle has a pattern of change.
- Fifth-grade students study an enlarged plastic model to identify the parts of the human outer and inner ear.
- Middle school students tour a cave to examine the development of stalactites, stalagmites, and columns.

Art and Language

- Students use real objects as the focus of a drawing exercise (e.g., a flower, an outdoor scene, a human model).
- Third-grade language arts students visit a museum's dinosaur exhibit to gain inspiration for creative story writing.

Math

- First-grade students manipulate apples, oranges, and pretzels to add or subtract and form equal or unequal sets.
- High school physics students use a combination of pulleys and weights to measure the different amounts of force needed to lift a specific item.
- Special needs students manipulate tangrams to construct patterns.

Social Studies

- Multicultural students discuss the impact of various artifacts (tools, weapons, etc.—real or replicas) on the lives of those from another culture.
- Students dress in clothes of another time period to role-play the differences of various lifestyles.

THE VALUE OF EXAMPLES

As illustrated in the section on real objects and models, examples are frequently used in instructional settings. Research has shown that examples are very effective in helping learners understand a concept and its application. Note how the examples here and throughout this chapter have been used to

- help you see how the media can be applied and generalized across different situations
- help make the information more relevant
- illustrate and highlight one or more important characteristics of each of the individual media
- make ready comparisons across the different media and their individual characteristics (this may help you begin to generate potential benefits and limitations of each form)

- Computer science students examine a vacuum tube, a transistor, and an integrated microchip as they discuss the main evolutionary steps of the computer.

Text

The term *text* refers to alphanumeric letters and characters, usually presented to students in the form of printed materials or on a computer screen. Examples include study guides, manuals, worksheets, textbooks, and computer displays. Textbooks have long been the foundation of the learning process. Many of the other media and computer formats discussed in this book can be used in conjunction with, and as supplements to, textbooks.

The most common application of text is the presentation of information. Students read text to learn the content presented. They are given reading assignments and held accountable for the material during class discussions and on tests. Text can also complement a teacher's presentation. Students may use study guides and supplementary worksheets to augment the information presented by the teacher or through other media. Worksheets allow students to practice what they have learned and to receive feedback from the teacher. Additionally, students may refer to text references in the library or media center or search computer databases to find information on a specific topic.

Instructional Applications

Science

- Students read an assigned unit in the science book discussing features of the earth's crust.

- Students complete worksheets about the workings of an artificial heart after having viewed a film on the topic.

Social Studies

- Students in the eighth-grade social studies class review old newspaper articles to learn about local fund-raising events that occurred during World War II.
- High school students research replicas of handwritten court records from the 1800s to discover information about their ancestors.
- Students read and study material on the U.S. civil rights movement during the 1950s and 1960s.

Language

- High school literature students read the classic works of Shakespeare and Voltaire before discussing similarities and differences in their works.
- Teacher education students use a computer database to review studies published by Ken Goodman involving the use of whole language learning.

General

- Elementary students review a poster describing the steps to be taken in case of an earthquake or tornado.
- A shipping intern uses a packing checklist to make sure all of the parts of a computer system were properly mailed.
- Technology students assemble a bicycle by following the directions in its accompanying pamphlet.

Visuals

Visuals are two-dimensional materials designed to communicate a message to students. They often include verbal as well as symbolic visual cues. Examples include photographs, study prints, drawings, charts, graphs, posters, and cartoons. Sources of visuals include textbooks, reference materials, newspapers, and periodicals, as well as visuals created by the teacher or student.

There are numerous applications of visuals. For example, photographs or drawings may be used to illustrate specific lesson topics, especially those involving processes. Visuals are helpful with objectives requiring the identification of people, places, or things. They may be used to stimulate creative expression such as the telling or writing of stories or the composing of poetry. They can provide an excellent means to review or preview experiences of past or future field trips. Visuals also serve to pique interest and curiosity and provide specific information for testing and evaluation purposes.

Textbook visuals are provided as aids to study, not as mere decorations, and students should be encouraged and taught how to "read" those visuals to aid their learning. Because of their important role, the quality and quantity of a textbook's illustrations should be a weighted priority during the textbook selection process.

Instructional Applications

Science

- Sixth-grade science students sequence the major steps involved in the production of iron using a set of drawings.
- Students use a simple cutaway drawing to point out the various parts of an acorn to illustrate the layers of a seed.

Art

- Students use photographs of local buildings to illustrate a unit on architectural styles.
- Art students use pictures of famous paintings to study and compare the styles of different painters.

Social Studies

- Middle school students generate a visual timeline depicting the main historical events that have occurred since their birth.
- Students view turn-of-the-century photographs to study and discuss the working conditions within a child sweatshop.

- High school history students use geography maps to point out the difficulties an army would have if it attempted to invade Switzerland.

Math

- High school business students generate a graph that depicts the rise and fall of several blue-chip stock prices over the past 18 months.
- Math students collect data and generate a pie chart to indicate the proportion of air pollution created by automobiles, airplanes, trains, trucks, and buses in the United States.
- Students use graphs to make cause-and-effect comparisons between increased reported cases of AIDS and the retail demand for condoms.

Display Boards

There are many surfaces in the classroom on which to display text and visual materials, including chalkboards, multipurpose boards, and bulletin boards. The most common medium in the classroom is the chalkboard. Once called blackboards, chalkboards, like chalk, now come in a variety of colors. Although the chalkboard is most commonly used as a medium of verbal communication, it can be used as a surface on which to attach or draw visuals. Pictures can be fastened to the molding above the chalkboard, taped to the board with masking tape, or placed in the chalk tray to help illustrate instructional concepts and support verbal communication. Visuals, such as sketches, diagrams, charts, and graphs, may be drawn on the chalkboard for display to the class.

Some classrooms are equipped with multipurpose boards instead of chalkboards. These are also called white boards or marker boards. As their name implies, they can be used for more than one purpose. Their smooth, white plastic surface requires a special erasable marker rather than chalk. The white surface is also suitable for the projection of films, slides, and overhead transparencies. Materials cut from thin plastic, such as figures and letters, will adhere to the surface when rubbed in place. Some of these boards have a steel backing as well and can be used as a magnetic board for the display of visuals.

A bulletin board's surface is made of a material that holds pins, thumbtacks, staples, and other sharp fasteners without damage to the board. In practice, bulletin board displays tend to serve three broad purposes: decorative, motivational, and instructional. The decorative bulletin board is probably the most common in schools. Its function is to lend visual stimulation to the environment. Displaying student work exemplifies the motivational use of bulletin boards. The public recognition offered by such displays can play an important role in the life of the classroom. It fosters pride in achievement, reinforcing students' efforts to do a good job.

The third purpose of bulletin boards is instructional, complementing the educational objectives of the formal curriculum. Rather than merely presenting static informational messages, displays can be designed to invite participation. Such displays ask questions and give viewers some means of manipulating parts of the display to verify their answers (e.g., flaps, pockets, dials, or movable parts). Learners can also take part in the actual construction of the display. For example, to introduce a unit on animals, an elementary teacher might ask each student to bring in a picture of a favorite animal. The students would then make a bulletin board incorporating all the pictures.

Instructional Applications

Math

- Elementary students use the chalkboard to practice multiplication problems.
- Geometry students use a chalk-holding compass and a large protractor to draw shapes and angles illustrating theorems on the chalkboard.

Spelling

- Students rearrange large, colorful magnetized letters to correctly spell weekly vocabulary words.

Social Studies

- Groups of students generate lists of the pros and cons of slavery for the economy of the pre–Civil War southern states using a large multipurpose board.

Science

- Students classify various types of igneous, metamorphic, and sedimentary rocks displayed on platforms secured to a bulletin board. Then they check their responses against the correct answer provided under a movable flap.
- Students view posters reminding them of the need for safety gloves and glasses.

Music

- Students sing the simple notes of the treble clef displayed on a multipurpose board. As sharps and flats are added, different colors draw students' attention to these special notes.
- Eighth-grade band students display award ribbons received at a recent competition on the "Hall of Fame" bulletin board.

Overhead Transparencies

Because of its many virtues, the overhead projector is widely used in classrooms. Basically, it is a box with a large "stage" on the top. Light from a powerful lamp inside the box passes through a transparency (approximately 8 inches by 10 inches) placed on the stage. A lens-and-mirror system mounted on a bracket above the box turns the light beam 90° and projects the image back over the shoulder of the teacher.

Overhead transparencies may be created from clear acetate, photographic film, or any of a number of other transparent materials capable of being imprinted with an image. In addition, a variety of materials can be projected, including cutout silhouettes, small opaque objects, and many types of transparent objects. Transparent plastic devices such as clocks, engines, geometric shapes, and the like are available. These can be manipulated by the instructor to demonstrate how the parts interact as they are displayed on the screen. Transparencies may be used individually or made into a series of images consisting of a base visual with one or more overlays attached to the base with hinges. Complex topics can be explained step by step by adding a series of overlays one at a time to the base diagram.

The overhead has a myriad of group-instruction applications. One indication of the breadth of applications is the fact that commercial distributors of transparencies have made materials available for virtually all curricular areas, from kindergarten through high school. These materials range from single, simple transparencies to elaborate sets with multiple overlays.

Instructional Applications

Math

- Students in a fourth-grade math class attempt to answer a projected math brainteaser before class begins.
- Kindergarten students classify various opaque, shaped items placed on the overhead as either circles, triangles, squares, or rectangles.

The overhead projector is an easy-to-use device for showing visuals to a group.

Science

- Fourth-grade students highlight a simple line drawing on a transparency with colored marking pens to depict the flow of electricity.
- Students show the relationship of the body's main organs to their protective skeletal structures using an overlay transparency set.
- Students illustrate the flow of information between a computer's central processing unit and its random-access and read-only memories by drawing arrows on the transparency.

Social Studies

- World history students use map transparencies of Europe and Asia to plot the travels of Marco Polo.
- High school students summarize and list on an overhead transparency the major points of a discussion regarding the impact of drugs and alcohol on the inner-city schools of large U.S. cities.

Language and Art

- Students in a seventh-grade English class use marking pens to write original paragraphs on clear pieces of acetate. Randomly selected paragraphs are projected for the class to critique.

Slides and Filmstrips

Slides are small, transparent photographs individually mounted for one-at-a-time projection. Like other forms of projected visuals, slides may be used at all grade levels and for instruction in all curricular areas. Many high-quality slides are available commercially, singly, and in sets. The fine arts, geography, and the sciences are especially well represented with commercially distributed slides.

A filmstrip is a roll of 35-millimeter transparent film containing a series of related still pictures designed to be projected one at a time. Commercially produced filmstrips typically contain roughly 20 to 60 images ("frames") and are stored in small plastic canisters. Because filmstrips are simply packaged and easy to handle, they are well suited for independent study. Filmstrips are popular items in study carrels and media centers. One major difference between slides and filmstrips is that slides lend themselves to teacher-made presentations, whereas filmstrips are better suited for mass production. Furthermore, slide sets tend to be used in a more open-ended fashion than filmstrips. Filmstrips are usually packaged as self-contained kits; that is, the narration to accompany the pictures is provided either as captions on the filmstrip or as an audiocassette sound track.

Recorded sound tracks that accompany the filmstrip can provide narration, music, and sound effects. The cassette tape is played on a regular cassette recorder or on a player built into the filmstrip projector. For most sound filmstrips and some slide sets, the tape contains not only the sound track but also a second track carrying inaudible signals that automatically trigger the projector to advance to the next frame. Depending on the capability of the projector, users generally can choose to manually advance the filmstrip according to audible beeps or set the projector to run automatically using the inaudible pulses.

As with slides and other types of projected visuals, filmstrips find appropriate applications in a wide variety of subjects and grade levels. Their broad appeal is attested to by the constantly growing volume of commercial materials available. A major directory of commercially available slides and filmstrips is the *Filmstrip & Slide Set Finder*, published by the National Information Center for Educational Media (NICEM).

Instructional Applications

Consumer and Family Science

- Students view a slide show of clothing articles that were designed, sewed, and modeled by fellow students.

Business

- College business students take a "slide tour" of a local business to examine the role of the production manager.

- Mechanical engineering students view a filmstrip showing the intricate steps involved in manufacturing computer hard drives.

Science

- Second graders watch a slide set of the different stages in the life cycle of a butterfly.

- Kindergartners watch a filmstrip demonstrating proper dental care.

Social Studies

- Students design and produce a slide show of the history of their community or school.

- High school students view a set of slides and listen to the synchronized audiocassette recording about the history of South Africa as supplemental materials to a class discussion on apartheid.

Audio

In addition to the teacher's voice, there are numerous ways to bring sound into the classroom. The most common is the audiocassette tape. A newer medium is the **compact disc (CD).** The cassette tape allows both students and teachers to make their own recordings to share with the class. The cassette is very durable. It is easy to use because it requires no manual threading. It can be snapped into and out of a recorder in seconds, and accidental erasures can be avoided by breaking out the small plastic tabs on the edge of the cassette. Storage is also convenient. A major directory of commercially available audiotapes and CDs is the *Audiocassette & Compact Disc Finder*, published by NICEM.

For hands-on learning, students can receive procedural instructions on an audiotape prepared by the instructor. To be efficient and effective in their work, these students must have both hands free and their eyes on their work, not on a textbook or manual. Audiotapes allow students to move at their own pace and leave the instructor free to circulate around the classroom and discuss each student's work individually.

Students with learning difficulties can revisit classroom presentations via audiotape. They can replay more difficult sections as often as necessary. The students practice their listening skills with

Students can share audio experiences.

tapes of recorded stories, poetry, and instructions. After the students have practiced their listening skills under teacher direction, they can be evaluated using a tape they have not heard before.

Instructional Applications

Speech

- Students in a middle school speech class use the tape recorder to practice the intonation needed to deliver a persuasive talk.
- Students in a foreign-language class listen, review, and mimic the correct pronunciation of new vocabulary words.

Language and Art

- Students with visual impairments listen to recorded versions of novels being discussed in literature class.
- Students complete an oral book report by recording responses to questions presented on an audiocassette.

Music

- Orchestra students individually record a familiar piece of music for critique by their conductor.

History

- Students practice interviewing techniques as they prepare the oral histories of their parents and grandparents.
- High school students interview local citizens regarding the history of their community. Excerpts are duplicated and edited into oral histories for use by other students.

Business and Training

- Marketing students learn how to increase levels of consumer motivation for buying a specific product by combining dramatic music with emotional oral testimonies of the product's effectiveness and value.
- A college student follows a set of recorded instructions to set up a computer system consisting of a printer, monitor, keyboard, computer, and mouse.

Video and Film

The recording of moving images has progressed from film to videotape, and now to videodisc and computer disk. All these formats offer ways to store and display moving images accompanied by sound.

As we will see, the formats differ considerably in cost, convenience, and flexibility.

Video is defined as the display of recorded pictures on a television-type screen. Any media format that employs a cathode-ray screen to present a picture can be referred to as video: videotapes, videodiscs, and CDs. The most common video formats are described in Table 4.1.

The VHS half-inch **videotape** is the preferred medium for commercial distribution of moving images. VHS is also the current preferred format for amateur production of video in education. Within the past decade, VHS has replaced 16-millimeter film as the format of choice for distribution of educational "film." VHS videotape is considerably cheaper than 16-millimeter film and has been so universally accepted that some companies now offer their productions *only* in VHS.

A **videodisc** resembles a large CD. Images and sound are recorded in a manner similar to that for the compact disc. A videodisc (CAV format) can hold up to 30 minutes of motion video images or up to 54,000 still images, or a combination of both motion and still images. As with the CD, the videodisc can be indexed for rapid location of any part of the material. However, indexing must be incorporated into the disc during production; it cannot be added by the user. When a videodisc playback unit is connected to a computer, the information on the disc can become an integral part of a computer-assisted instructional program. The computer program makes use of the index on the disc.

Both videotape and videodisc are more flexible for instruction than film. Both video formats have fast-forward and reverse search capabilities, while film does not. Video formats, particularly videodisc, can be indexed, making it possible to locate specific sections of a program. Certain special effects, such as slow motion, can be obtained during the video presentation. Because of ease of operation of the equipment, video lends itself to individual study much more readily than film.

A video copy of a program is less expensive than its film counterpart. Media centers have found that compared with film, purchasing, handling, storing, distributing, and maintaining video is a great deal easier on the budget and personnel. A major directory of commercially available videos and films is the *Film & Video Finder*, published by NICEM.

Instructional Applications

Social Studies

- Sophomore high school students in a government course view a film of a dramatic re-creation

Table 4.1 Common video formats

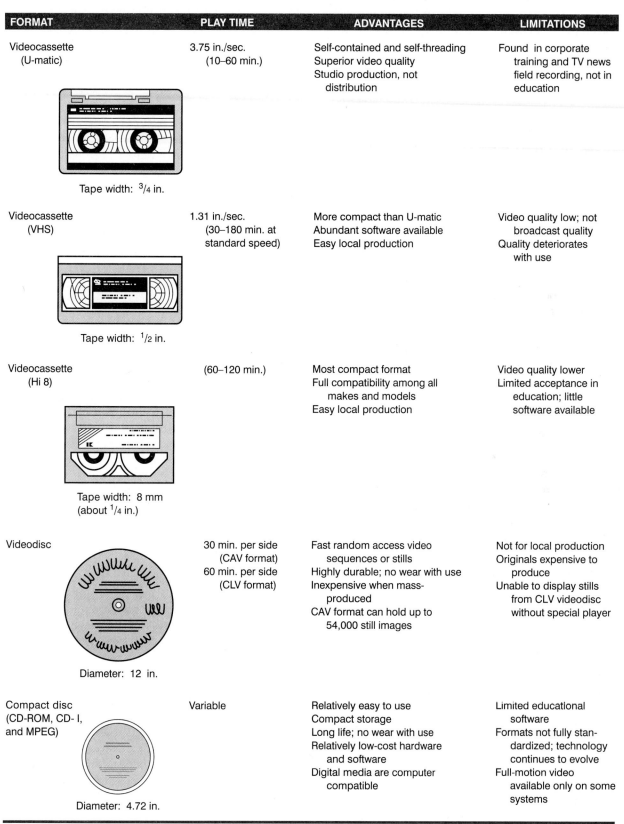

FORMAT	PLAY TIME	ADVANTAGES	LIMITATIONS
Videocassette (U-matic) Tape width: ³/₄ in.	3.75 in./sec. (10–60 min.)	Self-contained and self-threading Superior video quality Studio production, not distribution	Found in corporate training and TV news field recording, not in education
Videocassette (VHS) Tape width: ¹/₂ in.	1.31 in./sec. (30–180 min. at standard speed)	More compact than U-matic Abundant software available Easy local production	Video quality low; not broadcast quality Quality deteriorates with use
Videocassette (Hi 8) Tape width: 8 mm (about ¹/₄ in.)	(60–120 min.)	Most compact format Full compatibility among all makes and models Easy local production	Video quality lower Limited acceptance in education; little software available
Videodisc Diameter: 12 in.	30 min. per side (CAV format) 60 min. per side (CLV format)	Fast random access video sequences or stills Highly durable; no wear with use Inexpensive when mass-produced CAV format can hold up to 54,000 still images	Not for local production Originals expensive to produce Unable to display stills from CLV videodisc without special player
Compact disc (CD-ROM, CD-I, and MPEG) Diameter: 4.72 in.	Variable	Relatively easy to use Compact storage Long life; no wear with use Relatively low-cost hardware and software Digital media are computer compatible	Limited educational software Formats not fully standardized; technology continues to evolve Full-motion video available only on some systems

Note. Adapted with permission from *Instructional Media and Technologies for Learning* (5th ed.) (p. 199), by R. Heinich, M. Molenda, J. D. Russell, and S. E. Smaldino, 1996, Englewood Cliffs, NJ: Merrill/Prentice Hall. Copyright 1996 by Merrill/Prentice Hall.

of the signing of the Declaration of Independence to learn something about the individuals who participated in its signing.

- Eighth-grade students react to a film that incorporated the use of graphic footage and music in order to shape and influence their attitudes toward conservation and environmental issues.
- Students view short video clips of a typical school day for children from Taiwan, Germany, Ethiopia, Peru, and the United States in order to make comparisons.

Physical Education

- Physical education students use slow-motion and freeze-frame capabilities of the videodisc to practice imitating the grip and swing of a golf professional.

Speech

- Students use a film of the famous "I have a dream" speech by Martin Luther King Jr. to analyze the impact of body language and vocal intonation on his delivery.
- Participants in a junior high school speech contest videotape their practice speeches for replay and critique.

Language and Art

- The high school language class begins a unit on Shakespeare by viewing a film of *Romeo and Juliet*.
- Students write a position paper after viewing videos presenting the opposing positions of the lumber industry and environmentalists on retention of the virgin forests of the northwestern United States.
- Art students select works of art by Renoir from a videodisc containing pictures of thousands of pieces of art.

Business and Training

- Auto production assembly-line workers view a video of new production practices to determine how they differ from previous practices.
- New managers practice responding to employee problems presented via an interactive videodisc program. Based on the manager's response, the program provides visual feedback.

Television

In this book, television refers to *live* broadcasts, whereas video refers to images captured on tape or disc. Some schools use curriculum-based programs that are broadcast by school districts or carried on local cable channels.

Instructional Applications

Government

- Students in a high school government class view live congressional hearings on a recent Supreme Court nomination.
- Students watch television news reports covering a city council meeting to enhance discussions on the role of local government.
- Elementary school students view an inauguration ceremony of a newly elected president as they study a unit about the federal government.
- Students view congressional debates on foreign trade agreements and then discuss their potential impact on American workers.

Foreign Language

- Students in a high school Spanish Conversation class use Spanish news broadcasts to increase their listening and comprehension skills.

Science

- Students view television broadcasts to report on experiments being conducted on the space shuttle and the progress of the work.
- College physics students watch a live news conference announcing the development of a method to achieve cold fusion to begin a discussion on potential benefits from such a source of energy.
- College geoscience students tune to the television weather channel to gather information about an impending hurricane and how it is being tracked by the weather service.

Computer Software

The computer—with its virtually instantaneous response to student input, its extensive capacity to store and manipulate information, and its unmatched ability to serve many individual students simultaneously—has wide applications in instruction. The computer has the ability to control and manage a wide variety of media and learning material, including films, filmstrips, video, slides, audiotapes, and printed information. The computer can also record, analyze, and react to student responses

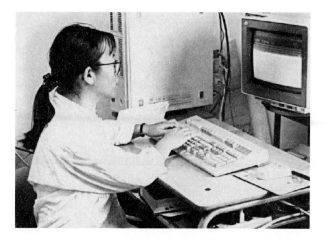

Computers are becoming pervasive at all levels of education.

that are typed using a keyboard or input with a mouse. Some display screens react to the touch of a student's finger.

Instructional Applications

Social Studies

• Ninth-grade students use a computer research database to locate recently published books and articles describing the impact of Germany's unification.

• Learners study the *Titanic* through the use of an interactive videodisc program that provides diagrams of the ship's structure, biographies of individuals sailing on the ship, information about rescue operations, and film footage of the exploration and discovery of the wreckage.

Science

• Students use a physics computer simulation to view how various changes in weight, velocity, and gravity impact a moving object.

Math

• Elementary students use a computerized instructional game that requires quick responses to simple multiplication and addition problems.

Reading

• First-grade students use a computerized storybook with colorful pictures and large words presented on a computer screen. The children choose whether to read the words alone or to have the

computer pronounce individual words or entire passages.

Language Arts

• Students use a literature computer program to read a passage and instantaneously receive definitions, explanations, or clarifications for any unknown word, name, or phrase specified.

INTEGRATING TECHNOLOGY
Investigating Media and the Computer

Recently, Janette shared with us some of her memories of the way teachers used media to effectively teach foreign-language courses when she was in high school. Language teachers were noted for capitalizing on the strengths of many of the media discussed in this chapter. Besides the use of authentic objects from foreign cultures, including foods, jewelry, clothing, and even games and toys, a variety of visuals were also displayed around the classroom. Ms. Moreno remembers brightly colored posters and maps, as well as wall hangings and brochures. As students' facility with the particular language increased, Spanish newspapers and magazines were read. Novels and textbooks written in the foreign language were read and discussed, and phonograph records were used to present popular music from other cultures. Occasionally even a foreign film was shown. Janette also described the yearly homemade slide shows that her language teacher would make following her most recent trip overseas!

One of the most innovative applications Janette experienced was the language laboratory, which was a great way to individualize language instruction for each student. Janette remembers working in small study carrels equipped with audiotape recorders and headphones, listening to passages in different languages. What was interesting about the setup of these laboratories was that, even though students' responses were not recorded on the tape being played, the teacher could listen in on the carrels and give students feedback. This kept students on track and also provided opportunities for teacher-student interactions based on specific learners' needs. This was a fairly popular approach at the time, and Ms. Moreno, as a student, appreciated the features of individual work, opportunities for practice, and tailor-made teacher feedback.

When Janette first started teaching she utilized many of the techniques she was familiar with (only

Media can be used to involve students in learning.

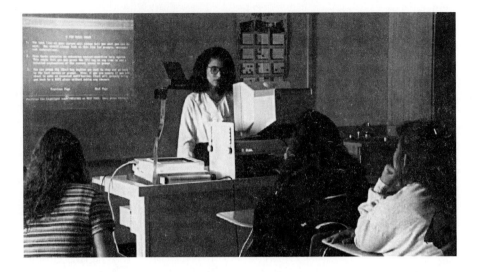

instead of creating a slide show, she used a video recorder when she traveled overseas). The traditional media and methods still had a lot to offer language students. Yet she began to experience some frustrations, due, in part, to the widening range of students enrolling in her courses. She needed to find ways to increase her own capacity to meet individual learners' needs. Janette described her initial hesitation and early frustrations in trying to use the computer to meet those needs. "It was awful. I was so afraid I was going to break something or mess up a program, or lose what I was working on. I knew nothing about the computer—I didn't even know what a disk or a hard drive was. I attended a workshop one summer that covered a lot of basic technical stuff, and I managed to hook up with another language teacher who was just a few steps ahead of me. The thing that saved me? I learned how to learn from my mistakes!"

Janette has grown a lot in both knowledge and confidence since she took that first computer course. As noted in Chapter 1, she continues to look for new ways to make learning meaningful and exciting for her students, and, as you might expect, many of Ms. Moreno's recent innovations revolve around some type of computer application. Yet what she is able to accomplish today still rests on the basic knowledge she gained during that summer workshop. Knowledge of computer basics is still foundational to effective computer use.

THE POWER OF COMPUTERS

At this juncture we are going to turn our attention away from media in general and focus more specifically on the computer as a uniquely powerful media platform. The computer is an instructional tool, and

oh, what an instructional tool it is! It brings to the teaching and learning environment capabilities that are unequaled. It can present text and visuals. Newer multimedia computer systems can also present high-quality audio and video. Thus the computer can employ and coordinate multiple media. Its capacity to accept, store, display, and manipulate information makes it a uniquely flexible and powerful teaching tool. The computer not only displays information in different ways, but also it processes information. It has the power to match its representational systems and processing to the needs of the individual learner and, thereby, enhance learning.

Yet the computer is more than an instructional delivery vehicle; it is a tool that can be used in many different ways. While it can be used to deliver prepared instruction, it can also assist the teacher or learner in performing routine tasks. What is more, the computer can act as a malleable "canvas" on which students express their ideas. It can interact with students in an individualized fashion, or, with an attached display device, it can be used as a large-group presentation tool. It can access instruction stored on a diskette in the computer, or it can reach across network or telephone lines to gather information from down the hall or from halfway around the world.

Computers in Education

This diversity of computer uses in education is reflected in a popular categorization scheme developed by Robert Taylor (1980). Taylor's model divides computer applications in education into three broad categories: the computer as a teacher, the computer as a tool, and the computer as a learner. In the first category, the computer presents instruction to the learner. In the second category, the computer aids the teacher or learner in performing routine tasks. In the final category, which Taylor dubbed the "tutee" mode, the computer becomes the "student" and the learner "teaches" the computer to perform some task. While new developments have somewhat blurred the distinctions between categories, this model remains a simple but useful way to look at different computer uses in education.

Computers as Teachers

Of course, the computer can be used to present instruction directly to students. In this mode, the computer engages in activities that have traditionally been associated with a human teacher or tutor. It presents instruction, provides instructional activities or situations, quizzes or otherwise requires interaction from the learner, evaluates learner responses, provides feedback, and determines appropriate follow-up activities. When used as a teaching machine, the computer can be highly interactive, individualized, and infinitely patient. Applications that utilize the computer for teaching are usually labeled **computer-based instruction (CBI), computer-assisted instruction (CAI),** or **computer-assisted learning (CAL).** Several instructional approaches are commonly used in CBI, including drill and practice, tutorial, simulation, problem solving, and instructional games.

Computers as Tools

In the tool mode the computer aids the teacher or the learner in performing routine work tasks. It can substitute for a typewriter, a manual filing system, a financial worksheet, an artist's canvas, a drafting table, and much more. As a tool the computer is a labor-saving device that can be applied in myriad ways. Teachers often employ the computer as a tool for the production of instructional materials (e.g., printed matter, graphics, interactive presentations). Of course, learners can also employ the computer as a tool for the production of materials. In addition, computer tools can be used in ways that help students learn. For example, students can develop their research and critical-thinking skills through work with computer databases. Thus computer tools may be used for production in support of teaching and learning or as a more direct vehicle for learning. Important computer tool applications for education include word processors, databases, spreadsheets and other numerical tools, graphics packages, computer communication tools, and integrated tools, which combine more than one of the preceding.

Computers as Learners

The third major category of computer uses in education is the learner or tutee mode. Here the traditional roles of computer and learner are reversed. The computer becomes the learner; the user becomes the teacher. The objective is for the user to "teach" the computer to perform some task. In order to achieve this objective, the user must come to an understanding of how to perform the task and then must be able to communicate this to the computer in a way that the computer will "understand." In other words, the user must learn to program the computer. This requires logical thinking and problem-solving skills, and, as a result, many experts believe that this is one of the most valuable ways to use a computer in education. The most commonly used computer languages for tutee activities include Logo, BASIC, and Pascal, as well as newer multimedia/hypermedia authoring tools such as *HyperCard, HyperStudio, Linkway,* and *Toolbook.*

Multimedia and Hypermedia

The term **multimedia** has been around for a while, although for many people it carries a connotation of a system composed of a bank of slide projectors dissolving one image into another and synchronized to a master audiotape. Today this term conveys the notion of a system in which various media (e.g., text, graphics, video, and audio) are integrated into a single delivery system under computer control. A modern **interactive multimedia** system may weave together text, graphics, animation, data, video, and audio from various sources, including a videodisc, a CD, and the computer itself.

Picture a foreign-language student in Ms. Moreno's class seated in front of a multimedia system. It looks pretty much like a computer system, perhaps with a few additional pieces of equipment connected to it via cables. The student reads the directions on the computer screen and clicks the mouse to get started. The lesson begins with a video clip, originating from a videodisc, which depicts a conversation between two native speakers of Spanish. The video not only allows the student to see and hear two native speakers, but it also provides a cultural backdrop, as it was shot on location overseas. As the lesson progresses, the student makes use of a Spanish dictionary that is stored on a CD-ROM. This provides definitions and translations, as well as the actual aural pronunciation of each word and phrase. The computer facilitates the student's access to all of this information and provides periodic review questions and feedback about the student's progress. This is just one example of what interactive multimedia can be like.

Hypermedia is a related but subtly distinct term. For many years there has been interest in the notion of an information-processing machine that could work by associations, as the human brain does. The term **hypertext** was coined to describe such an associational information-processing system in the text domain. In a hypertext system, text information is stored in nodes, and nodes are connected to other nodes of related information. Imagine that you are reading a text passage and you come to a section where you wish to know more about the topic. In a hypertext system, the passage could be linked to another reference that in fact does contain additional information about the topic. By traversing the link between these related nodes, you could instantly jump to the desired information following your own associational interests. This is the essence of hypertext. Hypermedia simply extends this notion to other media. In a hypermedia system, nodes of information may contain graphics, animation, video, or audio as well as, or instead of, text. Thus the term *hypermedia* describes a particular form of multimedia in which the information is stored in interconnected nodes.

Multimedia and hypermedia represent one of the most important developments in educational technology. For many years, various media developed along separate and independent lines. Today all media are converging in the personal computer. While the technology is still in its infancy today, within a few years we can expect to see all media integrated into a single, easy–to–use system. As a result, all of the advantages of the various media (text, visuals, audio, and video) are linked to the control and processing power of the computer and made available to teachers and learners simultaneously.

Interactive Multimedia Systems

Today, interactive multimedia comes in a variety of forms. The simplest forms use a relatively limited set of media and employ a level of interactivity that is rather low. More complex forms use a wide variety of media from a number of different sources and may be highly interactive. Today there are three common interactive multimedia systems: CBI, interactive videodisc, and CD-ROM and related digital technologies. While these can be viewed as separate forms of interactive multimedia, it is important to recognize that any or all may be present in a single interactive multimedia system. Figure 4.2 depicts a complex interactive multimedia system.

1. *Computer-based instruction.* As we noted above, CBI refers to the use of the computer in the delivery of instruction. Today, personal computers, even without sophisticated multimedia capability or access to other devices, can convey information through text, graphics, and simple sound effects. Computers are, in effect, interactive multimedia machines in themselves. In this way, CBI provides a baseline for interactive multimedia.

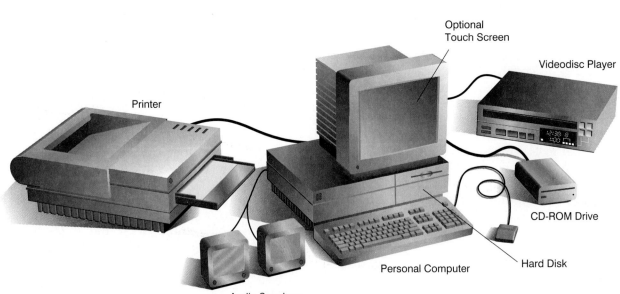

Figure 4.2   A pictorial representation of a complex interactive multimedia system

2. *Interactive videodisc.* **Interactive videodisc** refers to a system in which video from a laser videodisc is presented in response to choices made by the user. A simple interactive videodisc system consists of a laser videodisc player connected to a television or video monitor and controlled through the use of a handheld remote control. Such a system can provide a variety of media (text, graphics, video, and audio) with at least rudimentary interactivity. When a laserdisc player is linked to a computer, the result is a CBI system that also provides video and audio. Such an interactive video system begins to show the real potential of interactive multimedia.

3. *CD-ROM and related digital technologies.* The newest forms of interactive multimedia rely on various digital technologies. Computers are digital machines; therefore, digital multimedia technologies have built–in compatibility with the computer. **CD-ROM** (compact disc—read-only memory) is a technology in which computer data, text, and graphics are stored in digital form on a CD and retrieved by the computer. When combined with digital audio circuitry and speakers, a CD-ROM can turn a personal computer into a multimedia PC (MPC). Other forms of digital information storage are available as well. Some, such as Apple's *QuickTime* software, are able to store and retrieve digital video images using only the computer.

The products of the various forms of interactive multimedia, like the technologies themselves, can take many forms. A single CBI package or a single videodisc, for example, may be considered a multimedia product if it embodies multiple media. In the most complex cases, a multimedia package may involve a videodisc, a CD-ROM, and computer software controlled by hypermedia software such as *HyperCard.* There are many examples of interactive multimedia products today, ranging from overtly instructional programs to explorable interactive information resources such as multimedia encyclopedias.

CUE Computer Use ESSENTIALS

The following is the first in a series of explanations of how the computer can be used. Our goal here is to lay a foundation of basics about the computer system. While the number of terms introduced here may seem daunting, it is important at this point for us to establish the vocabulary needed for talking about computers in order to facilitate subsequent discussion. You may want to refer back to this CUE when questions occur to you as you learn about specific computer applications later in the book.

UNDERSTANDING COMPUTER SYSTEMS

The computer's capabilities are defined, enabled, and constrained by the hardware and software that comprise a particular computer system. The physical components of the computer system are termed **hardware.** The hardware sets absolute limits on what the computer can do. With only a monochrome display device, for example, a computer cannot display multicolor images. **Software** is the term for the programs or instructions that tell the computer what to do. It is the software that unlocks the capabilities of the hardware. A computer is a machine capable of performing an amazing variety of tasks, but each task requires appropriate software. Without the software, a computer is just a high-tech paperweight.

In popular terms, the word **computer** refers to a machine that processes information, usually numeric data, according to a set of instructions. When most people picture a computer, they think of a desktop (or maybe larger) device that has elements such as a keyboard, a disk drive unit, and a monitor. In reality, what most people are thinking of when they picture this thing is a **computer system,** a collection of components that includes the computer and all of the devices that people use with the computer. The computer itself is responsible for processing information. The other components are usually responsible either for putting information into the computer (input) or getting information out of the computer (output).

There are three generally recognized categories of computer systems. The members of the largest and most powerful class are known as **mainframe computers.** Mainframe computers have very large storage capacities and very fast processing speeds; often they are used to support large numbers of users simultaneously. Mainframes are very expensive and generally are used by large businesses, universities, and governments for large-scale processing tasks. The most powerful and fastest of the mainframes are called **supercomputers.** The members of the second class of computer systems, **minicomputers,** feature intermediate storage capacities and processing speeds and simultaneous use by several to dozens of users. They are often used by small businesses and larger schools.

The members of the third class, **personal computers** or microcomputers, are the smallest, least powerful, and least expensive. Personal computers are intended for use by individuals. Since their proliferation began in the late 1970s, they have become the focus of much of the computing industry. In addition, as personal computer capabilities have grown, the distinctions between personal computers and the more powerful classes of computers have begun to blur. We will focus our attention on personal computers because they are such useful and widespread tools for educators. As a basis for subsequent discussion, we will look at the components of a typical personal computer system and present some basic computer terminology. Figure 4.3 presents diagrammatic and pictorial representations of a computer system.

CPU

At the core of any computer system is the central processing unit, or **CPU.** The CPU is the "brain" of the machine. It controls the functions of the rest of the system, and it performs the calculations that make the computer a prodigious number cruncher. In personal computers, the CPU resides on a single computer chip, a little square of silicon with tiny electronic circuits etched onto it, called a **microprocessor.** Different personal computers are distinguished from one another, in part, by the particular microprocessor each uses. The more powerful versions found in newer personal computers today may have over one million electrical components and are capable of a large number of operations at very high speeds.

Most computers are digital machines; that is, they work with numbers. While there are such things as analog computers, they are far less common than their digital counterparts. At their most basic level, personal computers do their work using just zeros and ones. Zeros and ones are the language the computer "understands," that is, machine language. People represent this information using the binary numbering system.

Figure 4.3 Diagrammatic and pictorial representations of a computer system (*Note:* The dashed box represents the computer proper in the computer system.)

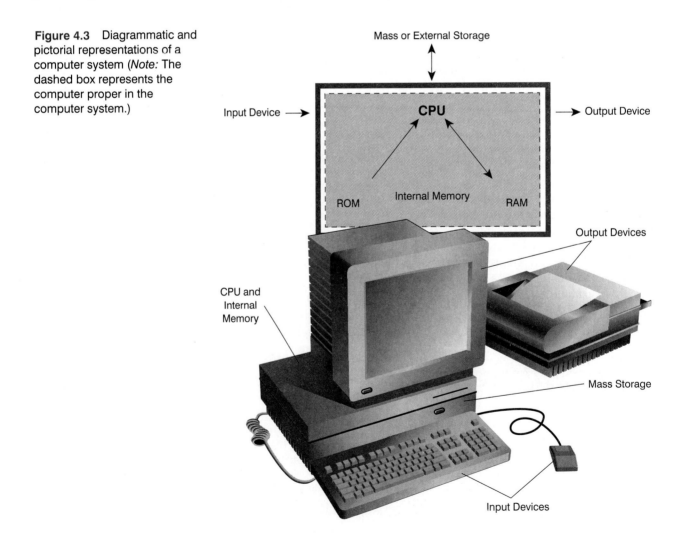

The smallest amount of information the CPU can deal with is a single zero or one, that is, a single binary digit, or **bit** for short. By itself, a single bit is not very exciting. However, put some bits together, and you've got something! A collection of eight bits is used by the computer to code each basic symbol needed to represent such things as a letter of the alphabet, a numeral, or a punctuation mark. In computer terminology, this collection of eight bits is called a **byte.** There is a unique byte for every letter, numeral, and symbol the computer can represent. In a way, bytes are the intelligible common denominator of the computer world.

Internal or Main Memory

In order to do its work, the CPU has to have information to process. This information is stored inside the machine in the **internal** or **main memory.** The CPU in a personal computer maintains an intimate working relationship with the internal memory of the machine. The CPU retrieves information from internal memory and deposits information there. There is a constant, ongoing exchange. Indeed, the computer proper inside a computer system is usually considered to be the CPU and its associated internal memory. There are two basic varieties of memory found in most personal computers: **read-only memory (ROM)** and **random-access memory (RAM).**

ROM

ROM is the permanent memory that is built into the computer at the factory. It contains the basic instructions that the computer needs to operate. ROM is referred to as "read only" because the computer can retrieve, that is to say, read, the information that is stored there, but it cannot change that stored information. Every time you turn on your computer, the information in ROM is accessed first to get things going.

RAM

RAM is the computer's working memory. When you use a personal computer, RAM is your personal work space. When you use a word processor, your word-processing program is typically copied from disk into a section of RAM to be used. The document that you write with your word processor occupies another block of RAM as you compose it. The beauty of RAM is that you can change its contents, as needed, to perform different tasks. Unfortunately, this is also its curse. Common RAM is volatile; that means that its contents disappear as soon as the power is turned off (or otherwise interrupted). Mass or external storage, which we will discuss shortly, is used to store the contents of RAM so that work is not lost between computer sessions.

It is useful to think of RAM as a long row of mailboxes. To the computer, each mailbox has a unique address, and the CPU can instantly go straight to the correct mailbox to put in or take out a piece of information. That is what is meant by "random access." Any memory location is immediately and directly accessible without having to go through all of the preceding mailboxes to get to it. In the computer, each mailbox holds one and only one byte. Imagine the number of mailboxes it takes to hold a single word-processing document!

Since each RAM location holds a single byte, the quantity of working memory in the computer is usually described in terms of the number of bytes available. Because it takes a lot of bytes to accomplish something useful, it is simpler to talk about thousands or millions of bytes of available RAM. The metric abbreviations K for kilo (thousand) and M for mega (million) have been adopted to describe the number of bytes of computer memory. So, a computer that has 640K of RAM can store roughly 640,000 bytes of information in working memory, while one with 8M (i.e., 8 **megabytes**) of RAM can store approximately 8 million bytes. To put these quantities in perspective, consider that a typical double–spaced, typewritten page requires about 2K of storage. Personal computers today come equipped with varying quantities of RAM. While older systems had relatively little RAM, many systems now require 8M or more for efficient operation.

Input Devices

In addition to its working relationship with internal memory, the CPU maintains contact with the various devices that connect to the computer. Collectively, these devices are referred to as peripherals. **Peripherals** include input devices, output devices (collectively referred to as **I/O devices**), and mass storage devices. The computer communicates with these devices through electronic go–betweens called **interfaces.** Let's begin by looking at input devices.

The CPU processes information that is in the computer. Somehow information has to get into the computer for processing. Information that goes into the computer is referred to as **input,** and a device that generates input is called an **input device.** Several types of input devices now are common on personal computers.

Keyboard

The most common input device is the **keyboard.** The computer keyboard resembles the keyboard of a typewriter. However, computer keyboards generally possess a few extra keys, such as Control and Escape, that provide for additional functions. When the user presses a key on the keyboard, such as the letter A, a signal is sent to the CPU, which processes it and responds in some way. Your word processor, for example, would then display the letter A on the computer's screen. Some keys are special. The Return (or Enter) key, for example, is similar to the carriage return on a typewriter and is often used to signal the computer to proceed or to perform some operation in an application. Keys with arrows allow one to move the **cursor,** a highlighted position indicator, around on the display screen.

Mouse and Pointing Devices

The **mouse** is a pointing device. When the mouse is moved along a flat surface such as a desktop, an arrow moves across the display screen in the same direction. The mouse typically has one to three buttons that may be used for selecting or entering information. Using a mouse, one can select and also move information on the display screen. On some computer systems trackballs, joysticks, and game paddles function in much the same manner as a mouse. Pointing functions can also be accomplished through the use of a light pen or a touch-sensitive screen.

Modem

Another important device is the modem. A **modem** is really a combination input and output device that allows a computer to communicate with another computer over telephone lines. A modem (short for modulator–demodulator) converts digital computer information into sound (and vice versa) for transmission over telephone lines. It is an increasingly important device because it gives personal computer users access to other computers and to huge databases all over the world.

Other Input Devices

A variety of other input devices are available. Oversized keyboards and special input pads are available for use with younger learners or those with impaired motor skills. For learners with severe impairments, there is a range of augmentative communication devices that can provide access to the computer. With the growth of multimedia, several other types of input devices have become popular computer accessories. **Graphics tablets** permit the development of sophisticated artwork. Musical instrument digital interface (MIDI) devices allow the exchange of input and output between the computer and electronic musical instruments. Optical **scanners** allow material from printed sources such as books to be entered into the computer. In somewhat similar fashion, video **digitizers** allow still or even motion video to be captured in a form that the computer can use. Audio digitizers do the same thing for sound.

Output Devices

If you can put information into the computer, you must also be able to get information out. Information that comes out of the computer is called **output.** Common **output devices** include the display screen or monitor, a printer, and speakers.

Display Screen or Monitor

The display screen or **monitor** is the most common output device on personal computers. Most desktop personal computers come equipped with television–like display screens called **CRTs** (cathode-ray tubes) or sometimes VDTs (video display terminals). This type of display functions very much like a television.

Laptop computers popularized the use of liquid crystal display (LCD) screens. **LCD screens,** unlike bulky CRT displays, are compact, flat units. In addition to serving as display screens for laptop computers, LCD panels are used in conjunction with overhead projectors as large-group display devices for computer output.

Computer displays, whether CRT or LCD, are distinguished from one another by two main characteristics: resolution and color capability. Resolution refers to the clarity of the image that can be displayed. The image on the computer screen is formed from a grid of tiny dots. Each dot is called a **pixel** (short for picture element). Higher-resolution monitors can display more pixels, resulting in sharper graphics and better text readability. Color capability varies considerably. On one end of the spectrum are monochrome (one-color) displays; these commonly use a black background with white, green, or amber text and graphics. At the other end of the spectrum are monitors that are capable of displaying millions of different shades of color. The actual resolution and color displayed depend both on the monitor or screen display itself (i.e., you cannot get color from a monochrome monitor) and on the display circuitry and memory built into the computer (i.e., the computer may not be able to produce all of the colors the monitor can display).

Printer

The **printer** provides printed output, commonly referred to as **hard copy.** Several types of printers are common in personal computer systems, including dot matrix, ink-jet, and laser printers.

Dot matrix printers are inexpensive and versatile. They are so named because a set of tiny pins strikes the page to form the image of each letter out of a matrix of dots. In draft mode, the dots often are visible, but in higher-quality modes the dots overlap to produce smoother letters. There are two basic types of dot matrix printers: 9-pin models and 24-pin models. The 24-pin models are capable of **letter-quality** (LQ), or typewriter-like, output, while the 9-pin models can only manage near letter quality (NLQ). Dot matrix printers are versatile because they can print text in various type fonts and sizes and can also print graphics. However, they are rather slow and noisy.

Ink-jet printers are a step up from dot matrix. These printers form letters on the page by shooting tiny electrically charged droplets of ink. Ink-jet printers can produce both text and graphics, and their prices have fallen to levels comparable to dot matrix printers. They have the added advantage of being faster and quieter than dot matrix printers, although operating costs (e.g., ink cartridges) are higher.

The cream of the printer crop are **laser printers,** which combine laser and photocopying technology to produce very high quality output, comparable to that produced in typesetting. They can produce text as well as high-quality graphics. Typical laser printers can achieve print densities of 300 to 600 dots per inch for very finely detailed images. Laser printers are also fast and virtually silent. Their chief disadvantage is cost; they are expensive to buy and to operate.

Most printers feature a single color, usually black print on a white page. However, color printers are available. The color versions tend to be more expensive than their black-print counterparts, and there is considerable variation in quality. However, the technology is there for those who need color output.

Other Output Devices

While display monitors and printers are the most common output devices, there are others. Plotters, like printers, are used for creating hard copy. Plotters are used mainly for drawings such as CAD (computer-aided design) blueprints. With the growth of multimedia, audio speakers have become an increasingly important output device. CBI today can speak to the learner as well as print instructions on the display screen. Sound can be either synthesized or stored in digital form. Some personal computers are even capable of outputting motion video images without the use of an external video player. The video is stored on the computer's mass storage device in digital form and played back on the display screen.

Mass Storage

Mass or **external storage devices** are considered I/O devices because they send information to and receive information from the CPU. Sometimes mass storage is also thought of as external or auxiliary memory. Regardless of the particular conception, the salient characteristic of mass storage is its ability to provide access to programs and other types of data that can be stored over a long period of time. RAM is volatile; its contents disappear when the power to the computer is turned off. Mass storage provides a means for keeping work from one computer session to the next. Most mass storage devices use magnetic means for storing the data, but newer technologies are emerging. Let's examine the most popular mass storage devices.

Magnetic Tape

Magnetic tape is one of the oldest of the mass storage media. Mainframe computers today, like their latter-day relatives, use reels of magnetic tape for large-scale storage needs. This approach was utilized in the first personal computers, which relied on audiocassette tape as a storage medium. While audiocassette tape storage has all but disappeared, magnetic tape systems are still used for large-scale storage needs, such as backing up the hard disks of computers, especially those that act as network file servers.

Floppy Disks

Almost all personal computers today rely on **floppy disks** (or **diskettes**) for mass storage. The typical personal computer system today comes equipped with one or more floppy disk drives. Like tape, the floppy disk is a magnetic storage medium, and the read/write head in a floppy disk drive works very much like the comparable part in a tape recorder. But, unlike linear tape, floppy disks can be randomly accessed, making storage and retrieval of information much easier. Floppy disks are so named because the medium itself is very flexible, although rigid cases sometimes disguise that fact.

Floppy disks and floppy disk drives are distinguished by size and storage capacity. Two sizes of floppy disks are widespread today: 5.25 inch and 3.5 inch. While the first personal computers used the 5.25-inch size, the 3.5-inch size is preferred for the latest generation of personal computers. Capacities of floppy disks have always been close to the typical RAM capacity of personal computers. Older personal computers with little RAM had low disk capacities. Today, 1.44M floppy disks are common, and 2.88M versions have been introduced. There is even a special kind of floppy disk, called a floptical, that has a capacity of 20M.

Hard Disks

Floppy disks are a convenient, portable storage medium for personal computers. They become far less suitable, however, when storage requirements are large. It usually takes a lot of floppy disks to store 100M of data! Large storage requirements call for a **hard** or **fixed disk.** Like magnetic tape, hard disks were first used as a storage medium on mainframe computers. Hard disks, which are also a magnetic storage medium, are so named because the disks are rigid, unlike floppy disks, so that they can be manufactured to very fine tolerances with large storage capacities. While floppy disks are removable, hard disks are fixed; they stay within sealed units that protect the disks from dust, smoke, and other harmful contaminants. Hard disk drives read and write data at a much faster rate than do floppy disk drives. Like floppy disks, they come in various sizes and capacities.

Most hard disks are made to fit into the space that would be occupied by a floppy disk drive inside a computer. So, there are 3.5-inch and 5.25-inch sizes of internal hard disks, as well as external units that sit in their own case outside of the computer. Capacities vary considerably. Today the low end of the spectrum is about 200M, with sizes ranging all the way up to **gigabytes** (or billions of bytes). Hard disks have become nearly essential for productive work on personal computers today.

Other Mass Storage Devices

While hard disk drives remain the primary mass storage device for personal computers, there are other options. These include other magnetic storage options as well as emerging optical and magneto–optical technologies. One drawback of hard disks is their lack of portability. This problem has been addressed in a couple of ways: cartridge hard disk systems and Bernoulli boxes. These systems use removable media and are often used for backup purposes or as auxiliary mass storage devices.

For exceptionally large storage requirements, optical storage technologies provide a solution. A single **CD-ROM,** a medium derived from the audio CD, can store about 600M of data. With the growing demands of multimedia, CD-ROM is becoming a popular mass storage peripheral, and many software programs are now distributed on CD-ROM. However, CD-ROM is a read–only medium; that is, the computer can retrieve prerecorded data from a CD-ROM but cannot record information onto it. This barrier has been overcome with the development of media that rely on a combination of laser and magnetic means to record, erase, rerecord, and play back information. These magneto–optical drives are now available. While expensive and comparatively slow today, such devices promise to be important mass storage devices for personal computers in the future.

Software

Finally, it is important to recognize that software is an essential component of any computer system. As we noted above, the software is what makes the hardware work. Software, within the limitations set by the capabilities of the hardware, determines what the computer can do. Like the music you play on a stereo system, it is the software that gives the hardware real meaning.

With a stereo system, software may consist of the individual songs that are recorded on a medium such as a tape or CD. In a computer system, software takes the form of **computer programs,** sets of instructions to the computer's CPU that tell it how to perform a particular task, such as processing text or presenting a computer-based lesson. Permanent programs are stored in the computer's ROM, while other programs may be loaded from disk into the machine's RAM for use as needed. There are two basic categories of software: systems software and applications software.

Systems Software

Systems software is the basic operating software that tells the computer how to perform its fundamental functions. For example, the computer has to be told what to do when the power is turned on, how to retrieve a program from disk, and how to save your word-processing document. These are all functions that are carried out by the systems software.

In most computers, the basic systems software is called the **operating system (OS).** Because the operating system often controls access to disks, the term disk-operating system (DOS) is also common. Regardless of the chosen term, the OS acts as the master control program for the computer. In some personal computers, part of the OS may be permanently stored in ROM. In others, only very rudimentary start-up instructions are kept in ROM, and the remainder of the OS must be loaded from disk into RAM.

Different computers use different operating systems, and the characteristics may vary considerably. The IBM–PC and compatibles use PC–DOS or MS–DOS. Newer IBMs and compatibles often use a graphical enhancement to DOS called Windows. Some computers in the IBM family sport operating systems called Windows 95 or OS/2, which completely replace the old DOS. The Apple Macintosh uses MacOS. Some personal computers even run versions of UNIX, an operating system popular on mainframe computers. The latest trend in operating systems is a move toward a **graphical user interface (GUI).** First popularized by the Apple Macintosh and now seen in Windows and OS/2, the GUI makes use of graphical symbols instead of text commands to control common machine functions such as copying programs and disks.

Applications Software

Applications software includes programs that are designed to perform specific functions for the user, from processing text to doing calculations to presenting a lesson on the computer. Thus, applications software includes the common computer tools (word processors, database management programs, etc.) as well as all educational software. Although applications software interacts frequently with the OS because of the OS's role in controlling the machine, it is through the applications software that the real work gets done.

Putting It All Together

When the computer operates, it carries out a complex set of actions that involves an interplay among the various components of the system, the software, and the person using the computer. Suppose that you wish to use your word-processing software to compose a letter. When you sit down at your personal computer and turn it on, the ROM is tapped to provide the basic start-up information for your computer. On many personal computers, a brief check of all systems is conducted to make sure everything is operating properly. Your operating system is then loaded into RAM, where it assumes control of your computer.

To begin your word-processing session, you might type the name of your word-processing program or use your mouse to click on the **icon** (pictorial representation) representing the software. This input passes to the CPU and on to the OS, which acts on this input by instructing the computer to copy the word-processing program from your computer's hard disk into working memory. The word-processing program then assumes control of your interactions with it.

As you begin to type, each keystroke sends a signal to the CPU. The word-processing software keeps the information in RAM and displays the contents of your letter on the monitor. When you finish, you select the print option from the word processor. A copy of your letter is sent to your printer, and a hard copy emerges. Finally, you save a copy of your letter to a diskette for later reference or editing. Again, the computer system, operating system software, and word-processing software work in concert to carry out the desired action. The whole process involves a complicated interplay of many different components. Fortunately, this process usually works so well that we never even notice it is happening.

SUMMARY

In this chapter we have explored different forms of instructional media. Similar to our coverage of instructional approaches in Chapter 3, it was our hope to give you exposure to the different types of media commonly found within the classroom setting. Each medium, with its individual characteristics, was shown to provide a means to carry an instructional message to a learner. It was also pointed out that, beyond the delivery function, the characteristics of the individual media can have a critical impact on the manner in which learning is constructed by the learner. It is our belief that familiarity with a number of different media, like familiarity with different instructional approaches, provides you with an increased repertoire of alternatives from which to select as you encounter varying learning situations.

Additionally, within this chapter we paid extended attention to the computer—its contributions to education, its power, and its basic functions. Because of its use as both a production technology and presentation technology, the computer will receive special attention throughout this text. In the first of our Computer Use Essentials (CUEs) you were exposed to the basic parts of the computer and how those parts interact with each other to form a useful system.

REFLECTIVE QUESTIONS AND ACTIVITIES

1. Think back to an instructional experience in which you felt you learned something of value. In what ways do you think the media helped deliver the instructional message? In what ways do you think the media facilitated the effectiveness of the message? How was the efficiency of the delivery impacted by the selected media? What role did the media have on the overall appeal of the instruction for you?

2. Regarding the same instructional experience, were there alternative ways in which the message could have been presented? What would have been the benefits and challenges incurred by attempting a different form of media?

3. Imagine that you are asked to submit a proposal to a school superintendent to teach four workshops, listed below, within the school district. Divide each workshop into the main topics you would cover and then select the form(s) of media you feel would be most appropriate for the presentation of each topic. Include a short written justification of why you feel your media is warranted and would benefit the learners.

   a. Basic games for the elementary school physical education class

   b. Instruction on conflict resolution in the high school classroom

   c. Effective study skills for the freshman high school student

   d. How to design and carry out a school-sponsored "Family Art Night"

4. For the next few weeks, keep a media reference notebook. In the notebook include a list of instructional media you encounter, how effective, efficient, and appealing you found them to be, what problems were encountered, and what alternatives could have been used.

5. Take a trip to the local computer store and ask a salesperson to explain the differences in computer models based on their internal memory, mass storage capabilities, monitors, keyboards, and printers.

6. Identify a company that has recently announced a new multimedia or hypermedia product. Write a letter inquiring about the product and request a demonstration version with accompanying literature. If possible, review the product and write a brief synopsis of your impressions of it. List how you may be able to use it at home, in the classroom, or in a training environment.

INTEGRATION AND SYNTHESIS

This chapter concludes the introductory section of the text. Following the foundational information presented in Chapters 1 and 2, the last two chapters have focused on giving you a solid background in the tools of instructional technology. Similar to the homebuilder who faces different challenges when constructing every new home, there is a need for knowledge and skill with a variety of instructional technology tools in order to be able to maximize learning given the different learners, content, and situations that will be encountered. This chapter was designed to introduce you to a variety of media, most of which you will use sometime during your career.

In Section II we begin to plan for our instruction. A key point within that plan will be the type of media formats that can be used to enable the instruction to be delivered and/or experienced optimally by the student. Without this initial knowledge of the media, such a selection process would have limited success. Chapter 7 will focus on when and why the various media should be selected, and Chapter 8 will give you information on how they can be most effectively used.

SUGGESTED READINGS

Heinich, R., Molenda, M., Russell, J. D., & Smaldino, S. (1996). *Instructional media and technologies for learning* (5th ed.). Englewood Cliffs, NJ: Merrill/Prentice Hall.

Kozma, R. (1991). Learning with media. *Review of Educational Research, 61*(2), 179–211.

Section II

Planning

Webster's *New World Dictionary* defines a *plan* as "any detailed method, formulated beforehand, for doing or making something." Planning is a natural part of life. We plan in order to exercise some influence over future events and to increase the likelihood that things will turn out the way we want. Although a plan doesn't guarantee success, not having a plan may sometimes ensure failure. Here are a few examples of the various forms plans can take:

- A recipe helps us make sure the food we are preparing includes the necessary ingredients and cooks for the right amount of time.

- An itinerary helps us make sure our vacation trip includes all the things we want to see and do, given a limited amount of time.

- A budget helps us make sure our income both covers our expenses and also allows us some spending money.

- A grocery list helps us make sure we purchase the necessary items when we go shopping.

This section is about planning for instruction and learning. Our purpose is twofold: to convince you that effective planning is a vital part of effective instruction, and to provide you with some practical guidelines for effective planning.

This is the first part of the PIE model described in Chapter 1. Your instructional plan directs what takes place during the implementation and evaluation stages of instruction. Once you have a plan for your instruction, you can move on to implement the instruction outlined in the plan. Once you have implemented the instruction, you can evaluate its effectiveness in helping your students learn. Planning instruction is made up of three parts (we've

emphasized the words beginning with *p* as a memory aid for this part of the model):

1. **Purpose, participants,** and **place:** this involves specifying the intended outcomes for the instruction, identifying the important characteristics of the students, and specifying the relevant features of the learning environment. We discuss purpose, participants, and place in Chapter 5.

2. The instructional **plan:** this is the written instructional plan itself. We've provided a format that's flexible enough to use in a variety of grade levels, content areas, and environments, yet structured enough to guide your planning while you gain teaching experience and develop your own instructional style. We discuss the instructional plan in Chapter 6.

3. **Producing** instructional materials: this refers to the process of assembling and/or developing the instructional materials that will be needed to carry out the plan. We discuss producing and selecting instructional materials in Chapter 7.

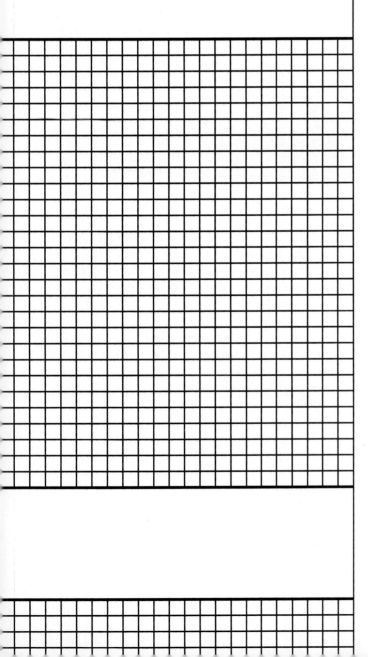

Chapter 5

Preplanning

KEY WORDS AND CONCEPTS

Instructional outcome	Prerequisites
Objective	Motivation
Performance	Learning environment
Conditions	Concept map
Criteria	

◀ COMPUTER USE ESSENTIALS (CUE)
Words and Concepts

Word processor	Undo
Word processing	WYSIWYG
Word wrap	Font
Cursor control	Type style
Insertion	Text justification
Deletion	Printer driver
Text selection	Spelling checker
Block operations	Grammar checker
Search and replace	ASCII format

OUTCOMES

After reading and studying this chapter, you will be able to:

■ State the purposes of preplanning for instruction.

■ List the three steps in the preplanning stage.

■ Describe the value of specifying lesson outcomes.

■ Specify the outcomes for a lesson on a topic of your choice.

■ Identify the important characteristics of a group of students.

■ Identify the relevant characteristics of a learning environment.

■ Define *word processor* and *word processing*.

■ Identify the benefits of using word processors.

■ Discuss the common features of word processors.

■ Describe the use of word processors as tools for teachers in the planning and development of instruction and for students in learning to write.

■ INTRODUCTION

The first step in solving any problem is figuring out just what the problem is. As an example, imagine that you're buying a car. Which car you buy (the solution) will depend on how you define your needs (the problem). For example, do you have a large family or go on frequent trips in the car? If so, then you would probably look for a full-size car with a lot of passenger room and luggage space—maybe even a car with a large towing capacity if you have a trailer or camper. Are you on a tight budget? If so, then you would probably look for a small, low-priced car that gets good gas mileage and is relatively inexpensive to maintain. Is

safety a priority consideration? If so, then you would probably look for a car that has a number of safety features, such as antilock brakes, air bags, and side-impact protection.

Now imagine that you're a teacher developing a political science lesson. You want your students to understand the differences between conservatism and liberalism. The lesson you create (the solution) will depend on how you define your needs and those of your students (the problem). For instance, do you want your students to be able to recognize examples of conservatism and liberalism in historical events and/or current news reports? If so, then you might provide definitions, along with a variety of examples of conservatism and liberalism, to point out the essential characteristics of both. Do you want your students to be able to describe the policy implications of conservatism and liberalism? If so, then you might provide several examples of conservative and liberal policies and ask your students to describe how these policies reflect a conservative or liberal perspective. Do you want your students to be able to argue an issue from either a conservative or liberal position? If so, then you might ask your students to debate an issue, by taking either a conservative or a liberal viewpoint.

The point is that the instructional approaches and media you choose, and the way you organize your lesson, will depend on how you define the "problem." This chapter is about defining the problem and getting the information needed to plan the instruction—or, as we refer to it in the chapter heading, preplanning. For teachers, this means identifying the purpose (specifying the lesson outcomes), the participants (describing the important characteristics of the students), and the place (describing the environment in which learning will occur). ■

PURPOSE: SPECIFYING LESSON OUTCOMES

Our discussion of preplanning for instruction begins with specifying the final outcomes of an instructional lesson. Regardless of when they are developed, specified outcomes form the foundation of a lesson. Outcomes give direction to those designing the lesson, those delivering the lesson, and those receiving the lesson. They help everyone understand when and to what degree the purpose of the instructional materials has been accomplished. **Instructional outcomes,** as we define them, are what the students should be able to do or what can be inferred that the students can do (based on the completion of specified performances) following their interaction with the instructional materials. Often compared to instructional, performance, or behavioral **objectives,** the term *outcomes* is used here to allow more flexibility in indicating not only what the students should be able to demonstrate following the instruction, but also what can be inferred about students' learning when the learning is of a more cognitive, less observable, nature.

The Importance of Specifying Outcomes

Alice, on her way to Wonderland, meets the Cheshire Cat, and they have the following conversation (Carroll, 1923, p. 69):

> "Would you tell me, please, which way I ought to walk from here?"
>
> "That depends a good deal on where you want to get to," said the cat.
>
> "I don't much care where—," said Alice.
>
> "Then it doesn't matter which way you walk," said the cat.
>
> "—so long as I get *somewhere*," Alice added as an explanation.
>
> "Oh, you're sure to do that," said the cat, "if you only walk long enough."

Their conversation illustrates what we call the "Cheshire Cat Rule": If you don't know where you're going, any road will get you there. But where is there?

Imagine that you are taking a vacation trip. You will want to know where you're going. Why? So you can

- make reasonable decisions about what routes and means of transportation to take, how long you will take to reach your destination, what you might want to see along the way, what you'll need to take with you, and so on
- manage your budget
- monitor your progress and manage your time
- tell concerned others (friends and family) where you're going.

A lesson is an instructional "trip," and, like a vacation trip, you'll want to know where you're going. Why? So you can

- make reasonable decisions about what instructional approaches and media to use, how long your students will take to reach the "destination," what else you might want them to learn along the way, what materials, facilities, and equipment you'll need, and so on
- manage your budget
- monitor the students' progress and manage the time allotted for the lesson

- tell concerned others (students, parents, principals, other teachers, etc.) where you're going.

So, outcomes are important because they define where "there" is—the knowledge or skills the students should have at the end of the lesson. Research on teacher planning indicates that teachers commonly specify and use outcomes, even when the outcomes aren't their first consideration (Reiser & Mory, 1991; Sardo-Brown, 1990). However, specifying outcomes, like specifying performance objectives, has its critics. Questions have been raised about the practical value of specifying outcomes in advance (Dick & Reiser, 1989; Yelon, 1991). Here are several of the most common criticisms, along with our responses.

Criticism: Outcomes dehumanize the instruction by focusing on the requirements rather than on the students.

Response: Contrary to this common misperception, the purpose of identifying and describing desired outcomes isn't to fit every round student into the same square hole. Rather, the purpose is to specify the knowledge and skills that are important for the students to achieve. Specifying the desired outcomes in advance will allow the teacher to plan a way for each student to achieve the learning goals and to help students learn at their own pace. In addition, clearly stated outcomes tell the students where they will be going. This helps motivate them, guides their studying, and allows them to monitor their own progress toward the goal. Specifying the desired outcomes also gives students something to reflect on. That is, they can compare their level of learning with the specified outcomes and generate questions, such as, How does what I have learned compare with what was desired? Are there any additional experiences that I need? How can my performance and experience be altered to gain additional insights? In what ways have I gone beyond what was desired? Such reflective questions help students monitor their own learning and adapt as is warranted.

Criticism: Specifying outcomes takes up valuable time.

Response: We prefer to think of the time spent specifying outcomes as an *investment* rather than an expenditure. As with any other investment, clearly stated outcomes have a significant dividend: they assure that your instructional plan (the solution) matches your students' needs (the problem).

Criticism: Outcomes can't be specified for complex or intangible skills, such as problem solving or critical thinking. The result is a focus on low-level skills, such as memorization, which are easy to describe and measure but not always the skills the students should be learning.

Response: It is easier to specify outcomes for low-level skills such as memorization. However, outcomes can be specified for all types of learning, including complex, high-level skills like problem solving or creative thinking. Consider the following examples:

- Using examples along with their notes, the students will be able to compose a haiku that conforms to the essential characteristics of this verse form.

- Given the necessary equipment and supplies, the students will be able to devise an experiment that demonstrates the operation of a semipermeable membrane. The experiment should clearly show the passage of some molecules, but not others, through the cell membrane.

In fact, because of the greater complexity of high-level skills, specifying outcomes for them may be more important than specifying outcomes for low-level skills. The more complex the skill, the more components there are to consider. Specifying the outcomes for these types of skills forces the teacher to identify which aspects of the complex skill are most important. Although specifying outcomes is more difficult and more time-consuming for high-level skills, the payoff is greater.

Criticism: Specifying outcomes in advance "locks in" the curriculum and makes it difficult to change.

Response: Explicitly stating outcomes doesn't necessarily mean they are written in stone. They can be modified as easily as they were written. The key is to review the outcomes periodically so you can modify those that are no longer relevant.

Criticism: Specifying outcomes in advance leads to a rigid, mechanistic approach to teaching that reduces the teacher's ability to respond creatively and spontaneously to the students and to the "teachable moments" that often occur in the classroom.

Response: At the beginning of this section we likened outcomes to the destination on a vacation trip. The analogy has particular relevance here. When you're taking a vacation trip, having a destination doesn't mean you can't or won't take side trips to explore other interesting places. In fact, you may know about some of these places in advance and plan to explore them when you get there, depending on how much time, money, and interest you have. You may also discover other places along the way and decide to explore them because they look interesting. Similarly, when you're taking an instructional "trip," specifying your outcomes in advance doesn't mean you can't or won't take side trips to explore other interesting outcomes. In fact, you may know about some of these outcomes in advance and plan to help your students explore them when they reach them, depending on your time and resources and the students' interest. Your students may also discover other outcomes along the way and want to explore them because they look interesting.

Criticism: Specifying outcomes in advance results in a tendency to "teach to the test."

Response: If the test assesses what is stated in the outcomes, as it should, then the instruction should be designed to help the students reach those outcomes measured by the assessment.

Table 5.1 summarizes the practical benefits of specifying the outcomes for a lesson. As the table shows, outcome statements provide a useful communication tool as well as practical guidance for teachers, students, and others.

Table 5.1 The practical benefits of specifying outcomes

	Communication	Guidance
Teacher	Reminds the teacher of what the expected outcomes are.	Guides selection and development of lesson content and activities. Guides selection and development of assessments.
Students	Tells the students what will be expected of them.	Guides the students' studying.
Others	Tells interested others (e.g., principals, parents, substitutes) what the students are learning and what is expected of them.	Guides the development of the overall curriculum into which the lesson or course fits. Guides the delivery of instruction by substitutes.

Sources of Lesson Outcomes

There are a number of sources that may help teachers identify the outcomes for a lesson. A teacher developing an instructional plan is likely to draw on one or more of these sources:

- *Curriculum guides.* Outcomes are often provided in curriculum guides, competency lists, and content outlines that are set forth by state education departments, school districts, or professional organizations. These may be written at the course level rather than the lesson level. The teachers' task then is to translate these course outcomes into outcomes for specific lessons.

- *Textbooks.* More and more textbooks are including outcomes at the beginning of each chapter. These are given either in the textbook itself or as part of an accompanying instructor's guide.

- *Activities.* Activities that are commercially produced are, like textbooks, likely to include suggested outcomes that identify what the students should learn from the activity. Also like textbooks, these outcomes may be presented as part of the activity or in an accompanying instructor's guide.

- *Tests.* Outcome statements can be derived from the tests used in a course. When the outcomes, instruction, and assessments are congruent, the test will indicate what the students should have learned. This is true for standardized tests as well as for tests developed by the teacher. The general principle is that if it is important enough to be on the test, it is probably important enough to be specified as an outcome of the instruction.

- *The teacher's own ideas.* Teachers often have their own ideas about what students should learn from a lesson, especially if they have taught the lesson before or are familiar with the particular students.

Specifying Lesson Outcomes

Outcomes define the desired results of the instruction. They specify what the teacher wants the students to learn. Various methods for specifying outcomes have been described (Jacobson, Eggen, & Kauchak, 1993). We suggest the method described by R. F. Mager (1984), in which outcomes include three components:

- **Performance:** what the students will do to indicate that they have learned
- **Conditions:** the circumstances under which the students are expected to perform
- **Criteria:** the standard that defines acceptable performance

Specifying the outcomes for a lesson involves identifying each of these three components.

Specify the Performance

What will the students do or say that will indicate they have learned? We suggest specifying the performance first because it's often the easiest component to identify. Teachers usually know what they want their students to learn in a lesson, even if they haven't thought out all the details. The key is to specify a performance that is an observable indicator of the students' capabilities.

Observability of the Performance.   Assessing student learning almost always involves inference. In some situations (e.g., learning to solve arithmetic problems) the inference is relatively small and straightforward, while in others (e.g., learning a new concept) the inference is greater and more difficult. But in virtually every situation the students must do something before their level of learning can be inferred. The outcome should specify the observable performance that would allow the teacher to make this inference. One way to ensure the specification of an observable performance is to use verbs that describe overt actions—things the teacher can see or hear the students doing. Table 5.2 lists some overt action verbs, along with some verbs that describe hidden actions—things students could do but which can't be seen or heard. This list isn't exhaustive, but it should give you an idea of the kinds of verbs to use when specifying lesson outcomes.

Capability of the Students.   Teachers are naturally focused on what is going to happen during the lesson (Sardo-Brown, 1990). One result of this is a tendency for the teacher's plans to focus on the activities (either the teacher's or the students') that will take place during the lesson or on the content that is to be covered. Each of these is an important aspect of planning. But the purpose of specifying lesson outcomes is to clearly identify the results, or destination, of the lesson rather than the route that will be followed to reach that destination. What should the students learn? One way to make sure you describe a student capability is to use the phrase "the student will be able to" before the action verb. Using this phrase will remind you that the desired outcome of the lesson is a future capability of the student.

Table 5.2 Use overt action
verbs in outcome statements

"Overt" Action Verbs			"Hidden" Action Verbs	
compare	construct	operate	understand	believe
translate	create	adjust	appreciate	become familiar with
describe	explain	replace	become aware of	think
measure	repair	compose	know	be comfortable with
identify	define	compute	recognize	
draw	administer	solve		

Specify the Conditions

What are the circumstances under which the students will be expected to perform? What will they be given to work with? The key is to specify conditions that will be in place *at the time* of the expected performance. One way to specify the conditions is to think about the questions the students are likely to ask about the expected performance (Yelon, 1991). Their questions can be grouped into four categories (Knirk & Gustafson, 1991):

- *Setting:* Where will they be expected to perform?
- *People:* Will they be working alone? With a team? Under supervision?
- *Equipment:* What tools or facilities will they have to work with?
- *Information:* What notes, books, checklists, or models will they have to work with?

For example, imagine that you want your students to describe the use of symbolism in *Macbeth*. The students might ask: Will we have to come up with the examples ourselves, or will we describe examples you give us (information)? Will this be an in-class assignment, or can we take it home (setting)? Can we use our books (information)?

As another example, imagine that you wanted your students to solve simultaneous algebra equations. The students might ask: Can we use our calculators (equipment)? Can we use our notes (information)? Can we work together (people)? As shown in the following examples, your responses to these questions can be included in the stated outcome by using a word such as "given" or "using":

- Given a scene from *Macbeth*, the students will be able to describe the use of symbolism in the scene.
- Using their calculators, the students will be able to solve simultaneous algebra equations.

Specifying the conditions may not seem important, but it often helps the teacher define the per-

formance. Thinking about the conditions helps identify what is important in the performance. For example, if you want your students to describe symbolism in *Macbeth*, you might consider the following questions: Is it important that they recall instances of symbolism, or is it enough that they can describe the symbolism that has been identified? Is it important that they be able to perform under pressure, as in the classroom, or is it enough that they can perform in the more private and relaxed setting of home?

Specify the Criteria

What is the standard that defines desired performance? How well must the students perform? Some might argue that specifying the criteria for students' performance is part of developing a test. However, criteria, like conditions, are an important component of an outcome because they help you identify what is important in the performance. Recall the example of wanting your students to describe symbolism in *Macbeth*. Will you accept just any description? Probably not. You want the students' answers to be "correct" in some way. Thinking about what "correct" looks like will help you devise a lesson that will guide the students to the desired outcome. There are a number of possible ways of defining a "correct" performance. As Table 5.3 indicates, these can be classified into three broad categories: time, accuracy, and quality (Mager, 1984; Yelon, 1991). Of course, not all of these criteria will be relevant in every situation. The key is to identify those that are critical for successful student performance in your particular lesson.

Of course, an outcome may use more than one type of criteria, as the following examples show:

- Given a "victim" with no pulse or respiration, the student will be able to administer one-person CPR at a steady rate of 12 compressions per minute (time: rate) according to the procedure described in the CPR manual (quality: source).

Table 5.3   Categories of criteria for defining acceptable performance

Category	Description	Example
Time		
Time limits	Specifies the time limits within which the performance must take place.	Given a "victim" with no pulse or respiration, the student will be able to begin one-person CPR within 15 seconds.
Duration	Specifies the length of the performance.	Given a "victim" with no pulse or respiration, the student will be able to maintain one-person CPR for at least 15 minutes.
Rate	Specifies the rate or speed at which the performance must take place.	Given a "victim" with no pulse or respiration, the student will be able to administer one-person CPR at a steady rate of 12 compressions per minute.
Accuracy		
Number of errors	Specifies the maximum number of acceptable errors.	Given a topic, the student will be able to compose a letter that contains no more that two errors in grammar or syntax.
Tolerances	Specifies the maximum measurement range that is acceptable.	With the aid of a dial gauge, the student will be able to measure the lateral roll-out on a disc to within 0.002 inch.
Quality		
Essential characteristics	Specifies the characteristics that must be present for the performance to be considered acceptable. Often signaled by words such as "must include."	Without reference to books or notes, the student will be able to describe the causes of the American Revolution. The description must include at least two of the significant events leading up to the war.
Source	Specifies the documents or materials that will be used as a gauge of the performance. Often signaled by words such as "according to" or "consistent with."	Given a computer with a hard drive and a new software application, the student will be able to install the software onto the hard drive according to the procedure described in the software manual.
Consequences	Specifies the expected results of the performance. Often signaled by words such as "such that" or "so that."	Given a flat bicycle tire, a patch kit, and a pump, the student will be able to patch the tire so that it holds the recommended air pressure for at least 24 hours.

- Given a topic, the student will be able to compose a letter that contains no more than two errors in grammar or syntax (accuracy: number of errors). The letter must be at least one page long (time: duration) and contain a combination of simple and complex sentences (quality: essential characteristics).

Composing Lesson Outcome Statements

Once you've considered each of the three components of an outcome, you can put them together. You can simply list the components of the outcome, as in the following examples:

Performance:	Solve simultaneous algebra equations
Conditions:	Graphing calculators
Criteria:	Accurate to two decimal places
Performance:	Describe the symbolism in *Macbeth*
Conditions:	From memory; can't use books or notes; will be given a copy of the lines from a scene
Criteria:	Must include the symbol, what it symbolizes, and its relationship to a major theme of the play

Performance:	Administer one-person CPR
Conditions:	A "victim," which may be a mannequin
Criteria:	Steady rate of 12 compressions per minute; must follow the procedure described in the CPR manual

Or you can combine the components into a coherent sentence or two, as in the following examples:

- With the use of graphing calculators, the students will be able to solve simultaneous algebra equations. Solutions must be accurate to two decimal places.

- Given a set of lines from *Macbeth,* the students will be able to describe the use of symbolism in those lines. The description must include the symbol, what it symbolizes, and its relationship to a major theme of the play.

- Given a "victim" with no pulse or respiration, the student will be able to administer one-person CPR at a steady rate of 12 compressions per minute, following the procedure described in the CPR manual.

PARTICIPANTS: IDENTIFYING IMPORTANT CHARACTERISTICS OF STUDENTS

This section is based on the premise that teachers are concerned with students as well as with outcomes. Specific outcomes are often mandated, and teachers are held accountable for them, but that accountability is defined in terms of the students. In other words, teachers aren't held responsible for a set of outcomes; they're held responsible for helping a particular group of students reach those outcomes. In fact, it is frequently the students who make the teacher's task an ill-defined problem. Students come to class varying in their knowledge, abilities, interests, and experience. Even when there is a "correct" way to help some students reach the outcomes, that way may not work for all the students. The teacher's ill-defined problem is to help *each* student reach the desired outcomes.

So, how do teachers solve this type of problem? Instruction, represented by an instructional plan, is the teacher's attempt to build a bridge between the curriculum, represented by the outcomes, and the students. The point we are making here is that the nature of this bridge depends on the particular students who will be using it. The critical planning task, then, is to make sure that the instruction matches the students in terms of their existing knowledge and skills and provides the proper motivation.

Existing Knowledge and Skills

Existing knowledge and skills refer to what the students already know. There are two related questions: Are the students ready to begin the lesson? and, Have they already achieved the desired outcomes? To understand the first question, it's important to understand the concept of **prerequisites.** Outcomes define the knowledge and skills the students should have at the *end* of the lesson. Prerequisites, on the other hand, define the knowledge and skills the students should have at the *beginning* of the lesson. When students don't have the necessary prerequisites, they will, at best, have a difficult time succeeding in the lesson. Learning is cumulative, and this means two things. First, it means that virtually every lesson has prerequisites. In fact, the outcomes of one lesson often form the prerequisites for the next lesson. Second, it means that, to be effective and efficient, instruction should build on what students already know.

The best way to explain the value of finding out whether students have the prerequisites for a lesson is through an example. Imagine that you are planning a lesson on long division. The prerequisites for long division are subtraction and multiplication. This means that in order to learn long division effectively and efficiently, students must be able to subtract and multiply. Students lacking these prerequisite skills will, at best, have a difficult time learning long division. Consider Figure 5.1, which illustrates the order in which these prerequisites lead up to long division. It represents three students who differ in what they already know. The first student, Tom, has mastered subtraction but not multiplication. Long division is over his head; he isn't ready yet because he doesn't have all the prerequisites. He's likely to feel frustrated and lost. The second student, Becky, has all the prerequisites. She knows how to subtract and multiply but doesn't yet know how to do long division. She's ready to begin. The third student, Polly, has gone beyond the prerequisites. She knows how to subtract and multiply, and she knows how to do long division, at least in some situations. Like Tom, Polly is likely to be frustrated, but for a different reason; she's likely to be bored. The instruction is redundant; it's presenting something she already knows.

This example shows that one way to bridge the gap between the students and the outcomes is to match the starting point of the instruction to the individual students, to start with what each student

Figure 5.1   An example of the concept of prerequisites

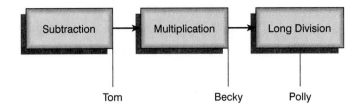

already knows. Students like Tom need some additional instruction. He needs to master multiplication before he can start long division. Students like Becky can start at the beginning of our lesson. Students like Polly can begin with more difficult problems in long division.

Motivation

Motivation refers to an internal state that leads people (like students) to choose to work toward certain goals and experiences. It defines what people *will* do, rather than what they *can* do (Keller, 1983). Motivation is a common influence on human activities. We are motivated to pursue certain relationships, to enter certain careers, to take up certain hobbies, to go to certain places, to read certain books, and so on. Motivation is, in turn, influenced by many variables, some internal (such as our perceptions, wants, and personal goals) and some external (such as opportunities and rewards).

There have been a number of attempts to describe the role motivation plays in learning (Stipek, 1993). But the most comprehensive effort to make motivation an integral part of instructional planning has been Keller's motivational design model (Keller, 1983). Keller's model is based on the premise that motivation influences students to choose learning goals and to work toward those goals. Three factors make Keller's model valuable for instructional planning:

1. *Keller's model categorizes motivational influences on instruction.* Keller distinguishes four major categories of motivational influences, identified by the mnemonic ARCS (the mnemonic has given its name to the model, which is often called the ARCS model):

Attention refers to whether the student's interest is gained and maintained throughout the instruction.

Relevance refers to whether the student perceives the instruction as meeting some personal need(s).

Confidence refers to whether the student expects to succeed based on his or her own efforts.

Satisfaction refers to the intrinsic and extrinsic rewards the student receives from the instruction.

The value of this model is twofold. First, it helps us look at existing instruction with an eye toward identifying the components of the instruction that will either increase or decrease student motivation. Second, it helps us consider the motivational factors that can and should be incorporated into our plans for new instruction.

2. *Keller's model identifies a set of motivational strategies within each of those categories.* Keller's model is based on the premise that instruction can be made more motivating by applying strategies related to these four categories. In broad terms, the strategies are (Keller & Strong, 1991) as follows:

Attention
- Perceptual arousal—capturing student interest
- Inquiry arousal—stimulating student inquiry
- Variability—maintaining student attention

Relevance
- Goal orientation—meeting student needs
- Motive matching—matching student interests and learning styles
- Familiarity—creating links to student experiences

Confidence
- Learning requirements—developing an expectation for success
- Success opportunities—supporting student belief in competence
- Personal responsibility—establishing effort as the basis for success

Satisfaction
- Intrinsic reinforcement—encouraging natural enjoyment of learning
- Extrinsic rewards—providing rewarding consequences

USING MNEMONICS

Mnemonics are defined as memory aids, and they are used to do just that—increase our ability to remember. There are several different kinds of mnemonics. The one just illustrated (ARCS) is commonly called an *acronym*. Acronyms are frequently used to help recall a list of items. The first letter of each item in the list is combined with the first letter of the other items in the list to form a word or phrase. Recalling the list is simplified by first recalling the acronym, which prompts the recall of each of the individual items of the list. Here are two well-known examples:

- HOMES stands for the first letter in the names of each of the Great Lakes: Huron, Ontario, Michigan, Erie, Superior.
- Roy G. Biv is a fictional name representing the colors of the prism: red, orange, yellow, green, blue, indigo, violet.

The reason acronyms are effective is that instead of needing to recall individual items and the order in which the items are to occur, only one item is recalled; then that item is used to prompt the recall of the entire list.

Similar to the acronym mnemonic is another memory technique known as *acrostics*. Acrostics make use of whole words, the first letter or letters of which are meant to indicate something. An example of an acrostic is "King Philip's class ordered a family of gentle spaniels" to help recall the names of the animal kingdom classification (kingdom, phylum, class, order, family, genus, species).

- Equity—demonstrating fair treatment among students

Keller (1983) has identified more detailed strategies within each category. The value of these strategies is that they are prescriptive; that is, they tell us what we can do to increase the extent to which our instruction motivates our students.

3. *Keller's model describes a process for incorporating these strategies into instructional planning.* During instructional planning, a main question to be answered about motivation is, How can the instruction be made more motivating to the students? Answering this question involves two basic steps. The first is to develop a motivational profile (Leshin, Pollock, & Reigeluth, 1992) by asking questions based on the four categories of motivational influences. The second step is to identify the motivational strategies that will be most useful with a particular group of students. These two steps are summarized in Table 5.4.

A lack of motivation in students is generally an ill-defined problem; that is, it may not have a single "correct" solution. Each group of students will present a different motivational profile and therefore require a different combination of motivational strategies. The teacher must create a unique solution for each unique problem. Keller's model doesn't give us a single "correct" way to motivate students.

Its value is in providing us with a framework for problem solving; it helps us identify all the factors that should be considered in order to effectively motivate our students.

As a brief example of this motivational design process, let's look again at our lesson on long division. Table 5.5 shows the motivational profile of our three students and identifies some motivational strategies that might be used. A second way, then, to bridge the gap between the students and the outcomes is to incorporate motivational strategies that match the motivational needs of the particular students—that is, to increase the motivational appeal of the instruction for the students. The example also illustrates the fact that different students have different motivational needs. The more clearly we can identify the motivational needs of our individual students, the better we can match the instruction to those needs, which will result in a greater likelihood of their reaching the desired outcomes.

Sources of Information about Students

The teacher's challenge, then, is to build an effective bridge that will help the students reach the outcomes. In order to do that, it's important to find out as much as possible about the students. Simply put, the more we know about the students the better we can match our instruction to their existing knowledge and motivation. In the absence of infor-

Table 5.4   Incorporating motivational strategies into a lesson

	Step 1: Motivational Profile	Step 2: Motivational Strategies
Attention	• To what extent are the students interested in the content?	• Create curiosity by using novel approaches, and injecting personal and/or emotional material.
	• How can I stimulate an attitude of inquiry?	• Increase levels of curiosity by asking questions, creating paradoxes, and nurturing thinking challenges.
	• How can I maintain their attention?	• Use a variation in presentation style, concrete analogies, human-interest examples, and unexpected events.
Relevance	• To what extent do the students perceive the instruction as meeting some personal need(s)?	• Provide statements or examples of the utility of the instruction, and match the instruction to students' personal needs, learning styles, and experiences.
	• In what way can I provide the learners with appropriate choices, responsibilities, and influence?	• Make the instruction responsive to learner motives and values by providing personal achievement opportunities, cooperative activities, leadership responsibilities, and positive role models.
	• How can I tie the instruction to the learners' experience?	• Make the materials and concepts familiar by providing concrete examples and analogies related to the learners' work.
Confidence	• In what way can I assist in building the students' expectations for success?	• Establish trust and positive expectations by explaining the requirements for success and the criteria for evaluation.
	• How will the learners clearly know their success is based on their efforts and abilities?	• Use techniques that offer personal control and provide feedback that attributes success to personal effort.
Satisfaction	• In what manner can students be helped to anchor a positive feeling about their accomplishments?	• Make performance requirements consistent with what is expected, and provide consistent measurement standards for all learners' tasks and accomplishments.
	• What will provide reinforcement for the learners' successes?	• Use verbal praise, real or symbolic rewards, and incentives, or have students present their work to others.
	• How can the learners be provided with meaningful opportunities for using their newly acquired skills and knowledge?	• Provide problems, simulations, or work samples that allow students to see how they can now solve real-world problems.

Adapted from J. M. Keller, 1987.

mation about the students, there is a natural tendency to assume that all students are alike and that they are like us. The risk in these "ethnocentric" assumptions (Smith & Ragan, 1993) is that we will create instruction that includes the information, examples, and activities that will help us learn but won't necessarily help students who are different from us. And since students represent a diverse group of individuals, it's likely that our students will differ from us in some important ways.

There are a number of ways to obtain information about students. Of course, some of these meth-

ods will work better in some situations than in others, and you might want to use more than one method to find out about your students. The point is to find out as much as you can about the students so you can match your instruction to their existing knowledge and motivation. There are three basic sources of information:

1. *The students.* The most direct way to get information about the students is from the students themselves. This is often the best, most valid source of information because it is the most direct source;

Table 5.5 An example of incorporating motivational strategies into a lesson

	Step 1: Motivational Profile	Step 2: Motivational Strategies
Attention	None of the students has any inherent interest in long division. Tom and Becky, in particular, have found arithmetic to be boring.	• Demonstrate the use of long division within an interesting situation. (Perceptual arousal) • Begin with a demonstration of how to do long division, then let the students work together on long division problems that increase in difficulty, then ask them to participate in a game in which they have to solve long division problems. (Variability)
Relevance	All three students see long division as the next part of learning arithmetic. But, beyond being the next thing they have to learn, they don't see much value in it.	• Identify some interests of the students (e.g., music, sports) and show how long division will help them with those interests. (Motive matching)
Confidence	Becky and Polly believe they will succeed in learning long division; their past experience in arithmetic has been positive. Tom, on the other hand, doesn't have as much confidence because he's had trouble with arithmetic in the past.	• Especially for Tom, begin with arithmetic problems he can solve (which may mean addition and subtraction problems) and work up to more difficult problems. (Success opportunities) • Help all the students develop study plans that will allow them to assess their own progress toward the outcomes. (Personal responsibility)
Satisfaction	Polly likes arithmetic and would probably choose it over other school subjects. However, Tom would rather be doing almost anything else, and Becky would also probably prefer other subjects.	• Help all the students use their long division skills with their particular interests as soon as possible. (Intrinsic reinforcement) • Use frequent praise. (Extrinsic rewards)

the information hasn't been filtered by anyone else, and you can draw your own conclusions. You can use any of these techniques:

- *Test the students.* Giving the students a test is an effective way to find out about their existing knowledge. The test can cover prerequisite knowledge and/or lesson outcomes. For example, results from previous instruction may provide information about whether the students have the necessary prerequisite knowledge.
- *Talk with the students.* Formal testing isn't always practical. As an alternative, you can talk with the students informally. Careful questioning can provide a wealth of information about the students' existing knowledge and motivation. Although it isn't necessary to talk with all of the students, it is important to talk with a representative sample. You're trying to avoid the assumption that all the students are alike, so talk with students who you think will represent the range in existing knowledge and motivation.
- *Watch the students.* Another informal way to obtain information about the students is to observe them in action. Careful observation can provide useful information about the students' prerequisite

knowledge and motivation. Again, it's important to observe a representative sample of students in order to make sure you obtain information about the range of existing knowledge and motivation.

2. *Others who know about the students.* Sometimes you can't get information directly from the students, or you want to validate information you got from the students, or you simply want another perspective. In these cases, talking with principals, other teachers, or other people who know the students will provide useful information about the students' existing knowledge and motivation. If possible, you should talk with several people in order to avoid any bias that might accompany a single perspective.

3. *Your own assumptions and guesses.* When you are familiar with the particular students, this is a quick, easy, and reliable source of information about the students' existing knowledge and motivation. However, when you aren't familiar with the particular students, relying on this source alone is risky. Whenever possible, you should obtain enough information from other sources to validate your assumptions.

PLACE: DESCRIBING THE LEARNING ENVIRONMENT

So far we have described the teacher's ill-defined problem in terms of the intended outcomes of the lesson and the characteristics of the students for whom the lesson is intended. There is one more aspect to defining the ill-defined problem: specifying the relevant features of the place or **learning environment.**

Simply stated, the learning environment is the setting or physical surroundings in which learning is expected to take place. At first glance this may seem obvious: learning takes place in the classroom. This is more complicated, however, for two reasons. First, classrooms are different; they vary in size, layout, lighting, and seating, among other things. Second, learning takes place in a variety of settings besides the classroom: the laboratory (computer lab, science lab, or language lab), gymnasium, playground, or field trip. In fact, learning typically involves some combination of environments.

We said earlier that instruction should match the students for whom it is intended. It is equally true that instruction should match the environment in which it will occur. If it doesn't, the instruction may be theoretically valid but practically impossible (Tessmer, 1990). That is, it may incorporate educational principles and instructional approaches that are sound but which can't be used in the anticipated environment. Sometimes this is obvious, as in the following examples:

- A history lesson on the American Civil War that includes showing parts of Ken Burns's *Civil War* video requires a video monitor and the electricity to run it. When there is no access to a video monitor, for whatever reason, the video cannot be used.

- A biology lesson that includes a laboratory experiment in which the students use microscopes to identify the structures of the cell requires enough lab equipment and supplies for the students. When lab equipment is limited, it may be necessary to change the experiment to a group activity. When lab equipment is severely limited, it may be necessary to use a demonstration as the instructional approach.

Sometimes this problem isn't as obvious, as in the following examples:

- A mathematics lesson on solving algebra equations that includes a commercial computer-based tutorial requires a site license authorizing use of the tutorial at multiple workstations. Without a site license, the students may have to use the tutorial one at a time, requiring a reorganization of the lesson.

- A social studies lesson that includes a small-group problem-solving activity requires a relatively quiet place for the students to meet in their small groups, apart from the distractions of the other groups. If this can't be done conveniently, it may be necessary to simplify the task so the groups can complete it successfully amid the distractions.

Defining the ill-defined problem, therefore, involves asking several questions about the setting:

- Where will learning occur? A classroom? A laboratory? Some other area of the school? On a field trip?

- What are the characteristics of the environment(s)? Just as the characteristics of the particular students are important, so too are the characteristics of the particular environment(s). How large is the space in relation to the number of students? How are the seats arranged? Can they be moved easily? What equipment is already in place? What equipment is available for use? How much noise do you anticipate in the setting? What other distractions are there? Is the lighting adequate? Can the lighting be adjusted?

- How will those characteristics influence the instruction? Can the setting(s) be modified to accommodate the instruction? If not, what constraints will the setting(s) impose on the nature of the instruction?

INTEGRATING TECHNOLOGY
Using Word Processing in Preplanning

We believe that one of the reasons Ms. Moreno is a successful teacher is that she spends time *outside* the classroom getting ready to teach. In Chapter 1 we described how Janette took time to determine (1) the purpose of the instruction, (2) the expected student outcomes following instruction, and (3) students' current levels of knowledge, skills, and motivation. The information gained during this preplanning stage enabled Ms. Moreno to competently and consistently develop and deliver effective instructional activities to her students.

As you might expect, Ms. Moreno is a busy professional who often finds herself with little time to preplan for her instruction. By using the word proces-

Ms. Moreno uses the word processor for planning.

sor, though, she has simplified many aspects of this process so that it is no longer the time eater it used to be. For example, she uses the word processor to draft and file ideas regarding potential lesson outcomes, to produce student questionnaires and pretests to determine current levels of knowledge, and to communicate with students and their parents about course goals and expectations. In addition, Ms. Moreno uses the word processor to generate outlines, create tables, and import and design graphics as illustrations for student handouts. These functions have all made Janette's work a lot easier and a lot faster.

Students in the Spanish Conversation class have also benefited from knowing how to use the word processor. For example, after students turn in required written assignments, Ms. Moreno grades them and returns them with specific comments and suggestions for improvement. Students are expected to redo these assignments, incorporating her ideas, and to return them for additional evaluation. In previous years this assignment required a great deal of student time and effort. By using a word processor, however, this can now be accomplished fairly easily. Student effort is directed toward making the needed changes rather than rewriting and retyping the entire document. According to Ms. Moreno, students seem to appreciate these evaluative comments and have started asking for opportunities to resubmit other work following her critiques. It's not too surprising that the final quality of most projects has improved.

CUE Computer Use ESSENTIALS

For many years, teachers have planned and developed instruction using the tools available to them. These tools have included the typewriter, pencil and paper, note cards, and lesson planning books. In many cases, these remain popular tools today. But we are going to take this opportunity to introduce some of the newer, computer-based tools that can facilitate the process of planning and preparing instructional materials and other written work. In particular, we will look at the word processor, the most popular computer tool of all. It is important to understand its basic functions, how it can be used, when and why it is important for both teacher and student, and some of the problems one may encounter when first using it in an educational setting.

WORD PROCESSORS

Word processors are generally conceded to be the most widely used computer tool for personal productivity. A **word processor** is a computer program for writing. Word processors support the entry, editing, revising, formatting, storage, retrieval, and printing of text. Many of the more capable word processors today also permit the inclusion of graphic images along with text. Popular word processors for personal computers include *WordPerfect*, Microsoft *Word*, *WordStar*, and *AmiPro*, as well as the word processors that are integrated into multifunction programs such as Microsoft *Works, Framework,* and *Appleworks.* **Word processing** is the term describing the use of a word-processing program.

Benefits of Word Processors

Word processors are tools for writing. As such, they are valuable aids in the development of written instructional plans. While we introduce them in that context, it is important to realize that word processors are generic tools that are beneficial for any task that involves writing. They do not assist the writer in conceptualizing the written work (e.g., when you make an instructional plan, you still have to decide what the outcomes will be), but they do help in the process of writing and revising. They offer some significant advantages when compared to traditional writing tools such as typewriters and pencil and paper. These advantages can be realized by both teachers and learners.

In a nutshell, word processors eliminate many of the difficulties associated with editing and producing a mechanically correct printed version of written work. As text is entered in a word processor, it appears on the computer's display screen. If an error is made, it is a simple matter to correct the error on the display screen before the written work is printed on paper. More complex editing, such as moving or inserting entire paragraphs, is not much more difficult than correcting a single mistyped letter. Text can be aligned and formatted as desired. The spelling of the words in the text can be checked. Finally, after the text is revised and laid out as desired, a "clean" copy can be printed. In addition, the word-processed text can be stored on computer disk for later retrieval, updating, and reuse.

Features of Word Processors

The most important word-processing functions can be divided into four basic categories: (1) text entry and editing, (2) text formatting and page layout for printing, (3) special assisting features, and (4) document storage and retrieval. Let's discuss each of these categories.

Text Entry and Editing

Word processors greatly simplify the process of entering and editing text. They do so through a number of features that are common to nearly all word processors:

- *Word wrap.* As text is entered, it is not necessary to press the carriage return key at the end of each line as it is with a typewriter. When a line of text is filled, the word processor automatically shifts the next whole word to the next line of the document (**word wrap**). The carriage return key (or the enter key on some computers) is used to signal the end of a paragraph.

- *Cursor control.* Position in a word-processing document is denoted with a lighted block or line called the cursor. **Cursor control** refers to the use of directional movement keys or a mouse to position the cursor anywhere within a document for the purposes of editing.

- *Insertion.* Most word processors are designed for automatic **insertion** of text at the cursor's location if one simply begins to type. Any text that follows is automatically shifted over to make room for the inserted text. Most word processors also allow one to switch to a typeover mode that allows one to replace existing text rather than insert new text.

- *Deletion.* Just as word processors allow for insertion of text, they also allow for **deletion.** The cursor is moved to the desired location, and the backspace or delete key is used to eliminate unwanted text.

- *Text selection.* Through the use of the cursor movement keys or the mouse, word processors allow portions of a document to be selected for subsequent editing. **Text selection** is sometimes called highlighting because selected text is usually denoted through the use of highlighting or special colors.

- *Block operations.* Once selected, blocks of text can be manipulated in several ways with **block operations.** A selected block can be deleted, moved to another location in the document, or copied to be inserted somewhere else. In addition, formatting commands, such as changing to italicized type, can be applied to a selected block of text.

- *Search and replace.* Word processors allow one to search for the occurrence of any word or phrase within a document. Further, the word or phrase can be replaced by something else. **Search and replace** comes in very handy if, for example, you have written a report about air travel and decide that you want to change your references from "blimps" to "dirigibles."

- *Undo.* This feature lets you recover from an error. Suppose you select and delete a block of text and then realize you did not mean to. The **undo** command let's you take back an action.

Text Formatting and Page Layout

Word processors provide a high degree of control over the appearance of the text on the printed page. Although the degree to which the text on the computer screen accurately reflects the appearance of the text on the printed page varies from one word processor to another, today nearly all aspire to a standard called **WYSIWYG** (*what you see is what you get*) (Figure 5.2). In other words, word processors today try to display exactly what you will see when the document is printed. Let's look at common formatting and page layout features.

- *Fonts.* The appearance of the text itself can be altered through the selection of various **fonts,** or typefaces, in various sizes. These include many of the fonts common to the printing field, such as Times, Helvetica, and Courier.

- *Type styles.* In addition to the application of various fonts, word processors allow **type styles** to be applied to any of these fonts. Type styles include **boldface,** *italics,* underline, SMALL CAPS, and others.

- *Margins and tabs.* Margins on all four sides of a document can be set. Tab stops can be set with respect to the margins.

- *Text alignment.* Text can be positioned in a variety of ways. Automatically centering is one option. Another option is **text justification,** that is, alignment with respect to the left and right margins. Left justification, the most common, aligns the text flush with the left margin, leaving a "ragged" right margin. Right justification does the reverse. Full justification pads the text with spaces to create fully aligned left and right margins, like most newspapers and magazines.

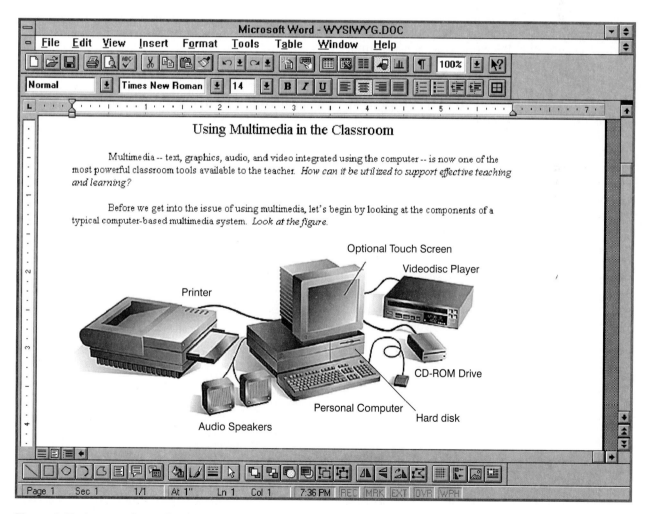

Figure 5.2 A screen from *Microsoft Word for Windows* showing WYSIWYG
Screen template and text reprinted with permission from Microsoft Corporation. Illustration by Tom Kennedy.

- *Line spacing.* Single and double line spacing, as well as half-line spacing, can be set easily.

- *Paging.* Typically, word processors automatically page the document. Many word processors automatically avoid leaving the first or last line of a paragraph at the top or bottom of a page. Page breaks, which define the start of a new page, can be added by the user.

- *Graphics.* As word processors have grown in sophistication, an increasingly common feature is the ability to embed graphics in documents. Many word processors today are moving toward the page layout standards first established by desktop publishing programs.

- *Other formatting features.* Most word processors support other formatting features, such as headers, footers, and footnotes.

- *Printing.* Of course, word processors allow for documents to be printed. Communication between the word processor and the printer is mediated by special software called the **printer driver,** which ensures that the word processor's formatting commands are correctly translated into actions by the printer. Most word processors provide a number of different printer drivers to support the different models of printers available.

Special Assisting Features

For the most part, word processors simplify the mechanical aspects of producing written work. But some of the features available in modern word processors go beyond the merely mechanical to provide assistance in the writing process. Let's examine some of these special features.

- *Thesaurus.* The thesaurus has long been a popular library tool for the writer in search of synonyms. Many of today's word processors include an on-line thesaurus that can be accessed at any time. The on-line thesaurus provides a list of synonyms from which the writer may choose. The built-in thesaurus gives the writer a tool for creating a richer vocabulary in written work.

- *Outliner.* Outlining is a common organizational technique for written material. Many word processors include an automatic outlining feature. The outliner allows the writer to generate an outline, with headings and indentations automatically provided.

- *Spelling checker.* A common ancillary feature of word processors is a **spelling checker.** The spelling checker searches through a document and reports any instances of text that do not occur in the program's built-in dictionary. The writer is then given options for dealing with these instances. True misspellings can be corrected; many word processors suggest possible corrections. Flagged words that are not actually incorrect, such as technical terms or proper names that do not appear in the dictionary, can be left as is. Many spelling checkers allow the writer to add new words to the dictionary or create a special supplementary dictionary so that those words will not be flagged in future occurrences.

- *Grammar checker.* A step beyond the spelling checker is the **grammar checker.** These ancillary programs identify a wide range of grammatical and format errors such as improper capitalization, lack of subject-verb agreement, split infinitives, and the like. They provide the writer with a check on many common problems, and they may be especially helpful for novice writers. However, grammar checkers are subject to problems, including limited capabilities, excessive suggestions, and sometimes even erroneous suggestions.

Document Storage and Retrieval

Another key benefit of word processors is their ability to store documents on and retrieve documents from disk. The implications for teachers are considerable. No longer must a course syllabus be created from scratch anytime there is a change in course content. The old version of the syllabus, saved on disk, can simply be retrieved from disk and edited to reflect the new content, and a new version can be printed. This also means that instructional plans, saved on disk, can be easily modified for subsequent use based on trials with students. These features of word processors support the thoughtful development of instructional plans based on revisions from student trials. Let's look at these features in more detail.

- *Storage.* Word processors allow documents to be saved to floppy diskette or hard disk. In this process, a copy of the document in the computer's working memory is transferred to disk. To save a word-processed document, the user must name it—preferably in a meaningful fashion that will facilitate later retrieval (e.g., BIOTEST is more sensible than XB34Z1 as the name of a biology test). When an existing document is altered, most word processors have a "Save As" option that permits the document to be stored using a different name (e.g., BIOTEST2 instead of BIOTEST).

- *Retrieval.* Just as documents can be stored on disk, they can also be retrieved from disk. In most cases, the user retrieves a document simply by entering the desired document name or clicking on the document name with a mouse. Retrieval or loading transfers a copy of the document from disk into the computer's working memory. The action of retrieving a document does not alter the copy on disk.

- *File import and export.* Most word processors support the importing of document files from other popular word processors. This capability facilitates document exchange among users of different word-processing programs. Likewise, many word processors permit documents to be exported, that is, stored in the format of another word processor. File storage capability for different computer platforms, such as Macintosh and IBM-PC, has become a common feature of word-processing packages that exist on both platforms. One type of exporting that is nearly universal in word processors is the ability to save a document in plain text, or what is called **ASCII format** (ASCII is an acronym for *American Standard Code for Information Interchange*; it is the standard way of representing text that allows different types of computers to "talk" to one another). Usually word-processing documents are stored with all of the formatting intact. However, for some types of document exchanges, especially those involving computer telecommunication, documents must be free of formatting. This feature permits the storage of plain text files.

Word Processors and Writing Instruction

We have introduced word processors as tools for the teacher, tools for creating instructional plans. There is no question that word processors are potent tools for the teacher. They can be used for the production of many kinds of written work: instructional plans, examinations, student handouts, letters to parents, and so on. But today even more attention is being focused on the role of word processors for learners. Word processors are emerging as an important tool in students' learning of writing.

Students' Writing with Word Processors

Writing today is viewed as a continuous process in which the writer generates ideas, creates drafts, revises, redrafts, and revises yet again. This process is characteristic of writing from the primary grades all the way to graduate school. The process approach to writing is perfectly suited to the capabilities of the word processor. With a word processor, the drudgery once associated with revising written work is removed. Therefore, word processors have become an integral part of the writing process in classrooms throughout the country.

Research supports the effectiveness of word processing in writing instruction. In a statistical review of 32 studies, Bangert-Drowns (1993) concluded that the use of word processors in writing instruction results in both longer documents and better-quality writing. Clearly, word processors can make a significant contribution to writing instruction in the schools. However, it should not be assumed that any use of word processors in a classroom will automatically result in student learning. Cochran-Smith (1991) cautions that the effects of word-processing instruction derive from the teacher's methods and the organization of the classroom as well as from the features of word processors. In other words, it is important for teachers to integrate word processors into a process approach to writing and to take into account the particular classroom environment where they are used.

Other Writing Tools

With emphasis on the process approach to writing, other tools have emerged to assist students with aspects of the writing process. For example, programs such as *Writer's Helper II* and *Writer's Workbench* provide students with prewriting activities designed to assist in the process of generating ideas. *Story Maker* permits students to use predefined story elements to write and illustrate their own stories. IBM's *Writing to Read* program makes use of technology to support reading and writing instruction in the primary grades. For younger students, especially, the use of word processors may be limited by poor keyboarding skills. Therefore, programs such as *Mavis Beacon Teaches Typing*, which introduces keyboarding technique, can be valuable additions to the use of word processing in the classroom.

Finally, an emerging class of programs allows both students and teachers to explore interrelationships among concepts. Programs such as *Inspiration, Semantic Mapper,* and *Semnet* allow individuals to build networks of interrelated concepts, terms, or ideas. As prewriting tools, these can be useful tools for students to "play with" the arrangements of various ideas. As review tools, they can help students organize information from a written passage or from instruction. For the teacher, these tools can be helpful in designing instructional plans. By developing a semantic network or **concept map** of key ideas, the teacher is forced to organize content in a logical fashion. This may transfer into a better instructional plan for student learning.

CONCEPT MAPS

Concept mapping is a visual organizational technique that can be used to facilitate learning and recall. The map is designed to help visualize two or more concepts and their relationships to one another. The visual representation may be effectively used to introduce a topic to students or as a review of the concepts and their relationships. Additionally, teachers may find concept mapping a useful organizational tool when planning instruction. Figure 5.3 is an example of such a map.

Figure 5.3
A concept map describing basic ways of controlling bleeding

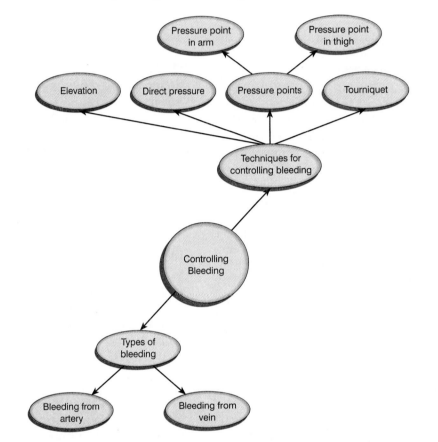

In order to develop a concept map, the following steps should be considered:

1. Select the major concepts to be included. These may be generated during brainstorming, from other knowledgeable individuals, or by using outside reference materials.

2. Cluster the concepts according to two criteria:

    • Group concepts horizontally if they function similarly (i.e., are at a comparable level of abstraction). In Figure 5.3 these would include the related concepts of "bleeding from artery" and "bleeding from vein."

    • Group concepts vertically if they are hierarchically related (e.g., techniques for controlling bleeding → pressure points → pressure point in arm).

3. Arrange the concepts in a way that depicts their individual relationships. This may require rearranging, rethinking, reclustering, and adding prior knowledge.

4. Connect the concepts with lines and, if needed, label the connections.

Note: Not only has concept mapping been found effective as a study aid, but also the building of concept maps by students has been shown to be an effective means for them to gain insights and understanding of the relationships between the different concepts (Ault, 1985; Barenholz & Tamir, 1992).

SUMMARY

In this summary we will use a series of visual concept maps of the main topics presented in this chapter. In this chapter we focused on gaining the foundational information needed to ensure that instruction will be properly selected, developed, and delivered. Additionally, we showed that the word processor is an effective tool to enhance the capabilities of both teachers and students.

The primary point in this chapter was that certain information is needed *before* an effective instructional plan can be developed. In order to develop instruction that will help your particular students meet their particular learning needs, it's important to gather information about the purpose (or outcomes) of the lesson, the participants (or students), and the place (the learning environment). These major preplanning elements are represented graphically in Figure 5.4.

The first preplanning element is what is to be learned—the purpose or outcomes. Outcomes specify the intended results of the instruction; they define what the students should be able to do following the instruction. Outcomes have three components: a performance, conditions under which the performance is expected, and the criteria that define acceptable performance. These components are represented graphically in Figure 5.5.

The second preplanning element is who will be learning—the participants. Students invariably bring to any instructional situation their unique sets of prior knowledge and motivations. A major part of the teacher's task is to fit the instruction to the students, and that means gathering information about what the students already know and about what their motivation for learning is. This is represented graphically in Figure 5.6.

The third preplanning element is the place or learning environment. Just as it's important to consider what is to be learned (the purpose) and who will be learning (the participants), it's also important to consider where the learning will occur—the place or learning environment. Effective instruction is matched to the learning environment as well as to the students. Some of the important aspects of the learning environment are represented graphically in Figure 5.7.

Finally, this chapter described the word processor as an invaluable tool that can be used in gathering and organizing preplanning information, as well as other aspects of planning, implementing, and evaluating instruction. The main functions of word processing are represented in Figure 5.8.

REFLECTIVE QUESTIONS AND ACTIVITIES

1. Read each of the following outcomes and determine whether each one contains the three components described in this chapter. Rewrite any outcome that doesn't include the three components.

   a. Identify the correct methods of financing the purchase of a new house.

   b. Summarize the benefits of specifying performance outcomes in instruction.

   c. Describe the relationship between f-stop and shutter speed. The description should include their effects on exposure.

   d. Explain why firms under competition will adopt least-cost technologies.

   e. Understand the importance of semiconductors in the microcomputer industry.

   f. Discuss from memory the five basic economic goals. The discussion should be consistent with the course textbook.

   g. Judge the extent to which the design for an electrode system meets a set of specifications.

Figure 5.4 The major elements of preplanning

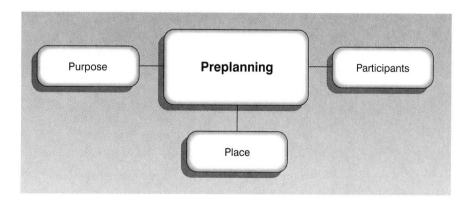

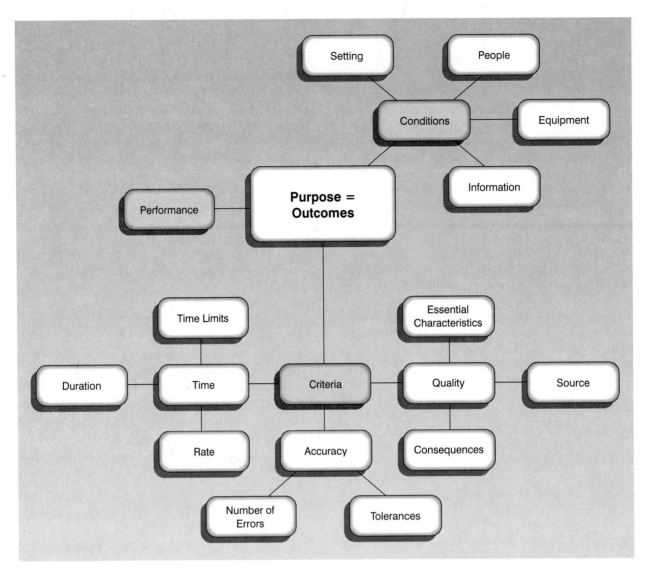

Figure 5.5 The components of instructional outcomes

Figure 5.6 Important characteristics of the students

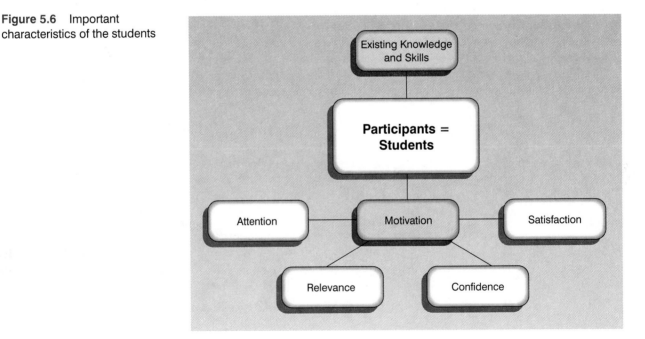

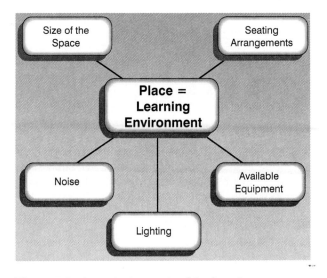

Figure 5.7 Important aspects of the learning environment

3. Reflect on what motivates you as you encounter a situation in which you need to learn. Think about how this could be classified based on any or all of the components of the ARCS model. From your perspective, which motivational components are most effective in increasing your level of motivation?

4. Consider a learning environment you have been in recently. Visit it if you can. What are the characteristics of that environment? How do you think those characteristics might influence a lesson presented in that environment?

5. Think about a recent writing assignment (e.g., a term paper). Did you use a word processor? If so, what specific features of the word processor did you find most useful? If not, what specific features of word processors would have been most useful?

INTEGRATION AND SYNTHESIS

In Chapters 3 and 4 we discussed basic background information on the instructional approaches and media one could employ to deliver instructional materials. In this chapter we have indicated certain critical pieces of information that are needed in order to prepare for the actual planning of the instruction. Those pieces (information about the instructional outcomes, the students, and the learning environment) will now be used as the main input for our discussion of the instructional plan in Chapter 6. This combined information will then be used to help you in the selection, adaptation, and development of the actual instructional materials in Chapter 7. The more information you have about

h. After completing the course, the student will be able to utilize a particular medium effectively.

i. Given a computer, the students will improve their computer skills.

j. Given a partner, an elastic bandage, and tape, the learner will be able to wrap his or her partner's ankle effectively.

2. Consider a class you have been in, either as a teacher or as a student. Write a brief motivational profile for the class, based on the ARCS model. Then identify the motivational strategies you think would be most useful for students in the class.

Figure 5.8 Primary features of word processing

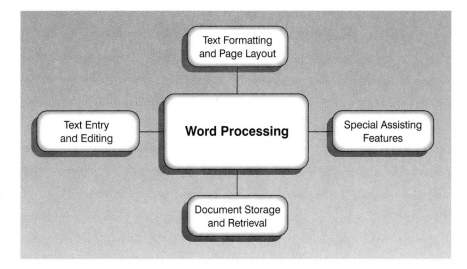

the approaches, possible media, the students, and the desired outcomes, the better position you're in to create an effective instructional plan.

As a learning tool, the word processor has been, and will continue to be, an invaluable assistant in the gathering, recording, and reporting of information; additionally, in the chapters to come we will discuss using the computer to find, gather, store, and retrieve huge amounts of information, which will be helpful for both teacher and student.

SUGGESTED READINGS

For objectives

Gronlund, N. E. (1995). *How to write and use instructional objectives.* Englewood Cliffs, NJ: Merrill/Prentice Hall.

Mager, R. F. (1984). *Preparing instructional objectives* (2nd ed.). Belmont, CA: Pitman.

Yelon, S. L. (1991). *Writing and using instructional objectives.* In L. J. Briggs, K. L. Gustafson, & M. H. Tillman (Eds.), *Instructional design: Principles and applications* (2nd ed.) (pp. 75–122). Englewood Cliffs, NJ: Educational Technology.

For motivation

Keller, J. M. (1983). Motivational design of instruction. In C. M. Reigeluth (Ed.), *Instructional design theories and models: An overview of their current status* (pp. 383–434). Hillsdale, NJ: Lawrence Erlbaum.

For student characteristics

Knirk, F. G., & Gustafson, K. L. (1991). *Instructional technology: A systematic approach to education.* Ft. Worth, TX: Holt, Rinehart & Winston. (See especially Chapter 7)

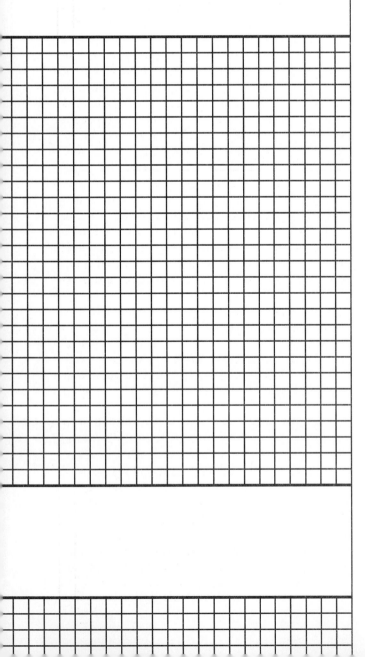

Chapter 6

The Instructional Plan

KEY WORDS AND CONCEPTS

Instructional event	Reinforcing feedback
Introduction	Corrective feedback
Content information	Assessment
Application information	Heuristic
Questioning	Congruence
Practice and feedback	

Words and Concepts

Database

Database management
system (DBMS)

Field

Record

Datafile

Flat filer

Relational database

Local-area network
(LAN)

Wide-area network
(WAN)

Server

Internet

Baud rate

Terminal emulation

Electronic mail

Bulletin board

Listserver

Telnet

ftp

Gopher

World Wide Web
(WWW)

OUTCOMES

After reading and studying this chapter, you will be able to:

- Outline the "ingredients" of an instructional plan.

- Describe the instructional events.

- Discuss what it means to say that an instructional plan is heuristic.

- Distinguish between congruent and incongruent instructional plans.

- Describe the practical benefits of an instructional plan.

- Develop an instructional plan for a lesson on a topic of your choice.

- Define *database* and *database management system.*

- Identify the advantages of computerized databases.

- Describe the structure of a typical computer database.

- Distinguish between flat filers and relational databases.

- Identify teacher and student uses of computer databases.

- Distinguish between a local-area network and a wide-area network.

- Identify the components needed for computer communication over telephone lines.

- Define *baud rate, terminal emulation, electronic mail,* and *electronic bulletin board.*

- Identify common applications of computer communication.

- Identify teacher and student uses of computer communication.

■ INTRODUCTION

An **instructional plan** is like a recipe. Allow us to explain. Most people cook from recipes. A recipe tells the cook what ingredients are needed and how to combine those ingredients to produce a particular dish. Cooks who don't have much experience, either in general or with a particular dish, tend to follow a recipe closely. They will carefully measure the ingredients, add them in the order listed on the recipe, and cook the dish for the prescribed length of time in order to make sure it turns out the way they want. On the other hand, cooks who have a lot of experience will often vary the recipe to fit the diners and what is known about their tastes and preferences. They may substitute ingredients, change the amounts of the ingredients, or cook the dish for a different amount of time. In addition, experienced cooks may make adjustments to the recipe "on the spot," based on their repeated taste-testing. Experienced cooks follow a recipe, but it may be in their heads or written in a shorthand form, and they use it as a flexible guide. They have cooked the dish often enough that they can prepare it without constantly referring to the recipe, and they've learned how they can modify the recipe without sacrificing the quality of the dish. For both novice and expert cooks, creating the dish involves identifying the ingredients and specifying how they are to be combined to produce a satisfying eating experience.

Most teachers have a plan. The plan tells the teacher what "ingredients" are needed and how to combine them to produce learning in a particular group of students. Teachers who don't have much experience, either in general or with a particular topic, will probably follow a relatively detailed plan. They will outline the content in detail, carefully describe any activities, and follow their plan closely in order to make sure their instruction turns out the way they want. On the other hand, teachers who have a lot of experience will often vary the plan to fit the students and what is known about their existing knowledge and learning preferences. They may substitute activities, rearrange the activities, or vary the amount of time spent on various activities. In addition, experienced teachers may make adjustments to the plan "on the spot," based on their repeated evaluation of how the students

117

are responding. Experienced teachers have a plan, but it may be in their heads or written in a shorthand form, and they use it as a flexible guide. They have taught the lesson often enough that they don't need to constantly refer to their plan, and they've learned how they can vary from the plan without sacrificing the quality of the instruction. For both novice and expert teachers, developing the plan involves identifying the "ingredients" and specifying how they are to be presented to ensure a satisfying learning experience.   ■

INSTRUCTIONAL PLANS
The Instructional Events

As a way of describing the ingredients in an instructional plan, we will use the concept of an instructional event (Gagné, Briggs, & Wager, 1988). Simply put, the term **instructional event** refers to something that is done during a lesson to help the students learn. Instructional events have been described and combined in various "recipes" (Dick & Reiser, 1989; Hunter, 1982; Kauchak & Eggen, 1989; Sullivan & Higgins, 1983). We believe there are six instructional events that should, at least, be considered in planning any lesson:

- Introduction
- Content information
- Application information
- Questioning
- Practice and feedback
- Assessment

Introduction

The **introduction** may be the most complex part of a lesson. It doesn't have to be long. In fact, good introductions are often quite brief, helping the students get into the substance of the instruction quickly. However, to be effective, an introduction should provide a hook, a purpose, and a context.

Hook.   An effective introduction should stir the students' interest in learning. A motivational profile of the students (see Chapter 5) will help identify the strategies that might be used to motivate them. Of course, the need to motivate the students goes beyond placing a "hook" in the introduction. Effective instruction also uses various motivational strategies to hold the students' interest throughout the lesson.

Purpose.   In general, instruction is designed to help the students reach some desired learning destination, defined as intended learning outcomes. Specifying the outcomes for a lesson was described in Chapter 5. An effective introduction should help the students understand what those intended outcomes are.

Context.   Any particular lesson fits into an overall learning context. That is, it naturally follows some lessons and leads to others. As an instructional event, an effective introduction should help the students understand the learning context by helping them see where they have been (what they have previously learned), where they are now (what they will learn in this lesson), and where they are going (what they will learn in the next lesson). To develop the introduction part of the instructional plan, consider questions such as these:

- How will the outcomes for the lesson be communicated to the students?
- What motivational strategies will be used throughout the lesson?
- How will the context in which the lesson fits be communicated to the students?

Content Information

Instruction generally includes some new content (facts, concepts, principles, etc.) and an opportunity for the students to practice using that content. The purpose of the **content information** part of the plan is to outline the content. The outline should include the sequence of major ideas and the example(s) that will be used to illustrate each major idea. To develop the content information part of the instructional plan, answer the following questions:

- What major content ideas (facts, concepts, principles, etc.) will be presented?
- In what sequence will those ideas be presented?
- What, and how many, examples will be used to illustrate each major idea?

Application Information

Just learning new content isn't enough; the students must be able to use that content. This requires knowing when to use the information as well as understanding why it should be used. The purpose of the **application information** part of the plan is to provide the students with this type of information. Application information helps the students internalize what they learn and transfer it to a variety of problems by telling them when the new content will be useful (the types of situations in which it can or should be used) and why the new content should be used (how it will help). To develop the application information part of the instructional plan, answer the following questions:

- What information will be presented about when and why to use the new content?
- When, and how, will that information be communicated to the students?

Questioning

Questioning is analogous to taste-testing a recipe as it is being prepared. For example, a cook preparing a spaghetti sauce will periodically taste it to determine what should be done next. Does it need more oregano? Is it thick enough? Is it done? Similarly, you should periodically ask yourself questions to determine what to do next in a lesson. Do the students understand the content information? Are they ready to practice? Do they need more information? Notice we say "periodically." Like taste-testing, questioning is a diagnostic tool used throughout a lesson to check the students' understanding of the content information. If their understanding is clear and sufficient, they can move on to the next instructional event, practice and feedback. If, on the other hand, the students don't understand the content information, you might need to go back over it to clarify specific points or present additional examples.

Questioning can be used in conjunction with other instructional events, and it often occurs more than once within a single lesson. For example, if the students are initially interested and motivated (introduction), it's possible to present the content information. If they aren't motivated, it will be necessary to find additional ways to make the lesson relevant or interesting to them. Additionally, if the students understand when and why they should use the new content (application information), it's possible to proceed with practice and feedback. If they don't understand when to use the new information, it will be necessary to find additional ways to illustrate this application information. Finally, if the students understand the feedback they receive following practice, it's possible to provide additional practice or proceed to assessment. If they don't understand the feedback, it may need to be

clarified. To develop the questioning part of the instructional plan, answer the following questions:

- How can questions be posed to properly measure the students' level of understanding?
- At what points will questioning be most effective for teacher and students?
- What information is needed at those points, and what questions will provide that information?

Keep in mind that questioning shouldn't be considered something generated and used solely by the teacher. Questioning is a powerful strategy that can be developed and used by the students to monitor and evaluate their own level of comprehension and understanding. Helping students learn how to generate questions and reflect on their potential answers can be shown to be a major step in the learning process (Ertmer & Newby, 1995).

Practice and Feedback

Instruction culminates in an opportunity for the students to try out what they are learning. The purpose of the **practice and feedback** part of the plan is to provide them with that opportunity. Like questioning, practice serves a diagnostic function. If the students practice successfully, they can move on to assessment. If, on the other hand, they have trouble with the practice, they might either repeat the practice, perhaps with simpler activities, or go back to the content information, clarifying the necessary information. In order for practice to serve as an effective diagnostic tool, it should be directly related to the established lesson outcomes. This means that, during practice, students should be asked to demonstrate the performance called for in the outcomes under the same conditions indicated in the outcomes.

Practice may include varying amounts of guidance. In guided practice the students are given clues that suggest how they should proceed. In unguided practice the students must decide for themselves how to proceed. In general, guidance is inversely related to difficulty; that is, practice that includes more guidance is generally less difficult than practice that includes less guidance. Because of this, guidance can be regulated to meet the needs of individual students as they progress through the lesson. Students who progress easily might benefit most from relatively unguided practice, while those who are having trouble might need much more structured guided practice.

Practice and feedback are inseparable, or at least should be. If practice refers to an opportunity for the students to try out what they're learning, then feedback refers to information about how well they're doing in that practice. Feedback comes in two forms: reinforcing feedback and corrective feedback. **Reinforcing feedback** is like the proverbial pat on the back. It's used to recognize good performance and encourage continued effort. **Corrective feedback,** as the name implies, tells the students specifically what they can do to correct or improve their performance. These two forms of feedback are often used together, reinforcing what the student has done well and correcting what the student could do better. Practice without feedback has limited value because it doesn't tell the students whether or not they're progressing toward the outcomes or what they can do to improve their progress. To develop the practice and feedback part of the instructional plan, answer the following questions:

- How will the students be encouraged to try out their new knowledge or skill?

- How much guidance will be provided?

- How will the students be given feedback about their performance during practice?

Assessment

The purpose of **assessment** in the instructional plan is to determine what methods will be used to evaluate how well the students have mastered the intended lesson outcomes. As with several of the previous events, assessment serves a diagnostic function. Students who "pass" the assessment are ready for the next lesson, while those who don't "pass" may need some additional instruction before they go to the next lesson. We have purposely put quotation marks around the word "pass" to make a point. We often think of assessment in terms of traditional paper-and-pencil tests. But, as we describe in Chapter 12, where we discuss assessment in more detail, there are a variety of ways to assess how well the students have learned, and the meaning of "pass" will be different for these different assessment methods. To develop the assessment part of the instructional plan, answer the following questions:

- How will it be determined whether the students have achieved the intended learning outcomes?

- How will the students be given feedback about their performance during the assessment?

These six instructional events are summarized in a generic instructional plan format, shown in Figure 6.1. The instructional plan includes space to describe both the instructional approach chosen for the lesson and the media and materials that will be needed for each event. (Chapter 3 described the instructional approaches and provided guidelines for selecting an instructional approach for a particular situation. Chapter 4 described instructional media, and Chapter 7 will provide guidelines for selecting media and materials.)

Instructional Plans as Heuristic Guides

Allow us one more reference to our recipe analogy as a way of making a point about the flexibility of instructional plans. Ask three people how they make spaghetti sauce. Chances are you'll end up with three different recipes. Now, ask three teachers to show you their instructional plans (they may call them lesson plans) for a given topic. Chances are you'll end up with three different plans, even if the content is the same.

We've suggested an instructional "recipe." But it's a recipe that's flexible and can be adapted to a wide variety of teaching and learning situations. Remember that an instructional plan, like a recipe, is a decision-making guide. It helps the teacher decide what ingredients to use and how to combine them to help the students learn. The instructional plan we have presented is designed to provide you with a set of **heuristic** guidelines; that is, it's a set of rules of thumb that can be adapted to fit each situation, rather than a rigid procedure that must be followed in the same way every time. Our goal is to provide you with guidelines that are flexible enough to use with a variety of situations, yet structured enough to provide practical guidance. However, it's important to keep in mind that there is no one "correct" instructional plan. Instructional situations differ in terms of the needs, interests, and experiences of the students; the structure of the content; the available resources; and the preferences, interests, and experiences of the teacher. The teacher's task is to create a unique solution for the unique problem of helping the students learn; that is, the teacher must develop a plan that helps the particular students learn the particular content. There are several ways in which instructional plans may vary from one situation to the next.

The order in which the events are presented to the students may vary. We've listed the instructional events in a common order, but that isn't the only "correct" order. For example, you may decide that the application information part fits best at the end of the les-

Figure 6.1   Sample format for an instructional plan

INSTRUCTIONAL PLAN

Class _____   **Topic(s) for this lesson** _____

Outcomes for this Lesson
- What are the intended outcomes?

Introduction
- How will the outcomes for the lesson be communicated to the students?
- What motivational strategies will be used throughout the lesson?
- How will the context in which the lesson fits be communicated to the students?

- What type of instructional approach could/should be used?
- What form of media and materials will be needed?

Content Information
- What major ideas (facts, concepts, principles, etc.) will be presented?
- In what sequence will those ideas be presented?
- What, and how many, examples will be used to illustrate each major idea?

- What type of instructional approach could/should be used?
- What form of media and materials will be needed?

Application Information
- What information will be presented about when and why to use the new content?
- When and how will that information be communicated to the students?

- What type of instructional approach could/should be used?
- What form of media and materials will be needed?

Questioning
- In what ways can questions be posed to properly measure the students' level of understanding?
- At what points will questioning be most effective for teacher and students?
- What information is needed at those points, and what questions will provide that information?

- What type of instructional approach could/should be used?
- What form of media and materials will be needed?

Practice and Feedback
- How will the students be encouraged to try out their new knowledge or skills?
- How much guidance will be provided?
- How will the students be given feedback about their performance during the practice?

- What type of instructional approach could/should be used?
- What form of media and materials will be needed?

Assessment
- How will it be determined whether the students have achieved the intended learning outcomes?
- How will the students be given feedback about their performance during the assessment?

- What type of instructional approach could/should be used?
- What form of media and materials will be needed?

son, when you're sure the students have mastered the new knowledge or skill. Alternatively, you may decide it fits best after the introduction, following naturally after the presentation of the purpose and context for the lesson. The idea is to develop a lesson that is coherent and has a logical flow to it.

The instructional events may occur separately or be combined. We think the six instructional events are basic ingredients and should be included in every lesson. However, that doesn't necessarily mean that each event must be a separate entity in every lesson. The instructional events may overlap one another, and when they do they may be combined. For example, the purpose of practice and feedback is to allow the students to try out their new knowledge or skill, and the purpose of assessment is to determine whether they have mastered the intended outcomes. It's possible to present a sequence of practice activities that will help determine whether the students have mastered the intended outcomes. In this case, assessment and practice have been combined. The point to keep in mind is that each instructional event has an important purpose in the lesson. Sometimes those purposes can be accomplished by combining two or more instructional events.

Which instructional events are emphasized may vary. The instructional events are not all necessarily of equal importance in every lesson. For example, one lesson may present a lot of content information and provide limited time for practice and feedback, while another lesson on the same content may present a small amount of content information and allow a lot of time for practice and feedback.

The manager of each instructional event may vary. The manager of an instructional event is the person or thing that is primarily responsible for carrying out that event, dictating the pace of the event, controlling the flow of information, and determining what to do next. We say "primarily" because learning is always a collaboration among the students, the teacher, and the instructional materials, and all are likely to influence each instructional event. However, it's possible to think of a continuum in the balance of power. To what extent are the students, the teacher, and the materials exercising control over the pacing, flow of information, and decision making? Note that the manager may vary from one event to the next. For example, the teacher may manage the introduction and the practice and feedback while the material manages the content information and the students control the application information.

Encouraging students to manage their own learning is a powerful learning technique (refer to the discussion of constructivist learning theory in Chapter 2). However, this is an acquired skill, and students—especially younger or less-sophisticated ones—may require instruction and practice before they are able to do it well. Although teaching students to manage their own learning is beyond the scope of this book, readers who are interested in learning more about this topic can refer to Derry and Murphy (1986), Palinscar (1986), and Schmitt and Newby (1986).

The amount of detail or structure in the description of each event may vary. The way an event is described within an instructional plan may be more or less detailed, more or less structured. This may depend on the teacher's experience with the technique being used. As indicated at the beginning of this chapter, a teacher who is relatively inexperienced or who is using a new technique may want the plan to provide a lot of structure and will, therefore, describe the content, activities, and materials for that event in great detail. On the other hand, a teacher who is using a familiar technique may need less structure and therefore sketch out the learning event rather than describe it in detail. Note that we're talking about individual events rather than an entire plan. Also, different events within a plan may be described at different levels of detail. For example, a teacher who is using a new beginning to a familiar topic may develop a detailed introduction while briefly outlining the familiar content information.

The order in which the instructional events are developed may vary. Our instructional plan sequences the instructional events as they might be presented to the students, but that doesn't mean the events are always developed in that order. In different situations, planning may begin at different points and follow a different sequence. While the possibilities are not exactly endless, there are more options than we can list here. As examples, consider possible beginning points alone. Developing an instructional plan might begin with any of the following steps:

- specifying the intended outcomes for the lesson
- determining the content to be covered
- identifying the assessment method to be used
- developing one or more practice activities for the students
- deciding on the instructional approach or media to be used in one of the events
- selecting particular instructional materials to be used in one of the events

To add to the complexity, the instructional events influence one another, and decisions made while developing one part of the plan will affect the decisions made in the other parts of the plan. This may mean changing decisions that have already been made. Again, the possibilities are virtually limitless. The point is that the instructional plan must be fluid as well as flexible.

Congruence in Instructional Plans

There's another important point to make about the instructional plan: it's critical that the plan be **congruent.** What does it mean to say that an instructional plan is congruent? It means that the components of the plan match. The outcomes should match the instructional events, and the instructional events should match one another. The outcomes should accurately represent the knowledge and skills described in the content information and measured in the assessment. Conversely, the assessment should measure the knowledge and skills described in the content information and represented by the outcomes. The introduction should motivate the students to learn the knowledge and skills they will be practicing, and the students should be practicing the knowledge and skills they will be assessed on. And so on through all the combinations of the instructional events.

To illustrate the concept of congruence, consider the brief examples in Table 6.1. In which example are the components congruent? The answer seems pretty clear. In Example A the outcomes, content information, practice and feedback, and assessment all match. They all relate directly to learning how to solve algebra equations. In Example B, however, the outcomes, content information, practice and feedback, and assessment are all aimed at different aspects of algebra. Although they are all important, they don't match one another.

Sample Instructional Plans

How might the instructional events be combined to form an instructional plan for a specific situation? The following two sample instructional plans (Figures 6.2 and 6.3) will help answer that question. Each problem is different, and the plans are different. Look over each of the two sample plans. What differences do you notice? How might you explain those differences? What does this suggest about the flexibility of the instructional plan?

Scenario A. Ms. Heinrich teaches a beginning Spanish class for fourth graders. A curriculum guide distributed by the school district specifies that the students should be able to carry on simple conversations in Spanish and be able to use Spanish greetings (see Figure 6.2).

Scenario B. Mr. Delgado teaches a beginning Spanish class for sixth graders in the same school district as Ms. Heinrich. He has read about cooperative learning techniques, and he likes what he's read. He wants to try cooperative learning in his class (see Figure 6.3).

PRACTICAL BENEFITS OF INSTRUCTIONAL PLANS

An instructional plan is a decision-making guide. It allows the teacher to make sensible decisions about how to carry out the instruction, respond to the changing needs of the students and the situation, and make continual improvements in the instruction provided to the students. The practical benefits of having a plan can be described in terms of the functions the instructional plan serves before, dur-

Table 6.1 Congruence in the instructional plan

	Example A	Example B
Outcome	Be able to solve algebra equations	Be able to solve algebra equations
Content information	Information on the notation that is used in algebra equations, followed by a demonstration of how to solve various types of algebra equations	Information on the historical development of algebra as a branch of mathematics
Practice and feedback	Problems asking the student to solve the types of algebra equations presented in the content information	Problems asking the student to interpret various types of algebraic notation
Assessment	A set of algebra equations to solve	Questions about the importance of knowing how to solve algebra equations

Figure 6.2   Instructional plan for teaching Spanish greetings and responses

> ### Instructional Plan
>
> Class: _Fourth-grade Spanish I_   Topic(s) for this lesson: _Greetings_
>
> **Outcomes for this Lesson**
> - _Say the Spanish equivalent to a given English greeting._
> - _Say the appropriate Spanish greeting when meeting someone._
> - _Say an appropriate Spanish response when greeted in Spanish._
>
> **Introduction**
> _Present a series of situations, in English, calling for a greeting—ask what they would say._
>
> _Show similar situations in Spanish on videotape. Present the lesson outcomes as steps toward being able to converse in Spanish. Emphasize the importance of practice._
>
> **Content Information**
> _Demonstrate common Spanish greetings and responses (both formal and informal) for morning, afternoon, and evening. Write the words on the chalkboard; say them several times._
>
> _Emphasize the greeting/response pairs._
>
> **Application Information**
> _During the demonstration, clearly explain when each greeting and response would be used._
>
> **Questioning**
> _Before starting the practice activity, ask the students when greetings are generally used and why. Then ask them when they would use the different types of greetings and why. Use this discussion to decide whether to review any of the previous information._
>
> **Practice and Feedback**
> _Pair the students up with an audiotape._
>
> _Instruct students to practice on the tape and to listen to the tape to see how they sound._
>
> **Assessment**
> _Spend a few minutes with each pair after they have recorded a practice greeting and response._
>
> _Listen to the taped practice with the students (ask them to evaluate what they hear on the tape). Point out specific strong points in their pronunciation and give specific pointers for improving pronunciation._

ing, and after the instruction (Borko & Livingston, 1992; Kauchak & Eggen, 1989; Reynolds, 1992).

Before the Instruction

Bridge.   The instructional plan serves two important linking functions. First, it is the link between the curriculum goals and the students. The plan is the vehicle teachers use to decide how to tailor the curriculum, which is often predetermined, to the needs of their particular students. Second, the plan is the link between the outcomes, instruction, and assessment. It is the means by which teachers can decide how to adapt the outcomes, instruction, and/or assessments to ensure that they match one another. The way these links are made depends on (1) the particular curriculum, (2) the students, and (3) the teacher's knowledge of the content, level of experience, beliefs about students and how they learn, and knowledge about the teaching methods that will help the students learn. By making these links, the teacher can make sure the prescribed

Figure 6.3 Instructional plan for teaching Spanish greetings and responses using cooperative learning

---

Instructional Plan

Class: _6th-grade Spanish_   Topic(s) for this lesson: _Spanish Greetings_

Outcomes for this Lesson
- *Say the Spanish equivalent to a given English greeting.*
- *Say the appropriate Spanish greeting when meeting someone.*
- *Say an appropriate Spanish response when greeted in Spanish.*

Introduction
Greet students in English—All languages use similar greetings.
Their task will be to learn greetings in Spanish.   *Written materials*
Each student will learn one greeting from audiotape and teach it to classmates.
This is the beginning of being able to talk with people in Spanish. Once they've learned the greetings, they will be able to move on to other parts of conversation.
Time: 5 minutes
Approach: Presentation

Content Information
Approach—Cooperative learning
Media—Audiotaped Spanish greetings
Divide class into 3 equal groups: Morning, Afternoon, Evening
Each group is to learn their greeting and response so they can teach it to 2 classmates — *Encourage students to help*
Time: About 2̶0̶ 15 minutes *1 another w/their groups*

Practice and Feedback   *Time: 15 minutes*
Reorganize class into groups of 3—from each of the previous groups.
Directions—Teach greeting to one another.
          Everyone must learn each greeting and response.
Circulate around the room—Keep students on track!
           — *NOTE: Find an alternative—students need more time*
Assessment   *for the practice activity.*
Call students to the front in pairs. Give 1st student an English greeting on a card.
Student is to greet partner with corresponding Spanish greeting. Partner is to respond in Spanish.
Media—Spanish/English flashcards
Time—15 minutes

Application Information
Debrief lesson—
- *Recall when each greeting and response is used.*
- *Ask who else students might teach these greetings to (parents, friends, etc.).*
- *Suggest using the greetings with one another around school.*

USING EMBEDDED QUESTIONS

As you have noticed, we often address questions to you, the reader. Questions such as these have been given the name "embedded questions" because they are embedded within the text material. Such questions, strategically placed within the text (or within an oral presentation, etc.) have several purposes:

- They are effective at focusing the reader's attention (e.g., as an advance organizer to cue the student regarding what warrants special attention).
- They encourage discussion and further inquiry of critical parts of the instruction that have already occurred or that are going to occur.
- They prompt student self-monitoring and self-assessment to ensure that critical information has been received, understood, and, in some cases, transferred.

    Examples would include questions such as the following:

- What do you think will happen next?
- Why is this considered true (false)?
- Can you explain this in your own words?
- What was the purpose of this?
- How is this relevant to you?
- How could you see this being used in other situations?

learning goals are met by the students, thus making the instruction more accountable.

Checklist. The instructional plan encourages the teacher to anticipate the specific materials, facilities, and equipment needed, as well as when they will be needed. This helps the teacher make sure that there will be enough materials on hand for all of the students.

Schedule. The instructional plan allows the teacher to decide what activities will be used to help the students learn, to put them in a logical sequence, and to allocate sufficient time to the different activities.

During the Instruction

Road Map. The instructional plan describes the destination the teacher wants to reach and the routes he or she plans to follow to get there. This road map function helps the teacher make adjustments in the plan. This is important for two reasons. First, interruptions in the classroom are inevitable (e.g., because of student absences or school assemblies). The instructional plan helps the teacher keep the instruction on track, monitor the students' progress toward the destination, and make sure the prescribed content is covered in the face of these inevitable interruptions. It does this by marking the

place for the teacher so he or she can return to the same place after the interruption. Second, students' needs and interests may change, and unanticipated learning opportunities may arise. The instructional plan allows the teacher to respond to these changing needs, interests, and opportunities while continuing to progress toward the destination. The plan is designed to be flexible, to allow the teacher to improvise based on the students' responses. In this way the plan is like a highway system rather than a slot car track. There are various destinations and various routes to any destination, all of which can be changed during the trip.

Outline. The instructional plan gives the teacher a set of guidelines to follow in the classroom. These guidelines may take the form of a brief agenda or a more detailed script. In either case, the teacher can concentrate on interacting with the students rather than trying to remember what comes next.

Compass. The instructional plan provides the teacher with a clear sense of direction, and this helps to increase the teacher's confidence and reduce the uncertainty and anxiety that often accompany not knowing where you're going. This may be especially important for teachers who are relatively inexperienced and need something to provide guidance.

After the Instruction

Diary. The instructional plan provides the teacher with a place to record what happened during the instruction (McCutcheon, 1980). It is also a place for the teacher to record his or her observations and comments about what worked and what didn't. These notes can then be used to improve the instruction.

Briefing Book. It is often important that others know what is happening in the classroom. The instructional plan provides a convenient way to do this. For example, the plan will tell substitute teachers what parts of a lesson have been completed and what is yet to be done. Similarly, the plan will help principals keep track of what is happening in the classrooms in their building.

INTEGRATING TECHNOLOGY
Managing Information within the Instructional Plan

Planning for instruction follows logically from the results obtained during the preplanning stage. After Ms. Moreno determined her course outcomes and her students' levels of knowledge, skills, and motivation, she began developing specific lesson plans. For example, one of her outcomes dealt with increasing students' facility with an increasing number of Spanish vocabulary words. Her first learning plan focused on simply introducing new words and using a computer drill-and-practice activity to increase retention. This plan incorporated only three events of instruction: introduction, content information, and practice and feedback. Based on student responses obtained during initial tryouts, two other events were added: application information and assessment. Application information was introduced in the form of instruction regarding when and why to use specific forms of words and particular oral expressions. Assessment was achieved by adding a question-and-answer section that allowed Ms. Moreno to confirm students' understanding before they moved on to the next lesson.

As Janette's instructional plan gradually incorporated a greater number of individualized components, she began to rely more and more on various computer capabilities. For example, the computer helped her solve a recent problem regarding managing an extensive amount of information in her Spanish course. Janette had wanted to create some type of file of vocabulary words that students could

Ms. Moreno is working on her plan for an upcoming lesson.

access whenever they needed a definition, an English translation, or examples of words or phrases in context. She toyed with the idea of making a large file of index cards, but she was daunted by the amount of time and energy that would take. After Ted Mellette, her student teacher, had demonstrated the benefits of hypermedia, she started thinking about the advantages that a computer filing system might offer. She remembered learning a little bit about databases in her first computer workshop, but she needed to refresh her memory regarding how to create and use them. She pulled out the textbook and her notes from that workshop, called her old lab partner, and got to work.

CUE Computer Use ESSENTIALS

In the last chapter we introduced one of the most important of all computer tools, the word processor. In this chapter we examine two other important computer tools: databases and computer communication. We introduce these computer-based tools in the context of instructional planning because they can assist the teacher and learners in finding and organizing information. As such, they can be very useful in the planning process. The teacher can use the tools to organize various instructional strategies and techniques, while learners can use them to improve information-acquisition skills. And, like the word processor, these too are flexible, powerful tools that can be used for a wide variety of instructional purposes.

COMPUTER DATABASES AND DATABASE MANAGEMENT

A **database** is nothing more than a collection of information. We are familiar with many examples of databases that are *not* computerized: a telephone book, a recipe file, a collection of old magazines, and so on. These examples of noncomputer databases may be organized to a greater or lesser extent. Telephone books are well organized if you know the name of the individual for whom you need a telephone number. A recipe file may be organized by type of dish: entrée, side dish, salad, or dessert. A stack of old magazines may be organized by date of issue. However, other ways of approaching this information may be very awkward. What if you have a telephone number and want to know what address it corresponds to? What if you want to know all of the recipes that involve a basic white sauce? What if you want to find all of the articles in your magazines that relate to a particular topic? These tasks are very difficult with a noncomputerized database, but when the database is computerized they become simple.

Benefits of Computer Databases

Computerized databases offer significant advantages compared to their noncomputer counterparts:

- *Flexible access.* While a telephone book is convenient if one knows the name of the person to be called, a computerized telephone directory can be searched by name, number, address, or any other information it contains. Any information in a database can be used for searching. For example, a library's electronic card catalog can be searched by title, subject, author, or key word without the need for separate catalogs.
- *Amount of information.* Electronic databases can provide access to huge amounts of information. In France, the entire country's telephone directory is now available electronically. CD-ROM databases can hold about 600 megabytes of information—enough storage space for an entire encyclopedia. One popular CD-ROM, Microsoft's *Bookshelf,* includes the *Concise Columbia Encyclopedia,* the *American Heritage Dictionary,* the *Ham-mond Atlas, Roget's Electronic Thesaurus, Bartlett's Familiar Quotations,* the *Concise Columbia Dictionary of Quotations,* and the *World Almanac,* complete with text, graphics, and multimedia elements including animation and audio.
- *Ease of manipulation.* Electronic databases also make it easy to work with the information they contain. Schools that maintain student records, grades, and other administrative information in electronic databases can quickly generate grade point averages by class, or identify all of the teachers who should be notified of student absences because of an upcoming band trip.

Database Management Systems

Computerized databases are commonplace. Most libraries now have electronic card catalogs. CD-ROM databases are proliferating rapidly. Electronic databases are also available on-line through commercial computer communications services as well as on the Internet, the network that links university and research computers throughout the world. (See the computer telecommunications section that follows for more information about these.)

A computer program that accesses a computer database is known as a **database management system (DBMS).** Database management software enables the user to enter, edit, store, retrieve, sort, and search through databases. To understand exactly what DBMSs do, let's examine the structure of a typical computer database.

Suppose you want to put the name and address information from your Rolodex (or from your address book) into computer form. How would it be organized? A computer database is organized in much the same fashion as the Rolodex itself. Each card in the Rolodex corresponds to an individual. On the card are various items of information: name, address, telephone number, and so on. In computer terminology, each individual category of information that is recorded is called a **field.** So there might be a name field, a street address field, a city field, a telephone number field, and so on. The whole collection of fields that corresponds to one Rolodex card—that is, to one individual—is called a **record.** Each record is designed to contain the same collection of fields. All of the records are collected into a **datafile.** The datafile corresponds to the entire Rolodex. In simple cases the database consists of only a single datafile. In other cases the database is a collection of datafiles that are interrelated in some way. For example, you might cross-reference your name-and-address file with your recipe file to make sure that you prepare a different dish the next time you have certain friends over for dinner. These components of a computer database are depicted graphically in Figure 6.4.

Database management software allows you to create a database like the one we have depicted. In most cases, the first step in the process involves defining the fields that will comprise a record. Because the capability to search is often linked to fields, it is important to decide exactly what fields each record will contain. While a single name field may be adequate for a Rolodex, you might want both a first-name field and a last-name field in a computer database so that you can search by either first or last name. After defining the fields, the actual data are entered into each record. After the data have been entered, the user can sort the information according to any field (e.g., alphabetically by last name). The information can be edited. In addition, it is possible to search through the infor-

mation (e.g., in a variety of ways, you can find all of the individuals in your electronic address book who live in a particular city). Of course, the database can be saved to, and retrieved from, disk.

There are two basic varieties of traditional database management programs: simple or **flat filers** and **relational databases.** Flat filers limit their work to a single datafile at a time. Popular flat filers include *Filemaker Pro* as well as the database components of integrated products such as Microsoft *Works* and *ClarisWorks.* Relational databases are more powerful but are usually more complex to use. They permit the interrelation of information across more than one datafile. Programs such as *Access, dBASE,* and *Paradox* fall into this category.

With the rapid growth of hypertext and hypermedia, more and more computerized databases are incorporating elements of these technologies. You will recall from our discussion in Chapter 4 that the terms *hypertext* and *hypermedia* refer to systems in

Figure 6.4 Components of a computer database

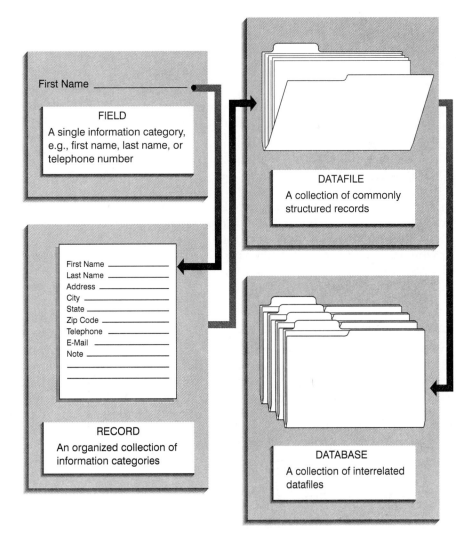

which information is stored in nodes that are inter-linked with other nodes in a nonlinear fashion. Linking is often accomplished by means of a button or "hot link" that the user activates by clicking with a mouse. In a computerized database on CD-ROM, for example, one might link from an article about the heart to one about the lungs simply by clicking on the word "lungs" in the text of the heart article. Hypertext and hypermedia links allow learners to explore information following their particular inter-ests. Popular hypermedia development packages such as *HyperCard* and *Toolbook* can be used to develop hypermedia database applications.

Teacher Uses of Computer Databases

We have introduced databases and database man-agement programs in this chapter because they are logical tools for the teacher to use in organizing information. Some examples of useful teacher data-bases include the following:

- basic information about students in classes
- bibliographic files of books and/or articles avail-able in the school that support the curriculum
- records of media and materials available in the classroom or resource center
- test or quiz questions referenced by topic, book chapter, objective, and possibly other identifiers such as level of Bloom's taxonomy
- compilations of teaching methods, strategies, and lesson plans

A number of projects have compiled successful teaching plans into databases. For example, Mary Budd Rowe gathered a number of the most suc-cessful science lesson plans developed as part of the curriculum reforms of the 1960s and 1970s on a CD-ROM called *Science Helper.*

Student Uses of Computer Databases

We live in what has been called the Information Age. As electronic databases and the means to access them proliferate, it is becoming increasingly impor-tant for students to understand how to find and interpret database information. Therefore, instruc-tion and use of databases is becoming an important part of the school curriculum. Students may use databases in the curriculum in several ways:

- *Simple location of information in prepared databases.* At a minimum, students need to be able to make use of database management software to locate

basic information in prepared databases. For example, a student should be able to locate a book in the school library's electronic card cata-log or find the name of the 19th president in a database of U.S. presidents. As students progress, they should learn to apply the Boolean (logical) operators AND and OR to narrow or expand searches, respectively.

- *Complex problem-solving and higher-order thinking skills.* Once students have mastered the basics of using database management software, databases make excellent tools for the development of problem-solving and higher-order thinking skills. The teacher can foster the growth of these skills through the use of open-ended questions. For example, using a database of U.S. presidents, one might ask questions such as the following: How does war impact presidential elections? Is there a relationship between the rate of increase of federal spending and the political party of the president?

- *Student development of databases.* Students can learn a great deal about research, information organization, and a particular content area by developing their own databases. For example, as a class project, students might develop a data-base of historical sites near their community. Not only would the development of the database be an excellent exercise for the students, but the resulting database would be a resource that could be used by others as well.

Problems and Pitfalls

There are several things to watch out for when using computer databases. Students—especially younger learners—need to have a good concept of research before using a computer database to find information. Poor library research skills can easily translate into poor computer search skills. Younger learners, especially, may need examples and assis-tance to understand Boolean logic and more com-plex search techniques.

When constructing databases, it is important to think about your information needs and to plan well. Some simple DBMSs do not allow changes to be made once the structure of the database has been defined. You don't want to start all over halfway into the data-collection process. Some programs are also limited in other ways. For example, the database components of many integrated packages permit only a limited view of the data when printed reports are being generated. While this can be a limitation, careful planning can help alleviate these problems.

INTEGRATING TECHNOLOGY
Using Computer Communication

Janette Moreno told us about an interesting thing that happened to her this past year. The school district she works for had just finished installing new phone lines in all of the high school classrooms so that teachers, students, and staff would all have access to local and worldwide telecommunications networks via their desktop computers. In-service training was provided to the teachers, and support staff was added to help teachers make effective use of the new technology. Janette attended the workshops, but she had yet to really use the network. However, when she attended a professional conference in the fall she had exchanged electronic mail addresses with another Spanish teacher, Ramona Sorelli, from a neighboring state.

Ms. Moreno was very excited as she described how this simple exchange had led to a unique source of ideas for enriching her Spanish course. For example, Janette had been brainstorming recently about how to teach a particularly challenging aspect of the curriculum, Spanish poetry and literature. Her past attempts had been unsuccessful; students had not been enthusiastic, and the overall benefits had been minimal. So she decided to tap some outside resources; maybe Ramona would have some ideas.

To get started, Janette turned on her computer and modem. She launched her telecommunications software program from the hard disk and opened its dialing directory. There she had already entered the telephone number for the commercial communication service that she and Ramona subscribed to. With a click of the mouse, the software signaled her modem to dial. She heard it dialing, and the high-pitched tone indicated that she was connected. Then the log-in screen for the communication service appeared. Janette typed in her ID and password and was soon on her way. Using the service's electronic mail function, she sent a message to Ramona asking for ideas.

The next day, Janette logged onto the service again. A reply from Ramona was waiting in her mailbox. Unfortunately, Ramona didn't have any new ideas; however, she did have a suggestion for accessing another electronic resource. Ramona knew about a database of lesson plans on the Internet and gave Janette instructions for how to access it. It was incredible. Janette accessed the Internet through a gateway in her telecommunication service and located the database with little trouble.

After entering "Spanish lesson plan" as a keyword search term, she was amazed to find a list of lesson plans that someone had previously compiled, including a lesson plan on the topic of Spanish poetry and literature, which she had been wrestling with. She followed the directions for downloading that she had received during the fall workshops and soon had a printed copy of the desired lesson plan. Janette became an instant believer in the value of computer communication and continues to tap this source on a regular basis.

COMPUTER COMMUNICATION

The development of the personal computer marked a dramatic turning point in the history of computers. Before the personal computer, computer power and information tended to be centralized in large computers operated by government, businesses, and universities. Terminals were "dumb"; that is, they lacked their own processing and information-storage capabilities. With the spread of personal computers, computing power and information has become much more broadly distributed. Today there are millions of "smart" personal computers, and they are becoming interconnected to other computers, both large and small, at an astonishing rate. We live in an era of global computer interconnectivity. As a result, there is literally a whole world of information available to the personal computer user through computer networking and telecommunication.

There are two basic categories of computer networks: **local-area networks (LANs)** and **wide-area networks (WANs)**. LANs cover a limited geographical area—often within a single building or even in a single room within a building. They are common in offices and in school computer laboratories. They permit the sharing of resources; for example, a single printer can be shared by many users via a LAN. In schools, many different software programs can be installed on the network **server**, the computer that manages the network, allowing users to easily access the software without having to fumble with floppy disks. See Chapter 11 for more about LANs.

Wide-area networks, as their name implies, cover a broad geographic area; in the most extreme case, the **Internet** is a conglomeration of computer networks that links computers worldwide (we discuss the Internet in more depth in a later section). In many universities and businesses today, high-speed network connections allow personal computers to act as individual nodes on WANs such as the Internet. However, for most users access to WANs occurs via telephone lines and a dial-up connection with a host computer. Let's examine the hardware and software requirements for dial-up access to computer services.

Computer Communication over Telephone Lines

Many computer communications services and networks now are available over telephone lines on a dial-up basis. What is required to connect to these services? In general, one must have a personal computer (usually equipped with a serial interface), a modem, communication software, and a clear telephone line. When two computers communicate, each one must be so equipped (Figure 6.5).

Telephone lines were designed to carry human speech (i.e., sound) between two points. In order for computers to use telephone lines for communication, they must adapt their information to this format. A modem converts a computer's digital information into sound (and vice versa) so that the information can be transmitted over telephone lines. Modems come in both internal (occupying an expansion bus or slot inside the computer) and external varieties. External modems must be con-

nected by a cable to the computer's serial port, because the information is sent to and from the computer as a series or stream of individual bits.

Modems are also distinguished by their maximum speed of transmission and by adherence to various communication standards. Speed of transmission is measured by the **baud rate,** which roughly indicates the approximate number of bits transmitted or received each second. Today a low-end standard is 2,400 baud, while the upper end for which clear standards have been established is 14,400 baud. Faster modems exist, but the industry has not agreed on the standards that govern their operation. Nearly all modems today adhere to a basic command set called Hayes-compatible (based on the set first used by Hayes modems). For example, in order to dial a touch-tone telephone, Hayes-compatible modems use the command ATDT followed by the telephone number.

Normally, communication with and control of the modem is accomplished by means of communication software. This software sets the baud rate and other communication parameters. In addition, communication software supports **terminal emula-**

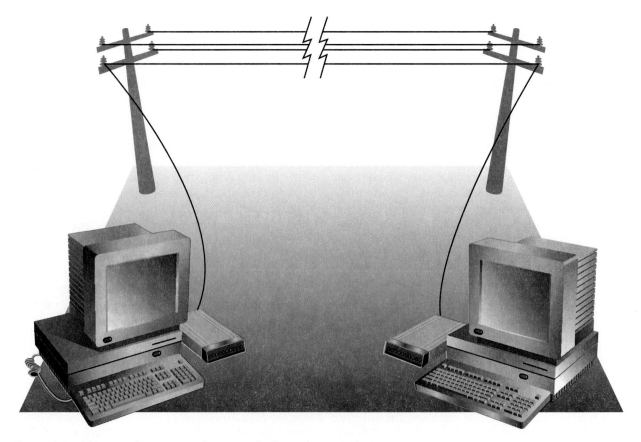

Figure 6.5   Diagram of computer telecommunication using a modem

tion. Many computer communication services are maintained on mainframe computers, which only know how to "talk" to terminals; terminal emulation software allows a personal computer to communicate as if it were a mainframe computer terminal. Most communication software also allows the user to maintain a directory of commonly dialed numbers along with the appropriate communication settings. Popular computer communication software packages include *Procomm, Crosstalk, Smartcom, QuickLink,* and *Microphone II.*

Applications of Computer Communication

There are a number of applications of computer communication that are common regardless of the particular system, including the following:

- *Electronic mail.* **Electronic mail** (e-mail for short) is analogous to postal mail but much faster. It allows private messages to be sent from individuals to other individuals or from individuals to groups. Messages are kept in a private electronic mailbox and can be accessed only by the user.

- *Bulletin boards and computer conferences.* **Bulletin boards** and computer conferences are computer services where individuals electronically post messages for others to read. Unlike e-mail, which is private, bulletin board systems are designed to be public forums. There are thousands of bulletin board systems available on many different topics of interest to numerous special-interest groups.

- *File exchange.* Because of incompatible disk formats, it is often difficult to exchange information directly between different computer brands. Although some computers, like the Apple Macintosh, can get information from diskettes that are formatted for IBM-PC computers, this is the exception rather than the rule. Computer communication, however, is a way to exchange information. If two computers, each with a modem and telecommunications software, connect with one another over telephone lines, they can exchange files that are stored in a standard format. In the personal computer world, standard text files (ASCII format) can be exchanged. Many bulletin board systems maintain libraries of text and program files that can be accessed.

- *Access to databases.* Many databases are accessible via computer communication. Some commercial information services specialize in making large databases available. In other cases, such as many Internet resources, there are huge quantities of information available, although that information is often poorly structured. When information is not well structured, it can be very difficult to locate exactly what you want.

A variety of commercial information services have emerged that offer some or all of the applications listed above. General-purpose information services include CompuServe, America Online, and Prodigy. For a fee—which can range from a flat monthly rate, to an hourly on-line rate, to some combination of the two—users can get dial-up access to these services. In addition to the applications listed above, these services include features such as up-to-the-minute news, stock market quotations, travel information and reservations, and home shopping via electronic catalogs. In addition to these general services, more specialized services such as DIALOG offer access to literally hundreds of commercial databases. DIALOG users can get bibliographic information about magazine articles, read the full text of some newspapers, and locate current medical reference information.

The Expanding World of the Internet

While commercial computer communication services have been expanding rapidly, so too has the Internet. Originally formed to link defense computers and scientists, the Internet has grown into a sprawling collection of computer networks that circles the globe. Today, millions of computers used by tens of millions of people are linked to the Internet. Although it tends to be much rougher around the edges, the Internet offers many of the same capabilities as the commercial services, particularly electronic communication and access to stores of information. While the Internet has traditionally been difficult to navigate, in recent years software has been developed that greatly simplifies the process of accessing information. Most universities already have Internet access, many companies are hooked to it as well, and an increasing number of K-12 schools are gaining access. It appears that the Internet will form the foundation, or a key part, of the "information superhighway" that will eventually connect all schools, businesses, and homes. Let's look more closely at some of the things the Internet has to offer.

Electronic Mail

E-mail is one of the simplest and most popular features of the Internet. It permits rapid communication between individuals; an e-mail note from the United States to Europe may be delivered in mere seconds, compared to the days required for postal mail. E-mail can also be used to communicate from one person to many others—something like bulk or mass mailing, but with much greater ease. It is a simple matter to broadcast a single e-mail message to a list of interested users. Automated facilities to perform mass mailings are common on the Internet. Called mailing lists or **listservers,** these facilities take any e-mail message sent to them and send it out to all of the persons on the mailing list. Listservers on a wide variety of special interests have sprung up, and interested individuals can join or subscribe to share ideas with others. They provide a mechanism for people from all over the world to share a common interest.

To send e-mail to someone on the Internet, you must have access to mail services on a computer linked to the Internet, and you must know the other person's e-mail address. Just as you have a postal mail address, everyone on the Internet has an e-mail address. The basic form of any Internet e-mail address is *userID@location.* The *userID* is usually the individual's assigned identifier on his or her computer system; this may be something simple like the person's name (e.g., lehman or newby), or it may be a relatively cryptic identifier (e.g., xvp2 or k0115), depending on the particular system. The *location* refers to the other person's computer system.

All computers on the Internet communicate via a common protocol known as TCP/IP, and every computer on the Internet has a unique IP (Internet protocol) address, usually represented as four numbers separated by periods (e.g., 140.147.254.3). Mail services maintain lists of names that correspond to these locations, or what are referred to as domains, so that you can mail to a location by name rather than by number. For example, three of the authors of this book (lehman, newby, and jrussell) can be contacted at the computer domain *vm.cc.purdue.edu.* The complete e-mail address for James Lehman is *lehman@vm.cc.purdue.edu.*

An *edu* at the end of a location name indicates an educational institution. Other common domain identifiers include *com* (company), *gov* (government), *mil* (military), *net* (network), and *org* (organization). All countries also have domain identifiers that are added to the end of the location name for international e-mail. Examples include *au* (Australia), *ca* (Canada), *fr* (France), *tw* (Taiwan), and *uk* (United Kingdom).

Remote Log-in

Another feature of the Internet is the ability to make a connection with a computer at a remote location. The standard Internet protocol for making a connection with a remote computer is called **telnet.** Similar to e-mail, the common syntax for establishing a remote connection, a telnet session, is *telnet location,* where *location* is an Internet domain name as discussed above.

The chief use of telnet is to gain access to information resources that reside on a remote computer. For example, the catalog of the Library of Congress and the library catalogs of many institutions of higher education are available on-line via telnet. One can connect to the remote computer and search the catalog just as though one were actually in the library. Freenets, community computer systems that are open to the public and free of charge, are also accessible in this manner. For example, the Cleveland Freenet, a pioneer of the community freenet concept, has a wide variety of information resources that can be accessed via telnet.

It is important to point out that only certain computer systems on the Internet are freely accessible via telnet. There are millions of computers on the Internet, and most require a bona fide user ID and password for access. Only certain systems have been established for open, public access via telnet; many of these provide instructions for use when you connect to them. It is also important for the user to bear in mind that telnet establishes a live connection to a remote computer. Attention should be paid to any directions or prompts from the remote computer, because operating commands may differ from the user's host computer. Further, telnet makes less efficient use of network resources than do many other forms of Internet access.

Information Retrieval

Information retrieval, especially for education, is becoming one of the most important uses of the Internet. Telnet is one way to retrieve information. There are several other sources of information, or ways to retrieve information, including usenet news groups, file-transfer protocol, Gopher, and the World Wide Web.

Usenet news groups are the Internet equivalent of bulletin boards. They are discussion groups on a wide variety of topics that are maintained by interchanges among a number of computers on the Internet. As with bulletin boards, individuals can contribute comments or news articles that can be read by anyone who belongs to the news group. Others can react to previous comments or post their own thoughts. Discussion topics are identified by a number of common abbreviations: comp (computers), misc (miscellaneous), sci (science), rec (recreation), and alt (alternative). Educators should be aware that the alt, especially, can contain topics that most people would consider unsuitable for school-age children.

The standard Internet method for exchanging files is called file-transfer protocol, or **ftp.** As with telnet, it is possible to establish a connection with a remote computer for the purpose of conducting a file transfer using the command *ftp location.* Many Internet sites support what is known as anonymous ftp. This system allows the public access to certain files without an individual having to possess a registered user ID and password for the computer. While the method can vary from computer to computer, many systems permit anonymous ftp when the user logs in using "anonymous" as the log-in ID and his or her own e-mail address as the password.

Many excellent resources are available on the Internet via anonymous ftp. However, finding resources on a particular topic can be a chore. To help individuals find files that may be accessed via ftp, a number of computers around the world maintain databases of ftp sites. A software system called Archie allows users to search the database for information of interest.

Unfortunately, even with available databases, standard telnet and ftp can be daunting for the uninitiated. The good news is that in recent years software has been developed that makes navigation and use of the Internet much easier. One of the foremost software tools for information retrieval on the Internet is **Gopher** (designed to "go for" informa-

tion), which was developed at the University of Minnesota, the home of the Golden Gophers. It employs what is known as a client-server model. Gopher servers, of which there are many worldwide, maintain collections of information and references to information located on other computers. Gopher clients—programs that can operate on large and small computers alike—find and retrieve information through communication with Gopher servers. A simple menu-driven system is used (Figure 6.6 shows a sample menu from the Gopher server operated by the Purdue University Libraries).

One real advantage of the Gopher software is that the user is shielded from knowing where information is located and how to get it. Gophers automatically locate information and retrieve it as needed. Further, the Gopher software uses resources only as needed. Gopher software does not maintain a connection as telnet does; it simply connects long enough to retrieve the requested information, and then the connection is freed for another user. This method makes for efficient use of computer resources. Users can use Gopher menus to browse for information, or they can conduct searches. Just as Archie provides for searches of ftp sites, a software system called Veronica is available that permits users to search Gopher databases for topics of interest.

The fastest-growing part of the Internet is called the **World Wide Web (WWW).** The WWW, with its access software Mosaic and Netscape, provides

Figure 6.6 Purdue University Libraries Gopher server menu

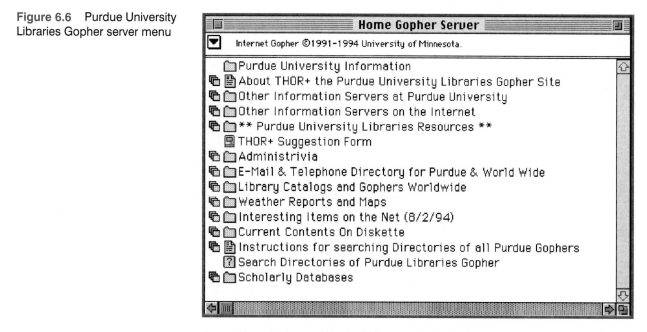

Source: Team Gopher and Purdue University. Reprinted with permission.

access to information on the Internet in the point-and-click hypertext format that is familiar to all users of the Macintosh or Microsoft Windows operating systems. Like Gopher, it uses an efficient client-server model. Unlike Gopher, which relies on a menu-driven system, the WWW has the simple mouse-driven interface that is already familiar to millions of computer users. To access a "hot link" to related information, usually represented by an icon or colored text, the user simply clicks on it with a mouse. There is no need to know where the link leads; the software will automatically make the appropriate connection and retrieve the information. As a result, this kind of interface is rapidly becoming the most popular way to access the Internet.

In addition, with appropriate software and a sufficiently high-speed connection, Mosaic and Netscape software can provide access to full multimedia resources, including text, graphics, audio, and even digital video. The Internet is going multimedia! Figure 6.7 shows a sample WWW resource, the home page of the White House WWW server established by the Clinton administration in 1994.

The phenomenal growth of the Internet, and the interest from the educational community in it, is not surprising. Here, at the touch of a button, are the resources that have accumulated over many years by millions of people on millions of computers worldwide. The sheer scope is staggering. It is not too much of an exaggeration to call the Internet

the brain and nervous system of the planet. The people of the world are interconnected, and information is available as never before. For educators, the challenge is to find the best and most productive ways to make use of this tremendous resource. Table 6.2 contains a number of Internet resources that may be of interest to educators.

Teacher Uses of Computer Communication

As with databases, we can cite numerous examples of how the use of computer communication is of benefit to teachers:

- e-mail to contact other teachers in similar positions to exchange ideas and reduce teacher isolation
- bulletin boards to solicit assistance with technical problems, teaching concerns, lesson ideas, and so on
- on-line databases of teaching methods, strategies, and instructional plans

Student Uses of Computer Communication

Many experiments involving student use of computer communication have been conducted over the past decade. These experiments suggest a number of productive ways that computer communication can be used in an instructional context:

Figure 6.7 Home page of the World Wide Web server for the White House

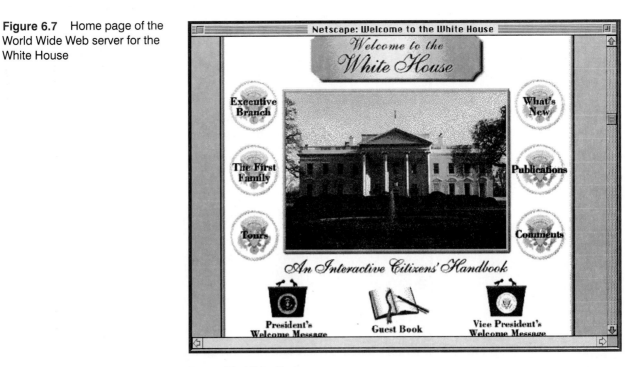

Source: The White House

Table 6.2 Internet resources for educators (Addresses as of August 1995)

Internet Resource	Description	Internet Address
Academy One	On-line K–12 resource from the National Public Telecomputing Network	freenet-in-a.cwru.edu
Big Sky Telegraph	K–12 curriculum/lesson plan clearinghouse for network projects	bigsky.bigsky.dillon.mt.us
Cleveland Freenet	Cleveland community freenet, featuring a wide variety of resources	freenet-in-a.cwru.edu
Educational Resources Information Center (ERIC)	ERIC databases and information services for educators	ericir.syr.edu
Info-Mac archives	Large ftp archive site for Macintosh freeware and shareware	sumex-aim.stanford.edu
Library of Congress catalogue	Searchable catalogue of the Library of Congress holdings	locis.loc.gov
NASA Spacelink	NASA bulletin board that includes current information and classroom activities	spacelink.msfc.nasa.gov
NASA Web Server	NASA's World Wide Web server accessing other NASA locations	http://hypatia.gsfc.nasa.gov
NCSA Web Server	World Wide Web server of the University of Illinois's supercomputer center	http://www.ncsa.uiuc.edu
White House Web Server	World Wide Web server for the White House	http://www.whitehouse.gov
WUARCHIVE	Washington University archives, one of the largest of all ftp archives	wuarchive.wustl.edu

- *Use of e-mail or bulletin board systems for pen-pal exchanges with students at other locations.* In the best cases, these can lead to the development of cross-cultural awareness through electronic exchanges involving students in other countries and cultures (Levin, Riel, Miyake, & Cohen, 1987).

- *Promotion of improved writing through the exchange of written work with students at other locations.* Students write better when they know there is a real audience that will read what they have written (Cohen & Riel, 1989).

- *Science experiments involving the sharing of data from many locations.* National Geographic's *Kidsnet Project* (Julyan, 1991; Tinker & Kapisovsky, 1991) has involved thousands of schoolchildren from across the United States and Canada in real experiments, including a survey of acid rain in North America.

- *Research involving databases and other resources available on-line.* Students can locate current information, often up-to-the-minute, through on-line database services like DIALOG, as well as through communication services maintained by the likes of NASA, the National Weather Service, and the National Earthquake Center.

Problems and Pitfalls

Computer communication opens many new and exciting avenues for teachers and students. But the information highway is not free of potholes! With its myriad of technical details, computer communication can be one of the most difficult computing areas to master. The basic problem is that computer communication requires many separate components to work in concert: the computer, modem, modem cable, communication software, telephone line, and the remote computer. Often they do not. It is important to read documentation carefully and follow the recommendations. If you cannot overcome a problem, call a help line or ask a knowledgeable friend for some assistance.

Many teachers are excited by the opportunities available through access to the Internet. But teachers need to be a little cautious. Simple pen-pal projects or aimless searching of the massive resources available may accomplish little educationally. Teachers need to think about productive ways to use the network, and they may want to locate useful resources in advance. Teachers also need to be aware that the Internet is unregulated. Material unsuitable for children is available on many computers on the Internet. In addition, there have been reported incidents of adults using electronic networks to stalk or lure children. If the Internet is available to students, close supervision is essential.

SUMMARY

An instructional plan is like a recipe. It describes the "ingredients" of instruction and indicates how those ingredients are to be combined for a particular lesson. The ingredients in the instructional plan are the instructional events. This chapter has identified six instructional events: introduction, content information, application information, questioning, practice and feedback, and assessment. These are represented graphically in Figure 6.8.

Like a recipe, an instructional plan is a flexible decision-making guide, and these instructional events can be combined in various ways, depending on the needs, interests, and experiences of the students, the structure of the content, the available resources, and the preferences, interests, and experiences of the teacher. Regardless of how the instruc-

tional events are combined, it's critical that the components of the plan are congruent with one another. An instructional plan that is congruent offers a number of practical benefits before, during, and after the delivery of the instruction. These benefits are represented graphically in Figure 6.9.

This chapter also described the value database management and telecommunications software have during instructional planning. The types of databases, their major components, and their practical benefits are represented in Figure 6.10. Figure 6.11 represents the basic types of telecommunications networks that exist and, more importantly, the various applications that can be used by the classroom teacher in order to access and transfer information.

REFLECTIVE QUESTIONS AND ACTIVITIES

1. Look back at the sample instructional plans in this chapter and think back to the discussion of motivation in Chapter 5. In each of the sample plans, what is being done to motivate the students?

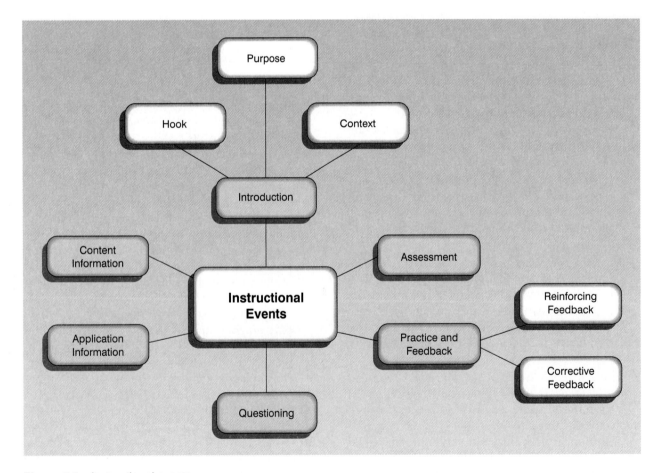

Figure 6.8   Instructional events

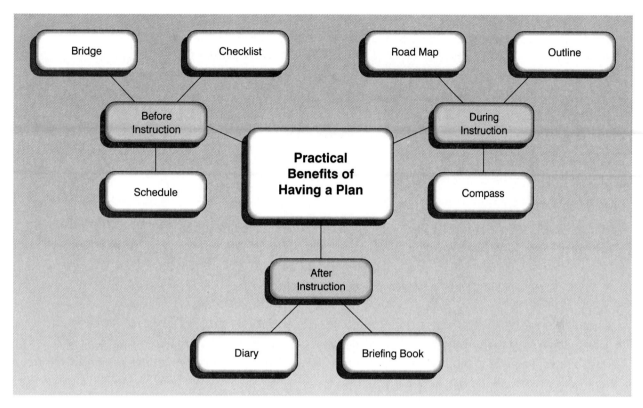

Figure 6.9   Practical benefits of instructional plans

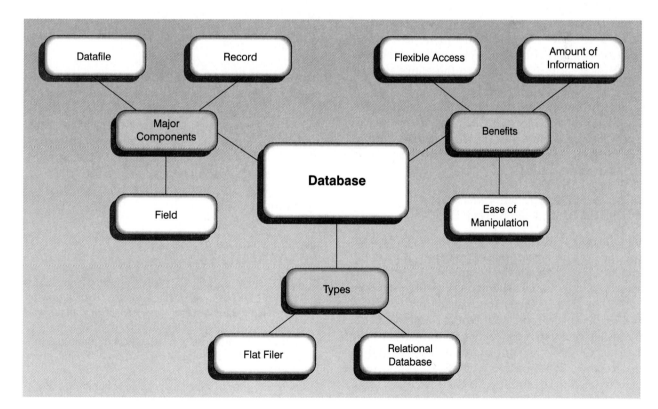

Figure 6.10   Database components, types, and benefits

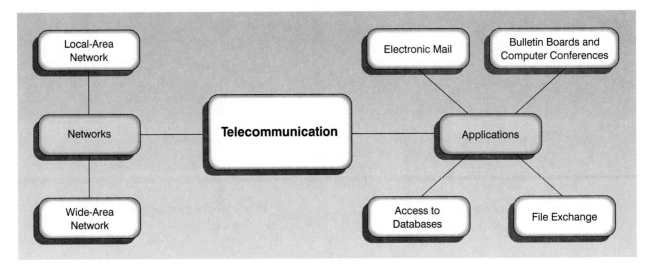

Figure 6.11   Applications and types of networks associated with a computer telecommunications tool

Use Table 5.4 to classify these strategies. What else might you suggest to motivate the students?

2. Review the two sample instructional plans in this chapter. Consider each plan in turn and identify the manager for each event. How might you shift the balance of power in each event?

3. Develop an instructional plan for a lesson. Briefly describe how each instructional event would be implemented. Give your plan to another student and ask for feedback. Does the plan make sense? Does it seem coherent? Are the instructional events clearly described? Are there any alternative ways of implementing each event?

4. For the sample instructional plans, review the different components in each and then describe the changes that would occur if one were to change the order of the events or the instructional approaches used.

INTEGRATION AND SYNTHESIS

In Chapter 5 the discussion concentrated on preparing and gathering information in order to effectively prepare for the instructional lesson. This information included where the students should be after they had received the instruction—the outcomes. In other words, what would the students do, or be able to do, to indicate that the proper learning had occurred? This information was needed in order to provide direction to the plan and to indicate when the destination of the instruction had been achieved. Additionally, we discussed the students themselves and the need to know their abili-

ties, experiences, and levels of motivation prior to receiving the instructional materials. This information, coupled with that from Chapters 3 and 4 concerning the instructional approaches and media, was used in the present chapter to help create the instructional plan. As we showed, the classroom teacher has a great need for access to additional information. Database management systems and computer telecommunications were presented as valuable tools for the teacher.

Chapter 7 will conclude the section on the planning phase of the instruction. Now that the instructional plan has been developed, it is important to select or create the desired instructional materials. As we will show, the focus is on carefully using and following the instructional plan to select the actual materials needed to achieve the desired outcomes. To facilitate this process of selecting or creating the actual instructional materials, the focus of the CUE will be desktop publishing, graphics, and other applications designed to help with such needs.

SUGGESTED READINGS

Borko, H., & Livingston, C. (1989). Cognition and improvisation: Differences in mathematics instruction by expert and novice teachers. *American Educational Research Journal, 26*(4), 473–498.

Clark, C. M., & Yinger, R. J. (1987). Teacher planning. In J. Calderhead (Ed.), *Exploring teachers' thinking* (pp. 84–103). London: Cassell.

Reynolds, A. (1992). What is competent beginning teaching? An overview of the literature. *Review of Educational Research, 62*(1), 1–35.

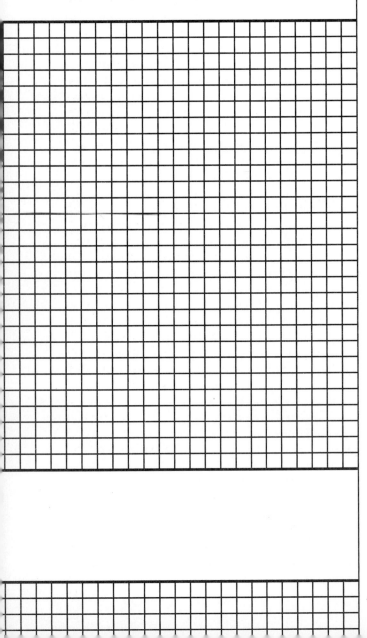

Chapter 7

Selecting, Modifying, and Creating Instructional Materials

KEY WORDS AND CONCEPTS

Instructional materials

Repurposing

COMPUTER USE ESSENTIALS (CUE)
Words and Concepts

Graphic

Bit-mapped graphics

Vector graphics

Clip art

PhotoCD

Video digitizer

Desktop publishing (DTP)

Authoring system

OUTCOMES

After reading and studying this chapter, you will be able to:

- Discuss the most important criteria used in selecting instructional approaches and media.
- Describe the considerations in selecting the optimum type of media (media format) for an instructional plan.
- Identify sources of existing instructional materials.
- Complete the media selection process for any instructional plan.
- Describe techniques for modifying available instructional materials.
- Modify existing instructional materials or design new ones.
- Define *graphic* and *pixel*.
- Distinguish between bit-mapped and vector graphics.
- Identify common types of graphics programs.
- List the hardware tools used for graphics production.
- Define *desktop publishing*.
- Identify the common features of desktop publishing software.
- Describe the continuum of options available for authoring computer-based instructional materials.
- Discuss classroom uses of authoring tools.

■ INTRODUCTION

For a few moments imagine that you are in charge of a large machine shop that produces various types, sizes, and quantities of metal machine parts. These parts might vary from tiny ball bearings, to 2-inch brackets, to 24-inch gear mechanisms. Parts are constructed from precision-made dies (manufacturing molds). Customers constantly bring you orders for their needed parts. It is your job to make sure that customers receive the desired number of parts, in the time allotted, and according to the given specifications.

If you were faced with such a task, the need for a clear production and product specification plan would be paramount. The plan would allow you to examine the specific requirements (e.g., size, tolerance) for the part and the end product's appearance. Then, to be as productive and cost-efficient as possible, you would need to ask the following questions:

1. Do we already have the dies in stock for making the needed parts? That is, can we use what has already been produced?
2. If the exact die does not exist, is it possible to adapt another part's die to make a part that meets specifications for this particular customer?
3. If adaptation is impossible, can we create a new die to produce the needed parts within the given time and monetary constraints?

These questions are sequenced according to cost—both in dollar amounts and in time. That is, the most cost-efficient manner in which to deliver the needed parts is to use ones that are already available. When that is not possible, the next alternative is to adapt existing parts according to the needed specifications. As a last alternative, you may have to actually manufacture the necessary products.

In this chapter we are going to discuss the use of an instructional plan as it pertains to the *acquisition* of instructional materials. We will begin by showing how the different sections of the instructional plan contribute to the selection and acquisition of the final instructional materials. Similar to the machine shop manager, the instructional plan should outline the needed specifications. Based on these specifications, the instructional materials will be acquired. Although at times this will require the actual development of materials, similar to the machine shop production manager, the first choice is to see if something already exists or if something can be adapted to meet current needs.

Following the information given in Chapter 6, it is possible that you have begun an instructional plan. To get to that point you have identified the content of the plan; analyzed your learners to determine what they already know, their styles of learning, and other relevant characteristics (e.g., levels of motivation); and considered the environment in which the learning will or should occur. Now you are ready to determine the media format and the actual instructional materials that will be needed.

143

To begin, let's distinguish between the terms *media* and *instructional materials* as they will be used in this book. In Chapter 4 we defined a *medium* as a channel of communication, that is, a means of carrying information between the teacher and the students. The types of media, or media formats, for learning include real objects and models, text, visuals, display boards, overhead transparencies, slides and filmstrips, audio, video and film, television, computer software, and multimedia. Descriptions of these media and examples of their use were also given in Chapter 4. **Instructional materials** are the specific items used in a lesson and delivered through various media formats; for example, a videotape titled *The Second Russian Revolution* may be used in a social studies class. The media format is video, and the instructional material is the information about the Russian Revolution found on that videotape. The instructional plan discussed in Chapter 6 is not complete until the instructional materials and their associated media formats have been determined.

Instructional materials can be incorporated throughout the instructional events outlined in the instructional plan, from the opening introduction event through the concluding assessment event. For example, if you were designing a physics lesson on the characteristics of light there may be several events requiring instructional materials, all of which may be presented via various media formats:

- *Introduction.* A videotape segment with animation could illustrate the behavior of light.
- *Content information.* Text and visuals could present information about the principles of light.

Instructional materials are used by the students and teacher to facilitate learning.

- *Application information.* Slides could be used to illustrate key points in a teacher-led discussion.
- *Questioning.* Overhead transparencies could be used to present self-examination questions about reflection and refraction.
- *Practice.* Real objects (e.g., lenses, mirrors, prisms) could be provided to allow student exploration of the behavior of light.
- *Assessment.* Paper-and-pencil tests could be used to determine students' level of mastery.

Once you have determined what instructional materials are needed or what media formats will be required, you must do one of the following: (1) identify and obtain already-existing materials that match your requirements; (2) identify existing materials that can be used if they are first modified to match your requirements; or (3) design and develop materials to match your requirements. For example, suppose you have a need for some instructional materials concerning chemistry laboratory procedures and you have decided that videotape would be an effective medium of communication. At that point you have three options: (1) select an existing videotape that appropriately addresses the chemistry laboratory procedures; (2) locate a videotape that comes close to meeting the needs of your students and modify it through editing until it meets the requirements for your instructional plan; or (3) start from scratch and create a videotape covering the needed content.

Instructional materials are an important aspect of any instruction. This chapter describes both the criteria used and the procedures needed to successfully acquire the needed instructional materials. The procedure we present can be used when selecting commercially available materials, modifying existing materials, or creating new materials for a specific instructional situation. By using the proper media format coupled with the instructional materials, you can assure the effectiveness and efficiency of your students' learning.   ■

THE INSTRUCTIONAL MATERIALS ACQUISITION PROCESS

Let's explore how to go about finding instructional materials for your lesson. Figure 7.1 identifies the major components of the instructional materials selection process and illustrates their relationships to each other. Note the input of the learners and the content or outcomes (as discussed in Chapter 5) to both the instructional approach and the instructional materials. As you go about selecting an appropriate approach and the appropriate materials, important information is needed about both the content to be taught and the individuals who will receive the instruction. These have already been determined in the instructional plan. Also note the doubled-headed arrows between the learning environment, instructional approach, and instructional materials components of Figure 7.1. These indicate that the components interact with and are affected by each other.

In the typical case, the manner in which targeted instructional materials are selected generally involves determining (1) where and under what conditions the materials will be experienced by the students (i.e., learning environment) and (2) what the optimal instructional approach (e.g., simulation, presentation, discussion, problem solving) would be, based on considerations of the learners, the content, and the setting. However, there are other times when it is appropriate or necessary to select the instructional approach or a set of instructional materials prior to the determination of the setting or other considerations. The following examples illustrate some of the possible scenarios.

Scenario A: Setting → Approach → Instructional Materials. Mr. Hughes wants to teach sentence structure to his eighth-grade English class, which meets right before lunch. He doesn't see a benefit or a need to move to another location, thus the learning environment will be his classroom. He decides

to use a game approach to make the topic interesting and to give his students a chance to practice the skills and receive feedback. Not able to find any instructional materials in his school, he decides to design his own game in the format of a board game in which students roll dice, draw a card, and advance if they can correctly identify the part of a sentence highlighted on the card.

Scenario B: Approach → Instructional Materials → Setting. The students in Pat Todd's social studies class are studying World War II. She decides to use the presentation approach to introduce the topic because this can provide the students with an overview of a critical event in history that occurred before they were born. In thinking about what media to use, Pat considers supplementing the textbook and presentation with visuals. She wants her students to have an image of the war to help them remember the content. With the help of the school library media specialist, Pat locates a series of slides with an audiotape. There are 80 slides in the set— far more than she wants to use to introduce World War II. She selects from the series a dozen slides that will highlight her key points. Because the level of the tape is too elementary for her students, she decides to substitute her own explanation for the less appropriate tape. The environment will be her classroom equipped with a slide projector.

Scenario C: Instructional Materials → Approach → Setting. Ms. Roth, a fifth-grade teacher in the Midwest, wants to increase her students' awareness of the ways in which living things affect each other. She recently found a piece of computer software titled *A Field Trip into the Sea* in the school library media center. After previewing it, she decided it matches the characteristics of her students and teaches the content she wants to cover. She is sure the software will motivate her students to develop an awareness of living things they have not seen. The computer software determines the approach— in this case discovery. Since Ms. Roth wants all twenty students to use the software simultaneously, the environment must be the school's computer lab.

Integrating Media and Instructional Materials into the Instructional Plan

In Chapter 6 we discussed an instructional plan that delineated several instructional events: introduction, content information, application information, questioning, practice and feedback, and assessment. As we showed, instructional materials may be deliv-

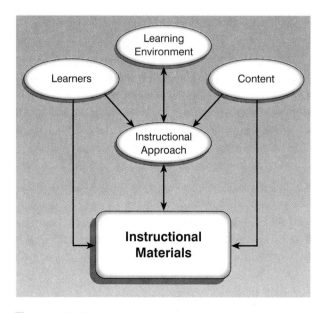

Figure 7.1 Components of the instructional materials acquisition process

ered through various types of media across all the different instructional events. For example, a videotape could be shown to get students' attention as part of the introduction before a lesson on tornadoes. Content information about parts of speech could be presented on a display board. Groups of students could prepare their own slides and audiotape presentations for the application information portion of a lesson on modes of transportation. The teacher could use overhead transparencies to stimulate questioning on the organization of governments. Practice and feedback for foreign-language or unfamiliar vocabulary could be provided by drill-and-practice computer software. Finally, real objects and models could help students and teachers in the assessment of math facts.

In the best of all possible worlds, the teacher's first choice should be to select instructional materials off the shelf, that is, to find exactly what is needed and use those materials. If materials cannot be found that will enable students to meet desired outcomes, however, a teacher's second choice should be to modify existing materials to facilitate learning. Only as a last resort should teachers create their own materials, since doing so is expensive and time-consuming. Most teachers do not have the time to create materials, and few teachers have the expertise to produce their own quality materials, especially videotapes and computer software. Let's now explore the options shown under instructional materials in Figure 7.2.

Select Optimum Type of Media Format

In Chapter 4 we introduced you to eleven types of media: real objects and models, text, visuals, display boards, overhead transparencies, slides and filmstrips, audio, video and film, television, computer software, and multimedia. The first step in selecting materials, as shown in Figure 7.2, is to select the optimum type of medium or media to teach the *content* to your *learners* using the *approach* previously selected in the *setting* available. What media characteristics will best teach the content to your learners—visual, color, sound, motion, interaction, or tactile (touch)? See Figure 7.3, which matches media characteristics with the various media formats. To make a good decision about the type of medium to select, you must be aware of the advantages and limitations of each. To help you in this selection process, Table 7.1 presents the main advantages and limitations of all the media described in Chapter 4.

Now that we've explored the advantages and limitations of the different types of media formats, let's look at the media selection checklist in Figure 7.4

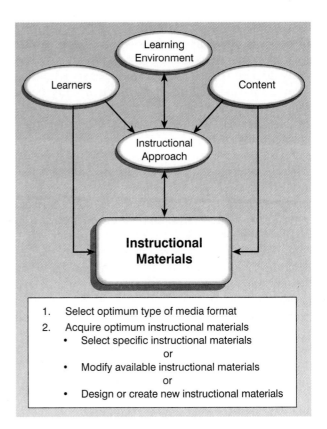

Figure 7.2   Instructional materials acquisition process

(on pages 154–55). It will assist you in selecting a medium to help your students master the content. Take some time to read and ponder each of the following three scenarios. Decide what would be the optimum media format for each situation. Make sure you refer back to Figure 7.1 and identify each of the main components (learners, content, instructional approach, and learning environment) found within each. After you have made those identifications, answer the following questions: What were the reasons you used to make your selection? Are there any potential problems with your selection? If so, what would those problems be? What other media formats could also have been selected? Under what conditions would you switch to those alternatives?

Scenario A.   The sixth-grade concert band instructor, Mr. Snyder, has decided that his students need to discriminate better between sharps and flats on the musical scale. To introduce the topic, he has decided to complete a demonstration that will emphasize differences between sharps, flats, and natural notes. Because he has 56 students currently in his band, his demonstration will have to take place in the band room, which is large enough to seat approximately 125 individuals.

Figure 7.3   Media characteristics

Types of Media	Visual	Color	Sound	Motion	Interaction	Tactile
Real objects and models	●	●				●
Text (books, handouts)	●	●				
Visuals (pictures, photos, drawings, charts, graphs)	●	●				
Display boards (chalk, bulletin, multipurpose)	●	●				
Overhead transparencies	●	●				
Slides and filmstrips	●	●	●			
Audio (tape, disc, voice)			●			
Video and film (tape, disc)	●	●	●	●		
Television (live)	●	●	●	●		
Computer software	●	●	●	●	●	
Multimedia	●	●	●	●	●	

Scenario B.   Within an advanced survival training course, there was a need to teach the six participants how to recognize edible versus nonedible desert plants found in the southwestern portion of the United States. Even though the course involved training for *desert* survival, it was being taught at a small college in Ohio.

Scenario C.   Mrs. Spence and her class of fourth-grade students have been working on a unit dealing with developing critical-thinking skills. One section of the content focused on methods used to solve ill-defined problems. To give students practice using the different techniques they studied, Mrs. Spence decided that a simulation would be the best approach to get the students actively involved in using the different techniques.

To help you understand the interrelationship between the learning environment, approach, and selected media, consider what would happen to your media format selection if the following alterations were made to the previous scenarios. Scenario A: Instead of being a band director, Mr. Snyder is a private flute teacher with 12 students who all come at different times during the day for individualized instruction. His goal is still to have the students increase their ability to discriminate between flats, sharps, and natural notes. Scenario B: The survival course took place at the University of Nevada, Las Vegas. Scenario C: The focus of Mrs.

Spence's class changed from simulation to cooperative learning.

Select Specific Instructional Materials

After determining the optimum type of medium or media for your instructional plan, you must select the specific materials to meet the needs and characteristics of your students. For example, if you decide that a videotape is the optimum medium for the lesson, you would look at sources of videotapes.

There are a number of sources of instructional materials. Check the listing of materials in your

Selecting the appropriate materials for instruction is an important process.

Table 7.1 Advantages and limitations of each media format

Media Format	Advantages	Limitations
Real Objects and Models	• *Less abstract and more concrete.* Real objects and models provide hands-on learning experiences and emphasize real-world applications. • *Readily available.* These materials are readily available in the environment, around school, and in the home. • *Attract students' attention.* Students respond very positively to both real objects and their models.	• *Storage.* Large objects can pose special problems. Caring for living materials such as plants and animals can take a lot of time. • *Possible damage.* Materials are often complex and fragile. Parts may be lost or broken.
Text	• *Readily available.* Printed materials are readily available in a wide range of topics and formats. • *Very flexible.* Printed materials may be used in any lighted environment. They are very portable. Properly designed text is very user-friendly and easy to use. It provides organization of the content. • *Economical.* Text can be used again and again by many students.	• *Reading level of learners.* Many students are non-readers or poor readers. Some critics say textbooks promote memorization rather than higher-level thinking skills. • *Passive.* Others contend that text promotes solitary learning rather than cooperative group processes. Textbooks may be used to dictate the curriculum rather than to support the curriculum.
Visuals	• *Realistic format.* Visuals provide a representation of verbal information. • *Readily available.* Visuals are readily available in books, magazines, newspapers, catalogs, and calendars. • *Easy to use.* Visuals are easy to use because they do not require any equipment. • *Relatively inexpensive.* Most visuals can be obtained at little or no cost.	• *Size.* Some visuals are simply too small to use with a large group, and enlarging can be an expensive process. However, the opaque projector can project an enlarged image before a class. • *Two-dimensional.* Visuals lack the three-dimensionality of the real object or scene. However, by providing a series of visuals of the same object or scene from several different angles, this limitation can be addressed. • *Lack of motion.* Visuals are static and cannot show motion. However, a series of sequential still pictures can suggest motion.
Display Boards	• *Readily available in classrooms.* Display boards do not usually have to be scheduled. • *Versatile.* Display boards can be used for a wide variety of purposes by both students and teachers. • *Colorful.* Display boards provide color and add interest to the classroom or hallway. • *Involvement.* Students can benefit from designing and using display boards.	• *Commonplace.* Instructors often neglect to give display boards the attention and respect they deserve as instructional devices. Displays can quickly lose their effectiveness if left in place too long. • *Not portable.* Most display boards are not movable and must be used where they are.

Media Format	Advantages	Limitations
Overhead Transparencies	• *Versatility.* The overhead can be used in normal room lighting. The projector is operated from the front of the room, with the presenter facing the audience and maintaining eye contact. All projectors are simple to operate. • *Instructor control.* Projected materials can be manipulated by the presenter, who can point to important items, highlight them with colored pens, add details by marking on the transparency with a pen, or cover part of the message and progressively reveal information in a step-by-step procedure. • *Instructor preparation.* Teachers can easily prepare their own transparencies. Information that might otherwise have to be placed on a chalkboard during a class session may be prepared in advance for presentation at the proper time.	• *Instructor dependent.* The effectiveness of overhead projection presentations is heavily dependent on the teacher. The overhead projector cannot be programmed to display information by itself. The overhead system does not lend itself to independent study. The projection system is designed for large-group presentation. • *Preparation required.* Printed materials and other nontransparent items, such as magazine illustrations, cannot be projected immediately but must be made into transparencies by means of some production process.
Slides	• *Flexibility.* Because slides can be arranged and rearranged into many different sequences, they are more flexible than filmstrips or other fixed-sequence materials. • *Easy to produce.* Cameras with automatic exposure controls, easy focusing, and high-speed color films allow teachers and students to easily produce their own high-quality slides. • *Ease of use.* Projectors offer the convenience of remote control, allowing the presenter to remain at the front of the room while advancing the slides via a push-button unit. • *Availability.* The general availability and ease of producing slides allows one to easily build up permanent collections for instructional purposes.	• *Lack of sequence.* Because slides come as individual units, they can easily become disorganized. Even when stored in trays, the slides can be spilled if the locking ring is loosened. • *Jamming.* Slides can be mounted in cardboard, plastic, or glass of varying thicknesses. This lack of standardization can lead to jamming in the slide-changing mechanism. Cardboard mounts become dog-eared; plastic mounts swell or warp in the heat of the lamps; thick glass mounts fail to drop into showing position. • *Damage.* Slides that are not enclosed in glass covers are susceptible to accumulation of dust and fingerprints. Careless storage or handling can easily lead to permanent damage.
Filmstrips	• *Cost.* Filmstrips are relatively low cost. A commercially distributed filmstrip costs substantially less per frame than a set of comparable slides or overhead transparencies.	• *Fixed sequence.* The main drawback is that it is not possible to alter the sequence of pictures without destroying the filmstrip. Backtracking to an earlier picture or skipping over frames is cumbersome.

Table 7.1 *Continued*

Media Format	Advantages	Limitations
Filmstrips, *continued*	• *Sequential.* The sequential order of frames in a filmstrip can be an advantage. A chronological or step-by-step process can be presented in order without fear of having any of the pictures out of sequence or upside down, as can sometimes happen with slides. • *Control.* The pace of viewing filmstrips can be controlled by the teacher or student. This capability is especially relevant for independent study but is also important for teacher-controlled group showings. • *Independent study.* Many types of tabletop viewers are made especially for individual or small-group use. Young children have no difficulty loading filmstrips into these viewers.	• *Damage.* Because the filmstrip is pulled through the projector by means of toothed sprocket wheels, there is the constant possibility of tearing the sprocket holes and damaging the filmstrip. Improper threading or rough use can cause tears, which are very difficult to repair.
Audio Tapes	• *Student and teacher preparation.* Students and teachers can record their own tapes easily and economically. When the material becomes outdated or no longer useful, the tape can be erased and reused. • *Familiarity.* Most students and teachers have been using audiocassette recorders since they were very young. • *Verbal message.* Students who cannot read can learn from audio media. For nonreading students, audio can provide basic language experiences. • *Stimulating.* Audio media can provide a stimulating alternative to reading and listening to the teacher. Audio can present verbal messages more dramatically than text can. • *Portable.* Audiocassette recorders are very portable and can even be used "in the field" with battery power. Cassette recordings are ideal for home study since many students already have their own cassette players.	• *Fixed sequence.* Audiotapes fix the sequence of a presentation, even though it is possible to rewind or advance the tape to a desired portion. It is difficult to scan audio materials as you would printed text materials. • *Lack of attention.* Students' attention may wander while they are listening to audiotapes. They may hear the message but not listen to or comprehend it. • *Pacing.* Presenting information at the appropriate pace can be difficult if your students have a wide range of skills and background experiences. • *Accidental erasure.* Just as audiotapes can be quickly and easily erased when no longer needed, they can be accidentally erased when they should be saved.
CDs	• *Locating selections.* Students and teachers can quickly locate selections on CDs and even program the machine to play in any desired sequence. Information can be selectively retrieved by students or programmed by the teacher.	• *Cost.* The cost of a CD and CD player has slowed its acceptance in the education market. However, when prices come down it will become a standard format for using audio in the classroom.

Media Format	Advantages	Limitations
CDs, *continued*	• *Resistance to damage.* There are no grooves to scratch or tape to tangle and break. Stains can be washed off and ordinary scratches do not affect playback of the recording.	• *No recording capability.* Students and teachers cannot produce their own CDs as they can cassettes.
Video and Film	• *Motion.* Moving images can effectively portray procedures (such as tying knots or operating a potter's wheel) in which motion is essential. Operations, such as science experiments, in which sequential movement is critical can be shown more effectively by means of motion media. • *Real-life experiences.* Video and film allow learners to observe phenomena that might be dangerous to view directly—an eclipse of the sun, a volcanic eruption, or warfare. • *Repetition.* Research indicates that mastery of physical skills requires repeated observation and practice; through the recorded media a performance can be viewed over and over again for emulation.	• *Fixed pace.* Film and video programs tend to run at a fixed pace; some viewers are likely to fall behind, while others are waiting impatiently for the next point. • *Expense.* The video version of a program is generally cheaper than the film version, and the combination of a video player and video monitor costs less than a film projector and screen. • *Scheduling.* Videos and films have to be ordered well in advance of their intended use. Arrangements also have to be made for the proper equipment to be available. The complexity of the logistics discourages some teachers.
Videodiscs	• *Storage capacity.* Videodiscs come in two formats: CLV (extended play) and CAV. The former stores up to one hour of video per side, while the latter stores up to 30 minutes of video per side. CAV videodiscs can also intermix short video sequences with still frames. One side of a CAV videodisc can store up to 54,000 still images, the equivalent of hundreds of slide projector carousels. • *Rapid access.* Videodisc players can rapidly access any still image or video sequence on a videodisc, usually in no more than a few seconds. Teachers or students can access the images using a remote control or bar code reader, or via computer connection. • *Dual audio channels.* Videodiscs can contain two to four audio channels. Many manufacturers include both English and Spanish audio tracks to make the videodiscs accessible to different audiences.	• *Expense.* Videodisc players are more expensive than VCRs and slide projectors. In addition, while the cost per image can be low, videodiscs can be expensive. Many better videodiscs cost several hundred dollars each. • *Limited play time.* When used strictly for video playback, the playing time of videodiscs is much less than videotape at only 30 to 60 minutes per side, depending upon format. With most videodisc players (there are some exceptions), the videodisc must be manually flipped over to access information on the second side.

Table 7.1 *Continued*

Media Format	Advantages	Limitations
Videodiscs, *continued*	• *Durability.* Videodiscs are exceedingly durable. Unlike videotape, videodiscs do not lose quality after repeated playing. There is no physical wear when the videodisc is played, and videodiscs are encased in a clear plastic coating that prevents damage during handling. • *Image quality and cost.* Videodiscs have high image quality, superior to that of most VCRs. In addition, because the cost of replicating videodiscs is relatively low, the cost per image can be very low compared to other media such as slides.	
Television	• *Instantaneous.* Television has the advantage of bringing actual world events into the classroom as they happen. Viewers across large geographic areas can experience a live event simultaneously. • *Cost.* By means of broadcasting, satellites, and cable, large audiences can be reached at a very low cost per student. • *Influence.* Television has the ability to affect the attitudes of students. The reality of current events and broadcast programs provides a basis for follow-up discussions.	• *Technical problems.* Television requires a production crew to match the quality of commercial networks and the expectations of students. Technical problems can be very frustrating and interrupt the learning process. There may be interruptions in the transmission of the television signal. In addition, classroom television receivers may malfunction. • *Cost.* Basic television equipment (cameras and receivers) is very expensive. Sophisticated equipment (satellite dishes and cable distribution systems) costs a great deal of money.
Computer Software	• *Interactivity.* The key element of computers is interaction with the user. The computer can present information, elicit the learner's response, and evaluate the response. • *Individualization.* The computer's branching capabilities allow instruction to be tailored to the individual. The computer can provide immediate feedback and monitor the learner's performance. • *Consistency.* Individualization results in different instructional paths for different learners. But it can be equally important to ensure that specific topics are dealt with in the same way for all learners. • *Motivation.* Many learners find computers to be motivating. Computers can provide variety through the use of varied feedback, different approaches to content, and, of course, multiple media.	• *Equipment requirements.* Although computers have become less expensive and more widely available in recent years, cost and access can still be barriers, especially with the limited budgets of many schools. • *Compatibility.* The lack of compatibility among the various brands of personal computers limits the transportability of CAI. Developers cannot create a single CAI package that will work across all types of computers. • *Start-up costs.* The cost of the computer itself and the necessary software may be limiting. Although delivery costs often are low, start-up and development costs for CAI tend to be high.

Media Format	Advantages	Limitations
Computer Software, *continued*	• *Learner control.* Computers can give the user control of both the pace and the sequencing of the instruction. Fast learners can speed through the program, while slower learners can take as much time as needed.	• *Limited modalities.* Most CAI relies on text and limited graphics. A heavy demand is placed on the learner's reading and visual skills. The visual and auditory cues that are common to live instruction tend to be absent from CAI. • *Limited intelligence.* Most computer software is limited in its capacity for genuine interaction with the learner. Much CAI relies on simple multiple choice or true-false questions for assessing the learner's progress.
Multimedia	• *Better learning and retention.* Interactive multimedia provides multiple learning modalities and actively involves the learner. • *Addresses different learning styles and preferences.* The incorporation of multiple modalities provides opportunities for teaching individual learners. For example, those with weak reading skills can use aural and visual skills to process verbal information. • *Effectiveness across learning domains.* Interactive multimedia instruction has been shown to be effective in all learning domains. It can be used for psychomotor training such as learning CPR techniques; to present simulations that provide opportunities for problem-solving and higher-order thinking skills; and even to address affective components of learning. • *Realism.* Interactive multimedia provides a high degree of realism. Instead of merely reading about a speech by Dr. Martin Luther King, students can actually see and hear the speech as originally presented. • *Motivation.* Learners show consistently positive attitudes toward interactive multimedia. For today's MTV-conscious youth, multimedia instruction represents a natural avenue for exploring the information revolution.	• *Equipment requirements.* The equipment requirements for multimedia can be an impediment. While basic systems may involve only the computer and its built-in components, more complex systems may involve external videodisc players, CD-ROM players, audio playback speakers, and so on. These can be difficult to hook up and maintain. • *Start-up costs.* Start-up costs can be high. The computer itself can be expensive. When additional components are added, thousands of dollars in additional costs can be incurred. • *Complexity and lack of standardization.* Interactive multimedia systems can be quite complex. Sometimes it is a challenge just to get the individual components to work together. The novice may become hopelessly lost. This is complicated by the fact that there is a lack of standardization today in many facets of multimedia.

Figure 7.4   Media selection checklist

Which Media Should I Choose?

As you begin planning your instruction, it is important to select a medium that will enhance your topic. The Media Selection Checklist will help you in the process.

Each type of media has a set of advantages (e.g., motion, realism) and a set of educational limitations (e.g., room size, group size). These specifications are listed in the first column of the table. There are nine columns next to the specifications. Place a ✓ in all the white spaces that best describe your instructional needs (or situations).

For Example

If it is important that you draw or write key words during your presentation, go to item #7 on the table and put "✓s" in the three columns to the right that are white. Continue the process for each requirement or item that best describes your instructional situation (needs).

When you have gone through the entire table, determine which column has the most "✓s" entered in the white spaces in the column.

If most of the "✓s" are in:	Select
RO	Real Objects (models)
PT	Printed Text (handouts)
CB	Chalkboard or White Board
OT	Overhead Transparencies
SL	Slides
VF	Video and Film (film, tape, disc, television)
V	Visuals (photos, charts, diagrams)
A	Audio (tape, CD)
CS	Computer Software

It is possible that you will have more than one column with most of the white spaces filled in. In that case you will need to choose which medium is best or consider using multiple media formats in your presentation.

Note. © Claranne K. English, 1995

school building. The librarian or media specialist can help you find materials. Most schools maintain a list of materials in a computer database in the media center, and some school districts maintain a central collection of instructional materials. Items from the collection can be scheduled in advance and delivered to the school when you need them.

Regional media centers and service centers serve many school districts in a several-county area. Schools pay a per-pupil fee to belong to the consortium, and a list of materials in the regional media center's collection is provided to each school. You can check the catalog to see if materials are available that might meet your needs.

Commercial companies that produce and/or distribute materials are another source. They publish a catalog that lists available materials. The media are available for purchase and sometimes for rental.

Additional sources of instructional materials are professional meetings and trade shows. These are held at the local, state, and national level. Talk with vendors and other teachers in your discipline to learn what is available and what materials they use.

A convenient computer-based technique for locating commercially available instructional materials is *A-V Online,* an automated index of nonprint educational materials. With *A-V Online* you can locate the distribution sources for thousands of educational, informational, and documentary materials recorded in a variety of media formats, including video, audio, film, filmstrips, slides, slide/tape programs, overhead transparencies, and multimedia kits. The database covers the entire spectrum of the educational field, from preschool to graduate and professional school levels. Librarians, media specialists, curriculum planners, vocational and technical skill developers, and teachers can select from thousands of materials supplied by a variety of producers and distributors. A wide range of subject areas is included, such as athletics, foreign languages, health and safety, history, psychology, science, mathematics, vocational and technical education, fine arts, geography, guidance and counseling, literature and drama, and sociology. *A-V Online* acquires information from producer and distributor catalogs (for nonprint materials), the

Media Selection Checklist

Student learning will be enhanced by media that:	RO	PT	CB	OT	SL	VF	V	A	CS
1. Enable students to see and/or touch actual objects		■	■	■	■	■	■	■	■
2. Allow materials to be taken from the classroom			■	■	■	■	■	■	■
3. Can be used after the lesson as a reference, guide, or job aid	■		■	■	■	■	■	■	■
4. Allow several participants to respond simultaneously	■		■	■	■	■	■	■	■
5. Can be easily erased/modified	■	■	■		■	■	■	■	■
6. Require minimal expense	■		■	■	■	■			■
7. Allow one to draw or write key words during the lesson	■		■	■					
8. Are appropriate for a small group (under 25)					■			■	
9. Can be used in a fully lit room		■	■	■					
10. Use visuals that are easy to prepare	■					■	■	■	
11. Allow advanced preparation of the visuals	■					■	■	■	
12. Present word cues or a lesson outline	■					■	■	■	
13. Provide portability	■		■			■	■	■	
14. Offer commercially prepared visuals	■				■	■	■	■	
15. Allow the order of the material to be easily changed	■					■	■		
16. Allow the user to control pacing and/or to replay a portion of the presentation	■	■	■						
17. Are appropriate for students who have difficulty reading or understanding English		■	■	■					
18. Reproduce an exact sound	■	■	■		■		■	■	
19. Are easily used by teachers or students	■	■	■			■			
20. Present high-quality, realistic images (color/graphics/illustrations/visuals)	■		■			■	■		■
21. Can be used independently of the instructor	■		■	■			■	■	
22. Show motion, including sequential motion	■	■					■		
23. Allow observation of a dangerous process; real-life reenactments	■						■		
24. Provide a discovery learning environment	■						■		
25. Present problem-solving situations that lead to group discussions	■						■		■
26. Shape personal and social attitudes	■	■	■	■	■		■	■	■

Library of Congress, media centers, libraries, and many other sources.

A comprehensive database that reviews computer software is *The Education Software Selector* (TESS), which includes reviews of educational software at every level, from preschool to college. Published biennially by the Education Product Information Exchange (EPIE), *TESS* has four volumes, each covering a different subject area. It is also available on computer disks. For each piece of computer software, the following information is included: title, subject area, type, grade level, producer, required hardware, citation of published reviews, and EPIE's own rating.

In all cases, once you've located potential media in your school's collection or through other sources, materials should be previewed *before* purchase to be certain they meet the needs of your students. In the Appendix we have included preview forms to help you in this selection process. Those forms can be used to evaluate a specific piece of instructional material or to compare two potential materials. In addition to checking against the criteria on the form, you want to make sure that the instructional material is appropriate for your learners, matches your desired outcomes, and can be used in your instructional setting. You should also determine the availability of the material.

If the content of the instructional materials doesn't match the goals of your instructional plan, you have two alternatives: (1) modify the instructional materials so they do meet your goals, or (2) design new instructional materials. We will discuss these options in the next two sections.

Modify Available Instructional Materials

If you cannot locate suitable materials and media, you might be able to modify what is available. This can be both challenging and an opportunity for you to be creative. In terms of time and cost, it is a more efficient procedure than designing your own materials. For example, assume the only available visual showing a piece of equipment being used in a middle school woodworking class is from a repair manual. The picture could be useful, but it contains too much detail and complex terminology. A possible solution would be to use the visual but modify the caption and simplify or omit some of the labels.

In another situation, the only videotape available shows a needed video sequence, but the audio is inappropriate because the vocabulary level is too high or low for the students. In such a case, you could show the videotape with the sound turned off and provide the narration yourself.

A similar approach may be used for filmstrips accompanied by audiotapes. You can record your own narration using the appropriate vocabulary level for your students. Another modification technique is to show just a portion of a videotape, stop the VCR, discuss what has been presented, then continue with another short segment, followed by additional discussion.

Modification can be made in the audio portion of foreign-language materials (or English-language materials for a bilingual class). Narrations can be changed from one language to another or from a more advanced rendition of a foreign language to a simpler one.

VCRs provide teachers with much flexibility in using television programs for instructional purposes. Recorded programs can be shown at whatever time best suits the instructional situation.

One frequently modified media format is a set of slides with an audiotape. If the visuals are appropriate but the language is not, it is possible to change the narration. It is also possible to change the emphasis of the narration. For example, the original audiotape might emphasize oceans as part of an ecosystem, whereas the teacher may want to use the slides to show various types of fish found in oceans. By rewriting the narration, the teacher could adapt the material to his or her purposes while using the same slides. By redoing the tape you can also change the level of the presentation.

Videodiscs, which are produced to teach specific content, lend themselves to a process called **repurposing**. Repurposing refers to creating a new computer program to control the videodisc. For example, *The National Gallery of Art* videodisc contains images of all the paintings in the National Gallery in Washington, D.C. An art teacher can design software that will direct students to specific paintings, ask questions about the art, and move to another piece when the student answers the questions correctly.

If you try out modified materials while they are still in more or less rough form, you can then make further modifications in response to student reactions until your materials meet their exact needs. A word of caution about modifying commercially produced materials: be sure your handling and use of such materials does not violate copyright laws and restrictions. If you're in doubt, check with your school media specialist.

Design New Instructional Materials

Teachers have long been known for their creative use of available tools and resources to produce instructional materials. Classrooms are usually filled

Designing instructional materials is an important and rewarding task.

with a wide variety of teaching materials, from concrete objects to posters, bulletin boards, and printed material of every kind. For several decades the tools for producing instructional materials changed relatively little, with typewriters and ditto machines doing the bulk of the work, but the times are changing.

Photocopying machines, which have long been commonplace in society at large, are becoming standard equipment in schools. Compared to a mimeograph or ditto machine, the process of preparing copies with a photocopier is much simpler. You just feed in the master and out come the copies. In addition, the tools for creating the master copies of instructional materials have improved by leaps and bounds. The reason, of course, is the computer. Computer-based tools make it much easier to produce high-quality, professional-looking materials.

Figure 7.5 presents guidelines for designing instructional materials. Because there is a need to be able to effectively design and develop instructional materials, we have listed important factors you should consider whenever you attempt to develop materials with any of the various media formats.

INTEGRATING TECHNOLOGY
Using DTP to Create Instructional Materials

We've spent a lot of time discussing Ms. Moreno's concern for helping her students increase their oral communication skills. As you have probably already noticed, this was not an isolated goal in Ms. Moreno's Spanish Conversation course. Rather, this goal was situated within the larger context of improving students' understanding of Spanish culture, including a knowledge of Spain's unique geographical features and an appreciation for its special customs, beliefs, and folklore. As students' communication skills increased, she decided that it might be interesting to have her students "own" a travel agency that was responsible for persuading Spanish travelers from northern Spain to visit towns and cities in the southern part of the country, and vice versa. Using the format of a travel brochure, students were asked to create an informative and captivating tri-fold (in Spanish, of course) that would introduce potential tourists to the people, culture, and attractions of the region.

Members of the class divided into teams and began researching a variety of information sources. Some went to the reference section in the school library; others visited local travel agencies and collected information about the northern and southern regions of Spain. A couple of class members contacted a local graphic artist to get some pointers on how to design brochures, that is, how to structure information so that the important parts are attended to by prospective customers. Students integrated this information using the word-processing program on their class computers and produced a rough draft. After getting feedback and suggestions for improvement, the final text materials were completed.

At this point, Ms. Moreno asked the computer coordinator to show the students how to take their word-processed document and import it into a popular desktop publishing (DTP) program. This program allowed students to transform and manipulate the simple text material into a layout that resembled

Ms. Moreno's students practice their computer and design skills while learning Spanish.

Figure 7.5 Guidelines for designing instructional materials

Real Objects and Models

Real objects do not lend themselves to design by teachers. However, there are some models available for purchase that can be assembled by teachers. There are plastic model kits of various animals, including dinosaurs, and of parts of the human body, such as the eye, ear, nose, and skull. These models can be modified and colored with paint to meet your needs.

Teachers can also make models for instruction from readily available materials. For example, small buildings can be used to make model cities. Various materials, such as athletic balls, can be used to model the solar system.

Text

As we saw in Chapter 5, the word processor is one of the most valuable tools a teacher can have. Word processors make it easy to produce printed materials and to revise them to meet the changing needs of your students. We have already examined the features and uses of word processors; in the CUE for this chapter we look at other tools that can be used for the production of instructional materials. We examine graphic tools and desktop publishing programs that can facilitate the production of high-quality printed materials.

Headings

- Headings and subheadings should be used to separate and identify sections and to show the organization of the content. Introductions may have to be written in order to relate a series of key ideas so there is a smooth transition from one section to the next one.
- Headings should be briefly worded and explicit so they communicate quickly and effectively. By glancing at a set of sequential headings, the student should gain a clear overview of the topic.
- Use side heads (e.g., words in left margin) to call attention to important concepts.

Writing Style

- State the main ideas or theme at the beginning of the text.
- Put topic sentences at the beginning of each paragraph.
- Use simple sentences and a clear writing style.
- Use active voice where possible.
- Include definitions with technical terms so they won't be misconstrued.

Page Layout

- Be clear and consistent in page layout (use the same type of text in the same typeface, size, and layout from page to page).
- Provide ample white space (use wide margins and uncluttered format) to facilitate reading, note-taking, and location of information for review. White space can separate elements and create a feeling of openness.
- Increase the space between lines in note-taking handouts to allow room for student notes.
- Use unjustified or ragged right margins. By justifying both margins, extra space is created between words, which makes text more difficult to read.

Type Style/Mechanics

- Choose typeface styles with simple designs.
- Use upper- and lowercase letters for ease and speed in reading. Use uppercase words only for emphasis and to attract attention.
- Use 9- to 12-point type for most text.
- If the material is typed, use a space and a half between lines for ease of reading.
- Avoid breaking words (hyphenating) at the end of lines.

Highlighting

- Highlighting techniques for printed materials include color, size of type, italics, and boldfacing. Do not use capitals, because they are difficult to read within text. Capitals are OK for short headings.
- Highlight important ideas to help students locate key points.
- Use bullets (•) to present ideas in a list (as used in this section).
- Avoid underlining except to point out negatives (e.g., not and except), as it has little or no effect on retention of content.

Visuals

Visuals include photographs, diagrams, posters, charts, and drawings. The CUE for this chapter describes how you can use computer graphics programs to produce high-quality visuals. The following guidelines apply to visuals for printed material, slides, overhead transparencies, and artwork for videotapes. They apply whether you are producing the visuals by hand or with the aid of a computer.

General

- Keep visuals simple (avoid too much realism in visuals).
- Place visuals as near the related text as possible.
- Use larger visuals if more detail is required.

Informational/Instructional Purposes

- Use drawings and diagrams whenever possible to illustrate ideas.
- Use graphs to present data.
- Present a single concept in each visual.
- Break down complex visuals into simpler ones or build them up step by step.

Graphic/Picture Elements

- Use visuals that are neither too abstract nor too realistic.
- Eliminate distracting backgrounds.
- If feeling of depth is important, use another object to create the foreground.

Text/Lettering Elements

- Center title at top of visual.
- Use short, concise, meaningful, descriptive titles that contain key words.
- Eliminate unnecessary words.
- Use italics, boldface, underlining, color, or a change in lettering style for emphasis.
- Minimize text on each visual; use a maximum of six words per line and six lines per visual.
- Spacing between lines should be 1½ times word height.

Color

- Use brightest and lightest color to focus attention on important elements.
- Use lettering and visuals that contrast with background color.
- Select colors that are harmonious.
- Use consistent background colors in a series of visuals.
- Limit the number of colors in a visual to five.

Layout

- Make visuals as simple as possible; avoid excessive detail.
- Use size, relationships, perspective, and such visual tools as color and space to emphasize important elements.
- Use a horizontal format for overhead transparencies and slides.
- Use a pleasing layout that appears balanced and orderly.

Display Boards

Displays may be created by students or the teacher. The following guidelines apply to chalkboards and especially bulletin board displays since they are prepared in advance and kept in place for days or weeks. Do not leave these displays in place too long, or they will lose their effectiveness.

General

- Limit the display to one topic.
- Generate a theme and incorporate it into a headline. It is a challenge to work out a catchy theme that will entice the viewer into further examination of the display. Wording should be simple, couched in the students' language, and visually integrated into the arrangement of the display.

Figure 7.5 *Continued*

Display Boards, General (continued)

- Work out a rough layout. The blueprint you develop should reflect these guidelines:

  Emphatic—conveys message quickly and clearly

  Attractive—color and arrangement catch and hold interest

  Balanced—objects arranged so stability is perceived

  Unified—repeated shapes or colors or use of borders holds display together visually

  Interactive—involves the student

  Legible—lettering and visuals can be read from across the room

  Lettered properly—spelled correctly, plain typeface, use of lowercase except where capitals are required

  Durable—well-constructed physically, items securely attached

Overhead Transparencies

When preparing your transparencies, keep in mind these guidelines based on research and practical experience.

General

- Present a single concept on each transparency. A complex transparency may be confusing and unreadable for the viewer. Design a series of transparencies rather than a crowded single transparency.
- Use transparencies to present visual ideas through the use of diagrams, graphs, and charts.
- Include minimum verbiage, with no more than six words per line and six or fewer lines per transparency.
- Avoid preparing a transparency directly from a paragraph of printed material. Select key points or concepts to summarize the information, and then elaborate on them verbally.
- Use key words to help the audience remember each point.
- Use letters at least ¼ inch high to ensure legibility. One quick way to check it is to lay the transparency on the floor over a piece of white paper. If you can read it from a standing position, your students should be able to read it when projected.
- Use a horizontal format to better fit the rectangular screen. Avoid mixing horizontal and vertical transparencies in a presentation, as this can be annoying to the students and bothersome to you.
- Simplify a complex diagram by dividing it into segments for separate transparencies or by using masking or overlay techniques. Overlays can explain complex ideas by adding information sequentially to the base transparency.

Slides and Filmstrips

You can produce your own slides, but producing your own filmstrips is impractical and unnecessary. Although principles of photography are beyond the scope of this book, we will describe some general guidelines for designing slides.

General

- Determine the topic for your slides.
- Prepare a list of the slides you need.
- Take several shots of the same scene at different angles and distances. It is cheaper to take several shots originally than to return to the location if none of the original slides meets your needs. If it is a special event that occurs only once, take extra shots in order to have enough slides for your instructional program.
- When your slides are returned, compare the multiple shots by projecting them or by viewing them with a light box.
- Select the specific slides you want to use, and put them in sequence.
- Prepare your narration on note cards (one card for each slide).
- Deliver the narration live by talking through the slides with your note cards. Don't read directly from the cards; make it conversational.
- As an alternative, record your narration on audiotape as described in the next section. Slide-and-audiotape combinations are great for self-instruction.

Audio

A major advantage of audiotapes is the ease with which they can be prepared by teachers and students. All that is needed is a blank audiotape, a tape recorder, and a bit of know-how.

Physical Environment

- Record in an area that is as free as possible from noise and sound reverberations. A small room such as an office is preferable to a normal-size classroom.
- Place the recording setup at least six feet from the chalkboard, windows, or hard walls.
- Have a glass of water nearby to "lubricate" your throat if necessary.

Tape Recorder

- Familiarize yourself with the operation of the tape recorder you intend to use.
- Advance the tape beyond the leader before recording (about ten seconds). You cannot record on the clear plastic, nonmagnetic leader of the tape.
- Record an excerpt of about a minute and play it back to make sure the recorder and microphone are operating properly.
- If an error is made while recording, stop the tape recorder, rewind to a segment of tape containing a natural pause, engage the record mode, and continue recording. It is unusual to make an entire tape without making mistakes or mispronunciations.
- Once the recording has been completed, play back the entire recording. Listen carefully for any errors. It is better to catch imperfections and correct them immediately than to redo the tape later.

Microphone

- Place the microphone on a desk or table with a sound-absorbing towel or other soft cloth under the microphone.
- Turn off fans and other sources of noise that may be picked up by the microphone.
- Handle note cards and pages quietly to avoid possible paper rustle.
- Maintain a constant distance from the microphone. As a rule of thumb, your mouth should be about a foot from the microphone.
- Speak over the top of the microphone, not directly into it.

Video and Film

Just as it is impractical to make your own filmstrips, it is impractical to make your own educational films. Both students and teachers can produce effective videotapes for instructional purposes. All that is required is a camera, a microphone (often built into the camera), and a videotape.

Camera

- Use a zoom lens rather than a fixed-focal-length lens to allow flexibility in selecting a view from a range of magnifications without having to move the camera closer to or farther from the subject.
- Do not aim the camera at the sun or other bright light, since that can damage the videotube.
- Turn the camera off when it will not be used for a period of time.
- Cap the lens when the camera is not in use.
- Keep the lens clean by dusting with a soft camel-hair brush.

Microphone

- Handheld cameras usually come with a microphone built into the front of the camera. This microphone has automatic level control, which automatically adjusts the recording volume to keep the sound at an audible level. At times this may cause problems.

Videotape

- Use high-quality, brand-name videotape. Other tapes may be manufacturer's seconds or tapes that were improperly stored.

Figure 7.5 *Continued*

Video and Film, Videotape (continued)

- Your video production may be preplanned or live action. If you are recording local landmarks for presentation in your classroom, determine what shots you will take before you go. If you are recording an event, simply videotape it as it happens.

- Planning a videotape recording is similar to planning other instructional materials. Organize the content and plan the method of visualizing the subject to be videotaped. Pay special attention to the *motion* involved. Movement is basic to successful videotape recordings—otherwise, use slides or overhead transparencies.

- When taping people, use a full-body shot for motion (e.g., athletics, dancing, etc.) and a head-and-shoulder shot for speaking.

Television

Teachers tend not to produce live television, so we will not discuss studio television production techniques here. If you ever produce live television, refer to a book on the subject.

Computer Software

The development of computer software may be too time consuming for most teachers. However, the most recent authoring systems make it possible for teachers to develop their own computer software without knowledge of computer programming. These authoring tools are described in detail in the CUE for this chapter. Here are some basic guidelines for developing computer software.

General

- Make good use of the computer's capabilities and employ a high level of interactivity.
- Allow for individualization through learner control, branching, and other appropriate techniques.
- Provide informative feedback to the learner. Tell the learner why particular responses are correct or incorrect.
- Keep screen displays simple. Usually, present only one major concept per screen.
- Follow the guidelines for textual material (on page 158) when presenting text via the computer.
- Use graphics where visual presentation is appropriate. Follow the guidelines for visuals (on page 159).
- Keep the learners informed of their progress and performance.

Multimedia

Even more complex and time consuming is the development of computer-based multimedia materials. The specifics of this process are beyond the scope of this book, but here are some guidelines to assist you if you decide to try your hand at the process.

General

- Follow the guidelines given above for computer software.
- Select the best media for addressing particular learning objectives. Whenever possible, provide for different learning preferences; that is, provide the same content via text, audio, and visual modalities.
- Ensure that different media are properly synchronized with one another.
- Keep navigation as simple and transparent as possible. Learners can become lost and confused in complex multimedia environments. Provide navigational aids such as maps and position markers.
- Use embedded cues to assist learners in locating and using information.

---

a travel brochure. Through the use of clip art and other graphics programs, pictures and figures were inserted into the document to add visual information and variety. Once they completed the brochure, the students made copies and mailed a few to the tourist bureaus of the cities they had mentioned in the tri-fold, requesting comments about their work.

CUE Computer Use ESSENTIALS

As we saw in Chapter 5, the word processor is probably the most valuable production tool a teacher can have. Word processors make it easier to produce written materials. Since we have already

STUDENT-GENERATED INSTRUCTIONAL MATERIALS

Instruction has traditionally been planned, designed, produced, and delivered by the instructional expert. There is good reason for this. The expert knows the content, knows how the subject matter should be sequenced, knows what prerequisite knowledge is necessary, and knows how the content can best be presented. But is it always better to have the teacher supply the instructional materials for the student? Could there be some advantages for having the student generate the instructional materials?

There are several advantages to having students participate in the design, development, and delivery of the instructional materials:

• Students bring their own experiences and backgrounds to the learning situation; therefore, they may tailor the instruction to their individual understanding, thus increasing the likelihood of effective encoding and retrieval.

• In most cases, for learners to be able to effectively design and develop instructional materials, a high degree of understanding of the subject matter must first be achieved.

• The process of planning and designing effective instruction constitutes a high-level problem-solving task. Not only do students learn subject matter, but they also gain experience analyzing and solving specific problems.

• Investing effort into relevant and creative endeavors can be highly intrinsically motivating. Students may increase their level of motivation and interest for content they help plan and develop.

• Students may learn additional skills as they produce the instructional materials. For example, if students create a multimedia presentation to help teach about different plant fauna of the intermountain Northwest, they may learn not only about plants but also about how *Hypercard* stacks are effectively designed and scripted.

---

examined the features and uses of word processors, in this chapter we will look at other tools that can be used for the production of instructional materials. We will examine graphics tools and desktop publishing programs, which can facilitate the production of high-quality printed material. In addition, we will look at available alternatives for the development of CBI. In Chapter 9 we will consider presentation software, which is computer software designed to support the development and presentation of instruction to large groups.

GRAPHICS PRODUCTION

Any pictorial representation of information in the computer—chart, graph, drawing, animated figure, or photolike reproduction—is a **graphic.** Graphics, of course, can convey important information and are often used to supplement text. They can be an important element in printed material and in CBI. In the past, teachers were forced to use traditional cut-and-paste methods or to draw graphics by hand for use in teaching materials. Today

there are powerful computer tools for working with graphics.

In the computer, graphics are usually one of two basic types: **bit-mapped graphics** or **vector graphics.** Graphic images on the computer screen are composed of myriad tiny dots, much like photographs in a newspaper. Each dot is referred to as a picture element, or pixel. In bit-mapped graphics (sometimes called paint or raster graphics), each pixel directly corresponds to—that is, maps—a spot on the computer's display screen. The computer must keep track of position and color information for each spot on the display screen. In vector graphics (also called draw graphics), on the other hand, the computer "remembers" the steps involved in drawing a particular graphic image on the screen. This information is independent of a particular screen location or a graphic's size. While this technique is more difficult to accomplish, vector graphics can be scaled without any loss of information. Bit-mapped graphics, when scaled to larger sizes, become jagged looking. Now that we understand the basics, let's look at some of the types of graphics programs available.

Types of Computer Graphics Programs

There is a wide variety of computer-based tools for working with graphics in various settings. Here are some of the most common examples.

Print Graphics

Although virtually all graphics programs support printing, this category refers to inexpensive programs that use built-in clip art to produce simple printed work such as signs and banners. Generally these programs are not designed for the development of original or complex graphics. The most well known product in this category is *Printshop,* which provides the user with a simple means to produce signs, greeting cards, and other graphically enhanced printed material.

Business and Scientific Graphics

Programs that produce graphics common to business or scientific environments—charts and graphs—fall into this category. These programs accept data, often from within the program or from another source (such as a spreadsheet program), and produce a chart or graph according to specifications set by the user. Business graphics often include bar charts, pie charts, and line graphs (Figure 7.6). Scientifically oriented programs focus on line graphs as well as mathematical functions such as trigonometric functions. Examples of programs in this category include *Cricket Graph, Harvard Graphics,* and *Graphical Analysis.*

Mechanical Drawing

Traditional drafting applications today rely on the computer. Computer-aided design (CAD) is used for the production of blueprints and factory floor layouts, for landscape architecture, for the design of machined parts, and so on. A popular program of this type is *AutoCAD.*

Creative Arts

A number of graphics packages are available that permit the user to produce original artwork or modify existing artwork. Most of these packages are used with a mouse and provide the user with a variety of tools that are intended to mimic what an artist might use, such as a pencil, a paintbrush, a color palette, and an eraser. In addition, they include computer-automated functions such as electronic cut and paste, and they have the ability to draw perfectly straight lines, squares, circles, and polygons, as well as curves and irregular shapes. Some graphics packages are designed for bit-mapped graphics, some are designed for vector graphics, and some are able to work with either kind. Popular graphics packages include *Corel Draw, Aldus Freehand, Adobe Photoshop, MacDraw, MacPaint,* and *Superpaint.* Figure 7.7 shows the bit-mapped graphics "canvas" from *Superpaint.*

Graphics Hardware

Most graphics programs today use the mouse as a drawing tool. However, there are alternatives. Graphics tablets are drawing devices that connect to the computer. Users commonly employ a pen or stylus that is pressed against the pad, much as artists use a sketch pad, and the resulting image is displayed on the computer screen. Light pens allow users to draw directly on the computer screen. Many people prefer graphics tablets and light pens because the act of drawing is more like using pencil and paper.

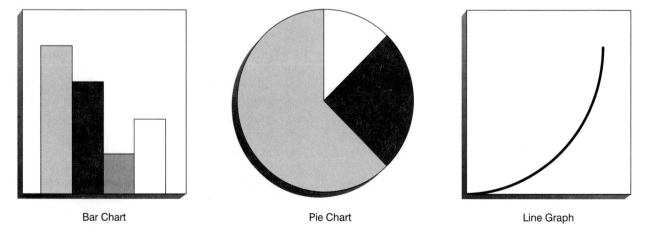

Bar Chart   Pie Chart   Line Graph

Figure 7.6   Common examples of business graphics

TECHNOLOGY INTEGRATION PROMPT

USING CLIP ART

For most learners, the old adage "a picture is worth a thousand words" holds true. Well-designed visuals can help clarify and facilitate understanding, as well as increase instructional appeal. With the development of the computer and graphics software, the inclusion of visuals within textual materials has become relatively easy.

One simplified way to incorporate visuals within your instruction is through the use of electronically stored clip art. **Clip art** refers to a collection of pictures. Whenever a picture is needed, it is selected from the collection, highlighted, copied, and pasted within the specific document. For example, if you were writing a paper on the history of air travel, you might locate a noncopyrighted picture of an airplane, copy it, and paste it within your document.

Electronic clip art has many advantages, including its ability to be

- easily stored. With the advent of the CD-ROM, several thousand pictures can be stored on a single CD. Once you have selected the picture you want, you can easily copy it and store it within your document.
- quickly retrieved. Most electronically stored clip art is categorized for easy identification and access. In many cases, the clip art comes with a printed catalog that allows you to review and make your selection and then retrieve it from the CD-ROM or diskette.
- easily altered. In most cases if a picture needs to be cropped (unnecessary pieces cut off) or sized (proportionately made larger or smaller) it can be completed with relative ease. Additionally, titles and labels can be added or deleted as desired.
- combined with other clip art pictures. For example, if you need a picture of a seashore with a specific type of shell lying on the beach, you may locate a good picture of the seashore and combine it with a separate picture of the desired shell.

Because of the popularity of clip art, many presentation programs (e.g., *PowerPoint, Astound*) now come with libraries of clip art. No longer do teachers have to try to draw freehand or to cut and paste with scissors and glue.

Because graphics usually require large amounts of disk storage space, developments in compact disc storage have made it possible to maintain large libraries of graphic images. CD-ROMs are often used to store clip art and other graphics that can be imported into graphics programs for manipulation and use. In addition, Kodak has developed a new CD format called the **PhotoCD**. A PhotoCD stores up to 100 high-quality images, in sizes and resolutions ranging from thumbnail pictures to large and very detailed images, which are made from 35-millimeter photographic negatives or slides. Many graphics programs now accept images stored in the PhotoCD format.

Probably the most significant developments in the area of graphics tools in recent years center around digitizing technologies. One such device is the optical scanner, which uses technology similar to a photocopying machine to take an image from a printed page and convert it into a form the computer can understand. Scanned graphic images can be manipulated for desktop publishing applications (see the next section) or imported into graphics software. Both black-and-white and color scanners are available. In somewhat similar fashion, **video digitizers,** add–on devices for the computer, take video from any standard video source (TV, VCR, videodisc, etc.) and capture a frame of that video as a computer graphic. Recently, still–picture cameras have come onto the market that fit into the process. The Canon Xapshot camera, for example, stores pictures as video images on a miniature floppy disk inside the camera. The images taken by the camera can be dumped to a digitizing board to create a graphic of the image in the computer. These tools make it easy to incorporate high-quality, realistic graphic images in the computer.

Finally, it is important to mention the printing of graphic images. As we have noted, nearly all graphics programs support the printing of graphic images. Most laser printers are capable of producing between 300 and 600 dots per inch. As a result,

Figure 7.7 Screen from
Superpaint graphics program

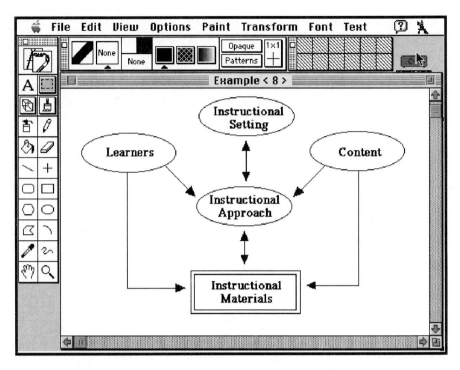

Source: Superpaint, Adobe Systems. Reprinted with permission.

very finely detailed graphic images can be printed. However, most printers produce only black-and-white output. For many applications this is satisfactory; however, it is often desirable to have color rendering of computer-generated graphics. Color printers are also available, although they tend to be somewhat more expensive than their black-and-white counterparts. The good news is that color printers based on ink-jet technology have fallen in price and now are available for only a few hundred dollars. Although they are not of the highest quality, they do a reasonable job of printing color graphics.

DESKTOP PUBLISHING

The word processor is the teacher's main production tool, and it does an excellent job with basic textual material—handouts, tests, worksheets, lesson plans, letters to parents, and so on. However, until recently, word processors were not capable of employing graphics. Because of this limitation, a new software category emerged in the mid-1980s—**desktop publishing (DTP).** Desktop publishing programs give the user a high degree of control over the composition and layout of material on a printed page, including both text and graphics. Desktop publishing programs immediately filled an important niche in the business sector; they allowed small publishing operations to produce very professional looking publications without the high cost

associated with commercial printing services. It didn't take long for DTP to enter schools as well.

Many schools now use high-quality desktop publishing software to produce school newspapers and yearbooks. In addition, inexpensive desktop publishing programs make excellent tools for producing all sorts of illustrated material in the classroom. Students can produce class newsletters, illustrated stories and poems, minibooks, and the like. Inexpensive desktop publishing software, primarily designed for school use, is now available and widely used.

Desktop publishing programs, unlike most word processors, focus on the layout of text and graphics elements on one printed page. Of course, multiple pages can be produced, but the focus is on composing each page. Page composition consists of identifying features such as the number of columns text will occupy, the size and positioning of headlines or titles, the text fonts used, the spacing of text (both between lines and between individual letters), the position of graphics, and the wrapping of text around graphics. Desktop publishing programs typically afford a much higher degree of control over the elements of the printed page than do word processors. However, it is important to bear in mind that this high degree of control is unnecessary for many applications.

Most desktop publishing programs include basic word-processing and graphics functions. However, high-end DTP packages, especially, are designed to import text and graphics from other sources, such as major word-processing and graphics programs. DTP packages are used for page layout rather than actual development. Major desktop publishing programs include Aldus *PageMaker, Quark XPress, Ventura Publisher,* and *Publish It!* Figure 7.8 shows a sample work screen from Aldus *PageMaker.* While desktop publishing programs continue to fill an important niche, it is important to note that word-processing programs are rapidly beginning to incorporate many of the features that were once considered exclusively DTP features. Major word-processing programs now allow the importing of graphics, column layouts, wrapping of text around graphics, and so on. While their level of functionality may not be as great as for desktop publishing programs, they may be more than adequate for many educational applications. Regardless of the particular package used, the computer tools exist to allow both teachers and students to produce very high quality, professional-looking printed materials.

AUTHORING COMPUTER-BASED INSTRUCTIONAL MATERIALS

Let's now consider the development of CBI. Most teachers obtain instructional software through software publishers, software exchanges, textbook pub-lishers, and the like. The development of CBI has long been recognized as a difficult and time-consuming task. It is not something most busy teachers will do routinely. But software that is appropriate to meet specific needs is not always available commercially. For example, while most school curricula include state and local history elements, these topics are too narrow for commercial software publishers. As a result, a specific need could be addressed through local software development. Fortunately, computer tools have emerged that make the development of CBI much easier and less time-consuming than it once was.

Authoring Tools

Options for developing CBI range along a continuum from authoring systems to general-purpose programming languages. **Authoring systems** are computer programs that permit the development of interactive computer-based applications without a need for programming knowledge. While easy to use, they often have limitations that may restrict their utility in some cases. In addition, high-quality authoring systems can be quite expensive. Examples of authoring systems are *Authorware Professional, IconAuthor, Quest,* and *TenCORE.*

On the other end of the continuum are general-purpose programming languages such as BASIC,

Figure 7.8 Screen from Aldus *PageMaker*

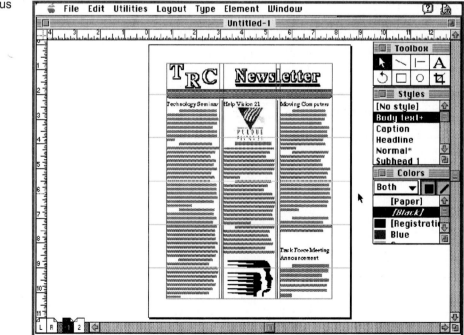

Source: PageMaker, Adobe Systems. Reprinted with permission.

Pascal, and C. In the past, all development of CBI was done using programming languages. They offer the greatest power and flexibility. But programming languages can be difficult to use and time-consuming. While programming languages are often used to develop commercial applications, most teachers avoid pure programming languages because they can be difficult to work with, since they demand knowledge of the programming language.

Between authoring systems and programming languages are hypermedia packages like *HyperCard, HyperStudio, Linkway,* and *Toolbook.* These hypermedia programs are built for developing multimedia applications. They are easier to use than general-purpose programming languages, and much of their flexibility comes from the fact that scripting (programming) languages are available as part of the program. They also tend to be reasonably priced. As a result, these programs have become very popular platforms for development in schools. Table 7.2 summarizes the available options for authoring tools and gives the advantages and disadvantages of each.

Using Authoring Tools in the Classroom

Teachers can make use of authoring tools to develop CBI for student use. As we have noted, one of the major justifications for such an activity would be to meet a specific local need that cannot be met with existing commercial software. In some cases it might be more economical to develop something locally than to purchase a commercial application. Of course, there are also some teachers who simply enjoy developing their own CBI applications.

It is important to recognize, however, that authoring tools are valuable for students as well as for teachers. Using authoring tools, students can produce computer-based reports, presentations, projects, and lessons. As a way of "killing two birds with one stone," students in programming classes at the secondary level can be encouraged to develop educational projects for use in other classes in the school. Students engaged in the development of multimedia projects must learn the content, locate and incorporate appropriate multimedia examples, and organize and present the material in a coherent way. Many educators believe that this is a very powerful learning experience for students.

SUMMARY

In this chapter you learned to complete an instructional plan by selecting appropriate instructional materials. After identifying the characteristics of your learners and the content to be learned, you must determine the learning environment, the instructional approach, and the instructional materials. These three components can be determined in any sequence, as we described, and deciding on one may affect the other two. The acquisition of instructional materials involves selecting the type of media or media format (slides, videotape, computer software, etc.) and the specific instructional materials. You should select existing instructional materials if they are available. If appropriate materials are not available, you should try to modify existing materials to meet the needs of your students. Only as a last resort should you attempt to design and develop new materials.

Table 7.2   Authoring options for computer-based instruction

Authoring Option	Advantages	Disadvantages
Authoring systems	• Easiest to use • Short development time • Little specialized knowledge needed	• Options may be limited; may lack power • Can be costly
Hypermedia programs	• Relatively easy to use • Short development time • Power available if needed • Relatively inexpensive	• Not as easy to use as authoring systems • Less powerful than computer languages
Programming languages	• Most powerful • Inexpensive	• Require specialized knowledge • Can be difficult to use • Long development time

REFLECTIVE QUESTIONS AND ACTIVITIES

1. Think back to the last time you were given the opportunity to teach. It may have been for a formal in-class setting (e.g., at school or church), or it may have been very informal (such as showing a friend how to program a VCR). Consider the approach you used and the media and instructional materials involved. Describe how that teaching/learning situation would have changed if the setting were different or if you had selected a different instructional approach. Explain why the format of the media selected is impacted by the instructional approach used and why an instructional approach can be constrained if a specific media format is required.

2. Using the preview forms in Appendix B, preview a number of sets of instructional materials delivered using the same media format. Select the best of those you preview and explain why you rated it higher than the rest.

3. Locate a textbook—other than this one—that you are currently using (or used recently). Select a chapter and compare the text design principles listed in Figure 7.5 with the layout of the chapter in your text. If you were the editor of the text, what suggestions would you make to the author for improvements in the text design before the next edition is printed?

4. Go to a school or university library media center and check out a number of different sets of instructional materials that cover the same topic but involve different media formats. Using the preview forms provided in Appendix B, review the different materials. Describe the major differences between them. If you were a student using these materials, which ones would be most effective for learning?

INTEGRATION AND SYNTHESIS

This chapter has focused on taking the blueprint (i.e., the instructional plan, Chapter 6) and actually assembling and putting together something tangible that can be delivered to and experienced by your students. In Chapters 3 and 4 you learned basic information about instructional approaches and instructional media; here in Chapter 7 we put that information to use. In this chapter we also showed how the computer's usefulness as a word processor can be expanded by incorporating graphics and desktop publishing functions. These, coupled with the database and telecommunications capabilities discussed in Chapter 6, begin to show how important a tool the computer is for the classroom teacher, especially when instructional materials have to be modified or created.

When the instructional materials have been selected, modified, or designed, your instructional plan is complete. You are then ready to implement the instruction with your students. To assist in this, Chapter 8's focus is on how to effectively prepare and utilize the various media formats. Chapter 9 provides guidelines for using instructional materials with large and small groups of students, and Chapter 10 describes principles for using instructional technology with individual students.

SUGGESTED READINGS

Brock, P. A. (1994). *Educational technology in the classroom.* Englewood Cliffs, NJ: Educational Technology.

Fleming, M., & Levie, H. (1993). *Instructional message design: Principles from the behavioral and cognitive sciences.* Englewood Cliffs, NJ: Educational Technology.

Heinich, R., Molenda, M., Russell, J. D., & Smaldino, S. (1996). *Instructional media and technologies for learning* (5th ed.). Englewood Cliffs, NJ: Merrill/Prentice Hall.

Kemp, J. E., & Smellie, D. C. (1994). *Planning, producing, and using instructional media.* New York: Harper & Row.

Romiszowski, A. J. (1988). *The selection and use of instructional media.* New York: Nichols.

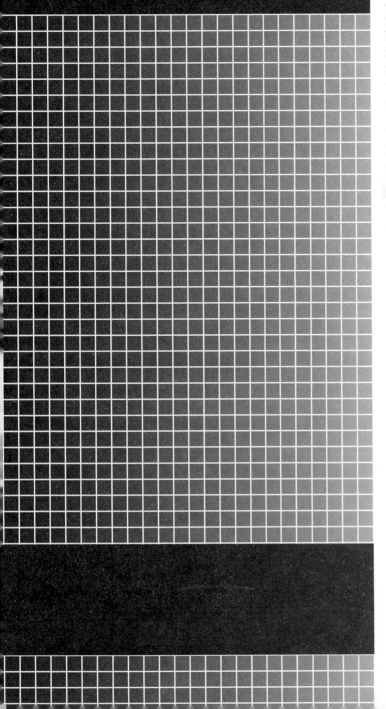

Section III

Implementation

In reviewing the first two sections of this textbook, you will note two key foundational components. First, in the introductory section, we provided a background and foundation for the broad topic of learning. Chapters 1 and 2 focused on instructional technology, including its components and definitions, and on how learning can be enhanced through the application of its important theoretical underpinnings. In Chapters 3 and 4 the emphasis was on providing an overview of the different approaches to learning and the various means by which the instructional message could be received and experienced by the learner. In the second section of the book, that background was used to design an instructional plan. Taking into consideration the participants, the setting, and the content to be learned, the plan was structured around specific instructional events. Finally, in Chapter 7 the actual materials, as well as the media to be used in delivering those materials, were identified and either assembled, modified, or developed.

Although a lot of ground has been covered to get us to this point, the question now is, If the students interact with these materials, will they learn? The answer is—"it depends." Moving to the "I" in the PIE model, the next section of this textbook will concentrate on how the instructional materials are best *implemented*. We will illustrate how an excellent plan and set of instructional materials *must* be coupled with good implementation strategies in order for learning to be maximized. Consider the last few times in which you experienced *poor* results from instruction. Was your learning inhibited by poorly planned materials, by the manner in which the materials were implemented, or by some of both? Were there, for example, distractions because of a poor-quality video, uninterpretable audio, or visuals that weren't relevant to the information being presented? What about discussions that were dominated by a single individual, group work that turned divisive instead of cooperative, or a game that had no perceivable instructional value or purpose? The point is, you may have the best instructional plan ever developed and a wonderful set of instructional materials, but if they are not properly implemented, learning can be restricted.

In this section we emphasize that learning is impacted not only by the instructional content but also by the manner in which the student interacts with the content. That is, there are principles of utilization that can help to ensure that learning occurs. These principles apply to both the specific media format (e.g., audio, projected visuals, video, computer software) and the particular instructional approach (e.g., discussion, cooperative learning)

that will be used with the instructional materials. It is not enough to know the different types of media and approaches that exist and the situations in which to use them; you must also know *how* to use them effectively.

To begin this section, Chapter 8 explores some general principles of preparation that ensure that all is in readiness before instruction begins. It includes a description of the utilization principles for a variety of media formats. In Chapters 9 and 10 we discuss how to implement the different instructional approaches we described in Chapter 3. One key feature in the use of these various approaches is the size of the group with which you are working. Some approaches are more readily utilized with large groups (e.g., presentation, demonstration), while other approaches work more effectively with smaller groups (e.g., cooperative learning, discovery learn-

ing) or with individuals (e.g., simulations, drill and practice, tutorials).

In terms of the computer, the previous sections focused on the computer's role as a production assistant through the use of word processing, database management, and telecommunications. In this section we consider the computer's role in the implementation of instructional materials. Here we focus on the computer as a way to deliver the instruction to individuals, small groups, large groups, and learners who are at a distance from the actual source. This will require a different set of skills for the instructor and may necessitate the addition of a different set of peripherals for the typical computer system. In the final chapter of this section, Chapter 11, we focus on managing instructional technology—especially that which falls within the computer environment.

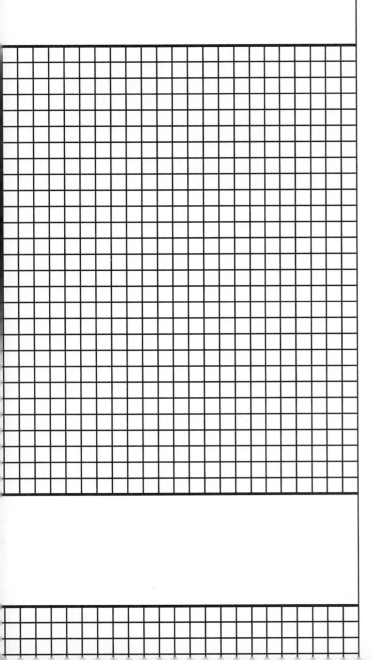

Chapter 8

Using Instructional Technology

COMPUTER USE ESSENTIALS (CUE)
Words and Concepts

Distance education

Audio teleconferencing

Video teleconferencing

Two-way interactive video

Audiographics

Computer-mediated communication (CMC)

Computer conferencing

OUTCOMES

After reading and studying this chapter, you will be able to:

- Generate examples of the four basic steps in preparing for instruction.
- Demonstrate the correct procedures for using real objects and models, text, visuals, display boards, overhead transparencies, slides and filmstrips, audio, video and film, television, computer software, multimedia, and various display devices.
- Define *distance education, audio teleconferencing, video teleconferencing, two-way interactive video,* and *computer-mediated communication.*
- Describe some examples of audio-based, video-based, and computer-based distance education technologies.
- Compare and contrast distance education technologies on the basis of capabilities, advantages, and limitations.

◼ INTRODUCTION

In today's fast-paced society, commercial airliners have become an almost routine mode of transportation. For many of us, both vacations and business trips begin and end with some kind of airline flight. Think back to the last time you took such a flight. As you boarded the plane and passed the formal greeting party of airline attendants, did you happen to peer into the pilot's cabin? Have you ever wondered what pilots do in there, especially before they actually begin flying the plane? If you've ever had the chance to peek, you may have noticed them going through a standard procedure of checking all the instruments that monitor the different processes, systems, and parts of the aircraft. Some of these pilots have flown hundreds, if not thousands, of times—one would think that they should know the routine well enough not to have to worry about using the same preflight checklist time and time again. However, the Federal Aviation Administration requires them to do so. In fact, pilots must demonstrate that they have attended to this set of written checkpoints prior to each and every flight. As one pilot explained, "Using the preflight checklist isn't the most exciting part of this job, but it sure provides a reasonable assurance that all systems are working properly and that in-flight surprises are minimized. It also allows for consideration of alternative plans of action in case certain problems do occur."

The preflight checklist helps pilots prepare for the proper use and management of their aircraft. Even though they have used the checklist hundreds of times, each flight is "new and different," thus requiring them to go over each component to confirm its proper functioning, as well as the functioning of its primary backup system. In much the same way, the instructional expert needs time to review and "check off" what is needed before the actual use of instructional materials. This chapter focuses on the preparation and use of different "hard" technologies, that is, how one prepares what is needed in order for students to "arrive" at desired learning destinations. Proper preparation helps to ensure that what is desired is actually achieved, and, if difficulties do occur, that backup systems can be activated so learning can still occur.

Now that your instruction has been planned and the materials assembled or produced, you need to get ready for your students to receive the instruction. This chapter focuses on preparation and utilization techniques for a wide variety of media and instructional materials. Proper use of media and materials can improve the effectiveness and efficiency of instruction and, consequently, increase student achievement. Many of the techniques described in this chapter apply to groups of all sizes. This chapter focuses on general media utilization guidelines.

First we describe preparation skills that are always necessary, both when you are presenting to your class and when your students are learning in small groups or studying individually. The remainder of the chapter explores specific techniques for properly using real objects and models, text, visuals, display boards, overhead transparencies, slides and filmstrips, audio, video and film, television, computer software, and multimedia. ◼

PREPARATION

To be a good teacher, you must know your content and present it effectively. There is a preparation phase and an implementation phase of instruction.

Preparation is an important aspect of success in the classroom.

You must prepare yourself, the materials, the environment, and the students for learning. Preparation for instruction is an important process. Without proper attention to it, your instruction may not be as effective as it could be.

Prepare Yourself

Plan what you are going to do and say. Follow closely the instructional plan you developed (see Chapter 6), and make sure you outline all of the instructional events that will occur during the lesson. Use key words or phrases and short descriptions of activities. Don't write out a script, since we don't talk like we write. Some teachers put their lesson outline on index cards, while others prefer letter-size sheets of paper. You can store your lesson outline in your computer and print out a copy whenever you need it. This allows for fast and easy adaptations and revisions.

Prepare Your Instructional Materials

You have already selected, modified, and/or developed the materials for your lesson. This may have been done some time ago. Now you need to gather all the media and materials you and your students will need during the lesson. Make sure everything is available. Some teachers have a list of necessary materials for each lesson. The list can be stored and updated in your computer.

Some materials, like audio- and videotapes, will need to be "cued up" prior to the beginning of the lesson. Other materials, like bulletin boards and displays, will need to be assembled and/or put up. You may also need to prepare the classroom or learning environment, as discussed in the next section.

Prepare Your Learning Environment

Wherever the instruction is to take place–classroom, laboratory, or playground–the facilities will have to be put in order. Certain factors are taken for granted for any instructional situation: comfortable seating, adequate ventilation, climate control, suitable lighting, and the like. Many media require a darkened room, a readily accessible power supply, and access to light switches. At the very least, you should check to see that the equipment is in working order and arrange the facilities so that all the students can see and hear properly.

Check your equipment setup in advance of your presentation. Change the arrangement, if necessary, to meet your needs. When the equipment is in place, make sure everything operates properly. For films, slides, and video projection, place the screen front and center. Place the overhead projector screen or flip chart at a 45° angle and near the corner of the room. Place the overhead screen to your right if you are right-handed, or to the left if you are left-handed. Place the flip chart to your left if you are right-handed, or to your right if you are left-handed. When you use a video monitor, place a single monitor front and center. If you are using two monitors, place one on each side of the front of the room. Position objects being studied in the front and center. Remove them when they're no longer being studied.

Prepare Your Students

As you begin the lesson, the first step is to prepare your students. Research on learning tells us very clearly that what is learned from a lesson depends on how well the learners are prepared for the lesson. You have probably noticed that entertainers are obsessed with having their audiences properly warmed up. Preparing the students is just as important when they are involved in a lesson. Chapter 6 discussed the components of an effective instructional introduction: hook, purpose, and context.

A proper warm-up, from an instructional point of view, generally consists of an introduction, which gives a broad overview of the content of the lesson. You should arouse interest in the lesson and motivate the students to learn (hook), create a need to know by telling the learners how they will profit from learning (purpose), and explain how the lesson relates to previous and future topics (context). Several of these functions—directing attention, arousing motivation, and providing a rationale— may be served by informing the students of the desired lesson outcomes.

In certain cases, other steps will be called for. For example, unfamiliar vocabulary may need to be introduced, or special visual effects, such as time-lapse photography, may need to be explained. Other preparation steps relevant to particular media will be discussed later in this chapter. Figure 8.1 summarizes the preparation guidelines to follow before presenting a lesson.

UTILIZATION OF MEDIA

Now that we've explored the necessary preparatory steps, let's look at specific procedures for increasing the effectiveness of commonly used instructional media and display devices. In Chapter 4 we introduced these media and display devices with descriptions and examples of their possible applications. Then, in Chapter 7, we discussed the advantages and limitations of each medium, as well as procedures for selecting, modifying, and creating these same media and display devices.

Figure 8.1 The four Ps of preparation

Prepare Yourself
- ❑ Plan
- ❑ Outline instructional events
- ❑ Practice

Prepare Your Instructional Materials
- ❑ Check list of materials needed
- ❑ Gather media and materials
- ❑ Check equipment
- ❑ Cue media and put up materials

Prepare Your Learning Environment
- ❑ Provide comfortable seating
- ❑ Provide adequate ventilation
- ❑ Control temperature
- ❑ Provide suitable lighting
- ❑ Arrange seating so all can see and hear

Prepare Your Students
- ❑ Arouse interest and motivate
- ❑ State purpose
- ❑ Present overview of content
- ❑ Relate content to previous and future topics
- ❑ Explain unfamiliar vocabulary

Real Objects and Models

There are countless things in the environment that can be used by you and your students—leaves, globes, dolls, Cuisenaire rods, tools, and so on. However, real objects and models will be effective only if they are used properly. To use them effectively, familiarize yourself with the object or model before using it in the classroom. Practice your presentation. If your object or model is a working one, know how it works and what might go wrong.

Instructional objects must be large enough to be seen by the class but not so big or heavy as to be distracting. If you have trouble moving and handling the object, students may laugh at your problems. As part of your preparation, handle the object and be certain you can manipulate it and show its important features.

Show or demonstrate an object by revealing it only when needed and covering it or putting it out of sight when it's no longer in use. Otherwise your students may continue to look at the object and be distracted from the rest of the lesson.

Be sure your students don't get the wrong impression of the size, shape, or color of the real object if the model differs from it in these respects. Use a size indicator, a color slide, or a visual to show size and color of the object the model represents. Whenever it is feasible to do so, encourage your students to handle and manipulate the objects or model under study before and after your presentation or during individualized or small-group instruction.

Generally you should avoid passing a single object around a classroom of students, since this takes time and distracts the students. Instead, walk around the classroom and briefly show the object to everyone. You can also make it available at the end of the lesson. If duplicate objects are available, it may be possible to pass them around without taking up an exorbitant amount of time.

Applied Example

Nancy Foust, an instructor at the local vocational-technical school, is demonstrating how automobile carburetors work so her students can adjust and repair them. She brings several different carburetors into the classroom to arouse interest at the beginning of the class. The students can handle and look at them before the class begins. Then the carburetors are put away.

Nancy uses a larger-than-life model of a carburetor to show how internal parts operate. Some of the parts are made of clear plastic, and many are color coded for easy identification. Having seen and manipulated the actual carburetors, Nancy's students know how big they are and what they look like. The enlarged model allows all of her students to see the various parts as she describes their functions.

Utilization Checklist: Real Objects and Models

- Familiarize yourself with the object or model.
- Make sure objects are large enough to be seen.
- Show objects only when needed.
- Indicate actual size, shape, and color of objects represented by models.
- Avoid passing a single object around class.

Text

Textbooks should be used to meet your students' needs rather than dictate what they do. As indicated in the PIE model, you should determine student outcomes and then select the materials that will facilitate your students achieving those outcomes. Too often textbooks are selected first and then what the students learn and do are determined by what is in the textbook.

Your students must know how to get the most from their textbooks. One technique is the SQ3R method (West, Farmer, & Wolff, 1991), which is made up of five steps: *Survey, Question, Read, Recite,* and *Review. Survey* requires the students to skim through the text, as well as to read the overview or summary. *Question* asks the students to write a list of questions to be answered while reading. In the *Read* step, students are encouraged to look for the organization of the material, put brackets around the main ideas, underline supporting details, and answer the questions written in the previous step. *Recite* requires students to test themselves while reading and to put the content into their own words. *Review* suggests that students look over the material immediately after reading it and then look it over again the next day, then a week later, and so on.

Even if you don't use this specific model with printed materials, you can still direct student reading by using objectives and/or questions. Provide students with specific questions to answer while they are reading. You can develop a worksheet if one isn't provided by the textbook.

Emphasize the use of visuals in textbooks. Teach your students to read visuals (photographs, drawings, charts, diagrams, maps) and discuss them in class. A lot of valuable information may be contained in the nontext material in textbooks.

Refer to the teacher's guide for supplementary materials and activities. You can also supplement the textbook with other media (videotapes, real objects, computer software) and approaches (discussion, role play) we have described elsewhere in this book.

Applied Example

Jean Montgomery's fourth graders are carefully studying the photographs in their textbooks as they read about the countries of Africa. Ms. Montgomery has taught them that photographs are an important part of their textbooks and all books. Students are working together in small groups, with each group studying a different country. Some students are referring to the encyclopedia on CD-ROM in the classroom to get additional information. Ms. Montgomery reminds them that the CD-ROM is just another "book" and should be used accordingly.

Student groups begin by surveying the material available on their assigned country, and then they develop a set of questions to answer. Following this, they individually read the material in their textbooks and encyclopedia. They return to their small groups to discuss (recite) the information they learned. The materials are reviewed the next day before they present their findings to the entire class. Note that the SQ3R approach was used to structure the learning process.

Utilization Checklist: Text

- Use textbooks to meet student needs.
- Encourage students to use the SQ3R or similar reading comprehension methods.
- Direct student reading with objectives and/or questions.
- Emphasize the use of visuals in printed materials.
- Check the teacher's guide for additional materials and activities.
- Supplement the textbook with other media.

Visuals

A wide variety of pictures, drawings, charts, and other visuals are available or can be prepared for classroom use. When using them in the classroom, you should use simple materials that everyone can see simultaneously. If you intend to display them at the front of the room, be certain they are large enough for group viewing. Lettering should be large enough to be seen by students in the back of the room.

Provide written or verbal cues to highlight important information contained in the visual. But don't include too much information; the visual will lose its effectiveness if it's crowded.

During a demonstration or presentation, limit the number of visuals used in a given period of time. It's better to use a few visuals well than to

VISUALS WITHIN TEXT

We live in a very visual society. From pictures in the morning newspaper, to signs on the roadway, to graphics downloaded from the Internet, we are bombarded with visuals each and every day. Why are visuals used so prominently? Because they work. Visuals can increase *effectiveness* by highlighting information, which increases viewers' comprehension and memory. For example, visuals can depict real or abstract items, illustrate procedures, provide examples, identify parts and pieces, and draw attention to similarities and differences among various objects. Additionally, visuals can increase *efficiency* by representing, in a single form, what may take hundreds if not thousands of words to explain. Finally, visuals can increase *appeal* by attracting attention, as well as stimulating thought and inquiry.

When adapting or creating instructional materials, the selection and use of visuals is important. Just as the proper visual may lead to increased instructional effectiveness, efficiency, and appeal, one that is not appropriate may cause learner difficulties and frustration. Consider the following questions when selecting visuals for use within your instructional materials:

- Is the visual relevant to the instructional outcomes?
- Is the information depicted accurately?
- Is the information current?
- Is the information presented in a clear and simple manner?
- Will learners comprehend what is depicted?
- Will it be big/small enough for the given purpose and size of audience?
- Is it aesthetically pleasing?

overwhelm your students with an abundance of insufficiently explained ones. A good guideline is to use about two visuals per minute. Display a visual only when it is needed. Use just one picture at a time except for purposes of comparison. As you finish discussing each visual, put it down on a table or desk, cover it, or put it away to direct attention back to yourself or another visual.

Add your notes to the back side of handheld visuals. As you teach, hold up the picture to your side, but out in front of you so that you can read the notes on the back. This technique contributes to a professional presentation and eliminates holding or glancing down at notes.

Hold visuals steady when you are showing them to a group by resting them against a desk or table or putting them on an easel. Freestanding or table-top easels are available. Be certain the easel is high enough to allow for unobstructed viewing by the students. Mount visuals on poster board, stack them in correct order, and place all of them on an easel. After you finish discussing each visual, flip it down onto a table in front of the easel.

Help students learn from a visual by asking direct questions about it. Talk to your students and not to the visuals.

Applied Example

Tom Keller selects one of his students' favorite books, Alexander and the Terrible, Horrible, No Good, Very Bad Day, *to read to a small group of second graders. Before beginning the story, he asks questions that the students should be able to answer after listening to the story.*

To enhance the students' interest and understanding, Tom uses study prints (large visuals) depicting parts of the story. He asks his students to discuss the characters shown in the study prints. After reading and discussing the questions related to the story, Tom has the students create their own stories based on one of the study prints.

Utilization Checklist: Visuals

- Use simple materials that everyone can see.
- Provide written or verbal cues to highlight important aspects of visuals.
- Use one visual at a time except for comparison.
- Hold visuals steady.

Display Boards

In the classroom, the most widely used (and abused) tool is the chalkboard. Although chalkboards have been replaced by dustless multipur-

Visuals help to clarify information for many students.

pose boards in some classrooms, the same simple techniques can be used to increase the effectiveness of both.

First, check the visibility of the board from several positions around the room to be sure that there isn't any glare on the surface. If there is, move the board (if portable) or adjust the window shades or blinds. Taking too much time to write or draw creates restlessness and may lead to discipline problems, so put extensive drawing or writing on the board before class. Cover material such as a test or extensive lesson materials with wrapping paper, newspaper, or a pull-down map until you are ready to use it.

Organize in advance *what* you plan to write on the board and *where* you plan to write it. Outline your drawings with barely visible lines before class and then fill them in with bold lines in front of the class. Your students will think you're an artist! Use drawing aids such as rulers, stencils, and templates (patterns) to save time and to improve the quality of your drawings. For frequently drawn shapes, use a template cut from wood or heavy cardboard. A dresser drawer knob or empty thread spool mounted on the template makes it easier to hold it in position while tracing around it.

Print neatly rather than using script. For 32-foot-long classrooms, the letters should be 3 to 3.5 inches high, and the lines forming the letters should be a quarter-inch thick. Hold the chalk or marker at an angle so it won't make scratching or squeaking noises. Use color for emphasis, but don't overuse it. Two or three different colors work best. If your printing normally runs uphill or downhill, use a water-soluble felt-tip marking pen and straightedge (e.g., a yardstick) to put guidelines on the chalkboard. The guidelines can't be wiped off with a

chalk eraser, but you can wash them off when you no longer need them.

Eye contact with students is important! Face the class when you're talking. Don't talk to the board. Avoid turning your back to the class any more than is absolutely necessary. Move around so you don't block what you've written on the board.

A multipurpose board will provide many years of use if it's cared for properly. The board should be completely erased with a felt eraser after each use. Don't let the marks remain on the board overnight. The longer the marks remain on the board, the more difficult they are to erase. However, old marks *can* be erased by tracing over them with a black erasable marker and erasing immediately.

For general cleaning, simply wipe the board clean with a soft, damp cloth. If further cleaning is necessary, use a mild spray cleaner. You can also apply a soapy detergent solution and rub briskly with a soft, clean cloth. Always rinse thoroughly with clean water and dry with a soft towel after cleaning.

The erasable markers also require some special care. They have a solvent base that dries quickly. This is the key to their erasability. The markers should be kept *tightly capped* and stored in a horizontal position to prevent them from drying out. If a cap is accidentally left off, the tip will go dry. When this happens, it *may* be possible to restore its usability. Cap the marker, turn it upside down, and shake it up and down vigorously for twenty seconds. Storing the marker overnight with the tip end down may also help.

Vary your presentation techniques. Do not overuse or rely entirely on the board. Use handouts, the overhead projector, and other media during instruction when appropriate.

Applied Example

The white marker board is a permanent fixture in Bonnie Johnson's computer classroom. Chalk dust would seriously damage the thirty computers and their associated disk drives. Her high school students are learning a variety of computer applications, such as spreadsheets and desktop publishing. She also uses the overhead projector when introducing specific programs, but she prefers the marker board when students are working on a variety of applications software.

Ms. Johnson uses the marker board and a variety of colored markers to diagram the relationships among the various components of each applications program. She leaves these diagrams on the marker board during class so students can refer to them. She also puts key commands on the board for easy reference by her students.

Utilization Checklist: Display Boards

- Check the visibility of the board from several positions around the room.
- Decide in advance how you plan to use the board.
- Use drawing aids or outlines to create visuals on the board.
- Use temporary guidelines to help you write in a straight line on the board.
- Print rather than write in script.
- Move around so you don't block what you have written on the board.
- Talk to your students, not to the board.

Overhead Transparencies

The overhead projector is one of the easiest presentation devices to use. With a little practice, anyone—including your students—can make a professional presentation using overhead transparencies.

Use the same frame size for all your transparencies. If you want to, you can tape a guide on the projector platform to assure that each image will project in the same screen area. Number your transparencies sequentially in the order in which they'll be used. Place your notes (key words) on the frame of the transparency.

When you prepare to use the overhead projector, close the blinds and use a medium room light. Focus the image so it fills the screen. You may want to start the lesson by projecting an outline to show your students what to expect. Plan ways to add meaningful details to the transparency as needed during the lesson; this infuses an element of spontaneity. Avoid using the projector as a doodle pad. If the basic transparency is valuable and will be reused, cover it with a blank acetate before drawing on it.

You can direct students' attention to parts of the transparency by using the following techniques:

- Point to specific portions using a pencil as a pointer. Lay the pencil directly on the transparency, because any elevation will put the pencil out of focus and any slight hand movement will be greatly exaggerated on the screen. Avoid pointing to the projection screen.
- Circle or underline specific items on the transparency. (*Note:* Make sure you use water-soluble overhead transparency pens.)
- Reveal information one point at a time to control pace and audience attention by placing a sheet of paper under the transparency. Mask unwanted portions by covering them with a sheet of paper or using cardboard windows to reveal one section at a time.

You can overlay new information in steps. You can build up a complex idea by superimposing transparencies one at a time. Up to four overlays can be used successfully.

Shift the audience's attention back to you by switching off the projector when you have finished referring to a particular transparency. However, don't turn the machine off and on so frequently that it becomes distracting (30 seconds is a good guideline).

Applied Example

The chalkboard and overhead projector made a good team for teaching problem solving in Dianna Williams's physics class. After she demonstrated how to solve acceleration problems, Dianna projected similar problems with the overhead projector. Prior to class time she prepared the problems on transparencies, using an 18-point font so all students would be able to see and read the problems. The screen was placed in the front corner of the room so it wouldn't block the chalkboard.

Several students were randomly selected to do the problem on the chalkboard. They were instructed to print large enough that everyone in the room could see their work. The other students worked on the same problem at their desks. When all students were finished, Dianna led a discussion on the various ways to approach the problem. Students indicated errors they found in the methods and calculations of each other's problems.

Utilization Checklist: Overhead Transparencies

- Use the same frame size for all your transparencies.
- Number your transparencies sequentially in the order in which they'll be used.
- Place your notes (key words) on the frame of the transparency.

- Focus the image so it fills the screen.
- Add meaningful details to the transparency as needed.
- Direct student attention to parts of the transparency.
- Overlay new information in steps.
- Shift the students' attention back to you by switching off the projector.

Slides and Filmstrips

When you use slides or filmstrips, the following techniques can add professionalism to your lessons. Make sure that the projector works and that the room is appropriately set up for viewing slides or filmstrips. Be sure everyone can see. If individuals or small groups are viewing the material, make sure that they will not distract or be distracted by other students working in the area. For a group showing, darken the room sufficiently but prepare a way to light your notes; a penlight or flashlight can serve this purpose. Begin and end the presentation with a black slide or frame, since a bright white screen can be irritating to the eyes. Stand facing the students and use a remote control to advance the slides or filmstrip. This will allow you to stand at the side of the room, where you can keep an eye on the material on the screen while maintaining some eye contact with the class.

Plan and rehearse your narration to accompany the slides or filmstrip if it isn't already recorded on tape. Limit your discussion of each slide or frame. Even a minute of narration can seem long to your students. Consider adding a musical accompaniment to your live or recorded narration. This can help to establish the desired mood and keep your class attentive. But don't have the music playing in the background when you're providing narration.

The following guidelines apply to the use of slides. If there is a "talky" section in the middle of your slide presentation, use a gray slide or turn off the projector rather than leaving an irrelevant slide on the screen. Gray slides can be produced locally or purchased from commercial sources. They let through enough light to allow you to be seen, avoiding total darkening of the room. Gray slides can also be used at points where an explanation is needed or where questions will be raised. Make certain that your slides are in sequential order and right-side up. Disarrangement can be an embarrassment to you and an annoyance to your students (see Figure 8.2 for a foolproof method of marking slides). If you need to use a slide twice, make a second slide of it. Use a Universal 80-slide tray (the one with the largest slots) instead of standard 80- or 140-slide trays, which have a high probability of jamming. Use slides to test visually the students' mastery of visual concepts. You can, for instance, project a slide and ask students to make an identification or discrimination.

The following techniques can add professionalism to filmstrip utilization. Don't feel compelled to run the filmstrip all the way through without stopping. You can show the filmstrip as an overview and then reshow it, pausing for discussion at key frames. Encourage participation by asking relevant questions during the filmstrip. You may want the students to read some of the captions. This is a particularly good reading activity for elementary students.

Applied Example

Instead of taking a field trip to the local food-processing plant, Ned Quinn's consumer science students are viewing a set of slides showing various operations within the plant. In previous years students actually toured the plant. However, with rising transportation costs and plant officials' increasing concern for students' safety, it was decided to discontinue the tours. As the last group of students prepared to take the tour, Mr. Quinn suggested that they capture the tour on slides. The school provided cameras and film, and the students eagerly took a wide variety of slides. Following the field trip, the class spent several weeks sequencing the most illustrative slides for use by future students.

Now students can view the slides as Mr. Quinn provides the narration from his notes and distributes literature provided by the food-processing plant. Students learn the processes and see the operations without actually leaving the classroom.

Utilization Checklist: Slides and Filmstrips

- Darken the room so all can see.
- Begin and end with a black slide or frame.
- Make sure slides are in the correct order and right-side up.
- Stand facing your class and use a remote control to advance the slides or filmstrip.
- Consider adding music before or after your live or recorded narration.
- Break up long presentations with a gray slide or turn off the projector.

Audio

In formal education, a lot of attention is given to reading and writing, a little to speaking, and essentially none to listening. Like all skills, listening can

There are eight possible ways a slide can be placed in a projector. Seven of them are wrong (e.g., upside-down, backwards, sideways). To avoid all seven mistakes a standardized procedure is recommended for placing a reminder spot on the slide.

❑ First, your slides should be arranged and numbered in the order in which they are to be shown.

❑ Then take each slide and hold it the way it is supposed to be seen on the screen, that is, right-side up with the lettering running left to right, just as it would be read. If the slide lacks lettering or other orienting information, hold it so that the emulsion side (the duller side) is toward the screen.

❑ Then simply place a spot (or number) on the bottom left-hand corner.

❑ This spot is referred to as a "thumb spot" because when the slide is turned upside down to be placed in the projector, your thumb will grip the slide at the point of the thumb spot, as shown.

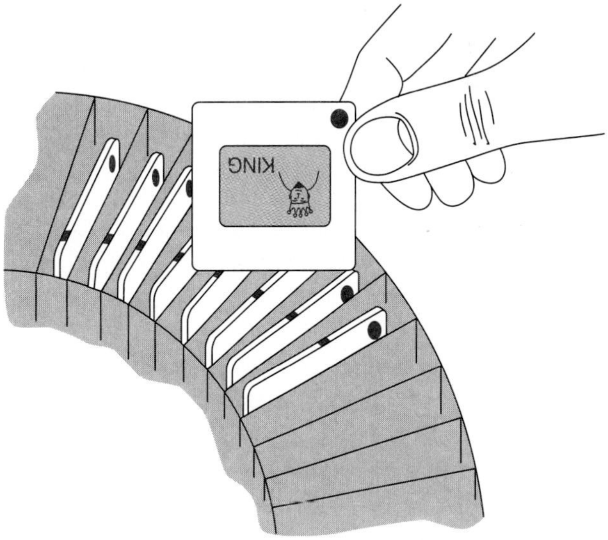

❑ Before all the slides are put in the tray in proper order, some users like to run a felt-tip pen across the tops of the slide mounts in a diagonal line. This way if some slides later get out of order, they can be replaced just by following the line.

Figure 8.2   Thumb spots: An effective procedure for making sure slides are properly projected
Note. From *Instructional Media and Technologies for Learning* (5th ed.) (p. 144), by R. Heinich, M. Molenda, J. D. Russell, and S. Smaldino, 1996, Englewood Cliffs, NJ: Merrill/Prentice Hall. Copyright 1996 by Merrill/Prentice Hall. Reprinted with permission.

WARM-UPS AND DEBRIEFINGS

One simple but effective training principle is, "Tell them what you are going to tell them, tell them, and then tell them what you told them." More than just for the purpose of repetition, this principle is useful because it illustrates the importance of both the "warm-up" and the "debriefing." The warm-up is basically a short introduction prior to an instructional activity or lesson that is designed to help students identify what they should attend to during the instruction. For example, prior to a slide presentation covering different works by a particular artist, the warm-up may consist of a simple statement such as "*Pay close attention to* the artist's use of color and how he expresses basic feelings through its use." The warm-up helps learners pick out and attend to key information.

The debriefing occurs shortly after an instructional lesson or activity and is used to help learners understand what they have just experienced. A simple debriefing may be in the form of a guided discussion or the posing and answering of a set of relevant questions. In most cases, the debriefing and the warm-up are coordinated and focus on the same key information. The benefits of using these two instructional techniques are, first, that students know what specific things to attend to during instruction, and second, that they then have the opportunity to compare the actual experience with the expected one.

Suggestions for implementing the warm-up:

- Preview the instructional materials to identify the key concepts.
- Ask guiding questions to help students think about the key concepts as they watch the video, listen to the tape, read the passage, participate in the computer simulation, and so on.
- Ask the students to determine what key concepts are to be gained from the experience. Depending on the audience, you may need to give them a hint or an example of what they should be looking for.
- Use the direct route—direct them to "pay attention to . . . " as they go through the materials. Although you may direct their attention, allow them to discover why the identified concept is relevant and important.

Suggestions for implementing the debriefing:

- Make sure the debriefing is connected with the warm-up; that is, follow up on the questions asked prior to using the instructional materials.
- Ask questions about how the key concept was understood. Was it what they expected? How did it differ? Why was it selected as a key concept? What was its importance?
- Ask them to relate the experience to other personal experiences. How could this information be important to them? Why?

Students are often overheard complaining that they "didn't get anything out of" an activity involving the use of software, videos, or other instructional media. This may be because students didn't identify the key concepts within the instructional materials. Warm-ups and debriefings are used specifically to help students overcome these problems. Prior to implementing your materials, think about how you are going to warm up and then debrief your students in order to ensure that they "get something out of it."

be improved with practice. When you're preparing to use audio materials, cue the tape or disc to the information you want to play. This will avoid delays and distraction for the students. Check the volume level in advance so you don't "blast" your students out of the classroom. Make sure all the students can hear. Try to minimize any noise and visual distraction for students using audio materials. The students using the audio materials shouldn't be distracted, and the audio activity shouldn't distract other students in the area who aren't participating.

Provide an introduction to the topic, and indicate why it is important. You might list key terms, major points, or important questions to be answered on the chalkboard or on an overhead transparency.

While the students are listening to the audio material, they may need a handout or worksheet in order to maximize their learning. If it is a class activity, you should participate as well so that your students know you think the materials are important. You may want to stop the audio presentation for discussion or other activities. In some cases you may even replay important parts.

As a follow-up activity to the audio lesson, you might want to use activities such as a teacher summary, class discussion, or student projects. Often the important learning from an audio activity comes from what the students do with the material after they've heard it.

Applied Example

The eighth-grade students at Fairfield Middle School are using cassette tape recorders to gather an oral history of their community. The project is a cooperative effort by all eighth-grade social studies teachers and their students. The teachers divided up various aspects of the community's history, such as transportation, government, business, industry, and recreation. Students spent many weeks deciding on important topics in the area assigned to their class. Then students worked together to develop a set of questions to be asked of each individual they would interview.

Armed with tape recorders, students interview people from the community. Some of the citizens come to the school; others are visited by the students. The individual tapes are then edited by the students into one tape that highlights important aspects of the community's history. The finalized copy will be available for use by community groups and organizations. Copies will also be available in the school and community libraries.

Utilization Checklist: Audio

• Cue the audio material before you and your students use it.

• Make sure that all students involved can hear and that other students aren't distracted.

• Provide an introduction to the topic and indicate why the topic is important.

• Use a handout or worksheet to maximize learning from audio media.

• Use a follow-up activity after an audio lesson.

Video and Film

Here are some general tips that apply equally to the enhancement of both video and film presentations. You should check lighting, seating, and volume controls to be sure that everyone can see and hear the presentation. Close the blinds. With videotape, use a medium light. With film, use either dim lights or no lights.

Prepare your students by briefly reviewing previous related content and by asking questions about the topic. List on the chalkboard or overhead transparency the main points to be covered in the video or film. Discuss any new vocabulary.

Get involved in the program yourself. Watch attentively, and respond when the presenter asks for a response. Be a good role model. Stop the video or film at appropriate points to discuss key ideas and to reinforce student learning. You need not show all of a film or video, just the most relevant parts. It's very easy to cue a videotape to the portion desired. You can highlight major points by listing them on the chalkboard during the lesson. The showing should be followed by meaningful follow-up activities.

There are showmanship tips that apply specifically to showing films. Many classrooms have a wall-mounted screen in the front of the room. In some classrooms, unfortunately, the door to the hallway is near the front of the room, and this door often has a large window in it or a window area beside it. If light from the hall interferes with the brightness of the projected image, you may have to cover part or all of the window area with poster board or butcher paper. If this isn't possible, move the projector closer to the screen to get a brighter picture. Remember that a smaller, brighter image is better than a larger, dimmer one.

Set the focus and note the correct sound level before the class arrives; then turn the volume knob back down to zero and run the film back to the beginning. Some films have focus and sound-level adjustment footage before the start of the film. When this is the case you can properly set focus and sound before you reach the beginning of the film. You shouldn't project the leader (the part of

Proper showmanship increases the effectiveness of media in the classroom.

the film with the number countdown on it). The first image the students see should be the title or opening scene of the film. When everyone is ready, start the projector, turn on the lamp, and turn the volume knob to the predetermined level (this is particularly important when the film has no introductory music). Adjust the focus and sound after you start the projector.

When the film is over, turn off the lamp, turn down the sound, and stop the projector. Run the rest of the film footage through after class. Rewind the film if you are going to show it again. If you are not showing it again, and if you used the same size reel the film came on, you need not rewind the film—the agency you got it from will rewind it during routine inspection. Before you put the film back in the container, fasten down the end of the film with a piece of tape. The film normally arrives with the film held down with tape. Peel it off and stick it on the projection cart so that you can use it later to hold the end down. The film is better protected when this is done.

Applied Example

Paige Ertmer's preservice teachers are viewing the acclaimed videotape Good Morning Miss Tolliver *in their mathematics methods course. The program was awarded the 1993 George Peabody Award, broadcast television's highest honor. Originally shown on PBS, the video is a captivating look at how Kay Tolliver, an East Harlem math teacher, combines math and communication arts skills to inspire and motivate her students.*

Dr. Ertmer is hoping this videotape will inspire and motivate her students, who will be doing their student teaching next semester. She has distributed a set of questions to direct her students' viewing of the videotape. The

students have been asked to look over the questions prior to seeing the tape and to take notes during the viewing. These questions will form the base of a whole-class discussion following the video.

Utilization Checklist: Video and Film

- Check lighting, seating, and volume controls before the showing.
- Prepare students by reviewing previously learned content and by asking new questions.
- Stop the videotape or film at appropriate points for discussion.
- Highlight major points by writing them on the chalkboard or overhead.
- Support the showing with meaningful follow-up activities.

Television

When you use live television in the classroom, you should attempt to find out about the content and objectives of the program from a printed program guide, since you will not be able to preview the program in advance. Decide if you should use the program during the broadcast time or record it for later use. The latter will also let you preview the program before you show it to the students. Record evening programs for use the next day to be certain that all students can see it.

You should check the equipment in advance. Test the receiver (TV set) and make necessary adjustments in volume and location so all can see and hear. Have some daylight and/or artificial light in the room, but avoid distracting glare on the screen.

Close the blinds to shut out disturbing glare. Turn off the lights above and behind the monitor, but leave room lights on so students can take notes and not be tempted to sleep.

Be sure to plan introductory and follow-up activities. Tell the students in advance what they will see, what they should learn from the program, and what they will be responsible for after viewing the program. Watch the television program and participate actively in it with your students. After the showing, you may answer student questions or ask students to react to the content of the program. Have the students do a project, either as a class, in groups, or as individuals. Help students articulate what they've learned from the experience.

Applied Example

At Pineview Elementary School, selected fifth and sixth graders prepare a live closed-circuit television news program each morning for all the students in the school. The news anchors and the support staff arrive at school early with newspapers and newsmagazines in hand to put together the five-minute broadcast. The roles of news reporters, anchors, and support staff rotate each month so that all students who want to can participate in the program. Other students wait anxiously in their classrooms to get the latest school, local, state, national, and international news. Teachers check the equipment in advance to be sure it's in operating order and to ensure that all students can see and hear the program.

The news program is also recorded on videotape so that teachers can provide follow-up activities in their classes. Students on the news team also look at the videotape to evaluate their individual and team performances. Teachers prepare their students by reviewing previous news events and new developments. The news video can be stopped at appropriate points for discussion. Major points are highlighted on the chalkboard or overhead.

Utilization Checklist: Television

* Determine the content and objectives of the program in advance, if possible.
* Check the equipment in advance to be sure it's in operating order.
* Be sure that all students can see and hear the program without interference.
* Plan introductory and follow-up activities.
* Participate actively in viewing the program with your students.

Computer Software

When you use computer software with a class, use a display technology that is appropriate for the size of the room (see the CUE in Chapter 9). Before using the software, check lighting and viewing angles to make certain that everyone can see the displayed image. You should position your computer so that you can face your class. If you place the computer to one side at a 45° angle, you can observe the computer's display and still maintain eye contact with your students.

Install and test in advance any software that you'll use in the presentation to make sure that everything works properly. When you use presentation software (see the CUE in Chapter 9 for a description), run the software from the hard drive rather than from a floppy. It will operate much more quickly. Keep the screen displays and program operation simple. Most presentation software can be set to advance at the press of a button or the click of the mouse. When possible, select a large font size to display text. This greatly increases readability, especially in large rooms.

Encourage participation by asking questions during the presentation. When you demonstrate software, have students suggest actions to take or allow them to take turns actually operating the computer. When you demonstrate software that students will eventually use, be sure to point out features they'll need to know and be able to use during subsequent hands-on activities.

Applied Example

A small group of students in George Matson's middle school mathematics class is using the computer simulation Hot Dog Stand *to develop a wide variety of mathematical and practical skills. The simulation requires planning and record keeping, as well as judgments based on computational skills, to make as much money as possible while managing a hot dog stand during a season of high school football games. The random generation of variables assures that the same students can use the program again and again.*

The students are gathered around a computer in the corner of the classroom while other students are engaged in different activities. Mr. Matson has checked to be sure that all can see the screen and interact without disturbing other students. He installed and tested the software before the class. The students record data that are put into spreadsheets and converted into graphs. There is friendly competition to see which group of students can "earn" the most money from its hot dog stand.

Utilization Checklist: Computer Software

* Use a display technology that is appropriate for the number of students.
* Check lighting and viewing angles to make certain everyone can see.

- Install and test software in advance of your presentation.
- Run the software from the hard drive rather than from floppy disk.
- Keep screen displays simple and use large font size for text.
- Encourage student participation through questioning and having students decide next steps.

Multimedia

When you use multimedia materials, you should assemble and test all of the components of the multimedia system well in advance of your presentation. Multimedia systems can be difficult to operate, and you want to make certain that everything will work when you are ready to use it. Connect all of the components with the power turned off. Never connect or disconnect components with the power on; doing so may result in damage to the computer or the components. When everything is up and running, gather cables together and tuck them out of the way to avoid possible tripping hazards or accidental disconnections.

In advance of your presentation, install and test any software that you will use. As before, operate from the hard drive rather than from a floppy disk for greater speed. Also remember to check lighting, viewing angles, and audio levels to make certain they are appropriate. Position the multimedia system so that you can face your audience. As mentioned earlier, if you place the system to one side at a 45° angle, you can observe the computer display and still maintain eye contact with your students. Additionally, plan follow-up discussions and activities to help students get the most out of the presentation.

Applied Example

Individual fifth- and sixth-grade students in Jim Crawford's bilevel Spanish class sit at a learning carrel and view slides that their teacher took during his trip to Spain last summer. Jim decided to use an audiotape to narrate the slides, which show various people, animals, and buildings in Spain. He recorded native Spanish speakers describing the scenes and objects shown in the slides, and he added Spanish music to set a mood before the recorded narration and during scenes showing folk dances.

The purpose of the slide-tape is to visually and aurally present basic vocabulary (the key vocabulary words are contained in a handout). Jim has checked to make sure his slides are in the correct order and right-side up. The slide-tape presentation begins and ends with a black slide. He cues the slides and tape before his students use

them. The students use headphones in order to not distract others in the classroom.

Utilization Checklist: Multimedia

- Assemble and test all components of the multimedia system in advance.
- Connect all components with the power turned off.
- Install and test all software in advance of presentation.
- Check lighting, viewing angles, and audio levels to make sure that all are appropriate.
- Plan follow-up discussions and activities to help students get the most from the presentation.

CUE   Computer Use ESSENTIALS

The use of media in support of classroom instruction has a long history. Real objects, pictures, and slides have been used in classrooms since the nineteenth century, and media are a staple of classrooms today. We have already examined appropriate classroom uses of media in this chapter. In this CUE we look at a somewhat different use of media, one that has a less lengthy history but which is growing in importance. Our focus here is the use of media not in a single classroom but in support of teaching and learning across distances. Distance education is growing, and computer and telecommunication technologies are helping to facilitate that growth.

Distance education refers to an organized instructional program in which the teacher and learners are physically separated. It addresses problems of educational access. Obviously, distance itself can be a major barrier to individuals seeking education. People in rural or remote locations are often at a disadvantage educationally compared with those in urban areas. Resources may be scarce, and, in the worst cases, there may not be enough teachers to reach the students. A small, rural school may not be able to justify the cost of a teacher to provide advanced physics instruction or teach Japanese to a handful of students. Problems of access may be manifested in other ways as well. For example, learners who are homebound due to illness or physical disability may not be located far from an educational institution, but they are effectively isolated. Adults who wish to pursue education may lack the time needed to pursue traditional coursework at a local school or college. For them,

Distance education can open the classroom to the world.

home study may be the only option. Distance education can overcome many of these problems of access and provide educational opportunities.

DISTANCE EDUCATION TECHNOLOGIES

The earliest efforts at distance education involved correspondence study in which individuals used self-study printed materials. While useful and still in existence today, print-based correspondence study is limited, especially because of the limited interaction between instructor and learners. Over the years, various technologies have been employed to enhance distance education, including radio, television, and the telephone. Today a variety of telecommunication technologies are available for support of distance education. Often, a key element of these technologies is their ability to enhance the communication between teacher and learners. We will look at three broad categories of distance education technologies: audio based, video based, and computer based.

Audio-Based Distance Education Technologies

Radio is an audio-based technology with which most of us are familiar. It has the capability to reach a relatively broad geographical region at relatively low (compared to television) cost. It can provide a standardized message to a large audience, and it has clear utility in areas such as music, discussion, dramatic presentation, and language learning. However, radio broadcasts adhere to a fixed schedule, and this can be a disadvantage compared with more flexible media such as audiocassettes. In addition, without special measures, radio is a one-way medium; it sends a message from the instructor to the learners, but it doesn't allow learners to send messages back to the instructor. Today radio rarely

plays an overtly instructional role in this country, although educational and informational programming are staples of the National Public Radio network. However, in some developing countries where schools are scattered across isolated geographical regions, radio is used successfully for instruction.

Audio teleconferencing is a distance education technology that overcomes the one-way limitation of radio. It is an extension of a basic telephone call that permits instruction and interaction between individuals or groups at two or more locations. By using a speakerphone or more sophisticated audio equipment (e.g., microphones, amplifiers, noise filters, high-quality speakers), members of the audience can both hear and be heard. This allows for true, live, two-way interaction between two or more physically separated sites.

Audio teleconferencing is a popular and convenient way to conduct meetings or simple instructional sessions in situations where the time and cost of travel cannot be justified. When only dialogue is needed—for example, for discussion or consultation—it is ideal. A literature teacher might use it to have her students interact with the author of a book recently read by the class. A foreign-language teacher might use it to permit students to interact with a native speaker of the language. Audio teleconferencing offers the advantage of true interaction; people can talk to one another. Its chief limitation is that it is an audio-only medium. Visual elements are absent, unless print-based or graphical materials are distributed to the participating sites in advance.

Video-Based Distance Education Technologies

Video overcomes the lack of visual elements in audio-based distance education technologies. Video may be delivered over distances using a variety of means, including broadcast television, satellite and microwave transmission, and closed-circuit and cable systems. The key distinction among the various delivery systems is the degree of interactivity afforded. Options include one-way video and audio, one-way video with two-way audio, and two-way, fully interactive video.

Video, like radio, often involves a one-way transmission of information, with limited opportunities for interaction. This mode of information delivery is typical of broadcast television, and experiments in the use of television for education date back many years. Today, many schools make use of programming developed by the Public Broadcasting System as well as special programming designed specifically for schools, such as Whittle Communication's *Channel One* and CNN's *CNN Newsroom*. The obvious advantage of one-way video for distance education is its ability to cost-effectively reach a mass audience with both video and audio information. Its chief limitations are time dependence (i.e., programs are broadcast at certain times, whereas videocassettes can be used at any time that is convenient) and the lack of interaction between the instructor and the learners.

One solution to the interactivity problem associated with one-way video is to provide two-way audio accompaniment. This approach is common where video is used to deliver formal instruction, as in video-based courses. **Video teleconferencing** is an extension of audio teleconferencing that uses this concept. Audio "talk-back" capability usually is added by means of a simple telephone connection, perhaps with a speakerphone, between the originating video location and the receiving sites. With this talk-back capability, students can call the instructor with questions or comments. In other words, talk-back capability allows students to be active participants rather than passive receivers of a video-based message. This is a significant advantage compared to one-way video. Limitations include the added cost of talk-back capability, the instructor's lack of visual contact with callers, and problems of access that can arise when there are many receiving sites attempting to call a single originating site.

The latest development in video-based distance education is **two-way interactive video.** With this technology, both sending and receiving sites are equipped with cameras, microphones, and video monitors. Some means of transmission—satellite, microwave, cable, fiber optic, or digital-grade telephone line—links the two (or sometimes more) sites together. As a result, a high level of interaction is possible, with audio and video information traveling in both directions. This is the closest approximation to face-to-face instruction yet achieved by technological means.

Clearly, two-way interactive video overcomes many of the limitations of one-way distance education technologies. It promises to offer situations where an expert teacher at one location can teach a class that is physically dispersed at many different locations, complete with visual feedback and interchange among sites. Experiments in the use of two-way interactive video in K–12 schools are under way at many sites, and considerable enthusiasm surrounds the potential of this medium. However, it is important to recognize that this technology is still in its infancy. Video compression, which is needed to support two-way video transmission over telephone lines, is technically difficult and can result in problems with picture quality. In addition, two-way interactive video equipment can be quite complex and expensive to set up and operate. Schools interested in exploring this technology should consult experts in the field for advice about the best ways to proceed.

Computer-Based Distance Education Technologies

Computers represent one of the newest tools for distance education. Just as audiocassettes and videocassettes can be used to supplement print-based correspondence study, computer diskettes with instructional software can be mailed to learners for correspondence study on home computers. However, this approach doesn't use computers as telecommunication tools. There are, however, ways that computers can be used to augment audio and video telecommunication, as well as ways that computers can be used as telecommunication tools in their own right.

Audiographics refers to the use of audio teleconferencing along with the transmission of still pictures and graphics. Several techniques can be used to accomplish the transmission of images to accompany an audio teleconference. These include slow-scan video, fax, and electronic graphics tablets. At heart, each of these is really a computer-based technology, and, in fact, the most sophisticated audiographics systems include an integrated computer. Audiographics enhances the basic audio teleconference by adding the capability for use of images. However, the addition of audiographics capability significantly increases the cost of audio teleconferencing equipment. Also, when images are transmitted over standard telephone lines, voice interaction is interrupted on most audiographics systems, and transmission time can be lengthy.

Computers can also be used to enhance both one-way and two-way video teleconferencing. With special computer-based hardware, a computer signal can be "gen-locked," or integrated into a video signal. This permits a computer to be used as a presentation tool in video-based distance education. (See Chapter 9 for a more detailed discussion of the use of the computer as a presentation tool.) With this technique, the computer can be used like a slide projector to present computer text and/or graphics, or it can be used like a sketch pad to dynamically create drawings. If the aim of the distance education is to teach or demonstrate a particular computer application, this too can be accomplished. Of course, this capability adds to the cost of a video conferencing system, and there is some loss of resolution when a computer display is converted into video.

Computers themselves can be used as devices for distance education. **Computer-mediated communication (CMC)** is the term given to the use of the computer as a device for mediating communication between teacher and learners and among learners, often over distances. Two types of applications commonly used in CMC are e-mail and computer conferencing. E-mail, as you learned in Chapter 6, is similar to postal mail but faster and more effective at delivering a message from one to many. It permits personal communication between teacher and learners and among individual learners. With the growth of computer networking—particularly the Internet—e-mail is becoming an increasingly valuable communication tool in education.

Computer conferencing systems have similarities with audio and video conferencing. They permit two or more individuals to engage in a dialogue. However, computer conferencing is an asynchronous communication medium; that is, people do not converse with one another at the same time. Instead, these systems allow individuals who have access to an appropriate personal computer or terminal to type messages and post them to the conference at any time and from any place that is convenient for them. The computer maintains and organizes the messages posted by the participating individuals. So, a computer conference resembles an ongoing conversation, in printed form, where participants can drop in and out at any time without missing anything.

Computer conferencing removes barriers both of distance and of time, and it has been used successfully for distance education, particularly at the college level. However, it requires computer access and familiarity for effective use. In addition, it is limited because it is not well suited to instructional formats other than discussion, and, like audio conferencing, it lacks visual elements. However, some distance educators have begun to explore the use of CMC in conjunction with other forms of distance education, such as video. As computer networks continue to expand, it is likely that increasing use will be made of computer-based distance education, both alone and in conjunction with other distance education media.

INTEGRATING TECHNOLOGY
Spanning Distances to Impact Learning

Janette Moreno recently made use of distance education technologies to provide her advanced Spanish students with a unique educational experience. As we mentioned in the last chapter, the class had spent several weeks studying the cultures of northern and southern Spain. The students had enjoyed reading about the different areas of Spain, so Janette decided to capitalize on their enthusiasm and provide them with the opportunity to directly interact with people living in those areas. How could she manage that? She recalled how when she was young she had a pen pal in Barcelona with whom she had corresponded, exchanging an assortment of interesting items, including coins, stamps, photographs, and postcards. Janette regretted that she never had the opportunity to actually meet her pen pal, Juanita, or to speak with her in person. Yet with recent advancements in distance education technology, it was now quite feasible that students in cities across the globe from each other could actually engage in interactive conversations. She decided to check into both audio and video teleconferencing as possible means of bringing Spain into her classroom.

First Ms. Moreno contacted, via e-mail, her former professor, Señor Diego, whose wife was a high school teacher in Seville. She solicited their help in planning for a "real-time" conversation between the students in Señora Diego's English class and Janette's students in the Spanish Conversation class. However, Ms. Moreno soon discovered, after talking with local experts and Señor Diego, that a video teleconference was not feasible, as it was simply too costly. So she decided to try an audio teleconference. She checked with her principal to make certain that the school would permit a transatlantic telephone call (the Spanish Club volunteered to pay for the call), and she set the date and time with

A speakerphone allows Ms. Moreno's students to interact with students in Spain.

Señora Diego, being sure to account for the significant time difference with Seville.

The next week, using a speakerphone borrowed from the school's technology center, Ms. Moreno placed a call to Señora Diego at the time that she was scheduled to be with her advanced English students. Ms. Moreno had asked her students to prepare questions for the Spanish students, and they all took turns asking and answering questions. Janette described the interesting conversation that ensued as her students practiced their Spanish and the Spanish students practiced their English! Yet somehow they all managed to understand each other, and both sets of students were excited about having the opportunity to meet and interact each other.

As a follow-up activity, Ms. Moreno's students initiated an electronic conversation with their new pen pals via e-mail on the Internet. Thus, students got to practice their writing skills as well as their speaking skills. What was most rewarding to Ms. Moreno, however, was the fact that several of her students continued to correspond with these new friends months after they were introduced using distance education technologies.

Uses of Distance Education Technologies

Distance education technologies can be used for almost any educational goal that one would have in a typical classroom. We have already suggested some uses in our discussion above and the example of Ms. Moreno. Some common applications of distance education technologies include the following:

- reaching individuals isolated by distance or geographical barriers
- reaching nontraditional populations of learners (e.g., adult learners, homebound individuals)
- providing instruction in specialized subject areas, such as advanced physics or foreign languages, for which a local teacher might not be available
- bringing experts or other special individuals into the classroom from a distance (e.g., having the author of a children's book interact with a class of elementary students who have just finished reading the book)
- linking two classrooms together so that students can interact with one another to learn, solve problems, and communicate
- allowing teachers to consult with experts at remote locations regarding teaching practices, curriculum, research, and so on

Problems and Pitfalls

Distance education technologies offer many exciting opportunities for educators and for learners. However, they are not without cost, both in monetary terms and in difficulty. All distance education technologies entail some real monetary cost. In the case of simpler technologies, such as audio teleconferencing, this may be only the cost of a long-distance telephone call. That alone, however, may be a problem in some schools. More advanced distance education technologies, such as two-way interactive video, can be very costly. The equipment needed is expensive, and the recurring costs associated with actually connecting two sites can be quite high. Distance education technologies can be technically complex as well. While an audio teleconference may not be too difficult to set up, video conferencing requires expert assistance and may involve the coordinated efforts of local personnel, vendors, telephone company technicians, and others.

Distance education requires careful planning. This is true even for simpler forms of distance education. Most distance education media require advance scheduling of equipment and facilities.

Materials may need to be prepared in advance and mailed to participants or remote sites. In many cases, teachers need to redesign curriculum and learning activities to accommodate or take advantage of the distance education medium. Teachers may need training to effectively use distance education technologies. Learners may need assistance in learning via these unfamiliar means, and provisions for assisting participants need to be made. These may involve on-site coordinators, telephone help, e-mail, and the like. In short, there is a lot to distance education, and teachers and schools shouldn't expect to engage in it without significant effort. As with any other educational enterprise, distance education requires time, effort, commitment, and resources. The technology is only a tool that helps schools meet existing needs.

SUMMARY

In reviewing this chapter, several points should be highlighted. First, preparation plays a key role in the learning process. Preparation of oneself, the materials, the environment, and the students can all impact the effectiveness of the instruction. Additionally, this preparation is important not only for traditional teacher-dependent instruction (e.g., lectures or demonstrations) but also for those materials designed for more independent use by the students.

Second, there are a number of ways in which different media formats may be implemented within the instructional setting; however, general principles for the correct utilization of all media do exist. These include (1) becoming familiar and comfortable with the media format (e.g., previewing the materials, making sure you understand how to run the necessary machines); (2) making sure all in the audience can see and hear; and (3) emphasizing the relevance of the media and, when appropriate, highlighting what the students should expect to gain from their experience with it.

Third, specific utilization principles for all of the different media formats were noted and discussed. Then applied examples were used to illustrate how the principles could be put into practice and what problems may be encountered during utilization.

Media can be used for distance education as well as within the traditional classroom. Three broad categories of distance education technologies were discussed: audio based, video based, and computer based. Each of these technologies has advantages and disadvantages, but all share the characteristic of increasing interaction between teacher and learners across distance.

REFLECTIVE QUESTIONS AND ACTIVITIES

1. Imagine you are a media specialist for Franklin Middle School. One of the eighth-grade students at the school, Joey Miller, has come to you and asked for help on an assignment he has recently received. The assignment requirements include giving a 7-minute oral presentation on a famous person or event of the 20th century. Joey has selected the 1969 moon landing as his subject matter. He has asked for your ideas on how different forms of media could be incorporated within his oral report to enhance his presentation. What would you suggest?

2. Prepare and deliver a presentation or demonstration that involves the use of media and have it videotaped (or videotape someone else's presentation). With a group of two or three individuals, review the video and discuss the following:

   a. How did the media enhance or detract from the presentation?

   b. Was the media effectively utilized? Could it have been improved? In what ways?

   c. What additional media could have been used to facilitate learning?

3. Reflect on a classroom experience in which you were involved in the planning and delivery process. How did you prepare yourself, your materials, your environment, and your students for the experience? If you were to do it again, would you modify your preparation in any way? Why or why not?

4. Observe or participate in a distance education experience. How is it similar to and/or different from a traditional course?

INTEGRATION AND SYNTHESIS

This chapter is the first within the implementation section of this textbook. Preceding it, the focus of Chapters 5, 6, and 7 was on creating the instructional plan and then assembling, modifying, and/or developing the needed instructional materials. With that information and the background on media formats provided in Chapter 4, this chapter focused on preparing for the implementation of the materials, as well as specifying what should be done to ensure proper media utilization. Chapters 9 and 10 will also focus on the implementation of the instructional plan—specifically, with groups of students, ranging from a single individual to a large number. Throughout those chapters, information will be incorporated concerning the need for media adaptation and utilization given additional implementation situations and constraints. It should also be noted that during the section on evaluation (Chapter 13) close scrutiny will be made of the manner in which the media have been utilized and specific ways in which techniques could be improved.

SUGGESTED READINGS

Heinich, R., Molenda, M., Russell, J., & Smaldino, S. (1996). *Instructional media and technologies for learning* (5th ed.). Englewood Cliffs, NJ: Merrill/Prentice Hall.

Kemp, J. E., & Smellie, D. C. (1989). *Planning, producing, and using instructional media.* New York: Harper & Row.

Satterthwaite, L. (1990). *Instructional media.* Dubuque, IA: Kendall/Hunt.

Teague, F. A., Roger, D. W., & Tipling, R. N. (1994). *Technology and media: Instructional applications.* Dubuque, IA: Kendall/Hunt.

Volker, R., & Simonson, M. (1995). *Technology for teachers.* Dubuque, IA: Kendall/Hunt.

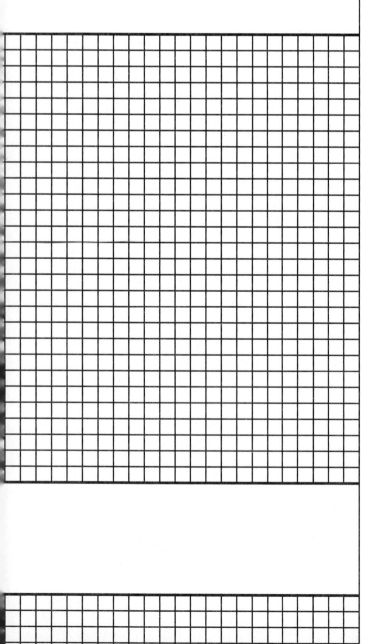

Chapter 9

Instructional Technology for Large and Small Groups

COMPUTER USE ESSENTIALS (CUE)
Words and Concepts

Composite video

RGB

Liquid crystal display
    (LCD)

Presentation software

One-computer
    classroom

OUTCOMES

After reading and studying this chapter, you will be able to:

- Describe the major utilization principles for various instructional approaches, including presentation, demonstration, discussion, cooperative learning, discovery, problem solving, and instructional games.
- Identify the benefits and challenges of working with large and small groups of students.
- Generate examples illustrating how different instructional approaches can be combined and integrated with different instructional media formats.
- Describe common types of presentation hardware and the circumstances under which each is appropriate for large-group instructional use.
- Distinguish between composite video and RGB monitors.
- Distinguish between CRT and LCD presentation devices.
- Define *presentation software* and identify its common characteristics.
- Discuss methods of using computers with small groups.
- Discuss methods of using one computer with a whole class, other than the use of presentation hardware and software.

■ INTRODUCTION

Recently a principal at Oakland Elementary stopped one of her teachers in the hallway and inquired about a series of in-service lessons she was giving for the school district. The lessons were about the integration of computers within the elementary classroom.

"So, tell me how your lessons have been going. How have they been received?" asked the principal.

"Well," replied the in-service teacher, "I've taught the class twice now, and both times the class went smoothly. It's kind of funny—even though both were about the same content, they seemed like two separate lessons. The first time I taught the lesson was during the spring in-service workshops put on by the district. There were lots of teachers attending, and I think I had over 60 come to my presentation. Typically I like to ask lots of questions and work closely with the teachers, but the sheer size of the class limited how much discussion we could have and how much time I could spend with the individual teachers. I was in a large lecture hall, and it was so big that many of the participants didn't really join in—it seemed to inhibit their asking questions and making comments. I spent most of my time demonstrating different pieces of software and lecturing on the various capabilities of the computer. Although they got the critical information, the amount of interaction wasn't what I like to have.

"During the last in-service things were quite a bit different. We held it here after school one day last week, so a much smaller number of people came to participate—only about a dozen. The smaller number of teachers allowed me to approach the content in a number of different ways. For example, at the beginning we discussed the relevant issues and information presented in the reading assignments I gave them to complete before they came. Instead of depending on me to present the information, they would discover and discuss the issues among themselves. They participated more freely, and I could prompt those who tended to hold back to join in and make a contribution. Because of the smaller numbers, they had the opportunity to experiment with different pieces of software. After previewing a specific program, they would share their critiques with the class and describe how they might apply it in their own teaching.

"Overall, I think both sessions went well. But you know, I have the feeling that those who were in the smaller class actually experienced and gained more. They seemed better prepared to apply the information in their own classrooms."

"Unfortunately, this lesson probably will continue to be taught in larger classrooms," mentioned the principal. "What do you think you might do within the larger classroom that could capture some of the experiences you had with the smaller group of students?"

"Well," replied the in-service leader, "I realize that certain bits of information can be presented quite efficiently through large presentations and demonstrations. But I'd like to find a way to use

These teachers have learned that instructional approaches may vary depending on the size of the audience.

more open discussion, more cooperative learning, and more discovery-type experiences with all of my in-service groups, regardless of their size."

Chapter 8 described ways to prepare to implement instructional materials and the manner in which different media formats are best utilized. In this chapter the focus is on another important aspect of implementation: how to effectively utilize a variety of instructional approaches.

The first questions you may ask are: Why do I need to know how to use different instructional approaches? Wouldn't it be better to learn one basic approach and be able to implement it effectively? Look back at the instructional plans outlined in Chapter 6. In each of those examples at least one type of approach was selected to be incorporated into each instructional plan. This selection was based on knowledge about the different types of approaches available (e.g., discussion, demonstration, case study, simulation, drill and practice), what they entail, and when they should be implemented. In Chapter 3 we compared the different instructional approaches to the different routes a delivery company may take to ensure that a package is delivered in the best manner. Packages are often routed in different ways because of various factors, including pickup and delivery locations, package contents, and the speed with which the package needs to arrive. A package delivery company that was restricted to a single route would be severely limited in its effectiveness. Likewise, if a teacher only knows a limited number of approaches (or routes), learning effectiveness may be severely limited. Remember that the only thing constant within education is that nothing stays the same. Learners, situations, and content are always chang-

ing, and this dictates that teachers know a variety of instructional approaches. Once we are familiar with different approaches, we can then begin to utilize the proper media formats to successfully stimulate the learning process. Integrating and coordinating the use of different media formats (Chapter 8) within the different instructional approaches (Chapters 9 and 10) are critical.

In this chapter we will look at the application of several different instructional approaches. You probably already have some experience with most of those described here—some perhaps from a teacher's perspective and others from the learner's viewpoint. It is important to remember that, just as with the selected media format, the best instructional materials will have limited effectiveness if improperly used. Throughout this chapter the emphasis will be on what should be considered in order for the approach to be most beneficial to the learner.

The selection of an appropriate instructional approach is based on several different factors. A critical factor is the size of the group that will receive the instruction. In some cases the group may be quite large (more than 25 individuals), while in other situations it may involve a smaller group (25 or fewer) or even just one person. Because the size of the group has such a large impact on the effectiveness of the selected approach, we have divided our discussion of the different approaches by the size of the group.   ■

LARGE VERSUS SMALL GROUPS OF LEARNERS: INSTRUCTIONAL IMPLICATIONS

The key advantage to delivering instruction to large groups is efficiency. With a large group, the amount of time (and the number of teachers) required to deliver instruction to a maximum number of individuals is typically reduced. By reducing the amount of time required to deliver instruction and/or the number of needed teachers, efficiency is generally increased. When efficiency is increased, the delivery cost is generally reduced. That is, if you don't have the personnel, time, or money available to teach additional classes, increasing the size of the groups receiving the instruction becomes a viable solution. For example, after the United States entered World War II, an immediate need was created for additional trained combat pilots. This problem was compounded by the lack of qualified instructors and the increased speed with which the new pilots needed to be trained. An immediate response to this need was to increase the size of the groups receiving the training. Today this same effect is seen at the school level when administrators attempt to diminish overall instructional costs by reducing the number of teachers. As teaching positions are eliminated (and the number of students remains constant or increases), the number of students within each class must increase.

If efficiency were the only instructional consideration, then most teaching situations would involve large groups of students. However, as shown by Kulik and Kulik (1989) and others (e.g., Geske, 1992; Gleason, 1986; Rivers, 1986), large-group instruction may not be as effective as instruction involving a smaller number of students. In many cases, for example, working with fewer students allows for additional approaches to be used, and this may prove more effective for student learning. In this chapter we begin with a discussion of approaches used with larger groups and describe how they are best utilized. This is followed by a section on implementing instructional approaches suitable for smaller groups of individuals. We conclude with an in-depth discussion of how the computer can be used to implement these approaches within both large and small groups of learners. In Chapter 10 our focus is specifically on approaches that work well with individuals.

WORKING WITH LARGE GROUPS OF LEARNERS
Challenges of the Large Group

When you are working with groups or classes of more than 25 learners, several things need to be considered. First is the sheer *number* involved. Increased

numbers magnify the physical demands of ensuring that all individuals can hear and see all that is being presented. Moreover, the difficulty of monitoring the level of understanding increases as the size of the group increases.

Second is the challenge of *time*. Although efficiency may increase when you present the instruction to more individuals at one time, learning can be impeded because individuals require varying amounts of time to understand what is being presented. In any teaching situation involving more than one individual, determining the optimal amount of time to devote to a specific topic or concept is difficult. This concern is magnified significantly as the number of individuals increases.

A third major challenge is the *amount of resources* required by a large group. Equipment, lab space, and handouts are just a few of the resources that can be impacted by large-group instructional situations. Advance planning is always important; however, it is compounded when the group size is increased. Groups of 20 or less, for example, usually can be accommodated within a K–6 elementary-level computer lab, but many such labs will have difficulty accommodating a class twice this size. This increased demand for resources, coupled with the additional time needed for production and distribution, can add problems and frustration to the situation.

Instructional Approaches for Large Groups
Presentation

The most common instructional approach is presentation. Standard lectures are an example of this

Classes with large numbers of students can offer special challenges to both teachers and students.

approach. Typically, in a presentation the instructional content is presented by the instructor verbally and the students listen and take notes. This approach is readily used with groups of various sizes and lends itself particularly well to larger groups of students. Moreover, video- and audiotaped presentations can also be used, either as the main way of presenting new material or as an ancillary approach for covering a specific topic in more detail.

Consider some of your own experiences with different types and qualities of presentations. First, recall a specific presentation that was a positive learning experience, and then think of one that wasn't. Compare the two and try to identify basic differences in the manner in which they were presented. What helped you learn from one presentation but impeded learning from the other? Was one easier to follow, to attend to, or to comprehend?

Consider the following list of utilization principles when you are employing the presentation approach. As you read each principle, reflect on your positive experience and determine if it was utilized in the presentation.

- *Organize in advance.* Presentations need to be organized in a logical fashion. Inform students of the purpose of the presentation. This can be accomplished by providing them with an agenda or outline of the presentation.

- *Highlight the critical points of the presentation.* This can be done in a number of ways, from showing a visual that illustrates a key point, to repeating the key points several times, to using voice fluctuation to emphasize important points, to merely declaring the point as one of central importance. Additionally, if you highlight these points early on, the audience is more apt to perceive them when they are addressed during the presentation (Fleming, 1987). These critical points will also provide a good basis for summarizing and concluding your presentation.

- *Make the presentation relevant.* Learners need to be able to relate the information from the presentation to their own experiences. This can be accomplished by asking questions such as the following: How does this relate to you? Have you ever had a similar kind of experience? How could you use this information now or in the future?

- *Involve your audience.* With large audiences, direct involvement is often difficult; however, through the use of questioning and other techniques, the audience can be encouraged to participate. For example, increase involvement by giving short in-class assignments for the students to complete

and turn in (e.g., "Write an example of what should be included in a persuasive speech."). Then pull several samples from the stack and use those as examples in your lecture. A similar technique involves the use of a "minute paper" (McKeachie, 1994). At the conclusion of your presentation give the students 1 to 3 minutes to jot down the main lecture points and to describe their perceived importance. Have students sign their papers and turn them in. This gives you a gauge of the audience's grasp of the critical points and also indicates to the learners their understanding of the content.

- *Use variety.* Attending to any one item for more than 15 to 20 minutes is difficult, even for highly motivated adult learners. Keeping things constant may be efficient, but it soon becomes boring. Variety helps to maintain attention. Variety can be added by introducing projected visuals or other forms of media, by asking questions, by incorporating relevant personal experiences, or even by making a simple change in your volume or rate of speech. But don't overdo it. Spending too much time making things "interesting" may cause the students to miss some important content.

Demonstration

Another common instructional approach used with both large and small groups is the demonstration. As we explained in Chapter 3, this is where an individual performs a procedure in order to highlight an important principle or process. For example, a cooking demonstration generally involves an individual measuring and mixing ingredients to show the steps involved in creating some type of culinary masterpiece. Other demonstrations may involve a poet reading some of her recent works, a cowboy demonstrating how to "cut" a cow from the herd, or a fifth-grade teacher demonstrating how to determine the volume of an object such as a refrigerator.

In most instructional situations, demonstrations don't stand alone; that is, they're used in conjunction with other approaches. For example, demonstrations may be incorporated into presentations. The demonstration adds variety to the presentation while at the same time providing insights into how a process is completed.

To effectively utilize the demonstration approach, follow these guidelines:

- *Plan, prepare, practice.* While planning, preparation, and practice are important for all instructional approaches, they are especially critical for demonstrations. Incomplete procedures, forgotten parts,

These students are observing a demonstration in a chemistry lab.

or a mixed-up sequence may lead to confusion instead of clarification. Students who attempt the procedure by themselves at a later time may not be able to discern if it has or has not been successfully completed. Before actually implementing the demonstration, it is wise to practice to make sure everything is in working order.

- *Ensure that all can see and hear.* With large audiences it is necessary to perform demonstrations so that all in attendance can see and hear. If materials are too small (e.g., folding of origami paper birds), the large group may have to be divided into smaller groups, the procedure may need to be repeated several times, or large-screen projection equipment with a video camera may be needed in order to enlarge the size so all can see.

- *Explain the purpose of the demonstration.* Indicate why time will be devoted to the demonstration and how it is relevant to the learners.

- *Present the demonstration in small, sequential steps.* If students are to master the steps involved and understand how they are related, it is important to break the larger process down into small, sequential steps. Use of too large or too complex steps can result in confusion and frustration.

- *Use a non-example.* An effective demonstration can be one that focuses on what *not* to do. By changing the ingredients or altering the procedures, you can quickly teach students the consequences of improper actions. This may be instructionally beneficial because it points out the differences in the overall results.

- *Conclude with a review.* Follow the demonstration with a reminder of its instructional purpose and a brief summary of how each step was completed. This will help to solidify the procedure in the learners' minds.

- *Allow the audience to practice.* It is often motivational for learners to watch a demonstration and then attempt to complete it themselves. Moreover, if those in the audience can see a successful completion by someone they perceive to be a peer, it can increase their confidence for successfully completing the task themselves.

WORKING WITH SMALL GROUPS OF LEARNERS
Benefits of the Small Group

You probably noted in the example cited earlier, when the principal was talking with the in-service teacher, that even when the content of a course remains constant, the instructional approaches may vary dramatically based on the number of students in the course. This is not to suggest that smaller groups will *always* produce greater amounts of learning. There are times when instruction to larger groups will achieve a more desirable result. However, in many situations, implementing instruction with a smaller number of learners has definite advantages.

First, from the instructor's perspective, when there are fewer students in the class you can become more familiar with them in less time. That is, you can get to know and understand the desires, goals, and needs of 20 students much more readily than you can get to know 35 or 40 students. This

USING EXAMPLES

In an earlier TIP (Chapter 4) we examined the importance of including examples within instructional materials. Let's expand on that to include some additional hints regarding how to use examples effectively.

- Begin with easy examples so students can readily identify the critical attributes of the example. Easy examples can also increase your learners' confidence.

- Present examples in different formats, such as flowcharts, pictures, live demonstrations, and real objects.

- Use non-examples (negative examples) to help highlight the critical attributes of the examples. Non-examples may have some of the same attributes of the examples but vary on those features that make the critical difference. For example, to teach the concept "red" you may present the learner with an example of a red ball. To make sure the learner understands the critical attribute of color, non-examples such as a blue ball and an orange ball may be introduced. All of the attributes in the examples and non-examples are the same, *except* for the critical attribute of color. The non-example helps to identify that critical attribute.

- Gradually increase the difficulty level of the examples until you end with more difficult ones that approximate the real-world cases that students will encounter.

familiarity allows you to monitor the progress and level of understanding achieved by each student. By knowing where individual students are in terms of their existing knowledge and where they need to be, you are in a better position to provide relevant and timely prompts, practice and appropriate feedback, and personalized encouragement. As mentioned by the in-service teacher in our introductory example, a significant difference between the two classes was the speed and degree to which she "got to know" the 12 students in her small class compared to the 60 students in her larger class.

Second is the instructor's ability to monitor the whole group's level of understanding. It is important to know when additional information is needed, when more practice is required, when the group

needs more time for projects, or when enough time has been given and it's time to move on. The larger the class, the more difficult it is to accurately infer whether the optimal time and effort on each topic have been reached. Giving too little attention to a topic can lead to misunderstanding and frustration; too much can lead to boredom.

Third, from the students' perspective, being a member of a smaller group is usually less intimidating than being part of a large group. As students become more familiar and comfortable with other members of the group, they may increase the number of comments and questions they are willing to make during the class. Moreover, they may perceive that the instructors of such groups are more approachable, so students may more readily ask for further insights and clarification.

Fourth, from a logistical standpoint, the coordination of learning experiences for a small number of students is often easier than with larger numbers. For example, requiring all participants to individually operate a piece of equipment or software requires less time and/or equipment for smaller groups than for larger ones. Within her after-school course, the in-service teacher in our example was able to give each student a piece of software to experience firsthand. Because of a shortage of time and a lack of legal copies, the students in the larger workshop only saw the software demonstrated and didn't get the chance to use it personally. The learning experience for both groups varied; for some students this would not make a noticeable differ-

Increased levels of student interaction frequently occur within smaller groups.

ence, but for others a significant difference in learning could have resulted.

Finally, there are additional instructional approaches that can be more readily used with smaller groups. In particular, the smaller group is amenable to the use of group discussion, cooperative learning, discovery learning, problem solving, simulations, and instructional games. Some of these will be explained in further detail in the next section of this chapter, while others will be expanded on in Chapter 10.

Instructional Approaches for Small Groups

As we pointed out at the beginning of Chapter 8, there are general preparation skills required before implementing instructional materials. These preparation skills are just as important for small groups as they are for large-group presentations. With each of the small-group instructional approaches listed below, you must prepare yourself, your materials, your environment, and your students before presenting the lesson. Throughout each of the following sections on the individual approaches, the manner in which this preparation must be made will be discussed.

There are several approaches that can be used effectively with small groups. These were introduced in Chapter 3, but here we will focus on how they are utilized and implemented. Specifically, we will focus on discussion, cooperative learning, discovery learning, problem solving, and instructional games.

Discussion

As defined in Chapter 3, discussion is an instructional approach that involves a group of individuals sharing information about a topic or problem. A major benefit of the discussion approach is the amount of interaction that occurs and the learning that results from that interaction. For example, in a large group the instructor may pose a question about a specific topic, and then one or two individuals may have the chance to respond. A good discussion, however, involves all of the members of the group, so that each participant has the opportunity to describe his or her thoughts on the subject, to be challenged by the thoughts of others in the group, to evaluate the responses of others, and to make further comments and share insights on the issues. The overall assumption behind the discussion approach is that interaction and active participation increase not only student content knowledge of a specific topic but also help participants develop critical-thinking and problem-solving skills.

Several different types of discussion have been found to be effective. Figure 9.1 indicates the types of discussion formats, the number of students typically involved, and how the specific format is carried out. An example of each type is also provided.

A common discussion approach is to have students debate an issue.

Figure 9.1   Discussion formats

Whole-class discussion

Number involved: An entire class of individuals (*Note:* If the size of the class goes beyond 30 individuals, it will be very difficult to get all involved and maintain their involvement to any significant degree.)

Main points:

- Generally, this is more formal, where the teacher directs a discussion by asking questions, clarifying student comments, and summarizing the students' understanding of the topic of discussion.
- In some cases, increased student interest and thinking can be achieved by presenting a unique, unusual, or opposing viewpoint for discussion. Often this can lead into other small-group debates or buzz sessions, listed below.

Example: Whole-class discussion on the effectiveness of the word processor on the enhancement of writing capabilities with elementary schoolchildren. For an opposing viewpoint, introduce some data that indicate the problems created by elementary students use of word processors.

Debate

Number involved: Two small groups (typically not more than six individuals within each group)

Main points:

- Introduce a topic for discussion—usually one that is controversial and that can be discussed from pro and con positions.
- Divide the group into two teams, with each focusing on a different side of the issue.
- Require each team to work independently to develop its position and to prepare a persuasive argument for its position.
- Allow a specific amount of time for presentation of the different positions.
- Once each side has presented its position, allow time for rebuttals.
- Once the debate has concluded, resume discussion with the whole group. Another effective technique is to have the groups switch positions after the initial debate and to argue the issues from the opposite side.

Example: Debate concerning the use of government-imposed controls for Internet information access.

Media can be used in a number of specific ways within the small-group discussion:

- *Inspiration/motivation.* Before beginning a discussion, use a still picture, an audio recording, or a short video to secure the interest and attention of the participants. For example, showing a picture of a mangled car resulting from an auto accident involving a drunken driver can be very effective in gaining the group's attention before discussing the problems of drug and alcohol abuse.

- *Presentation of information.* Different media formats can be used to open a discussion by presenting new information or by demonstrating upcoming procedural changes. Slides or overheads of last year's productivity plus company projections for the next two years can be used to effectively begin discussion or convey the information gained from smaller groups.

- *Summarization tool.* Some forms of media can be used to summarize and/or synthesize the different viewpoints of various small groups discussing aspects of a specific topic. For example, the research from several related small-group buzz sessions could be assembled into a single text format and distributed to all group members as a summary to the discussion.

The following are several important principles that need to be considered in order to ensure the successful use of the discussion format with small groups:

- *Format of the discussion.* It is important to realize that a discussion needs three basic components in order to be an effective instructional approach: (1) an introduction that helps the students determine the purpose and direction of the discussion; (2) an interactive exchange period in which all participants are encouraged to take part; and (3) a summarization and evaluation of the information and ideas discussed.

- *Adequate preparation.* Consider the following questions pertaining to preparation: How will the

---

Buzz sessions

Number involved: Small groups of four to eight individuals

Main points:

- Divide a larger group into several small groups.
- Give a specific topic to be discussed within each of the buzz sessions (the topics for each group should be related, but they do not have to be the same).
- Allow a specific amount of time.
- Instruct the groups to discuss the topic and develop a report of the results of the discussion.
- Have each group report its individual results.
- Use the reports to stimulate large-group discussion.

Example: Ask different buzz groups to discuss the various types of instructional approaches and how they could best be utilized in different types of learning situations.

Forums and Panels

Number involved: Usually two to eight individuals

Main points:

- In both cases, small groups are given a topic to research, discuss among themselves, and develop a presentation about for the whole class.
- In the forum, each individual within the group may research a separate section or subtopic within the general topic.
- During the presentation, each member of the forum presents his or her own portion of the topic and later fields questions from the listeners about his or her individual research.
- In the panel format, each member may research the same topic and present his or her own view of the topic. These different views can be used to stimulate large-group discussions.

Example: Forum discussion involving three individuals discussing the potential impact of Internet access on teachers in elementary, secondary, and postsecondary education.

---

groups be introduced to the topic and motivated to discuss it? How will participants be assigned to their individual small groups? How will participation be monitored and encouraged throughout the discussion process? What will be done to make sure that the discussion groups are striving toward the specific learning goal? If they become sidetracked, what can be done to get them back on track?

- *Active participation.* The exchange of ideas among group members is a critical factor in learning from discussion, so the participation of each group member should be strongly encouraged, if not required. To facilitate this you should try to keep the size of the small discussion groups to between four and eight individuals. As group size increases, individual members may begin to withdraw from active participation. Additionally, the members are more likely to participate when they understand the purpose and goals of the group and when they have specific background and experiences related to the topic.

- *Acceptance of ideas.* As individuals participate in discussions, differences of opinions naturally occur. Such differences should be encouraged by the instructor and respected by other members of the group.

- *Goals of the discussion.* Often the goals of the discussion go beyond simply learning new content. This approach may also be used to (1) arouse interest for a new topic; (2) explore ideas and ways to identify and/or solve problems; (3) improve leadership, organization, verbal communication, and listening skills; and (4) develop acceptance and tolerance for other viewpoints.

Other factors to think about:

- Consider the age and maturity levels of the students. Typically, the lower the levels, the more structure and guidance needed within the discussion.

- Questions are often needed to stimulate the discussion, so prediscussion questions should be prepared.

- Discourage dominance of the discussion by a few students.
- Impose time limits to keep the group on task.
- Include follow-up activities that enhance the main topics of the discussion.

Cooperative Learning

Cooperative learning refers to a small group of individuals working toward a common goal or task. This approach is specifically designed to encourage students to work together, drawing on their individual experiences, skills, and levels of motivation to help each other achieve the desired result. The central idea is that cooperation and interaction allow students to learn from several sources, not just the teacher, while also providing opportunities for sharing one's own abilities and knowledge. Most forms of cooperative learning are implemented with groups of three to seven members. Research results indicate that cooperative learning leads to increased levels of student interaction and academic achievement, as well as improved student behavior and attitudes toward class (Johnson & Johnson, 1984; Qin, Johnson, & Johnson, 1995; Slavin, 1990a).

When cooperative learning is chosen as the optimal approach for teaching a specific topic, implementing and utilizing this approach require forethought and practice for maximum effectiveness. Several key implementation principles should be noted before utilizing cooperative groups:

- *Build an atmosphere that encourages participation and cooperation.* Help the students realize the advantages of working together as a team. This can be facilitated by requiring that all members of the group have roles to fill that are necessary for the group's success. Some possible roles may include being the group recorder, the observer, the materials monitor, the encourager, and so on. Stress the importance of the need to support others within the group and the interdependence of the group members. Help students understand that everyone's role is important and that they are responsible for carrying out their assigned tasks. Create a physical environment (e.g., pushing the desks together) in which students come to view themselves as a single group. Structure the task in such a way (e.g., a single paper or presentation) that all group members must be involved with the same production.
- *Teach group processes to the students.* Effective group cooperative efforts do not happen by chance. To increase the likelihood of the group's success, members should be taught to seek clarification and justification when needed; to offer to explain and clarify; to criticize ideas, not people; and to summarize out loud in order to check the understanding of other group members.
- *Learn to facilitate, not dominate.* It is important for the teacher to take on the role of monitor, facilitator, and guide instead of director. Groups will need more guidance during the initial stages, but as the group progresses you should pull back and let the cooperation and interdependence among the individual group members develop.

Cooperative groups have several uses, including facilitating learning about a specific topic, promoting positive interactions and interdependence among groups of students, and teaching important social and communication skills. Another important reason for using such an approach is to teach individual accountability. When the input of each individual within a group is needed for the success of the group as a whole, individuals learn to be accountable for their actions. Finally, cooperative groups teach the value of group processing and the ability to generate and work together to achieve a better answer to various problems or tasks.

Review the following two examples and consider the things that could be learned by using a cooperative learning approach.

Example 1: Recently the four members of the fifth-grade Elementary Ecology Club and their advisor went on a field trip to view a creek near their school. Upon close observation of the creek, the students noticed patches of oil floating in the slow-moving water. After further investigation the club advisor decided it would be a good project for the group to research what was occurring and to determine what could be done about it. Each group member was given a specific task. One student was to determine who should be contacted at the public health department. Another was to find out what the oily substance was and determine how it could have been introduced to the creek. Still another was in charge of identifying potential ways of publicizing what was occurring and determining the potential impact on the animals and community. The fourth was to review what could be done to raise public awareness.

Example 2: In a high school art appreciation class, several groups of students were assembled to learn about the different forms of creative art. Each group was composed of three students: one who was accomplished at a musical instrument, another who had the ability to paint, and a third who had the

(a)   (b)

Fifth graders in this cooperative group are working (a) to gather data and then (b) complete their individual roles.

ability to sculpt. The group's task was to learn about the different art forms and their relationships.

Review these two examples and ponder the practical implementation challenges that had to be addressed in order for the cooperative group exercises to be effective. Consider the following questions in order to ensure the effectiveness of this approach:

- How will the learners be informed of the task? Will they see the need to work together as a group?
- How will group cohesiveness be achieved? What will be done to make sure all group members participate and feel needed?
- In what ways can the group be assembled?
- How will the roles within the individual group be distributed and completed?
- How will the directions be relayed to the group?
- How will the group members be monitored, and how will they be guided to remain on task?
- What measures will be taken to make sure that all individuals carry their fair share of the work and that no one will be allowed to "hitchhike" through the project?

As more and more information becomes available for our use, and as more information is required to make proper choices and judgments, businesspeople and educators alike are realizing the need for students to be able to work cooperatively in groups. As this trend continues, the need for the use of cooperative learning—both as an approach to learning content and as an approach to improving communication—will be increased.

Discovery

In many situations, student learning can be achieved by simply hearing or reading the needed information. To learn about ecosystems, for example, a biology student may read a text, listen to a teacher, or view a video. Implementing a discovery instructional approach, however, places students in the actual situation so that they can learn through personal experience. The biology student in this case could learn about an ecosystem by actually walking the shoreline of a nearby marsh to see, hear, feel, and smell firsthand the relationships among the plants, animals, and physical features of the landscape.

Such experiences generally require learners to develop and use observation and comparison skills. Moreover, like a detective, the student must learn to follow leads and clues and record the findings in order to generate an explanation of what was experienced. This approach has been shown to be highly motivational, because students experience firsthand how things work, how features are related, and how potential explanations can be formulated and revised. In many cases, the "discoveries" made are directly tied to the world of the student (e.g., taking apart a toaster to see how the heating elements are structured to cook the toast evenly; building a rope bridge to cross a mountain stream), where they are more relevant and thus can be easily remembered.

Even though the emphasis of this approach may be on the development of critical thinking through a comparative type of learning, it can be useful for groups of all ages. For example, the kindergarten child may find it fascinating to "discover" the utility of wheels and how they can make pulling and pushing easier. When faced with the job of pulling a box of wood blocks across a carpeted floor, the 5-year-old may discover what happens when wheels are attached to the bottom of the box. In a similar way, a high school physics student may design an experiment to "discover" the relationship between mass, force, and friction and how the relationship is altered through the use of rollers or wheels. In both cases, the students are given the opportunity to experience what is occurring—to observe, draw conclusions, and make inferences.

When you are implementing this approach, pay attention to several key principles:

- *Thorough and detailed planning is required.* Think about Christopher Columbus, Marco Polo, Marie Curie, Neil Armstrong, and other explorers. In all cases, long hours of planning and preparation were required before discoveries could be made. Similarly, it is important to remember that this approach to learning will require advance planning and preparation in order to allow the learner/discoverer to be in a position to discover. Such planning may require a determination of the general purpose of the exercise, the conditions that need to exist, the types of equipment and other resources that need to be available, and the potential types of guidance, help, or encouragement needed. In many cases this planning and preparation should be an important part of the learning experience for the student. In other cases, efficiency may require that the advance planning be completed by the teacher. For example, the biology teacher who walks through the marshlands prior to taking her class on a discovery field trip may find certain areas more accessible and thus better for observing the inner workings of the different ecosystems. Additionally, noting the different types of equipment (e.g. nets, binoculars, shovels, boots) that may be needed by the students will facilitate the discovery process and optimize the educational experience.

- *Be prepared for all types of "discoveries."* Combining unique students with unique learning environments often leads to unique results. Be prepared for all types of standard and not-so-standard findings when students are allowed to make their own observations and draw their own conclusions. A goal of discovery learning is to create a situation in which students can explore events and check out different explanations. Discouraging students from alternative findings or explanations may inhibit their future desire and motivation for exploration.

- *Encourage students to share their discoveries.* Through the experience of discovery, students often gain both great insights into their subject and great enthusiasm for what they have learned. These important insights and feelings should be shared with other individuals. Encouraging peer or reciprocal teaching may facilitate learning in a couple of ways (Brown & Palincsar, 1987). First, it helps those making the original discoveries to think through and further analyze what they experienced. Teaching other learners about their discovery requires additional thought about their own methodology, results, and conclusions. That is, they must fully understand what they have done before they can adequately explain it to others. Second, those individuals receiving the information from the original discoverer have the opportunity to not only learn about the discovery but also to hear it from the one who made it. This often creates a sense of excitement for the subject matter that may not be generated by reading a book or watching a video. Moreover, levels of confidence in one's abilities may increase by observing a peer successfully complete a task. The old adage "If he (she) can do it, I can do it" can be generated through peer teaching.

When implementing the discovery approach, you should take the following factors into consideration:

- Setting up the full experience is generally easier to accomplish for a small number of students (less than 12) than for larger groups. Many different discoveries can be made with larger groups, but with more individuals involved at any one time more difficulties are possible.

- Students can be placed in pairs or trios to work together on tasks. This encourages them to question each other and help each other "see" what has occurred or what needs to be explained.

- This approach takes more time than others do.

- Make sure that the students understand that "one right answer" does not exist. They may need instruction and examples on how to observe, compare, and evaluate phenomena.

- Constantly encourage and reward students for being inquisitive, for asking questions, and for trying new approaches.

- Remember that this approach, when successfully implemented, will produce unforeseeable situations and results. Be prepared to examine situations you may not have thought about previously.

Problem Solving

The real world is filled with problems that need resolution. Some problems may be very well defined (e.g., determining if purchasing a new outfit is within one's current monetary means; finding the best route to travel to a nearby art museum), while others may be somewhat ill-defined (e.g., determining how to increase neighborhood safety; finding the "best" postsecondary education). To fully participate in this world, learners need to be able to analyze problems, form tentative hypotheses, collect and interpret data, and reach some type of logical conclusion about how the problem might be solved. The instructional approach of problem solving focuses on developing and enhancing these abilities in students.

Most of the instructional approaches previously discussed are primarily designed to assist learners in learning some type of content. With the problem-solving approach, the focus is somewhat altered. In problem solving the emphasis is on teaching the learner how to learn (Orlich, Harder, Callahan, Kauchak, & Gibson, 1994, p. 296). Because we are faced with novel problems throughout our lives, an important skill is knowing how to approach problems and how to increase the probability that a good solution will be selected. In many cases the problem posed to the learners (as they are learning how to problem-solve) is not of critical importance; however, the process of reaching the solution is. For example, many of us have encountered contrived problems such as the following:

> Three tennis professionals—Larry, Arthur, and Don—are counting up their money for the year. Arthur is a bachelor. The oldest of the three has a daughter learning to play tennis. Larry earns the least money but is not the youngest. The largest income is earned by the oldest. List the tennis professionals in order of increasing age.

The instructional goal for using this problem generally doesn't concern how much money Larry, Arthur, and Don actually make, or even how old they are. What is instructionally important is how one perceives the problem, identifies the important information, eliminates possibilities, and generates and tests potential conclusions. Problem solving requires higher-level cognitive functioning, including analyzing, generalizing, and synthesizing.

To fully utilize this approach, the following implementation principles should be considered:

- *Clarify the problem when necessary.* Especially with less mature learners, one of the most difficult parts of problem solving is getting a true, accurate picture of the problem itself. In the initial stages of problem solving the teacher's role often involves providing assistance in identifying and outlining the specific problem. One should be wary, however, not to overdo the clarification. If the problem is explained too thoroughly, the answer doesn't require any thought or work by the student.

- *Present problems in the proper sequence.* Beginning with more defined, easier, or familiar problems and then adding successively more difficult or less-defined problems can facilitate the learning process.

- *Make sure problems fit the skill and maturation level of the students.* For example, asking elementary students to review the trade differences between the United States and Japan and suggest ways to improve trade relations may be beyond their scope of understanding and definitely beyond their desire for understanding. However, presenting the students with a scenario involving a group of children who are learning to trade baseball cards, toys, or candy will be more relevant and appropriate.

- *Use additional resources and materials when necessary.* It is important that students have access to additional resources, as well as instruction on how those resources can be used most effectively.

- *Keep groups small.* Because of the uniqueness of the potential solution paths to the problems and the time required to complete the various steps, a smaller number of students is often essential.

- *Help students understand the need for generalization.* Students must recognize that problem solutions are generally unique and that no single answer works for all problems. This connotes an emphasis on learning general problem-solving strategies and procedures and adapting them as each new situation dictates.

To review and synthesize how these principles of utilization and implementation can be incorporated, read the following example of a classroom teacher who successfully integrated a problem-solving approach.

Sister Anne is a sixth-grade science teacher at St. John's Catholic School. During a recent unit in science, she wanted her students to directly experience the impact of human population on the environment. She posed the following problem to her group of students: "Does acid rain have an impact on the environment?" She quickly felt the need to clarify and redefine the question at her students' level, so she revised her question to "In what ways does acid rain impact the growth patterns of common outdoor plants?" She asked her students to design an experiment that would provide an answer to that question. To guide their work Sister Anne gave them a handout that explained the list of problem-solving steps:

Step 1: Identify all of the major components within this problem.

Step 2: Define each of those major components.

Step 3: Break the problem down into subparts and visualize (draw) components and their relationships.

Step 4: Determine how to examine the important relationships.

Step 5: Collect data.

Step 6: Evaluate and synthesize the data for meaningful relationships.

Step 7: Draw conclusions based on the data.

Step 8: Explain your conclusions to other class members.

In addition, Sister Anne took the time to go to the school and city libraries to review the information available on acid rain. With those additional references, she was in a position to refer her students to several areas of research if they needed them. She realized that this task would be teaching more than a single skill and that it would take additional time and effort by both the students and herself. The benefit of this approach was that the students were able to investigate, in depth, a specific topic (acid rain) while engaging in an investigative process by which they could look at different relationships and determine potential solutions. It was anticipated that this process would transfer to other problems that the students would subsequently encounter in other courses.

Instructional Games

Read the following two learning situations and reflect on the subsequent questions.

Situation A: A group of high school chemistry students is given the assignment to memorize 15 element names and their associated numbers and symbols from the periodic table. The teacher has given each student a set of flash cards with the element's name and number listed on one side and the symbolic label listed on the other.

Situation B: A similar assignment has been given to another group of students. In this group, how-

ever, the teacher explains that all individuals who can demonstrate the completion of the task with 100% accuracy within a 30-minute time limit will get 10 points added to their next exam score.

If you watched these two groups perform this activity, do you think that those in one group would invest more effort than those in the other? Would one group of learners rate this activity as more appealing than the other group would? If you were confronted with this task and had the chance to select which group you worked with, which would it be? Why?

From past experience we have learned that Situation B is generally preferred. Why? Are the extra points really that important? What caused the possibility of receiving the extra points to take on such a high value?

As we pointed out in Chapter 3, whenever you deal with the topic of games, motivation is quickly brought to the forefront. Games have certain attributes and qualities that can increase our motivation for a task. The two situations mentioned above illustrate this. Although both present the same basic learning task, in one situation the overall task challenge was increased by establishing a specific performance criterion goal coupled with a reward for the successful completion of that goal. Both the extrinsic reward and the setting of the attainable goal are attributes that have been shown to increase students' level of challenge and thus their level of motivation.

Games have two key attributes: first, a clearly defined set of rules that outline how the game will be played, what actions are and are not allowed, what constitutes winning the game, and what the end result will be for a winning performance; and second, elements of competition or challenge wherein players compete against themselves, against other individuals, or against a standard of some type (Merrill et al., 1992, p. 109). These attributes can be incorporated into many instructional situations in order to increase student motivation and levels of effort for specific learning tasks. Many different types of games exist, and these can be adapted to include relevant content. The hope, therefore, is to capitalize on the benefits of the gaming elements so as to increase the amount or quality of learning that occurs. To increase this likelihood, the following implementation strategies should be considered:

- *Make sure that you fully understand the abilities of the members of the target audience and their level of rule comprehension.* Instructional games are not effective if the players do not or cannot comprehend how the game is to be played. Often practice or trial games—with an emphasis on rule understanding—need to be attempted before the actual game is started.

- *Have a clear concept of the instructional goal of the game.* Ask yourself, What do the students need to learn, and how will a game help accomplish that? Make sure to communicate the answer to these questions to the learners.

- *For games to be motivational, they need to be challenging but not impossible.* Make sure that all participants perceive that their efforts could produce the desired result.

- *Match the content to be taught with an appropriate game format.* For example, for memorization-type tasks a relevant game would be one that included high amounts of repetitive practice (e.g., math drills with a timer and accuracy scorecard). Likewise, for a skill such as learning to shoot a foul shot in basketball, a contest for shooting free throws would be an appropriate match. Many familiar games (e.g., tic-tac-toe) can be effectively adapted for instructional situations.

- *Develop the procedures and rules for how the game should proceed and how all scoring should occur.* With a new game it always helps to have written rules. If possible (and especially with a new game), have a pilot group of students try out the game to see if there are any problems or if further clarification is needed.

- *Make sure the game is structured so active involvement is maintained at the highest possible level for all participants.* If groups are too large and long waits occur between "turns," the effectiveness of the game will wane.

- *Allow enough time to play but not so much that students grow tired of the game.*

- *Make sure the game is not creating additional problems.* For example, response speed can be an important element within a game. However, if speed requirements lead to decrements in the quality of student responses (e.g., sloppy handwriting), adjustments to the game are needed.

- *Include a debriefing or discussion following the conclusion of the instructional game.* This should focus on the instructional content and value of the game and why it was completed. Make sure the students understand that their participation in the game had an instructional purpose, and summarize what they should have learned from it.

INTEGRATION: INCREASING VARIETY AND EFFECTIVENESS

Combining Instructional Approaches

At this point in the chapter we would like to reemphasize the complexity of learning. As we stated in the initial chapters, learning is not easily identified, measured, or designed. Because of the variations one encounters with different individual learners, with different settings, and with different types of content, it is important to realize that the implementation of any one approach doesn't exclude other approaches. That is, once one approach is selected, it doesn't mean that another approach may not be equally effective, and it also doesn't mean that these approaches cannot be combined. Some of the most powerful instruction is that which accounts for the various needs of the learners and incorporates a number of approaches within the same materials. For example, imagine placing students within cooperative learning groups with the task of researching and collecting data on a specific problem (i.e., combining cooperative groups and problem solving). Then expand this experience by having the different groups discuss and/or debate their findings with other groups that have carried out their own investigations. In another situation, you might expand your presentation to a large group by demonstrating a specific procedure and then dividing students into smaller groups to play a game that requires use of the new concepts and procedures introduced during your presentation and demonstration. Again, combining the approaches can lead to a more powerful learning experience for the students.

Combining Instructional Approaches and Media

Just as it is important to combine different instructional approaches, it is also important to consider how media might be combined with the various instructional approaches. Across the different approaches, one or more different types of media may be needed. Each medium has its own advantages and limitations (see Chapters 7 and 8), and, based on the activity, learners, situation, and content, the selection of medium may vary. Table 9.1 lists the approaches discussed in this chapter and gives several examples of how media could be incorporated.

INTEGRATING TECHNOLOGY
Videodiscs and Classroom Presentations

People of all ages love to tell jokes, and students in Ms. Moreno's class are no different. Janette

Table 9.1   Examples of combining instructional approaches and media

Approach	Example of combining media with approach
Presentation	• Audiotape of John F. Kennedy's inaugural address for a high school history course • Taped video presentation on the topic of weightlessness given by shuttle astronauts while on a shuttle mission
Demonstration	• Video of steps involved in making a model rocket • Slides of finished products that show the end result of a wood-carving demonstration • Use of a cadaver to demonstrate how leg muscles are attached to bone
Discussion	• Review of a television documentary on the problems created by illegal immigration, followed by a debate on the issues involved • Use of a visual depicting an abused child to stimulate buzz group discussions on ways to eliminate child abuse
Cooperative learning	• Small-group development and demonstration of a filmstrip showing how balloons are manufactured • Use of overhead transparencies to present results of a group research project involving how to feed and care for exotic zoo animals
Discovery	• Use of an interactive video multimedia program investigating all aspects of the *Titanic*—its voyage, crew, and passengers • Dissection of a sheep brain to locate and identify the different lobes and fissures
Problem solving	• Use of a software package to present logic problems and then provide specialized feedback as each section is attempted • Display of math story problems and possible solution techniques on a classroom bulletin board
Instructional games	• Use of audiotaped instructions on how to play a game involving the rescue of members of a disabled space station • Use of a computer game that tracks a criminal across several countries and cultures of the world

often uses jokes and humorous stories to catch her students' attention and to help them notice subtle differences in meaning, especially those due to the context and manner in which a particular message is delivered. Recently, Janette acquired a wonderful videodisc that includes numerous excerpts from a couple of popular Spanish sitcoms. Her students love to watch these excerpts and try to figure out why a particular clip is so funny. This usually involves stopping the videodisc to examine the speakers' body language and facial gestures, as well as the general context.

Ms. Moreno's class is incorporating the use of videodisc technology to study nonverbal communication.

Just last week, Ms. Moreno used these clips as the basis for a cooperative group activity. She divided her students into groups of three and sent them to the computer lab to view different segments of the disc in order to determine what was funny about their particular clip. Students had to focus not only on the words being spoken, but also on the surrounding situation, the obvious and subtle movements of the speakers, and facial expressions and hand gestures. Group members were required to come to consensus on an interpretation of the situation and then to present the clip and their explanation of it to their classmates. This activity had the effect of directing students' attention to some of the subtleties of the Spanish language while involving them in a very enjoyable group activity.

Computer Use ESSENTIALS

In the last chapter you learned about using many of the common tools available for instructing groups of learners: the chalkboard, the overhead projector, the slide projector, video and film, and so on. Like many of the other traditional tools we have examined in this book, these have been available to teachers for many years. Today, as in so many other spheres, things are beginning to change because of the computer. The computer, when used in conjunction with a large-screen monitor or projection device, is emerging as a powerful group presentation tool that combines many of the features and capabilities found in traditional presentation tools. In this CUE we will examine the hardware and software that support the computer as a group presentation tool.

As we have seen, one of the real strengths of the computer is its flexibility. Using the computer as a presentation tool is not the only way that it can be used with groups. The computer can be the focal point of small-group cooperative learning activities. In addition, in many school settings today, only a single computer may be available for in-class use. Besides whole-class presentations, are there other ways that a single computer can be used with a classroom full of students? Certainly, the answer is yes! In the latter part of this CUE we will examine some of the ways that a single computer can be used with groups.

COMPUTERS AS PRESENTATION TOOLS

The basic concept behind the use of the computer as a presentation tool is quite simple. Normally a personal computer is designed to be used by an individual. Display screens are of a size that is appropriate for viewing by an individual, although small groups of students (typically no more than two to four) may be able to work productively when clustered around a single personal computer. In order to use the computer as a presentation tool for a large group, some mechanism is needed for making the screen image larger so that it can be comfortably viewed by the group. This necessitates special hardware—a large monitor or display device.

With special hardware, the computer's display screen can be effectively shown to a group. Regular computer software can be displayed. For example, a teacher can demonstrate how to use the key functions of a database program to her students, or she might run through an educational program with the entire class. In addition, a special category of software called presentation software is now available. A teacher can use presentation software on the computer in lieu of overhead transparencies, slides, or other more traditional presentation tools to create engaging and even interactive presentations for classes or other groups.

Computer Presentation Hardware

In order to make the computer's display visible to a group, one of several special hardware options is required. The choices include use of a large computer monitor, a large television or video monitor (usually requiring special computer-to-video conversion hardware), a video projector, and a liquid crystal display (LCD) projector or panel. Let's look at each of these options.

Large Computer Monitors

As you learned in Chapter 4, the display screen or monitor on desktop personal computers is often called a CRT (cathode-ray tube); it is based on the same fundamental technology as a television set. The dimensions of CRT screens, like those of televisions, are measured along the diagonal. On most personal computers the CRT is relatively modest in size. Typical display screens on desktop computers measure from 12 to 15 inches (laptop computers have even smaller screens). While sufficient for individual work, these are not big enough for large-group presentations. However, larger computer monitors, ranging from 16 to 21 inches, are available. On the upper end, these rival the dimensions of many home and classroom television sets but have much better resolution.

These oversized monitors are designed primarily for individuals who want a lot of personal com-

Large-screen monitors can facilitate presentations, demonstrations, and other classroom activities.

puter screen real estate. For example, they can be used with word-processing software to display two pages of a document at once. However, they can also be used for presentations to groups. These monitors can be utilized effectively with some groups when larger type fonts are displayed, although it is important to keep in mind that even the largest of these monitors cannot be used effectively with groups of more than about 20 or 25. Like large television sets, these oversized monitors are big, heavy, and not particularly portable. In addition, they can be quite expensive—in some cases thousands of dollars—and may require that a special video board (at additional expense) be added to your computer. So, although a large monitor may be an option in some circumstances, it is typically one of the least desirable ones.

Large Televisions or Video Monitors

Most schools possess large televisions or video monitors, often mounted in classrooms or available on carts, for use with VCRs or other video programming. For classroom use, monitor sizes begin at 21

inches and go on up; 25-, 27-, and 30-inch monitors are common. Large-screen televisions, although less common, can also be used for group presentations.

For many years, schools have been interested in using existing televisions or video monitors with computers for large-group presentations. Interestingly, with one of the first personal computers, the Apple II, this was a snap. The Apple II computer used what is known as **composite video,** a system commonly used on VCRs and other video equipment, in which all of the video information is carried by one signal that is sent to the monitor through a single cable. This meant that Apple II output could be fed directly into any video monitor, and it required only an inexpensive adapter to connect to a standard television set. Thus many schools were able to use their Apple II computers with large video monitors or televisions in their classrooms.

Newer personal computers, in the quest for better screen resolutions and control of color, adopted a different way of generating screen output. Called **RGB,** this system used three separate signals to control display of the three primary colors (red, green, and blue) in the monitor. This resulted in sharper images and better color, but it required special RGB monitors. Consequently, personal computers quickly became incompatible with ordinary video monitors.

Today most personal computers are incapable of working with standard video monitors or televisions without special hardware. (Two exceptions are the Commodore Amiga and Apple's Macintosh AV.) That's the bad news. The good news is that a number of vendors are now supplying the special hardware needed to convert the computer's output to standard video. These devices, which can be plug-in boards for the computer or external boxes that connect to the computer and its regular monitor, convert the computer's RGB signal into video (often referred to as NSTC, the U.S. video standard). Most of these products, which have prices starting at a few hundred dollars, provide composite video output, and some have S-video (super VHS video) output as well. This output can be directed to a large video monitor or video projector for group presentations.

These computer-to-video conversion devices provide one convenient option for teachers who wish to display computer images in the classroom. However, they have a disadvantage. Standard video cannot reproduce the high resolutions found on most personal computers today. As a result, when the computer image is converted to video there is some degradation of the image. Images may become somewhat fuzzy, and small text fonts are likely to become completely unreadable. To compensate for this loss of resolution, large text fonts (e.g., 18 point) should be selected when the computer is used with a video monitor.

Video Projectors

Video projectors provide the capability to project a video image onto a screen, much like a motion picture projector projects an image onto a screen. Because video projectors are capable of producing very large images—in some cases 20 feet or more across—these devices provide an excellent option for very large groups. Indeed, they are popular in university lecture halls, auditoriums, and other facilities that seat large numbers of people.

The capabilities and costs of video projectors vary considerably. On the low end are single-lens units that are capable of accepting composite video. Such units can be used with the computer-to-video conversion hardware described above. Better projectors use three separate lenses (one each for red, green, and blue) and are capable of accepting computer RGB output directly (usually with some sort of adapter). These better projection units are capable of faithfully reproducing the computer's output

on a large screen. As such, they are one of the best options when computer projection is needed with very large groups. However, these devices can be very expensive (many thousands of dollars), and sometimes frequent maintenance is required to keep the image well focused. All video projectors function best in darkened rooms, although many are sufficiently bright for use in subdued lighting.

Liquid Crystal Display (LCD) Panels and Projectors

As you learned in Chapter 4, laptop computers do not use CRT displays; they use **liquid crystal display (LCD)** technology. This technology relies on special materials that can transmit or block light based on the application of an electrical signal to the screen location of a single pixel. This technology has been adapted to produce large-group display devices. LCD panels are compact, flat units that mount on top of overhead projectors. LCD projectors use the same basic technology but include a built-in light source. These are the newest, and in many ways the most desirable, of the hardware options for large-group presentations.

A variety of LCD panels and projectors, distinguished by a number of features, are now available. There are both monochrome (black and white) and color units. Like monitors, color units are quite a bit more expensive than their monochrome counterparts. Color units are distinguished from one another by the number of colors supported, screen resolutions, and the underlying technology. LCD panels

An LCD projector can be used to display computer output to large or small groups.

and projectors use either passive matrix or active matrix technology. Active matrix, the more costly of the two, produces a brighter image that is refreshed (updated) more rapidly. This feature is important when tracking rapid motion such as the movement of a mouse cursor on the computer screen. The best LCD units today can reproduce both IBM-type and Macintosh screens (adapters may be needed to connect to specific computer models) as well as full-motion video.

LCD panels are made to work with overhead projectors, one of the most common of all educational tools. The image from an LCD panel can be projected to any size that the overhead projector will support, so, in image size, LCD panels rival projection systems. In addition, they are clearly the most portable of all of the large-group presentation options. A laptop computer and an LCD panel make for a completely portable computer presentation tool package. Further, LCD panels are frequently less expensive than video projection units; costs range from several hundred dollars for basic monochrome panels to several thousand for color panels.

However, LCD panels do have some limitations. Image brightness is not as good as with video projectors. Even when LCD panels are used with the recommended extra-bright overhead projectors, mostly darkened rooms are needed for optimal viewing. In addition, LCD panels suffer from thermal sensitivity. On a hot overhead projector, the image can become "washed out" or the panel damaged with extended exposure to heat. Most LCD panels use fans and/or specially treated glass to minimize the effects of heat. Their portability, while usually an advantage, can create problems. Because LCD panels are handled, there is a greater likelihood that one could be dropped and damaged, and their portability makes them a ready target for theft.

LCD projectors tend to be brighter than LCD panels, so they are more effective in better-lit rooms. While bulkier than panels, LCD projectors are nonetheless portable. Like panels, LCD projectors are made to be computer-compatible; other than adapters, special hardware is not normally required for computer connection. Because they include the light source, LCD projectors are somewhat more expensive than comparable LCD panels. Both LCD panels and LCD projectors offer attractive options for classroom display of computer images.

Computer Presentation Software

As we noted above, with proper presentation hardware any computer image can be displayed to a group. Many teachers demonstrate the use of specific pieces of software using some kind of display hardware. However, as computer display devices have proliferated, a special class of computer software has emerged to take advantage of this capability. **Presentation software** is computer software designed for the production and display of computer text and images. It is intended primarily to replace the functions typically associated with traditional presentation tools such as the slide projector and the overhead projector. Popular presentation packages include Microsoft PowerPoint, Aldus Persuasion, Lotus Freelance Graphics, IBM Storyboard Live, Asymetrix Compel, WordPerfect Presentations, Harvard Graphics, and Gold Disc's Astound. The following are some common features of presentation software:

- *Slide format.* Most presentation software packages are organized around the concept of a slide, analogous to a photographic slide. What appears on a single computer screen is treated as though it were a photographic slide. Individual slides may have any of a number of elements, including text, graphics, bullets for emphasis, and multimedia elements (see Figure 9.2). Once individual slides have been created, the set of slides can be arranged—just as a photographer would order his or her slides—to create the presentation.

- *Slide templates.* In order to simplify the process of creating the slides, slide templates are usually provided. These templates have preselected formatting, artwork, fonts, text styles, bullets, special effects, and so on. The user simply selects the desired template and enters the information; the program automatically applies the template's formatting.

- *Slide special effects.* To make for an engaging presentation, text can be bulleted. In many cases, bullets or text can be animated or made to appear point by point. When going from one slide to another, presentation packages allow for any one of a number of special effects, including dissolving, wiping, and fading.

- *Printing.* Presentation packages usually allow the user to create a printed copy of the slides, either full size (one slide per page) or in a reduced-size format that permits multiple slides to be printed on each page.

- *Disk storage and retrieval.* Of course, like other computer tools, presentation software allows information to be stored on, or retrieved from, disk.

- *Text entry and editing.* Because text is usually an integral element of most presentations, presentation packages provide basic text entry and edit-

Figure 9.2 Screen from Microsoft *PowerPoint*, a presentation program

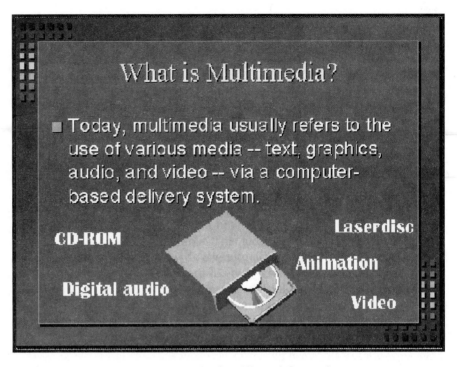

Note. Screen shot reprinted with permission from Microsoft Corporation.

ing features. A wide variety of fonts and type styles is generally included. Basic word processor–like functionality is provided. Some packages provide a "chalk" function that allows the user to write on a slide during a presentation by using the mouse like chalk on a chalkboard.

- *Graphics.* Graphics, too, are an important part of most presentations. Typical packages provide a basic set of drawing or painting tools. Chart- and graph-production capabilities are common. In addition, most presentation packages permit the importing of graphics created in other packages.

- *Multimedia elements.* The latest trend in presentation packages is the inclusion of multimedia elements. These may include digitized audio, digitized video, hypermedia links, and control of external devices such as audio CDs. With full multimedia capability, presentation packages now include the functions of slide projectors, overhead projectors, tape recorders, and VCRs all rolled into one.

Using Presentation Hardware and Software in the Classroom

We have introduced presentation hardware and software here because they are excellent tools for the teacher to use in large-group instruction. Obviously, a major use of these tools is in support of lectures or other presentations to groups. In addition

to presentations in the classroom, these are excellent tools to employ for presentations to school boards, at professional meetings, and the like. In addition, there are other ways that the tools can be used. When doing brainstorming or other development activities with an entire class, for example, presentation software is an excellent tool for recording thoughts and ideas. It can be used in place of the chalkboard or overhead projector for drawing or writing information. A real advantage is that the information can be saved to disk for later reference. Furthermore, students can use these tools to generate their own presentations.

USING COMPUTERS WITH SMALL GROUPS

Presentation hardware and software are important tools for using computers for group instruction. Unfortunately, because of the expense and/or newness of this product technology, presentation hardware and software are not yet available in many schools. Are there other ways to use computers with groups? Of course, the answer is yes! There are a number of ways to use computers with groups, especially with small groups of learners.

Group Work

Many times, educational software that is aimed primarily at the individual user can be adapted for

TECHNOLOGY INTEGRATION PROMPT

PROGRESSIVE DISCLOSURE

Have you ever experienced "information overload"? It may have happened while listening to a lecture on genetics, during a discussion with your counselor, or while trying to figure out how to become the next *Reader's Digest* grand sweepstakes winner. In any case, you came to a point where you couldn't handle any more information. Receiving too much information at any one time can be frustrating and overwhelming and can block effective thinking.

Students are constantly faced with this problem of information overload. One instructional technique that can help reduce the effects of dealing with too much information is called progressive disclosure (also known as successive disclosure). For example, instead of presenting an entire list of information all at once, the list is presented one item at a time. After one item has been discussed, the next item is presented. Learners are less likely to feel overwhelmed, because new information is presented in a way that builds on the previous information.

The use of the overhead and a cover sheet provides an ideal setup for the implementation of this technique. By placing the sheet under the transparency (thus blocking projection of any of the information) and then slowly pulling the sheet down to reveal each additional item, information can be presented (and digested by students) in manageable chunks. With the advent of presentation software, such as PowerPoint and Astound, a series of projected slides can be made so that points can be added one after another until all the items have been projected. In this way, the overall information is slowly revealed and discussed. This technique helps individuals focus on each individual item, yet it doesn't allow them to become overwhelmed while learning the entire list.

group instruction. Simulation and problem-solving programs are especially well suited to this kind of approach. Suppose that your class is studying the growth of plants, and you have a computer program that simulates the effects of a number of different factors (e.g., light, water, temperature) on plant growth. The class can be divided into teams, each of which is given one factor to explore. Groups can take turns exploring the effects of their assigned factors using the computer program. Afterwards, the groups can come together to share their results and draw overall conclusions.

The same approach can be utilized in science with a microcomputer-based laboratory (MBL), a special hardware and software combination that turns the computer into a laboratory data-collection instrument. MBLs allow students to collect data (e.g., temperature, the position of a moving cart over time) and display a real-time graph of the data as they are being collected. Again, groups of students can take turns using the equipment to conduct experiments. When each group performs the same basic experiments, data can be pooled, sources of variation analyzed, and so on. The coming together of the whole class affords an opportunity to consider the importance of replication of experiments in science. Alternatively, different groups

can do different experiments that collectively provide a fuller picture of a particular phenomenon.

Groups can also make use of software tools for learning activities. For example, in a social studies class, a learning activity might involve the construction of a database about the U.S. presidents. The class could be divided into work teams. Each team of students would be assigned particular presidents to research. After completing its research, each team would enter its information into the database. The result would be a complete database of the U.S. presidents that the entire class could use for research and problem solving.

Cooperative Learning Activities

In problem-solving situations on the computer, groups can be especially beneficial. Sometimes individual learners encounter difficulties when confronted with problem-solving situations. When working in groups, the interaction among students becomes a valuable aspect of the learning, in addition to the interaction with the computer. By discussing problems among themselves and reaching consensus for a course of action, groups of learners can often accomplish more than individuals. Cooperative learning with computers offers benefits over both individual and competitive learning situations (Johnson, Johnson, & Stanne, 1985). There is clear rationale for using group and cooperative activities with the computer.

Some educational software producers, notably Tom Snyder Productions, have even developed computer programs that are designed to take specific advantage of what the computer can do to assist in the instruction of groups. Snyder's *Decisions, Decisions* series features whole-class problem solving and decision making in a variety of content areas. The programs are designed to manage role-playing simulation games that focus primarily on fostering student dialogue about important problems. The computer plays the role of the game coordinator and referee, giving students their assignments, providing feedback, and leading groups through the steps in the decision-making process. Groups of students work with one another playing particular roles to try to solve problems. While this process could be managed by the teacher, having the computer manage the game frees the teacher to work directly with the groups as they discuss the ideas underlying the simulation.

THE ONE-COMPUTER CLASSROOM

Classrooms with a single computer are common in schools across the country. In fact, despite the fact that millions of computers are now installed in U.S. schools, the **one-computer classroom** remains a fixture of the educational landscape. What can be done with a single computer in the classroom? The answer is, a lot.

All of the methods of using computers in the classroom that we discussed above can apply to the one-computer classroom. The computer can be used as a presentation tool either by the teacher or by students wishing to demonstrate their own work. Students can work with software in groups. Cooperative learning activities can be used. In addition, there are ways to use computers effectively with individuals in a whole-class setting.

One simple but useful approach to utilizing limited hardware is to provide access to individual students in rotation. We will look at the options for individual use of the computer in the next chapter, but we consider this approach here as one way of working with a large group. The rotation model is especially popular at the elementary level, where the computer is often established as one of a number of learning centers through which students rotate. For example, primary-age learners working on basic arithmetic skills might rotate through several related learning stations featuring concrete manipulatives, traditional flash cards, and a computer drill-and-practice game on arithmetic skills. While time on the computer is necessarily limited in this approach, it does provide one mechanism for giving an entire class at least some access to the computer. A key concern with both individual and small-group use of a single computer is that the teacher must effectively manage students' access to the computer to avoid conflicts and to keep those students who are not working on the computer productively engaged in other activities. While this can be a challenge, it is one that teachers successfully meet in classrooms all across the country every day.

Various multimedia packages are included in the Decisions, Decisions *series by Tom Snyder Productions.*

These students are using the one computer in their classroom.

Finally, one should not overlook the use of a single computer in the classroom as a tool for the teacher. For example, as noted in Chapter 5, word processing is a great tool for producing printed material. With a single computer equipped with word-processing software and attached to a printer, the teacher can produce printed instructional materials that can then be copied for use by an entire class. Some software produces printed output. If time doesn't allow for student use, the teacher can generate printouts of key problems or situations and duplicate those for classroom study. Similarly, many textbooks today come with computerized question banks; the teacher can make copies of selected questions to help guide review activities. Of course, the teacher can use the computer for many other functions, such as maintenance of student grades, other record keeping, and computer telecommunication. As some experts have argued, if you only have one computer in a classroom, the most useful place for it is on the teacher's desk!

SUMMARY

This chapter focused on the implementation of instruction with groups of varying sizes. Group size was shown to be important because it often allows, or limits, a specific type of instructional approach to be employed. In the case of the larger group, presentations and demonstrations were shown to be commonly used. In addition, discussions, cooperative learning, discovery, problem solving, and instructional games were shown to be effective approaches with smaller groups. In all cases the emphasis was on how to effectively utilize the approaches, as well as how to integrate the use of media within each approach. Key principles of utilization within each of the approaches centered on completing adequate preparation and planning, helping the students understand the purpose and relevance of the instruction, and emphasizing how the learning can be transferred to other situations.

When using a computer with a group, display options include a large television or video monitor, a video projector, or an LCD panel or projector. Presentation software is designed to facilitate the use of the computer as a group presentation tool. Computers can also be used in other ways with groups, even in a one-computer classroom.

REFLECTIVE QUESTIONS AND ACTIVITIES

1. Spend a few minutes thinking about the last presentation and/or demonstration you attended. Jot down the main points that you remember from the experience. Also list your general feelings about the presentation. Did you enjoy it? If you were to make some suggestions to the pre-

senter for improvement, what would you select as the three most important things the individual should do?

2. Think back to a formal experience (e.g., school classroom, training session) in which you learned a lot. Review it in your mind and identify the instructional approach used. Was more than one approach used? If so, in what ways were they combined? What types of media formats were incorporated? Were different formats used with the different approaches? Were the approaches and media used during this learning experience important to its success? Why or why not?

3. What is the value of knowing how to use different instructional approaches?

4. Visit a vendor or a school site that uses different kinds of large-group computer display devices. Under what conditions do they work well? How do costs compare? What do you like or dislike about them?

5. Go to a local elementary, middle, or high school. Interview the school's computer technologist and examine the available hardware. Ask about their use of the presentation software and what pieces the teachers have found most beneficial.

INTEGRATION AND SYNTHESIS

This chapter's focus was on the implementation of various instructional approaches with different sizes of groups. This information is directly tied to Chapter 3, where we introduced the instructional approaches, and to Chapter 6, where we showed the approaches to be an integral part of the instructional plan. Likewise, Chapter 10 will continue to discuss instructional approaches—specifically, those that are best implemented with individual learners. It is important to remember the role of the instructional plan in the selection and implementation of a proper instructional approach. Correct implementation is influenced by the participants, the context, and the content—all of which were discussed in the planning section (Chapters 5–7) of this text.

SUGGESTED READINGS

Johnson, D. W., Johnson, R. T., & Scott, L. (1978). The effects of cooperative and individualized instruction on student attitudes and achievement. *Journal of Social Psychology, 104,* 207–216.

Lyman, L., Foyle, H. C., & Azwell, T. S. (1993). *Cooperative learning in the elementary classroom.* Washington, DC: National Education Association.

McKeachie, W. J. (1994). Why classes should be small, but how to help your students be active learners even in large classes. In W. J. McKeachie (Ed.), *Teaching tips* (pp. 197–210). Lexington, MA: Heath.

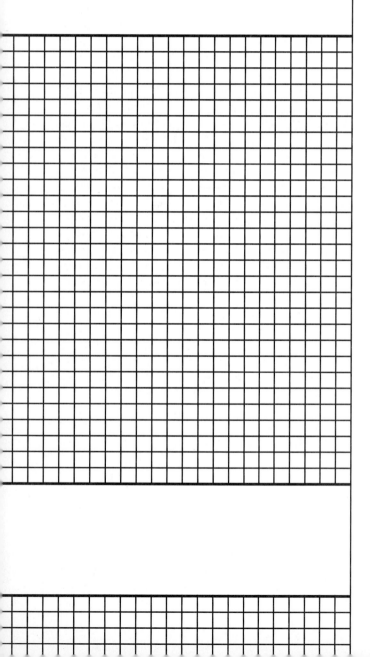

Chapter 10

Instructional Technology for Individuals

KEY WORDS AND CONCEPTS

Individualized instruction

Systems of instruction

Peer tutoring

Mastery learning

Audio-tutorial instruction

Personalized system of instruction (PSI)

Individualized education program (IEP)

Problem-solving software	Syntax
	Top-down approach
Programming	Structured programming
Programming language	
Machine language	Logo
Low-level language	BASIC
High-level language	Variable
Interpreter	OOPS
Compiler	Event-driven
Algorithm	

OUTCOMES

After reading and studying this chapter, you will be able to:

- Define *individualized instruction.*
- Describe the basic instructional approaches that are most appropriate for use with individuals.
- Describe some specific systems of instruction for individuals.
- Select an appropriate approach to individualized instruction for a given instructional goal, given the attributes of the approaches described in this chapter.
- Identify common approaches used in computer-assisted instruction.
- Discuss a rationale for teaching computer programming in the schools.
- Define *computer program, programming language, algorithm, syntax,* and *structured programming.*
- Identify computer languages that are commonly associated with education and discuss the characteristics and typical applications of each.

■ INTRODUCTION

Do you know the old expression "Too many cooks spoil the broth"? Imagine what it would be like to have a group of cooks preparing a soup. One might like salty tastes, another sweet. One might like carrots, another beets. If each cook added his or her own favorite ingredient, the clash of different tastes might indeed spoil the broth. Or, perhaps more likely, the group might discuss the ingredients and prepare the soup as a committee. In this case the tendency would probably be for the group to eliminate all of the flavors not favored by the majority. The result would be a soup inoffensive to most but lacking the unique character of fine cuisine—sort of a common denominator of broths. Prepackaged foods that you buy at the supermarket often seem just like this.

Learning can sometimes be like that. This is not to say that learning in groups is bad; as you learned in the last chapter, there is much to be said for learning in groups and many ways to conduct group learning activities. However, learning in groups may fail to take into account the unique instructional "tastes" of individual learners. Instructional approaches for large groups—lecture presentations, for example—usually expose all of the students to the instructional material at the same pace and in the same way. Lecturers usually try to aim their presentation toward the "typical" student. In most cases there is little consideration of the differences among individual learners. More capable or knowledgeable students may become bored, while those who are less capable or knowledgeable may become lost. Small-group approaches are more flexible and allow for greater variation, which may better accommodate the needs of individual students. However, these approaches, too, may fail to account for particular learners' needs. The educational ideal has long been to provide instruction that is truly individualized. **Individualized instruction** refers to instruction in which the content, pacing, instructional sequence, and (often) media and approaches are determined by the individual student's learning needs, abilities, and attitudes. In this chapter we examine approaches and instructional systems that are most appropriate for individualized instruction.

Each student brings to the learning task a unique set of experiences, abilities, and attitudes. A student who lives on a farm may have developed considerable knowledge of plant and animal biology, diesel engines, hydraulics, and the like. The student whose mother is an accountant may come to school with a particularly positive attitude toward mathematics. One who has visited a state historic site may have gained a firsthand perspective on its significance. Each student brings unique strengths to the classroom. Of course, students also have their unique weaknesses. Ideally, instruction should be tailored to each and every student's background and needs.

For a variety of reasons, truly individualized instruction is rarely achieved. First, it can be difficult to determine exactly what understandings and attitudes an individual brings to a particular learning task in order to appropriately tailor instruction for that individual. Second, economics makes it unfea-

221

sible to provide a personal tutor for every student; the demands of the classroom make it difficult for a single teacher to design and manage a truly individualized program of learning for a whole class of students. Despite these realities, there are instructional approaches that provide a measure of individualized instruction. As you learned in Chapter 3, instructional approaches that can be used with individuals include drill and practice, tutorial, simulation, problem solving, discovery learning, and instructional games.

In the last two chapters, you learned that a number of approaches are most often used with large or small groups (e.g., discussion, presentation, cooperative learning). In this chapter we will focus primarily on those approaches that are commonly used with individuals: tutorial, drill and practice, and simulation. In addition to these basic approaches, however, we will examine more complex approaches to the instruction of individuals. These might best be termed **systems of instruction,** as they typically involve more than one basic approach. However, all of these systems or complex approaches share the characteristic that they are intended primarily for individualized instruction. In this category, we will consider programmed instruction, audio-tutorial instruction, the personalized system of instruction, individualized education programs, computer-assisted instruction, and the use of the computer as learner. The latter two categories, those involving the computer, are the focus of this chapter's CUE.   ■

BASIC APPROACHES TO INDIVIDUALIZED INSTRUCTION

Presentation and Demonstration

Presentation and demonstration, as you have learned, are approaches that are primarily used with large and small groups. Of course, they can be used with individuals as well. For example, demonstrations are an integral part of apprenticeship training. A teacher in a woodworking class may do a one-on-one demonstration to show a student how to use a miter box to cut a piece of wood at a 45° angle. However, because these approaches are more commonly used with groups in most school settings, we will not consider them further in this chapter.

Instructional Games, Problem Solving, and Discovery Learning

While presentation and demonstration are mainly large-group approaches, instructional games, problem solving, and discovery learning are most com-

monly used with small groups. As you saw in the last chapter, there are benefits to having small groups of students work together to solve problems using the discovery approach. Gaming, problem solving, and discovery are possible approaches for individuals, and—as we will see later in this chapter—they are important ways to use the computer with individuals. However, for now we will move on to those general approaches that are more commonly used with individuals.

Tutorial

In many respects, the ideal form of individualized instruction is one-to-one tutoring. When time and resources permit, a single teacher or teacher's aide can work with a single student to help that student learn. However, because typical class sizes make it difficult for a teacher to spend much individual time with one student, alternatives have been sought. For example, students can tutor one another. **Peer tutoring** is the term used to describe the technique of having students tutor one another. Students from the same class can tutor one another, or, in cross-age grouping, older students can tutor younger ones. A review of relevant research on peer tutoring suggests that it is beneficial for both the student being tutored and the student doing the tutoring (Cohen, Kulik, & Kulik, 1982).

Tutorials are instructional approaches designed to embody the role of the tutor. They introduce content to the learner and assess the learner's progress. The typical tutorial introduces a well-defined body of content, which is usually broken up into blocks or chunks that may be delivered via almost any medium, although most tutorials involve text and graphic information. When concepts are introduced,

Peer tutoring can be effective for both the student being tutored and the student doing the tutoring.

examples and non-examples are often presented to help the learner understand the concepts. Questions are embedded after content blocks to ensure that the learner is mastering the material. In addition, larger content units become the focus of questioning at various points in the tutorial. Students' responses to questions can be used to guide branching within the tutorial.

Tutorials can be delivered by a live teacher or tutor, or they can come in printed form or in other mediated forms such as audiotape, videotape, or computer-assisted instruction (CAI). They may be used in the classroom in a variety of ways and for almost any subject matter. In many cases, tutorials may be used for enrichment or for remediation. An advanced student who is not being challenged by the regular classroom mathematics curriculum could use a tutorial to learn new mathematical concepts. Likewise, students who miss class due to an illness could catch up with their classmates, without occupying teacher time, by studying a tutorial on the topics missed. As with any instructional activity, it is important that students have the appropriate background knowledge and skills to use a tutorial. In addition, as with any individualized form of instruction, the teacher needs to plan for varying rates of completion. Some students will proceed quickly and others will need more time.

Utilization Principles: Tutorial

Planning

- Use tutorials for verbal and conceptual learning.
- Use them for introducing new information, for remediation, or for enrichment.
- Be certain that the student has the necessary prerequisite knowledge and skills.
- Make sure all materials and equipment are available.

Implementation

- Present an overview of the material to be covered.
- Present content or skills one step at a time.
- Ask questions of the student and encourage the student to ask questions.
- Prompt students through content or skills, then release them to demonstrate content or skills on their own.
- Plan for varying rates of completion.
- Be aware of potential discipline problems when the teacher is not present.

Evaluation

- Monitor students' progress regularly to ensure that they are on task and learning.
- Provide opportunities for students to apply what they have learned.

Tutorial Examples

- Mr. Day, an industrial arts teacher, uses a video-based tutorial on shop safety as a prelude to having his students work with power equipment.
- Ms. Johnson uses a tutorial, in the form of an illustrated storybook on local history, as a makeup activity for her fourth-grade students who were absent when the topic was covered in class.

Drill and Practice

Drill and practice is a common classroom technique for helping individual learners master basic skills or knowledge through repetitive work. Drill and practice is not designed to introduce new content. It is assumed that the skill or knowledge has already been introduced, and thus its purpose is to give learners the opportunity to master the material at their own pace.

A common form of drill and practice in the classroom is seatwork. Seatwork usually involves printed worksheets that provide practice problems covering recently introduced knowledge and skills in areas such as mathematical computation, language arts, reading comprehension, basic science facts, history, and geography. Most of us associate drill and practice with basic skill-building approaches such as the use of arithmetic flash cards. However, drill and practice can also come in other forms. For example, as we note below, drill-and-practice programs are among the most popular forms of CAI.

Utilization Principles: Drill and Practice

Planning

- Use drill and practice for basic skills and knowledge where rapid or automatic student response is desirable (e.g., basic arithmetic skills, letter and word recognition, discrimination of geometric shapes).
- Introduce content prior to the use of drill and practice.

Implementation

- Provide a level of difficulty appropriate for the individual learner.

FEEDBACK

We are all familiar with the phrase "practice makes perfect," but is it true? By attaching a short addendum we can capture a more accurate picture—that is, "Practice makes perfect, *as long as feedback is provided.*" Feedback, according to Rothwell and Kazanas (1992, p. 13), is "a continuous process of providing information about an activity, sometimes during the activity itself." Feedback can serve two functions: (1) it can inform students about *how much* of the task they have completed, thus encouraging them to continue working; and (2) it can inform students *how well* they are performing and indicate what they can do to improve their performance.

As instruction is designed and implemented, it is important to make provisions for delivering feedback to the students. Without timely, reliable feedback, students may not know if their work is correct. Potentially, without some form of feedback, students could continue practicing errors over and over. When designing practice and feedback exercises, the following guidelines should be considered (adapted from Leshin, Pollock, & Reigeluth, 1992):

- Effective feedback should be delivered immediately (or as soon as reasonably feasible) after practice is completed.
- Well-designed feedback can motivate students to greater levels of performance.
- Informative feedback should function like a good example.
- Corrective feedback should require learners to think. Give hints but don't provide the correct answer immediately.

- Use many short drill-and-practice sessions instead of a few longer ones.
- Use both individual and group drill-and-practice activities.
- Use competition (against self or others) to make drill more interesting.
- Make sure students are practicing the correct information or procedures. Only correct practice makes perfect!
- When feedback is not built into the drill-and-practice activity, the teacher should provide it quickly.

Evaluation

- Check students' performance to adjust the level of difficulty as needed.
- Encourage periodic review. Repeatedly check student performance over different periods of time to ensure that they retain what they have practiced.
- Provide opportunities for students to apply that which is mastered through drill and practice.

Drill and Practice Examples

- Ms. Owens uses arithmetic flash cards to work individually with her first graders on basic addition skills.
- Students in Ms. Groves' seventh-grade geography class work on their map-recognition skills using printed worksheets.

Simulation

Simulations approximate real-life (or sometimes imaginary) situations or phenomena. They give learners the opportunity to interact with these situations or phenomena without the danger, expense, or difficulty associated with the real things. Simulations are widely used by businesses and the military for training tasks such as flying an airplane or maneuvering a tank in battle. In the classroom, some simulations are designed for group instruction. Role-playing activities are a good example. As we will discuss in more detail in the CUE, most simulations that are designed for individuals are computer based. Using the computer, students can experience phenomena as diverse as the operation of a nuclear power plant or the economics of running a hot dog stand. In general, simulations are designed to promote students' abilities to apply previously learned concepts and to invoke higher-order thinking skills.

Utilization Principles: Simulation

Planning

- Use simulations for promoting students' conceptual understanding as well as thinking and problem-solving skills.
- In most cases, prior introduction to the concepts is important for successful use of simulations.
- Explain the purpose, procedures, and/or rules for the simulation.

Implementation

- Limit the scope of the simulation to critical aspects of actions or processes.
- Make students aware of oversimplifications implicit in the simulation.
- Explain the goal to be achieved and, where appropriate, the role of each student.
- Simulations can be confusing, and students may need guidance or direction in order to benefit from them. Questions, activities, and scenarios can fill this guidance role.
- Allow participants to play out their roles with minimum input from the teacher.

Evaluation

- Provide feedback following the simulation (some simulations provide feedback during their use).
- Conduct follow-up discussions or debriefing with students so they gain the most from the simulation.
- Develop generalizations and/or summarizations at the conclusion of the simulation.

Simulation Examples

- Students in Mr. Morales' social studies class learn about the operations of government by participating in a role-playing simulation about the creation and passage of new legislation.
- The sixth graders in Ms. Krajcik's class learn about ecology by playing a computer simulation about life in a lake.

SYSTEMS OF INSTRUCTION FOR INDIVIDUALS

The approaches to individualized instruction that we discussed above are all general approaches that can be used in a variety of contexts. As we noted, tutorial materials may be print-based, audiotaped, videotaped, or computerized. Drill and practice may involve written seatwork, classroom activities, or computer interaction. Simulations may be in-class exercises or computer based. Each approach can be used in different contexts, and, often, each of these basic approaches is part of a larger classroom system of instruction. Now we are going to turn our attention to other, more complex, approaches to individualized instruction. We refer to these approaches as systems of instruction because they often involve more than one of the basic approaches discussed above. Some of them may involve approaches for

small- and large-group instruction as well. But they all share the characteristic that they are intended primarily for the instruction of individuals.

At the root of many of these complex approaches to learning is the idea of mastery learning. **Mastery learning** derives from the conviction that learners of different abilities can learn or master a particular learning task or body of content if given enough time and opportunity. In most cases, the mastery approach involves clear specification of a series of learning outcomes through which students progress at their own pace. Criteria for specific levels of mastery are preestablished. For example, the student may have to achieve 90% correct in order to proceed. While a mastery approach to learning can be used in settings that are not strictly individualized, the concept of mastery implies individualization because each student is individually accountable for mastering the content. Mastery learning is not one approach; rather, it forms the foundation for many of the systems of individualized instruction we will discuss.

Programmed Instruction

Programmed instruction is a form of independent learning based on the mastery approach. It can be used in a variety of content areas, at educational levels from elementary school through college, either in addition to other methods or as a primary means of content delivery. Derived from behavioral learning theory, programmed instruction is characterized by a sequence of small segments of instruction, called frames, combined with opportunities for frequent learner interaction. Following a short instructional segment, the learner is asked to respond to a question about the content. Reinforcement, in the form of the correct answer to the question, is provided. Learners proceed at their own pace.

Books that adopt this approach, called programmed texts, are often used for practicing or remediating basic skills. A student using a programmed text first reads a short instructional passage, typically only a few lines or a paragraph or two in length. A question about that instructional passage follows. The student writes the answer to the question in the book in the space provided. Then the student checks the answer by uncovering a strip along the side of the page, where the correct answers are written. This process continues over and over until the student has progressed through the entire book. Content is slowly built up from simple to complex, and questions on previously introduced content are interspersed with questions on new content to maintain the student's performance.

While many programmed texts are linear—that is, follow a specific sequence of instruction from start to finish—some provide branching or alternate pathways through the material, depending on the answers to specific questions. With a branching text, the student is simply directed to a particular page based on his or her response to a key question. Programmed instructional materials are intended for self-study, although in the classroom the teacher or peers can provide support for students using them. Many CAI programs base their approach of using small blocks of content and frequent review questions on the model of programmed instruction. A review of research on programmed instruction with secondary learners found that it was slightly more effective than conventional instruction (Kulik, Schwalb, & Kulik, 1982).

Audio-Tutorial Instruction

Audio-tutorial instruction relies on the use of audiotapes to guide students through individualized learning activities. Like programmed instruction, the audio-tutorial approach relies on mastery learning and can be an instructional supplement or a primary means of content delivery. Originally developed by Sam Postlethwait at Purdue University (Postlethwait, Novak, & Murray, 1972), the audio-tutorial approach provides students with considerable flexibility in independent study. Rather than being tied to lecture-based content delivery, students can learn at their own pace and often according to a preferred schedule. Largely at their own convenience, students come to an instructional laboratory equipped with audiotape players to learn the basic course content. The audiotapes tutor the students through particular content units. If a stu-

Audio-tutorial instruction supports self-paced, individualized instruction through the use of audiotapes.

dent has difficulty with a particular portion of the content, the tape can be stopped, rewound, and replayed as many times as the student needs.

During the independent study, printed materials and real objects related to the content are often used with the audiotapes. In addition, an instructor or proctor may be available to assist learners. Thus the sessions often take on the flavor of one-to-one tutoring or laboratory sessions, yet, with sufficient audiotape equipment, many learners can be accommodated simultaneously. Often, independent study sessions are complemented by small- and/or large-group meetings, which extend or reinforce concepts introduced in the independent study. Research has generally supported the achievement benefits of audio-tutorial instruction in comparison with traditional methods (Kulik, Kulik, & Cohen, 1979b).

Personalized System of Instruction

The **personalized system of instruction (PSI)**, developed by Fred Keller (1968), is a system for managing individualized instruction. PSI, also known as the Keller Plan, makes use of a variety of instructional materials—potentially including programmed texts, readings, videotapes, audiotapes, filmstrips, and computer software—in a mastery context. The instructor assembles instructional materials for each unit of content and students study these materials independently. For one unit of instruction the materials may include a reading and an audiotape; for another they may involve a videotape and a computer program. The intent is to assemble materials that provide the best coverage of the content to be addressed.

After studying the materials, students must demonstrate mastery by satisfactorily passing a test before going on to the next unit of content. Assistance during the independent study and administration of tests are handled by proctors, who may be advanced students. When assistance is needed, the proctors provide one-to-one tutoring for the learners. Large-group lectures and demonstrations by the instructor are rare in PSI and are used primarily for motivational purposes. Because of its emphasis on content mastery with regular assessments of progress, PSI heads off problems that could arise when students' failure to master material early in a course leads to compounded difficulties later on. Reviews of research on the achievement effects of PSI have strongly favored it in comparison with traditional approaches (Kulik, Kulik, & Cohen, 1979a).

Individualized Education Programs

Considerable attention has been given to the needs of exceptional students in our schools. Once students with special needs were separated from their peers and placed in special programs. Today the emphasis is on including exceptional students in regular classroom settings—what has been termed the "educational mainstream"—to the greatest extent possible. An important element of the education of exceptional students is the **individualized education program (IEP)**. The IEP is an instructional plan for an individual student and is developed through a conference with the student's parents, his or her teachers, and other appropriate individuals. Most IEPs describe the student's current level of proficiency and set short- and long-term goals and objectives. In other words, the IEP is an individualized plan for the education of each student. While the concept of the IEP arose as a result of the needs of exceptional learners, there is growing interest in many schools in extending the concept of the IEP to all learners in the school. One day, every school learner may have an IEP that sets out a truly individualized program of study.

As we noted earlier, today the computer is one of the main tools for individualized instruction in the schools. In this chapter's CUE we discuss two ways that the computer can be used for individualized instruction: computer-assisted instruction and the use of the computer as learner. These two approaches are both common ways that computers are used with individual learners in the schools. Let's

An IEP is an important element of the education of students with special needs.

look more closely at computer-based approaches now, beginning with another visit with our friend Ms. Moreno.

INTEGRATING TECHNOLOGY
Structuring for the Individual Learner

Every classroom teacher, including Ms. Moreno, faces the challenge of finding a way to use class time so that all students are learning information and skills that are relevant to their individual needs. Students in any class tend to represent a wide range of skill levels: what Reina needs most is much too basic for Justin; what Yolanda finds useful is way above Bethany's head. Ms. Moreno had struggled for a long time trying to meet all the individual needs of her students, and she indicated that she finally met with some success after she started relying on some materials for individualizing instruction. Furthermore, her choices became more effective after she learned how different instructional approaches were more or less appropriate for different types of learning outcomes.

For example, Reina seemed to need a lot of repetitive practice recognizing and using the growing list of vocabulary words that Ms. Moreno had introduced. What methods do you think Ms. Moreno considered as being particularly suited to Reina's needs? If you recalled the drill-and-practice program mentioned in Chapter 1, you're thinking the same way she did. This specific program had been installed on the school's computer network after a site license had been obtained from the producer. Reina had the opportunity to work with this program during study hall and during the computer lab's open hours before and after school. Reina could work on her vocabulary skills on her own time and at her own pace, and she didn't have to worry about taking up other students' time during regular class meetings.

Yolanda had a fairly good handle on Spanish vocabulary and was particularly interested in learning new things about the people and culture of Spain, as she was planning on participating in the Spanish exchange program during her senior year. What methods would be well matched to Yolanda's needs? Of course, you don't know what Ms. Moreno had available to her, but if you considered audio-tutorials or simulation games you're on the right track. In fact, Ms. Moreno used both of these approaches. Yolanda used the audio-tutorial materials on her own time and participated in a role-playing simulation/game during class time. The game was designed so that students took turns playing the role of a tourist or a Spaniard. The object of the game was for the native to give directions to the tourist to get him or her from the airport to some landmark in the shortest time. This game allowed students to practice speaking and understanding Spanish; it also required that they become familiar with Spanish landmarks and Spanish maps. The best part about the game, according to Ms. Moreno, was that students forgot that they were learning "Spanish" throughout the entire process. They just enjoyed the game.

By using a variety of instructional materials and methods to individualize instruction for her students, Janette found that class time could be spent in ways that increased benefits for all class members.

 Computer Use ESSENTIALS

COMPUTER-ASSISTED INSTRUCTION

As you learned in Chapter 4, any instructional use of the computer in which it assumes the role of a teacher or tutor can be labeled computer-assisted instruction. CAI is the oldest of the instructional uses of the computer. The first uses of CAI date to the 1950s and 1960s and involved the use of basic computer drills and tutorials to instruct individual learners. Over the years, CAI has remained one of the predominant uses of computers in education.

The chief advantage of the computer is its interactivity. Whereas a printed worksheet or programmed text may leave space for a student's answer, there is no guarantee that the student will in fact write one. The computer can require the active involvement of the learner. Research analyses of studies comparing CAI with traditional methods suggest that CAI produces slightly superior achievement, usually requires less time, and may produce improved attitudes toward computers and sometimes the subject matter itself (Kulik & Kulik, 1991; Niemiec & Walberg, 1987). The positive effects of CAI are somewhat greater in the lower grades.

Since the first uses of CAI, there has been an enduring myth that computers will become perfect teaching machines and will replace human teachers. Computers have not yet evolved into perfect teaching machines, nor does it seem likely that they will anytime in the near future. While there have been advances in software design and artificial intelligence techniques, few computer programs have been produced that even approach the capa-

bilities of a human tutor. We see little evidence to suggest that the computer will ever replace the teacher. CAI is merely one more tool at the teacher's disposal for individualizing instruction in the classroom.

As you learned in the last chapter, there are many ways that the computer can be used with both large and small groups. Although CAI can be used in those ways, it is usually associated with the instruction of individuals. Applications of individualized CAI can be categorized in a number of ways. The most common categories of software fit within our basic instructional approaches: drill and practice, tutorial, simulation, instructional games, and problem solving. Let's examine each of these in more detail.

Drill and Practice

As we have noted, a drill-and-practice application is designed to help the learner master some basic skill or knowledge through repetitive work. Compared with noncomputer drill and practice, the computer offers some significant advantages:

- *Interactivity.* The computer can present many problems and require student responses.

- *Immediate feedback.* The computer can immediately inform the learner if an answer is right or wrong, and, in a well-designed program, tell the learner why.

- *Infinite patience.* A computer drill-and-practice program can go all day without getting tired or irritable.

- *Variable level of difficulty.* The computer can adjust the level of difficulty. This might be set by the teacher or by the learner, or the program may adjust automatically based on the student's performance. Well-designed drill-and-practice programs automatically recycle missed items until they are mastered.

- *Motivation.* Through the use of challenge and gaming elements, or just because it is on the computer, a computer drill-and-practice program may be more motivating to the student than similar paper-and-pencil exercises.

These characteristics make the computer an excellent tool for drill-and-practice applications and explain why they are among the most popular of all computer applications in education, especially in the elementary grades. Drill-and-practice programs tend to be used for basic information and skills in a variety of subject areas. *Stickybear Math* and *Reader*

Rabbit are examples of computer drill-and-practice programs (in the content areas of arithmetic computation and beginning reading skills, respectively) that are popular in the elementary school. In *Stickybear Math,* students are drilled on basic arithmetic facts (e.g., 3 + 1 = ?). As each question is answered, reinforcement is provided, and after accumulating a number of correct answers the student is able to help Stickybear (a cartoon bear) get out of some kind of jam. *Reader Rabbit* helps students practice beginning word-recognition and word-construction skills. Figure 10.1 shows a sample screen from the program in which the student must select the correct letters to form simple words.

Students can usually gain some benefit from drill-and-practice programs even with relatively little exposure per session. As a result, drill-and-practice programs are a popular option when computer hardware is scarce. A common strategy is to rotate individual students through the drill program so that each student is able to get 15 or 20 minutes of practice at a time.

Tutorial

In a tutorial application, the computer assumes the primary instructional role of teacher or tutor. It presents new content and assesses learning. A tutorial typically contains an organized body of knowledge, one or more pathways through that knowledge, specific learning objectives, and built-in tests of student learning. Computer-based tutorials offer a number of advantages:

- *Embedded questions.* Like computer drills, tutorials on the computer have the advantage of being interactive. Students must take an active role by answering embedded questions. As with drills, immediate feedback is provided.

- *Branching.* While programmed texts can incorporate branching by directing the learner to a particular page, computer tutorials can automatically branch according to the learner's responses to embedded questions. Remediation or advancement can be built in to meet the needs of the individual learner.

- *Dynamic presentation.* The power of the computer can be used to present information dynamically. Important text can be highlighted on the screen to capture the learner's attention. Processes can be depicted through animated graphics. With a multimedia computer system, audio and video can also be employed.

- *Record keeping.* Computer tutorials can automatically maintain student records. These can be used to inform the learners of their progress. In addition, the teacher can check the records to ensure the students are progressing satisfactorily.

While a poorly designed tutorial may be little more than an electronic page-turner, a well-designed

Figure 10.1 Screen from *Reader Rabbit*, a drill-and-practice program

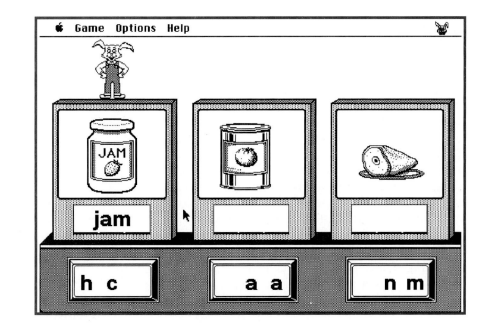

one can be a highly interactive and effective form of instruction that responds to the needs or wants of the individual learner. Tutorials are available for a wide range of subject matter and at all grade levels. *Mavis Beacon Teaches Typing* is an example of a tutorial program designed for use in schools and homes. Also, most popular computer tool packages (e.g., Microsoft Word, a word processor) come with associated tutorials that provide instruction on how to use the tool. In most cases, computer tutorials in the schools are used to supplement regular instruction rather than to replace it. Because many tutorials require a significant time commitment (a student may require hours to complete an extensive one), it's difficult to use tutorials effectively with large numbers of students without access to a computer laboratory. Where computer hardware is limited, computer tutorials may be used with selected students for remediation, enrichment, or makeup work.

Simulation

As we noted earlier, a simulation is a representation or model of a real (or sometimes imaginary) system, situation, or phenomenon. In most cases, this representation is simplified to make learning easier. Simulations make excellent use of the computer's capabilities:

- *Control of multiple variables.* Computers can manage multiple variables simultaneously. As a result, they can realistically depict complex phenomena, such as the growth and change of a city. Learners can manipulate these variables to observe their effects on the system being modeled.

- *Dynamic presentation.* As with tutorials, the computer's ability to dynamically present information is important in simulation. Simulated instrumentation can change like the real thing, and processes such as plant growth can be graphically depicted.

- *Time control.* The computer can contract or expand time to allow study of phenomena that are too slow (e.g., population growth) or too fast (e.g., chemical reaction) for normal classroom observation. Alternatively, the computer can depict a particular time in history (e.g., a 19th-century wagon train).

- *Effects of chance.* Many simulations include an element of chance or randomness that makes them even more realistic, allowing students to interact with them differently on different occasions.

Simulations have found their greatest use in the natural and social sciences. There are many good examples of educational simulations, including *SimCity* (management of a growing city), *CatLab* (simulated cat breeding), *Decisions, Decisions* (social studies role-playing simulation series), and *The Oregon Trail* (travel by covered wagon). Most simulations are designed to promote thinking and problem-solving skills. They tend not to teach basic concepts. As a result, it is usually important that students be well grounded in the underlying concepts of the simulation before use, and guidance is often needed during use. For example, *The Oregon Trail* simulates pioneers crossing the United States in the 19th century. Students must make decisions about the amount of food and ammunition to take at the start, and they must decide what to do when they encounter various problems and opportunities along the trail. But, to make the experience meaningful as an historical exercise, students need some background about the westward expansion and the factors that promoted it. Figure 10.2 shows a sample screen from *The Oregon Trail.*

Simulations vary in their time requirements. Simple simulations of some processes may require only a few minutes of student time; others may demand hours. Although we have discussed simulations from the standpoint of individual instruction here, small-group work is a common application of simulations in the classroom.

Instructional Games

Instructional games add an element of fun to CAI. In most cases, games are simply modified versions of other types of CAI, such as drill and practice or simulation. Games are distinguished by the elements of motivation and clear rules of play:

- *Motivation.* The chief advantage of computer games is the variety of motivational elements that may be employed. These may include competition, cooperation, challenge, fantasy, recognition, and reward.

- *Game structure.* The game structure means that there are rules of play and an end goal.

- *Sensory appeal.* Games on the computer also achieve some of their appeal through the use of graphics, animation, sound, and other enhancements.

Computer games tend not to fit into a unique CAI category. As noted above, they are usually modified forms of other types of CAI. A game may have begun as a drill-and-practice, problem-solving, or simulation program to which gaming ele-

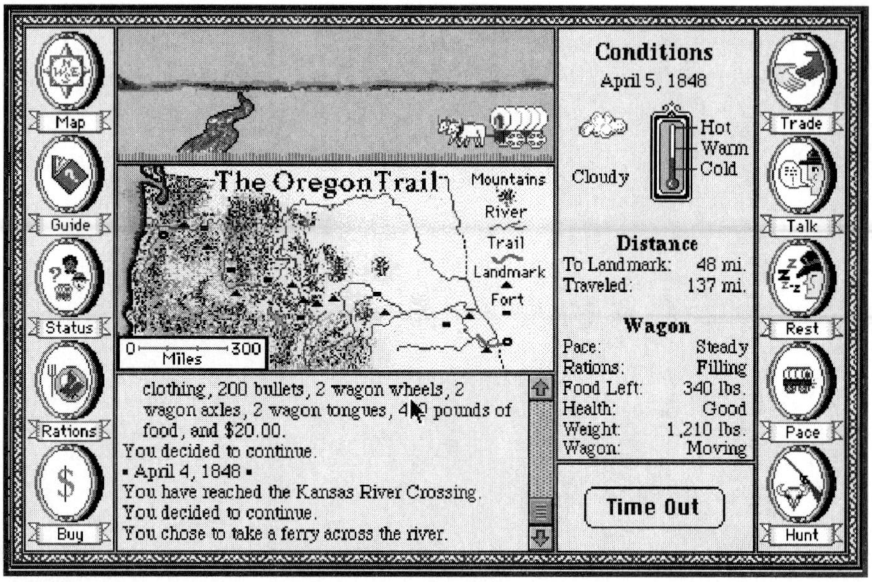

Figure 10.2 Screen from *The Oregon Trail*, a popular educational simulation

Source: The Oregon Trail, Copyright MECC. Used with permission. All rights reserved.

ments were added. One of the most popular CAI programs is a geography computer game called *Where in the World is Carmen Sandiego?* In this simulation game, students play the role of a detective who must use geography clues to track a thief around the world. By being placed in the role of a detective chasing an international thief, the student experiences an element of fantasy. There is challenge in that the thief must be located within a set amount of time by using the clues embedded in the game. Students may compete against one another for the best times, or students may cooperate with one another to help catch the villain. All of these elements make the program a terrific game. The program has proven so popular that is has spawned a series of other similar computer games, a line of merchandise, and a television series. Figure 10.3 shows a sample screen from *Where in the World is Carmen Sandiego?*

Computer games vary in their time requirements. Some may require only a few minutes. More complex games may extend over hours or even days. Probably the biggest concern about educational computer games is that the education should not take a backseat to the game. As a result, care should be taken when instructional computer games are integrated into the curriculum.

Problem Solving

Some CAI applications are designed to foster students' problem-solving skills but don't fit into any of the categories given above. These programs are categorized as problem-solving applications. Again, computer problem-solving applications have certain advantages:

- *Problem focus.* Specific problem-solving programs often focus on specific problem-solving skills (e.g., spatial ability, logic).
- *Quantity.* The computer can provide the student with practice over a large number of problems in a short period of time, requiring interaction and providing feedback as in other forms of CAI.
- *Variety.* The computer is capable of presenting a wide variety of problems. This helps students to generalize their problem-solving skills.

Problem-solving applications are designed to promote students' higher-order thinking skills, such as logic, reasoning, pattern recognition, and strategies. **Problem-solving software** often helps students by providing concrete representations of abstractions. Examples of problem-solving programs include *The King's Rule* (mathematical patterns), *The Factory* (spatial orientation, strategies, and reasoning), and *Geometric Supposer* (geometry). Some teachers use problem-solving software to enhance students' problem solving-skills for their own sake. Others link the use of problem-solving software to relevant curricular areas such as mathematics.

Most problem-solving programs, like drill and practice, require relatively short stretches of time for use. As a result, programs can often be used by rotating individuals or small groups of students when computer hardware is limited.

Figure 10.3 Screen from *Where in the World is Carmen Sandiego?*, a popular educational computer game

Source: Where in the World is Carmen Sandiego? ®, © 1985, 1995, Broderbund Software, Inc.

Other CAI Applications

There are many other possible applications of computers that do not neatly fit into any of the preceding categories. These may include demonstrations, content review or testing programs, dialogues, context-sensitive help systems, and many others. It is important to recognize that categories are a useful place to begin discussions, but they should never be allowed to restrict one's thinking about computer applications in education. There are many forms of CAI and many ways to view the role of the computer in education. As software and our knowledge of human learning evolve, we may invent new categories or change old ones to better reflect the reality in the classroom.

Problems and Pitfalls

We have emphasized the many advantages of CAI, and rightly so. CAI has much to offer. However, there are concerns that must be considered as well. Critics charge that CAI is a low-level use of the computer that simply puts a new face on old busywork and which is not consistent with a view of learning as knowledge construction. In some cases this charge is surely justified. Some drill-and-practice programs are little more than electronic worksheets. Some tutorials are mere electronic page-turners. There is a tendency for the first uses of a

new technology to be simply re-creations of older forms. For example, many early television programs were just stage plays performed in front of a camera; it took a while for the medium to develop its own unique forms. In similar fashion, many early CAI programs were simply adaptations of older instructional forms such as programmed instruction. But that is changing. Newer software releases tend to make better use of the computer. However, it remains the teacher's responsibility to see that CAI is used productively in the classroom to help students construct new knowledge and is not used as simply busywork.

Classroom management is also an important consideration in the use of CAI. Effective use of CAI often requires special classroom management strategies. With only a single computer in the classroom, a teacher must devise mechanisms to ensure that each student gets access. This may involve a rotation schedule, sign-up sheets, a learning station approach, or some other technique. If a computer laboratory is available in the school, the teacher must plan computer activities well in advance in consultation with the school's technology or media coordinator. Laboratory settings, too, have the potential to become chaotic as many students forge off in their own directions. Careful planning and structured activities are often needed to provide the direction required to keep students productively on task.

THE COMPUTER AS LEARNER

In computer-assisted instruction, the computer assumes the role of teacher. It presents content, poses questions, provides the opportunity for student responses, gives feedback, and so on. In most cases, the student simply responds to whatever has been built into the software. Given that only so much can be included in any one CAI program, that is a limitation. Many computer educators advocate an alternative use of the computer, one in which the student becomes the "teacher" and the computer plays the role of the "learner." This is a more open-ended approach and relies on the students' abilities to construct their own understanding. In order to teach the computer to do something, the student must learn the subject at hand *and* learn to communicate with the computer in a way that it understands. In short, the student must learn to program the computer.

When personal computers first emerged in the late 1970s, considerable attention in education was focused on computer programming. In large part, this was simple necessity. Virtually no tool or CAI software was available for the first personal computers. Practically all one could do with them was programming. As a result, there was a lot of early emphasis on programming. As time went on and both tool and CAI software became available, many educators began to question the need to teach programming. Today it is clear that programming receives much less emphasis than it once did, and there are many educators who feel that today it has *no* place in the curriculum at all.

However, advocates of the use of programming in education remain, and many are quite vocal. Indeed, those who support this form of computer use, such as Seymour Papert, the inventor of the computer language Logo, feel that it is one of the best ways, probably *the* best way, to use the computer with learners. Why? Several rationales can be put forth:

- *Problem solving.* At its core, computer programming is a problem-solving activity. One cannot program the computer to perform some task without applying logical thinking and problem-solving processes. In a sense, programming is a tool to think with.
- *Constructing knowledge.* Computer programming is consistent with the view of learning as knowledge construction. In order to program the computer to perform a task, the learner must come to understand that task very well.
- *Computer understanding.* By programming the computer, one gains a deeper understanding of the computer itself, what it can and cannot do, how it functions, and how it can be controlled.
- *Preparation.* Because computer programming remains an important part of many postsecondary curricula and because a number of jobs involve programming, the teaching of programming—at the secondary level—can serve as preparation for future study and employment.
- *Usefulness.* Finally, knowledge of programming can be useful in performing other tasks. A person with programming knowledge may be able to solve some problems by writing a program. In addition, knowledge of programming can be helpful when working with the command elements of some computer tools, such as spreadsheets and databases. Indeed, software giant Microsoft now uses a form of BASIC, Visual BASIC, as a common applications language in all of its major products.

Programming Fundamentals

Before we proceed with our examination of how the computer can become the "learner" for individualized instruction, we need to establish a few fundamentals. A computer program is a set of instructions that tells the computer how to do something. **Programming** is the process of creating a computer program. Programs are written in a **programming language,** a set of instructions that can be assembled, according to particular rules, to create a working program.

Types of Computer Languages

The most basic language of any computer, called **machine language,** is the binary code that controls the device at the level of its circuits. Because machine language amounts to nothing more than a long stream of zeros and ones, no one actually attempts to program computers in machine language anymore. People have invented computer languages that are more accessible to humans.

Some languages are **low-level languages;** that is, they remain close to machine language. Assembly language is an example. It uses alphabetic representations of basic computer instructions, which are translated by a special program (called an assembler) into machine language. Assembly language is very powerful, and programs written in assembly language are capable of working at blinding speeds. However, using assembly language requires an intimate knowledge of the workings of a particular computer's central processing unit. As a result, it is rarely used by anyone except professional programmers.

The really people-friendly languages are called **high-level languages.** High-level languages contain instructions that more closely resemble natural language (e.g., FORWARD and PRINT). They don't require knowledge of the inner workings of the computer. As a result, they are much easier for people to understand and work with. There are many high-level languages, including Logo, BASIC, HyperTalk, Pascal, C, FORTRAN, LISP, and COBOL. The most prominent languages in schools are Logo, which is popular at the elementary level; BASIC, which is widely used from the middle school level on up; and the languages underlying hypermedia development tools, such as HyperTalk, the language that undergirds *HyperCard.*

In order to function, the computer must translate all high-level languages into machine language. There are two basic kinds of high-level language translators: interpreters and compilers. High-level languages commonly use one form of translator or the other. **Interpreters** translate the program into machine language as the program is operating. That is, they do it "on the fly." The computer languages Logo and BASIC are commonly (but not always) interpreted. **Compilers,** on the other hand, translate an entire program into machine language before the program will operate. The computer languages Pascal and C are commonly compiled.

It tends to be easier to develop and modify programs that are written in interpreted languages. If you make an error in a program in an interpreted language, the program will work up to the point of the error. You can then fix the error and immediately launch the program again. However, interpreted languages are usually comparatively slow, and the interpreter must be present on a particular computer for it to operate an interpreted-language program. Programs that are written in compiled languages must be free of all gross errors in order to get through the compilation process. That alone can be difficult. If an error is discovered when the program is operating, the error must be corrected and the whole program recompiled before it can be tried again. While this makes for a more difficult development process, the net result is a faster program and one that is easier to transport to other computer systems.

The Programming Process

Like other disciplines, computer programming involves basic concepts that tend to apply regard-

less of the particular environment or the particular programming language used. As you learned in Chapter 4, computer systems involve three basic functions: input, processing, and output. Computer programs control one or more (usually all three) of these basic functions. Programming involves specifying, in a way that the computer understands, exactly how this is to occur.

The first step in the programming process is determining how to tackle a particular problem or task. In most programming languages, the programmer must define a series of steps for the computer to follow to reach the solution. The series of steps needed to solve a particular problem or perform a particular task is called an **algorithm.** Thus, in order to properly control the machine, the programmer really has a two-part chore. The first part is figuring out the steps needed, that is, devising the algorithm. This is not a programming task per se but rather a problem-solving task. The second part is coding the algorithm in a computer language.

Defining the algorithm for a particular problem involves specifying, often in exacting detail, the steps needed to obtain a solution. Let's consider a simple example. Suppose that you want your computer to act like a rudimentary adding machine by having it add two numbers that you enter from the keyboard. A basic algorithm for this task might look like this:

1. Accept one number entered from the computer's keyboard (input).
2. Store the number in the computer's memory (processing).
3. Accept a second number entered from the computer's keyboard (input).
4. Store the number in the computer's memory (processing).
5. Retrieve the two numbers from the computer's memory and add them together (processing).
6. Display the resulting sum on the computer's screen (output).

Once the algorithm has been clearly specified, the programmer must translate these steps into commands that the computer can follow. This part of the task demands that the programmer use the proper statements from a particular computer language and the proper **syntax,** the rules for using the computer language. This can be a complex and demanding process. The need for planning and a methodical approach cannot be overstated. As a result, most programmers adopt what is called a top-down approach and rely on structured programming techniques.

The **top-down approach** is an approach to problem solving and programming characterized by beginning with the "big picture" or basic problem. The basic solution is outlined at a fairly high level of abstraction. The basic problem is then broken down into its major parts, and the parts are further broken down until they can be coded. So, one can characterize the top-down approach as one that begins globally and is refined progressively until the desired goal is reached. In practice, the top-down approach looks like this:

1. Begin with the problem or task at hand.
2. Generate a plan or solution (the algorithm) in your own words; that is, start by describing what you want the program to do in English (or another language if you prefer).
3. Translate your plan into a more structured form (see the following discussion).
4. Code the program.
5. Debug the program; that is, locate and fix any errors.
6. Test, revise, and implement the program.

Software designers and computer programmers often use one of several techniques in step 3 above. Most programmers describe the logic of the program using flowcharting. Flowcharting is a graphical means of representing the steps and logic involved in the problem's solution. A clearly written flowchart will simplify the process of writing the program. Software designers often use a technique called storyboarding, originally borrowed from animators. Storyboarding is a technique for illustrating, on paper, what all of the computer screen displays will look like in a program. The paper representations can be redesigned and rearranged before the program is actually coded. Finally, many programmers use a technique called pseudocoding to translate the algorithm into the coded program. Pseudocoding involves writing the steps of the algorithm in English that resembles computer code. This process simplifies the task of translating the written steps into actual computer code by providing an intermediary form.

Structured programming embraces the top-down approach as one element of an overall strategy of computer programming designed to result in organized, easy-to-read, and correct programs. In addition, structured programming relies on modular program design (involving well-tested

subprograms or procedures), a limited set of program constructs (sequencing of program steps, decision points, and loops or repeated sets of statements), and careful documentation of the program. Structured programming is now accepted as the standard approach in the data-processing industry, and considerable criticism has been leveled at schools that teach programming without adhering to this approach. We strongly recommend that the structured approach be central to any computer programming instruction in the schools, at least at the secondary level.

Programming Languages
Logo

Let's turn our attention now to the computer programming languages that are particularly prominent in education. The first one we will consider is Logo. **Logo** was developed by Seymour Papert and his associates at the Massachusetts Institute of Technology (Papert, 1980). Use of Logo is widespread in schools, particularly at the elementary level. It's a popular vehicle for introducing young students to computer programming and for exploring many aspects of mathematics, particularly geometry.

The development of Logo was influenced by Papert's work with famed cognitive psychologist Jean Piaget. Piaget's belief that learning results from one's interaction with the environment was critical in the development of Logo. Piaget saw learning as a constructive process that results from a learner's activity. Papert sought to construct a computer environment that could actively engage the learner.

Papert was also influenced by his association with the artificial intelligence community at MIT. Logo's roots lie in the computer language LISP, a mainstay of artificial intelligence programming. What resulted from this fusion of Piaget's psychology and artificial intelligence programming was Logo, a programming language simple enough even for young children yet with sufficient power for complex programming tasks.

Logo Programming.   The first experiments with Logo involved using the computer to give simple commands such as FORWARD, LEFT, and RIGHT to a small, mobile robot connected to the computer. This robot, which could be made to draw designs on sheets of butcher paper by means of an attached pen, was dubbed a "turtle." The robot turtle evolved into a graphic figure on the computer's screen which could be commanded to draw geometric designs. This figure became the basis of "turtle geometry" or "turtle graphics," one of the most popular uses of Logo.

In turtle graphics mode, the Logo turtle starts in the center of the computer's display screen, an area that adheres to the Cartesian coordinate system familiar to us from mathematics. A number of built-in commands, known as primitives, are available to cause the turtle to act. The most common of these are FORWARD (FD), BACK (BK), LEFT (LT), RIGHT (RT), PENUP (PU), and PENDOWN (PD). The student can use these to steer the turtle around on the display screen and create geometric designs.

For instance, a square can be drawn on the screen by using the following sequence of commands:

FD 50 RT 90 FD 50 RT 90 FD 50 RT 90 FD 50 RT 90

FD 50 commands the turtle to move forward on the screen 50 "turtle steps" or pixels. RT 90 commands the turtle to turn to the right 90°.

As students' knowledge of Logo grows, they are able to accomplish drawing functions by putting the commands in procedures or miniprograms. A more sophisticated way of drawing a square, using REPEAT—Logo's way of performing looping—is shown in Figure 10.4. Once defined, procedures such as SQUARE behave like primitives. Thus they can be used to build even more complex designs. By spinning the square about one corner, a pinwheel shape can be created, as shown in the procedure and resulting design in Figure 10.5.

Logo in the Classroom. Logo can be used for a variety of educational activities or learning objectives in the classroom:

- *Introductory computer programming.* As we have noted, Logo is a popular tool for introducing com-

puter programming to elementary-age students. Simplified versions of Logo have even been used successfully with preschool learners. The appeal of the language should be obvious. Because of its simplicity, a student can actually be doing things with Logo only moments after being introduced to it. Yet it has a richness that can permit problem solving and exploration as far as the student wants to take it.

- *Problem solving.* Using Logo, students can become acquainted with the computer and the control of the computer through a programming language. This involves problem solving, and the procedural orientation of Logo encourages students to adopt a top-down approach. Logo also teaches students that there is more than one way to solve a problem and encourages them to view mistakes as steps on the path to a correct solution.

- *Geometry.* Turtle graphics introduces students to many geometric concepts at a much earlier age, and in a much different way, than has been the case in the past. An elementary-age learner may not understand the concept of degrees in the Logo command RIGHT 90, but before long that student begins to acquire an intuitive sense of degrees and other geometric concepts.

- *Art.* Turtle graphics in Logo can provide a natural linkage to art and demonstrate the geometric underpinnings of many designs. Many people liken complex Logo patterns to those produced by the child's art toy, the Spirograph.

- *Microworlds.* Logo can be used to explore small, well-defined environments, called microworlds, in a variety of subject areas, from mathematics to language to physical science. Microworlds afford the learner the opportunity to gain a rich understanding of one small, well-developed environment.

Figure 10.4 A procedure for drawing a square in Logo

```
TO SQUARE
    REPEAT 4 [FD 50 RT 90]
END
```

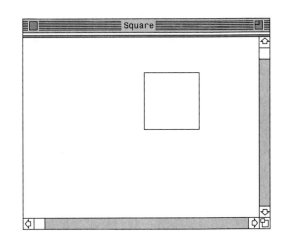

Figure 10.5 A pinwheel design in Logo built from the square procedure

```
TO PINWHEEL
        REPEAT 12 [SQUARE RT 30]
END
```

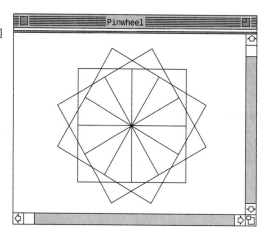

In addition to these applications, Logo has now been extended in ways that afford further opportunities. *LogoWriter* is one of the most popular of the current school implementations of Logo. It combines Logo with a basic word processor for children. Lego Logo, in some ways, takes Logo back to its roots. Students use Lego building blocks and small electric motors to construct simple machines that can be controlled via Logo in much the same way that the original Logo turtle was controlled. In addition, a number of foreign-language versions of Logo have been produced. These allow students whose native language is not English to use and learn with Logo just like English-speaking students.

There is no one right way to use Logo in the classroom. Like the computer itself, it is a flexible tool that can be used in myriad ways. However, advocates of Logo argue that it should be introduced in a social environment where children are free to explore, discover, and invent their own ways of doing things. Most Logo purists argue against any formal computer programming instruction with Logo. Certainly, the concepts of structured programming that we discussed earlier do not mesh well with the open-ended explorations of Logo. Instead, students should be introduced to a new Logo primitive or guided toward more sound programming practices only when they have confronted a problem that demands it. For those teachers who consider this approach to be too inefficient, some balance should be struck between formal instruction and discovery.

BASIC

BASIC (Beginner's All-purpose Symbolic Instruction Code) was developed by John Kemeny and Thomas Kurtz at Dartmouth University in the 1960s. It ranks as one of the oldest computer languages and has a long association with personal computers. BASIC was designed to be used interactively. It is a small, concise language that can be learned quickly. When the first personal computers were developed in the late 1970s, internal memory was limited and very costly. BASIC, because of its compact size, was a natural choice to include with these machines. As a result, BASIC was included on all of the early personal computers, and it developed into the lingua franca of the personal computer world.

Today, because of its relative ease of use and its historical association with the personal computer, BASIC remains an important programming language. While the first versions of BASIC on personal computers were interpreted and not very powerful, newer and more powerful compiled versions of the language are available today. These include Quick-BASIC, True BASIC, and Future BASIC. One of the newest versions of BASIC, Microsoft's Visual BASIC, is a popular Windows development tool and an application-development language underlying Microsoft *Office*, the suite of popular productivity applications. In schools, BASIC continues to be taught as a programming language, usually from the middle school level on up through college.

BASIC Programming.   BASIC has achieved its popularity primarily because of its ease of use. Most of the fundamental commands in the BASIC language are familiar English words. For example, to display information on the computer's screen, BASIC uses the command PRINT, as in

> PRINT "Whatever you want to appear on the screen"

Other BASIC commands similarly rely on familiar words, although the syntax and usage of these words is often different from spoken English.

Because BASIC was designed to be interactive, it includes commands that permit the program to interact with the individual operating the program. A simple example of an interactive BASIC program and the resulting output is shown in Figure 10.6. The key to interactivity in this example is the BASIC command INPUT. This command instructs the program to stop and wait for information to be entered from the keyboard. The UserName$ following INPUT in the third line of the program is called a variable; variables are an important feature of computer languages. A **variable** is a label used to denote a storage area in the computer's memory. It is a way the computer program can keep track of information that does or may change.

In this case, UserName$ is the label given to whatever the user types in response to the question "What is your name?" In our example, the user types "Susan," so "Susan" is stored away in memory with the label UserName$. Once stored in memory, the variable can be used to retrieve the information. In our example, the information is retrieved so that the computer can respond with "Hello Susan!!" Later in the program, Number is another variable used to store the user's response to the arithmetic question. The number can then be checked against the correct answer. This is basically how drill-and-practice programs function.

BASIC in the Classroom.   Like Logo, BASIC has several potential uses in the classroom:

- *Computer programming instruction.* BASIC remains one of the most popular languages for programming instruction. Many school districts offer BASIC programming classes at the middle school and high school levels. BASIC offers a good bridge between the relatively unstructured Logo and the languages more commonly associated with computer science instruction, such as Pascal and C.

- *Problem solving.* BASIC, like other programming languages, can be a useful tool for doing many types of problem solving. For example, students using BASIC programs can explore aspects of mathematics that would be difficult to study otherwise. While a student may be able to identify all of the prime numbers less than 20, going much beyond this can become quite a chore. But it is a relatively simple task to produce a BASIC program that can identify all of the prime numbers below 100, 1,000, or even 1,000,000.

- *Graphics.* Personal computer versions of BASIC provide access to the graphics capabilities of the computers. Having students write programs to create graphics designs teaches them about programming in a way that can be highly motivational.

Hypermedia Scripting Languages

Because of the growing popularity of hypermedia packages, such as *HyperCard* for the Macintosh, *Linkway* and *Linkway Live* for MS-DOS machines, and *Toolbook* for the Windows environment, many schools are now concentrating on the scripting languages that underlie these packages. These scripting languages include HyperTalk, the language in *HyperCard,* and OpenScript, the language in *Toolbook.* Scripting languages are programming languages that are usually interpreted, relatively easy to learn, and easy to use.

Figure 10.6   A simple interactive BASIC program

```
Untitled

BASIC Program                          Example Output
CLS
PRINT "What is your name?"             What is your name?
INPUT UserName$                        ? Susan
PRINT "Hello ";UserName$;"!!"          Hello Susan!!
PRINT "What is 9 times 7?"             What is 9 times 7?
INPUT Number                           ? 63
IF Number = 63 THEN                    You are right!
    PRINT "You are right!"
      ELSE
    PRINT "The answer is 63."
END IF
END
```

Programming in hypermedia packages is often different from traditional programming languages such as BASIC and Pascal. For one thing, scripting languages have characteristics of what are known as object-oriented programming systems (**OOPS**). Each thing that one sees on-screen (card or page, button, text field, etc.) is treated as an object, and each object can have programming code associated with it. Hypermedia packages are also **event-driven,** which means that programs respond to events in the environment. For example, when the user clicks on a button, this triggers a mouse action event. A program written in the scripting language can respond to this event to cause some action to occur.

Figure 10.7 shows a simple example from *Hyper-Card* and its scripting language, HyperTalk. The script (program) shown corresponds to the Continue button used for navigating in the *HyperCard* stack. In this case, if the mouse button is released while the mouse is over the Continue button, a mouseUp event is triggered. The script then directs the computer to go to the next card in the stack.

While much can be done in hypermedia packages like *HyperCard* and *Toolbook* with only minimal programming, the scripting languages unlock the real power of these programs for dealing with many useful tasks. Because hypermedia packages have become popular in schools, many schools now teach these packages and their scripting languages in place of or in addition to the more traditional languages such as BASIC. As a result, students from the upper elementary grades on up through high school and college may be exposed to scripting language programming.

Other Programming Languages

There are hundreds of other computer programming languages. Some, such as FORTRAN and COBOL—which are used for scientific and business programming purposes, respectively—are well known. However, they have little impact in education circles. There are a few other languages, however, that do play a role in education. We briefly mention three here.

Pascal. Pascal, named for the 17th-century Frenchman who developed one of the first mechanical calculating machines, was invented by Swiss computer scientist Niklaus Wirth in the late 1960s and early 1970s. Pascal was designed with structured programming in mind. To use Pascal, one must plan carefully and program in structured fashion. As a result, Pascal has become popular as a programming language in college computer science programs. This influence has spilled over into the secondary schools. When the College Board developed an advanced-placement examination for high school students planning to pursue computer science in college, Pascal was selected as the basis for the examination. So, many high schools now teach Pascal programming to prepare students for postsecondary education.

Pilot. Pilot is an example of what is called an authoring language. It is a computer language designed for the development of educational software. As a result, some teachers use Pilot to develop programs for their students. A language that is commonly interpreted, Pilot is easy to learn and to use. In addition, most versions of Pilot have built-in capabilities for handling tasks that are common in educational software programs. For example, in Pilot it is relatively easy to check the accuracy of a student's typewritten response to a question. In addition, text handling, graphics handling, and branching tend to be easier than in other programming languages. There are versions of Pilot available for many personal computers.

Figure 10.7 Sample HyperTalk script in *HyperCard*

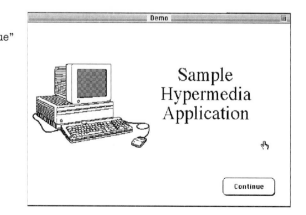

```
Script of button "Continue"

on mouseUp

    go to the next card

end mouseUp
```

Sample Hypermedia Application

C and C++. The C language was developed at the Bell Laboratories in the early 1970s. It features a blend of high-level and low-level language characteristics. This makes it relatively easy to use but quite powerful. In addition, C programs can be quite portable; they can be compiled to run on everything from mainframe computers to personal computers. Today C is the language that is most commonly used for writing systems software and major application programs such as commercial word processors. C++ is a recent extension of C that adds OOPS features. Because of their popularity with professional programmers, C and C++ are being taught more widely at the college and even secondary levels.

Problems and Pitfalls

Programming is, and probably will remain, a controversial aspect of computers in education. Detractors point out that tool applications become more powerful every day and that few students will ever become professional programmers. So, they say, we shouldn't be wasting our time teaching kids to program computers. Proponents, on the other hand, stress the problem-solving and practical benefits of learning to program. The debate seems likely to continue for some time to come.

Individual languages, too, have their advocates and their critics. Many see Logo as an excellent tool for doing numerous problem-solving activities and for teaching children about computers. However, investigations of the problem-solving claims of Logo's supporters have led to some questions, and it is difficult to prove that learning to use Logo results in students' enhanced problem-solving abilities. BASIC, while among the most widely used computer languages, is often criticized because older versions lack structure. Students who learned to program in older versions of BASIC, without attention to structured programming principles, may have actually been harmed by this experience. They may have to "unlearn" bad habits later on. While this isn't the fault of BASIC per se, BASIC is often the object of the blame.

When you use the computer as the "learner," it is important to keep the goals of the activity in mind and to pay heed to what the experts say about using the programming language. The developers of Logo stress the importance of having an open, exploratory classroom environment. Students need time and opportunity to explore and learn, so adequate time must be set aside, and too much structure may be harmful. Additionally, the teacher needs to realize that there are many ways to solve particular problems. Some teachers are uncomfortable with the open-endedness of computer programming. Yet this is an essential element of using the computer as "learner." The teacher needs to adopt the role of a guide helping the learner to learn.

At the secondary level, the focus in computer programming should shift to the application of structured programming principles. At this level, while there are still many ways to solve particular problems, not all solutions may be equally valid in terms of their adherence to proper programming principles. Even scripting languages, such as HyperTalk, which may appear not to require much structure, can be approached from a structured programming perspective. Teachers should help students begin to develop proper habits early on. To be properly prepared for postsecondary education and computer vocations, students must know how to properly design and test computer programs.

SUMMARY

In this chapter we examined approaches to the instruction of individuals. While many of the approaches previously examined can be used with individuals, three are particularly appropriate: tutorial, drill and practice, and simulation. In addition to these basic approaches, a number of more complex approaches or instructional systems are designed primarily for individualized instruction. Most of these complex approaches take a mastery learning perspective. These complex approaches include programmed instruction, audio-tutorial instruction, the personalized system of instruction (PSI), individualized education programs (IEPs), computer-assisted instruction (CAI), and using the computer as "learner." The last two were the subject of the chapter CUE.

Computer-assisted instruction involves the use of the computer in delivering instruction to the student. Many basic approaches may be embodied in CAI. When the computer plays the role of the "learner," it is the student who must "teach" it through the use of a programming language. Programming requires students to do problem solving. Three programming languages are especially prominent in education: Logo, BASIC, and hypermedia scripting languages.

REFLECTIVE QUESTIONS AND ACTIVITIES

1. Think about the times you experienced individualized instruction. What approaches were used? How did you react to these approaches? How did you like individualized instruction as compared with small- or large-group instruction? Why?

2. Arrange a visit to a school, university, or business that is using one of the specific systems of instruction mentioned in this chapter. Take notes about your impressions of the visit. What basic approaches were embodied in this system?

3. Find an advertisement for a CAI program in a magazine or catalog. Write to the company for more information or for a demonstration or preview copy of the software.

4. Preview several examples of CAI software. Write down your reactions to the programs (use the appropriate checklist in Appendix B). Make a list of how you might use them in the classroom for individualized instruction.

5. Think about your feelings concerning the computer programming debate. Do you think computer programming should be part of the school curriculum? Why or why not?

INTEGRATION AND SYNTHESIS

In Chapters 8 and 9 we examined instructional approaches that are appropriate for large and small groups of learners. In this chapter we examined approaches and systems of instruction that are most appropriate for individualized instruction. You now can see the range of instructional approaches that can be applied to instructional settings involving any number of students. The computer, of course, can play an important role in many of these instructional approaches. In this chapter we focused on two of the most common uses of computers in schools: CAI and the computer as "learner." In Chapter 11 we will look further at computers in the classroom by examining some of the integration and management issues associated with computers and other instructional technologies.

Chapter 11 concludes Section III, the implementation of instruction. Immediately thereafter we begin the final section of the book: evaluation. In that section we will explore the effectiveness of the instructional materials that were designed (Section II) and implemented (Section III), the learning of our students, and ways in which both can be increased through the use of instructional technology.

SUGGESTED READINGS

Kulik, C. C., & Kulik, J. A. (1991). Effectiveness of computer-based instruction: An updated analysis. *Computers in Human Behavior, 7,* 75–94.

Papert, S. (1980). *Mindstorms: Children, computers, and powerful ideas.* New York: Basic Books.

Russell, J. D. (1978). *The audio-tutorial system.* The Instructional Design Library (Vol. 3). Englewood Cliffs, NJ: Educational Technology.

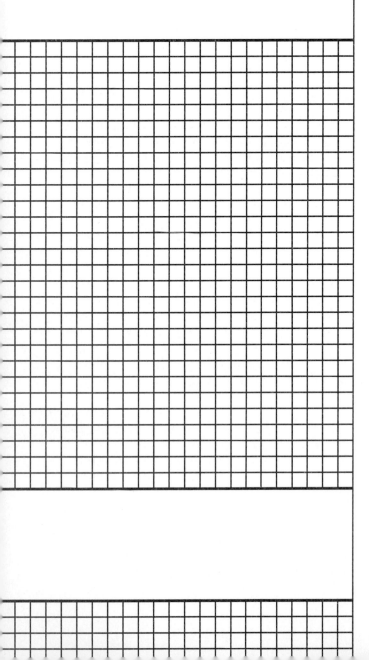

Chapter 11

Managing Instructional Technology

KEY WORDS AND CONCEPTS

File server	Copyright
Ergonomics	Technology coordinator
Virus	

OUTCOMES

After reading and studying this chapter, you will be able to:

- Discuss the importance of planning in the technology implementation process.
- Describe how technology integration in the schools can meet students', teachers', curricular, and societal needs.
- Identify the elements of a school's technology program that should be evaluated during technology planning.
- Discuss criteria for the evaluation of computer hardware systems.
- Discuss factors that should be considered when planning a computer facility.
- List preventative maintenance measures for computer hardware and software.
- Discuss factors that should be addressed by school policies and procedures related to access to technology, rules for use of computer facilities, and software usage.
- Outline a step-by-step procedure for evaluating and selecting computer software.
- Discuss the implications of copyright law for the use of computers and multimedia in the schools.
- Describe the role of a technology coordinator in a school.
- Identify basic principles for conducting technology in-service training.
- Discuss basic strategies for classroom management and describe how they can apply to the use of technology in the classroom.

■ INTRODUCTION

We know of a woman who, not long ago, turned her hobby of making jewelry into a lucrative business. How did this come about? Well, in the beginning, Mary just made jewelry in her spare time for fun. Friends and relatives admired her work, so she began to make pieces for others. Before long, word started to spread, and Mary realized that she could probably sell her work for profit. So she set about to turn her jewelry making into a business.

At first things didn't go particularly well. Mary found herself jumping from one thing to another and having difficulty finding the time to make new pieces. After a while she realized that she needed to get organized, so she set aside a regular time to work on her jewelry business and established a plan for producing various items. Her time management and production-schedule planning paid off. It didn't take long for things to start clicking, and soon people began placing more orders. Her business was on its way!

Mary's jewelry was stylish and tremendously popular. After a while, orders began to flood in. She hired another jewelry maker, and then another, and then another, to help her turn out more pieces. Before long, Mary and a large workforce were busy making jewelry. Then disaster struck. Market conditions changed, and Mary and her employees were so busy creating pieces that they failed to take notice. Orders plummeted, and Mary's business quickly fell into dire financial straits. Without clear direction and plans for handling problems, Mary and her business were floundering. Realizing that she couldn't work out the problems on her own, Mary called on a management consulting firm for help.

The management consulting firm began by helping Mary and her employees develop a business plan. The plan laid out a course for the business to follow, including a company vision, development and marketing plans, methods for making effective use of equipment and inventories, and ways to appropriately use company personnel. In addition, because Mary lacked much business background herself, the consulting firm recommended that she hire a business expert to handle day-to-day operations. Mary incorporated all of the suggestions, and today her jewelry company is thriving and stable.

What does this story have to do with instructional technology in the schools? There are parallels. When computers and allied technologies first came into the schools, just as when Mary first started her business, there was freedom to do almost anything. However, this lack of organization hampered effectiveness. As technology grew in the schools, just as when Mary's business grew, things looked good at first. Then problems arose that made the need for planning and management more evident. Just as Mary's business was at economic risk, so too are the tremendous investments in money, time, and effort that schools make in new technologies every year. Planning and management are just as important in schools as in a business. In large and complex organizations such as schools, the key to realizing the full benefits of "hard" technologies such as computers, multimedia, and other allied technologies is proper application of the "soft" technology of instructional design and delivery. A key aspect of this is careful planning and management.

This chapter explores some of the important integration and management considerations that are associated with the acquisition, use, and maintenance of instructional technology—particularly computers and related technologies—in the schools. ■

PLANNING FOR TECHNOLOGY INTEGRATION AND MANAGEMENT

To begin, we want to emphasize the importance of planning for technology integration. The need for technology planning cannot be overstated; it is critically important! Just as individual teachers need to plan their teaching and learning activities for the classroom, so do teachers, schools, and school districts all need to plan for technology implementation (Dyrli & Kinnaman, 1994).

Not so long ago, when computers were first finding their way into classrooms, affairs were pretty much catch as catch can. One teacher might use one brand of computer with a particular software package in a favorite curriculum area, while a teacher down the hall might use a different brand of computer with different software to study the same subject in a different way. Computers were used by only a few interested teachers, and there was a complete lack of hardware, software, and curriculum planning. When the number of computers in schools was still small, this situation wasn't a big problem. However, as schools invested more and more money in computers and related technologies, it began to become apparent that planning and cen-

tralized administration were necessary. Gradually, schools began to form technology committees and to designate knowledgeable individuals as technology coordinators to make decisions and manage resources. Today most schools have reached the point where at least minimal technology planning is conducted. However, schools today vary widely in the extent and sophistication of their technology planning and management, and many remain relatively ill-prepared to deal with increasingly important technology issues.

Forming a Technology Committee

For those schools that have not yet begun to consider, or that are preparing to revisit, technology issues, the first step is to create a district-level (or sometimes building-level) technology committee. The committee should have representation from all of the constituent groups that have a stake in the committee's work. Clearly, it should include teachers, and the teachers should be representative of the various grade levels, disciplines, and schools involved. It should also include administrators. Adequate communication with, and support of, school administration is essential. Representation from other important constituent groups such as parents, the community, and the school board should also be included. Even student representation, assuming an adequate level of understanding and maturity, should be considered. The committee would also benefit from the presence of at least one educational technology expert to serve as a consultant.

A technology planning committee should have representation from all key constituencies.

Developing a Vision

The first task of any school's technology committee is to develop a vision of education and to articulate a role for technology in that vision. Many schools make the mistake of jumping on the technology bandwagon simply because it's there. Technology concerns, or the desire to put computers in classrooms simply because others are doing it, should not be allowed to cloud the issue. Educational considerations must come first. Often, insufficient attention is paid to clarifying the educational mission, in general, and the role of technology in achieving that vision, in particular. This is an all-important first step and shouldn't be overlooked.

The committee should begin by asking fundamental questions about education. How do the school and community view education? What are the general educational goals for all students? Can a brief statement be drafted that captures the school's educational mission (see Figure 11.1)? Once the committee establishes a general education mission and basic goals, it can consider the role of technology, at least in a broad context. When is the use of technology appropriate? Are there aspects of the education vision—distance education, for example—that clearly suggest the need for technology? In general, the justifications for technology integration can be viewed from four broad perspectives: meeting students' needs, meeting teachers' needs, meeting curricular needs, and meeting societal needs. A technology plan may reflect any or—more likely—all of these. Let's consider each one.

- *Meeting students' needs.* In most cases, the first and most powerful justification for integrating technology in the schools is that of meeting students' needs. While this may seem obvious, it's worth examining. For example, most schools agree that helping students learn to read and write effectively is one of the most important goals of education. Today's technology can help achieve that goal. Using a word processor can help students write longer and better compositions, thus offering a compelling reason for using technology in writing instruction (Bangert-Drowns, 1993). When a school's goals relate to specific student needs, specific applications of technology can be identified to help achieve those goals. The school's technology plan should also be sensitive to meeting students' needs equitably. All students can benefit from access to technology, and schools must take measures to avoid possible inequities (e.g., haves vs. have-nots, boys vs. girls, regular students vs. those with special needs).

- *Meeting teachers' needs.* If meeting students' needs is obvious, then so too is meeting teachers' needs. However, this category is often overlooked. It's sometimes said that education is the only business that provides technology to the clients (students) before the employees (teachers). Unfortunately, it's often true that schools purchase computers for student use long before they purchase them for teacher use. As we have emphasized in this text, computers are powerful tools for both teachers and students. Computers can help teachers accomplish a variety of tasks more effectively and efficiently. Furthermore, teachers who use computers for their own purposes tend to become more confident and capable in using them to help students accomplish learning tasks. Generally, those schools that have provided computers to teachers for their personal use have found that the dividends ultimately extend to the students and the school as well (McCarthy, 1993).

- *Meeting curricular needs.* Of course, technology can also be of benefit in meeting specific curricular needs. Perhaps the most obvious example is the secondary business education curriculum. Because computers are commonplace in the business world, it is important for schools to use computers in business education in order to properly prepare students for the workplace. There are many other examples, from practically every content area, of specific curricula that could benefit from the use of computer-related technology.

- *Meeting societal needs.* Technology is a fundamental part of our lives today, meeting many broad societal needs. Many jobs involve the use of technology, and most experts predict that in the future even more jobs will involve technology. Many of the issues that our legal system must deal with (e.g., privacy, copyright) relate to the use of new "hard" technology. In order to prepare students for participation in our democratic society and for the realities of life and work in the 21st century, schools need to integrate technology throughout the curriculum.

By considering these four areas of need in broad terms, a school's technology committee can begin the process of outlining a plan for integrating and managing technology in the schools. However, this is just the beginning. The next steps involve getting more specific about what sorts of technology should be implemented, at what grade levels, in what curricular areas, and how.

Figure 11.1 Excerpts from two school technology plans, one articulating a vision for instructional technology and the other showing the action agenda for one year of a multiyear plan

---

Philosophy of Instructional Technology

Instructional technology in the Tippecanoe School Corporation will provide and encourage an atmosphere for life long learning. Technology strives to meet the educational goals of the corporation, supports the curriculum, and provides avenues for assessment of student progress. Technology should facilitate creativity and productivity as well as expand communication. Learning opportunities for staff and students involving technology are provided on a regular and ongoing basis. TSC maintains a standard of equal access for all and legal use of all forms of media.

Adopted by the TSC Technology Council, April 1993

This document is to serve as a road map for technology in the Tippecanoe School Corporation. The plan is developed by teachers, administrators and patrons of the Tippecanoe School Corporation. It is intended to be an ever-changing plan which will be shaped by both the needs of the school district and the emergence of new technologies. Guided by the above philosophy, this course of action addresses both the instructional and administrative needs of our schools.

Since 1987, it has been the intent of TSC to integrate technology into the curriculum. Our belief is that technology is not an end in itself, but rather a tool for learning to be used in all subject areas. The TSC model for instructional computers continues to be that each school contains at least one networked lab as well as networked classroom machines. This goal should be realized during the life of this 4-year plan. Additional technologies have and will continue to be integral parts of our educational program as well. Among these are CD-ROM, telecommunications, videodisc players, and other multi-media. As technology grows, so must we too. (*Source:* Tippecanoe School Corporation, Lafayette, IN)

YEAR THREE
1996–97

Goal	Strategy	Action
III	3	Increase number of laserdisc (2) and CD-I players (2), and purchase portable, networkable computer notebooks (2)
III	4	Provide large screens in needed classrooms and add two mobile I.CD/projection systems (elem. and jr-sr h.s.)
III	1	Expand phone system for integrated information system (IIS)-infrastructure to establish school-wide communications, initiate homework hotline, voicemail, telecommunications, and distance learning (DOE grant w/WCIESC allows one Parke Co. school to be local # hub for InterNet)
V	4	Establish voice mail, homework hotline, and parent/school communication system accessible at all hours
I	5	Assess need for additional K-12 curriculum software, purchase upgrades
III	4	Begin replacement of 45 original IBM Model 25s/30s/50s in elem/h.s./bus/cad (will be 9–10 yrs old—**replace 10 per year w/3 printers**)
III	1	Establish networked computer mini-labs (workstations w/printer) in both elementary (4) and jr-sr h.s. (6) libraries
IV	4, 5	Provide intensive and on-going staff development training in elem and jr-sr h.s. for all staff and administration (budget for in-service subs, trainers, wkshops)
I	4	Evaluate staff development, usage, implementation, application, and results of present technologies
I	5	Evaluate, revise, and continue implementation of long-range technology/curriculum plan

(*Source:* Turkey Run Community Schools, Marshall, IN)

Evaluating the Status of Technology Implementation

Before a technology committee can get specific about its technology implementation plan, it's important for it to assess the current status of the district's technology implementation efforts. Billings (1985) has suggested that some of the important steps are:

- *Catalog hardware and software resources.* Future efforts must build on the existing base of resources, so it is important to identify those hardware and software resources that are already available in the school district.

- *Identify current uses of technology.* In addition to cataloging the physical resources, it's important to find out how these resources are used. What technology implementation goals are being pursued? In what manner? With what resources?

- *Assess faculty and staff proficiency.* How technologically literate are the faculty and staff? Who uses technology, and for what purposes? Which faculty members and staff might be able to lead technology implementation efforts? What kinds of in-service training have been done in the past? What appears to be needed?

- *Evaluate students' use of technology.* Do students have the opportunities to acquire the technology-related knowledge and skills they are supposed to learn? Are technology-related knowledge and skills routinely assessed? How do students perform? Are their needs for future schooling, employment, and daily life being met?

Various methods can be used to collect the information that is needed. One of the most effective means to get this information is through questionnaires completed by teachers and other appropriate individuals. An example of a faculty/staff questionnaire is shown in Figure 11.2. In addition, the committee may want to make classroom observations and conduct interviews with key personnel to get in-depth information and to verify whether or not survey results accurately reflect actual practice. Student achievement data can be collected. In addition, the committee may want to include input from parents or other community members. Interviewing or sending a questionnaire to recent high school graduates may help to determine how well prepared those students were to use technology in college or on the job.

The information that is collected should be summarized in a report on the status of technology implementation. This report should organize the information in such a way that the committee can see what is currently going on, how present efforts might be extended, and what new efforts may be needed in the future.

Considerations in Technology Integration

The technology committee's final task is to develop a framework for integrating technology that has sufficient detail to permit measurable outcomes. To accomplish this, specific technology objectives must be associated with the general goals outlined by the committee. Technology implementation efforts should be planned over a reasonable, short-term period. In most cases, a three- to five-year plan is desirable. This looks far enough into the future to provide useful guidance, but not so far that conditions are likely to change dramatically because of changes in the technology. In order to ensure that the plan stays on course, however, it's important to have clearly achievable objectives for each year of the multiyear plan. Observable progress is the key to the success of the plan.

Let's consider an example. A general technology goal of the district might be to use technology in ways that model uses of technology in the workplace. A specific objective that addresses this goal might be the following: *Students in all secondary science classes will have experience using the computer as a data-collection and data-analysis device in the science laboratory.*

Actual implementation of particular objectives is best left to the discretion of local committees of teachers. In our example, a committee of teachers from the science department would be best qualified to identify ways to actually accomplish the objective. They might decide to use microcomputer-based laboratory (MBL) sensors in some instances, spreadsheets in others, and graphing calculators in still others. Any attempt to centrally mandate particular approaches would likely be doomed to failure. Teachers have a tremendous amount of autonomy in their classrooms—their own ways of doing things. A decentralized approach that emphasizes shared leadership in achieving technology goals and objectives generates a sense of ownership and involvement across a broad base of faculty.

In identifying ways to implement particular objectives, teachers need to take into consideration several factors:

- *Availability of hardware.* Of course, one important factor is the availability of hardware. A nationwide survey of technology-using teachers found that access to technology, along with motivation and a supportive environment, was critical to

Figure 11.2   Sample faculty/
staff questionnaire

Faculty/Staff Computer Survey

Rate yourself on the following statements according to the scale:

A – never   B – rarely   C – occasionally

D – fairly often   E – extensively

	Never				Extensively
1. I have participated in technology-related in-service training offered by my school, regional training center, or other organization.	A	B	C	D	E
2. I have taken college-credit courses in computer education or computer science.	A	B	C	D	E
3. I have pursued coursework towards computer teaching certification.	A	B	C	D	E
4. I have served on local, regional, or state educational technology committees.	A	B	C	D	E
5. I have participated in hardware or software purchasing decisions for my school.	A	B	C	D	E
6. I have used computers or related technologies (e.g., CD-ROM) for instructional purposes in my teaching.	A	B	C	D	E
7. I have used other advanced technologies (e.g., videodiscs, satellite video) for instructional purposes in my teaching.	A	B	C	D	E
8. I have used computers or related technologies for management or personal productivity purposes.	A	B	C	D	E
9. I have encouraged my students to use computers and other technologies.	A	B	C	D	E

How have you used technology? Please describe any software/hardware used.

Are there ways you would like to use technology in the future? If so, what are some of these?

What kinds of technology in-service training would you find beneficial?

success (Hadley & Sheingold, 1993). If the science department has only one set of MBL sensors, that may dictate the use of a demonstration approach, at least initially. However, if the science committee feels that use of MBLs is very important for all science students to experience, then a recommendation to purchase additional sets of MBL sensors may become a part of the technology plan.

- *Availability of software.* Software availability is another key aspect of integration planning. What software is available? Are sufficient copies, or appropriate licenses, owned to support the planned integration activities? Is the software up to date? Again, if appropriate software isn't available for key parts of the technology plan, a

recommendation to purchase needed software or to upgrade existing software may be added to the plan.

- *Curriculum.* The curriculum itself is another important consideration. It's important to examine the curriculum from the perspective of technology fit. What aspects of the curriculum would benefit from the use of technology? While it's best to begin with the curriculum and look for technology fits, in some cases technology may suggest curriculum revisions. For example, widespread availability of graphing calculators might lead to completely different ways of approaching some topics in science and mathematics.
- *Individual's teaching styles.* Of course, individual teachers have their preferred ways of teaching

and managing the classroom. Hadley and Shein-gold's (1993) study found that no one profile could adequately characterize teacher accomplishment with technology. Individuals need to find ways to use technology that work with or complement their teaching styles. In addition, just as technology may suggest new ways of approaching the curriculum, it may also suggest new ways for approaching teaching. While generalization is always difficult, it is a common belief that computers and related technologies can help create a more learner-centered classroom in which the teacher acts as a guide and coach. So, while technology can support lecturing, it can also lead to a classroom less focused on lecturing and other teacher-centered methods. Teachers often need help in finding the most appropriate ways to use technology. Therefore, staff development and support are critical elements to include in a technology plan for a school district.

Thus, we see that there are a number of considerations in planning for technology implementation, from the school district level down to the individual teacher. All are important, and all affect the likelihood of success in efforts to integrate technology in teaching and learning. Now let's look in more detail at some of the important issues related to hardware, software, and personnel.

HARDWARE ISSUES

In the best of circumstances, hardware is the last thing teachers should have to worry about. Ideally, teachers should begin by identifying what they want to be able to do. Then instructional materials (software) should be located to support this objective. Finally, the hardware to support the software should be identified. For example, if a social studies teacher wants her class to learn about the American civil rights movement of the 1960s, and a good videotape is in the school's media center, a VCR to play that tape should be the least of her concerns. In most U.S. schools today, this would be a relatively minor concern; VCRs are commonplace, and VHS tapes are an accepted standard. In the computer arena, however, things can be more complicated.

With computers, at least, the ideal is rarely possible anymore. Most schools already have established a substantial base of both software and hardware. Therefore, issues of compatibility with the installed base often come to the fore and color subsequent decisions. While many popular software packages today are available on multiple computer platforms, many programs remain available on only

one. The teacher who locates a great software package for the Macintosh, but teaches in a school with all IBMs, is out of luck. He or she would have to convince the school to change, or at least diversify, its hardware base in order to make use of the software package. Of course, particular hardware platforms often have their own advocates (or in some cases zealots) who argue for the merits of one or the other. For these reasons, hardware selection decisions are often at the core of many schools' plans for technology integration.

Computer Hardware Evaluation and Acquisition

Today, three computer models dominate the installed base in U.S. schools: the Apple II family, the MS-DOS family, and Apple Macintosh computers. Apple II–family computers (including the Apple II, II+, IIe, IIc, and IIgs) are still fairly widespread in the schools. One of the earliest personal computers, the Apple II came to dominate the education sphere because of its color capability and easy expandability. However, the technology underlying the Apple II eventually became outdated, and the manufacture of the Apple II family was finally discontinued. As a result, the choice today is largely between Windows and MS-DOS–family computers (IBM-PCs and compatibles from companies like Tandy, Compaq, Dell, Gateway, etc.) and Apple Macintoshes (including the LC, Powerbook, and Quadra). Recently, IBM and Apple have cooperated on the development of a new generation of computers, called PowerPCs, that can support software from both platforms. This development may considerably alter hardware selection decisions in the future. For now, though, Macintosh and MS-DOS machines are the two main personal computer options.

The PowerPC is a new type of personal computer resulting from the cooperation of IBM and Apple.

Let's look at the factors you should consider when selecting a personal computer hardware system:

- *Software availability.* Clearly, software is one of the most critical considerations. Without the right software, even the best hardware is worthless. Be sure to consider both systems software (the software that operates the machine) and applications software, including standard tools and educational software. The Apple Macintosh is known for very easy-to-use systems software. The Macintosh popularized the graphical user interface (GUI) and use of a mouse. There is good availability of tool applications and a growing selection of educational software for the Macintosh. The MS-DOS family is considered to be somewhat less easy to use, although Microsoft Windows has helped MS-DOS computers become more user-friendly. There is excellent availability of tool software and a reasonably good base of educational software.

- *Processor.* The microprocessor, at the heart of the computer, determines much about the computer's performance. Newer processors are capable of more processing power than their predecessors (e.g., 32-bit operations vs. 8-bit operations), and they work at faster speeds (more megahertz). The Apple Macintosh line is based on processors made by Motorola, while MS-DOS computers are based on processors made by Intel. IBM and Apple's new PowerPCs are based on a new processor from Motorola that uses a new design that promises to support both MS-DOS and Macintosh software. While the latest and greatest is rarely necessary for school applications, schools should look for newer processor models in order to reduce the potential for obsolescence.

- *Screen display.* Most personal computers today are designed for GUIs. Graphics capability varies widely and can significantly affect the cost of a computer system. The original Apple Macintosh was black and white only, but today's models support varying levels of color. Low-end Macintoshes support what is called 8-bit color, which results in up to 256 simultaneous screen colors, while high-end Macintoshes support 24-bit "true" color, capable of millions of hues. More color requires more display memory and higher processing speeds. The MS-DOS family has gone through numerous graphical standards, including CGA, EGA, mCGA, and VGA. The standard today is VGA, and many machines support even better Super VGA or XGA graphics. These, like the Macintosh, can support full 24-bit color.

- *Sound.* Sound can be a useful feature, and with the growth of multimedia applications it's becoming increasingly important. Apple Macintoshes all have built-in digital audio playback and recording capability. For most MS-DOS computers, digital audio capability is not built in but must be added through an expansion board (e.g., Sound Blaster).

- *Keyboard.* The keyboard is the basic input device, and having a good one is very important. The Apple Macintosh family has two options, a standard keyboard and an extended keyboard. The standard keyboard is sufficient for basic uses but lacks many special function keys. The extended keyboard is preferable for higher-level uses such as terminal emulation when communicating with a mainframe computer. MS-DOS computers almost always come with full keyboards, as they pioneered keyboards with function keys, numeric pads, and separate cursor-control keys. When you are shopping for portable computers, ease of use and functionality of the keyboard can be an especially important consideration.

- *Internal memory.* Memory demands have increased dramatically over the past few years. It's important to plan for a lot; memory is relatively inexpensive. For both Macintosh and MS-DOS computers, 8M of RAM is probably the minimum needed today. Special applications, such as multimedia development, may require much more.

- *External storage.* Today's applications also demand a great deal of external storage. In addition to one or more floppy drives, a hard disk is essential. Both Macintosh and MS-DOS computers rely primarily on 3.5-inch floppy disk drives with a capacity of at least 1.44M. Many MS-DOS machines still support 5.25-inch floppy disks with a 1.2M capacity. Today hard disk capacities start at around 200M and go up into the gigabytes.

- *Peripherals.* Consider the availability of other peripherals for the system. For example, almost all systems today come equipped with a mouse. A printer is an important peripheral for most systems. With the growth of multimedia, you will probably want to consider acquiring at least some CD-ROM drives and videodisc players. For development work, scanners and digitizers allow images to be imported into multimedia applications. While all of the computer brands support a variety of peripherals, specific brands of peripherals may work only with specific computers; it's important to thoroughly research compatibility issues prior to purchase.

- *System expandability.* As your needs change, it's useful to be able to upgrade your system to meet those needs. Built-in system expandability provides this capability. Most personal computers have one or more expansion slots for add-in boards and support additional memory without modification. Some computers are designed to accept newer processors to upgrade performance.

- *Service.* Service options are available on all machines. One option is a service contract or extended warranty that covers future repairs, but this is often costly. IBM is known for its high-quality, on-site service. Another option—offered by many computer stores—is carry-in service. Tandy Corporation has been successful, in part, because of its numerous stores. If no other options are available, you can ship your computer back to the manufacturer for service.

- *Cost.* Cost is always an important consideration. Today systems can range anywhere from a few hundred dollars to more than $10,000. A good basic computer system for school use can generally be purchased for between $1,000 and $2,500.

In most cases, at least for volume purchases, schools must go through a bid process in order to acquire computer systems and other hardware. In this process, specifications for the equipment are detailed. Bid specifications must be written carefully to ensure that only the desired equipment will be obtained. These bid specifications are then sent to a number of vendors for bids, and the vendor submitting the lowest bid is awarded the contract to fill the order.

When a hardware order begins to come in, deliveries must be checked against the purchase orders for accuracy. New equipment must be checked to make certain that it operates, and it must be inventoried. Proper record keeping is essential, especially in larger school districts. Finally, the equipment must be distributed to the proper locations and set up for operation. This can be a difficult and time-consuming task. Many schools have technology coordinators who perform this service. If no technology coordinator is available, a computer-using teacher should be given release time to inventory and set up equipment.

Planning Computer Facilities

Acquisition of hardware suggests the need for facilities planning and management. As with everything else that we have discussed, it is important to carefully consider needs and to plan in advance in order to make the most of computers and other technology-related equipment. Many factors need to be considered. Let's examine some of the most important ones.

Concentrate or Disperse?

One of the most basic decisions regarding technology is whether it should be concentrated in one or more locations (e.g., a computer lab) or dispersed throughout a school. There are pros and cons associated with each approach, and the decision often has as much to do with philosophy as with practical considerations. Concentrating computers in a laboratory may provide a sufficient "critical mass" to allow entire classes of students to work on computers at one time. Peripherals, such as printers, can be shared. Security is enhanced, and it's easier to house and maintain software and other resources in one central location. But when computers are concentrated in one or two locations, conflicts and scheduling problems are common. Simply getting access to the facilities can be a barrier to use. On the other hand, when computers are dispersed—by putting one or more computers in each classroom, for example—they are readily accessible, and the teacher or students in a class can use them every day. However, using one or two computers with an entire class requires creativity and classroom management. Unless the computers are networked, each teacher must have copies of software available in the classroom. Resource management becomes complicated, and security is decreased.

Laboratories tend to be preferred in many secondary schools, where simultaneous use of computers by many individuals, such as word processing in English class, is more common. Dispersal of individual computers into classrooms is preferred in many elementary schools, where the computer is often treated as one of several learning stations through which students rotate. Some schools have taken a hybrid approach by establishing mobile minilabs. In this approach, several computers are placed on carts that can be wheeled into a particular classroom to create a small laboratory for one or more days. The use of mobile stations is also a common strategy for sharing resources such as VCRs and videodisc players. Of course, as numbers of computers in a school increase, it's possible for the school to get the best of both worlds by establishing laboratories and by placing computers in classrooms.

Locating a Computer Facility

Assuming a school decides to establish a computer facility, where should it be located? Of course, for many schools the answer to this question is already fixed. If space is at a premium, the computer laboratory may have to go anywhere there's room for it. When choices are available, however, an interior, centrally located room is preferred. A central location makes for easy access, and an interior location usually provides better security and climate control. Many schools place a computer laboratory adjacent to, or in, the school's library or media center. This is usually a good choice, although a large concentration of computers inside the library may be disruptive because computer labs are often busy, noisy places.

Room Arrangement

A number of different room arrangements are common for computer labs. While there is no single correct way to set up a computer facility, certain arrangements are preferable for particular uses. Figure 11.3 shows some of the most common computer laboratory layouts. Let's consider the benefits of each of these arrangements.

The peripheral arrangement is common in many schools. Where rooms have been converted to computer labs without major renovations, this arrangement provides convenient access to wall outlets. It also works well for monitored laboratory situations. As students work at computers, the teacher can sit or stand in the center of the room and scan around the room to observe what each person is doing. The center of the room can be used as a common work area, for resources, or for cooperative learning activities. This arrangement doesn't work well for group presentations, because some students must always turn around to see what is being presented.

The classroom-style layout is designed to function as a teaching laboratory. This arrangement is excellent for teaching students to use computer applications. The teacher's station is located at the front of the room. Using an LCD panel, video projector, or large monitor, the teacher can demonstrate software features to the entire class, and students can immediately try the same thing at their stations. However, this laboratory layout doesn't work as well for independent learning situations, because observation of and access to individual stations is more difficult than in the peripheral layout.

The arrangement with back-to-back rows works well for independent learning-laboratory situations. Its chief advantage is that it allows for the maximum number of computers in a given space. It doesn't work well for group presentations because of the different orientations of student stations. In addition, it's difficult for the teacher to observe and access individual stations. Therefore, it works best when students know what they need to do and can work relatively independently.

The cluster arrangement is often used in libraries, learning centers, and individual classrooms. A sin-

Figure 11.3 Common computer laboratory layouts

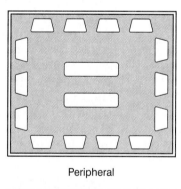

Peripheral

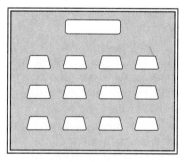

Classroom

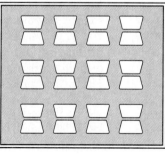

Back-to-back rows

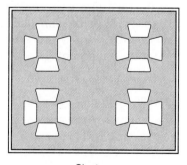

Clusters

gle cluster of computers can be placed in the corner of a room without dramatically impacting the rest of the room. This arrangement works well for cooperative learning activities. Students can easily group around particular clusters to work. This layout, like the back-to-back layout, is not conducive to either group presentation or easy observation of student stations. However, it is a great way to facilitate "islands of activity" in the classroom.

Electricity

Needless to say, computer systems must be supplied with adequate electricity. While a single personal computer doesn't require much electricity, a room full of 20 or 30 computer systems may overload circuit capacity. When a room in an older school building is converted into a computer laboratory, some upgrading of electrical service is often necessary. If a new facility is being designed, it's important to provide sufficient circuits and outlets for the computers and peripherals.

While exact requirements will vary with the particular computers, monitors, and peripherals placed in a laboratory, it's usually safe to connect 10 to 15 stations to an individual electrical circuit. A laboratory of 20 or 30 stations, then, could operate on two or three circuits. An advantage of the use of multiple circuits is that, in the event of disruption of power to one circuit, the entire laboratory isn't disabled. For ease of use and added control, it's also useful to control power to the individual circuits through a set of master switches.

Normally a minimum of two electrical outlets is needed for a single computer station (one for the CPU unit and one for the monitor). However, with the addition of powered peripherals such as CD-ROM drives, videodisc players, scanners, and printers, two outlets may be insufficient. Planners should consider the need for providing additional outlets at the time of the design of the laboratory. When sufficient wall or floor outlets are not available, multiple-outlet power strips can be used. Such devices should always be plugged directly into a wall or floor outlet; they should not be "daisy chained" from one strip to another. Because electrical surges and spikes can be a problem for computer equipment, surge-suppressing outlet strips should be used.

The proliferation of wires in a computer laboratory can be a problem. If care is not taken, a student may trip over a loose wire and be injured or cause damage to the equipment. At a minimum, wires should be gathered together and tucked out of the way. Whenever possible, wiring trays and electrical conduits should be used to keep wires safely out of the way. If a laboratory is being designed from scratch, it may be possible to specify under-the-floor channels to safely hide the wiring and cabling going to the computer stations.

Networking

One of the most important decisions to be made related to a computer facility today is whether or not to network. Local-area networks (LANs) are much more common than they once were, and, depending on the type of network, they can offer varying advantages. Simple networking options, such as Windows for Workgroups and Apple's LocalTalk, rely on what is known as a peer-to-peer model. These networks connect individual computers to one another to permit the exchange of files and the sharing of some resources. For example, a laser printer connected to one computer can be used by all of the computers on the network. Peer-to-peer networks are relatively easy to set up and maintain, but they aren't very powerful.

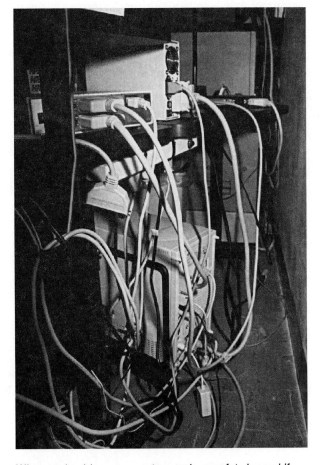

Wires and cables can create a serious safety hazard if they are not properly bundled and stored.

Other networks use what is called a client-server model. In these networks, a computer called the network **file server** is dedicated to managing the network and providing resources to the other computers on the network (the clients). Figure 11.4 shows a diagrammatic representation of a client-server network. The file server is usually faster and has larger storage capabilities than the client machines. Client-server networks usually require special hardware and cabling and may operate with software such as Novell Netware running over Ethernet. These networks are more complicated to set up and maintain than peer-to-peer networks, but they yield more benefits. In addition to permitting file exchange and shared printers, a file server can be loaded with a large collection of software to provide software access to an entire laboratory or school building. This eliminates the need to handle diskettes and provides enhanced security. Such networks can also support compliance with copyright law because they can be equipped with software that ensures that no more than the appropriate number of copies of a particular software title are used at one time. Also, because of the resources available through the file server, individual stations on the network may not require as much memory or hard disk space as they would if they were stand-alone machines. This cuts costs.

However, networks do have certain disadvantages. As we noted, networks often require special adapters for each computer, as well as cabling, networking software, and, in the case of a client-server network, a dedicated computer to act as the file server. These costs may offset the savings realized on individual stations. Some software won't work on a network. Network "crashes" or failures can disable an entire laboratory or even a whole school if there is a single server. In addition, the complexities of a network often require that someone knowledgeable be available to install software and maintain the network.

In most schools today, the advantages of networks are thought to outweigh the disadvantages. The decision then becomes which particular type of network to employ and how to manage it. Networking issues become even more complex if a school considers going beyond LANs, for example, by establishing a connection to the Internet. Schools considering networking should consult with networking experts and thoroughly research the available options before committing to a particular network solution.

Room Environment

Several environmental factors related to the specific computer facility need to be considered. Lighting should be indirect to avoid glare on monitors. If the room has windows, blinds or shades should be provided to block sunlight. Variable lighting is desirable; if a projection device is used, for example, visibility is increased if the lights are dimmed.

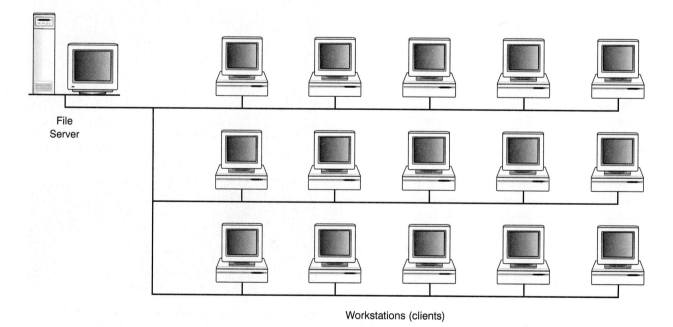

File
Server

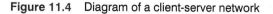

Workstations (clients)

Figure 11.4   Diagram of a client-server network

Temperature regulation is a near necessity for most computer facilities. Although most computers don't generate large amounts of heat, a room full of computers is a lot like a room full of people. Enough heat is generated to raise the temperature noticeably. Of course, computer labs have both computers *and* people! They do heat up. In extreme cases, such as a classroom in the summer without air conditioning, equipment failures can result. The fine tolerances of devices such as hard disk drives can be thrown off by temperature swings. Schools must plan on regulating the temperature of computer laboratories. If the entire building isn't air-conditioned, air-conditioning should be provided for the computer laboratory separately.

Dust can act as an insulating blanket on electrical components and create temperature problems. As a result, computer laboratories should be designed to be as free of dust as possible. One of the best ways to reduce dust is to replace chalkboards with white boards.

Carpeting reduces room noise and enhances the appearance of a computer laboratory. However, it often introduces an unwanted and potentially damaging problem—static electricity. Static electricity can damage the tiny electrical circuits in computer chips and can cause data loss. To avoid these problems, use carpeting that is designed to reduce static, apply an antistatic spray to the carpet, or use static mats or grounding devices at each computer station.

Ergonomics

The study of the physical interaction of machines and humans is called **ergonomics.** When a computer facility is being designed, it's important to take ergonomics into consideration. The tables on which computers are placed should be at a proper height for typing. Some tables are adjustable or have adjustable trays on which the keyboard is placed. Wrist rests can also be employed to minimize possibly harmful effects (e.g., carpal tunnel syndrome—a very painful wrist injury caused by repetitive motion) that can result from long sessions at the computer keyboard. Adequate space is needed not only for the computer system itself but also for using a mouse and for placing work materials. In general, computer stations need about twice the amount of space as the typical student desk. Monitors should be placed for comfortable viewing, slightly below eye level. In addition, because of concern about the possible effects of radiation from computer monitors, monitors should be placed at least 18 inches away from users. If lighting is a problem, antiglare screens can be mounted over the monitor; these can help to reduce eye fatigue as well. Adjustable monitors are preferred, as are adjustable-height chairs that allow individuals to sit comfortably.

Meeting Special Needs

When you are planning a computer facility, it's important to consider the needs of special students. Computers can empower students with special needs, and access to the technology can be provided in various ways. For example, a wheelchair-bound student can easily be accommodated through the use of an adjustable-height computer table in a laboratory. Various forms of adaptive technology are available to assist students with particular disabilities. For visually impaired learners, for example, there are numerous solutions, including text-enlargement software, text-to-speech converters, and Braille printers. For physically challenged learners, solutions include special keyboard-control software, modified keyboards, speech-recognition software, adaptive hardware for controlling software, and various types of switches designed to work with adaptive hardware. Availability of these technologies can make a world of difference to a student with special needs!

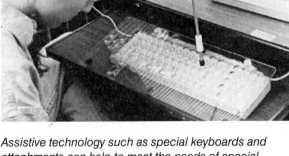

Assistive technology such as special keyboards and attachments can help to meet the needs of special learners.

Maintenance and Management

Of course, there is more to a computer facility than simply putting a bunch of machines in a room and forgetting about them. Equipment must be maintained, and the facilities must be managed. Let's examine some of the considerations involved.

Maintenance

The maintenance of computers and other equipment is an ongoing concern for schools. While personal computers tend to be reasonably reliable, problems inevitably arise over time and with sufficient quantities of hardware. What can be done? Schools need to establish an overall maintenance program that includes preventative maintenance, in-house repair, and outside repair.

One of the most important steps that can be taken is an active program of preventative maintenance. Heading off problems before they begin saves time and money in the long run. Basic preventative measures include

- use of electrical surge protection
- use of antistatic devices
- regular external cleaning of keyboards and monitors
- regular internal cleaning by blowing out dust with compressed air or by vacuuming
- cleaning of disk drives, printer heads, and so on, if problems arise

Simple repairs and maintenance can often be handled in-house. Diagnostic diskettes can be used to help pinpoint difficulties. These may come with some computers or may be purchased separately. If a component such as a disk drive appears to fail, the source of the problem can be localized by substituting known working parts until the problem is found. Then the faulty part can be replaced. Schools should maintain a supply of spare components such as disk drives, keyboards, mice, and power supplies in order to be able to replace faulty parts quickly. Larger school systems often maintain their own repair staffs to handle problems internally. Even in smaller schools, when an internal repair program is undertaken it's important that a staff member be provided with sufficient release time to work on the repairs. Broken computers don't fix themselves, and it's unfair for schools to expect the local expert to assume repair responsibilities without some compensation.

When problems are too difficult for in-house repair, most schools go to an outside repair service via a maintenance contract or on a piece-by-piece basis. Maintenance contracts provide for repairs on a continuing basis for a set fee. They usually provide a cost-effective option when the volume of repairs is sufficiently large. Otherwise, repair services can be obtained as needed. Often local computer stores work with area schools to provide piece-by-piece repair services. Regardless of the particular method, it's important for schools to plan and budget for repairs in advance.

Management

Management of computers and other equipment is a concern for schools as well. There are two important considerations: Who has access to the equipment, and what are the rules that govern its use? Let's look briefly at some of the issues involved.

In most schools, common classroom media equipment (e.g., VCRs, large TVs or monitors, overhead projectors, and cassette tape recorders) is handled by the school's media specialist or librarian. Often this equipment is available on carts that can be wheeled into the classroom for use. Teachers wishing to use this equipment simply contact the media specialist to schedule the equipment for use in the classroom at the appropriate time. Some schools have sophisticated media-retrieval systems that are capable of electronically delivering video or other media into individual classrooms from a central location. Many of these systems give the classroom teacher access to the media via a remote-control device or an intercom system that connects with the media center. However, even in these cases it is important for the teacher to schedule access well in advance to ensure that equipment and materials are available.

Computer access is often more complicated than access to other media. As we have noted, when a school decides to centralize its computer resources into a laboratory setting, access to that equipment can become a problem. In many schools, computers are used primarily for teaching computing (e.g., programming and computer application classes). Although this is natural, demand for computing resources increases as teachers in other curricula areas become familiar with computers and their capabilities (e.g., word processing in support of language arts classes). One obvious solution to this problem is to increase resources, and most schools are doing just that. However, even with increased resources, access frequently remains a critical issue that must be addressed in school policies and procedures.

Schools must establish access policies and procedures that align with their technology plans. We know of one school where the computer laboratory was designated as the place where students did remedial work. Certainly this is one reasonable use of resources. However, in practice the laboratory was booked every hour of every day for remediation alone, and students and teachers with other legitimate needs couldn't gain access. Consideration needs to be given to providing sufficient access to support all of the components of the technology plan.

Some means of scheduling computer laboratories should be established, and it should provide at least some opportunity for a broad range of uses. There is also the issue of unscheduled or out-of-class time. In many cases, students need out-of-class access to computers to work on projects and assignments. Some consideration should be given to this need. If computers are always scheduled during the school day, before- or after-school hours might be set aside for unscheduled use. Teacher access should also be considered. If teachers are encouraged to use computers, they need access to prepare materials and try things out. As we have already noted, some schools have made the decision to provide computers specifically for teacher use. Otherwise, special computers or special hours (e.g., a block of time before or after school) should be set aside in the computer laboratory for teachers. Schools also need to be sensitive to the problem of student "haves" and "have-nots." While some families can afford to have a computer at home, many cannot. Schools have a responsibility to provide some equality of access for students. Some schools have established computer checkout programs to allow students to take computers home.

Rules also need to be established for the use of computer facilities. The following are some of the factors that are commonly considered in setting rules for computer use:

- *Food or drink.* Because of the risk of damage to the equipment, prohibition of food and drink is a nearly universal rule in computer laboratories.

- *Method of access outside of class.* When open access is allowed, is it on a first-come, first-served basis, or can students reserve times?

- *Requirements for access.* What criteria govern open access to computers? Must students be in a class that uses the laboratory? Must students complete a proficiency checkout before use?

- *Types of applications permitted.* Are students restricted to specific programs? Can they play games on school computers?

- *Procedures for software access.* If software is not on a file server, what procedure governs how students get access to needed software?

- *Limits on access.* Are students limited to a certain amount of time per session? Is the number of sessions per week limited? How many students are permitted to work around a single computer station?

- *Materials usage.* Are students charged for the use of expendable supplies such as printer paper? If not, what limits are imposed?

- *Use of nonschool software.* Many schools prohibit use of nonschool software because of copyright issues and the potential for introduction of computer viruses, and to avoid the possibility that students might bring undesirable software to school.

SOFTWARE ISSUES

Hardware issues certainly are important. They must be adequately addressed if a school is to be successful in implementing its technology plan. However, software issues are arguably even more critical. Without appropriate software, hardware is worthless. Let's examine some of the issues that surround the integration and use of computer software.

Software Evaluation and Acquisition

In Chapter 7 we examined issues related to the selection of instructional materials in general and of different media in particular. Because we've given special attention to computers throughout this text, let's revisit the evaluation and selection of computer software here.

In most school districts today, hardware decisions are centralized. An individual teacher cannot go out and select just any computer for the classroom. However, software decisions often are made by individual teachers. There is commonly an approval process that involves the technology coordinator, a technology committee, or an administrator, but software purchasing usually begins with the individual teacher. It's important for teachers to know how to go about evaluating and selecting software. What are the steps involved?

1. *Determine needs.* As in any instructional activity, it's best to begin by assessing what it is that is needed. What needs might be addressed through the use of the computer?

2. *Specify desired software characteristics.* From a specification of needs, you should be able to come up with a general idea of what you want. For example, if your students are having trouble adding mixed fractions, you may decide

COMPUTER VIRUSES

In the biological realm, viruses are tiny particles that infect organisms; they can be benign or disease-causing. A virus invades a cell, takes over the cell's own production machinery, and then subverts it into making copies of the virus. When the copies are released, another cycle of infection begins. In the computer world, the term **virus** refers to a computer program that functions in a manner similar to a biological virus. A computer virus invades software, usually without any overt sign, and directs the computer to copy the virus and pass it on. Like natural viruses, computer viruses can have effects ranging from fairly benign (e.g., a prankish message appears on the infected computer's screen) to quite serious (e.g., the contents of the computer's hard disk are erased).

Computer viruses have become widespread. They are a common problem in many computer laboratories and are often spread through networks. A few years ago, many computers throughout the world were temporarily crippled when a virus, released by a student at Cornell University, spread throughout the Internet. What can schools and individuals do to protect themselves? To reduce potential problems, institute the following practices:

- Use antivirus software (e.g., Disinfectant, Norton AntiVirus, Virex, VirusScan) on your computers to check for and eliminate known viruses. Regularly update this software, because antivirus programs have limited effectiveness against new or unknown viruses.

- Avoid downloading software from bulletin boards; this is a common source of infection. While major on-line services (e.g., CompuServe, America Online, Prodigy) do check for viruses, many smaller bulletin boards do not. If you must download software, download to a floppy disk rather than to your hard disk. Scan the floppy disk with antivirus software before use.

- In computer laboratories, establish practices that reduce the spread of viruses. Discourage or prohibit students from bringing their own software into the laboratory. Reboot each computer between users, and set up your antivirus software to perform a scan automatically when the computer boots up. These techniques will help reduce the spread of viruses within a laboratory.

---

that you want a drill-and-practice program on this topic.

3. *Obtain or construct an evaluation form.* Many useful software evaluation forms are available from a variety of sources. We provide one simple example of a software preview form in Appendix B. Your school may have its own evaluation form. Alternatively, you could design one geared to your specific needs.

4. *Survey available sources of software.* Software can be obtained from a variety of sources. Look through publishers' catalogs. Read software evaluations published in journals and magazines. Talk to your colleagues. Visit vendors' booths at professional meetings. Check collections of shareware. All of these sources may help you to identify possible software.

5. *Obtain software for preview.* Many software companies now provide special demonstration disks for preview. Some are also providing demonstrations on CD-ROM. With these, if you like the software and go ahead and buy it, the company provides you with a password that unlocks full access to the software on the CD-ROM. Alternatively, you can often preview software via delayed-purchase-order billing. In this case, a purchase order for the product is submitted with the specification that it is for preview purposes. The company delays billing for a set period, usually 30 days. If you decide against purchase, simply return the software within the grace period, and the purchase order is canceled. Otherwise, keep the software, and the purchase order will be processed at the end of the grace period.

6. *Read the documentation.* While there is a temptation to simply jump into a software program, you should always read the documentation

first. It should indicate the recommended audience for the program, and it will provide directions for how to properly use the software.

7. *Run through the software several times.* The first time you go through the software, simply concentrate on using the program correctly. How does it work? For a second pass, make certain that the software is "bombproof"; that is, make certain it doesn't fail when something unexpected happens. Purposely test for problems; if the program indicates "Enter a number between 1 and 4," see what happens if you enter 5. Finally, run through the program with a pedagogical eye. Is the educational approach sound? Is it appealing? How does the software rate on the criteria given on your evaluation form? Have some students try out the program. How do they like it? Do they learn from it?

8. *Complete the evaluation form.* Using the information gained from your review of the software, complete the evaluation form.

9. *Repeat the process for any competing products.* If you have more than one possible purchase, look at each competing product in the same way.

10. *Make your selection.* Select the desired software package. File your evaluation with the school, and be sure to enclose a copy of your evaluation with any product that is returned to the publisher.

Software Management

Software, like hardware, must be managed effectively if it is to be of use to teachers and students. Several factors should be considered, including preventative maintenance, storage, and cataloging/circulating.

Just as hardware benefits from preventative maintenance, so too does software. Computer disks are vulnerable to damage from a variety of sources. It is important to protect them by taking some basic precautions:

- Keep diskettes away from magnetic fields, X-rays, and other potentially damaging sources of radiation.
- Avoid exposing diskettes to temperature extremes (below about 50°F or above about 125°F).
- Keep diskettes away from dirt, dust, or other contaminants.
- Do not open the metal shutter on 3.5-inch floppy diskettes; that exposes the disk surface to contaminants.

- Avoid dropping 3.5-inch floppy diskettes; the plastic case can break, and the metal shutter can pop off.
- Never touch the exposed surfaces of floppy diskettes; fingerprints are damaging.
- Do not bend floppy disks.
- Write on 5.25-inch floppy disks only with soft, felt-tip pens.
- Never force diskettes into or out of disk drives.
- Keep disks write-protected when copying.
- Maintain at least one backup copy of all diskettes.
- When diskettes are not in use, store them in boxes or cases made for that purpose.

Schools must routinely manage storage of computer materials and provision of access to them. When the school has a central file server, the problem is not severe. A copy of the software is placed on the file server, and the appropriate number of licenses is set to limit access through the file server's controlling software. The original copy of the software is then filed away in a secure location in case of future need. Documentation can be made available through the school's library, media center, or computer laboratory if students or teachers need to look up information about a particular function or feature. Networks eliminate much of the diskette-handling problems that arise in non-networked settings.

For schools that do not have a network with a central file server, some method is needed for storing computer materials in a way that affords access. Several approaches are common. Some schools separate diskettes from documentation. The diskettes are placed in storage cases and kept in a secure location, while the documentation is shelved separately. Students or teachers who want to work with a particular program must check out the diskette. The documentation, if needed, must be obtained separately. Alternatively, the diskettes and documentation can be kept together. One way to accomplish this is by shelving the materials in the original packaging. Unfortunately, computer software packaging is often bulky and can be highly variable in shape and size, so this can be awkward. In addition, shelving the complete materials leaves them vulnerable to theft or unauthorized copying unless they are all kept in a secure location. An alternative is to put diskettes and documentation in uniform file folders. Folders can be kept in file cabinets. They then can be checked out by students or teachers wishing to use the product. This method works

Software can be shelved in a library or media center to provide for access by students and teachers.

well as long as the documentation is not so extensive that the sheer bulk becomes a problem.

Of course, filing or shelving computer materials implies the ability to retrieve those materials when needed. Several methods can be used for cataloging materials. Libraries often use the Dewey decimal system. This approach has the advantage that it is well known to librarians and has established categories for materials. Many computer programs now come with Dewey decimal numbers. To novices, however, the Dewey decimal system can be confusing, and seemingly related materials can be cataloged using widely separated numbers. Alternatively, some other organizational scheme can be used. Some schools separate software by basic type: word processor, spreadsheet, computer language, CAI package, and so on. Others catalog software by order of acquisition, title, publisher, or some other scheme. Any method can work as long as there is a way to conveniently locate the materials. It's particularly helpful to establish a computer database of the software collection to provide a fast way to locate particular titles.

Finally, schools need to establish policies and procedures governing software use similar to those governing hardware use. Just as a teacher may want to reserve a VCR and a large monitor for use in the classroom, a teacher may want to reserve a computer software package for use in the classroom. Schools need to set up mechanisms for providing such access. Software checkout might be handled through the library, media center, or computer laboratory. Regardless of the particular location, basic rules for use need to be established. How does a teacher reserve software? What is the checkout procedure? How long can a package be checked out? Can students check out software? If so, under what circumstances? These questions should be addressed in policies and procedures governing software utilization.

Copyright Issues

One of the most important issues involving computers and multimedia is copyright. **Copyright** refers to the legal rights to an original work. Schools have an obligation, both under the law and from an ethical standpoint, to adhere to the law themselves and to instruct students in proper behavior. The penalties for violation of copyright law can be severe, and, as a number of schools and businesses have found, publishers' groups are willing to take action against organizations that are in violation. To avoid problems, schools need to establish clear copyright policies and make those policies known to both teachers and students. Although a complete discussion of copyright law is beyond the scope of this book, in this section we provide some basic guidelines. For more information, contact your school's library or media specialist or consult reference books on the subject.

Let's discuss some of the most important points of copyright law:

- *What are copyrighted materials?* Copyrighted materials are original works of authorship in any tangible medium of expression. This includes such things as written works, works of art, music, photographs, and computer software. Basically, any tangible authored work qualifies. Ideas, concepts, and procedures cannot be copyrighted.

- *Rights granted to copyright owners.* Copyright owners hold the rights to reproduce (copy) the work, create derivative works, sell or distribute the work to the public, and perform or display the work. These rights are exclusive to the copyright owner, except for certain allowances permitted by copyright law. These allowances are spelled out in the next three items.

- *Face-to-face teaching.* Educators are permitted to publicly display legally purchased works that may not have been licensed for that purpose (e.g., a videotape purchased with a FOR HOME USE ONLY notice) as long as they do so as part of a course of instruction in a classroom setting.

- *Software backup.* Computer software may be duplicated when such duplication is essential to the use of the software on a particular computer or to create an archival backup copy of the software to be used if the original fails. Other copying of computer software, except as may be allowed by the license for a particular software product, is illegal. This applies to networks as well as to stand-alone computers. While a network file server actually holds only one copy of a particular program, multiple copies can be operated on the network. This is illegal if only a single copy of that software was purchased. Schools must purchase network licenses or multiple copies of the software to run multiple copies on a network, and the network must monitor use to prevent violations if the license is restricted to a specific number of copies.

- *Fair use.* Fair use applies to situations involving criticism, comment, news reporting, educational use, and research associated with copyrighted material. A researcher, for example, can make single copies of articles as part of his or her research. A critic can excerpt dialogue from a book as part of a published review of the work. These are examples of fair use. What about educational use? Several factors affect whether a use is considered fair use: its purpose, the nature of the copyrighted work, the amount of the work involved, and the effect on the potential market for the work. While interpretations vary, guidelines on the subject suggest that educational use of a copyrighted work can meet fair-use guidelines if the following criteria are met: only a brief excerpt is used (e.g., an excerpt of less than 1,000 words or less than 10% of the whole written work), it is a spontaneous use (e.g., a whole article could be copied

for a class if the decision to use it was a spur-of-the-moment decision by the teacher), and there is no cumulative effect (e.g., the use doesn't occur in more than one course, it isn't repeated, and it doesn't serve as a substitute for purchase). Rules governing certain media, such as taped television broadcasts, vary but place significant limitations on what is considered fair use.

With the advent of digital media and distance education, copyright issues have become even more important and difficult to sort out. It's possible to digitize audio and video and incorporate the digital representations into multimedia presentations. However, is it legal? The use of media in the classroom as part of face-to-face instruction is often considered fair use, but what happens when distance education is employed and the instruction is no longer face-to-face? Unfortunately, the answers to these questions are not altogether clear today.

The best advice is probably that digital media should be considered according to the established fair-use guidelines. That is, use of small excerpts (less than 10%) of images or sounds from media such as videodiscs or audio CDs probably constitutes fair use when part of classroom instruction (including student-created projects) and when credit is given to the source of the materials. However, use or distribution beyond the classroom often is not allowed. A distance education setting may qualify as a "classroom" if the information is not publicly available. However, this is not completely clear; explicit permission may be needed to transmit materials over distances. Permission to use materials should be sought. Probably the most important consideration is this: Will the use adversely impact the author's potential to profit from the work or a derivative of the work? If the answer is yes, the use doesn't qualify as fair use and, therefore, is illegal. For example, a teacher who digitized images from a videodisc and placed them in a multimedia program that he or she distributed (even at no cost) to other teachers would be in violation of copyright law. Such use might adversely impact the author's potential profits and might also impinge on the author's exclusive right to make derivatives from the original work. Future legislation in copyright law may help to clarify the issues being raised by the advent of digital media. Until then, we must do our best to adhere to the intent of the copyright law as it exists today.

PERSONNEL ISSUES

To this point, we have discussed the "nuts and bolts" side of technology management in the schools—

the hardware and software. Now let's turn our attention to the human side of things. We will examine three personnel-related issues: technology specialists, in-service training, and management issues for the classroom teacher.

Technology Specialists

Until recently, most of the specialized work related to instructional media in the schools was performed by librarians and media specialists. Because of their expertise, these individuals were called upon to assist teachers with a variety of information-retrieval and media-usage tasks. As instructional media have changed, so has the task of media specialists. In many instances, the job has become much more technical and much more computer oriented. In fact, some media specialists today function as their school's technology expert as well as an expert on other, more traditional, forms of media. However, over the past decade or so a new category of specialist has also emerged in the schools— the computer or technology coordinator. The **technology coordinator** is a specialist and resource person who handles computers and related technologies for a school building or district.

In larger school districts, the position of technology coordinator is usually a full-time post. Indeed, some school districts even employ technology support staff consisting of several individuals. Many schools today also support building-level coordinators. At the building level, and at the district level in smaller school districts, it is common for the technology coordinator to be a teacher who has expertise in the use of computers and who assumes these duties on a part-time basis. Part-time coordinators usually receive some release time or extra compensation for their activities.

The job of a technology coordinator varies considerably from school to school. In some cases,

responsibilities are distributed among a number of persons, while in other cases one person does it all. It is common for a technology coordinator to do the following:

- work with teachers to support and promote technology integration
- provide in-service training for faculty and staff
- plan and oversee hardware and software purchases and installations
- install and maintain the school's computer network
- maintain up-to-date records of the school's hardware and software
- arrange for, or conduct, repairs of equipment
- assemble and disseminate information about computer education
- write grants to seek support for the school's technology activities
- work with administrators and the district's technology committee to develop and implement a technology plan

In-service Training

Of course, not every teacher will become a technology specialist. However, computers and other educational technologies have become so pervasive and so important to education that it is incumbent upon every teacher to become an effective user of educational technology. This is no small feat. Even the teacher who has been involved in technology can quickly find his or her knowledge and skills outdated by the rapid changes that occur in hardware and software. Regular in-service training is needed to keep teachers abreast of the latest developments and trends in educational technology.

A school technology coordinator is a specialist who takes care of computers and related technologies.

As we already mentioned in the discussion of technology planning, it is important for schools to plan for in-service training as part of the overall technology-planning process. In-service training in educational technology should be regular and ongoing. It should derive from the school's technology plan. It should help teachers to utilize technology effectively within the framework of the plan.

Several approaches may be used for in-service training. Single, focused presentations or workshops on a topic (sometimes referred to as "one-shot" in-service sessions) can be useful for raising faculty awareness and stimulating interest, but they are unlikely to have a long-term impact without follow-up activities. More successful programs involve a series of activities, with opportunities for guided practice, exploration, and feedback. Extended summer workshops can provide an intensive experience in a relatively short period of time. Teachers who desire advanced training may want to seek out courses available from local colleges or universities.

No one approach to in-service is right for everyone. However, some general principles can help to make in-service activities successful:

- *Use local computer experts and teachers,* rather than outside consultants, whenever possible. Teachers are more apt to believe in their own ability when the presentation comes from someone they know and can relate to. In addition, local people are available for follow-up support after the in-service.

- *Provide hands-on experience.* When people are learning about computers and related technologies, hands-on experience is essential. People don't learn to ride bicycles from lectures or books, and they don't learn to operate computers that way either.

- *Provide a nonthreatening environment.* Many people are afraid of, or intimidated by, computers. Fears range from a fear of breaking the machine to a fear of appearing stupid in front of students or peers. It is essential that computer in-services be conducted in a friendly and supportive atmosphere that encourages experimentation and mutual support.

- *Present information in steps,* with opportunities for practice and mastery. Too much information at the beginning can be overwhelming. Teachers need opportunities to learn, practice, and master new skills. This process can take weeks or even months. In most cases, teachers will indicate their readiness to move on by exploring and asking questions about new areas.

- *Provide follow-up support and feedback.* Going hand in hand with the step-by-step presentation of information, it is important for teachers who are learning new computer skills to get help when needed and to receive feedback about the use of their new skills.

- *Schedule in-service sessions at convenient times.* Teachers are busy people. In-service sessions should be scheduled at the most convenient times—scheduled in-service days, after school, or over the summer. School systems that are really serious about in-service opportunities for their teachers sometimes hire substitutes to release teachers for in-service training during regular school days.

Classroom Management

Ultimately, the success or failure of any technology innovation in the classroom depends on the classroom teacher. Of course, the teacher's knowledge, skill, and motivation all play a role. The use of technology in the classroom also requires a degree of classroom management that may not be demanded in other circumstances. Effective use of technology often involves a balancing act.

In general, classroom management refers to a set of skills and tactics that a teacher employs in order to keep students on task and to keep the classroom running smoothly:

- *Preparing in advance.* While this may seem obvious, one of the best tactics for making the classroom run smoothly is to prepare materials and activities well in advance.

- *Giving clear instructions.* Students who don't know what to do are apt to get off task. Teachers can minimize problems by providing precise instructions and then checking for student understanding of those instructions.

- *Setting a learning tone.* At the outset of a learning activity, the teacher should set a learning tone. This can be accomplished by removing potential distractions, presenting the goals of the activity, relating it to previous work, or presenting a puzzle or story designed to stimulate the students' thinking.

- *Maintaining attention.* In order to learn, students must attend to the task at hand. Teachers can maintain students' attention by varying tasks and classroom activities, encouraging student interaction and involvement, varying pacing, and calling on students.

- *Questioning.* Frequent questioning is an essential technique that teachers can use to maintain students' involvement, promote students' thinking, assess students' learning, and verify that students understand what they are to do.
- *Providing feedback.* Timely feedback is essential to students' learning. Teachers should provide frequent feedback about student performance in the classroom. This includes feedback on learning processes—not just learning outcomes.
- *Making smooth transitions.* Classroom activities are constantly changing. A skillful teacher makes the transitions from one activity to another as smoothly as possible. This can be accomplished through the use of posted schedules, clear directions, and appropriate physical arrangement of the classroom, and by orchestrating the assistance of the students.

While these are general classroom management skills and tactics, they can be especially important when educational technology is involved. Let's consider an example from a recent lesson taught by our friend, Ms. Moreno.

INTEGRATING TECHNOLOGY
Managing Instructional Technology in the Classroom

Have we told you yet about how Janette helped her students learn the rules of Spanish grammar? Again, this was an area in which students'

skill levels varied dramatically, from fairly low levels to moderately high ones. Ms. Moreno believed that students needed a lot of individualized instruction, coupled with a lot of practice, if they were going to show improvement in their knowledge and use of grammatical rules. Janette also knew from her experience that this kind of work could get tedious, so she purchased a computer program that combined tutorial instruction with a number of gamelike features. It was informative, interesting, challenging, and innovative. Called Tele-Grams, this program embedded small tutorials within a larger game format to help the students learn and practice a variety of grammatical rules in the context of deciphering humorous telegrams. As students correctly answered questions based on different grammatical rules, they would obtain small parts of the code needed to decipher the cryptic telegram messages (somewhat like a "Grammar Hangman").

When Janette came to the part in her course that dealt intensively with rules of grammar, she made plans to incorporate this tutorial/game into her instruction. A couple of weeks before she introduced the topic to her class, she reserved lab time with the school's technology coordinator. Even though Ms. Moreno had seen a demonstration of the program prior to purchasing it, she reviewed the software program the week before the lesson. She went through the program to remind herself of the content that was covered and to make a list of the things that students were expected to do. After previewing the program, she prepared a one-page summary of instructions for her students regarding

Providing students with instructions for operating software and with activities or questions to pursue can help to structure work in the computer laboratory.

how to operate the program. The day before the class was going to use the program, Janette demonstrated the software to her class, using a computer and an LCD panel in the classroom. This way students were well aware of what they would be doing, as well as why Ms. Moreno thought it was a valuable activity.

When students came to Ms. Moreno's classroom on the first day of the activity, she had already written a class schedule on the board. Before the class went to the laboratory, she spent a little time explaining the goals of the tutorial/game. She handed out the instructions and a response sheet to each student. The sheet included a number of questions that students were to address during the computer activity. During the lab period she circulated around the room to help the students, asking questions and checking progress. At the end of the class period, she collected the response sheets and dismissed the class.

The next day, Ms. Moreno returned the response sheets with her comments. She spent a few minutes summarizing and debriefing the previous day's activity, then continued on with the next part of her lesson.

This example illustrates how basic classroom-management skills and techniques can be applied to educational technology. Use of technology often involves more advance preparation than for other types of instruction. In our example, Ms. Moreno previewed the software program that she intended to use. Provision of clear instructions can be very important, since students can easily become confused by operating systems, computer menus, and the like. Ms. Moreno demonstrated proper use of the software and also prepared instructions for its use.

In many cases, it's possible for students to "go through the motions" with a piece of computer software without really attending to its content. To help keep students on task and to provide an assessment tool, many teachers, like Ms. Moreno, find it helpful to design their own worksheets or activity sheets that students must complete while using a particular computer program. When used in concert with the software itself, these provide a method of auxiliary questioning. Teachers can give students feedback by grading or commenting on them.

Finally, educational use of computers and other technologies involves working with the equipment. Ms. Moreno had to move her class to the computer lab in order to make use of the software. That required advance scheduling and some classroom management. A teacher who has one computer in the classroom has to work out rotation schedules so that students can have access. Using technology in the classroom can be a lot of work! However, it can also be very rewarding!

SUMMARY

In this chapter we examined issues related to the management of technology in schools. Schools planning for technology should form a technology committee with representation from all key constituencies. This committee should begin by outlining its vision of education and articulating a role for technology in that vision, taking into account the needs of students, teachers, the curriculum, and society. Next, it should evaluate the status of technology use within the school district. Finally, it should work with teams of faculty to develop detailed plans for integrating technology into the curriculum, taking into account available hardware, software, the curriculum, and individual teaching styles.

Evaluation and acquisition of computers and peripherals by schools involve consideration of many factors. Once computers are acquired, schools must be concerned with their placement within a building, arrangement of computer facilities, networking, and other factors. Ongoing management and maintenance of computer equipment must also be considered. Likewise, teachers and schools must be concerned with the evaluation, selection, and management of computer software, and with issues related to copyright law. Finally, there are issues related to personnel. Many schools now have technology coordinators, specialists who act as computer resource people. Other personnel issues include in-service training and the classroom management of individual teachers.

REFLECTIVE QUESTIONS AND ACTIVITIES

1. Contact schools in your area to find out how many of them have technology planning committees. Arrange to sit in on a committee's planning session, if permitted. Who participates on the committee? What kinds of issues does the committee address?

2. Identify the schools in your area that have written technology plans. Arrange to get copies of the plans from as many of the schools as you can. What are the common elements of the plans? How do individual plans differ?

3. We noted that the secondary business curriculum is obviously well suited to the integration of technology. What are some others?

4. Visit a local computer store. Cost out examples of computer systems that might be appropriate for school use. Investigate the availability of special pricing, discounts, or other incentives for purchases by schools or by individual educators.

5. Make arrangements to visit one or more area schools to investigate their computer use. Are the computers in the schools concentrated or dispersed? Are laboratories used? What rationale do school officials give for the placement of computers in the building? How do they manage hardware and software?

6. Survey area schools regarding their technology coordinators. How many have district-level technology coordinators? How many have building-level technology coordinators? Arrange to meet with a local technology coordinator. What does the job entail? What special compensation, if any, is received? What special training or qualifications does the individual possess?

INTEGRATION AND SYNTHESIS

In Chapter 8 we examined media utilization, both in the classroom and as applied to distance education. In Chapters 9 and 10 we looked at instructional technology for groups and for individuals, respectively. These three chapters provided a broad perspective of the techniques and principles involved in actually doing instruction. In this chapter we looked at implementation issues by focusing on the management of instructional technology—particularly computers—not just from the point of view of the individual teacher but also from that of the school and school district as well. In the school setting, the management of instructional technology involves many issues and requires the vision, commitment, and efforts of many people. In Chapter 12 we will turn our attention to the final element of the PIE model—evaluation.

SUGGESTED READINGS

Dyrli, O. E., & Kinnaman, D. E. (1994). Districtwide technology planning: The key to long-term success. *Technology and Learning, 14*(7), 50–54, 56.

Geisert, P. G., & Futrell, M. K. (1995). *Teachers, computers, and curriculum: Microcomputers in the classroom* (2nd ed.). Boston: Allyn & Bacon.

Hadley, M., & Sheingold, K. (1993, May). Commonalities and distinctive patterns in teachers' integration of computers. *American Journal of Education,* 261–315.

Section IV

Evaluation

Evaluation is, and probably always will be, anxiety-provoking. That is, most of us feel a little nervous when someone says, "Next week, you will be tested on . . . " or "It's time to assess your skill level in . . . " or even "Demonstrate how well you've mastered the goal of . . . " Why? Because evaluation is the major way we receive information about our levels of competency and skill—and that information may reveal some of our inadequacies. In a commercialized world that constantly promotes perfection, being shown that you have more to learn is about as much fun as a two-hour root canal procedure.

If evaluation is that unpleasant, why bother with it? Although many students may think that tests are created merely as a way for teachers to inflict pain and suffering, in most cases there is a good reason for their use. That reason centers around the *feedback* they provide. By obtaining feedback about one's current level of performance, changes can be made so a specific goal can be reached. This can be illustrated with a simple example. To earn a rowing merit badge in the Boy Scouts of America, young people learn a simple procedure to help steer a straight course while rowing a boat. Unlike a canoe or kayak, a small two-oar row boat generally requires the rower to sit with his or her back to the destination. This often leads rowers to either be frequently off course or, at the least, to be constantly turning around to see if they're still heading in the right direction. If, however, a passenger is along in the boat, he or she can use a simple procedure to keep the rower on course. The passenger sits facing the rower (and the desired location), and then simply puts both hands together with his or her fingertips pointed directly at the destination. The rower soon realizes that as long as the passenger's fingertips

are pointed directly at the rower's chest (and consequently the front of the boat), the boat is on course. Any differences require only a slight adjustment by the rower to get the boat on the right heading. The direction of the fingertips provides important feedback.

When individuals realize the value of feedback, evaluation becomes a desirable tool for facilitating improvement. Recall the opening pages of Chapter 1, where we described a master craftsperson and explained some of the differences between expert cabinetmakers and common laborers. One of the critical differences mentioned was the way experts constantly engage in self-evaluation. It's their goal to change and alter the little imperfections early on, so they wouldn't become big problems later. This is the true essence of evaluation—helping learners to assess where they are and then envisioning what the next steps might be.

In Chapters 12 and 13 the focus is on evaluation as a tool for improvement. Chapter 12 looks specifically at student evaluation, whereas Chapter 13 considers the evaluation of the instructional materials. In both cases you will be shown various instruments that can be used to supply feedback *as* learning is occurring (or supposed to be occurring) as well as *after* learning has occurred. Additionally, you will see how the computer can be an important assistant in the evaluation process. Computer-managed instruction can be used both to generate and score evaluation instruments and to provide critical feedback to students. Powerful spreadsheet programs are useful tools for the calculation of evaluation and other data, as well as for completing estimations and projections for potential changes.

This section on evaluation completes our discussion of the phases of the PIE model. Remember that this is not a linear model, such as shown in Figure A.

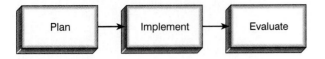

Figure A   A linear representation does not appropriately depict the interdependence of the different phases of the PIE model

All of the phases are highly interactive; each has an impact on the others. Information from both the planning and the implementation phases directly impact both the type of instrument(s) that should be developed and used and the type of evaluation that is constructed. Likewise, information obtained from the evaluation phase should have a direct impact on how future iterations of the materials are designed and carried out. Figure B illustrates the highly interdependent nature of the different PIE phases.

Chapter 14 concludes the text with a look at the past, present, and future of instructional technology. The highlights of the past help to illustrate how we have progressed to this point, but even more importantly, they help us to project the changes that are on the horizon. This is a great asset as we envision and plan for the future.

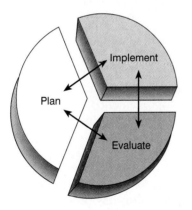

Figure B   A different representation of the PIE model that illustrates the high amount of interdependence of the phases

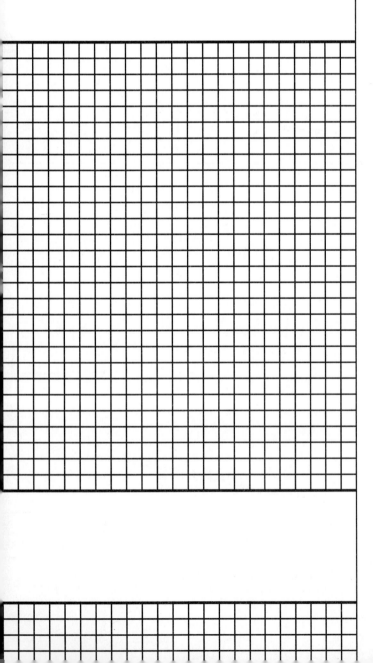

Chapter 12

Evaluating Student Learning

KEY WORDS AND CONCEPTS

Pretest	Validity
Formative evaluation	Stem
Summative evaluation	Distractor
Transfer	Foil
Reliability	Portfolio

COMPUTER USE ESSENTIALS (CUE)
Words and Concepts

Computer-managed instruction (CMI)

Test generator

Computer gradebook

Integrated learning system (ILS)

Electronic spreadsheet

Cell

Label

Formula

Template

Macro

OUTCOMES

After reading and studying this chapter, you will be able to:

- Describe the purposes of student evaluation and the need for it to occur before, during, and after instruction.
- Discuss standard and alternative evaluation instruments and identify the advantages and limitations of each type of instrument.
- Construct and/or assess a set of standard evaluation instruments using a list of development guidelines.
- Describe the general steps involved in planning a student evaluation.
- Define *computer-managed instruction* (CMI).
- Identify the types of software commonly associated with simple CMI.
- Discuss the common features of electronic spreadsheets, including their key advantages.
- Identify teacher and student uses of electronic spreadsheets.
- Distinguish between sophisticated CMI and simple grade-management applications.
- Define *integrated learning system* (ILS) and identify the common features of ILSs.

■ INTRODUCTION

During a recent parent-teacher conference, Ms. Powley, the ninth-grade English teacher at Mt. Vernon High School, explained some of the assignments and tests her students had completed recently. Many of her comments focused on the first essay examination. She explained that, for many students, this was the first exam they had taken that relied entirely on essay questions. She described how well the students had done and to what extent the test had achieved the intended outcomes. This particular evaluation method, Ms. Powley explained, had

been helpful in a number of different ways. First, she thought that the test had served as a great motivator. The students knew it was important. It gave them a reason to reflect on what had been discussed in class and to assimilate information from many different topics. Second, the exam served as a measurement of students' ability to recall, analyze, and integrate critical information. Third, students' answers provided an indication of their writing skills. Fourth, the exam gave students the chance to determine the effectiveness of their study habits. By comparing *how* they had studied with *what* had been asked on the test, they could judge if their efforts (methods) had been fruitful. Finally, the exam provided a means for Ms. Powley to give useful feedback. Extended teacher comments highlighted strengths and weaknesses of students' work.

Ms. Powley also commented that the test provided information of a different nature. From her perspective, it indicated how well the class as a whole was doing, which individuals needed remedial work, and which needed more challenge. Results from this exam influenced and guided her subsequent instructional plans. With both strong and weak aspects of her instruction highlighted, Ms. Powley could target areas for modification prior to teaching similar lessons in the future.

As you can see from this example, there may be several reasons for conducting an evaluation. In one case, student learning may be the focus; in other situations, the focus may be directed to the quality of the instructional approaches and materials. In this chapter our focus is on the student. Chapter 13 will be devoted to the evaluation of instructional materials, including all of the approaches and media that are utilized.

Before we begin our discussion of the evaluation of students, it's important to understand the need for evaluation. What are its purposes, and how can they be achieved? The next section of this chapter addresses these issues. This is followed by a look at the different means used to assess student learning, and the relative importance of each. When, why, and how should they be constructed, and how can they be used in an optimal fashion? The CUE for this chapter deals with computer-managed instruction and spreadsheets and indicates how these tools can be used within the realm of student evaluation. ■

PURPOSES OF EVALUATION

The reasons for completing an evaluation can be quite varied. From the perspective of assessing student knowledge and skills, evaluation can be helpful before, during, and after instruction.

Before instruction, evaluation can serve as a means to

- identify students' preinstructional knowledge and skill levels. This indicates (1) whether students have the prerequisite skills and knowledge they need to begin the instructional materials, or (2) whether they already know the content they're slated to learn. In the former instance, a lack of prerequisite skills requires that students receive remedial instruction in order to attain the entry skills and knowledge necessary to learn the new information. In the latter case, evaluation indicates if instruction is even needed, or if a review will suffice. This form of evaluation is often referred to as a **pretest** or a preinstructional evaluation.

- focus learners' attention on the important topics that will be covered in the upcoming instruction. By completing an evaluation prior to instruction, the learner is primed to perceive those important topics when they are later experienced within the instructional materials (Fleming, 1987).

- establish a baseline of performance that can be used as a comparison with postinstruction performances. This can indicate progress and may motivate students when they see what has or hasn't been accomplished since the preinstructional assessments. One word of caution: students need to be informed of the value of pretests. It should be explained that a pretest merely establishes a baseline—a base point from which the work will *begin.* Lower levels of performance prior to the instructional materials are expected.

For example, Ms. Powley could have given her English class an essay test similar to the one discussed *before* the unit was presented. This could have shown the students how much they were expected to learn and what key elements would be covered, as well as what information would be a prerequisite for learning the new material. For those students who had already mastered the content, additional enrichment instruction might have been provided.

During instruction, evaluation serves as a means to

- demonstrate what has been learned to that point. It supplies information about students' learning that indicates whether or not they have learned what is needed to progress to the next portion of the instruction. This form of assessment is frequently referred to as **formative evaluation** of students. This information may be used by either the teacher or the student to determine if new instruction should be introduced or if additional practice and feedback is needed.

- supply corrective feedback as the learning process occurs—that is, identify and correct mistakes and problems *before* they become thoroughly ingrained and practiced in an incorrect fashion. In a similar manner, formative evaluation can increase students' confidence by indicating that the content has been mastered to that point.

- identify when, where, and what type of additional practice may be needed. At this point in the instruction, evaluation ensures that the new knowledge and skills are being integrated with previously learned information and that they can be recalled when needed.

- refocus attention on the desired outcomes. Because it's easy to lose sight of one's reasons for learning, it's helpful to be reminded of the expected outcomes during the learning process. An evaluation during the instruction is an effective tool for refocusing learners' attention on the purpose of their efforts.

Ms. Powley frequently felt the need to measure how well the students were learning new information throughout the course. Her formative evaluations often consisted of asking students to write a paragraph or two summarizing a topic recently discussed. At other times she simply asked them to verbally answer questions posed about new information they had encountered. As Ms. Powley pointed out, her reasons for frequent questioning and evaluation during instruction were twofold: first, she wanted to know how well students were assimilating the information; and second, she wanted to model this form of interim evaluation so students could learn to do it for themselves. That is, she wanted her students to understand the value of constant personal monitoring and evaluation and to develop the skills needed to evaluate their own progress as they proceeded through any instructional materials.

After the instruction, evaluation serves as a means to

- measure what students have learned. This is the most frequent use of formal evaluation and is commonly referred to as **summative evaluation** of students. It gives students the opportunity to demonstrate what they have learned after they have experienced all of the instruction. Because this evaluation generally comes at the conclusion, or summation, of the instruction, students frequently prepare for it by devoting time and effort to study outside of the classroom. It can be a period of reflection and/or additional practice that leads to a synthesis of the separate parts of the instruction.

- make decisions about student accreditation, advancement, or remediation. In many cases the results of summative evaluations are used to make specific decisions. For the medical student there is a medical board exam, for the law student there is a bar exam, for those wishing to drive a car there is a driver's license exam. These assessments are used to make decisions about a person's level of skill and knowledge. In some cases students' performances will produce accreditation and advancement, while at other times further study and remediation will need to be provided.

- review important information and prepare for **transfer** of the information to new and different situations. Learning new information and/or skills is important, but the value of this learning increases when it is shown to be useful in a variety of contexts. This form of evaluation can be used as a review and as a preparation for transferring and generalizing to new situations.

Ms. Powley used the essay exam to determine how well her students could perform following instruction. The exam indicated how the students were progressing, how much improvement they had made, and whether they needed additional remediation or advancement. Additionally, she was able to show parents the level at which their son or daughter was performing and to indicate whether a recommendation could be made to proceed to the next unit of instruction. In some cases this information may have helped the parents decide what type of additional help, reinforcement, or encouragement their child should receive.

Table 12.1 summarizes the different kinds of evaluations that focus on students, when they are generally conducted, and the purposes of each. Remember, the focus of our discussion has been on students. In Chapter 13 the emphasis will change to the evaluation of instructional materials.

EVALUATION INSTRUMENTS

Now that we've discussed why evaluations of student learning are conducted, it's important to look at the specific instruments you can use to conduct the actual assessments. Remember the "learn-o-meter" we discussed in Chapter 1? Wouldn't it be great if our learners could be plugged into a machine that would overtly indicate when learning had occurred? Although it isn't quite as easy as shown in Figure 12.1, there are means that can be used to help identify when, and to what degree, learning has occurred.

Table 12.1 Types of student evaluations and their purpose

Type	When It Is Carried Out	Purpose
Pretest	*Before* the instruction	• to identify preinstruction skill and competency levels • to focus learner attention on important topics to be learned • to establish a performance baseline
Formative Evaluation	*During* the instruction	• to diagnose student progress to that point in the instruction • to supply corrective feedback • to determine whether additional practice is needed • to refocus attention on the desired outcomes
Summative Evaluation	*After* the instruction	• to measure student learning • to make decisions about student accreditation, advancement, or remediation • to prepare for the transfer of what was learned to other situations

Figure 12.1 Evaluation would be much easier if student learning could be overtly measured by a "learn-o-meter"

Think for a moment about the wide variety of musical instruments in the world today. Each is used for the general purpose of producing music, but each variety is quite distinctive in the way it's used and in the sound it produces. The quality of the music produced is dependent on a number of factors: how well the instrument is tuned, the competency with which it is played, the work or musical score that is being performed, and the place in which it is played. Similarly, there are many evaluation instruments, each of which can be used to gather information about student learning. As with the musical instruments, the quality of results may vary dramatically based on the type of instrument selected, how it is developed and tuned for the specific audience, and where and when it is used.

Before we begin our discussion of the different types of evaluation instruments, there are a couple of important concepts for you to understand. To illustrate, put yourself in the following situation. Suppose you are a concert flautist who has just flown into town for an evening concert. Unfortunately, neither your instrument nor your music arrived with you. Frustrated, you go to a local music store in search of a replacement flute and copies of the needed music. You ask to try out a couple of their flutes with copies of the appropriate sheet music. As you practice the warm-up scales with the first instrument, you immediately notice that even

though you have your fingers positioned to play a C, the note sometimes sounds closer to a C-sharp. This flute doesn't consistently produce the sound it's supposed to produce. Disappointed, you lay it down and pick up the second. This one, thankfully, is consistent in its sound. However, as you open up the sheet music to begin your practice you notice a slight problem. The music is for the correct piece, but for a different instrument. Although it may be fun to try and use the flute to play the sousaphone part, it really isn't made to do so. You begin to laugh and cry at the same time.

Why is this discussion about your predicament as a flautist important here? First, the experience with the initial instrument illustrates the need for consistency. For the flute, *as for any evaluation instrument,* there is a great need for **reliability**. If the evaluation instrument cannot produce similar results over and over, the information it gives cannot be trusted. Whenever you deal with an evaluation instrument, an important consideration is the degree to which it is reliable. Evaluation reliability is "the degree to which a test instrument consistently measures the same group's knowledge level of the same instruction when taking the test over again" (Gentry, 1994, p. 383). Unreliability is often created when assessment items are ambiguous and thus lead to significant amounts of guessing.

In the second instance, you found that the flute wasn't the correct instrument for playing the given sheet music. Similarly, an evaluation instrument must be shown to have **validity** for what it is supposed to measure. Just as the flute was not the right instrument to use with that particular version of the music, there are times when certain types of evaluation instruments will not be valid measures for specific types of performances. For example, a valid evaluation instrument for a band member may be to play several measures from a specific piece of music; it would not be valid to have him or her recite a Robert Frost poem. Throughout the process of student evaluation, ensuring reliability and validity of the instruments is necessary if results are to be worthwhile and meaningful.

The following section will give you an overview of different evaluation instruments, some of their advantages and limitations, some guidelines for their selection and use, and a number of examples. The first group of instruments will focus on the traditional means of gathering evaluation data (e.g., multiple-choice, essay, and true-false items), and the second will be devoted to alternative assessment forms (e.g., portfolios, logs, journals). We have included both types for a very important reason: different instruments will give different types of feedback. Just as we have shown the need for knowledge of a variety of instructional approaches and media in order to ensure the appropriate learning of individual students, knowledge of different forms of evaluation instruments is needed in order to be able to discern which will deliver the best possible information. You must understand the types from which to choose and under which conditions each is most appropriate. For example, many educators feel that standard evaluation instruments (e.g., multiple choice, true-false) will not always produce the full information about student learning that is needed during the learning process. In some cases, then, alternative forms (e.g., portfolios, journals) may prove more beneficial. Again, you must understand the learners, the situation, and the type of outcome (feedback) that is needed before a proper evaluation instrument can be selected. In all cases, however, you're in a much better position when you know the different varieties and their individual strengths and limitations.

Standard Evaluation Instruments
True-False

Figure 12.2 presents a set of guidelines and suggestions that should be considered when developing true-false evaluation items.

Review the following statement pertaining to U.S. history:

Slavery was the main cause of the American Civil War.

Is this statement true or false? Do you agree or disagree? Statements such as this are the focus of the "true-false" evaluation instrument. This instrument consists of statements in which a choice is made between two alternatives. Generally the student responds by signifying either *true* or *false*, *agree* or *disagree*, or even *yes* or *no*. Here are some additional examples:

True or False   The solar system in which we live consists of a sun and nine planets.

True or False   In the sentence "The old woman and her husband walked slowly up the stairs," the word *slowly* is an adjective.

True or False   The following musical excerpt illustrates a "fugue" (play the recorded musical selection).

Advantages of true-false instruments:

- These items and their answers tend to be short, so more items can be asked within a given time period. This is particularly helpful when a large amount of subject matter must be covered.
- It generally takes less time and effort to construct this type of item than multiple-choice or essay items.
- Scoring is relatively easy and straightforward.

Limitations of true-false instruments:

- There is no real way to know why the student selected the incorrect answer, thus it is difficult to review students' responses and diagnose learning problems.
- With just two possible answers, there is a 50% possibility of guessing the correct answer.

Figure 12.2 Development guidelines for true-false items

❏ Relate all items to an appropriate instructional outcome or objective.

❏ Provide clear, unambiguous directions.

❏ Select items that are unequivocally true or false. Words such as *always*, *all*, and *never* should be avoided. Sweeping generalizations are most likely to be false.

❏ Avoid multiple negatives (e.g., "It was not undesirable for the First Continental Congress to meet in response to the Intolerable Acts of the British Parliament.").

❏ Make sure the evaluation has approximately the same number of true and false answers. Questions with true answers are generally easier to write and have a tendency to be more readily produced on evaluations.

❏ Paraphrase items taken from the text—do not list them verbatim.

- There is a tendency to emphasize rote memorization. It is difficult to design true-false items that measure comprehension, synthesis, or application.
- True-false evaluation items presume a world that is composed of right and wrong and do not consider intermediate values.

Matching

Refer back to the question about the Civil War listed at the beginning of the section on true-false instruments. A simple adaptation and expansion of that item would be to ask the students to match various wars with their causes, as in the following example:

Wars

_____ 1. American Revolutionary War
_____ 2. American Civil War
_____ 3. Spanish-American War

Main Causes

a. Failure of the British to sign commercial agreements favorable to the United States.

b. Use of yellow journalism to sway public opinion about the need for humanitarian intervention and the annexation of Cuba by the United States.

c. The Nullification Controversy, in which South Carolina declared the U.S. tariff laws null and void.

d. Imposition of taxation without proper representation of those being taxed.

Part of this example requires students to have a similar kind of knowledge as that needed to successfully complete the original true-false question. However, additional information is required of the student here. In this case, students must make a choice between a number of different alternatives. This type of instrument is one in which students associate an item in one column with a number of alternatives in another column. Additional examples include the following:

Directions: Column A is a list of three famous explorers. Column B is a list of geographic landmarks that were explored by different individuals. Match the name of explorer to the landmark by placing the letter of the landmark in Column B on the appropriate line next to the explorer in Column A. One answer in Column B will not be used.

Column A	*Column B*
_____ 1. Champlain	a. Florida Everglades
_____ 2. Coronado	b. Grand Canyon
_____ 3. De Soto	c. Lake Huron
	d. Ozark Mountains

Directions: Column A is a list of common devices that are applications of specific simple machines. Column B is a list of simple machines. Match the simple machine in Column B with its example in Column A by placing the letter of the simple machine on the appropriate line next to the example given in Column A. Items listed in Column B may be used more than once.

Column A	*Column B*
_____ 1. loading dock	a. inclined plane
_____ 2. wheelbarrow	b. lever
_____ 3. broom	c. pulley
_____ 4. doorknob	
_____ 5. pliers	
_____ 6. escalator	

Advantages of matching instruments:

- This type of instrument helps to minimize guessing on the part of students.
- Matching items are well suited for measuring students' understanding of the association between pairs of items (e.g., objects and their functions, items and their locations, events and their dates, terms and their definitions).
- Students can rapidly respond without writing out their answers, thus allowing for more content coverage.
- Scoring is relatively easy and straightforward.

Limitations of matching instruments:

- An unknown answer may be determined through the process of elimination.
- They are frequently used to associate trivial information.
- Memorization skills are often emphasized, although more complex cognitive matching items can be constructed.
- They measure students' ability to recognize, rather than recall, the correct answer.

Figure 12.3 presents a set of guidelines and suggestions that should be considered when developing matching evaluation items.

Figure 12.3 Development
guidelines for matching items

❏ Explain to students the basis for matching and whether options may be used more than once or if more than one option is given for any of the questions. Additionally, instructions should advise students *how* to respond.

❏ Provide extra alternatives in the answer column to avoid selection by elimination.

❏ Provide homogeneous statements or terms in each column in terms of grammatical structure and conceptual content. Otherwise students may eliminate irrelevant options and obtain higher scores than warranted.

❏ Provide between six and eight associations within a single question. This may vary according to the level of the learner.

❏ Arrange the answer choices in a logical manner (alphabetical, chronological, etc.) to aid students in finding the keyed response easily.

❏ Place the shorter answers in Column B. This reduces the time needed to scan the potential answers.

❏ Make sure that all of the options are located on the same page.

Multiple Choice

Examine the following evaluation item:

Which of the following was a major cause of the American Civil War?

a. Failure of the British to sign commercial agreements favorable to the United States.

b. Use of yellow journalism to sway public opinion about the need for humanitarian intervention and the annexation of Cuba by the United States.

c. The Nullification Controversy, in which South Carolina declared the U.S. tariff laws null and void.

d. Imposition of taxation without proper representation of those being taxed.

How does this item differ from the similar ones mentioned in the previous two sections? One major difference is that students must discern the "most correct" or "best" answer from a number of plausible alternatives. This is an example of a multiple-choice item.

The multiple-choice instrument is one of the most frequently used assessment tools. Each item is made up of basically two parts: a stem and a number of options or alternatives. The **stem** sets forth a problem, and the list of alternatives contains one option that is the correct or "best" solution. All incorrect or less appropriate alternatives are called **distractors**, or **foils**. Here are some additional examples of multiple-choice items:

Which of the following is the simplified version of $(42 + 18) \div 5$?

a. 10

b. 12

c. 24

d. 300

If one frequently raises the cover of a container in which a liquid is being heated, the liquid takes longer to boil because:

a. boiling occurs at a higher temperature if the pressure is increased.

b. escaping vapor carries heat away from the liquid.

c. permitting the vapor to escape decreases the volume of the liquid.

d. the temperature of a vapor is proportional to its volume at constant temperature.

e. permitting more air to enter results in increased pressure on the liquid.

Advantages of multiple-choice instruments:

• They can be effectively used to measure objectives ranging from simple memorization tasks to complex cognitive manipulations.

• Student writing is minimized, so a substantial amount of course content can be covered in a limited amount of time.

• Similar to true-false and matching items, scoring is relatively straightforward.

- This format can be used to diagnose student learning problems if incorrect alternatives are designed in order to detect common errors.
- With three to five options, this instrument reduces the potential for guessing.
- This format can be constructed to require students to select between alternatives that vary in degree of correctness. Thus students are allowed to select the "best" alternative and aren't left to the absolutes required by true-false or matching instruments.

Limitations of multiple-choice instruments:

- They are often difficult and time-consuming to write. Determining three or four plausible distractors is often the most arduous part of the task.
- Students may feel there is more than one defensible alternative. This may lead to complaints of the answer being too discriminating or "picky."

Figure 12.4 presents a set of guidelines and suggestions that should be considered when developing multiple-choice evaluation items.

Completion and Short Answer

The following is an example of a short-answer item:

The Nullification Controversy was a major cause of which American war? _____

Unlike the earlier items regarding the Civil War, this item requires students to recall a particular short answer or phrase. Completion and short-answer instruments are similar. A completion instrument requires students to finish a sentence with a word or short phrase; a short-answer instrument poses a question that can be answered in a word or phrase. Here are examples of completion items and their corresponding short-answer items:

Completion	**Short Answer**
• Tiny bits of soil picked up and then deposited by the water in rivers and streams are known as _____.	• What is the term used to describe tiny bits of soil picked up and then deposited by the water in rivers and streams?
• The slow wearing away of rock and soil by water, wind, or ice is called _____.	• What do you call the slow wearing away of rock and soil by water, wind, or ice?

- An 1831 invention that consisted of a horse-drawn machine used to cut grain was the _____.
- What was the 1831 invention that consisted of a horse-drawn machine that could be used to cut grain?

Advantages of completion and short-answer instruments:

- Items are relatively easy to develop.
- These instruments are well suited for situations in which students are expected to recall specific facts such as names, dates, places, events, and definitions.
- The possibility of guessing a correct answer is eliminated.
- More items can be used because this type of item usually takes less time to read and answer than other types. This allows for a larger amount of content to be covered.

Limitations of completion and short-answer instruments:

- It is difficult to develop items that measure higher-level cognitive skills.
- Extended use of this type of instrument may place an overemphasis on memorization.
- They can be difficult to score. For example, which is the correct answer for the following item: Abraham Lincoln was born in _____ (Kentucky, a bed, a log cabin, 1809).

Figure 12.5 presents a set of guidelines and suggestions that should be considered when developing completion or short-answer evaluation items.

Essay

Before beginning this section, consider all of the different forms of evaluation items involving the American Civil War presented in the previous sections. Now think about what is required for correct responses in those versions, and compare that with what would be required of students responding to the following item:

Why does the simple cause of slavery fail to explain the emergence of the American Civil War?

A response to this question obviously requires students to be more thorough, work at higher cognitive levels, and take more time to respond.

Figure 12.4 Development guidelines for multiple-choice items

Full item

❏ Make sure the directions and the manner in which the items will be scored are understood.

❏ Make sure the vocabulary is suitable for students' reading level.

❏ Use items to measure skills other than just recall. To this end, avoid lifting a statement verbatim from the instructional materials.

❏ Avoid items measuring opinions. Opinion questions are neither correct nor incorrect, and all may be equally defensible.

❏ Include graphics, charts, and tables within items whenever possible.

Stems

❏ Present one problem or question in the stem, and make sure it presents the purpose of the item in a clear and concise fashion.

❏ Make sure the stem contains as much of the question or problem as possible. Do not repeat words in each option that could be stated once in the stem.

❏ Eliminate unnecessary material in the stem.

❏ Use negatives sparingly. If the word *not* is used in the stem, it should be underlined to make sure it is not overlooked.

❏ Make sure the stem is clear and grammatically correct and that it contains elements common to each alternative.

Alternatives

❏ Provide only one correct or clearly best answer. Unless given other directions, students will assume that only one of the alternatives is to be selected.

❏ Avoid irrelevant grammatical cues. All alternatives should be homogeneous in content and length and grammatically consistent with the stem.

❏ Provide three to five alternatives for each item.

❏ Write alternatives on separate lines beginning at the same point on the page.

❏ Ensure that all alternatives are plausible.

❏ Make sure that the correct answer is not highlighted by being excessively long or short.

❏ Compose incorrect alternatives by including common misconceptions. One good approach is to first use the item as a short-answer question and later make it into a multiple-choice item using the best "wrong" answers as alternatives.

❏ Arrange the correct alternative for multiple-choice items randomly.

The essay evaluation instrument is one that requires students to write a response to one or more questions. For elementary students an answer may consist of a single sentence. For older students the responses may range from a couple of sentences to several pages. Essay instruments can be used to compare, justify, contrast, compile, interpret, or formulate valid conclusions—all of which are higher-level cognitive skills.

Other examples of essay-type items include the following:

Why did the Pilgrims come to the New World?

Why do Amish people choose <u>not</u> to use motorized machines on their farms?

There were a number of social, economic, political, and military events that led to the launching of the cultural revolution in the People's Repub-

Figure 12.5 Development guidelines for completion and short-answer items

❑ Design items so that answers correspond with the main points of the content rather than to minor aspects.

❑ Write the item specifically enough that there is only one correct answer.

❑ Omit only key words from the completion items.

❑ Put the blanks near the end of the statement rather than at the beginning.

❑ Avoid writing items with too many blanks. This leads to confusion and guessing.

❑ Require a one-word response or at most a short phrase of closely related words.

❑ Use "a(n)" if the answer blank is preceded by the article "a" or "an" to avoid giving grammatical clues as to the correct answer.

❑ Use blanks of the same length to avoid providing clues as to the length of the correct response.

❑ Plan how the scoring will occur as the items are being developed.

lic of China. Select events in *two* of these four areas and evaluate Mao Tse-tung's actions in light of them.

Explain the function of neurotransmitters in the synapses of the body.

Advantages of essay instruments:

- They can be used to measure the desired competency at a greater depth and in greater detail than most other instruments.

- They give students the freedom to respond within broad limits. This can encourage originality, creativity, and divergent thinking.

- They are best used when dealing with outcomes that focus on written skills, interpretation and use of data, creative expression, and/or organization of ideas.

- Generally, they require a shorter amount of time to construct.

- They effectively measure students' ability to express themselves.

- The opportunity for guessing a correct response is severely limited.

- Knowledge of an upcoming essay evaluation has the tendency to motivate students to study more thoroughly.

Limitations of essay instruments:

- Since only a few essay items can be administered during a given period of time, the sampling of topics and behaviors is usually quite small.

- They provide more opportunity for bluffing.

- Essays are difficult and time-consuming to score, and scoring can be biased, unreliable, and inconsistent.

- Essays may be difficult for students who misunderstand the main point of the question, who tend to go off on tangents, or who have language and/or writing difficulties.

Figure 12.6 presents a set of guidelines and suggestions that should be considered when developing essay evaluation items.

Performance

The purpose of a performance instrument is to measure skills (usually psychomotor or physical) needed to accomplish a specific task. Within a performance situation, students are required to perform some feat or demonstrate some skill they have learned, such as delivering a persuasive speech, calculating an arithmetic average, performing a successful ceiling shot in racquetball, or parallel parking a car. Unlike the previous instruments, learners in this situation must demonstrate not only that they know *what* to do but also that they know *how* to do it. Regarding the Civil War topic previously presented, for example, a student may be asked to present a persuasive speech explaining why the Southern states were justified in seceding from the Union.

Advantages of the performance instrument:

- This instrument allows for the objective evaluation of a performance or product, particularly when a checklist is used.

- Students actually get to demonstrate, rather than simply describe, the desired performance.

Figure 12.6 Development guidelines for essay items

❑ Phrase each question so students clearly understand what is expected. For example, include specific directions using terms such as *compare*, *contrast*, *define*, *discuss*, or *formulate*. Without enough structure, students may miss the intent of the question or may attempt to bluff if they are not prepared to answer it.

❑ Provide as many essay items as students can comfortably respond to within the time allowed. Give students suggestions for distributing their time.

❑ Avoid using items that focus on opinions and attitudes—unless the goal is to formulate and express opinions or attitudes.

❑ Begin, when possible, with a relatively easy and straightforward essay item. This helps students gain composure and confidence.

❑ Minimize scoring subjectivity by preparing a list of key points, assigning weights to each concept, scoring all papers anonymously, and scoring the same question on all papers before moving on to the next question.

• With the use of a performance checklist, students can practice the performance before the test and receive reliable feedback from other students, parents, teachers, or themselves.

Limitations of the performance instrument:

• This format can be very time-consuming to administer (usually one at a time).
• It can be difficult to develop reliable checklists.
• It may require several individuals or judges (e.g., skating and diving competitions) to assess the abilities of the performers.
• Materials and equipment other than paper and pencils may be required.
• Specialized apparatus or location may be needed.
• Increased setup time is often required.
• Discipline problems can arise, since individuals are generally evaluated one at a time, leaving others to wait or be occupied with other activities.

Figure 12.7 presents a set of guidelines and suggestions that should be considered when developing performance evaluation items. Figure 12.8 is an example of a performance checklist used by water safety instructors to evaluate swimming performance.

Alternative Evaluation Instruments

In addition to the traditional types of evaluation instruments described above, there are a number of other instruments that can be utilized to effectively monitor and assess the learning of students. The portfolio instrument is one such method which has

gained popularity in recent years. As with the previous assessment instruments, we will outline the portfolio's purpose, its advantages and limitations, and some guidelines for its use. Following this we will describe a number of other instruments, including interviews, journals, writing samples, open-ended experiences, and long-term projects.

Portfolios

Arter and Spandel (1992) define the student **portfolio** as "a purposeful collection of student work that tells the story of the student's efforts, progress, or achievement" (p. 36). The portfolio is a rich collection of work that demonstrates what students know and can do. For years, artists have used portfolios to highlight the depth and breadth of their abilities. Similarly, students may use portfolios to illustrate their unique problem-solving or critical-thinking skills, as well as their creative talents (e.g., writing, drawing, design). Additionally, portfolios can be used to demonstrate the evolution students went through to achieve their current performance level. Unlike the end-of-the-unit objective evaluation, the portfolio is designed to capture a greater range of students' capabilities and to indicate how those capabilities developed and grew over time. Not only does the portfolio convey to others the students' progression, it also serves as a vehicle for students to gauge their own development and to envision what additional things they might learn.

In our discussion of constructivist theory in Chapter 2 we explained that this theory deals with the creation of meaning and understanding by the student. Portfolios (as well as journals, logs, long-term projects, etc.) can be effectively used to show how

Figure 12.7 Development
guidelines for performance tests

❏ Specify exactly what learners are to do (through a demonstration and/or
explanation), the equipment and materials that will be needed, and how
performances will be assessed.

❏ Develop and use a checklist based on acceptable performance standards.
In most cases, the checklist should include some type of scoring system.

❏ Make sure the checklist outlines all the critical behaviors that should be
observed. Behaviors that should *not* be observed should be listed on a
separate part of the checklist.

❏ Be sure that, if a sequence of behaviors is needed to complete a task
successfully, it is highlighted in some way.

❏ Keep the scoring system as simple as possible.

❏ Give a copy of the checklist and scoring system to students before they
begin to practice the skill. Have them refer to it as they are learning the skill.

❏ Prepare for the evaluation by having all required apparatuses ready.

❏ After the performance, explain to learners the strengths and weaknesses
of their performances.

❏ Use video- and/or audiotape to record performances. This may be ex-
tremely helpful when behaviors occur very quickly or in rapid succession.
The tapes are also an effective means for supplying feedback to students.

and to what degree that meaning and understanding have developed. Moreover, the portfolio itself offers a means by which learners can reflect and gain greater insights as they think about what they have accomplished and what additional things they can do.

As suggested by D'Aoust (1992), portfolios may be structured around the exemplary "products" of students' work (i.e., including only those of the best quality) or around the "process" by which students arrived at current levels of performance (i.e., pieces from the beginning, middle, and end of the course that show the progression of students' abilities), or

they could include a mixture of both. In either case, a major benefit comes from actually putting it together. "Students cannot assemble a portfolio without using clearly defined targets (criteria) in a systematic way to paint a picture of their own efforts, growth, and achievement. This is the essence of assessment. Thus, portfolios used in this manner provide an example of how assessment can be used to improve achievement and not merely monitor achievement" (Arter & Spandel, 1992, p. 37).

Within the classroom setting, the portfolio is becoming more and more accepted as a means of student assessment. Some states (e.g., Vermont) now

Figure 12.8 Performance
checklist for evaluating the front
crawl swimming stroke

Swimming stroke: **Front Crawl**

Component	Level V
Body Position	❏ Body inclined less than 15°
Arms	❏ Elbow high during recovery ❏ Hand enters index finger first ❏ Arm fully extended at finish of pull ❏ Arms pull in "S" pattern
Kick	❏ Emphasis on downbeat ❏ Relaxed feet with floppy ankles
Breathing/Timing	❏ Head lift not acceptable during breathing ❏ Continuous arm motion in time with breathing

Source: Courtesy of the American Red Cross.

By reviewing a student's portfolio, one can see how learning has occurred over a period of time.

have a mandated statewide portfolio assessment program. Other states (e.g., Indiana) will invoke similar programs in the near future.

Advantages of the portfolio instrument:

- It provides a broad picture of what students know and can do.
- It can be used to demonstrate student growth.
- It can portray both the process and the products of student work.

- It provides something tangible as a basis for discussion between student and teacher, teacher and parent, and student and parent.
- It actively involves students in assessing their own learning and actively promotes reflection on their work and abilities.

Limitations of the portfolio instrument:

- The work in the portfolio may not be representative of what students know and can do.
- The criteria used to critique the product may not reflect the most relevant or useful dimensions of the task.
- The quality of the work in the portfolio may make the viewer wonder about its authorship.
- There may be aspects of the portfolio process that don't allow students to demonstrate the extent of what they know or can do.
- The conclusions drawn from the portfolio can be heavily influenced by the person doing the evaluation.

Figure 12.9 presents a set of guidelines and suggestions that should be considered when developing portfolios.

Figure 12.9 Portfolio development guidelines

❑ Many different skills and techniques are needed to produce an effective portfolio. Students need models of finished portfolios as well as examples of how others develop and reflect on them.

❑ Students should be involved in selecting the pieces to be included in their portfolios. This promotes reflection on the part of students.

❑ A portfolio should convey the following: *rationale* (purpose for forming the portfolio), *intents* (its goals), *contents* (the actual displays), *standards* (what are good and not-so-good performances), and *judgments* (what the contents tell us).

❑ Portfolios should contain examples that illustrate growth.

❑ Student self-reflection and self-evaluation can be promoted by having students ask, What makes this my best work? How did I go about creating it? What problems did I encounter? What makes my best piece different from my weakest piece?

❑ All pieces should be dated so that progress can be noted over time.

❑ Students should regularly be given time to read and reorganize their portfolios.

❑ The portfolio should be organized, inviting, and manageable. Plan a storage system that is convenient for both you and your students.

❑ The portfolio should be evaluated as a whole using criteria such as flexibility, problem solving, improvement over time, and reflection.

❑ Students should be aware of the criteria used for evaluating the portfolio.

Other Alternative Instruments

Interviews and Oral Evaluations.   Interviews and oral evaluations are generally conducted face-to-face, with one person asking questions and the other responding. To conduct an interview or oral evaluation, a set of questions is designed covering a specific set of outcomes. The questions may be very structured (i.e., requiring a specific response) or fairly unstructured (i.e., open-ended questions that allow for lengthy, detailed answers). As with the questions for an essay evaluation, the person conducting the interview or oral evaluation asks a question and allows the student to respond. For purposes of clarification, students may take (or be asked to take) the opportunity to explain their answers in more depth and detail. The response may be recorded on video- or audiotape, or the gist may be written down by the interviewer. Because this form of evaluation is conducted orally between two or more individuals, it can be conducted over the telephone. As our expertise with e-mail increases, adaptations that incorporate this technology will become more prevalent. Interviews allow for more in-depth on-the-spot questioning if needed. However, they can take a lot of time to complete and they may be somewhat unreliable.

Logs and Journals.   Logs and journals are written records that students keep as they work through a long-term experience. For example, students in a discussion group might take time at the end of each session to write out their thoughts and experiences about what happened in the group. How well was the topic covered? What feelings did the discussion provoke? There is value in organizing one's thoughts and presenting them logically in writing. There is also value in rereading the journal later and reflecting on what one experienced. Just as students can reflect on their experiences, so too the journal or log can be used as a means to evaluate what was experienced. This is a good instrument to use during the formative stages of learning.

Writing Samples.   This evaluation tool is frequently combined with the portfolio. It generally consists of the student (or teacher) selecting one or more samples from different writing assignments and submitting them for evaluation. The samples may be selected as the students' "best work" as a means to demonstrate the progression that has occurred over a specific period of time. This type of instrument is frequently used by businesses and by graduate school selection committees. Table 12.2 gives several application examples of this and the other alternative evaluation instruments.

Open-Ended Experiences.   This type of evaluation instrument generally is not focused on a single "correct" answer. Here the students are placed in a novel situation that requires a performance, and that performance is judged by how they respond and react. Many results from a wide continuum of possible "correct" outcomes may be produced. Examples include mock trials, debates, and different types of simulated experiences.

Long-Term Projects.   Term papers, science fair projects, and unit activities (e.g., mini-societies, dramatic reenacts, trade fairs) are all examples of long-term projects. They can require extended research and library work and often involve the use of cooperative groups. As stated by Blumenfeld et al., "Within this framework, students pursue solutions to nontrivial problems by asking and refining questions, debating ideas, making predictions, designing plans and/or experiments, collecting and analyzing data, drawing conclusions, communicating their ideas and findings to others, asking new questions, and creating artifacts" (1991, p. 371). The evaluation instruments generally require the use of checklists with important attributes that must be exhibited within the project. Frequently, the effectiveness of this project is enhanced through the use of journals or logs.

PLANNING THE EVALUATION

After considering all of the different types of evaluation instruments, we are now ready to plan the manner in which students' learning will be evaluated. Think back to Chapter 6 and the instructional plan we discussed. Evaluation is an integral part of that plan. During Chapter 6 we emphasized the importance of planning in order that the final instructional materials accomplish the desired learning goals. Likewise, forethought and planning are required for learning to be properly measured. The following suggestions outline important considerations that should be undertaken while you are planning and constructing an evaluation. Do not interpret the following to be a "cut-in-stone" prescription of exact steps to be followed. These are merely guidelines and suggestions that have proven helpful in the past. Your specific situations will require some adaptation and alterations in order for the final product to be optimal.

1.   Ask yourself the following question: What is it that students are supposed to have learned? The easiest and quickest way to answer this question is to refer to the intended instructional outcomes. As

Table 12.2 Examples of the application of different alternative evaluation instruments

Alternative Evaluation Instrument	Application Examples
Portfolio	• Evaluate the improvement of writing skills over the course of a semester by having 11th-grade English students create a portfolio of their best writing samples at the end of the first week, at the end of the first 9 weeks, and at the end of the semester.
	• Have student teachers compile a portfolio of their teaching philosophy with accompanying documents and examples to illustrate the implementation of their philosophy during the semester of classroom teaching.
Interviews and Oral Examinations	• Interview third-year Spanish students about different cultural aspects of Mexico. All questions and responses are to be given in Spanish.
	• Ask preschool children to complete a sorting task and then explain how they actually accomplished the task.
Logs and Journals	• Have students within a fifth-grade "Conflict Resolution" program keep a journal about what they learned in class and how they used the main techniques with their family and friends.
	• Have students in a high school psychology class keep a daily journal of interactions between themselves and their friends, including descriptions of the "most significant interaction to happen each day" and thoughts on why it was important.
Writing Samples	• Evaluate potential graduate student applicants' writing and organizational skills by having them submit three or four papers from their undergraduate classes.
	• Assess the abilities of candidates for the school newspaper by having them submit short articles about recent school events.
Open-Ended Experiences	• Evaluate students on their ability to research and then debate the pros and cons of corporal punishment (e.g., spankings) used within the school systems of other countries.
	• Assess student understanding of the concept of supply and demand by having them set up a classroom store and demonstrate what would happen given different conditions (e.g., competition from other classes, lack of product, increased costs of product).
Long-Term Projects	• In a project on the Native American tribes of Indiana, group students into tribes of Miami, Potowatami, and Delaware Indians and have them develop reports and skits on the village life of their tribe. This could include designing a model of the village, preparing food similar to what their tribe would eat, and dressing in authentic attire.
	• After a science unit on sound, have students in a fourth-grade class develop different ways in which the principles of frequency and pitch can be demonstrated.

we explained in Chapter 5, the instructional outcomes, materials, and evaluations should all be congruent. This means that the evaluation instruments need to measure what was taught during the instruction and that instruction should have been developed from the expected outcomes.

2. Determine the relative importance of each outcome and how much emphasis was given to each during instruction. Make decisions on how many questions to ask related to the different outcomes and how much time is needed to evaluate each one. In most cases, those decisions are closely aligned with the relative importance of each outcome.

3. Based on the outcomes, select the most relevant evaluation instrument(s) and construct the evaluation items. These items need to reflect the

principles of good evaluation item construction discussed earlier. In Figure 12.10, several outcomes are listed with accompanying example and non-example evaluation items. Read through the outcomes and compare the example/non-example versions. Reflect on why the non-examples are not congruent with the intended outcome. It is critical that the conditions and the behaviors mentioned in the outcomes match those within the evaluation instrument. Be sure to consider other instruments that could be used to evaluate the given outcome.

4. Assemble the complete evaluation. As you bring together all of the individual items, it is important to consider the following:

a. Group questions according to item type (e.g., multiple choice, true-false) so students don't have to continuously shift response patterns.

b. Do not arrange items randomly. Try to list items in the order the content was covered or in order of difficulty. When possible, place easier

Figure 12.10 Examples and non-examples of evaluation instruments based on instructional outcomes

Outcome: Without reference to books or notes, the student will be able to describe the causes of the American Revolution. The description must include at least two of the significant events leading up to the war.

Example 1: (Essay) Without using your book or notes, describe at least two significant events that led up to the American Revolutionary War.

Example 2: (Oral) "Rachel, can you describe two or more of the significant events that led up to the American Revolutionary War?"

Non-example: (True-False) The American Revolutionary War began with the signing of the Declaration of Independence in 1776.

Outcome: Given a simple line drawing of the computer's central processing unit (CPU), RAM, ROM, and external memory devices, the student will recognize each of the parts and their functions and will illustrate how information passes between the parts.

Example 1: (Multiple Choice) An important component of a computer system is the permanent internal memory, which contains the basic instructions that the computer needs to operate. This part of the system is known as the:

a. central processing unit (CPU)

b. external memory

c. random-access memory (RAM)

d. read-only memory (ROM)

Example 2: (Matching) Column A lists different parts of the computer system. Column B is a list of their corresponding functions. Select the appropriate function description from Column B and put its corresponding letter in the blank by the proper part listed in Column A.

Column A	Column B
_____ 1. CPU	a. volatile working memory that contains contents that can change, as needed, to perform different tasks
_____ 2. ROM	b. controls the functions and calculations of the computer
_____ 3. RAM	c. permanent internal memory, which contains the basic instructions the computer needs to operate
	d. a device that generates input

Non-example: (completion) The first central processing unit (CPU) was designed by _____.

DEVELOPING EVALUATION INSTRUMENTS

Although it seems that the sequence of planning, implementing, and evaluating dictates that evaluation items be created during this final phase, this may not be the most effective or efficient time to do so. Most instructional design models suggest that one should design evaluation items at the same time one is developing the instructional outcomes—during the planning phase (Dick & Carey, 1990; Kemp, Morrison, & Ross, 1994; Smith & Ragan, 1993). Why? Because in both cases the focus is on the resulting performances of students and the conditions and criteria under which they will perform. It is imperative that these outcomes and evaluation items match. Evaluation items must measure the desired outcome of the instruction. By developing them simultaneously, there is a greater likelihood that they will match.

questions first to give students confidence at the outset of the test.

c. Avoid using a series of interdependent questions in which the answer to one item depends on knowing the correct answer to another item.

d. Reread the examination and make sure some items don't provide clues or answers to other items.

5. Construct the directions for the complete evaluation and any subparts. Make sure you include the full directions on the type of response that is required. It may also help to include information regarding the value of each item or subpart of the evaluation. This is useful to students as they determine how much emphasis they should place on any one item.

6. If possible, have a content expert check the items to be sure they are accurate and valid. For example, a fifth-grade teacher may ask another fifth-grade teacher to review the evaluation and make suggestions. This is helpful in terms of both the items and the directions.

7. If possible, try out the exam on a few students who are similar to the ones who will be receiving the evaluation. This tryout will ensure that the directions are clear, that the vocabulary is at the correct level, that the test length is appropriate, and that the scoring system is adequate.

8. Finally, consider what will occur after the evaluation is over. It's often useful to evaluate the evaluation. You may want to ask yourself the following questions: How well did the students do? Were there any particular problems? What should be changed before this evaluation is used again? How should this evaluation and the suggested changes be filed and retrieved when it is needed in the future?

CUE Computer Use ESSENTIALS

COMPUTER-MANAGED INSTRUCTION

Computers are excellent tools for working with all kinds of information—text, graphics, and data in various forms—so it should come as no surprise that computers can be very valuable teacher tools for managing the information associated with student progress. **Computer-managed instruction (CMI)** is the term given to the use of the computer in the management of the instructional process. While CMI can vary from simple grade keeping to quite complex applications, any form of CMI has something to do with student record keeping, performance assessment, monitoring of student progress, or evaluation. Let's begin by looking at some simple tools for evaluating student progress.

Test Generators

As described earlier, testing is usually an important aspect of the evaluation of student progress. Computer programs that are used to create tests are called **test generators.** Most test generators use a database of prepared test items; many textbooks now come with such databases to help teachers prepare tests. The database of test items may be coded into various categories, including book chapter, topic, objective, level of difficulty, type of item, and so on. Alternatively, the software allows teachers to create their own test items. Most test-generator programs accommodate different question types, including multiple choice, true-false, matching, and even essay. Examples of test generators include *Quiz Writer Plus, Test Quest,* and *Test Writer.*

The chief advantage of test-generator programs is that teachers can easily create multiple forms of the same test. With a sufficiently large database of items, the program can select from among several items for a given chapter and objective to create multiple unique forms of a test. This is useful to discourage students from cheating or when there is a high level of individualization in the classroom. In the latter situation, students working toward mastery may take exams at different times, and a single student may need to take a test over a particular content area several times before achieving mastery. The test generator can easily create the various versions needed. With an already-prepared database, test generators can be significant time-savers. However, teachers need to check the items in prepared databases carefully to ensure that they are accurate and appropriate for use with the class. When an already-prepared database isn't provided, the teacher must be willing to invest considerable time to develop the database before the test generator can begin to pay real timesaving dividends.

Test Scoring

Another area where computers can save time in the testing process is in test scoring. For some time, colleges and universities have utilized test-scoring services. With the advent of personal computers and readers designed to accommodate computer scoring sheets, test scoring capability has come to K–12 schools as well. Most test-scoring devices use special scoring sheets or cards, often called scan sheets or bubble sheets, on which students mark their answers to multiple-choice or true-false items. By optically scanning the sheets and comparing the students' selections to the key entered by the teacher, the machine can identify whether items are answered correctly or incorrectly. Simple test-scoring machines scan each sheet and print the student's score on the sheet itself. More sophisticated machines can feed the results to an attached personal computer. The computer then can provide additional information, such as a list of student names and their scores, descriptive statistics such as the class average and range, more sophisticated statistics such as t scores (scores adjusted for the variation within the class), and an item analysis of the test items used. These can assist teachers in evaluating both the students and the test itself.

Gradebook Programs

One of the most widely used of all basic CMI applications is the **computer gradebook** program. Computer gradebook programs are designed to resemble their paper-based kin, but with greater capability. Essentially, computer gradebooks are database programs that can store and manipulate students' grades. Most gradebook programs allow the teacher to work with a variety of common functions, such as creating a new class, entering student names for a class, adding categories of grades, entering student scores for particular categories, editing entries, calculating grades, printing reports, and saving to and retrieving from disk. Good gradebook programs allow categories of grades to be weighted to suit the teacher's grading scheme. Most accept either letter grades or numerical scores. Some include additional features such as attendance tracking, the ability to add comments to students' records, and even the capacity to print seating charts.

Computer gradebooks offer some significant advantages over their paper-based counterparts. One is time savings. Although it may take a little more time to set up a computer gradebook, this is more than offset by the time savings later. At the end of the grading period, grades can be generated at the touch of a button without the need for tedious manual calculations. Student records are also readily available at any time. If a student's parents stop by for a conference, it is a simple matter to retrieve the records and get an exact, up-to-the-minute picture of their child's status in the class. Finally, computer gradebooks offer the advantage of accuracy. As long as the program is set up correctly, the computer will not make errors in calculation (as the teacher might) that could result in an erroneous grade. Stand-alone computer gradebook programs include *Grade Machine, Gradebook Plus, Making the Grade,* and *Classmaster* (Figure 12.11 shows a sample screen from *Making the Grade*). Gradebook programs are also part of more comprehensive student management systems such as *Columbia* and *MacSchool.*

Sophisticated CMI

The applications of computers to the evaluation of student progress that we have examined so far have all been simple, single-purpose applications. Test generation, test scoring, and grade keeping are all useful functions in and of themselves. However, they can be combined in a single, sophisticated system. Sophisticated CMI systems include testing, record keeping, report generation, and often diagnosis of individual student's performance and prescriptions for learning activities. Several companies market sophisticated CMI systems for schools.

The rationale for sophisticated CMI systems can be found in the quest for individualized instruction and mastery learning, which we discussed in Chapter 10. In order to truly individualize instruction, the teacher must manage classroom learning

Figure 12.11 Screen from *Making the Grade,* a commercial gradebook program

ASSIGNMENT NUMBERS---->	27	28	29	30	31	32	33	34	35	36	CURRENT
ASSIGNMENT CATEGORIES->	LIT	PAR	SPL	QFT	ORL	LIT	LIT	WRT	QFT		STUDENT
ASSIGNMENT VALUES----->	58	25	30	182	50	100	✓	100	200		TOTALS
1 ARCHER, DENNIS E.	44	25	23	121	DRP	76	✓	80	92		75.2=C
2 BOWLES, CHARLES A.	82		20	103	30	70	✓	74	120		62.5=D
3 CHANCELLOR, JAMES L.	42	DRP	23	168	40	86	✓+	79	164		86.5=B
4 DICKERSON MICHAEL R.	35	25	27	156	45	78	✓	87	120		79.7=C+
5 GARCIA, EUGENE F.	24	25	29	107	40	72	✓	82	164		74.1=C
6 GLENN, HELEN B.	EXC	EXC	29	164	45	DRP	✓+	96	172		90.0=A-
7 GRAY, KATHLEEN R.	39	25	30	68	35	72	✓	78	92		70.6=C-
8 HOWARD, STACEY E.	DRP		18	152	40	80	✓	88	156		80.0=B-

FIND [ ] SCORES

	ASSIGNMENT TITLES	POINTS	ITEMS	X-FACTORS
34	COMPOSITION 1: The Nature of Man [10/28]	100	100	1.000
35	QUARTER I: Spelling Final Test [10/28]	200	100	2.000
36				

Source: Making the Grade, Jay Klein Productions. Reprinted with permission.

activities and assess the progress of a classroom full of students, all of whom are at different points along the learning path. This is a daunting challenge and is beyond the capability of most teachers. This is where the computer can help.

Most sophisticated CMI systems rely on a well-articulated curriculum and clearly defined, hierarchical objectives. Students are tested regularly, either on the computer or via paper examinations with computerized scoring sheets. The test data are fed into the computer, which then prepares a progress report on each student. The teacher uses the progress report and any prescriptive information provided to guide students' subsequent efforts. Of course, data from individual students, classes, and schools can be compiled to provide teachers and administrators with progress reports about entire school districts. Sophisticated CMI systems can help schools move a step closer to truly individualized instruction.

Integrated Learning Systems

The most widely used implementations of sophisticated CMI in the schools today can be found in **integrated learning systems (ILSs)** which combine sophisticated CMI and computer-assisted instruction (CAI) into a single computer delivery system. They are designed to provide a cycle of instruction, assessment, and prescription—all on the computer.

ILSs are usually supplied by a single vendor that provides all of the hardware and software necessary. The leading ILS producers today are Jostens

Learning Corporation, Computer Curriculum Corporation, and Wasatch Educational Systems. While ILSs are expensive, they provide a lot for the money. The hardware consists of a local-area network of computers that operates from a large file server that maintains all of the software. The software includes a fully articulated curriculum in particular subject areas such as mathematics and language arts as well as CMI software.

Students in schools that have ILSs typically use the system on a regular basis, ranging from daily to once or twice per week. Instruction, testing, and test scoring are all managed by the system. Because the curriculum is well integrated and spans a number of grade levels, students may work on the ILS over a period of years and progress at their own rate. Teachers like the fact that the instruction is individualized. In addition, because the computer handles both the instruction and the assessment, the teacher is freed to provide individualized assistance, plan ancillary learning activities, and guide the learning process. Administrators like ILSs because they provide detailed information about the levels of mastery of the student body. A study by the Education Products Information Exchange (1990) found a high level of satisfaction among adopters of ILSs.

Problems and Pitfalls

Some potential problems are associated with computer-based evaluation of student progress. Computer-based test generation and test scoring are sometimes criticized for their limited view of evaluation. Some test generators produce only a limited variety of item types, and automated scoring is almost always limited to multiple-choice and true-false items. Teachers shouldn't fall into the trap of using these approaches exclusively just because they're convenient. This is especially true with the increased attention being paid to alternative forms of assessment, such as student portfolios, in the schools today.

When maintaining grades on the computer, a couple of commonsense warnings are particularly appropriate. First, always maintain a paper-based backup of students' grades. Computers can fail, and you don't want to lose your only set of records if your hard disk unexpectedly quits the day before grades are due! Second, make sure that grades are maintained in a secure manner. Students should never be able to gain access to your electronic gradebook.

CMI shows great potential for helping teachers to individualize instruction. However, it is not without controversy. For one thing, considerable teacher time can be needed to properly manage the management system. Teachers need to set up student rosters, define learning activities, and track progress. When testing is not on-line, the teacher must manage the administration of tests. ILSs remove some of this burden. However, they have their critics as well. Some criticize the quality of the CAI component of ILSs. It can be pretty basic. There is also a philosophical debate about ILSs. While some schools embrace ILSs with open arms, others feel that this approach is too restrictive, takes too much control away from the teacher, and discourages more open-ended, creative uses of the technology. Critics charge that the ILS is simply a well-integrated version of a "cookie cutter" approach to education, stamping out students according to one narrow curriculum. Schools interested in adopting an ILS need to seriously evaluate their own goals and objectives as well as the ILS itself before deciding to choose this option.

INTEGRATING TECHNOLOGY
Creating an Electronic Gradebook

At the end of last school year, Ms. Moreno decided she needed to computerize her gradebook. Between a rush of end-of-semester assignments and some family obligations on the weekend, she found herself up until 3:00 A.M. the night before grades were due trying to figure out students' averages with a pencil and a calculator. She realized this was no way to run a class!

So over the summer Janette began looking into computer gradebooks. After some preliminary research, she went to see her school's technology coordinator, Maggie Crandall, and explained that she wanted to get one of the stand-alone computer gradebook programs she had researched. Maggie said, "Well, I sure can understand. I keep all of my grades on the computer. But I really don't want to approve the purchase of a gradebook program for you at this time. You see, the district technology committee is looking into getting a student management system for the whole district. When we get the new system, everyone will use the same gradebook program; one comes as part of the system. But the committee hasn't made its decision yet. We probably won't have the new system in place for another year or two. I really don't want to buy you one program when I know we're going to turn around and get another one. Have you thought about using a spreadsheet? That's what I use now."

"A spreadsheet?" asked Janette. "I don't even know what that is!"

"Well," explained Maggie, "a spreadsheet is a tool that businesses use to keep track of all their financial information. It's really just a general-purpose calculating tool. It's pretty easy to set up a gradebook in a spreadsheet. We already have the spreadsheet program here at school, and I have a template you can use. Come on! I'll show you!"

So Maggie showed Janette her spreadsheet gradebook. As it turned out, it was just fine for what Janette wanted to do. Since the program was already available in the school it didn't cost anything extra, and it avoided problems with the district's plans for the new student management system. Starting this past fall, Janette has been using a spreadsheet program to keep track of her students' grades. Let's learn more about this approach.

ELECTRONIC SPREADSHEETS

Electronic spreadsheets are general-purpose computer calculating tools derived from the paper worksheets used by accountants for many years. A spreadsheet is like a large piece of paper that has been marked off into rows and columns to form a grid. Each intersection of a row and column, a single block in the grid, is called a **cell**. Individual columns and rows are labeled for reference. In the most common scheme, columns are lettered and rows are numbered. Thus each cell can be uniquely identified by its column and row reference (see Figure 12.12).

Figure 12.12 Sample gradebook spreadsheet in Microsoft *Works* (cell H2 is highlighted)

File Edit View Insert Format Tools Window							
H2		=Average(B2:E2)*.5+F2*.2+G2*.3					

Example (SS)

	A	B	C	D	E	F	G	H
1	Name	Quiz 1	Quiz 2	Quiz 3	Quiz 4	Exam 1	Final	Overall
2	Butcher, Cheryl	83	76	91	94	86	90	87.20
3	Doe, Jane	98	89	94	100	95	92	94.22
4	Doe, John	73	60	86	89	77	74	76.10
5	Ferkis, Mary Ann	100	93	93	100	98	96	96.65
6	George, Ed	62	55	79	84	68	73	70.50
7	Lin, Ella	78	80	84	88	76	79	80.15
8	Mandell, Susan	91	90	95	95	89	94	92.38
9	Taylor, Dave	87	81	91	95	88	90	88.85
10	Ward, Aggie	76	65	82	80	75	81	77.18
11								
12	Class Average	83.11	76.56	88.33	91.67	83.56	85.44	84.80

Screen shot reprinted with permission from Microsoft Corporation.

An individual cell normally contains one of three types of information: a number, a textual label, or a formula. Since spreadsheets are fundamentally calculating tools, it makes sense that cells can contain numbers. Numbers are the basic stuff that spreadsheets work with. Textual **labels**, as the name implies, are used simply to label parts of the spreadsheet. From the standpoint of calculations, they are ignored. **Formulas** are mathematical expressions that direct the spreadsheet to perform various kinds of calculations on the numbers entered in the spreadsheet. Formulas work on values in the spreadsheet by referring to the cells where the values are located.

Spreadsheets offer several advantages over older paper-and-pencil methods of manipulating numbers. These advantages have been recognized by people in business for some time. In fact, VisiCalc, the first electronic spreadsheet program, is widely credited with transforming personal computers from hobbyists' toys into serious workplace machines. Spreadsheet programs today are indispensable computational tools. Popular spreadsheets include Microsoft *Excel, Lotus 1-2-3, Quattro Pro,* and *Wingz.* In addition, spreadsheets are found in integrated packages such as Microsoft *Works, ClarisWorks, Framework,* and *Appleworks.*

Benefits of Computer Spreadsheets

As we illustrated in our example of Ms. Moreno, spreadsheets can be used by teachers for management tasks such as grade keeping. Because most schools already have spreadsheet programs, they offer a convenient way for teachers to computerize their grade keeping. Let's look at the sample gradebook spreadsheet in Figure 12.12 as we discuss the advantages of electronic spreadsheets.

- *Formulas.* As we noted, spreadsheets make use of formulas to direct calculations on the numbers entered in the spreadsheet. Once a formula has been entered, the user is freed from the chore of performing the calculation. Our example in Figure 12.12 shows the formula used to calculate Cheryl Butcher's overall grade average. Here is what it does. The expression AVERAGE (B2:E2)*.5 takes the average of cells B2 through E2 (the four quiz scores) and weights that as 50% of the overall score. F2*.2 weights the score for Exam 1 as 20% of the overall score, and G2*.3 weights the score for the Final Exam as 30% of the overall score. These values are summed to give Cheryl's overall score in cell H2.

- *Replication.* Once a formula is created for a single case, it can be replicated or copied to similar cases in the spreadsheet. In our example, once the formula is created for the first student, it is simply replicated down the column for each student. The spreadsheet automatically adjusts the cell references in the formula, so that row 3 values are used for the second student, row 4 values for the third, and so on. Fixed values—ones that don't change with position on the spreadsheet—can also be used when necessary.

- *Automatic recalculation.* A powerful feature of electronic spreadsheets is their ability to quickly recalculate values based on a change in a formula or a number. For example, suppose the teacher decides that John Doe (row 4) deserves an extra five points on Quiz 2, raising his score from 60 to 65. The moment 65 is entered in cell C4, the values in H4 and C12, which depend on C4, are automatically recalculated and displayed.

- *Templates.* A **template** is a spreadsheet "shell" with all of the appropriate labels and formulas in place but without the data. By using a template, individuals who may not have used a complex spreadsheet application before can still use the spreadsheet program for computational tasks. In our earlier example, the technology coordinator gave Ms. Moreno a gradebook template, a spreadsheet already set up to do grades but without the student names and scores. Janette could get started just by entering her students' names and scores. Templates for popular spreadsheet programs are available from a number of sources and for many different kinds of computational tasks. They make it easier for people to get started using spreadsheets for useful tasks.

Features of Spreadsheet Programs

We have already noted many of the most common features of spreadsheet programs: row and column layout, ability to enter numbers or labels, formulas, and automatic recalculation. In addition to these, a number of other features are common to most spreadsheet programs:

- *Formatting.* The information entered in the spreadsheet can be formatted in a variety of ways. Text labels or numbers can be right justified, left justified, or centered. Numbers can be expressed to a certain number of decimal places or in different forms (e.g., dollar amounts or scientific notation). Different fonts and type styles can be applied.
- *Mathematical functions.* In our example above, AVERAGE is a built-in mathematical function that is used in the grade-calculation formula. Spreadsheet programs support a wide range of built-in mathematical functions, usually including simple statistics, logarithmic functions, trigonometric functions, and common financial functions. These greatly simplify the building of formulas.
- *Graphing.* Most spreadsheet programs have graphing capability. After selecting appropriate parts of the spreadsheet, the program will produce a graph of the data in the highlighted cells. This feature provides a way to easily visualize the data.

- *Database elements.* Although spreadsheets are basically calculating tools, many spreadsheet programs also include some database elements. For example, simple databases can be created in a portion of the spreadsheet by treating the cells in a particular column as a database field. The entries in the database then can be linked to calculations performed by the spreadsheet.
- *Macros.* A **macro** is a shortcut for encoding a series of actions in a computer program. While not unique to spreadsheets, macros are very commonly used with spreadsheet programs. Macros provide a means of performing a number of separate steps through a single command. They simplify the process of performing complex actions. For example, in a gradebook spreadsheet, a macro might be created to automatically copy end-of-quarter grades to a new location, keep students' names, and blank out the grades area in preparation for the start of a new grading period.
- *Disk storage.* Like any other modern computer program, spreadsheets allow storage to and retrieval from disk.
- *Printing.* Of course, spreadsheets also support printing. Because spreadsheets can grow quite large (e.g., tens of thousands of cells), some spreadsheet programs support a horizontal or sideways printing to better work with continuous-form printer paper.

Teacher Uses of Spreadsheets

We have introduced the computer spreadsheet in this chapter because, as you have seen, the teacher can use one to create a basic gradebook application. Certainly this is one of the most popular ways for a teacher to use a spreadsheet. A teacher might also use a spreadsheet to

- maintain nongrade information about students (e.g., a physical education teacher might maintain student performance in various exercises or sporting activities)
- track costs of classroom materials (e.g., a chemistry teacher could maintain information about the costs of chemicals used in laboratory exercises)
- demonstrate complex calculations to a class (e.g., a business teacher might build loan amortization tables varying by interest rate as a class illustration)

Student Uses of Spreadsheets

Students can also use spreadsheets for various purposes, such as to

- maintain financial records of a student organization (e.g., tracking candy sales by members of the pep band)
- set up and maintain a personal budget
- enter and analyze data from science experiments
- perform "What if?" simulation or hypothesis-testing activities

The last category listed above is one of the most frequently cited instructional uses of spreadsheets. Because of rapid recalculation, spreadsheets are well suited to having students test the effects of changes in variables. As a result, they can be used by students to investigate how changes in one factor can impact other factors. Using a template or a spreadsheet of their own construction, students in a high school business class, for example, might examine the effects of changing insurance rates on the cost of owning and operating a car. Students in a biology class could explore the effects of changing birth and death rates on the growth of populations. Students in geometry class could examine the relationship between perimeter and area in various geometric shapes. This type of use of spreadsheets allows students to concentrate on real-world problems without becoming bogged down in the calculations.

SUMMARY

This chapter focused on the importance of student evaluation, not only at the conclusion of a learning exercise but also prior to and during the learning process. We discussed the different evaluation instruments that can be used (Figure 12.13), presented guidelines for development and examples of each, and described how the computer can be used in the evaluation and management process. To select the proper evaluation instrument, it is important to know each instrument's advantages and limitations, as well as the unique content, students, and learning situation being addressed.

Finally, the CUE for this chapter concentrated on computer-managed instruction (CMI) and the use of spreadsheets. CMI was shown to be directly related to student record keeping, performance assessment, and the monitoring of student progress—all important topics when attempting to manage the evaluation of students. Additionally, spreadsheet applications and their potential classroom uses were explored. In particular, it was shown how spreadsheets are adaptable for use as gradebooks and for other needed classroom functions.

REFLECTIVE QUESTIONS AND ACTIVITIES

1. Review an examination that you took recently. Select one of the evaluation questions and then ask yourself the following questions:

   a. Does this question relate to the desired learning outcomes? If not, describe why you think this question was included in the evaluation.

   b. Do you think this question has or has not been constructed in a proper fashion? What would be your suggestions for improvement?

   c. Could the same type of information be attained through another type of evaluation instrument? If yes, describe the possible alternatives and your rationale for such a selection.

2. Form a small group and discuss the advantages and limitations of the standard evaluation instruments. Once that is complete, discuss the advantages and disadvantages of the alternative instruments.

3. As stated in the text, some states are now requiring the use of portfolios as the key measure of student achievement. With another individual, debate the pros and cons of such a requirement.

4. Reflect on a current class you have either taught or attended. How could CMI, sophisticated CMI, or even ILSs be used effectively?

5. Think about spreadsheet programs and their value. What would be the advantage of elementary or secondary teachers knowing the basics of a common spreadsheet program? How could their students benefit from learning about spreadsheets?

INTEGRATION AND SYNTHESIS

To this point, we have focused on how instruction can be planned and implemented so that student learning is impacted positively. One critical aspect of that planning was the development of instructional outcomes, as explained in Chapter 5. The current chapter, with its focus on the evaluation of student learning, uses those same outcomes as the basis for determining both the type of assessment instrument to use and the contents of the specific assessment items. We have also noted within this chapter the need to evaluate learning both during and after instruction. This same philosophy of evaluation will be used as we turn our focus in Chapter 13 to the evaluation of instructional materials. We will describe instruments that can be used to assess

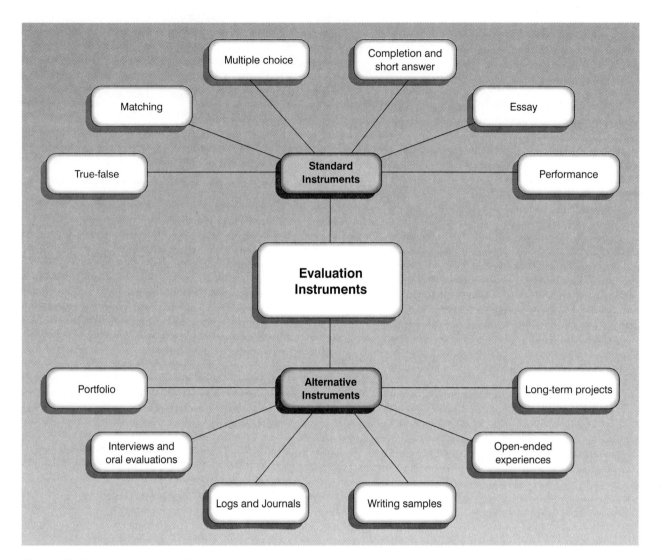

Figure 12.13   Types of evaluation instruments

the value of the materials, both during the development process and following its completion.

As a tool used in the development, storage, and use of student evaluation instruments, the computer has become invaluable. Sections of Chapters 5, 6, and 8, covering word processing, databases, telecommunications, and distance education, provided information on tools that can significantly impact the evaluation of students.

SUGGESTED READINGS

D'Aoust, C. (1992). Portfolios: Process for students and teachers. In K. B. Yancey (Ed.), *Portfolios in the writing classroom* (pp. 39–48). Urbana, IL: National Council of Teachers of English.

Herman, J. L., & Winters, L. (1994, October). Portfolio research: A slim collection. *Educational Research,* 48–55.

Rief, L. (1990). Finding the value in evaluation: Self-assessment in a middle school classroom. *Educational Leadership, 47*(6), 24–29.

Sax, G. (1989). *Principles of educational and psychological measurement and evaluation.* Belmont, CA: Wadsworth.

Other Suggested Resources

Portfolio Assessment Newsletter. Five Centerpointe Dr., Suite 100, Lake Owege, OR 97035. (Published five times a year by the Northwest Evaluation Association to support an information network for educators interested in portfolios and portfolio assessment)

Portfolio News. San Dieguito Union High School District, 710 Encinitas Blvd., Encinitas, CA 92024. (Published by the Portfolio Assessment Clearinghouse to report on individual projects and discussion of concern in portfolio assessment)

Portfolio News-Letter. English Department, University of North Carolina at Charlotte, Charlotte, NC 28223. (Published as a vehicle for teachers to share what they have tried with portfolios and with students)

Chapter 13

Evaluating the Instructional Process

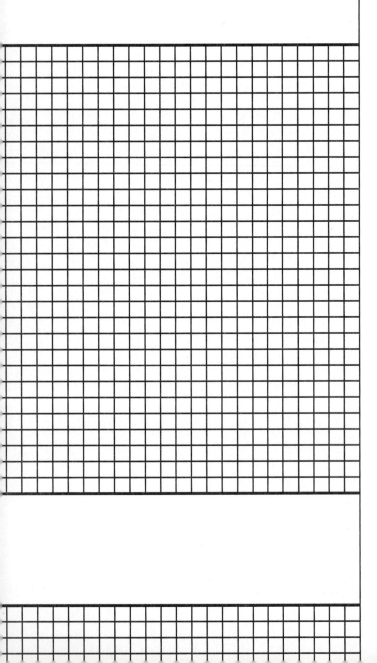

KEY WORDS AND CONCEPTS

Evaluation of instruction

Cycle of continuous improvement

Student tryout

Direct observation

Peer review

Classroom observation

Preview

Triangulation

OUTCOMES

After reading and studying this chapter, you will be able to:

- Identify how a continuous cycle of evaluation is different from formative and summative evaluation.
- Outline the benefits of evaluating instruction throughout a continuous cycle.
- Identify a variety of techniques for evaluating the instructional process and describe their advantages.
- Use a set of guidelines and a checklist to plan and implement an evaluation of instruction.
- Describe three principles that should guide the use of evaluation techniques as a part of a continuous cycle of improvement.
- Describe triangulation and its importance in the evaluation of instruction.
- Identify ways the computer can be used in the evaluation of instruction.

■ INTRODUCTION

Lisa Bell is shopping for a new car. She knows what features she wants in the car and what she can afford to pay. After some initial window-shopping at various dealers, she has narrowed her choices to three cars. At this point she checks the write-up on each car in the current issue of the *Consumer Reports Buying Guide,* paying particular attention to the "frequency of repair" information. She reads the warranty information for each car, finds out how much each dealer will give her for her present car, and takes each car out for a test drive. Lisa is gathering as much information as she can about each car as a way of assessing its value to her in order to decide which car to buy. Lisa is involved in the process of evaluation.

People commonly act as evaluators, and evaluation is part of many everyday activities. For example, we are involved in evaluation when we

- try on several coats in the store before buying one
- read over the menu of a new restaurant before going in for dinner
- listen to traffic reports on our way to work
- taste something we're cooking before taking it off the stove
- think about how reliable our television has been over the years before buying another piece of electronic equipment from the same company

Like Lisa and her new car, the essential feature in all of these situations is the need to make a decision, based on perceived value, which is, in turn, based on information.

Evaluation is also a common part of teaching. We most commonly think of teachers as evaluating students in order to give them a grade or certify their knowledge and skills in some way. But teachers evaluate much more than their students. They naturally evaluate their own instruction. For example, at the beginning of Chapter 12 you were introduced to Ms. Powley and her ninth-grade English class. Ms. Powley had given her class an essay test, and she noted that the test had been a valuable part of the lesson. She used it to motivate students, to measure how well they had learned, and to provide students with feedback that helped them understand how well their study habits had worked. In addition, Ms. Powley noted that the test gave her valuable information about how well her instruction had worked for individual students in the class. It allowed her to identify the parts of the instruction that didn't work as well as expected and, therefore, needed improvement.

Like Lisa Bell and others involved in the everyday situations mentioned earlier, Ms. Powley is making a decision, based on how valuable she thinks the various parts of her instruction had been and based on information about how well students had learned. The decision-making aspect of each of these situations is illustrated in Table 13.1 (the final row describes evaluation in Ms. Powley's English class).

This chapter, then, is about evaluating the instructional process. The **evaluation of instruction** can be described as a systematic method used to gather information to determine the value of the instruction in order to make a decision about its use (Worthen & Sanders, 1987).

Evaluation has been described as a tool that provides feedback that leads to continuous improvement. In Chapter 12 we focused on how evaluation is used with students. We described a range of techniques that could be used before, during, and after instruction to assess students' continuing learning needs and provide them with feedback about how to improve their performances. This chapter will continue to describe the use of evaluation with the same general purpose—to provide feedback that leads to continuous improvement. However, the focus of this chapter will be on the instruction rather than on the students. We will describe a range of techniques that can be used before, during, and after the instruction to assess how well the instruction is working and to provide the teacher with feedback about how it can be improved.

Table 13.1   Evaluation as a decision-making activity

Decision	Perceived value	Information Source
Which coat should I buy?	Which coat fits most comfortably?	Try the coats on.
	Which coat is the best bargain?	Compare the prices of the coats.
Should I stay and have dinner?	Are the selection and prices reasonable?	Read over the menu.
		Compare prices to similar restaurants.
Should I take an alternate route to work?	Is the usual route congested?	Listen to commuter traffic reports.
	Is an alternative route available?	
Should I add more spices?	Is the dish spicy enough?	Taste-test the dish.
Should I buy another piece of electronic equipment from the same company?	Has the television been costly to maintain over the years?	Think back over problems with the television.
		Look at any repair records.
Which parts of the instruction should be improved?	Which parts of the instruction worked? Which ones didn't?	Review results from the essay test.

In our discussion of the PIE model in Chapter 1, we described evaluation as a time to reflect on the successes achieved and problems encountered, resulting in a description of the strengths and weaknesses of the program that can be used to improve the materials. Seen in this way, a thorough evaluation necessarily considers all of the components of the instruction—approaches, media, goals, plans, activities, and materials—as well as the way these components are combined and presented to students to help them learn. This is a tall order and not always one that is eagerly carried out. Just as students don't always look forward to receiving information about their inadequacies as learners, teachers don't always look forward to getting information about their inadequacies as instructional experts. However, keep in mind that the essence of evaluation is continuous improvement, and continuous improvement depends on feedback that helps individuals see where they are and what the next correct avenue should be. This feedback will help the teacher plot and maintain a course, increasing the probability that the instruction will continue to meet the changing needs of individual students.   ■

EVALUATION BEFORE, DURING, AND AFTER INSTRUCTION

Traditionally, the evaluation of the instructional process has been separated into formative and summative evaluation (Worthen & Sanders, 1987). **Formative evaluation** has been defined as evaluation done *during* the planning or delivery of an instructional program as a way of identifying ways to improve the program. **Summative evaluation** refers to evaluation done *after* an instructional program has been completed as a way of deciding whether to use the program again.

We believe, however, that the distinction between formative and summative evaluation is largely arbitrary. In practice, all evaluation is formative, part of a "continuing system of self-renewal" (Worthen & Sanders, 1987) in which ongoing instructional programs evolve over time. This is true because instruction is often repeated. Teachers commonly teach the same lessons from one year to the next. Students change, but the basic content remains essentially the same. As a result, the challenge for the instructional expert is to continuously improve the instruction—before it is implemented, while it is being implemented, and after it has been implemented.

This translates into a **cycle of continuous improvement,** represented graphically in Figure 13.1. There are two important characteristics of this cycle. First, evaluation is an integral part of planning and implementing the instruction, rather than something that gets tacked on to the end of the process. Evaluation is an important part of "reflection in action" (Schön, 1983), in which instructional experts continuously monitor their efforts to help their students learn, looking for and incorporating ways to better match their instruction to their students. Second, evaluation done *after* instruction becomes, in practice, part of the evaluation done *before* instruction is delivered the next time.

Throughout the cycle, the consistent purpose of the evaluation is to increase the amount of student learning that takes place by continually evaluating the instruction in terms of its effectiveness (Does it

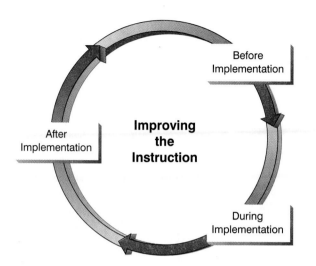

Figure 13.1 The cycle of continuous improvement

lead students to their learning goals?), efficiency (Does it make good use of available time and resources?), and appeal (Does it hold students' interest and maintain their motivation?). As the cycle is repeated the evaluation gains power, like the proverbial snowball rolling downhill. It should come as no surprise that instruction that has been used (and evaluated) several times often works better than instruction that is being used for the first time. Through repeated evaluation, information accumulates and trends—both positive and negative—can be identified. Based on the emerging trends, content can be updated; approaches, activities, and materials can be revised or eliminated; and new approaches, activities, and materials can be added. Thorough and continuous evaluation contributes to this by

- identifying areas of instruction that are unclear, confusing, dated, or otherwise not helpful to students
- identifying the areas of instruction that have the highest priority for revision because they (1) are the most critical aspects of the content, (2) present the most trouble for students, or (3) are likely to have the greatest impact on student learning
- providing a rationale and evidence in support of making specific revisions to the instruction

Naturally, evaluation takes a somewhat different form at different points in the cycle. Evaluation *before* instruction has a future orientation: How will it work? This encourages *pre*planning by providing a framework for making conscious estimates about the effectiveness, efficiency, and appeal of the instruction. Evaluation *during* instruction has a present orientation: How is it working? Continuing

the evaluation during the lesson allows for the revision of instruction in time to benefit current students. Evaluation after the instruction has a past orientation: How did it work? This encourages conscious reflection about the effectiveness, efficiency, and appeal of the instruction so it can be improved for the next time it's used.

As an example of evaluation throughout the instructional process, consider the following high school history class. Each semester, Mrs. Singleton teaches a 12th-grade U.S. history course to about 25 students. One of the units in the course focuses on the broad impact of various social issues that took shape during the 1960s, including desegregation and civil rights, the Cold War, poverty and the Great Society, and the space race. As part of her research, Mrs. Singleton previewed the "American History Videodisc" produced by the Instructional Resources Corporation. The videodisc contains a collection of photographs and short video clips that can be randomly accessed with a bar code reader and shown on a monitor connected to a videodisc player. The photographs and video clips are arranged chronologically and described in an accompanying catalog. Mrs. Singleton thinks the visual images that can be presented by the videodisc will help make her presentation of the events of the 1960s less abstract and will stimulate discussion among the students.

Before the lesson, as part of her planning, Mrs. Singleton discusses the visual images she has selected with Ms. Fellows, who also teaches history at the school. They discuss which issues might be most interesting to students, which are most likely to be confusing to students, and what possible directions students might take in their discussion of the issues. Based on this conversation, Mrs. Singleton decides to add a few images to her initial presentation and to identify a second set of images that matches the directions students are likely to take in their discussion.

During the lesson, Mrs. Singleton begins by showing a few selected images related to each issue, briefly describing each image. She begins the discussion by asking, "Which of these events had the greatest impact on American society during the 1960s?" Mrs. Singleton closely monitors the discussion as it progresses. She uses images from the videodisc, including the second set she had selected, to focus the discussion when it gets off track, to provide additional information when requested by students, and to provide visual support to students making critical points.

After the lesson, Mrs. Singleton assigns students the task of selecting one of the issues presented in class and writing an essay about the breadth and

The use of videodisc technology can enhance learning in the classroom.

depth of its impact. As she reads the essays, she notes that, in general, they are thoughtful and insightful and that they include more specific references to people, places, and events than had been the case when she had taught the lesson without the videodisc. She determines from this that the videodisc presentation is worth trying again, and she decides to expand its use. She decides to consider using the videodisc to link the social issues of the 1960s and the 1930s to encourage students to compare the two periods. Using her lesson plan as a diary, she notes the issues and questions that generated a lot of discussion, the types of images that might help bridge the two periods, and possible adaptations to the essay assignment.

Before she teaches the lesson during the next term, Mrs. Singleton reviews her notes and incorporates them into a revised instructional plan, emphasizing the link between the 1960s and the 1930s. She selects a new set of photographs and video clips to show to students, revises the question she will ask to begin the discussion, and modifies the essay assignment.

One final point should be made about the cycle of evaluation. We most often think of evaluation as being done by the teacher. Teachers, as instructional experts, are responsible for evaluation—of the instruction as well as of the students. However, throughout the cycle of evaluation, students can often evaluate their own learning and the instruction implemented to help them learn. They may need help in identifying the best techniques to use, and guidance in how to use those techniques, but they can often be effective evaluators.

Before the lesson, students can ask, What will work best for me? This will encourage them to think

strategically, identifying the instructional approaches, media, activities, and materials that are most likely to help them achieve the learning goals. *During* the lesson, students can ask, Is this working for me? This will encourage them to think about what they're learning and what they're having trouble with, thus helping to identify where additional information and/or different study techniques are needed. *After* the lesson, students can ask, Did this work for me? This will encourage them to think about their own skills as learners and about the learning strategies they use. They can then make a conscious effort to add to their repertoire of learning strategies and become more effective learners. Finally, *before* the next lesson, students can ask, What will work best for me now? This will encourage them to think ahead about their newly developed learning skills and strategies, identifying ways the instructional approaches, media, activities, and materials can be matched to their particular skills and strategies.

EVALUATION TECHNIQUES

This section of the chapter will describe a collection of techniques that can be used to generate information in order to evaluate the instructional process. The techniques are divided into three categories, according to the primary source of the information:

Information from students

- Tests
- Student tryout
- Direct observation
- Talking with students

TECHNOLOGY INTEGRATION PROMPT

REFLECTION

In 1933 Dewey characterized reflection as a special form of thinking that enables effective problem solving to take place. Whenever a teacher evaluates any of the components of an instructional lesson—the learners, the materials, himself or herself—he or she is engaged in a form of problem solving. Reflection can facilitate the evaluative process by focusing teachers' attention on the effectiveness, efficiency, and/or appeal of instructional materials and events.

Instructional experts who are skillful at self-reflection are able to adapt their instructional plans to fit the changing needs of their students, the content, and/or the learning context. As a central component of the continuous cycle of improvement, reflection fosters both self-evaluation and self-improvement.

Reflection is easily conceptualized and achieved through the technique of self-questioning. Consider using questions similar to the ones below to facilitate your own cycle of improvement.

Before the lesson ask yourself:

- How will this lesson work?
- Will these activities lead students to their learning goals?
- Will this lesson hold students' interest and attention?
- Is there a different way to structure this lesson to optimize students' time?

During the lesson ask yourself:

- How is this lesson working?
- How can I keep students focused on the important learning tasks?
- Are students remaining actively engaged in the lesson?
- How can I overcome the obstacles we are encountering?

After the lesson ask yourself:

- How did this lesson work?
- Were the selected materials and approaches effective in leading students to their goals?
- Did students find the lesson interesting, valuable, and meaningful?
- What can I do to improve students' learning the next time I use this approach?

Although these questions are posed from the instructor's point of view, students can also use reflective questions to evaluate and adjust their own learning strategies before, during, and after learning activities. If teachers model the use of these types of questions as they plan for and implement instructional lessons, students may be better able to utilize similar questions to assess their own learning strengths and weaknesses.

Information from colleagues

- Peer review
- Classroom observation

Information from yourself

- Preview
- Reflection

Tests

We're using the term *test* here in a generic sense to refer to any of the variety of standard and alternative evaluation instruments, described in Chapter 12, that can be used to assess students' knowledge and skills. As noted in Chapter 12, evaluation instruments can identify what students know before beginning the instruction, assess their growing knowledge and skills during instruction, and measure what they have learned at the end of instruction. Since evaluation instruments focus primarily on student learning, which is invariably the purpose of instruction, they provide a direct measure of the effectiveness of the instruction. As a result, it is usually a good idea to use test results as a part of evaluating the instructional process. The strengths, limitations, and development considerations for different types of evaluation instruments are described in detail in Chapter 12. They won't be repeated here.

For example, Ms. Estes has her fourth-grade students play the computer game *Where in the World is Carmen Sandiego?* (described in Chapter 10; see Figure 10.3). At the beginning of the lesson, Ms. Estes gives students a pretest—made up of an assortment of matching, multiple-choice, and short-answer items—to find out how much they already know about geography. Then, at the end of the lesson, when all the students have completed the game, she gives them another test (a posttest) to find out how much their knowledge of geography has grown. Ms. Estes finds that virtually all of the students scored much higher on the posttest than on the pretest. She determines from this that the game has been a valuable part of the lesson and decides to use it again the next time she teaches the lesson to similar students.

Student Tryout

A **student tryout** refers to a "test run" of some instructional activity, approach, media, or materials with a small group of students before using it on a large scale (Mager, 1988). In a sense, a tryout is a rehearsal or practice run-through intended to identify any problems that might come up when the instruction is used. A tryout has two distinct advantages. First, it's an opportunity to test our assumptions about the usefulness of the materials. Typically we select or develop instructional materials because we think they'll work with our students. A tryout provides a direct test of this hypothesis. Second, it helps us find any problems in the materials that can be "fixed" before the materials are used in the "real" classroom.

As we learned in Chapter 7, Mr. Hughes has developed a board game to use in his eighth-grade language class. However, before he uses the game in the class, he decides to try it out. He enlists the help of his 14-year-old daughter and several of her friends, asking them to play the game as though they were students in the class. He notices from this that the rules of the game are clear and that the game seems to engage their interest. However, he also notices that his tryout learners seem to become bored with the game as soon as it slows down for any reason. He determines from this that the game is potentially useful as long as it doesn't go on for a long time, so he decides to use it as a relatively short review activity.

Figure 13.2 presents a set of guidelines and suggestions that should be considered when trying out instructional materials.

Direct Observation

As may be clear from the term, **direct observation** refers to watching students as they go through some

Figure 13.2 Guidelines for student tryout

❑ Prior to the tryout, identify anything that is of particular interest in your evaluation of the materials. For example, if you are particularly interested in finding out whether the materials will hold the students' interest, make a note to watch for signs of boredom during the tryout. You'll want to pay particular attention to these aspects of the materials during the tryout.

❑ Try out the materials with students who are as much like the actual students as is practical.

❑ Give the students complete materials. Even when a small part of the materials is being tried out or when the materials are in draft form, give students everything they will need to complete the activity.

❑ During the tryout, use procedures, rules, or guidelines that reflect actual classroom use as much as practical.

❑ Observe students during the tryout and, rather than trust your memory, make notes about what does and doesn't seem to work well.

❑ Talk with students afterward. Ask them for their reactions to the materials. Clarify any notes made during the tryout.

part or parts of the lesson, often when group activities are involved. The primary advantage of observing students is that it provides information about the process of the instruction as well as products of the learning. Careful observation will provide information about how the materials are actually used, indicate how students are responding to the different parts of the lesson, and identify places where they may need more information or guidance.

As we discussed in Chapter 9, students in Mr. Lockwood's high school art appreciation class are learning about the different forms of creative art through a cooperative learning activity. Mr. Lockwood has divided the students into groups. Each group contains a student who plays a musical instrument, a student who paints, and a student who sculpts. The students' task is to use research as well as their own experience to identify the similarities and differences among these art forms. From this they are to identify the essential characteristics of the concept "art." Much of their research is done outside of class, but the groups meet during the class period to discuss what they have found. As they talk, Mr. Lockwood routinely listens to the groups, making sure that he spends time with each group. For the most part, he lets the students do their work. However, since the students have somewhat different experiences, each group is examining somewhat different issues and coming to somewhat different conclusions. As a result, Mr. Lockwood is making some modifications in the activity "on the fly" and pushing the groups in somewhat different ways. He challenges some groups to incorporate a broader range of creative arts to test their emerging definition of the concept. At the same time, he helps other groups narrow their focus on the important similarities among the arts as a way of developing a definition.

Figure 13.3 presents a set of guidelines and suggestions that should be considered when observing students during a lesson.

Talking with Students

Talking with students may take a wide variety of forms. It may involve a relatively formal discussion with a student or group of students, or it may consist of a relatively informal chat with the students. Whether it's formal or informal, talking with students has the advantage of going straight to the source to find out what they think about the instruction. As a result, it is an excellent source of information about the appeal of the materials. The idea is to find out as much as possible, from the students' perspective, about how well the materials worked and how interesting they were. This encourages students to reflect on their own learning and to think about what helps them learn. It also helps communicate the teacher's interest in his or her students. Students get the message that the teacher is committed to helping them learn.

As we described in Chapter 9, the fifth-grade Elementary Ecology Club took a field trip to a creek near the school, and the club's advisor decided to ask the club members to research the source of oil floating in the water and to determine what could be done about it. Each member of the group was given a specific task to perform. After the research had been completed and a report prepared and delivered to the public health department, the advisor decided to spend a club meeting discussing the project with the members. Specific questions were asked to identify which parts of the project had been easy and challenging, fun and boring, informative and uninformative. Based on the discussion, the advisor determined that the project had been a useful learn-

Figure 13.3 Guidelines for direct observation of students

❏ Prior to the observation, identify anything that is of particular interest in your evaluation of the materials. You'll want to pay particular attention to these aspects of the materials during the observation.

❏ Observe a range of students. Although it's relatively easy to observe students who ask for help, or who are particularly active, it's important to observe as many different types of students as is practical.

❏ Be as unobtrusive as possible; avoid letting your observation interfere with students' use of the materials.

❏ Rather than trust your memory, make notes about what seems to work well, what doesn't seem to work well, and for what types of students it seems to work or not work.

ing experience for students and decided that the club should do similar projects on a regular basis.

Figure 13.4 presents a set of guidelines and suggestions that should be considered when talking to students.

Peer Review

Peer review refers to asking a colleague or colleagues to examine all or part of the materials for a lesson, comment on their usefulness, and suggest ways the lesson could be improved. This is a little like getting a second opinion before having surgery. The idea is to have another set of eyes look at the materials. This has two distinct advantages. First, it helps identify trouble spots that you may miss. Sometimes, when a lesson is relatively new to us, we aren't sure what to look for. On the other hand, sometimes we're so familiar with a lesson that we look past existing problems, just as we sometimes read past our own spelling errors. In either case, we may overlook inaccuracies, inconsistencies, and other potential problems. Second, a review by a colleague will provide a fresh perspective on the materials, offering new insights on student responses to the lesson, ways to update the content of the lesson, and so on.

As we learned in Chapter 8, Mr. Crawford had developed a slide-tape presentation for his fifth- and sixth-grade Spanish class. He took the slides during his trip to Spain, and he had added Spanish music and his own narration describing the various people, places, and activities shown in the slides. Before showing the slides to his class, Mr. Crawford invited Mrs. Hunt, who also teaches Spanish, to review the slide-tape presentation. Mr. Crawford was particularly interested in whether the slides he has selected would be interesting to students, whether the slides and his narration were ade-

quately matched, and whether the technical quality of the slides and the tape was sufficient. Mrs. Hunt agreed that the slides add a personal touch to the lesson, which would increase its relevance to the students; however, in some parts she felt the students would become confused by the lack of explanation about the locations and landmarks. Based on this review, Mr. Crawford decided to rearrange the slides and to add more narration at several points.

Figure 13.5 presents a set of guidelines and suggestions that should be considered when asking colleagues to review instructional materials.

Classroom Observation

Classroom observation refers to inviting a colleague into the classroom to watch the lesson in process, comment on how well the materials and activities work, and suggest ways to improve the lesson. Like asking a colleague to review the instructional materials, classroom observation provides another set of eyes that can offer a different perspective and help find problems in the implementation of the instruction that may otherwise be overlooked.

As we learned in Chapter 8, Nancy Foust used a presentation with a larger-than-life model to teach her vocational school students how an automobile carburetor works. Because this was a relatively new part of the lesson, Nancy was interested in getting some feedback, so she asked Ted Morrison to observe her presentation. Ted, who teaches construction methods, frequently used models in his classes, and Nancy was particularly interested in how effectively she used the model carburetor during her presentation. After observing Nancy's class, Ted made a number of suggestions that allowed Nancy to improve this specific presentation and her use of models in general.

Figure 13.4 Guidelines for talking with students

❑ Prior to talking with students, identify anything that is of particular interest in your evaluation of the materials. You'll want to pay particular attention to these aspects of the materials during the discussion.

❑ Talk with a range of students. Although it's relatively easy to talk with students who express themselves easily or who are opinionated, it's important to talk with as many different types of students as is practical.

❑ Keep the discussion short and focused. To keep the discussion on track, ask about specific aspects of the materials.

❑ Use your listening skills. Try to avoid being defensive about the instruction. Remember that you're trying to find out what students think. Use open-ended questions, paraphrasing, and other active listening techniques to encourage students to talk. Clarify their comments when necessary.

Figure 13.5 Guidelines for
peer review

❏ Prior to asking a colleague to review your materials, identify anything that is of particular interest in your evaluation. Give this information to your colleague; you'll want him or her to pay particular attention to these aspects of the materials during the review.

❏ Ask colleagues who are familiar with the topic, the students, and/or the approaches or media in the lesson.

❏ Try to get a perspective that is different than your own by (1) asking more than one colleague to review the materials, when practical; (2) asking someone who is likely to hold a view of the content, the students, instructional approaches, and so on, that is different than yours; and (3) asking the colleague(s) to make a conscious effort to look at the materials in different ways.

❏ Use your listening skills. Explain your rationale, when necessary, but try to avoid being defensive about the materials. Remember that you're trying to get a second opinion. Use open-ended questions, paraphrasing, and other active listening techniques to encourage your colleague(s) to talk. Ask for clarification when necessary.

Figure 13.6 presents a set of guidelines and suggestions that should be considered when using classroom observation.

Teacher Preview

Regardless of the content area, a large variety of instructional materials is already available, from several different sources. Some have been produced commercially, some have been produced by teachers and published in professional journals or on the Internet, and some you may have produced yourself during previous terms. **Previewing** materials refers to the process of reading or working through some specific instructional materials prior to using them (Heinich, Molenda, Russell, & Smaldino, 1996). Chapter 7 described the instructional materials acquisition process, noting that the students, content, instructional approach, and instructional setting are all important considerations in selecting the instructional materials. A thorough preview is the necessary first step in determining how well specific materials match these considerations and, therefore, in deciding whether to use the materials as they are, use a part or parts of them, use them with some modifications or adaptations, or not use them at all.

For example, Mr. McCormick has found a piece of computer software titled *Discover—A Science Experiment,* which he thinks would be useful in his first-year high school biology class. However, before he makes a final decision he previews the software by working through the entire program himself. As he works through the exercises in the program, he makes notes on a preview form for computer software (see Appendix B). He is particularly interested in how well the program matches the objectives he has for the lesson, encourages collaborative hypothesis testing, and presents realisti-

Figure 13.6 Guidelines for
classroom observation

❏ Prior to asking a colleague to observe your classroom, identify anything that is of particular interest in your evaluation. Give this information to your colleague; you'll want him or her to pay particular attention to these aspects of the materials during the observation.

❏ Ask colleagues who are familiar with the topic, the students, and/or the approaches or media used in the lesson.

❏ Arrange to talk with the observer after the lesson. Make this conversation unhurried.

❏ Encourage the observer to use a "good news–bad news" format to make it easy to consider both the strengths of the lesson and the areas that could be improved.

cally complex problems, as well as how likely it is to hold the interest of his students. Based on his preview, Mr. McCormick determines that the exercises in the software match his learning objectives and are engaging, interesting, and reasonably complex. He decides to use the software in class, adding only his own introduction to the lesson and the software.

Figure 13.7 presents a set of guidelines and suggestions that should be considered when previewing instructional materials.

Reflection

In many cases, experience is the best gauge of whether something worked. As described in Chapter 1, reflection refers to the process of thinking back over what happened during a lesson, using your own experience and expertise to identify the parts of the lesson that did and didn't work.

For example, in a middle school U.S. history class, Mrs. Chan used a debate as part of a lesson. She selected two teams of students and asked them to debate the question, "Were the causes of the Civil War primarily economic or political?" The rest of the class observed the debate, evaluated the two teams on their presentation of facts and arguments, and selected a "winner." Later in the term, Mrs. Chan reflected on this activity. She reviewed the notes she had made on her lesson plan, specifically considering the clarity and scope of the debate topic, the time allotted to the debate, and the amount of participation of students who weren't on one of the debate teams. From her reflection, Mrs. Chan determined that, while it had been interesting, there had been too many students in the class who weren't involved in the debate. She concluded that this activity wasn't a good match for the large classes she often teaches, so she decided to save the activity for a time when she has a smaller class.

Figure 13.8 presents a set of guidelines and suggestions that should be considered when reflecting about the instructional process.

Guiding Principles

There are three principles to keep in mind as you select and use these techniques to evaluate your instruction. First, continuous improvement requires continuous information. Recall that the purpose of evaluation is to increase the amount of student learning through the ongoing self-renewal of the instruction as it evolves over time. To be effective, therefore, evaluation isn't simply tacked on to the end of the instruction. Instead, refinement of the instruction depends on a steady stream of information flowing before, during, and after the instruction each time it is used. Over time this information may become increasingly detailed and the refinements in the instruction may become increasingly small, but these small refinements are no less important to student learning than the earlier, larger refinements.

Second, selecting techniques to use will be based, in large part, on where you are in the cycle of continuous improvement. Figure 13.9 shows the techniques that might be most useful before, during, and after the instruction is implemented.

Third, information will carry more weight when it has been "triangulated" (Kemp, Morrison, & Ross, 1994). **Triangulation** refers to the process of obtaining information from multiple techniques or sources. All information is useful. However, information is strengthened when it's supported by information from other techniques or sources. Similarly, information is weakened when it's contradicted by information from other techniques or sources. Therefore, rather than relying on a single source of information, generate information from several different sources. Some of the techniques naturally seem to fit together. For example, as illustrated in Figure 13.10, it seems natural to preview the instructional materials yourself, ask a knowledgeable colleague to review them, and try them out with a small group of students. However, virtually all of the techniques can be combined in various ways to increase the power of the instruction.

Figure 13.7 Guidelines for previewing instructional materials

❏　Prior to previewing the materials, identify anything that is of particular interest in your evaluation. You'll want to pay particular attention to these aspects of the materials during the preview.

❏　Use a preview form (see Appendix B) to ensure that you consider all the important factors, provide the same information on different materials so they can be compared, and have a record of your preview.

❏　Read or work through the materials as completely as possible. For example, avoid basing your evaluation of the materials on the introduction alone.

Figure 13.8 Guidelines for reflecting about the instructional process

❏ Use a "now and later" process to guide your reflection. Record your immediate impressions as soon as is practical, even if you only have a few minutes. Then think about the lesson in more depth and detail when you have more time.

❏ Make notes on your instructional plan. Use the plan as a diary (see Chapter 6) to record opinions about what worked and suggestions about what to do differently the next time.

❏ Use a "strengths and suggestions" format to make sure you consider both the strong and weak points of the lesson. Include in your reflection thoughts about how to increase the strengths and reduce the weaknesses.

❏ Focus on specific modifications. It's okay to begin with general impressions, but gradually move to specific ideas about how to improve the lesson—the more specific, the better.

❏ Share your reflections with colleagues. Discussing your experience with knowledgeable colleagues will provide another perspective on the lesson and offer an opportunity for brainstorming ways in which the lesson can be improved.

CUE Computer Use ESSENTIALS

USING THE COMPUTER TO MANAGE EVALUATION

As noted earlier, the continuous improvement of instruction involves a continuous stream of information resulting in the gradual refinement of the instructional materials. For years, this process has involved a variety of tools—including typewriters and pencil and paper with which to develop the materials, and file cabinets in which to store them. Unfortunately, using these tools was often cumber-some and costly, in terms of both time and money, because the instructional materials had to be completely reproduced in order to revise them. In recent years, however, the use of the computer has greatly facilitated this process. Two computer applications are particularly useful tools in the continuous improvement of instructional plans and materials: word processing (described in Chapter 5) and databases (described in Chapter 6). With these tools, revisions can be made easily, quickly, and at little or no cost. As a result, instructional materials can easily be customized for groups of students, or even individual students, based on their particular

Figure 13.9 Evaluation techniques and the cycle of continuous improvement

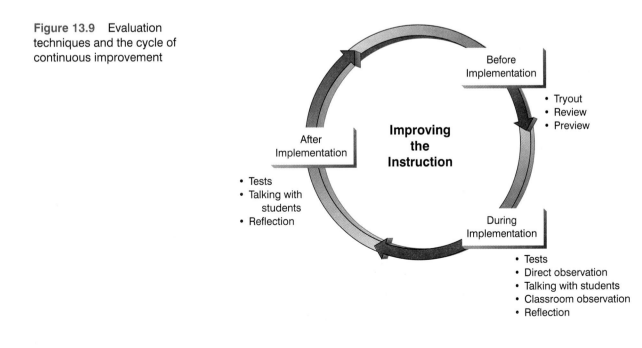

Before Implementation
• Tryout
• Review
• Preview

Improving the Instruction

During Implementation
• Tests
• Direct observation
• Talking with students
• Classroom observation
• Reflection

After Implementation
• Tests
• Talking with students
• Reflection

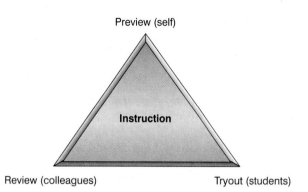

Figure 13.10   An example of triangulation

learning needs. Let's take a closer look at each of these computer tools.

Word Processors

Word processors are tools for writing, with features that support the entry, editing, revising, formatting, storage, retrieval, and printing of text. Word processors are valuable tools for the production of instructional plans, evaluation instruments, and other types of instructional materials. However, the focus in this chapter is on the continuous improvement of the instruction. So, we will focus here on the value of word processing in the *revision* of instructional materials.

A major disadvantage of the traditional tools that have been used to produce instructional materials (e.g., the typewriter) is that a document (e.g., an instructional plan or a handout) must be completely retyped every time it is changed in any way. This makes revision a costly and time-consuming process that might be justified when major changes are required but not when the changes are the kinds of minor refinements that are more common in the continuous-improvement cycle. Word processing solves this problem because, once a document has been retrieved from the disk, it can be updated quickly and easily by retyping only those parts of the document to be revised, often using only a few keystrokes. A clean, revised copy of the document can then be printed out ready for use. This revised copy can then be stored for later retrieval and revised again when additional refinements are made. As a result, it's easy to make major revisions. Just as importantly, it is even easier to make the kinds of minor refinements in the materials that will contribute to the gradual evolution of the instruction. This means that the instructional expert can easily

- update the list of equipment, supplies, and facilities needed for a lesson

- add or eliminate content and/or practice activities
- modify the sequence of a lesson, rearranging the order in which the content and/or practice activities are presented
- change the instructional approach and/or instructional media used to present the content to the students or add alternative approaches and/or media
- revise the handouts to be used during a lesson (these may be produced with a desktop publishing program, described in Chapter 7)
- modify the overhead transparencies and other types of visuals to be used during a lesson (these may be produced with a presentation program, described in Chapter 9)

Databases

A major disadvantage of the traditional tools that have been used to catalog and store instructional materials (e.g., card files and file cabinets) is that a document (e.g., an instructional plan or a handout) can be indexed only one way. Cross-referencing is, at best, cumbersome. This often makes finding and retrieving relevant materials difficult because it depends on knowing, or guessing, how they have been indexed. This may not seem difficult if you are looking for a particular document (assuming that your materials are filed according to a consistent system and that your file cabinet is in order), because you would probably know where it's filed. However, imagine that you were looking for ideas. For example, imagine that you want to incorporate a cooperative learning activity into your high school literature class. Where might you find potential activities? Under a content heading (19th-century American novelists), under the class or grade heading (Introduction to Literature—week 4), or under an instructional approach heading (cooperative learning activities)? In addition, potential activities might also be found under other content headings (19th-century short stories, British novelists, etc.) or class headings (Introduction to Poetry, Creative Writing, etc.).

A database solves this problem by cataloging documents and filing them in a way that allows flexible access. Documents can be indexed according to a variety of fields, making it easy to search for, and find, relevant materials. For the examples in the previous paragraph, the teacher would be able to use the "instructional approach" field and search the database for "cooperative learning activities." The result would be a collection of potentially useful activities, drawn from a variety of topics and classes. In this way, the instructional expert can use a variety of fields, including subject-matter topics (science, history, language, etc.), course or grade level, instructional approach (game, tutorial, discovery, etc.), and instructional media (video, slides, software, etc.) to catalog and store a variety of instructional materials, including handouts, activities and exercises, specific items for an evaluation instrument, instructional plans, instructional approaches, and media materials—commercially or locally produced.

INTEGRATING TECHNOLOGY
Evaluating for Continuous Improvement

In previous chapters we have illustrated the gradual evolution of Janette Moreno's high school Spanish class. As her course has evolved through the years, Ms. Moreno has incorporated a number of activities involving a variety of instructional technologies. These have included

- audio, then videotaped practice (Chapter 1)

- a computer drill-and-practice program, upgraded to a hypertext tutorial (Chapter 1)

- cooperative learning projects, including writing a persuasive brochure for potential tourists (Chapter 7) and interpreting the nonverbal and situational aspects of comedy excerpts presented on videodisc (Chapter 9)

- an audioteleconference with a high school class in Seville, followed by additional conversation carried out over e-mail (Chapter 8)

- a role play in which students are asked to give and receive directions in Spanish (Chapter 10)

All of these activities have been planned and implemented to help students increase their written and conversational skills in Spanish while maintaining a solid foundation of vocabulary, grammar, and punctuation basics. This is a complex and difficult goal but Janette has been able to accomplish it by taking a continuous-improvement approach to the class. She continues to generate an ongoing stream of information about the effectiveness, efficiency, and appeal of her instructional approaches. In addition, she triangulates that information through the use of a variety of techniques before, during, and after an instructional activity is implemented.

As one example of how her continuous-improvement approach has contributed to the success of the class, consider the evolution of the vocabulary- and grammar-building activities. It begins *during*

the use of vocabulary flash cards and involves evaluation techniques *before, during,* and *after* the use of computer drill-and-practice software.

During. Through direct observation (and perhaps by talking to students), Ms. Moreno quickly realized that vocabulary flash cards were boring and inefficient. She decided that although a drill-and-practice approach was a useful one, a computerized version might make it more interesting, efficient, and meaningful for individual students.

Before. As a result, Ms. Moreno initiated a conversation with the school's technology coordinator regarding available software. She found that another teacher had previously purchased such a program and that it was available for individual student use. However, Ms. Moreno took time to preview the program herself before recommending it for student use. In addition, to make it more accessible to a greater number of students, she asked the technology coordinator if a school site license could be obtained so that the program could be installed on the school's computer network. This allowed students more flexibility regarding when, where, and with whom they could work. Of course, Ms. Moreno made sure that she spent some time demonstrating the program in class and that she set aside time for the whole class to work in the computer lab when she was first introducing the program.

During. In the lab, students completed response sheets regarding the assigned activities. While students were working, Ms. Moreno circulated around the room, checking on their progress, helping them with any problems they were having, and asking questions to assess their understanding of the words included in the software program.

After. At the end of each lab period, Ms. Moreno collected the response sheets. She made comments on them and gave them back to students the next day as a way of providing them with feedback about their work. She also used the response sheets to obtain feedback regarding the effectiveness of each lab activity. Based on the feedback, she made notes on her instructional plan for additional activities that would give students more practice on troublesome vocabulary and/or grammar rules. In addition, Ms. Moreno reflected on how well the drill-and-practice and tutorial/game programs were meeting her goal of individualizing the instruction for her students. Based on a few comments regarding some shortcomings of the drill-and-practice program, she decided to have the vocabulary words placed into a hypertext program that allowed students to examine the definition of a particular word and see both an example of its use and its correct pronunciation.

Ms. Moreno's class continues to evolve. However, the class uses available computer technology to provide students with vocabulary- and grammar-building practice that is designed around the progress of each student. With this in place, Ms. Moreno can concentrate on using other instructional approaches in the classroom to help students develop their Spanish conversation skills.

SUMMARY

Like Chapter 12, this chapter focused on evaluation, not only after a lesson, but also before and during the lesson. However, while Chapter 12 focused on evaluating the students, this chapter focused on evaluating the instruction, including the approaches, media, goals, plans, activities, and materials used in a lesson. In this context, evaluation was described as a cycle of continuous improvement in which decisions are made about how to revise the instruction based on information from several sources. We discussed a variety of techniques, shown in Figure 13.11, that can be used to gather information from these sources before, during, and after the instruction. Each technique was described in terms of its advantages, and a set of practical guidelines was provided for its use.

Finally, the CUE in this chapter described the advantages that computers have over tools that have traditionally been used to revise and store instructional materials. Word processors facilitate the process of continuous improvement by allowing the teacher to quickly and easily make both major and minor revisions in the instructional materials. Databases facilitate the process of continuous improvement by allowing the teacher to store and retrieve materials in a flexible manner, making it easy to find and incorporate additional or alternative approaches, media, goals, plans, activities, and materials into the lesson.

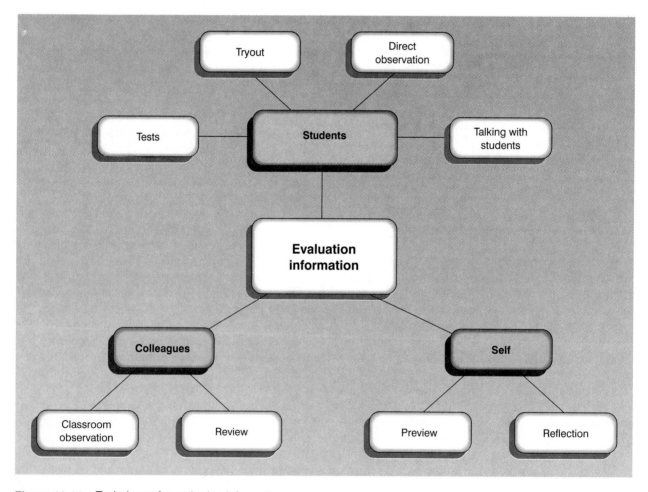

Figure 13.11   Techniques for gathering information

REFLECTIVE QUESTIONS AND ACTIVITIES

1. Think about the evaluation techniques described in this chapter. Which do you think would be the easiest or most natural for you to use as a teacher? Why? Which would be the most difficult for you to use? Why?

2. Think back on some recent instruction you have experienced as a student. What would you have identified as the strong points of the instruction? What suggestions would you have made for improving the instruction?

3. Talk to several teachers about how they evaluate their instruction. Do they evaluate before, during, and after the instruction? What techniques do they use? How does their evaluation help them in their role as instructional experts?

4. Think about a major purchase you have made recently. Did you use the principle of triangulation? What were your sources of information? What contribution did each of those sources make to your decision?

INTEGRATION AND SYNTHESIS

The focus in this chapter was on evaluating the instructional process. This is directly tied to several previous chapters. Chapters 9 and 10 described a variety of ways to implement instruction that was put together in an instructional plan (described in Chapter 6) in which instructional materials are selected, modified, or designed (Chapter 7) and presented using various instructional approaches (Chapter 3) and media (Chapter 4) to help particular students meet particular learning goals (Chapter 5). Chapter 12 described a variety of techniques that can be used to assess students' knowledge and skills before, during, and after the instruction. Chapter 13, then, described a variety of techniques that can be used before, during, and after the instruction to determine its contribution to student learning.

SUGGESTED READINGS

Kemp, J. E., Morrison, G. R., & Ross, S. M. (1994). *Designing effective instruction.* Englewood Cliffs, NJ: Merrill/Prentice Hall. (Especially Chapter 15)

Worthen, B. R., & Sanders, J. R. (1987). *Educational evaluation: Alternative approaches and practical guidelines.* New York: Longman. (Especially Chapters 1 and 3)

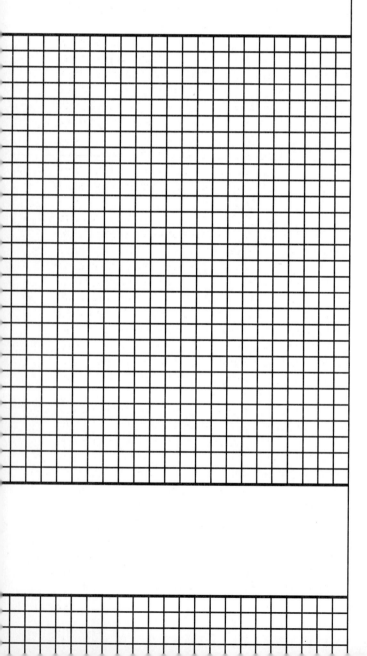

Chapter 14

Directions in Instructional Technology

KEY WORDS AND CONCEPTS

Artificial intelligence (AI)   Virtual reality (VR)

Intelligent tutoring
   system

OUTCOMES

After reading and studying this chapter, you will be able to:

- Describe the contributions of prominent individuals or projects to the development of the fields of instructional design, instructional media, and instructional computing.

- Discuss the evolution of instructional design, instructional media, and instructional computing from the beginning of the 20th century to the present.

- Describe the status of instructional design, instructional media, and instructional computing today.

- Identify the significant trends in instructional technology that seem likely to continue in the future.

- Speculate about the future of the instructional technology field.

- Speculate about the future of education and schooling, based on the changes now occurring in technology.

■ INTRODUCTION

One of the most enduring legends of the old West is that of the Pony Express. Most of us have images of daring young Pony Express riders, braving the elements and Indian attacks, racing across the plains to deliver the mail. Leaping from exhausted horses to fresh ones along the trail, the riders battled time and their own exhaustion to carry the mail from Missouri to California in a record-breaking 6 to 10 days. The Pony Express was truly a marvel of its day.

Do you know how long the Pony Express actually operated? It was just 18 months. Why did this legendary mail service exist for such a short time? In order to understand what happened to the Pony Express, we need a little historical perspective. Prior to the creation of the Pony Express, communication between the east and west coasts of North America was slow indeed. Ships had to travel the long route around South America or transport materials overland across Panama (the canal was not yet built) to another waiting ship. Stagecoaches, though faster, still required 20 days to carry mail from Missouri to California. The Pony Express, with its relays of riders, was a much faster way to deliver the mail. For a time, at least, it fulfilled a need. But, in 1861, the whole concept of communication was radically altered; overland telegraph connections across America were

completed. In a flash, technology transformed life. Communication was achieved in a whole new way, and the Pony Express faded into memory.

The story of the Pony Express has lessons for us. Just as a historical perspective helps us understand what happened to the Pony Express, a historical perspective allows us to better understand instructional technology and its role in education. The saga of the Pony Express underscores the importance of knowing where you are and where you might be going. Had the owners of the Pony Express realized that their business was really communication (not just mail delivery), they might have predicted how the telegraph would impact that business and taken steps to adapt. We are in the business of teaching and learning. Today, new technologies have the potential to transform that business. If we are to avoid going the way of the Pony Express, we need to understand what is happening in order to prepare for the future.

In this text, we introduced you to the concept of instructional technology, a systematic approach to planning, implementing, and evaluating instruction. Along the way we stressed the importance of the appropriate application of media in instruction, and we examined various media and how they can be used in the classroom. We also focused a great deal of attention on instructional computing, because the personal computer is a powerful tool not only for delivering instruction but also for helping teachers plan and evaluate instruction.

As with almost any field of study, there is a tendency for beginning students to view the discipline in static terms—as an established body of knowledge, practices, rules, and procedures. Of course, no discipline, including instructional technology, is static. As with any other field, what we know today has accumulated over many years as the result of the dedicated work of many individuals. Instructional technology has a past! Likewise, the discipline isn't standing still. Like any other field, it's growing and evolving. Undoubtedly, instructional technology will be different in the future than it is today.

The purpose of this chapter is to provide a historical perspective on instructional technology. We examine the roots of instructional design, instructional media, and instructional computing. Then, we turn our attention to the present. What is the status of instructional technology today? Can we identify trends and/or new directions? After examining the past and current trends, we attempt to extrapolate to the future. What changes might we reasonably expect? How might these changes affect education and schooling in the future? Finally, we turn our attention back to you, the teacher. ■

INSTRUCTIONAL TECHNOLOGY IN THE PAST

The roots of instructional technology run deep, and a complete exposition of the history of the field is well beyond the scope of this text. For the historical account that follows, the authors are indebted to the work of Anglin (1991), Gagné (1987), Shelly and Cashman (1984), and particularly Saettler (1990). Interested readers are encouraged to consult these references for more information.

The beginnings of instructional technology can be traced back as far as the ancient Greeks. Indeed, the word *technology* comes from the Greek *technologia,* meaning systematic treatment or craft. The Sophists, from whom we derive the term *sophisticated,* were a group of Greek teachers who were known for their clever arguments and oratorical style. Sophists often tutored groups of youths using a formal rhetorical style and thus can probably lay claim to being the first instructional technologists. Sophist teachings influenced the likes of Socrates, Plato, and Aristotle and, as a result, influenced the basic philosophical foundations of Western thought.

While we can see the bases for instructional technology in the ideas of the ancient Greeks, the modern history of instructional technology is one that falls largely within the 20th century. Let's begin by looking at the modern foundations of instructional design.

Instructional Design Roots

While many early contributions might be cited, probably the single most influential figure in the early history of the instructional design field was Edward L. Thorndike, who joined the faculty of Teachers College of Columbia University in 1899. Thorndike conducted scientific investigations of learning, first on animals and then on humans. As a result of his experiments, he developed what is considered by many to be the first scientific theory of learning. Thorndike's view of learning was founded on the basic notion that organisms establish a connection between stimulus and response. Every action has a consequence, and that consequence influences whether or not the action will be repeated. In a nutshell, when a particular action yields a satisfying result, it is more likely to be repeated in similar circumstances. When an action leads to a dissatisfying or unpleasant consequence, it is less likely to be repeated in the future.

From an educational standpoint, Thorndike's work suggested that teachers need to make explicit appropriate connections (e.g., between the stimulus 2 + 2 and the response 4), reward students for mak-

Edward L. Thorndike (left) developed one of the first scientifically based theories of learning and is often viewed as the "father of instructional technology."

ing the proper connections, and discourage inappropriate connections. These concepts are evident in classrooms even today. Thorndike's work had implications not only for classroom teaching but also for the social aspects of learning. In addition, he did pioneering work on educational measurement and the design of educational media. E. L. Thorndike cast a long shadow on the history of the instructional design field.

In the 1920s, Thorndike's idea of applying empirical methods to educational problems was expanded. Franklin Bobbitt, an advocate of schooling for practical ends, suggested that the goals of schooling should be based on analysis of the skills necessary for successful living. This laid the foundation for the practice of analyzing tasks in order to design better instruction. Further, it clearly established the link between instructional outcomes and instructional practices.

The early part of the century also gave rise to a number of efforts to individualize instruction. Frederic Burk began developing individualized instruction programs at the San Francisco State Normal School in 1912. Two of Burk's associates, Carleton Washburne and Helen Parkhurst, went on to develop their own well-known individualized instruction systems around 1920. Washburne developed the Winnetka Plan, a system that utilized self-instructional workbooks, simple record keeping, and diagnostic testing, features that now are commonly associated with mastery learning. Parkhurst developed the Dalton Plan, which made use of self-instructional practice materials, differing assignment difficulties adjusted to learners' levels, and what is today known as contract learning. These projects helped to lay the foundation for instructional methods that would become very influential in later years.

In the 1930s the concept of instructional outcomes was refined by Ralph W. Tyler at The Ohio State University. As part of his now famous Eight-Year Study, Tyler examined the notion of educational outcomes, which he termed *objectives.* He found that schools, even when they did specify objectives, often did so poorly. Resolving to address this problem, he refined the process of specifying instructional outcomes. By the end of his study, Tyler established that instructional outcomes could be clearly stated in terms of student behaviors and that the use of clearly specified outcomes made it possible to formatively evaluate instructional materials.

World War II gave a big boost to the field of instructional design. The need to rapidly train tens of thousands of new military personnel created a heightened interest in applying educational research in a systematic way. Many educational researchers participated in the war training effort, and this helped to propel forward systematic efforts to design instruction. During the war, the fruits of this effort were seen primarily in increased use of educational media to train military personnel. However, after the war, interest in instructional design greatly increased.

The 1950s and 1960s were a period of intense activity in the emerging field of instructional design. In 1956 Benjamin Bloom and his colleagues published the *Taxonomy of Educational Objectives,* a hierarchical scheme for categorizing educational outcomes that is now familiar to most students of education. Bloom's taxonomy proved to be very useful for specifying instructional outcomes and for designing instruction to attain those outcomes. During this time the concept of task analysis was also refined and became part of the lexicon of the field. Robert B. Miller, working for the U.S. military, is credited with developing the first detailed task-analysis procedures.

B. F. Skinner's theory of operant conditioning, commonly referred to as behaviorism, was one of the dominant views in instructional design in the 1950s and 1960s. As we mentioned in Chapter 2, Skinner's approach, which was an extension of the ideas originally put forth by Thorndike, focused on the role of reinforcement in connecting stimulus and response. Skinner maintained that by carefully controlling reinforcement, learning could be maximized. These ideas gave rise to programmed instruction (see Chapter 10) and a systematic approach to designing, developing, evaluating, and revising instruction. Although enthusiasm for programmed instruc-

tion waned in the 1960s, its influence on the field of instructional design was considerable and can still be seen today in many computer-assisted instruction (CAI) programs.

In the 1960s the field moved forward on several fronts. Work by Robert Gagné and other cognitive scientists helped to bring a more cognitive orientation to instructional design. Gagné specified the instructional conditions necessary for learners to achieve specific outcomes and focused more attention on understanding what happens inside the minds of learners. Robert Glaser coined the term *criterion-referenced measures* to refer to tests designed to measure the achievement of specific competencies. In addition, the term *instructional system* began to be used to describe systematic instructional design efforts. Because the federal government provided significant support for research and development in the field during this period, instructional design became much more widely used and studied.

By the end of the 1960s, instructional design was established as a discipline in its own right. The decades since the 1960s gave rise to refinements and expansions of the field. Cognitive theories of learning became increasingly influential. Instructional design degree programs were developed on many college campuses. Models of instructional design were developed and tested by various theorists in the field. Instructional design proliferated in military and business training, and there were efforts to promote its use in K–12 teaching.

Instructional Media Roots

In many ways, instructional media and instructional design developed along separate but converging pathways. Although the use of real objects, drawings, and other media have been a part of instruction at least since the dawn of civilization, the history of instructional media, like that of instructional design, is mostly confined to the 20th century. Explorations in the use of media took place at the beginning of the century. The field received a significant boost from World War II training efforts and began to diversify after the war. Subsequent developments led to a maturation of the discipline and increasing links with the field of instructional design.

In America, museums were one of the most significant early influences on instructional media. While this may seem odd, museums have a long history of cooperating with schools and assuming a clear instructional role in their communities. In 1905 the St. Louis Educational Museum became the first school museum to open in the United States. A

The St. Louis Educational Museum first used a horse and wagon to deliver instructional materials to teachers.

forerunner of what is now called a media center, the museum housed collections of art objects, models, photographs, charts, real objects, and other instructional materials gathered from collections from around the world. These materials were placed at the disposal of the St. Louis schools. The basic idea was to bring the world to the child. Weekly deliveries of instructional materials to the schools were first accomplished by horse and wagon and later by truck. A catalog of materials, organized by course of study, was even provided to teachers so that they could request specific materials. In 1943 the museum was renamed the Division of Audio-Visual Education for the St. Louis schools. Similar initiatives were undertaken in other U.S. cities.

Even before the beginning of the 20th century, there was widespread interest in what was then called visual instruction or visual education. The principle behind this movement was that pictures more closely represent real objects than do words; therefore, in school settings dominated by verbal information, pictures should make many topics more accessible to learners. Magic lanterns to project slides, and stereopticons, an early visual display device, were popular means of illustrating public lectures and could be found in schools prior to the start of the 20th century. In 1904 the state of New York organized the first visual instruction department, which was responsible for collecting and distributing lantern slides to schools. By 1920 a number of visual instruction departments had been formed at universities. These were the beginnings of what later became audiovisual and media science departments.

Films also came into classrooms early in the 20th century. Indeed, pioneers of the motion picture

viewed the medium primarily in educational terms, although films soon gravitated toward the theatrical and entertaining. Thomas Edison developed a series of historical and scientific films for school use. Some theatrical films were also used educationally—for example, to show productions of dramatic plays. The first educational film catalog to be published in the United States appeared in 1910,

The magic lantern was an early audiovisual device used in schools.

and later that same year the first public school system (Rochester, New York) adopted films for regular instructional use. Although the medium suffered some growing pains, particularly during the emergence of "talking" pictures and the economic trials of the Great Depression, film continued to evolve as an educational medium throughout the 20th century.

There were also early efforts by schools to use audio as an instructional medium. During the 1920s and 1930s, radio was the focus of a number of educational experiments. In 1929, one of the first major initiatives, the Ohio School of the Air, was launched with the cooperation of the state, The Ohio State University, and a Cincinnati radio station. Although it survived for less than a decade, it established a model for similar efforts in other locations and demonstrated that radio could be a useful educational medium. During this period a number of universities also launched educational radio stations. Typical educational fare included broadcasts of lectures and performances by campus bands and orchestras. Although not widely successful, these early efforts had their advocates, who were convinced of the potential of educational radio. Much later, in the 1960s and 1970s, audio returned to classrooms in the form of cassette tapes as part of audio-tutorial and related instructional systems.

During World War II, educational films and other media became an integral part of the training effort for the war. During the war years, the U.S. government produced over 800 training films and filmstrips, purchased tens of thousands of projectors, and spent about one billion dollars on training films. This rapid deployment of large quantities of mediated instruction certainly influenced the field and contributed to the perception that media can be very useful for education and training.

Following World War II, the educational media field began to shift its focus from hardware to the role of media in learning. Systematic studies were undertaken to establish how the attributes or features of various media affected learning. Various theories or models of communication were developed that incorporated the role of media. Over the years, many different models were proposed, considered, refined, and revised. These models helped to move audiovisual specialists beyond consideration of the hardware alone to a consideration of all of the components involved in the communication process. As a result, audiovisual studies began to be conceptualized as something broader than just media. A convergence of audiovisual sciences, communication theories, learning theories, and instructional design began. This marked the beginnings of instructional technology as we have defined it in this book.

In the 1950s, television took center stage as an important new medium on the educational scene.

Training of U.S. military personnel during World War II made extensive use of media such as film.

The first non-experimental educational television station was launched by Iowa State University in 1950. Others quickly followed suit. In 1952 the Federal Communications Commission set aside 242 television channels for public (then called educational) television stations. This action helped to spur an already growing interest in the use of television for education. Considerable financial support was also provided by the Ford Foundation for early educational television efforts.

Educational programming on television has been a fixture since television's earliest years. Today we see educational television in the form of the latest National Geographic special, newsmagazines, the Discovery channel, and similar programming. Instructional television, which refers more specifically to the use of television to deliver a specific body of content as part of a formal course of instruction, is less widespread. Although there have been notable successes and large projects, such as the *Sesame Street* program for early learning, instructional television has never achieved the success that was predicted by its early advocates. Nonetheless, instructional television has remained an available medium for use by educational technologists.

In the 1970s and 1980s, video came into school classrooms, but not in the form of television. The proliferation of VCRs in homes led to their widespread use in classrooms as well. To a large extent, the use of videotapes displaced the use of films in the classroom. In addition, other types of video media, such as laser videodiscs, became available. Newer video technologies, such as satellite-based video and two-way video conferencing, were also introduced into schools. Video continues to evolve and affect schooling, although not in the ways predicted by the original advocates of instructional television.

Of course, one of the most significant media developments of the 1970s and 1980s was the invention of the personal computer. The first personal computers began to arrive in schools in the late 1970s, and significant investments in computers were made during the 1980s. We will consider the impact of the personal computer and the roots of instructional computing in more detail in the next section.

As media use increased during the 1970s and 1980s, the field continued to change as well. While interest in new forms of media continued, the movement to redefine the nature of audiovisual sciences and media studies, which began at the end of World War II, continued. Media came to be viewed not in isolation but as one part of a larger educational technology process. As instructional design developed into a field of study, media sciences matured in ways that increasingly acknowledged their link to instructional design and communication.

Instructional Computing Roots

Computers are relatively recent innovations. The first all-electronic digital computer was invented in 1939 by John Atanasoff and Clifford Berry at Iowa State University. The first large-scale, general-purpose electronic digital computer, called ENIAC, was put into service by John W. Mauchly and J. Presper Eckert at

ENIAC was the first large-scale, general-purpose electronic digital computer.

the University of Pennsylvania in 1946. It was used to calculate trajectory tables for military artillery. By today's standards, ENIAC was huge. It included some 18,000 vacuum tubes, weighed 30 tons, and took up the space of a small house. It was capable of multiplying two numbers in about 3 milliseconds, a performance easily surpassed by today's personal computers.

Following ENIAC, computer technology developed at a dizzying pace. The history of computer development has been divided into four generations, with each generation being based on a different underlying technology. First-generation computers, like ENIAC, relied on vacuum tube technology. The second generation, which emerged in the late 1950s and early 1960s, was based on transistors, devices that replaced vacuum tubes and were smaller, faster, cheaper, and more reliable. The third generation followed rapidly on the heels of the second in the 1960s; it used solid-state technology or integrated circuits (ICs). ICs replaced discrete transistors and other electrical components with circuits etched onto tiny wafers of silicon called chips. The fourth generation, which arrived in the 1970s, relied on large-scale integration (LSI) and very large scale integration (VLSI). Perhaps the most significant development of the fourth generation was the invention of the microprocessor, a single silicon chip that included all of the key functions of a computer. It was created in 1969 by Ted Hoff of Intel Corporation. This development made possible the invention of the personal computer. In 1977 the Apple II, Commodore PET, and Radio Shack TRS-80 computers all came onto the market as ready-to-run personal computers. They began a revolution in the computer industry.

Actually, the first efforts to use computers for education came in the early 1960s, well before the personal computer. At Stanford University, Patrick Suppes and his associates initiated a CAI project. Working with elementary students, the Stanford team developed drill-and-practice and tutorial applications, first in mathematics and then in a number of curricular areas, that ran on mainframe computer terminals. These carefully developed and researched programs became models for many later developers of instructional computer software.

Also in the early 1960s, the PLATO project was initiated at the University of Illinois. Probably the best-known and largest CAI effort ever, PLATO (Programmed Logic for Automatic Teaching Operation) resulted in the development of hundreds of quality software programs in a wide variety of subject areas. Many courses at the University of Illinois relied on PLATO for instruction. High costs proved

to be a barrier to extension of the PLATO project to other institutions, and, while evaluation results were positive, they were not as positive as many had hoped. However, much of the courseware developed for PLATO was ultimately adapted for personal computers, and PLATO continues today as a corporate training system. The authoring language used with PLATO, called TUTOR, was used as the basis for subsequent personal computer authoring packages. IBM's Coursewriter authoring system, also developed in the 1960s, was similarly used as a model for later personal computer products.

The TICCIT (Time-shared Interactive Computer-Controlled Information Television) project, begun at Brigham Young University in the early 1970s, adopted an approach similar to that of the PLATO project. It focused on CAI aimed at community college learners. Like PLATO, TICCIT received positive evaluations, and many of the programs developed for TICCIT subsequently were adapted for personal computers. TICCIT was also significant because it marked one of the first attempts to merge instructional computing and instructional design. It was based on the notion of learner-controlled instruction, and the software for the project was created using basic principles of instructional design.

The impact of these early computer projects was limited, in part, because these projects were initially conducted using large mainframe computers, which were not widely accessible. The emergence of the personal computer in the late 1970s promised

A PLATO terminal gave the user access to a wide variety of CAI in one of the largest instructional computing projects ever.

to change that. Indeed, some developments in instructional computing did come about as a result of a successful transition from mainframes to personal computers. For example, Seymour Papert and his associates at MIT began work on the Logo computer language in the 1970s on large computers. Logo was quickly adapted for personal computers and became one of the early successes in instructional computing. The Minnesota Educational Computing Consortium (MECC), one of the first large-scale state initiatives involving educational uses of computers, also began with large computers and terminals. MECC quickly moved into the personal computer arena, however, and was instrumental in helping to spur and shape the early growth of instructional computing. Although MECC continues to this day, it is now an independent organization.

Personal computers were sufficiently inexpensive that they could readily be acquired by schools. As a result, the 1980s saw a dramatic rise in the number of computers in U.S. schools. Between 1981 and 1987, the percentage of U.S. schools with one or more computers earmarked for instruction rose from 18% to 95% (U.S. Office of Technology Assessment, 1988). By 1995 there were an estimated 5.8 million computers in U.S. schools, with a student-to-computer ratio of about 9 to 1 (U.S. Office of Technology Assessment, 1995). Furthermore, nearly every school had at least one personal computer available for instructional use.

However, the influx of computers into schools was not accompanied by equally rapid and trouble-free curricular integration. The first personal computers were not very powerful. They were capable of presenting only text and limited graphics, and the practice of networking personal computers was unknown. In addition, in the beginning there was very little prepared software of any kind. However, the first personal computers did come with a built-in programming language, BASIC. As a result, the first major use of computers in education focused on programming. This led to the mistaken perception by many people that instructional computing was highly technical and closely allied with mathematics.

Computer literacy was first defined as a body of knowledge and a set of computer skills, including the ability to communicate with the computer through programming. Early computer literacy courses and curricular integration plans focused on the development of computer knowledge and programming skills among students. Some authorities in the field predicted that a new discipline, computers and programming, would soon be taught alongside reading, writing, and arithmetic in the schools. While this view didn't prevail, the rapidly growing interest in computers and their educational applications gave impetus to the development of instructional computing programs of study at many colleges and universities.

As the use of personal computers proliferated and their capabilities grew, more and more software became available. Many of the early software packages were CAI programs in mathematics and other subject areas, mainly because of the ease with which such software could be developed. Software quality was frequently a topic of early debate. However, as the number of available titles expanded and the quality improved, the emphasis in computer education began to shift. The focus shifted from teaching about computers and programming for their own sake to using CAI software in support of traditional curricular areas such as mathematics, language arts, science, and social studies. In many ways, this shift mirrored the early mainframe efforts of projects like PLATO. Indeed, as we pointed out, many personal computer programs were derived from their mainframe project predecessors.

As personal computers continued to become more powerful and software continued to improve, other shifts began to occur. Powerful productivity applications such as word processors, electronic spreadsheets, and database managers were developed for personal computers. As a result, more attention was focused on the use of the computer for personal productivity. By the end of the 1980s, most experts in instructional computing had moved away from isolated computer study and the use of simple CAI for supporting the curriculum to a more comprehensive view of curricular integration that included the use of computers in authentic subject-area contexts. Thus greater attention was given to those uses of the computer that were carefully integrated into specific subject areas—for example, the use of word processing to support the teaching of writing, and the use of the Logo computer language as part of the study of elementary mathematics.

The capabilities of personal computers continued to develop as well. In 1984 Apple introduced a dramatically redesigned personal computer called the Macintosh. It featured a graphical-user interface (GUI) instead of a text-based operating system of the type used since the early mainframe days. This concept proved very popular, and with the development of Microsoft Windows, a GUI for IBM-type computers, the GUI concept began to dominate personal computing.

Experiments linking personal computers to other media were conducted in the late 1970s and early 1980s. For example, laser videodisc players were interfaced to personal computers. Networking and interconnecting computers became popular. Modems were developed for use with personal computers, and local- and wide-area networks spread. Personal computers emerged as the dominant form of computer technology.

From its inception in the late 1970s to the 1990s, the personal computer underwent a remarkable transformation from a novelty that could only be used for simple programming to a widespread, multipurpose, powerful personal productivity and educational tool. Instructional computing as a field of study was transformed along with the personal computer. It changed from a narrow focus on computers and programming to a broader perspective of the computer as a tool to be integrated into the instructional process. Like instructional design and media sciences, instructional computing emerged as a discipline in its own right.

INSTRUCTIONAL TECHNOLOGY IN THE PRESENT

In the previous section we gave you a sense of where educational technology has come from. The component disciplines that we discuss in this book—instructional design, instructional media, and instructional computing—are all relatively new. Instructional design and instructional media are only about a century old, and instructional computing is only a few decades old. Yet all have histories. All have evolved to become the unique fields of study that they are today. So, let's shift our focus to the present. Where is instructional technology today?

Instructional Design Today

In some ways, describing the state of instructional design today is a difficult task. Indeed, a criticism that is sometimes leveled at the field, both from inside its ranks and from the outside, is that there is no common core of understanding of what the discipline encompasses. While this may be a bit of an overstatement, it is probably fair to say that there is a degree of ambiguity surrounding the discipline. Within the instructional design community, there is a healthy, ongoing debate about the field and its role in education.

Part of this debate is just a matter of definitions and backgrounds. The core of the debate lies in the roots of the field as we described them in the previous section. Instructional design is, to a large extent, tied up in the work of psychological researchers who study basic processes of learning. Yet instructional design attempts to apply the theoretical work of psychological researchers to the real tasks of instruction. The field is also intertwined with the study of audiovisual media. As we noted earlier, World War II was a catalyst that blurred the distinctions between instructional design and instructional media. More recently, the emergence of the personal computer as a potent force in education blurred the boundaries among fields even more. One of the trends that we can see today is the growing interconnectedness of instructional design, instructional media, and instructional computing.

There is also much debate about the impact of instructional design. On the one hand, the instructional design field and its influence have never been greater. Instructional design programs in colleges and universities have shown steady growth since the 1960s, and there are many highly successful programs throughout the country. There are a number of professional organizations devoted strictly to the issues and concerns that confront instructional designers (Table 14.1). In the military and in business training settings, the systematic design and implementation of instruction has been widely embraced. Huge numbers of military personnel and business trainees benefit from instructional design practices every year. Most individuals in the field believe these approaches have been very successful.

On the other hand, systematic instructional design is only beginning to make a significant impact on K–12 education. Whereas instructional design as a field emphasizes the links among planning, implementing, and evaluating learner-centered instruction, much of K–12 education has overlooked these approaches in the past and remained entrenched in the teacher- and textbook-centered approaches that have dominated classrooms for over a century. Yet instructional design clearly has much to offer, and the foundations have been laid for it to play a greater role in schools in the future. Today much of the debate in the instructional design field centers around the potential role that instructional design might play in reforming or restructuring K–12 education. As you continue your own growth and development in the field, look to professional organizations, periodicals, user groups, books, and local colleges and universities for the latest information about the field.

Instructional designers are also in the midst of a significant debate over which theoretical perspectives should guide the field (see Chapter 2 for a discussion of these theoretical perspectives). As noted earlier, the field was founded on the works of Edward L. Thorndike and B. F. Skinner, researchers who took a behavioral approach to learning. Thorndike and Skinner regarded the learner as a black

Table 14.1   Professional organizations in the field of instructional technology

Organization	Description	Address
AACE	Association for the Advancement of Computing in Education. This group is concerned with the uses of computers and allied technologies in education. It publishes the following journals: *Journal of Computers in Mathematics and Science Teaching, Journal of Educational Multimedia and Hypermedia, Journal of Technology and Teacher Education, Journal of Computing in Childhood Education,* and *Journal of Artificial Intelligence in Education.*	AACE P.O. Box 2966 Charlottesville, VA 22902
AECT	Association for Educational Communications and Technology. This organization is concerned with all aspects of instructional technology. It publishes *Tech Trends* and *Educational Technology Research and Development.*	AECT 1025 Vermont Avenue, NW Suite 820 Washington, DC 20005
ASTD	American Society for Training and Development. This group focuses primarily on issues related to training. It publishes *Training and Development Journal.*	ASTD Box 1443 1630 Duke Street Alexandria, VA 22313
IICS	International Interactive Communications Society. This group focuses on communications and interactive multimedia technologies in industry and education.	IICS P.O. Box 1862 Lake Oswego, OR 97035
ISPI	International Society for Performance Improvement. This organization focuses broadly on performance and instructional technologies. It publishes *Performance and Instruction* and *Performance Improvement Quarterly.*	ISPI 1300 L Street, NW Suite 1250 Washington, DC 20005
ISTE	International Society for Technology in Education. This group focuses on the uses of computers and allied technologies in education. It publishes *Learning and Leading with Technology* and the *Journal of Research on Computing in Education.*	ISTE 1787 Agate Street Eugene, OR 97403

box. To them it didn't really matter what went on inside the black box as long as the learner gave the desired response. However, in the 1960s and 1970s, more and more attention was paid to cognitive theories of learning. Cognitivism, in contrast to behaviorism, stresses the importance of what happens inside the black box (i.e., the learner's mind). Cognitivists focus on the mental constructs learners bring to an instructional situation and the mental processes that occur during learning.

Today one of the most popular variations of the cognitive perspective is constructivism. The basic concept of this theoretical perspective is that knowledge cannot be transmitted to learners; rather, they must construct knowledge for themselves. Some constructivist schools of thought focus on the process of knowledge construction within the individual's mind, while others focus on the construction of knowledge within a social context, such as a school setting. These theoretical perspectives are among the most influential in education today.

Although instructional design remains linked in many people's minds to its behavioral roots, it is safe to say that the great majority of instructional designers accept the cognitive view. The constructivist perspective is also widely discussed and accepted in many quarters. However, the application of these theories to the practice of instructional design is far from clear and has sparked considerable debate within the field. What do these perspectives tell us about the practice of planning, implementing, and evaluating instruction? These issues are at the heart of an ongoing discussion in the field today.

In summary, instructional design today can be described as an established and reasonably successful field of study. But it is one that is in the midst of intense self-examination. This self-examination focuses on issues regarding the nature of the discipline, its role in K–12 education and reform, and its response to differing theoretical perspectives on the nature of learning.

Instructional Media Today

Like instructional design, the media field is also enjoying considerable success while undergoing significant change. Today there are more media available for education than ever before. The traditional media available to educators for many years—real objects, visuals, films, chalkboards, bulletin boards, and overhead projectors—remain important classroom tools. Videotapes and VCRs are also now common in classrooms. Newer media, such as the laser videodisc, CD-ROM, digital audiotape (DAT), and satellite TV, are finding their way into classrooms at an increasing rate.

Among the most significant changes in educational media today is the use of video. Once considered disappointing for its lack of impact, instructional television has reemerged as an important force in the classroom. In 1989 Whittle Communications launched its *Channel One* initiative, which delivers a daily news program into classrooms. Although it generated a furor in the educational community because of its inclusion of advertising, *Channel One* has nonetheless survived and has become widely distributed in U.S. classrooms. The Cable News Network (CNN) launched a similar program, the *CNN Newsroom,* in 1989. By the mid-1990s these programs reached many classrooms throughout the country.

Video is having an impact in other ways. VCRs are now among the most common of classroom tools, and they have all but replaced films in most schools. As of 1991, the typical school had six VCRs and seven TVs (U.S. Office of Technology Assessment, 1995). Laser videodiscs are becoming more common. This video medium offers capabilities—rapid random access, clear still picture, multilingual audio, and lack of wear—not available with videotapes and VCRs. Many schools are connected to local cable television systems, and some use the capability of the cable for their own communication needs. Satellite video capability is also becoming more common in schools. With access to satellites, schools can receive a broad range of programming, from commercial channels to NASA broadcasts. Finally, many schools are beginning to explore the use of video for distance education (see Chapter 8). Using standard broadcast methods or, in the most advanced cases, two-way interactive video, schools are able to provide specialized courses (e.g., college credit, foreign-language instruction, or advanced-placement mathematics/science courses) to students. Today video is enjoying a significant classroom renaissance.

The role of the school media specialist is also changing to keep pace with the changes in the field. Spurred by the success of media during World War II and, later, in response to the launch of the Russian Sputnik satellite, interest in school media services grew during the 1960s. At first, because they tended to be centralized in the library, media fell under the auspices of the school librarian, so library or information sciences influenced media sciences (and continue to do so today). As media grew in importance and became more widespread during the 1970s and 1980s, the role of the media specialist expanded. Today the school media specialist is often called on for a variety of functions: library circulation, acquisition and maintenance of media collections, curriculum planning, teacher inservice, instructional design support, and, in some cases, computer management and use.

Computers are having a major impact on the media field today. In fact, we are in the midst of what is probably the most profound change in media in history. Where once media developed separately—each with its own technological basis, vocabulary, and experts—today all media are merging in the computer. All media are going digital!

It's difficult to overstate the significance of the digital revolution. Traditional ways of handling text—typing, mimeographs, and printing—are giving way to word processing and desktop publishing. Computer graphics and newer technologies such as Kodak's PhotoCD are turning traditional visuals digital. Audio CDs, DAT, and computer audio digitizers are making sound digital. Telephone networks are converting to digital. Even video is being digitized. The advantages of this approach are considerable. Digital media can be reproduced flawlessly. They can be recorded on computer-readable media such as diskettes and CD-ROMs. They can be sent anywhere in the world by computers over telephone lines without loss of information. Additionally, computers can be used to process, transform, or otherwise manipulate the media in a myriad of ways. The information superhighway is being built on the foundations of digital multimedia!

Instructional Computing Today

Like instructional design and media, the field of instructional computing is changing today. Changing technology has much to do with this change. It has been said that if the automotive industry had advanced as rapidly as the computer industry over the past half century, you would be able to buy a car today that would travel at the speed of a jet, get a million miles on a gallon of gasoline, and cost only a few dollars! The changes in computers have indeed been dramatic. Since the emergence of the personal computer in the late 1970s, the capabilities of these machines have increased enormously. Today's personal computers are many times more powerful than the first models, and development continues. Remarkably, personal computers continue to become more powerful, more compact, and less expensive all at the same time!

The increasing capability of the personal computer has made possible the movement toward digital media. While digital media have many desirable characteristics, they place significant demands on computer resources. As computers have become more powerful and as memory and storage capacities have increased, it has become easier for them to handle digital media. However, we are not yet at the point that personal computers can readily handle the demands of all digital media. Audio and video, in particular, require resources that still limit what personal computers can do. However, the trend is clear, and it's easy to see that in the future the world of media will be all digital.

Networking is another trend that is clearly evident today. While personal computers were once isolated desktop machines, networking is common today and on the increase. Many personal computers are equipped with modems for dial-up access to other computing resources. Local-area networks are common in schools and offices. Wide-area networks are growing. The Internet, the mother of all networks, continues to expand at an exponential rate, and schools across the country and around the world are connecting to it. This vast interconnecting of computers is making enormous resources almost instantaneously available to people all over the world. Table 14.2 lists some Internet resources specifically related to instructional technology.

As a result of changes in technology, such as networking, the role of the computer or technology specialist is changing too. While once the computer specialist may have been responsible for teaching a little programming, today the technology specialist may have to manage many facets of educational technology: purchasing, hardware installation, software integration, teacher training, local- and wide-area networking, distance education technologies, and more. The job is getting much more complex and often falls to more than one person.

Computers are widespread in education today. There are millions of computers in U.S. schools, and the student-to-computer ratio is dropping steadily. Three brands of computers dominate the educational scene: the Apple II family, IBM-PC and compatible computers, and the Apple Macintosh. The Apple II computer, one of the first personal computers, has long dominated the K–12 market. The number of Apple II computers in schools is fairly large, but because the manufacture of these machines has been discontinued they are being replaced by newer, more capable models. Current sales figures

Table 14.2   Selected instructional technology resources available on the Internet

Instructional Technology Resource	Internet Location
World Wide Web	
Instructional Technology and Training	http://www.yahoo.com/Education/Instructional_Technology_and_Training
Office of Instructional Technology (University of Michigan) web site	http://www.oit.itd.umich.edu/
Netwatch Top Ten—Education	http://www.pulver.com/netwatch/topten/tt3.htm
Gopher	
AACE gopher	gopher aace.virginia.edu 70
AECT gopher	gopher sunbird.usd.edu 72
Distance Education clearinghouse gopher	gopher bluto.uwex.edu 70
Institute for Academic Technology gopher	gopher isaac.engr.washington.edu 70
ISTE gopher	gopher iste-gopher.uoregon.edu 70
E-mail list	
Computer Networks in Education list	CNEDUC-L@tamvm1.tamu.edu
Distance Education forum list	DEOS-L@psuvm.psu.edu
Educational Internet uses forum list	EDNET@NIC.UMASS.EDU
Educational Technology forum list	EDTECH@MSU.EDU
Media in Education list	MEDIA-L@bingvmb.cc.binghamton.edu
World Wide Web in Education list	WWWEDU@k12.cnidr.org

Note: All locations are current as of August 1995. Be aware that locations are frequently altered.

indicate that IBM and compatible computers and Apple Macintosh computers each account for about half of the new sales in education. The first joint efforts of Apple and IBM to develop a common personal computer platform, called the PowerPC, began to appear in the marketplace in 1994.

Software today is a far cry from the early days of personal computers. The GUI, embodied in the Macintosh operating system, Microsoft's Windows, and IBM's OS/2, dominates the way that users interact with personal computers. Other ways of interacting with computers—pen input, speech recognition, and virtual reality—are being refined and hold promise for education. Powerful tool applications—word processors, spreadsheets, databases, graphics programs, telecommunication packages, authoring programs, and so on—are widely available. Good educational software in a variety of content areas is available. Quality, once a major issue, is improving all the time. Programs making use of developments in the field of artificial intelligence are emerging. CD-ROM, because of its large capacity and ability to deliver multimedia, is becoming a common vehicle for delivering educational software.

Instructional computing as a field is also changing. As we noted earlier, instructional computing began with a focus on the computer as the object of instruction—computer literacy and computer programming. As software became available, attention turned to the use of CAI to support curricular areas. Today most of the attention is given to the use of computers as a genuine tool within particular subject areas. In addition, as developments in multimedia and networking continue, the focus of instructional computing and the role of the school computer

specialist continue to expand. The computer is the focus of much that is happening in education, including efforts to reform or restructure the educational process.

INSTRUCTIONAL TECHNOLOGY IN THE FUTURE

Predicting the future is always a risky business. Conditions change, new developments occur, and old patterns fail to hold true. Nonetheless, developments in the fields of instructional design, media, and computing over the past 100 years certainly do suggest some trends. If we assume that these trends will continue, then we are able to make some predictions about the future. The implications of these trends may not always be clear, but it is possible, at least in some cases, to see the direction in which we are headed. And knowing the direction in which we are going helps us to chart our future course.

One of the important trends that we see is the convergence of disciplines. When we looked at the past of instructional technology, we examined its three component disciplines—instructional design, instructional media, and instructional computing—separately. We did so because these three disciplines arose and, to a large extent, developed separately. When we looked at the present, we again looked at the three component disciplines separately, although we acknowledged that there were areas in which the fields were beginning to overlap. In this section we will consider instructional technology as a whole, because we believe the three component disciplines will come together even more in the future. This concept is illustrated in Figure 14.1.

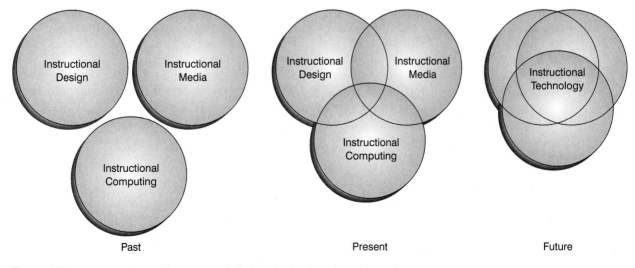

Figure 14.1 Intersections of instructional design, instructional media, and instructional computing in the past, present, and future

Instructional design, media, and computing began as separate disciplines, yet instructional design and media began to merge with Thorndike's experiments on the impact of textual presentations. As a result of the demand for effective and efficient training during World War II, this overlap increased. Media became incorporated into instructional design models, and there is considerable overlap between instructional design and media utilization today. Instructional computing was implicitly linked to instructional design and media from its inception. Explicit connections were made in early projects such as TICCIT, but, especially after the invention of the personal computer, many developments in instructional computing occurred separately.

With the development of digital media, the fields are coming closer together. Computers are important tools for instructional planning, implementation, and evaluation. Media are moving toward a digital future. Everything is coming together. Indeed, much of the rationale for this textbook was the need to treat these three previously separate disciplines as components of one integrated topic, that is, instructional technology as we have defined it. In the future, we see even greater overlap of instructional design, media, and computing.

In the future, the design of instruction is likely to focus increasingly on the use of computers and multimedia. These powerful tools offer tremendous flexibility both to the designer and to the learner. From a theoretical perspective, it seems likely that the attention given to cognitive approaches will continue to increase. By understanding learners and learning processes better, instructional designers will be able to design better instruction. As the networking of resources continues, the accumulated knowledge of humankind will become available electronically from anywhere in the world. As a result, instructional design approaches are likely to shift toward facilitating and assisting learners in sifting through and learning from many information sources and away from packaging and delivering discrete sets of information, as has characterized the field in the past.

A greater emphasis is likely to be placed on distance education in the future. As the technologies for delivering information over distances continue to improve and become more widespread, more and more people will seek the opportunities available through distance education. As the "information superhighway" spreads to homes, schools, and businesses, it will be easier than ever before for education and training to be delivered to individuals when and where they need it. As a result, instructional designers and media specialists with expertise in the field of distance education will likely be in greater demand in the future.

Technological advances also suggest other trends that are likely to impact education in the future. The developments that led to the personal computer and to the increases in computer capability that have occurred over the last two decades seem likely to continue unabated for a number of years. This means that personal computers will continue to become more powerful, faster, smaller, and less expensive. Eventually the laws of physics will slow the progress of the electronics industry. The tiny circuits that are packed onto computer chips can only get so small. But these fundamental obstacles have not yet caused significant problems, and researchers are already at work on ways to get around some of the problems that are beginning to loom. This means that we can look forward to more, and better, computer technology into the future.

The developments in computer power will support the continuation of media convergence that is under way today. It seems likely that, in the near future, computers will readily support audio and full-screen, full-motion video as well as text and true-color graphics. Functions that are now managed by separate devices—television, radio, telephone, fax machine, and so on—are likely to be merged into a single, multipurpose information machine, the computer of the future. Indeed, your grandchildren, or perhaps even your children, are likely to view today's many different machines as odd relics of a bygone era.

With declining size and cost, computers will become more portable and more commonplace. Most experts foresee a future in which small but powerful computers will become standard school equipment for every learner. While it's impossible to predict features accurately, it is likely that these computers will be far more capable than today's personal computers. These portable computers will probably be no larger than a textbook. Network connections wired into the school or home, or wireless connections of some kind, will allow these computers to stay tapped into the global information network. Such devices may completely replace textbooks, paper, and pencils in the future.

Software will continue to improve and become more sophisticated. For example, with software improvements, pen or speech input may come to replace the keyboard as the primary means by which users interact with the computer. Operating systems are likely to better reflect the ways that people work and how they use computers. In the near future, at least, we are likely to see even greater use of optical storage technologies—the underpinnings of laser videodisc and CD-ROM—for software dissemination. In addition, performance support or help systems that provide "just in time" information and training will become more widespread.

Software based on artificial intelligence is likely to become more commonplace in the future. **Artificial intelligence (AI)** is a branch of computer science concerned with the design of computers and software that are capable of responding in ways that mimic human thinking. Several branches of AI have already shown success. Expert systems are programs that embody the knowledge and skills of an expert in a particular discipline. They have already proven to be successful in fields as diverse as oil exploration and medical diagnosis. Robotics, machine vision, and speech-recognition technologies all rely on AI. In addition, intelligent software agents are being developed; someday such tools may be able to perform tasks such as searching the Internet for information tailored to your own needs. In education, **intelligent tutoring systems**—sometimes called intelligent computer-assisted instruction (ICAI) programs—have been developed in mathematics, geography, and computer science, to name just a few areas. Intelligent tutoring systems usually combine detailed information about the subject area and common student mistakes with a model of student performance to diagnose a given student's level of understanding and provide instruction designed to meet that student's needs.

Another emerging area of computer development is virtual reality. **Virtual reality (VR)** is created by a computer system that projects before the user a three-dimensional visual representation of an environment and responds to the user's motion within that environment. Today VR systems consist of a computer linked to special headgear and bodysuits or gloves worn by the user. The headgear projects the image of a three-dimensional world before the user and senses the motion of the user's head so that as the head turns, the image being projected for the user also turns. Sensor-equipped bodysuits or gloves can also be worn by the user. With the glove, for example, the user can reach out and touch or grab objects in the virtual environment. While the technology is fairly crude now, as it improves it may be possible for students to take virtual field trips—re-creations of historical events, travel to faraway places, journeys inside the human body—or perform virtual tasks such as mixing dangerous chemicals or practicing welding. The possibilities are truly exciting.

The networking of computers will continue in the future. The United States is already at work trying to plan and implement the information superhighway, which promises to bring information to everyone's fingertips. It's not hard to imagine that in the future every school and perhaps every home in the country will be connected to a high-speed, global information network. Even portable personal computers will be able to link to this network via plug-in connections or via wireless satellite or cellular phone–type connections. This global network will make information of all kinds immediately accessible to individuals and to schools.

So, we foresee a future in which the electronics technology that is driving many of the dramatic changes today will continue to develop. Powerful multimedia computing devices will become commonplace, and they will not be isolated. Computers worldwide will be linked by an information superhighway. In many ways, the planet will have developed a brain and nervous system. It seems certain that this will change the ways that we work, play, and learn.

EDUCATION AND SCHOOLING IN THE FUTURE

How will these predicted changes affect education and schooling in the future? This is the hardest thing of all to predict; our crystal ball is rapidly fading to black! The difficulty lies in the fact that education is a complex social, cultural, and political phenomenon. While it is relatively simple to predict that present technological trends will one day result in a computer that is capable of interacting with humans via speech, it is far less certain how, if at all, such a development may impact the educational enterprise. However, with trepidation, we will forge ahead.

Public education in the United States has been a tremendous success. Yet despite this success—or perhaps because of it—the history of education and schooling shows remarkable resistance to change. If you ever saw a picture of a 19th-century classroom, you probably noticed a teacher in the front of the room, students with books at neat rows of benches and work tables, and a potbellied stove in the corner. Except for the use of individual desks and radiators, not a lot has changed in present-day classrooms. Classrooms today still look like and to a large extent function as they did over 100 years ago. Even the summer vacation common to most school calendars is a vestige of a bygone era when children were needed during the summer to work on the family farm. Do schools today prepare students for the information age that is upon us?

Over the years, many educational innovations with promises of dramatic change have come and gone. Instructional television is certainly a case in point. During the 1950s, advocates of instructional television envisioned a radical change in education and schooling as a result of this innovation. Although instructional television didn't disappear, it never lived up to the expectations created by early advocates. Today some people think that the computer and its allied technologies represent a similar "flash in the pan" for schools. Critics charge that despite investments of huge sums of money, computers have not delivered the educational improvements that were expected. Perhaps, say some, computers will simply fade into a minor role in the classroom, as did instructional television. Education and schooling will continue on unaffected. This is one extreme position.

Yet it would be foolish to deny that dramatic changes are taking place in society. The information age is here now. Computers have brought about significant changes in the workplace, and they are becoming more common in homes every day. The beginnings of media convergence are here, and there is no denying that major corporations are investing significant sums of money in preparing for the expected information superhighway. Major changes *are* occurring!

Lewis Perelman, the author of the controversial book *School's Out*, makes a strong case for educational transformation. He suggests that schools and education today are already obsolete and that the only way to proceed is to scrap the current system altogether. He argues that with computers, knowledge acquisition and storage is no longer simply a human process. Whereas learning was once thought of as something that happens only in school, now it occurs everywhere, and it is a lifelong process. Further, with the growth of the information superhighway, learning is something that can happen anytime and anywhere. To put it simply, according to Perelman, schools are no longer needed, and, to make matters worse, they are getting in the way of the real changes that are needed. This is another extreme position.

So it seems that we have two possibilities before us for education and schooling in the future. On the one hand, perhaps the status quo will continue; nothing will change. On the other hand, changes may be so dramatic that they completely alter what we think of as education and schooling today. What will happen?

While either of the extremes described here might come to pass, we envision a more moderate course. It is clear that learning is already developing into a life-long commitment. The days when a person could expect to get a high school diploma, go to work for the local company, and retire 45 years later without ever having cracked a book again are long gone. It is also clear that the tools are here now, or will be here soon, to free learning from the confines of the school building. Soon the world's knowledge may be traveling into every household via a thin fiber-optic cable or through the airways. Will this mark the demise of schooling and education as we have known it? While it could, the social and political ramifications of such an eventuality would be considerable. Alternatively, this may provide the impetus needed to truly change schools to become centers of lifelong learning for the information age.

We envision a future between the two extremes. We envision a future where teachers and learners embrace and integrate instructional technology and use it to improve the teaching and learning processes. To be sure, this will mean that there must be some significant changes in the educational process. Here are some of the things we see as possible outcomes of this process of change:

- Multimedia learning resources, available via information networks, will proliferate and become a central feature of education.

- Teachers will change their role from "the sage on the stage" to the "guide on the side." Instead of conveying information, they will help learners make use of the new information tools to find, analyze, and synthesize information; to solve problems; to think creatively; and to construct their own understandings.

- Education will become a lifelong process, one that is important and accessible to all, and schools will become centers of learning—not just for children but for all members of the community.

- The boundaries separating schools from each other and from the community will blur or disappear. Using distance learning technologies, students may learn from teachers at other locations and collaborate with students at other locations. Teachers will learn alongside students. Students will learn from other students or from members of the community. Communities themselves will change as technology enables collaboration over distances.

- The artificial divisions of grade levels will disappear. Education will focus on mastery of appropriate learning outcomes and the uses of authentic means of assessment. Students will be judged by their ability to find and use information to solve genuine problems.

This is a future that's not just about instructional technology. Education and schooling are bigger than that. However, without instructional technology, it will be very hard for us to get where we need to go. We see a future that is *enabled* by instructional technology.

INTEGRATING TECHNOLOGY
One Teacher Looks to the Future

As we approached the end of this chapter (and this text), we wondered how we should wrap up our story about Ms. Moreno. Certainly, her story is not finished. As we mentioned many times throughout this book, Janette's teaching, and thus her story, continues to evolve. Since this chapter is about the future of instructional technology, we thought it might be fitting if Janette shared her personal vision for the future of instructional technology. We didn't want to ask her to write about the technical advances she might envision; we hope we have already done that. Rather, on a more personal note, we hoped Janette might share her vision for her own classroom and her future students. Here is what she wrote in response to our request:

"I have wonderful ideas for my future students. Some, I am sure, are just dreams, but dreaming is where the rest of this story began! So, why not dream? You know, I used to dream about all the wonderful things I would teach my students when I found time, or when they were ready to learn it, or when I had more resources, and so on and so forth. I finally realized that I'll never be able to teach my students everything they need to know! We just can't keep up with all the information that's out there anymore. But I *can* help my students become good learners—expert learners, even—by showing them all the possible ways they can learn and by exciting them about learning. And that's where technology comes in. It's so easy now for students to explore what's interesting, relevant, and meaningful to them and to do so in exciting and challenging ways. If I can excite my students about learning now, they won't be thinking about the day they can stop! They won't *want* to stop learning.

"Another dream that's already coming true is being able to include every student in every learning activity I design. In the past, I've been frustrated when a few students in the school couldn't be included in certain activities and learning projects because of handicaps, language differences, or disabilities. But technology is starting to eliminate those differences. Computers with touch screens, specialized keyboards, speech synthesizers, voice recognizers, and other amazing capabilities are reaching more and more students. It's becoming possible to give all students opportunities to work at their own pace on problems that have relevance in their own lives.

"I also look forward to accessing an ever-expanding number of information resources across the world. I've only started using distance education technologies to introduce my students to other students, teachers, researchers, and community leaders. I'm excited about increasing the frequency and range of these interactive exchanges even more. I'm especially hopeful that these interchanges will help expand my students' understanding of both the amazing similarities and the wonderful differences between themselves and others.

"I used to worry that all this powerful technology would eventually just replace me, but I really don't think that anymore. My role is changing, certainly, but it's become more meaningful rather than more mundane or rote. I actually feel like I have *more* opportunities to be a good teacher, as well as an amazing range of choices for reaching students. Technology has definitely increased the potential I have for helping all my students!

"Isn't it amazing how quickly we become comfortable with newfangled tools and devices? I remember how scared I was even turning the computer on, but now I can't imagine being without one. It's my all-purpose information tool—worldwide resources at my fingertips! And kids today hardly blink an eye at all these capabilities. They seem as natural to them as the telephone was to me and videotape and CD players are to you.

Janette Moreno reflects on the future of instructional technology and its role in education.

"It's exciting dreaming about our future classrooms and the growing possibilities for our future students. What do you think it will be like for you and your students in the next 10 or 20 years? Whatever changes you foresee, be sure you're a part of them. Don't be afraid to jump in!"

SUMMARY

In this chapter we examined the past, present, and future of instructional technology. The modern era of instructional design and media began near the start of the 20th century with the work of pioneers such as Edward Thorndike and with the school museum movement. Because of the need for effective and efficient training of military personnel during World War II, the fields received a major boost. Following the war, instructional design and media became established fields of study. Instructional computing began with early computer-assisted instruction experiments on mainframe computers, such as the PLATO and TICCIT projects. Computers proliferated in education following the development of the personal computer in the late 1970s.

Today, instructional design, instructional media, and instructional computing are all established disciplines and are converging through the capabilities of the computer. Media are becoming digital, and the computer offers new capabilities for planning, implementing, and evaluating instruction. Trends that we see today are likely to continue in the future. There will be even greater convergence of instructional design, media, and computing. Computer networking will expand, and computer capabilities will grow. While education and schooling may ignore these innovations or become totally transformed by them, we see a middle course that would allow instructional technology to empower teachers and learners.

REFLECTIVE QUESTIONS AND ACTIVITIES

1. Visit a museum or read a book that includes displays, photographs, or other information about schools and classrooms of the past. For contrast, visit a classroom today. What similarities do you see between past classrooms and those of today? What differences do you see?

2. What is the value of studying the history of the instructional technology field?

3. What evidence do you see for a convergence of instructional design, instructional media, and instructional computing today?

4. How do you think computers will be different in 5 years? 10 years? 50 years?

5. Create a scenario for a day in the life of a restructured school in the future. What will it be like? How will education and schooling be different in an ideal future?

6. Write to one of the professional organizations listed in Table 14.1 and request information about the organization and its membership.

7. Think about your own future and instructional technology. What resources can support your personal growth and development?

INTEGRATION AND SYNTHESIS

This chapter's focus was on the past, present, and future of instructional technology. This information is intended to focus on the field at large—where it has been and where it is going—as a way of wrapping up the information from this entire text. The past shows us that instructional technology developed out of several interrelated but initially separate fields of study. Today we see evidence that the fields are converging. In addition, they are changing and evolving in other ways. We expect current trends to continue in the future. Instructional design and media will converge further in the powerful new tool of the computer. Changes to the enterprise of education and schooling are being wrought by this technology as well as by increased use of multimedia and distance education, an emphasis on lifelong learning, and changes in our approaches to teaching and learning.

SUGGESTED READINGS

Perelman, L. J. (1992). *School's out.* New York: Avon Books.
Saettler, P. (1990). *The evolution of American educational technology.* Englewood, CO: Libraries Unlimited.

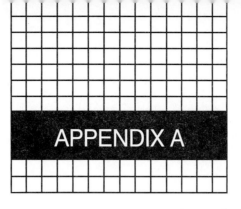

Checklist for Evaluating Instruction

Modify the questions asked in the first column based on whether the evaluation is being done before, during, or after the implementation of the instruction. Be as specific as possible about the sources of the information and any suggested revisions.

Course: _____

Lesson: _____   **Circle one:**   Before   During   After

Evaluation Criteria	Yes	No	Sources and Suggested Revisions
(Will, Are, Did) the students master their learning objectives?			
(Are, Were) students able to apply what they learned?			
(Is, Was) the information accurate, complete, and up to date?			
(Are, Were) the instructional approaches useful?			
(Are, Were) the instructional media useful?			
(Are, Were) the learning activities clear and congruent with the learning goals?			
(Will, Did) the sequence of the activities lead students to the learning goals?			
(Are, Were) the assessments valid?			
(Are, Were) the costs (both initial and continuing) within reason?			
(Is, Was) the amount of time required within reason?			
(Are, Were) the needed supplies, facilities, and equipment within reason?			
(Will, Are, Did) the students' interest and motivation remain high?			

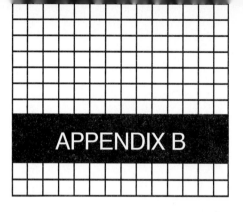

Preview Forms for the Review of Instructional Materials

Preview Form: Real Objects and Models		

Title/Description_____ Producer_____

Source_____ Date_____ Cost_____

Criteria   *Comments*

Relevance to objectives

Likely to arouse/maintain interest

Sturdy, stable, not easily broken

Ease of use, manipulable

Ease of storage

   Not dangerous (real objects)

   Shelf life (real objects)

Degree of realism (models)

Accuracy (models)

Preview Form: Text

Title_____ Producer_____

Source_____ Date_____ Cost_____

Criteria   *Comments*

Photographs, diagrams, drawings

Use of color, layout

Relevance to course objectives

Up to date, accurate (copyright date)

Free of objectionable bias

Reading level (easy to read)

Likely to stimulate/maintain student interest

Table of contents, glossary, index

Special features

Adjunct materials (student manual, teacher's guide)

Organization, scope, and sequence

Chapter summaries/reviews

Study questions

References (complete and up to date)

Preview Form: Visuals

Title _____ Producer _____

Source _____ Date _____ Cost _____

Criteria   *Comments*

Relevance to objectives

Authenticity/accuracy of visual

Likely to arouse/maintain interest

Likely to be comprehended clearly

Technical quality (durability)

Legibility for use (size and clarity)

Simplicity (clear, unified design)

Appropriate use of color

Appropriateness of accompanying verbal information

Timeliness (avoids out-of-date elements, such as dress)

Preview Form: Overhead Transparencies

Title _____   Producer _____

Source _____   Date _____   Cost _____

Criteria   *Comments*

Relevance to objectives

Accuracy of information

Likely to arouse/maintain interest

Likely to be comprehended clearly

Technical quality

Promotes participation/involvement

Evidence of effectiveness (e.g., field-test results)

Free from objectionable bias

Provisions for discussion/follow-up

Preview Form: Slides and Filmstrips

Title _____   Producer_____

Source _____   Date_____   Cost_____

Length _____   Frames _____   Minutes _____

Criteria   *Comments*

Relevance to objectives

Accuracy of information

Likely to arouse/maintain interest

Likely to be comprehended clearly

Technical quality

Promotes participation/involvement

Evidence of effectiveness (e.g., field-test results)

Free from objectionable bias

Provisions for discussion/follow-up

Preview Form: Audio

Title _____ Producer_____

Source _____ Date_____ Cost_____

Format _____ Length _____ Minutes _____

Criteria   *Comments*

Relevance to objectives

Accuracy of information

Likely to arouse/maintain interest

Technical quality

Promotes participation/involvement

Evidence of effectiveness (e.g., field-test results)

Free from objectionable bias

Pacing appropriate for audience

Clarity of organization

Appropriate vocabulary level

Preview Form: Video and Film

Title _____   Producer _____

Source _____   Date _____   Cost _____

Format _____   Length _____   Minutes _____

Criteria   *Comments*

Relevance to objectives

Accuracy of information

Likely to arouse/maintain interest

Technical quality

Promotes participation/involvement

Evidence of effectiveness (e.g., field-test results)

Free from objectionable bias

Pacing appropriate for audience

Use of cognitive learning aids (e.g., overview,
    cues, summary)

Preview Form: Computer Software

Title _____   Producer _____

Source _____   Date _____   Cost _____

Format _____   Length _____   Minutes _____

Criteria   *Comments*

Relevance to objectives

Accuracy of information

Likely to arouse/maintain interest

Ease of use

Appropriate color, sound, graphics

Frequent, relevant practice (active participation)

Feedback provides remedial branches

Free of technical flaws (e.g., dead ends, infinite loops)

Clear, complete documentation

Evidence of effectiveness (e.g., field-test results)

Preview Form: Multimedia

Title _____   Producer _____

Source _____   Date _____   Cost _____

Format _____   Length _____   Minutes _____

Equipment Required _____

Criteria   *Comments*

Relevance to objectives

Accuracy of information

Likely to arouse/maintain interest

Ease of use

Level of interactivity

Appropriate use of color, graphics, sound

Appropriate use of individual media

Coordination of visuals, sound, text

Technical quality

Evidence of effectiveness

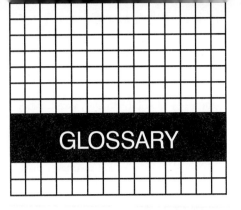

GLOSSARY

Algorithm   A series of steps needed to solve a particular problem or perform a particular task.

Analogizing   An instructional technique designed to facilitate learning by comparing a new concept with something that is more familiar or concrete. Analogizing includes the creation and use of similes, metaphors, and analogies.

Analogy   A statement that likens something new to something familiar. Analogies are typically used either to make abstract information more concrete or to organize complex information.

Antecedent   An event, object, or circumstance that prompts a behavior.

Application information   The part of the instructional plan that explains to students how information being learned will be useful as well as when and why it will be used. Helps students transfer what they learn to new situations.

Applications software   All software designed to perform a specific function for the user, such as processing text, performing calculations, and presenting content lessons.

Artificial intelligence (AI)   A branch of computer science concerned with the design of computers and software that are capable of responding in ways that mimic human thinking.

ASCII format   American Standard Code for Information Interchange; the standard way of representing text, which allows different computer brands to "talk" to one another. Sometimes referred to as plain text or unformatted text.

Assessment   An instructional event in which one determines what methods will be used to evaluate how well the students have mastered the intended lesson outcomes.

Attention   The process of selectively receiving information from the environment.

Audiographics   The use of audio teleconferencing accompanied by the transmission of still pictures and graphics via slow-scan video, fax, or an electronic graphics tablet.

Audio teleconferencing   A distance education technology that uses a speakerphone to extend a basic telephone call and permits instruction and interaction between individuals or groups at two or more locations.

Audio-tutorial instruction   A form of independent learning based on the mastery approach and characterized by the use of audiotapes to guide individual students through a series of learning activities.

Authoring systems   Computer programs that permit the development of interactive computer-based applications without a need for programming knowledge.

BASIC   Beginners' All-purpose Symbolic Instruction Code; one of the oldest computer languages that can be used with personal computers. A small, concise language that can be learned quickly.

Baud rate   The communication speed between a computer and a device (such as a modem), roughly equivalent to bits per second.

Behavior   A response made by an individual.

Bit   The smallest amount of information that the CPU can deal with; a single binary digit.

Bit-mapped graphics   Sometimes called paint or raster graphics, in which each pixel directly corresponds to a spot on the display screen. When scaled to larger sizes, this type of graphic looks jagged.

Block operations   The ability to manipulate blocks of text that have been selected in a document being word-processed. For example, a selected block can be deleted, moved to another location in the document, or copied and inserted somewhere else. In addition, formatting commands, such as changing to italicized type, can be applied to a selected block of text.

Bulletin board   A computer service designed as a public forum, allowing individuals to post messages for others to read.

Byte   A collection of eight bits, equivalent to one alphanumeric character.

CD   See **Compact disc.**

CD-ROM Compact disc—read-only memory. A CD used to store computer data. It can store approximately 600 megabytes of data.

Cell A single block in a spreadsheet grid, formed by the intersection of a row and a column.

Classroom observation A form of evaluation that involves having a knowledgeable person come into the classroom to watch a lesson in process, to comment on how well the materials and activities work, and to make suggestions for improvements.

Clip art Already-created graphics designed to be added to word-processing or desktop publishing documents or to computer-based instruction.

Cognitive domain The type of learning involving intellectual skills, such as assimilation of information or knowledge.

Communication "The process of creating a meaning between two or more people" (Tubbs & Moss, 1994, p. 6). Communication is said to occur when two or more individuals send messages to one another and receive messages from one another, using one or more methods or channels to carry the messages.

Compact disc (CD) A 4.72-inch-diameter disc on which a laser has digitally recorded information such as audio, video, or computer data.

Compiler A high-level computer language translator that translates entire computer programs into machine language before the program will operate. Computer languages that are commonly compiled include Pascal and C.

Composite video A video format commonly used by VCRs and other video equipment in which all of the video information is combined into one signal that is sent to the video monitor through a single cable.

Computer A machine that processes information, usually in the form of numeric data, according to a set of instructions.

Computer-assisted instruction (CAI) See **Computer-based instruction.**

Computer-assisted learning (CAL) See **Computer-based instruction.**

Computer-based instruction (CBI) The use of the computer in the delivery of instruction.

Computer conferencing An asynchronous communication medium in which two or more individuals exchange messages using personal computers that are connected via a network or telephone lines.

Computer gradebook A computer database program that can store and manipulate students' grades.

Computer-managed instruction (CMI) The use of the computer in the management of the instructional process, including applications such as student record keeping, performance assessment, and monitoring of students' progress.

Computer-mediated communication (CMC) The use of the computer as a device for mediating communication between teacher and students and among students, often over distances. Electronic mail and computer conferencing are two types of application software commonly used in CMC.

Computer program A set of instructions that tells the computer how to do something.

Computer system A collection of components that includes the computer and all of the devices used with the computer.

Concept map A graphical representation of interrelated concepts that can be used by students as a learning aid or by teachers as an aid in content organization.

Conditions A portion of the instructional outcome that indicates under what circumstances students are expected to perform.

Congruence The degree of match among the components of an instructional plan. Outcomes, content, and assessments must work together to create an effective plan.

Consequence An event, object, or circumstance that comes after a behavior and is attributable to the behavior.

Content information An instructional event that details the sequence of major ideas and outlines examples that will be used to illustrate each major idea.

Contingencies The environmental conditions that shape an individual's behavior.

Cooperative learning An instructional approach that involves small heterogeneous groups of students working toward a common academic goal or task. Its use promotes positive interdependence, individual accountability, collaborative/social skills, and group processing skills.

Copyright The legal rights to an original work produced in any tangible medium of expression, including written works, works of art, music, photographs, and computer software.

Corrective feedback Feedback that tells students specifically what they can do to correct their performance.

CPU The central processing unit, or brain, of the computer, which controls the functions of the rest of the system and performs all numeric calculations.

Criteria A portion of the instructional outcome that indicates the standards that define acceptable performance.

CRT Television-like display screen that uses a cathode ray tube.

Cursor A highlighted position indicator used on the computer monitor screen.

Cursor control The use of directional movement keys or a mouse to position the cursor anywhere within a document for the purposes of editing.

Cycle of continuous improvement The continuous evaluation of instruction—before, during, and after implementation—which leads to continual revision and modification in order to increase student learning.

Database An organized collection of information, often stored on computer.

Database management system (DBMS)   Software that enables the user to enter, edit, store, retrieve, sort, and search through computer databases.

Datafile   The collection of all of the related records in a database.

Deletion   The ability to remove text from a document being word-processed.

Demonstration   An instructional approach that involves showing how to do a task as well as describing why, when, and where it is done. Provides a real or lifelike example of the skill or procedure to be learned.

Desktop publishing (DTP)   Computer application software that gives users a high degree of control over the composition and layout of material on a printed page, including both text and graphics.

Digitizer   A device that allows audio or still or motion video to be captured in a form that the computer can use.

Direct observation   A form of evaluation that involves watching students as they work through some part(s) of the lesson.

Discovery   An instructional approach that uses an inductive, or inquiry, method to encourage students to find "answers" for themselves through the use of trial-and-error problem-solving strategies.

Discussion   A dynamic instructional approach in which individuals talk together, share information, and work cooperatively toward a solution or consensus. This approach encourages classroom rapport and actively involves students in learning.

Distance education   An organized instructional program in which the teacher and learners are physically separated by time or by geography.

Distractors   The incorrect or less appropriate alternative answers for a given multiple-choice question. Also called **foils.**

Dot matrix printer   A low-cost, versatile printer in which a set of tiny pins strikes the page to form the image of each letter out of a matrix of dots.

Drill and practice   A series of practice exercises designed to increase fluency in a new skill or to refresh an existing one. Use of this approach assumes that learners have previously received some instruction on the concept, principle, or procedure that is to be practiced.

Electronic mail (e-mail)   A computer communication application that allows private messages to be sent from individuals to other individuals or groups.

Electronic spreadsheet   A general-purpose computer calculating tool based on the paper worksheet used by accountants.

Encoding   The process of translating information into some meaningful form that can be remembered.

Ergonomics   The study of the physical interaction of machines and humans.

Evaluation   The third phase in the Plan, Implement, Evaluate model. Focus is on assessment techniques used to determine the level of learning achieved by learners and/or the effectiveness of the instructional materials.

Evaluation of instruction   A systematic method used to gather information to determine the value of the instruction in order to make a decision about its use (Worthen & Sanders, 1987).

Event-driven   Computer programs, such as hypermedia software, that respond to events in the environment; for example, when the user clicks on a button, a mouse action event occurs.

Feedback   Information provided to students regarding how well they are doing during practice.

Field   Each individual category of information that is recorded in a database.

File server   A computer dedicated to managing a computer network and providing resources to other computers on the network (the clients). The file server is usually faster and has larger storage capabilities than the client machines.

Filter   Anything that distorts information as it is sent and received. Distortion can occur in the sender in the form of inadequate vocabulary, biases, and so on, and can occur in the receiver in the form of fatigue, daydreaming, limited knowledge, and so on.

Flat filer   A type of DBMS that works with a single datafile at a time.

Floppy disk/diskette   A magnetic storage medium for computer data that allows users to randomly access information.

Focusing question   A question typically used at the beginning of a lesson to direct students' attention to particularly important aspects of the new information.

Foils   See **Distractors.**

Font   The appearance of the text itself, which can be altered through the selection of various typefaces and sizes of type. These include many typefaces common to the printing field, such as Times, Helvetica, Geneva, and Courier.

Formative evaluation   A form of assessment that indicates whether or not students have learned that which is needed before progressing to the next portion of the instruction.

Formula   A mathematical expression that directs an electronic spreadsheet to perform various kinds of calculations on the numbers entered in it.

Frame   A small portion of information presented to the learner, followed by a question or problem that requires a learner response, followed by feedback based on the response.

ftp (file transfer protocol)   The standard method for sending or retrieving electronic files on the Internet.

Gigabyte   Approximately a billion bytes, or 1,000 megabytes.

Gopher   Software, invented at the University of Minnesota, for accessing information resources on the Internet. Gopher software relies on a client-server model and a hierarchical menu system to permit users to easily "go for" information located on many computers throughout the world.

Grammar checker Ancillary feature of word processors that identifies a wide range of grammatical and format errors such as improper capitalization, lack of subject-verb agreement, split infinitives, and so on.

Graphic Any pictorial representation of information in the computer, such as charts, graphs, animated figures, or photolike reproductions.

Graphical user interface (GUI) The use of graphical symbols instead of text commands to control common computer functions such as copying programs and disks.

Graphics tablet A computer input device that permits the development of graphic images by translating drawing on the tablet into on-screen images.

Hard copy A printed copy of computer output.

Hard disk A large-capacity magnetic storage medium for computer data. Also called a fixed disk, it remains sealed within the case of most computers to protect it from dust, smoke, and other contaminants.

Hardware The physical components of the computer system.

Heuristic A rule of thumb or flexible guideline that can be adapted to fit each instructional situation.

High-level language A computer language that contains instructions that resemble natural language and does not require knowledge of the inner workings of the computer.

Highlighting Various techniques designed to direct attention to certain aspects of information, including the use of **bold,** underlined, or *italicized* print; color, labels, and arrows for pictorial information; and speaking more loudly or more slowly to highlight verbal information.

Hypermedia Extends the notion of hypertext to other media besides text. In a hypermedia system, nodes of information may contain graphics, animation, video, and audio as well as text.

Hypertext An associational information-processing system in the text domain. In a hypertext system, text information is stored in nodes, and nodes are interconnected to other nodes of related information.

Icon A small pictorial or graphical representation of a computer hardware function or component, or a computer software program, commonly associated with a graphical user interface.

Implementation The second phase of the Plan, Implement, Evaluate model. Focus is on the use of instructional materials and activities designed to help students achieve the outcomes specified in the instructional plan.

Individualized education program (IEP) An instructional plan for an individual student (usually one with special needs) that describes the student's current level of proficiency and also establishes short- and long-term goals for future focus. An IEP is typically developed through a conference with the student's teachers and parents and other appropriate individuals.

Individualized instruction Instruction in which the content, pacing, instructional sequence, and often media and methods are determined by an individual student's learning needs, abilities, and attitudes.

Ink-jet printer A type of printer that forms letters on the page by shooting tiny electrically charged droplets of ink.

Input Information entered into the computer for processing.

Input device The hardware that is used to pass information into the computer.

Insertion The ability to add text to a document being word-processed.

Instruction The selection and arrangement of information, activities, approaches, and media to help students meet predetermined learning goals.

Instructional appeal The interest, or value, that instructional materials or activities have for the learner.

Instructional approaches The procedures, or methods, of instruction that are selected to help students achieve the stated outcomes or to understand the content or message of the instruction (e.g., presentation, simulation, drill and practice, cooperative learning).

Instructional computing The use of the computer in the design, development, delivery, and evaluation of instruction.

Instructional design "The systematic process of translating principles of learning and instruction into plans for instructional materials and activities" (Smith & Ragan, 1993, p. 2).

Instructional effectiveness A measure of the difference between what learners know before and after instruction; for example, Posttest – Pretest = Achievement.

Instructional efficiency A measure of how much learners achieve per unit of time or dollar spent; for example, (Posttest – Pretest) ÷ Time, or (Posttest – Pretest) ÷ Cost.

Instructional event What is done during a lesson to help students learn.

Instructional games An instructional approach that provides an appealing environment in which learners invest effort to follow prescribed rules in order to attain a challenging goal.

Instructional materials The specific items used in a lesson and delivered through various media formats, such as video, audio, print, and so on.

Instructional media Channels of communication that carry messages with an instructional purpose; the different ways and means by which information can be delivered to a learner.

Instructional outcomes What students should be able to do following their interaction with instructional materials or activities; also includes what can be inferred about students' learning when the learning is of a more cognitive and less observable nature.

Instructional plan   A blueprint for instructional lessons based on analyses of the learners, the context, and the task to be learned. Planning involves "the process of deciding what methods of instruction are best for bringing about desired changes in student knowledge and skills for a specific course content and a specific student population" (Reigeluth, 1983, p. 7). The instructional plan also includes the selection of appropriate media.

Instructional program   The arrangement and presentation of learning contingencies in the form of a series of frames.

Instructional technology   "Applying scientific knowledge about human learning to the practical tasks of teaching and learning" (Heinich et al., 1993, p. 16).

Integrated learning system (ILS)   Combines sophisticated computer-managed instruction (CMI) and computer-assisted instruction (CAI) into a single delivery system to provide a cycle of instruction, assessment, and prescription.

Intelligent tutoring system   Combines detailed information about a subject area and common student mistakes with a model of student performance to diagnose a given student's level of understanding. Also provides instruction designed to meet that student's individual needs. Sometimes called intelligent computer-assisted instruction (ICAI).

Interactive multimedia   Multimedia that allows user interactions so that the user can determine the direction of the program or presentation.

Interactive videodisc   A video playback system involving computer control of a videodisc player, where video is displayed in response to user choices.

Interface   An electronic go-between by which the computer communicates with a peripheral device.

Interference   Distortion of a message as it passes from the sender to the receiver; including such things as distracting noises or harsh lighting.

Internal memory   Information stored inside the computer. The CPU in a personal computer retrieves and deposits information in the computer's internal memory. Also called main memory.

Internet   A network of computer networks that links computers worldwide.

Interpreter   A high-level computer language translator that translates computer programs into machine language as the program is operating. Computer languages that are often interpreted include Logo and BASIC.

Intrinsic motivation   The desire to invest effort in a task because participation in the task is itself rewarding, that is, wanting to do something (e.g., a hobby) for its own sake.

Introduction   An instructional event that serves three instructional purposes: providing a motivational hook, stating the purpose, and putting the lesson into a context of previous and future lessons.

I/O device   Any computer input or output device.

Keyboard   The most common input device; resembles the key layout of a typewriter.

Kilobyte   Approximately 1,000 bytes.

Label   Text used to name parts of an electronic spreadsheet.

Laser printer   A printer that combines laser and photocopying technology to produce very high quality output, comparable to that produced in typesetting. Laser printers can produce text as well as high-quality graphics and can achieve print densities of 300 to 600 dots per inch for very finely detailed images.

LCD screen   Liquid crystal display screens are commonly used in laptop computers and also in conjunction with display panels and projectors as large-group display devices for computer output.

Learning   "Learning is an enduring change in behavior, or in the capacity to behave in a given fashion, which results from practice or other forms of experience" (Shuell, 1986, p. 412). To change (or have the capacity to change) one's level of ability or knowledge.

Learning environment   The setting or physical surroundings in which learning takes place, including the classroom, science or computer laboratory, gymnasium, playground, and so on.

Learning theory   A set of related principles explaining changes in human performance or performance potential in terms of the causes of those changes.

Letter-quality printer   Any printer capable of typewriter-like output.

Liquid crystal display (LCD)   See **LCD screen.**

Listserver   Also called a mail server, this is the computer or software that operates an e-mail discussion list on the Internet. Interested individuals subscribe to the list and subsequently receive all e-mail that is sent to the listserver.

Local-area network (LAN)   A computer network covering a limited geographical area, such as a single building or even a single room within a building.

Logo   A computer language developed by Seymour Papert and based on the learning theories of Jean Piaget; it is widely used in schools, particularly at the elementary level.

Low-level language   A computer language closely related to the workings of a particular computer's CPU. More difficult to understand and use than high-level language.

Machine language   The binary code that controls the computer at the level of its circuits.

Macro   A shortcut to encoding a series of actions in a computer program. Provides the means to perform a number of separate steps through a single command.

Mainframe computer   The largest and most powerful class of computers; these have very large storage capacities and very fast processing speeds, and they are often used to support large numbers of users simultaneously.

Mass storage   Input/output devices that provide for storage and retrieval of programs and other types of data that can be stored over a long period of time. Also referred to as external or auxiliary memory.

Mastery learning   An instructional technique that involves clear specification of a series of learning objectives through which students progress at their own pace. Criteria for specific levels of mastery are preestablished.

Medium   A channel of communication. Derived from the Latin word meaning "between," the term refers to that which carries information between a source and a receiver. Examples include slides, videotapes, diagrams, printed materials, and computers.

Megabyte   Approximately a million bytes, or 1,000 kilobytes.

Microprocessor   A single silicon chip that contains all of the CPU circuits for a computer system.

Minicomputer   A member of the second class of computers; features intermediate storage capacities and processing speeds and simultaneous use by several dozen users.

Mnemonic   Any practical device used to make information easier to remember, including rhymes, acronyms, and acrostics.

Modem   A combination input and output device that allows a computer to communicate with another computer over telephone lines. A modem (short for modulator-demodulator) converts digital computer information into sound (and vice versa) for transmission over telephone lines.

Monitor   A video or computer display device. The most common output device on personal computers.

Motivation   An internal state that leads people to choose to work toward certain goals and experiences. Defines what people will do rather than what they can do (Keller, 1983).

Mouse   A pointing device used to select and move information on the computer display screen. When the mouse is moved along a flat surface such as a desktop, an arrow moves across the display screen in the same direction. The mouse typically has one to three buttons that may be used for selecting or entering information.

Multimedia   Sequential or simultaneous use of a variety of media formats in a single presentation or program. Today this term conveys the notion of a system in which various media (e.g., text, graphics, video, and audio) are integrated into a single delivery system under computer control.

One-computer classroom   Classroom equipped with a single computer.

OOPS   Object-oriented programming systems where each thing that one sees on the computer screen is treated as an object, and each object can have a programming code associated with it.

Operating system   The master control program for a computer system.

Outcome   A statement of what learners will be expected to do when they have completed a specified course of instruction, stated in terms of observable performances.

Output   Information that comes out of the computer.

Output device   The hardware that receives and displays information coming from the computer.

Peer review   A form of evaluation that involves asking a colleague to examine all or part of an instructional lesson and make suggestions for improvement.

Peer tutoring   Teaching technique in which students teach one another, possibly from the same class, but often involving cross-age groupings.

Performance   A portion of the instructional outcome that indicates what students will do to demonstrate that they have learned.

Peripheral   Any of various devices that connect to the computer, including input devices, output devices, and mass storage devices.

Personal computer   Members of the third class of computers; these are the smallest, least powerful, and least expensive, intended for use by individuals.

Personalized system of instruction (PSI)   A system for managing individualized instruction, also known as the Keller plan. PSI arranges a variety of instructional materials (e.g., programmed texts, video- and audiotapes, computer software) into sequential order and expects students to master one unit before going on to the next.

PhotoCD   A CD format developed by Kodak that can store high-quality images made from 35-millimeter photographic negatives or slides.

Pixel   A single dot, or picture element, on the computer screen.

Planning   The first phase of the Plan, Implement, Evaluate model. Focus is on the design of instructional materials based on the learners, content, and context.

Portfolio   "A purposeful collection of student work that tells the story of the student's efforts, progress, or achievement" (Arter & Spandel, 1992, p. 36).

Practice   An instructional event that asks students to demonstrate the performance called for in the outcomes under the same conditions indicated in the outcomes. Can serve a diagnostic function, indicating to the teacher whether students are ready to move on or if they need more practice.

Prerequisites   The knowledge and skills students should have at the beginning of a lesson.

Presentation   An instructional approach involving a one-way communication controlled by a source that relates, dramatizes, or otherwise disseminates information to learners, and which includes no immediate response from, or interaction with, the learner (e.g., a lecture or speech).

Presentation software   Computer software designed for the production and display of computer text and images, intended to replace the functions typically associated with the slide projector and overhead projector.

Pretest   Preinstructional evaluation of students' knowledge and/or skills to determine students' level of performance before instruction.

Preview A form of evaluation that involves reading, viewing, and/or working through specific instructional materials prior to using them (Heinich et al., 1996).

Printer A device that provides printed output from the computer.

Printer driver Software that ensures that the word processor's formatting commands are correctly translated into printer actions. Most word processors provide a number of different printer drivers to support different models of printers.

Problem solving An instructional approach in which learners use previously mastered skills to reach resolution of challenging problems. Based upon the scientific method of inquiry, it typically involves the following five steps: (1) defining the problem and all major components, (2) formulating hypotheses, (3) collecting and analyzing data, (4) deriving conclusions/solutions, and (5) verifying conclusions/solutions.

Problem-solving software Computer applications designed to foster students' higher-order thinking skills, such as logical thinking, reasoning, pattern recognition, and use of strategies.

Programmed instruction A form of independent learning based on the mastery approach and characterized by a sequence of small segments of instruction and frequent opportunities for learner interaction.

Programming The process of creating a computer program.

Programming language A set of instructions that can be assembled, according to particular rules and syntax, to create a working computer program.

Questioning A diagnostic tool used throughout a lesson to check students' understanding of the content. Can be used in conjunction with other instructional events.

RAM Random-access memory—the computer's working memory. In a personal computer, RAM provides a temporary work space that allows you to change its contents, as needed, to perform different tasks. Common RAM is volatile, which means that its contents disappear as soon as the power is turned off (or otherwise interrupted).

Record A collection of related fields that is treated as a logical unit in a database.

Reinforcing feedback Feedback used to recognize good performance and encourage continued effort from students. Takes the form of verbal praise or a pat on the back.

Relational database A type of computer database that permits the interrelation of information across more than one datafile.

Reliability "The degree to which a test instrument consistently measures the same group's knowledge level of the same instruction when taking the test over again" (Gentry, 1994, p. 383).

Repurposing Creating a computer program to control a videodisc so that the content can be used in ways other than originally intended.

Retrieval The process of identifying and recalling information for a particular purpose.

RGB A system for generating computer screen output that uses three separate signals to control display of the three primary colors (red, green, blue) in the monitor.

ROM Read-only memory—the permanent memory that is built into the computer at the factory, referred to as "read only" because the computer can read the information that is stored there but cannot change that stored information. ROM contains the basic instructions the computer needs to operate.

Scanner Uses technology similar to a photocopying machine to take an image from a printed page and convert it into a form the computer can manipulate.

Search and replace A common feature of word processors that allows the user to locate the occurrence of any word or phrase within a document and substitute something else.

Server See **File server.**

Simulation An instructional approach involving a scaled-down approximation of a real-life situation that allows realistic practice without the expense or risks otherwise involved. Similar to problem solving, simulations often include case studies and/or role plays.

Software The programs or instructions that tell the computer what to do.

Spelling checker A common ancillary feature of word processors that searches through a document and reports any instances of text that do not match a built-in dictionary.

Spreadsheet See **Electronic spreadsheet.**

Stem The part of a multiple-choice assessment instrument that sets forth the problem that will be "answered" by one option from a list of alternatives.

Structured programming Uses the top-down approach as one element of an overall strategy of computer programming. This type of programming is designed to result in organized, easy-to-read, and correct programs. It relies on modular program design, a limited set of program constructs, and careful documentation of the program.

Student tryout A "test run" of an instructional activity, approach, media, or materials with a small group of students before using it on a large scale (Mager, 1988).

Summative evaluation Assessment that occurs after instruction and measures what students have learned.

Supercomputers The most powerful and fastest of the mainframe computers.

Syntax Rules for using computer languages.

System A set of parts that depend on one another and work together toward a common goal.

Systems of instruction Complex approaches to individualized instruction, including programmed instruction, audio-tutorial instruction, and the personalized system of instruction.

Systems software The basic operating software that tells the computer how to perform its fundamental functions.

Technology   "The systematic application of scientific or other organized knowledge to practical tasks" (Galbraith, 1967, p. 12). Technology performs a bridging function between research and theory on one side and professional practice on the other.

Technology coordinator   A specialist and resource person who handles computers and related technologies for a school building or district.

Telnet   The standard method for directly connecting to and using the resources of a remote computer on the Internet.

Template   A spreadsheet "shell" with all of the appropriate labels and formulas in place but without the data.

Terminal emulation   Computer software that allows personal computers to communicate as if they were mainframe computer terminals.

Test generator   A computer program used to create assessment instruments.

Text justification   The positioning of text in a word-processed document. This includes text that is centered, aligned with respect to the right margin (right justified), and aligned with respect to the left margin (left justified). Left justified, the most common, aligns text flush with the left margin, leaving a "ragged" right margin.

Text selection   The ability to choose portions of a document that is being word-processed for subsequent editing through the use of cursor movement keys or the mouse. Selection is sometimes called highlighting because selected text is usually denoted through the use of highlighting or special colors.

Theory   A set of related principles explaining observed events/relationships. Theories typically make predictions in the form of "If . . ., then . . . " statements that can be tested.

Top-down approach   An approach to problem solving and computer programming that begins by outlining the basic solution at a fairly high level of abstraction and then breaks that outline down into its major parts, which are further broken down until they can be coded.

Transfer   The use of prior knowledge in new situations or as it applies to new problems.

Triangulation   The process of obtaining information from more than one technique or source in order to strengthen individual findings.

Tutorial   An instructional approach in which a tutor—in the form of a person, computer, or special print materials—presents the content, poses a question or problem, requests learner response, analyzes the response, supplies appropriate feedback, and provides practice until the learner demonstrates a predetermined level of competency.

Two-way interactive video   A distance education technology in which sending and receiving sites are equipped with cameras, microphones, and video monitors and are linked via some means of transmission (e.g., satellite, microwave, cable, fiber-optic cable).

Type style   The ability to apply different features to any word-processing font, including **boldface,** *italics,* underline, and others.

Undo   A software feature that allows the user to recover from an error; for example, if you select and delete the wrong block of text, the undo command allows you take back the action.

Validity   The authenticity of a measurement instrument; its ability to measure whatever it is intended to assess.

Variable   A label used in a programming language to denote a storage area in the computer's memory. Used by the computer to keep track of information that changes.

Vector graphics   Also called draw graphics, in which the computer "remembers" the steps involved in creating a particular graphic image on the screen, independent of a particular screen location or the graphic's size.

Video   The display of recorded pictures on a television-like screen. Includes videotapes, videodiscs, and CDs.

Video digitizer   An add-on device for the computer that takes video from standard video sources and captures a frame of that video as a computer graphic or motion video.

Videodisc   A video storage medium composed of recorded images and sound similar to the CD. Depending on format, a videodisc can hold up to 30–60 minutes of motion video images, up to 54,000 still images, or a combination of motion and still images. As with the CD, the videodisc can be indexed for rapid location of any part of the material.

Videotape   A video storage medium in which video images and sound are recorded on magnetic tape. Popular sizes include one-inch commercial tape, three-quarter-inch U-matic, half-inch VHS or S-VHS, and 8-millimeter.

Video teleconferencing   A distance education technology that combines one-way video with two-way audio by means of a telephone connection between the originating video location and the receiving sites.

Virtual reality (VR)   A computer interface that simulates an interactive environment that appears to the observer as another reality. A VR system uses special hardware and software to project a three-dimensional visual representation of an environment and responds to the user's motion within that environment.

Virus   A computer program that infects a computer system, causing damage or mischief. Like a biological virus, it causes the host computer to make copies of the virus, which can then be spread to other computers over networks, through online services, or via infected diskettes.

Wide-area network (WAN)   A computer network covering a broad geographical area, such as between buildings, campuses, or even across hundreds or thousands of miles. Often involves the interconnection of multiple local-area networks.

Word processing   The use of a word processor.

Word processor   A computer program for writing that supports the entry, editing, revising, formatting, storage, retrieval, and printing of text.

Word wrap A feature of a word processor that automatically shifts the next whole word to the next line of the document when a line of text in a computer document is filled.

World Wide Web (WWW) An information system on the Internet that relies on a point-and-click hypertext navigation system similar to a graphical user interface.

Like Gopher, the WWW is accessed via a client-server model, but, unlike most Gophers, it provides access to multimedia, including various type fonts, color, graphics, and even audio and video.

WYSIWYG (What you see is what you get) The standard in word processors—displays exactly what you will see when the document is printed.

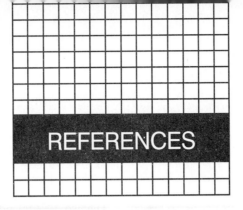

REFERENCES

Anglin, G. J. (Ed.). (1991). *Instructional technology: Past, present, and future.* Englewood, CO: Libraries Unlimited.

Arredondo, L. (1991). *How to present like a pro.* New York: McGraw-Hill.

Arter, J. A., & Spandel, V. (1992). Using portfolios of student work in instruction and assessment. *Educational Measurement: Issues and Practice, 11*(Spring), 36–44.

Asimov, I. (1966). *Asimov's guide to science.* New York: Basic Books.

Atkinson, R. C. (1975). Mnemotechnics in second-language learning. *American Psychologist, 30,* 821–828.

Ault, C. R. (1985). Concept mapping as a study strategy in earth science. *Journal of College Science Teaching, 15*(1), 38–44.

Ausubel, D. P., Novak, J. D., & Hanesian, H. (1978). *Educational psychology: A cognitive view.* New York: Holt, Rinehart & Winston.

Baine, D. (1986). *Memory and instruction.* Englewood Cliffs, NJ: Educational Technology.

Banathy, B. (1968). *Instructional systems.* Palo Alto, CA: Fearon.

Bangert-Drowns, R. L. (1993). The word processor as an instructional tool: A meta-analysis of word processing in writing instruction. *Review of Educational Research, 63*(1), 69–93.

Barell, J. (1995). *Teaching for thoughtfulness: Classroom strategies to enhance intellectual development.* White Plains, NY: Longman.

Barenholz, H., & Tamir, P. (1992). A comprehensive use of concept mapping in design instruction and assessment. *Research in Science and Technological Education, 10*(1), 37–52.

Bell-Gredler, M. E. (1986). *Learning and instruction: Theory into practice.* Englewood Cliffs, NJ: Merrill/Prentice Hall.

Billings, K. J. (1985). *An evaluation handbook for a computer education program.* Eugene, OR: ICCE Publications.

Bloom, B. S., Hastings, J. T., & Madau, G. F. (1971). *Handbook on formative and summative evaluation of student learning.* New York: McGraw-Hill.

Blumenfeld, P. C., Soloway, E., Marx, R. W., Krajcik, J. S., Guzdial, M., & Palincsar, A. (1991). Motivating project-based learning: Sustaining the doing, supporting the learning. *Educational Psychologist, 26,* 369–398.

Borko, H., & Livingston, C. (1992). Cognition and improvisation: Differences in mathematics instruction by expert and novice teachers. *American Educational Research Journal, 26,* 473–498.

Brock, P. A. (1994). *Educational technology in the classroom.* Englewood Cliffs, NJ: Educational Technology.

Brooks, J. G., & Brooks, M. G. (1993). *In search of understanding: The case for constructivist classrooms.* Alexandria, VA: American Society for Curriculum Development.

Brown, A. L., & Palincsar, A. S. (1987). Reciprocal teaching of comprehension strategies: A natural history of one program for enhancing learning. In J. D. Day and J. G. Borkowski (Eds.), *Intelligence and exceptionality: New directions for theory, assessment, and instructional practice.* New York: Ablex.

Brown, J. S., Collins, A., & Duguid, P. (1989). Situated cognition and the culture of learning. *Educational Researcher, 18*(1), 32–42.

Bruner, J. S. (1961). The act of discovery. *Harvard Education Review, 31*(1), 21–32.

Carroll, L. (1923). *Alice's adventures in Wonderland.* Chicago: J. C. Winston.

Clark, R. E. (1983). Reconsidering research on learning from media. *Review of Educational Research, 53*(4), 445–459.

Cochran-Smith, M. (1991). Word processing and writing in elementary classrooms: A critical review of related literature. *Review of Educational Research, 61*(1), 107–155.

Cognition and Technical Group at Vanderbilt. (1993). Designing learning environments that support thinking: The Jasper series as a case study. In T. M. Duffy, J. Lowyck, & D. H. Jonassen (Eds.), *Designing environments for constructive learning* (pp. 9–36). Berlin: Springer-Verlag.

Cohen, M., & Riel, M. (1989). The effect of distant audiences on students' writing. *American Educational Research Journal, 26,* 143–159.

Cohen, P. A., Kulik, J. A., & Kulik, C. C. (1982). Educational outcomes of tutoring: A meta-analysis of findings. *American Educational Research Journal, 46,* 355–385.

Collins, A., Brown, J. S., & Holum, A. (1991). Cognitive apprenticeship: Making thinking visible. *American Educator, 15*(3), 6–11, 38–46.

Dallmann-Jones, A. S. (1994). *The expert educator: A reference manual of teaching strategies for quality education.* Fond du Lac, WI: Three Blue Herons.

D'Aoust, C. (1992). Portfolios: Process for students and teachers. In K. B. Yancey (Ed.), *Portfolios in the writing classroom* (pp. 39–48). Urbana, IL: National Council of Teachers of English.

Derry, S., & Murphy, D. A. (1986). Designing systems that train learning ability: From theory to practice. *Review of Educational Research, 56*(1), 1–39.

Dewey, J. (1897). My pedagogic creed. *School Journal, 54,* 77–80.

Dick, W., & Carey, L. (1990). *Systematic design of instruction* (3rd ed.). Glenview, IL: Scott, Foresman.

Dick, W., & Reiser, R. A. (1989). *Planning effective instruction.* Englewood Cliffs, NJ: Prentice Hall.

Driscoll, M. P. (1994). *Psychology of learning for instruction.* Boston: Allyn & Bacon.

Duffy, T. M., Lowyck, J., & Jonassen, D. H. (1993). Introduction. In T. M. Duffy, J. Lowyck, & D. H. Jonassen (Eds.), *Designing environments for constructive learning* (pp. 1–5). Berlin: Springer-Verlag.

Dyrli, O. E., & Kinnaman, D. E. (1994). Districtwide technology planning: The key to long-term success. *Technology and Learning, 14*(7), 50–54, 56.

Educational Products Information Exchange. (1990). *Report of computer-based integrated instructional systems.* Water Mill, NY: Author.

Ertmer, P. A., & Newby, T. J. (1993). Behaviorism, cognitivism, constructivism: Comparing critical features from an instructional design perspective. *Performance Improvement Quarterly, 6*(4), 50–72.

Ertmer, P. A., & Newby, T. J. (1995). The expert learner: Strategic, self-regulated, and reflective. *Instructional Science, 21*(4), 1–24.

Fleming, M., & Levie, H. (1993). *Instructional message design: Principles from the behavioral and cognitive sciences.* Englewood Cliffs, NJ: Educational Technology.

Fleming, M. L. (1987). Displays and communication. In R. M. Gagné (Ed.), *Instructional technology: Foundations.* Hillsdale, NJ: Lawrence Erlbaum Associates.

Gagné, R. M. (Ed.). (1987). *Instructional technology: Foundations.* Hillsdale, NJ: Lawrence Erlbaum Associates.

Gagné, R. M., Briggs, L. J., & Wager, W. W. (1988). *Principles of instructional design* (3rd ed.). New York: Holt, Rinehart & Winston.

Galbraith, J. K. (1967). *The new industrial state.* Boston: Houghton Mifflin.

Gardner, H. (1985). *The mind's new science: A history of the cognitive revolution.* New York: Basic Books.

Geisert, P. G., & Futrell, M. K. (1995). *Teachers, computers, and curriculum: Microcomputers in the classroom* (2nd ed.). Boston: Allyn & Bacon.

Gentry, C. G. (1994). *Introduction to instructional development: Process and technique.* Belmont, CA: Wadsworth.

Geske, J. (1992). Overcoming the drawbacks of the large lecture class. *College Teaching, 40*(4), 151–154.

Gleason, M. (1986). Better communication in large courses. *College Teaching, 34*(1), 20–24.

Hadley, M., & Sheingold, K. (1993, May). Commonalities and distinctive patterns in teachers' integration of computers. *American Journal of Education,* 261–315.

Heinich, R., Molenda, M., Russell, J. D., & Smaldino, S. (1996). *Instructional media and technologies for learning* (5th ed.). Englewood Cliffs, NJ: Merrill/Prentice Hall.

Honebein, P. C., Duffy, T. M., & Fishman B. J. (1993). Constructivism and the design of learning environments: Context and authentic activities for learning. In T. M. Duffy, J. Lowyck, & D. H. Jonassen (Eds.), *Designing environments for constructive learning* (pp. 87–108). Berlin: Springer-Verlag.

Hunter, M. (1982). *Mastery teaching.* El Segundo, CA: TIP Publications.

Jacobson, D., Eggen, P., & Kauchak, D. (1993). *Methods for teaching: A skills approach* (4th ed.). Englewood Cliffs, NJ: Merrill/Prentice Hall.

Johnson, D. W., & Johnson, R. T. (1984). *Circles of learning.* Alexandria, VA: Association of Supervision and Curriculum Development.

Johnson, R. T., Johnson, D. W., & Stanne, M. B. (1985) Effects of cooperative, competitive, and individualistic goal structures on computer-assisted instruction. *Journal of Educational Psychology, 77*(6), 668–677.

Jonassen, D. H. (1991). Evaluating constructivist learning. *Educational Technology, 31*(9), 28–33.

Julyan, C. L. (1991). Getting connected to science. *HANDS ON! 14*(1), 4–7.

Kauchak, D., & Eggen, P. D. (1989). *Learning and teaching: Research based methods.* Boston: Allyn & Bacon.

Kearny, C., Newby, T., & Stepich, D. (1995, March). *Building bridges: Creating instructional analogies.* Presentation at the Annual Convention of the National Society for Performance and Instruction, Atlanta, GA.

Keller, F. S. (1968). Good-bye, teacher . . . *Journal of Applied Behavior Analysis, 1,* 79–88.

Keller, J. M. (1983). Motivational design of instruction. In C. M. Reigeluth (Ed.). *Instructional-design theories and models: An overview of their current status* (pp. 383–434). Hillsdale, NJ: Lawrence Erlbaum Associates.

Keller, J. M. (1987). Strategies for stimulating the motivation to learn. *Performance and Instruction, 26*(9), 1–7.

Keller, J. M., & Strong, L. (1991, March). *Applications of the ARCS Model of motivational design.* Presentation at the Annual Conference of the National Society for Performance and Instruction, Los Angeles, CA.

Kemp, J. E., Morrison, G. R., & Ross, S. M. (1994). *Designing effective instruction.* Englewood Cliffs, NJ: Merrill/Prentice Hall.

Kemp, J. E., & Smellie, D. C. (1994). *Planning, producing, and using instructional media.* New York: Harper & Row.

Knirk, F. G., & Gustafson, K. L. (1991). *Instructional technology: A systematic approach to education.* Ft. Worth: Holt, Rinehart & Winston.

Kozma, R. (1991). Learning with media. *Review of Educational Research, 61*(2), 179–211.

Kulik, C. C., & Kulik, J. A. (1991). Effectiveness of computer-based instruction: An updated analysis. *Computers in Human Behavior, 7,* 75–94.

Kulik, J. A., & Kulik, C. C. (1989). Meta-analysis in education. *International Journal of Educational Research, 13,* 221–340.

Kulik, J. A., Kulik, C. C., & Cohen, P. A. (1979a). A meta-analysis of outcome studies of Keller's personalized system of instruction. *American Psychologist, 34,* 307–318.

Kulik, J. A., Kulik, C. C., & Cohen, P. A. (1979b). Research on audio-tutorial instruction: A meta-analysis of comparative studies. *Research in Higher Education, 11,* 321–341.

Kulik, C. C., Schwalb, B. J., & Kulik, J. A. (1982). Programmed instruction in secondary education: A meta-analysis of evaluation findings. *Journal of Educational Research, 75,* 133–138.

Lashley, K. S. (1960). In search of the engram. In F. A. Beach, D. O. Hebb, C. T. Morgan, & A. W. Nissen (Eds.), *The neuropsychology of Lashley: Selected papers of K. S. Lashley* (pp. 478–507). New York: McGraw-Hill.

Leshin, C. B., Pollock, J., & Reigeluth, C. M. (1992). *Instructional design strategies and tactics.* Englewood Cliffs, NJ: Educational Technology.

Levin, J. A., Riel, M., Miyake, N., & Cohen, M. (1987). Education on the electronic frontier: Teleapprentices in globally distributed educational contexts. *Contemporary Educational Psychology, 12,* 254–260.

Lockard, J., Abrams, P. D., & Many, W. A. (1994). *Microcomputers for twenty-first-century educators* (3rd ed). New York: HarperCollins.

Mager, E. W. (1985). *Classroom presentation skills workshop.* Carefree, AZ: Mager Associates.

Mager, R. F. (1984). *Preparing instructional objectives* (2nd ed.). Belmont, CA: Pitman.

Mager, R. F. (1988). *Making instruction work: Or skillbloomers.* Belmont, CA: Lake.

Mandel, S. (1987). *Effective presentation skills: A practical guide for better speaking.* Los Altos, CA: Crisp Publications.

Mayer, R. E. (1982). Learning. In H. E. Mitzel (Ed.), *Encyclopedia of educational research* (pp. 1040–1058). New York: Free Press.

McCarthy, R. (1993). A computer on every teacher's desk. *Electronic Learning, 12*(7), 10–14.

McCutcheon, G. (1980). How do elementary school teachers plan? The nature of planning and influences on it. *Elementary School Journal, 81*(1), 4–23.

McKeachie, W. J. (1994). Why classes should be small, but how to help your students be active learners even in large classes. In W. J. McKeachie (Ed.), *Teaching tips* (pp. 197–210). Lexington, MA: Heath.

Merrill, P. F., Hammons, K., Tolman, M. N., Christensen, L., Vincent, B. R., & Reynolds, P. L. (1992). *Computers in education* (2nd ed.). Boston: Allyn & Bacon.

Niemiec, R., & Walberg, H. J. (1987). Comparative effects of computer-assisted instruction: A synthesis of reviews. *Journal of Educational Computing Research, 3*(1), 19–37.

Orlich, D. C., Harder, R. J., Callahan, R. C., Kauchak, D. P., & Gibson, H. W. (1994). *Teaching strategies: A guide to better instruction.* Lexington, MA: Heath.

Ormrod, J. E. (1989). *Using your head: An owner's manual.* Englewood Cliffs, NJ: Educational Technology.

Ormrod, J. E. (1995). *Educational psychology: Principles and applications.* Englewood Cliffs, NJ: Merrill/Prentice Hall.

Palinscar, A. S. (1986). Metacognitive strategy instruction. *Exceptional Children, 53*(2), 118–124.

Papert, S. (1980). *Mindstorms: Children, computers, and powerful ideas.* New York: Basic Books.

Perelman, L. J. (1992). *School's out.* New York: Avon Books.

Postlethwait, S. N., Novak, J., & Murray, H. (1972). *The audio-tutorial approach to learning.* Minneapolis, MN: Burgess.

Qin, Z., Johnson, D. W., & Johnson, R. T. (1995). Cooperative versus competitive efforts and problem solving. *Review of Educational Research, 65,* 129–143.

Reigeluth, C. M. (1983). Instructional design: What is it and why is it? In C. M. Reigeluth (Ed.), *Instructional-design theories and models: An overview of their current status* (pp. 3–36). Hillsdale, NJ: Lawrence Erlbaum Associates.

Reiser, R. A., & Mory, E. H. (1991). An examination of the systematic planning techniques of two experienced teachers. *Educational Technology Research and Development, 39*(3), 71–82.

Reynolds, A. (1992). What is competent beginning teaching? A review of the literature. *Review of Educational Research, 62*(1), 1–35.

Richey, R. (1986). *The theoretical and conceptual bases of instructional design.* London: Kogan Page.

Rivers, W. M. (1986). Comprehension and production in language learning. *Modern Language Acquisition, 70*(1), 1–7.

Robinson, P. W. (1981). *Fundamentals of experimental psychology.* Englewood Cliffs, NJ: Prentice Hall.

Rogoff, B. (1990). *Apprenticeship in thinking: Cognitive development in social context.* New York: Oxford University Press.

Romiszowski, A. J. (1988). *The selection and use of instructional media.* New York: Nichols.

Rothwell, W. J., & Kazanas, H. C. (1992). *Mastering the instructional design process: A systematic approach.* San Francisco: Jossey-Bass.

Saettler, P. (1990). *The evolution of American educational technology.* Englewood, CO: Libraries Unlimited.

Sardo-Brown, D. (1990). Experienced teachers' planning practices: A U.S. survey. *Journal of Education for Teaching, 16*(1), 57–71.

Schmitt, M. S., & Newby, T. J. (1986). Metacognition: Relevance to instructional design. *Journal of Instructional Development, 9*(4), 29–33.

Schön, D. A. (1983). *The reflective practitioner: How professionals think in action.* New York: Basic Books.

Schramm, W. (1954). How communication works. In W. Schramm (Ed.), *The process and effects of mass communication* (pp. 3–26). Urbana: University of Illinois Press.

Schunk, D. H. (1991). *Learning theories: An educational perspective.* Englewood Cliffs, NJ: Merrill/Prentice Hall.

Shannon, C. E., & Weaver, W. (1949). *The mathematical theory of communication.* Urbana: University of Illinois Press.

Shelly, G. B., & Cashman, T. J. (1984). *Computer fundamentals for an information age*. Brea, CA: Anaheim Publishing.

Shuell, T. J. (1986). Cognitive conceptions of learning. *Review of Educational Research, 56*, 411–436.

Simonson, M. R., & Thompson, A. (1994). *Educational computing foundations*. Englewood Cliffs, NJ: Merrill/Prentice Hall.

Skinner, B. F. (1945). *Walden two*. Englewood Cliffs, NJ: Merrill/Prentice Hall.

Skinner, B. F. (1968). *The technology of teaching*. New York: Appleton-Century-Crofts.

Skinner, B. F. (1984). The shame of American education. *American Psychologist, 39*, 947–954.

Slavin, R. E. (1990a). *Cooperative learning: Theory, research, and practice*. Englewood Cliffs, NJ: Merrill/Prentice Hall.

Slavin, R. E. (1990b). Research on cooperative learning: Consensus and controversy. *Educational Leadership, 47*(4), 52–54.

Smith, P. L., & Ragan, T. J. (1993). *Instructional design*. Englewood Cliffs, NJ: Merrill/Prentice Hall.

Stepich, D. A., & Newby, T. J. (1988a). Analogical instruction within the information processing paradigm: Effective means to facilitate learning. *Instructional Science, 17*, 129–144.

Stepich, D. A., & Newby, T. J. (1988b). Analogizing as an instructional strategy. *Performance and Instruction, 27*(9), 21–23.

Stipek, D. J. (1993). *Motivation to learn* (2nd ed.). Boston: Allyn & Bacon.

Sullivan, H., & Higgins, N. (1983). *Teaching for competence*. New York: Teachers College.

Taylor, R. P. (Ed.). (1980). *The computer in the school: Tutor, tool, tutee*. New York: Teachers College Press.

Tessmer, M. (1990). Environment analysis: A neglected stage of instructional design. *Educational Technology Research and Development, 38*(1), 55–64.

Thorndike, E. L. (1931). *Human learning*. New York: Century.

Tinker, R. F., & Kapisovsky, P. M. (1991). Telecomputing: Linking for learning. *HANDS ON! 14*(2), 15–17.

Trenholm, S. (1991). *Human communication theory* (2nd ed.). Englewood Cliffs, NJ: Merrill/Prentice Hall.

Tubbs, S. L., & Moss, S. (1994). *Human communication* (7th ed.). New York: McGraw-Hill.

U.S. Office of Technology Assessment. (1988, September). *Power on! New tools for teaching and learning* (Report No. OTA–SET–380). Washington, D.C.: Government Printing Office.

U.S. Office of Technology Assessment. (1995, April). *Teachers and technology: Making the connection* (Report No. OTA-EHR-616). Washington, D.C.: Government Printing Office.

Wasserman, S. (1992). *Asking the right question: The essence of teaching*. Bloomington, IN: Phi Delta Kappa.

Watson, J. B. (1924). *Behaviorism*. New York: Peoples' Institute.

Weinstein, C. E., & Van Mater Stone, G. (1993). Broadening our conception of general education: The self-regulated learner. *New Directions for Community Colleges, 81*, 31–39.

West, C. K., Farmer, J. A., & Wolff, P. M. (1991). *Instructional design: Implications from cognitive science*. Englewood Cliffs, NJ: Merrill/Prentice Hall.

Wittrock, M. C. (1990). Generative processes of comprehension. *Educational Psychologist, 24*, 345–376.

Woolfolk, A. E. (1990). *Educational psychology* (4th ed.). Englewood Cliffs, NJ: Merrill/Prentice Hall.

Worthen, B. R., & Sanders, J. R. (1987). *Educational evaluation: Alternative approaches and practical guidelines*. New York: Longman.

Yelon, S. L. (1991). Writing and using instructional objectives. In L. J. Briggs, K. L. Gustafson, & M. H Tillman (Eds.), *Instructional design: Principles and applications* (2nd ed.) (pp. 75–122). Englewood Cliffs, NJ: Educational Technology.

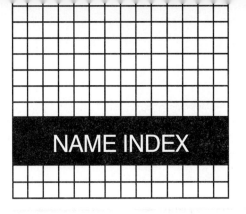

NAME INDEX

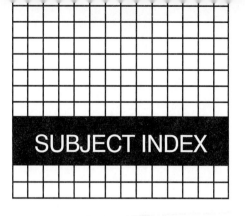

SUBJECT INDEX

We need your help . . .

Chapter 13 emphasized the need for continuous improvement of instructional materials. Although we all like to think our work is perfect, we understand that there will be some things that need modification. Now we need your help to improve this text. Would you please take a couple of minutes to express your opinion? We have two ways in which you can help.

First, e-mail us with your specific questions and comments. The address is: Newby@sage.cc.purdue.edu
One or more of the authors will personally respond to your questions. You can be very specific about a particular item within the text and/or very general with overall comments.

A second way to help us would be to complete the short form below, cut it out, and mail it directly to us at the address listed at the bottom of the form. We will compile this information and incorporate the suggestions in future editions of the text. We appreciate your using this text—and we really value your help in reviewing it so the needed changes can be identified and made. Thanks!

Background information

- Your major _____
- Your class rank: ❑ Freshman ❑ Sophomore ❑ Junior ❑ Senior ❑ Graduate student
- Was this a required course? ❑ yes ❑ no
- The course using this text was considered a course in: ❑ ed. methods ❑ media
  ❑ ed. computing ❑ instructional technology ❑ other (give type) _____
- Did you have a computer lab component with this course? ❑ yes ❑ no
- What type of computer do you use? ❑ Macintosh ❑ IBM compatible ❑ both

Specific information about the textbook

- Were the following topics covered sufficiently?

Topic	More info. needed	About right	Too much given
Learning	❑	❑	❑
Planning instruction	❑	❑	❑
Theory	❑	❑	❑
Computer applications	❑	❑	❑
Instructional approaches	❑	❑	❑
Motivation	❑	❑	❑
Uses of media	❑	❑	❑
Integration and management of computers	❑	❑	❑
Evaluation of students and materials	❑	❑	❑
Future instructional technologies	❑	❑	❑

- Overall, do you feel the CUE sections adequately introduced you to the essentials of computers and how they could be used by the classroom teacher? ❑ yes ❑ no ❑ not sure
- What additions or changes to the CUEs would you like to see?

- Did the TIPs help? ❑ yes ❑ no ❑ not sure
- What additions or changes to the TIPs would you like to see?

- Did you find the on-going extended example of Janette Moreno: ❑ effective ❑ okay ❑ waste of space
- What would help the Janette Moreno sections to be more effective?

- Were there enough examples in the text?

- What additional comments/suggestions/problems do you have about the text? Feel free to write on the back or send extra pages.

Send your comments to:

Dr. Tim Newby, 1442–LAEB, Purdue University, W. Lafayette, IN 47907-1442

Thanks again—this helps!